KU-115-050

Company Law

AUSTRALIA
The Law Book Company Ltd.
Sydney : Melbourne : Perth

CANADA AND U.S.A.
The Carswell Company Ltd.
Agincourt, Ontario

INDIA
N. M. Tripathi Private Ltd.
Bombay
and
Eastern Law House Private Ltd.
Calcutta and Delhi
M.P.P. House
Bangalore

ISRAEL
Steimatzky's Agency Ltd.
Jerusalem : Tel Aviv : Haifa

MALAYSIA : SINGAPORE : BRUNEI
Malayan Law Journal (Pte.) Ltd.
Singapore

PAKISTAN
Pakistan Law House
Karachi

Charlesworth and Cain

Company Law

TWELFTH EDITION

by

GEOFFREY MORSE, LL.B.

Barrister, Reader in Law at the University of Liverpool

SCOTTISH EDITOR

ENID A. MARSHALL, M.A., LL.B., Ph.D.

*Solicitor, Reader in Business Law
at the University of Stirling*

ACCOUNTING EDITOR

RICHARD MORRIS, B.A., M.Sc., F.C.A.

Professor of Accounting at the University of Liverpool

LONDON
STEVENS & SONS
1983

First Edition	(1932)	By His Honour Judge Charlesworth
Second Edition	(1938)	,, ,, ,, ,,
Third Edition	(1940)	,, ,, ,, ,,
Fourth Edition	(1946)	,, ,, ,, ,,
Second Impression	(1947)	
Third Impression	(1948)	
Fifth Edition	(1949)	,, ,, ,, ,,
Second Impression revised	(1950)	
Sixth Edition	(1954)	,, ,, ,, ,,
Second Impression revised	(1956)	
Seventh Edition	(1960)	By T. E. Cain
Second Impression	(1962)	
Eighth Edition	(1965)	,, ,, ,,
Ninth Edition	(1968)	,, ,, ,,
Tenth Edition	(1972)	,, ,, ,,
Eleventh Edition	(1977)	,, ,, ,,
Second Impression	(1980)	
Twelfth Edition	(1983)	By Geoffrey Morse

Published by Stevens & Sons Ltd.
of 11 New Fetter Lane, London
Printed in Great Britain by
Richard Clay (The Chaucer Press) Ltd.,
Bungay, Suffolk

British Library Cataloguing in Publication Data

Charlesworth, John
  Company law.—12th ed.
  1. Corporation law—Great Britain
  I. Title   II. Cain, Thomas Ewan
  III. Morse, Geoffrey   IV. Marshall, Enid A.
  344.106'66   KD2079

  ISBN 0-420-46030-6
  ISBN 0-420-46040-3 Pbk

All rights reserved.
No part of this publication may be
reproduced or transmitted, in any form
or by any means, electronic, mechanical, photocopying,
recording or otherwise, or stored in any retrieval
system of any nature, without the
written permission of the copyright
holder and the publisher, application
for which shall be made to
the publisher.

©
Stevens & Sons
1983

PREFACE

The development of company law since the previous edition of this work has been of a magnitude unprecedented in recent years. United Kingdom membership of the European Economic Community which required compliance during that time with two harmonising directives, provided the *raison d'être* for the Companies Acts of 1980 and 1981. Opportunity was taken on both occasions, however, to amend the existing law in many areas not required by the directives. Two examples, the regulation of insider dealing and the disclosure of substantial interests in shares, suffice to show that the scandals of the 1970s provided this further impetus for reform, once the EEC requirements had persuaded the Government to allow company law legislative time. The result is that company law has a far more statutory basis than it used to have—and, what is more, a basis founded not on one statute but on nine. It is therefore imperative that the consolidation of the legislation into one or more coherent statutes, promised for 1984, actually appears, whatever the political situation then appertaining.

This trend from case to statute law would appear to be irreversible in modern society, but there are many other important areas of company law, still untouched by statute, which have not stood still. In particular, the Court of Appeal has further examined the rule in *Foss* v. *Harbottle* in the case of *The Prudential Assurance Co. Ltd.* v. *Newman Industries Ltd.* (*No.* 2), and there have been important developments in the law of *ultra vires* and the duties of majority shareholders.

The present edition attempts to incorporate these developments into what remains, hopefully, a basic framework for those wishing to study company law. Because there is now simply more company law, the length of the book has increased but some attempt has been made to keep it within reasonable bounds by omitting the chapters on foreign companies and taxation which appeared in the previous edition. Instead references to tax law are made in the text where appropriate and readers are referred to Pinson, *Revenue Law* for further study.

There are four new chapters, reflecting in the main the new legislation. Chapter 12 is concerned with the revolutionary new powers of purchase and redemption by a company of its own shares. Chapter 13 sets out the new, complex, rules on the giving of financial assistance by a company for the acquisition of its shares by another. This topic was formerly incorporated in Chapter 10 but is now thought to merit specific consideration. Chapter 21 sets out the new criminal sanctions for the much publicised topic of insider dealing. Finally, Chapter 31 on take-overs has been separated from the chapter on re-constructions and amalgamations. The new chapter takes into account the development of self-regulation in the securities industry by the Council for the Securities Industry and the City Panel on Take-overs and Mergers. There are also many other changes too numerous to mention.

One important new development, however, has been the appointment of a specialist accounting editor. The events of the 1970s proved above all that lawyers could not just leave everything to the accountants and wash their hands of the consequences. In the light of the many changes introduced by the 1981 Act it is now more than ever essential for those wishing to claim a knowledge of company law to have a grasp of the accounting rules both in the legislation and in practice. The chapter on accounts has accordingly been rewritten and expanded by the Professor of Accounting at Liverpool, Richard Morris. I owe him a great debt for his ability to find in the mire of accountancy a path that even an innumerate lawyer may follow.

I also owe a considerable debt to my Scottish Editor, Dr. Enid Marshall, of Stirling University. In addition to providing an update on Scots law, and incidentally keeping within the bounds of reasonableness in the process, she has also corrected many of my errors and infelicities of style with a modesty I found impossible to resent. Scottish cases are, of necessity, for the most part mentioned only by way of footnotes; for fuller treatment of most of these cases the reader is referred to Dr. Marshall's *Scottish Cases on Partnerships and Companies* published by W. Green & Son Ltd. (1980).

Other contributors require a mention. My colleague, Christopher Ryan, being a specialist in criminal law as well as company law, was, I felt, in an ideal position to contribute the new chapter on insider dealing, and I am most grateful to him for that. He also contributed the section on the disclosure of substantial share interests in Chapter 10, having annotated that part of the 1981 Act for me in the Current Law annotations. He has not let me down. To my colleagues, Robert Upex, who assisted me on points involving labour law, and Ann Arora, who read the page proofs and corrected yet more errors, I am also in debt and tender my thanks. The secretaries in the Faculty of Law at Liverpool, in particular Mary Jenkins, also deserve my thanks for translating parts of my manuscript from hieroglyphics into legible English.

Finally I must, on behalf of a generation of law students, pay tribute to Tom Cain, whose work on this book now ends. He has achieved the difficult task of maintaining the essential character of a successful book developed by another. It is that task which now falls to me.

To my wife Christine, and children, Nigel and Carolyn, I owe a debt for their support, encouragement and patience, and, above all perhaps, for their ability to bring me down to reality whenever that appeared to them to be necessary.

The final responsibility for all errors and defects is of course mine. The law is stated as known to me on March 1, 1983.

Liverpool,
April 1983.

GEOFFREY MORSE

CONTENTS

TABLE OF CASES

Table of Cases

TABLE OF STATUTES

TABLE OF STATUTORY INSTRUMENTS

TABLE OF RULES OF THE SUPREME COURT

REFERENCES TO CITY CODE ON TAKEOVERS AND MERGERS

Chapter 1

NATURE OF REGISTERED COMPANIES

This book is mostly concerned with registered companies, whether public or private, limited by shares.[1] The term "registered company" means a company incorporated or formed by registration under the Companies Acts, the latest Acts being the Companies Acts 1948 to 1981. The 1948 Act has been added to and amended by the 1967, 1976, 1980 and 1981 Acts together with section 9 of the European Communities Act 1972, but it may still be regarded as the principal Act and in this book, unless it is otherwise stated or the context otherwise requires, references to sections and Schedules are to those of the Companies Act 1948 and references to the "Act" are to the Companies Act 1948. The sources of company law being so varied there are plans for a consolidation of all these Acts scheduled for 1984.[2]

The Companies Act 1948[3] provides that for the purpose of the registration of companies under the Act there shall be offices (Companies Registration Offices in England and Scotland) at such places as the Board of Trade (now the Department of Trade) think fit, and that the Board may appoint such registrars, assistant registrars, clerks and servants as they think necessary for the registration of companies and may make regulations with respect to their duties.

Section 1(1) enables two or more persons associated for any lawful purpose to form an incorporated company with or without limited liability, by complying with the requirements of the Acts in respect of registration. As is explained later in this chapter, the requirements are that certain documents be delivered to the appropriate Registrar of Companies and certain fees and stamp duties paid. Under section 12, for example, a memorandum of association and, usually, articles of association must be delivered to the Registrar, who must retain and register them.

The rest of this chapter attempts first of all to give a simple answer to the question "what is a registered company?" and then to trace briefly

---

[1] In general terms commercial companies.
[2] See the 1981 Act, s.116, for the procedure to be adopted.
[3] s.424.

the history of the registered company. After that there is a note on some of the proposals and influences on company law reform which have produced the recent spate of legislation and will continue to do so. Finally, the following topics are dealt with: the procedure to obtain the registration of a company; the effect of the registration of a company—this is that the company is a corporation with a legal existence separate from that of its members, who usually have the privilege of limited personal liability; the management of registered companies; a registered company's securities—these are the shares and debentures which it issues; registered companies and partnerships contrasted—a partnership is not a corporation and the partners do not have limited liability.

What is a Registered Company?

A registered company, *i.e.* a company incorporated by registration under the Companies Acts, is regarded by the law as a person, just as a human being, Mr. Smith or Mr. Jones, is a person. This artificial or juristic person can own land and other property, enter into contracts, sue and be sued, have a bank account in its own name, owe money to others and be a creditor of other people and other companies, and employ people to work for it. The company's money and property belong to the company and not to the members or shareholders, although the members or shareholders may be said to own the company. Similarly, the company's debts are the debts of the company and the shareholders cannot be compelled to pay them, although if, for example, the company is being wound up and its assets do not realise a sum sufficient to pay its debts, a shareholder whose liability is limited by shares is liable to contribute to the assets up to the amount, if any, unpaid on his shares. A company, of course, can only act through human agents, and those who manage its business are called directors. But the directors are only agents of the company, with the powers of management given by the company's articles of association and usually with power to delegate any of their powers to a managing director. The company is also liable for torts[4] and crimes committed by its servants and agents within the scope of their employment or authority. This conception of a company as a corporation, *i.e.* a person separate and

---

[4] Or, in Scots law, delicts.

distinct from the other persons who are its members and directors, is the fundamental principle of company law.

A company must have members, otherwise it would never exist at all, and in the case of a company with a share capital these members are called shareholders (or, if the shares have been converted into stock, stockholders). The shareholder's position with regard to the company itself and to his fellow shareholders is regulated by the Companies Acts and by the memorandum and the articles of association, and also by the principle that controlling shareholders, *i.e.* those with sufficient votes to pass a resolution in general meeting, must act bona fide for the benefit of the shareholders as a general body. The memorandum and articles vary considerably among different companies, but in every case the shareholder's position is that of the owner of one or more shares in the company, which shares usually carry a right of voting at general meetings, and, if profits are made, he may receive dividends on his shares. His shares are something which he has bought—perhaps from the company, or perhaps from somebody else—and something which he can sell or give away, either in his lifetime or by his will. The general rule is that he cannot get his money back from the company, so long as the company is in existence, because his position is not that of a person who has lent money to the company or has deposited his money as with a bank or a building society—it is that of the owner of property, namely, his shares, which can only be turned into money if a buyer can be found to pay for them. Shares may be fully paid or partly paid. When the shares are only partly paid the shareholder can be compelled to pay them up fully if called upon by the company or, if the company is being wound up and its debts exceed its assets, by the liquidator. In any event it is the general policy of the Companies Acts to see that the issued share capital is maintained intact, except for losses in the way of business, so that it may be available to satisfy the company's debts. Accordingly, while the company is a going concern the general rule is that no part of the paid-up capital may be returned to the shareholders without the consent of the court, or by following strict procedures intended to protect creditors.

A company may be formed to acquire and carry on an existing business, which may or may not belong to the promoters, or to start some new business. However, a company is commonly formed as a private company to acquire the promoters' business. In this case a price is put on the business and paid by the issue to the promoters of shares credited as fully or partly paid in the company. Most of the price will be left owing to the promoters so that if the company is later wound up they will rank for repayment of it as unsecured creditors otherwise if they take the whole price in the form of shares credited as fully paid they will rank for repayment of capital after the unsecured creditors. If a company is formed to acquire a business which does not belong to the promoters they may provide the necessary funds for the company by taking shares in the company for cash.

A company can also raise money by borrowing.[5] Persons who lend money to a company may be issued with debentures to show that they have lent money and are entitled to interest on their loans. Unlike shareholders, they are not members of the company and they have no right to vote at general meetings.

Shares in, and debentures of, public companies are extensively bought as an investment by people who want to derive an income from their capital but who are unable, for reasons of inclination, business, age, health or lack of opportunity, to take any part in the management of the company. To protect investors from dishonest or incompetent people who form companies in which the investors are likely to lose their money, disclosure of such things as the company's past financial record and the benefits of being a director, is required in the prospectus on the strength of which the public is invited to subscribe for shares or debentures of the company. Provision is also made for a company's accounts and the balance sheet and profit and loss account to be audited every year by auditors appointed by the shareholders and for the balance sheet and the profit and loss account and certain other documents to be circulated to every shareholder and debenture holder. With the exception of small companies and unlimited companies a copy of the balance sheet and the other documents must also be lodged with the Registrar of Companies.

The directors of a company, who are usually appointed by the members at their annual general meeting, have wide powers to manage the company's business conferred upon them by the articles. The members cannot control the exercise of these powers, although they can, *e.g.* alter the articles. The directors owe certain duties of good faith and care to the company.

---

[5] Money borrowed by a company is sometimes called "loan capital." It should not be confused with "share capital": Chap. 11.

A registered company is capable of perpetual succession but it may become insolvent or it may decide to retire from business. In such a case it is wound up, *i.e.* it is put, or it goes, into liquidation, and a person, called a liquidator, is appointed to wind up its affairs. He sells the company's property and pays as much of its debts as he can do out of the proceeds of sale. If there is a surplus, he distributes it among the shareholders. When the liquidation is completed the company is dissolved and ceases to exist.

The Acts have increasingly required disclosure by companies, their directors and substantial shareholders of many financial and other particulars. Usually this will be to the Registrar who will keep the information on the company's file. Such information is then available to anyone who makes a search of that file and is seen as one of the prices of incorporation.

THE HISTORY OF THE REGISTERED COMPANY

The modern commercial company, incorporated by registration under the Companies Acts, is the result of the fusion of two different legal principles. A registered company, like a statutory company or a chartered company, is a "corporation,"[6] *i.e.* in the eyes of the law it is a person, capable of perpetual succession and quite distinct from the natural persons who are its members at any given moment.[7] However, the expression "company" is not confined to a corporation but includes a partnership, which is not a corporation but, at least in the case of an English partnership,[8] is merely the aggregate of the individual partners, and the present-day registered company represents the fusion of the principle of incorporation with that of partnership.

At common law the Crown has always had the right of granting charters of incorporation.[9] Non-trading companies, such as the Law Society and the Institute of Chartered Accountants, are the kind of company now incorporated by charter but trading companies have in the past been formed in this way. The right was first used for creating commercial corporations at the end of the sixteenth and the beginning

[6] Companies Act 1948, s.13(2), *post*, p. 21.

[7] *Salomon* v. *Salomon & Co. Ltd.* [1897] A.C. 22, *post*, p. 22.

[8] A Scottish partnership, although not a corporation, is a legal person distinct from the partners of whom it is composed: Partnership Act 1890, s.4(2).

[9] A chartered company is sometimes referred to as "a common law corporation."

of the seventeenth centuries, when such companies as the Levant Company, the East India Company, the Hudson's Bay Company, and the notorious South Sea Company (afterwards incorporated by special Act of Parliament), were incorporated. As these corporations were legal entities quite distinct from their members, it followed that at common law the members were not liable for the debts of the corporation, and, indeed, the Crown had no power to incorporate persons so as to make them liable for the debts of the corporation.[10] In a partnership, on the other hand, the partners were always liable for all the debts of the firm and their liability was unlimited.

In England trading companies were originally regulated companies, that is, companies in which each member traded with his own stock subject to the rules of the company, but towards the end of the seventeenth century the joint-stock company emerged,[11] and this is the form of the company in common use today. In a joint-stock company, the company trades as a single person with a stock which is jointly contributed by its members. Such companies could only be formed by special Act of Parliament or by charter but, as the advantages of the joint-stock form of trading became better known, these methods proved too expensive and dilatory to meet the growing commercial needs of the nation. Accordingly there grew up a new type of company based upon contract. This contract took the form of an elaborate deed of settlement containing provisions regulating the relations of the members among themselves and providing for the transfer of shares. A body formed in this way was only a partnership in the eyes of the law and the liability of the members was unlimited. This type of unincorporated company fell into disfavour with the legislature, largely owing to the activities of fraudulent promoters and unscrupulous share dealers, and in 1720 the Bubble Act was passed to deal with it. Unfortunately, that Act had the effect of suppressing unincorporated companies without satisfying the want which had given rise to their existence, so that "joint-stock" enterprise had to wait till the middle of the nineteenth century before corporateness "for any lawful purpose" could be obtained by the simple process of registration, and personal liability be limited by "one magic word."[12]

---

[10] *Per* Lindley L.J. in *Elve* v. *Boyton* [1891] 1 Ch. 501 at p. 507 (C.A.).
[11] Holdsworth, *History of English Law*, Vol. 8, pp. 206–222.
[12] Carr, *Select Charters of Trading Companies*, Selden Society, Vol. 28, p. xx.

The origins of company law in Scotland were distinct from those in England, although regulated companies and joint-stock companies did exist from at least the later years of the seventeenth century. The common law of Scotland sanctioned the formation of companies with transferable shares and under the management of directors, and recognised such companies as having a personality separate from that of their members.[13] In Scotland common law companies constituted under contracts of co-partnery corresponded to the English deed of settlement companies. The Bubble Act extended to Scotland but, because of the common law companies, probably had no legal effect there.[14]

In 1825, by the Bubble Companies, etc., Act, the 1720 Bubble Act was repealed and the Crown was empowered in grants of future charters to provide that the members of the corporation should be personally liable for the debts of the corporation to such extent as the Crown should think proper. This was the beginning of "limited liability." By the Chartered Companies Act 1837 the Crown was empowered to grant letters patent, *i.e.* to grant the advantages of incorporation *without* granting a charter, to a body of persons associated together for trading purposes. The persons in question had to register a deed of partnership dividing the capital into shares and providing for transfers, and satisfy the other requirements of the Act; limited liability was then granted to them. The association to which the letters patent were granted did not become a body corporate and the grant of limited liability was an advantage to which they would otherwise not have been entitled.

By the Joint Stock Companies Registration, etc., Act 1844 provision was made in England for the incorporation of companies by registration without the necessity of obtaining a Royal Charter or a special Act of Parliament. The peculiarity of this statute was, however, that, instead of allowing the usual common law consequences of incorporation to follow, it proceeded on the lines of the Chartered Companies Act 1837 and merely gave a corporate existence to a body which it still evidently regarded as a partnership, because it imposed much the same

---

[13] The decision in *Stevenson & Co.* v. *Macnair and others* (1757) M. 14, 560 and 14, 667; 5 Brown's 340 suggests that Scottish courts might even, under continental influence, have developed a principle of limited liability in relation to these companies.

[14] An Act of 1825 (6 Geo. 4 c. 131) mentioned with approval the practice which had prevailed in Scotland of forming joint-stock companies with transferable shares.

liability on the members for the debts of the company as they would have had for the debts of a partnership. This Act also made it compulsory to register as companies all partnerships with more than 25[15] members. Liability limited by shares, *i.e.* where a member's liability is limited to the amount, if any, unpaid on his shares, was introduced in the case of registered companies by the Limited Liability Act 1855, and the Joint Stock Companies Act 1856 substituted two documents, the memorandum of association and articles of association, for the deed of settlement.

In Scotland the registered company was not introduced until the Act of 1856: neither the 1844 Act nor the 1855 Act applied to Scotland.

The Companies Act 1862 repealed and consolidated the previous Acts. It also established liability limited by guarantee and, in general, prohibited any alteration in the objects clause[16] of the memorandum of association. This prohibition remained until the Companies (Memorandum of Association) Act 1890 enabled the objects to be altered for some purposes, with the leave of the court, after a special resolution[17] had been passed by the members in general meeting. The Companies Act 1867 contained a power to reduce share capital. The Directors' Liability Act 1890 introduced the principle of the liability of the directors to pay compensation to persons who have been induced to take shares on the strength of false statements in a prospectus. The Companies Act 1900 contained the first provisions relating to the contents of prospectuses, the compulsory audit of the company's accounts and the registration of charges with the Registrar.

The Companies Act 1907 made provision for the private (as opposed to the public) company, *i.e.* a company which is prohibited from inviting the public to subscribe for its shares or debentures,[18] and relieved it from the necessity of making its balance sheet public (the public company had to lodge its balance sheet with the Registrar of Companies). The Companies (Consolidation) Act 1908 consolidated the 1862 Act with the various Acts amending it, and this was followed by the Companies Act 1929. The Companies Act 1948, which came

---

[15] The maximum number of members for a partnership is now 20, except in the case of certain professional firms: Companies Acts 1948, s.434; 1967 Act, s.120, *post*, pp. 34, 35.

[16] Dealt with *post*, p. 71.

[17] *Post*, p. 87.

[18] *Post*, p. 45.

into operation on July 1, 1948,[19] introduced the exempt private company, *i.e.* the "family" private company (as opposed to a private company which was, *e.g.*, a subsidiary of a public company) and called an exempt private company because it was the only kind of private company which was exempt from the necessity of making its balance sheet and profit and loss account public.

The 1948 Act also made far-reaching changes in the law relating to company accounts. As the Cohen Report[20] (on which the 1948 Act was based) said, "The history of company legislation shows the increasing importance attached to publicity in connection with accounts. The Act of 1862 contained no compulsory provisions with regard to audit or accounts, though Table A[21] to that Act did include certain clauses dealing with both matters. In 1879 provision was made for the audit of the accounts of banking companies, but it was not until 1900 that any such provision was made generally applicable. It was only on July 1, 1908, when the Companies Act 1907 came into force, that provision was made for including a statement in the form of a balance sheet in the annual return to the Registrar of Companies, and that provision exempted private companies from this requirement." The Companies Act 1929 required a balance sheet and a profit and loss account to be laid before the company every year, while the present Acts set out in great detail the contents of these accounts, with stringent provisions for their audit. The 1948 Act also for the first time required the auditor of a public or a private company to have a professional qualification.[22]

The present Acts are the Companies Act 1948, the Companies Act 1967, the Companies Act 1976, the Companies Act 1980 and the Companies Act 1981. The 1948 Act, Parts I and III of the 1967 Act, the Companies (Floating Charges and Receivers) (Scotland) Act 1972, section 9 of the European Communities Act 1972, sections 1 to 4 of the Stock Exchange (Completion of Bargains) Act 1976, section 9 of the Insolvency Act 1976, the Companies Act 1976, the Companies Act 1980, and the Companies Act 1981[23] are cited as the Companies Acts 1948 to 1981.[24] In Part I of the 1967 Act, the 1948 Act is referred to as "the principal Act."[25]

---

[19] s.462.   [20] (1945) Cmd. 6659, para. 96.

[21] A model set of articles of association.

[22] For a fuller treatment of the history of company law, see Gower, *Modern Company Law* (4th ed. 1979), Chaps. 2 and 3.

[23] Except for ss.28 and 29.   [24] 1981 Act, s.119.   [25] 1967 Act, s.1.

A number of the recommendations contained in the Jenkins Report[26] were given effect in the 1967 Act which amended the 1948 Act in a number of respects and came into operation on various dates between July 27, 1967, and July 27, 1968.[27] The status of exempt private company was abolished[28]—the definition of such a company in the 1948 Act was devised to save the small family business from disclosing its affairs to the public but many exempt private companies were not small either in membership or in capital or in the extent of their undertakings. There were important new provisions in connection with a company's acounts. For example, a subsidiary company's accounts were required to disclose the name of its ultimate holding company,[29] all accounts were required to give particulars of the directors' emoluments[30] and of the salaries of employees earning more than £10,000 a year[31] and the turnover for the year had to be stated.[32] Other important new provisions were: (1) The provisions in connection with the directors' report. For example, the principal activities of the company and its subsidiaries during the year were required to be stated.[33] The idea was to ensure that shareholders were kept more fully informed of the company's activities. (2) The provisions penalising the dealing by directors, their spouses or children, in certain options to buy or sell shares or debentures of the company or associated companies quoted on a stock exchange, and for securing the disclosure of certain material facts concerning directors.[34] (3) The provisions for securing the disclosure of a person's beneficial ownership of 10 per cent. or more of the shares in the company carrying unrestricted voting rights.[35] Part III of the 1967 Act gave the Department of Trade wide powers to compel companies to produce books and papers for inspection.[36] Many of these provisions have since been amended or replaced but the principles thereby established remain.

---

[26] (1962) Cmnd. 1749.
[27] 1967 Act, s.57.
[28] *Ibid.* s.2.
[29] *Ibid.* s.5.
[30] *Ibid.* s.6.
[31] *Ibid.* s.8.
[32] *Ibid.* s.9.
[33] *Ibid.* s.16.
[34] *Ibid.* ss. 25–32.
[35] *Ibid.* ss. 33 and 34.
[36] *Post,* pp. 429 *et seq.*

The Companies Act 1976 enacted the Companies (No. 2) Bill 1976 which itself reproduced a number of the clauses and schedules of the abortive Companies Bill 1973. The 1976 Act amended the law relating to the filing of company accounts and the keeping of accounting records. It provided for the disqualification of persons taking part in the management of companies if they were persistently in default in complying with the requirements to deliver documents to the Registrar. The Act also made new provision with respect to the qualifications, appointment, resignation and powers of auditors. It also required a statement of the first directors and secretary and of the intended situation of the registered office to be delivered to the Registrar on an application for registration of a company, and provided for the regulation of the names of oversea companies.

The Companies Act 1980 provided for the first time a major distinction between public and private companies, including minimum financial requirements for the former. It also contained new provisions relating to the issuing of shares and the payment for them. Payment of dividends became the subject of statutory rules. Tighter restrictions on directors were imposed following the many "unacceptable faces of capitalism" which manifested themselves in the 1970s. Insider dealing,[37] one of the most obvious of those, became a criminal offence. This Act was inspired by an EEC Directive of 1976 regulating the control of public companies.

The 1981 Companies Act was likewise prompted by an EEC Directive, this time of 1978, on company accounts. It provided a new format for accounts and for the public disclosure of them. In addition, however, new rules for company names, the purchase and redemption by a company of its own shares and for more stringent disclosure of shareholdings were included. Various other reforms were also appended.

Companies incorporated by registration under earlier Companies Acts are, of course, just as much subject to the provisions of the Companies Acts 1948 to 1981 as companies registered under the 1948 Act or the 1948 to 1981 Acts.[38]

Other relevant legislation includes section 9 of the European Communities Act 1972 which more or less gave effect to a recommendation

---

[37] See Chap. 21.
[38] 1948 Act, s.377; 1967 Act, s.53; 1976 Act, s.40; 1980 Act, s.83; 1981 Act, s.116.

of the Jenkins Committee[39] and brought United Kingdom company law into line with that of the EEC when, among other things, it modified the *ultra vires* doctrine.

The Companies (Floating Charges and Receivers) (Scotland) Act 1972 modified the law of Scotland in relation to floating charges and made provision for the appointment of receivers.

The Companies Bill 1973 attempted to give effect to other recommendations of the Jenkins Committee but lapsed on the dissolution of Parliament in February 1974 and many of the recommendations still have not been given effect to.

Part II of the Industry Act 1975 gives the Secretary of State power to prohibit transfers of control of important manufacturing undertakings to non-residents, and under Part IV manufacturing undertakings can be required to provide information about specified activities to the appropriate minister and, unless, *e.g.*, he decides that it would be contrary to the national interest or to statute, to trade unions recognised by the undertaking.

No attempt has been made to codify company law, *i.e.* to reduce to a code all the statute law and common law on the topic. Unlike Acts such as the Partnership Act 1890, the various Companies Acts generally have simply consolidated provisions previously in several other Acts. Consequently a significant part of company law is comprised of decided cases. Both the 1980 and 1981 Acts on the other hand contain many technical and complex provisions replacing case law decisions, often of long standing. This trend, from cases to statutes, is now firmly established and likely to continue in the future. The legislation, unlike case law, applies in general to both England and Scotland.

One final development has been the emergence of the Council for the Securities Industry, incorporating the City Panel on Take-overs and Mergers. These are self-regulating bodies operating codes without the force of law but of great significance in certain areas such as the acquisition of shares and take-overs in the public company sphere. These are mentioned, as appropriate, in the text.

TAXATION OF COMPANIES

Since 1965 companies have been subject to corporation tax on their profits and capital gains. The basic law is contained in the Income and

[39] Para. 42.

Corporation Taxes Act 1970 but significant amendments were made by the Finance Act 1972. Subsequent Finance Acts have also amended the law. In essence a company pays a flat rate of tax (currently 52 per cent.) on all its taxable profits, whether or not those profits are distributed to the shareholders. There is a reduced rate for small companies.

No attempt is made in this book to provide a comprehensive guide to tax law; instead, where tax considerations may affect the operation of company law an appropriate reference is made to *Pinson on Revenue Law* (15th Edition).

Proposals and Influences on Reform of the Law Relating to Registered Companies

Remaining recommendations of Jenkins Committee 1962

Although a number of recommendations contained in the Report of the Jenkins Committee[40] were implemented in the Companies Acts of 1967, 1976, 1980 and 1981[41] there has been no overall implementation of the Report as a whole and the remaining recommendations have not yet been adopted, although the Companies Bill 1973 attempted to give effect to many of them. Some of them are referred to at the appropriate places in the text.

The Report of the Committee of Inquiry on Industrial Democracy[42]

Following pressures both from the EEC and within the U.K. the Government appointed a committee under the chairmanship of Lord Bullock to inquire into the possible forms of industrial democracy for incorporation into the U.K. company structure. The majority of its members were opposed to the introduction of a two-tier board of directors system (as found in W. Germany). That system separates the management board from the supervisory board, the latter responsible for supervising the former. Employees would have the right to membership of the supervisory board. Instead they recommended the retention of the present single board but with modifications in the case of large companies, *i.e.* the ultimate holding company of a group which

[40] (1962) Cmnd. 1749.
[41] *Ante*, p. 8.
[42] (1977) Cmnd. 6706.

in toto employs two thousand or more people in the U.K. or any
individual company which employs two thousand or more people in
the U.K., whether or not it is part of a group. Before a company is
required to accept employee representatives on its board, a secret
ballot of its employees should be held and the majority required should
be a simple majority representing at least one-third of the eligible
employees. Where the conditions for employee representation are
met, the company's board should be reconstituted so as to be composed of three elements—an equal number of employee and
shareholder representatives plus a third group of co-opted directors.
The additional directors should be co-opted with the agreement of a
majority of each of the employee representatives and the shareholder
representatives, be an uneven number greater than one and form less
than one-third of the total board (the formula would be $2x + y$, x
representing the number of employee representatives and also the
number of shareholder representatives and y representing the number
of co-opted directors, so there would be minority but equal representation of shareholders, and employees). The co-opted directors should
be composed of various elements, *e.g.* senior or middle managers in
the company or people from outside the company who are at present
non-executive directors. Lastly, directors should continue to be required to act in the best interests of the company but in doing so they
should take into account the interests of its employees as well as its
shareholders. This report met with a lukewarm response from both
employers and employees and so far nothing has been done to provide
a formal structure of employee participation in the management of
companies although several companies do have some provision. The
only legal advances have been the encouragement of employee
shareholding by tax incentives[43] and two, rather weak, provisions in
sections 46[44] and 74[45] of the 1980 Act. The Fifth EEC Directive, noted
below, will have to tackle this difficult problem.

Measures of the European Community

There are a number of measures of the European Community
aimed at the harmonisation of the company laws of the Member

[43] See Finance Act 1978, ss.53–61; Finance Act 1980, s.47 and Sched. 10.
[44] See p. 371.
[45] See p. 85.

States. The First Directive of the EEC Council of Ministers was given effect to in the United Kingdom by the European Communities Act 1972, s.9, which among other things, modified the *ultra vires* doctrine and is dealt with in a number of places in the text. The Second and Fourth Directives have been implemented by the 1980 and 1981 Companies Acts, but there are others in the pipeline, some in draft form, others awaiting implementation. Even without United Kingdom pressures these will ensure a continuation of company law reform for the duration of the United Kingdom's membership of the EEC.

The following are currently on the pending list:

Third Directive on Mergers; Fifth Directive on the Structure and Administration of Public Companies; Sixth Directive on International Mergers; Seventh Directive on Group Accounts; Eighth Directive on the Qualifications of Auditors; Directive on Prospectuses; Directive on Stock Exchanges; Directive on Groups.

Convention for the mutual recognition of companies, firms and legal persons.

Draft regulation on European groupings.

Draft regulation containing the statute for the European company.

Draft Directive on mutual recognition of accountancy qualifications.

Most of the above proposals will be found set out, together with an introductory explanation, in *European Company Law Texts* by Professor Clive M. Schmitthoff.

Other proposals

There have been other white and green papers on aspects of company law such as the incorporation of the small firm—*i.e.* a new form of very small company—and securities regulation. No major legislation is likely however before the proposed consolidation promised for about 1984.

PROCEDURE TO OBTAIN REGISTRATION OF A COMPANY

To obtain the registration of a company certain documents must be delivered to the appropriate Registrar of Companies and certain fees and stamp duties must be paid. If the registered office is to be situate in England or in Wales,[46] the appropriate registrar is the Registrar of

[46] See *post*, p. 68.

Companies for England,[47] and his address is now Companies Registration Office, Crown Way, Maindy, Cardiff, CF4 3UZ.[48] If the registered office is to be situate in Scotland[49] the appropriate registrar is the Registrar of Companies for Scotland[50] and his address is Companies Registration Office, 102 George Street, Edinburgh, EH2 3DJ.

Documents which must be delivered to the Registrar

The following documents must be delivered to the Registrar of Companies:

(1) A memorandum of association[51] stating, *inter alia,* the objects of the company and if, as is common, the company is a limited company with a share capital, the amount of share capital with which the company proposes to be registered and its division into shares of a fixed amount,[52] *e.g.* £10,000 divided into 10,000 shares of a nominal amount of £1 each. If the company is a public company this figure must be not less than the authorised minimum,[53] currently £50,000.[54]

(2) Usually, printed articles of association[55] providing for such matters as the transfer of shares in the company, the holding of general meetings, *i.e.* meetings of the members or shareholders, the directors' powers of management and the extent to which they can delegate their powers to a managing director, and dividends.

(3) If the memorandum states that the registered office is to be situated in Wales and the memorandum and articles are in Welsh, a certified translation in English.[56]

(4) A statement in the prescribed form of the names of the intended first director or directors, and first secretary or joint secre-

---

[47] s.12 of the 1948 Act as amended by Sched. 2 to he 1976 Act and s.3 of the 1980 Act.
[48] The main part of the Companies Registration Office is now in Cardiff. There are microfilm reading room facilities in London at Companies House, 55–71 City Road, London, EC1Y 1BB.
[49] See note 46 above.
[50] See note 47 above.
[51] s.12. The memorandum is dealt with in Chap. 3.
[52] s.2.
[53] 1980 Act, s.3.
[54] 1980 Act, s.85.
[55] ss.6, 9, 12. Articles are dealt with in Chap. 4.
[56] 1976 Act, s.30(6).

taries, and the particulars specified in section 200(2) and (3) respectively.[57] Such statement must be signed by or on behalf of the subscribers of the memorandum and must contain a consent to act signed by each of the persons named in it. Where the memorandum is delivered for registration by an agent for the subscribers, such statement must specify that fact and the name and address of that person.[58] The statement must also specify the intended situation of the company's registered office.[59]

(5) A statutory declaration, by a solicitor engaged in the formation of the company or by a person named as director or secretary of the company in the statement delivered under (4) *ante,* of compliance with the requirements of the Acts in respect of registration.[60]

(6) A statement of capital (Form PUC1), unless the company is to have no share capital.

Form PUC1 will bear Inland Revenue capital duty[61] if the subscription shares are being paid for by the subscribers on incorporation.

For the purpose of ensuring that documents delivered to the Registrar are of standard size, durable and easily legible, the Secretary of State for Trade may prescribe such requirements as he considers appropriate. If a document delivered to the Registrar does not, in his opinion, comply with such requirements, he may serve a notice on the person or persons by whom the document was required to be delivered, whereupon, for the purposes of any enactment which enables a penalty to be imposed in respect of an omission to deliver a document to the Registrar, the duty to deliver is not discharged but the person subject to the duty has 14 days after the date of service of the notice in which to discharge it.[62]

The Registrar may, if he thinks fit, accept, under any provision of the Companies Acts requiring a document to be delivered to him, any material other than a document which contains the information in question and is of a kind approved by him. Thus the Registrar has power to accept information on microfilm.[63]

[57] *Post*, pp. 336, 390.
[58] 1976 Act, s.21.
[59] *Ibid.* s.23(2).
[60] 1980 Act, s.3(5).
[61] p. 19.   [62] 1976 Act, s.35.   [63] *Ibid.* s.36.

The duty of the Registrar on receiving the above mentioned documents is to examine them to see whether the statutory requirements have been complied with, but in exercising his duty he has no power to hold a judicial inquiry on evidence.[64] Among the statutory requirements to be observed are:

(1) That the memorandum is signed by at least two persons, and, if the memorandum is accompanied by articles, that the articles are signed by the same persons.[65]
(2) That the company is being formed for a lawful purpose.[66]

If the company is being formed for a purpose prohibited by law, *e.g.* to act as auditor of companies,[67] or for the sale of tickets in a lottery illegal in the United Kingdom, such as the Irish Sweep,[68] the Registrar will decline to register it.

(3) That the other requirements of the Act, *e.g.* as to the contents of the memorandum and articles, are complied with.[69]
(4) That the proposed name is not one which is absolutely, or conditionally, prohibited.[70]
(5) That the memorandum and articles are in the statutory form.[71]

Any person may inspect a copy[72] of the documents or other material kept by the Registrar relative to individual companies on payment of a fee, and may require a copy or extract of them on payment of the current fee.[73]

Fees and stamp duties

Registration fees

Section 37 of the Companies Act 1976 empowers the Secretary of State, by regulations made by statutory instrument, to require pay-

---

[64] *R.* v. *Registrar of Companies, ex. p. Bowen* [1914] 3 K.B. 1161.
[65] ss.1(1), 3, 6, 9, *post*, pp. 56, 104.
[66] s.1(1).
[67] s.161, *post*, pp. 517, 518.
[68] *R.* v. *Registrar of Companies, ex p. More* [1931] 2 K.B. 197 (C.A.).
[69] ss.1(1), 2, 3, 6, 9; 1980 Act, s.3, *post*, pp. 55, 56, 103, 104.
[70] 1981 Act, s.22, *post*, p. 59.
[71] s.11, 1980 Act, s.2, *post*, p. 56.
[72] s.426, as amended by s.98 of the 1981 Act. See also 1981 Act, s.100.
[73] 1948 Act, ss.424(5), 426; 1976 Act, ss.36(3), 38(3), as amended by 1981 Act, s.99.

ment to the Registrar of such fees as may be specified in the regulations in respect of the performance by the Registrar of such functions under the Companies Acts as may be specified, including the receipt by him of any notice or other document which the Acts require to be given or delivered to him.

Stamp duties

(1) On the formation of a company with limited liability, capital duty at the rate of £1 per £100 or part thereof is charged on the greater of the nominal value of the shares issued or allotted on incorporation and the actual value of assets of any kind contributed less any liabilities which have been assumed or discharged by the company in consideration of the contribution.[74]

The duty is impressed on return of allotments Form PUC2 if the allotment is for cash or Form PUC3 if the allotment is for a consideration other than cash.

(2) Conveyance or transfer duty on the transfer of property attaches, *e.g.* when a company is formed to acquire an existing business.[75] An *agreement* in writing for the sale of property (even to a company which is made up of vendors of the property) is, under section 59 of the Stamp Act 1891, as amended, liable to such duty on the consideration for the property, except in so far as that property consists of land, goods and merchandise, ships, stocks, shares or marketable securities. (When any land is *conveyed,* duty will be payable.) This duty is now £2 per £100 except that there are reduced rates where the consideration does not exceed £30,000 and the instrument is certified.[76]

It is no longer necessary to stamp the memorandum and articles with a deed stamp.[77]

---

[74] Finance Act 1973, ss.47–49 and Sched. 19. This complies with EEC Directive 69/335.

[75] *Post,* p. 117.

[76] Finance Act 1974, s.49 and Sched. 11; *Pinson on Revenue Law* (15th ed., 1982), para. 32–01.

[77] Finance Act 1970, Sched. 7, para. 1; *Pinson op. cit.* para. 34–11.

CERTIFICATE OF INCORPORATION

On the registration of a company the Registrar gives a certificate, either authenticated by a seal prepared under section 424(5) of the 1948 Act or under his hand, that the company is incorporated, in the case of a limited company that it is limited and, if it is a public company, that the company is a public company: section 13(1) of the 1948 Act[78]; s.38(2) of the 1976 Act.[79] The certificate of incorporation, which may be described as the company's birth certificate, is in the following form for private companies[80]:

CERTIFICATE OF INCORPORATION

I HEREBY CERTIFY that   , Limited, is this day Incorporated under the Companies Act 1948, and that the Company is Limited.

Given under my hand at Cardiff this   day of   .

Section 9(3) of the European Communities Act 1972 requires the Registrar to publish in the *Gazette* notice of the issue of a certificate of incorporation.

Section 3(4) of the Companies Act 1980 provides that the certificate is conclusive evidence that all the requirements of the Acts in respect of registration and of matters precedent and incidental thereto have been complied with, and that the association is a company authorised to be registered and duly registered. If the certificate states that the company is a public company it is conclusive evidence that it is such a company.

It is thought that the subsection means that it cannot be argued that a company is not validly incorporated, *e.g.* because the memorandum of association was not subscribed by two persons except where a statutory provision as to substance invalidates the registration.[81] In *Cotman* v. *Brougham*[82] Lord Wrenbury criticised[83] "the pernicious practice of registering memoranda of association which, under the clause relating to objects,[84] contain paragraph after paragraph not specifying or

---

[78] Taken with s.3(3) of the 1980 Act.

[79] Until 1981 a seal was compulsory—s.99 of that Act allows for the simpler procedure.

[80] A public company would have a different name and the additional declaration that it is a public limited company.

[81] *Per* Megarry J. in *Gaiman* v. *National Association for Mental Health* [1971] Ch. 317, at p. 329.

[82] [1918] A.C. 514.

[83] At p. 523.

[84] *Post*, p. 71.

delimiting the proposed trade or purpose, but confusing power with purpose and indicating every class of act which the corporation is to have power to do." He went on to say: "Such a memorandum is not, I think, a compliance with the Act" but that if the Registrar registers the memorandum the court "must assume that all requirements in respect of matters precedent and incidental to registration have been complied with and confine [itself] to the construction of the document." The certificate of incorporation has been held to be conclusive as to the date of incorporation.[85]

The reason for section 3(4) of the 1980 Act is that once a company is registered and has begun business and entered into contracts it would be disastrous if any person could allege that the company was not duly registered.[86]

The certificate will not be conclusive if a trade union should be registered as a company[87]—the registration of a trade union under the Companies Acts is void by statute.[88] Again, the certificate is not conclusive as to the legality of a company's objects—proceedings may be brought to have the registration cancelled where objects are illegal.[89]

The Registrar will allocate to each registered company a registered number, which must be disclosed on all its business letters and order forms.[90]

EFFECT OF REGISTRATION OF A COMPANY

From the date of incorporation mentioned in the certificate of incorporation, the subscribers of the memorandum, together with such other persons as may from time to time become members of the company, form a body corporate by the name contained in the memorandum, capable forthwith of exercising all the functions of an incor-

---

[85] *Jubilee Cotton Mills Ltd.* v. *Lewis* [1924] A.C. 958, where it was also held that "From the date of incorporation" in s.[13(2)] included any portion of the day on which the company was incorporated.

[86] *Per* Lord Cairns in *Peel's Case* (1867) L.R. 2 Ch.App. 674, at p. 682.

[87] *British Association of Glass Bottle Manufacturers Ltd.* v. *Nettlefold* (1911) 27 T.L.R. 527.

[88] Trade Union Act 1871, s.5; Companies Act 1948, s.459(9).

[89] *Per* Lord Parker of Waddington in *Bowman* v. *Secular Society Ltd.* [1917] A.C. 406, at p. 439.

[90] 1981 Act, s.97; E.C.A. 1972, s.9(7)(*a*).

porated company, but with such liability on the part of the members to contribute to the assets of the company as is mentioned in the Act: section 13(2).

The registered company is a body corporate, *i.e.* a legal person separate and distinct from its members.

S. had for many years carried on business as a boot manufacturer. His business was solvent when it was converted into a company, *i.e.* a company limited by shares was formed, the subscribers to the memorandum of which were S. and his wife, daughter and four sons (for one share each), and the business was sold to the company at a price of £39,000. The terms of sale were approved by all the shareholders. £9,000 was paid in cash. 20,000 fully paid shares of £1 each were allotted to S. so that S.'s wife and children held one share each and S. held 20,001 shares. S. left the rest of the price on loan to the company and for this sum of £10,000 he was given debentures secured by a charge on the company's assets. It seems that the directors were S. and his sons and that S. was appointed managing director. After a depression the company went into liquidation. The assets were sufficient to satisfy the debentures, but the unsecured creditors, with debts amounting to £7,000, received nothing. *Held,* that the proceedings were not contrary to the true intent and meaning of the Companies Act; that the company was duly registered and was not a mere "alias" or agent of or trustee for the vendor; that he was not liable to indemnify the company against creditors' claims; that there was no fraud upon creditors (or shareholders); that the company (or the liquidator) was not entitled to rescission of the contract of purchase: *Salomon* v. *Salomon & Co. Ltd.* [1897] A.C. 22.[91]

"The company is at law a different person altogether from the subscribers to the memorandum; and, though it may be that after incorporation the business is precisely the same as it was before, and the same persons are managers, and the same hands receive the profits, the company is not in law the agent of the subscribers or trustee for them. Nor are the subscribers as members liable, in any shape or form, except to the extent and in the manner provided by the Act": *per* Lord Macnaghten at p. 51.

One effect is that the property of the company belongs to the company itself and not to the individual members, so that even the largest shareholder has no insurable interest in the property of the company.[92] The managing director, even if he owns all the shares except one, cannot lawfully pay cheques to the company into his own

---

[91] Although *Salomon's* case is now generally accepted in Scots law, the Scottish courts were, about the same time and independently of that authority, giving effect to the same principle, *e.g. Henderson* v. *Stubbs' Ltd.* (1894) 22 R. 51, *Grierson, Oldham & Co. Ltd.* v. *Forbes, Maxwell & Co. Ltd.* (1895) 22 R. 812 and *John Wilson & Son Ltd.* v. *Inland Revenue* (1895) 23 R. 18.

[92] *Macaura* v. *Northern Assurance Co. Ltd.* [1925] A.C. 619.

banking acount or draw cheques for his own purposes upon the company's banking account.[93] It also means that the company's debts are the obligations of the company alone and normally cannot be enforced against the members, however many shares they may own.[94]

This principle of the independent corporate existence of a registered company is of the greatest importance in company law. As we shall see, it is this which mainly distinguishes a registered company from a partnership, which is the relation which subsists between persons carrying on a business in common with a view of profit. A partnership is not a corporation but, at least in the case of an English partnership,[95] is only the aggregate of the partners, *i.e.* a partnership has no legal existence but is merely the association of two or more persons carrying on business together. The property of the firm belongs to the partners and the firm's debts are the debts of the partners, *i.e.* the partners are personally liable for the firm's debts, whereas in a registered company the assets and liabilities are those of the company and not of the members.

A registered company is capable forthwith of exercising all the functions of an incorporated company, *e.g.* it can hold land and other property, and it can sue and be sued. If the company is a public company it cannot commence business until the requirements of section 4 of the 1980 Act have been complied with.[96]

The liability of a member of a company limited by shares to contribute to the company's assets (for the purpose of enabling its debts to be paid) is limited to the amount, if any, unpaid on his shares.[97] Thus if he has taken one thousand shares of £1 each in the company and the shares are fully paid up he is normally under no further liability to contribute to the assets. In the case of a partnership every partner is jointly liable with the other partners for all the firm's debts.[98]

---

[93] *A. L. Underwood Ltd.* v. *Bank of Liverpool & Martins Ltd.* [1924] 1 K.B. 775 (C.A.); *cf. Thompson* v. *J. Barke and Company (Caterers) Ltd.*, 1975 S.L.T. 67 (O.H.) (Company's cheques used to repay loan made to director held *ultra vires*).

[94] *Post*, p. 24. Two related companies are separate entities: *Taylor, Petitioner*, 1976 S.L.T. (Sh.Ct.) 82.

[95] A Scottish partnership or firm has a separate legal existence and is not merely the association of two or more persons. The property of the firm belongs to the firm, and the firm's debts are primarily those of the firm, although each partner may ultimately be made personally liable for the firm's debts.

[96] *Post*, p. 183.   [97] s.1(2).

[98] Further differences between registered companies and partnerships are dealt with later in this chapter.

The veil of incorporation

It was established in *Salomon* v. *Salomon & Co. Ltd.*, *ante*, that a registered company is a legal person separate from its members. This principle may be referred to as "the veil of incorporation." In general, the law will not go behind the separate personality of the company to the members, so that, *e.g.* in *Macaura* v. *Northern Assurance Co. Ltd.*, *ante*, it was held that the largest shareholder had no insurable interest in the property of the company. However, there are exceptions to the principle in *Salomon's* case where the veil is lifted and the law disregards the corporate entity and pays regard instead to the economic realities behind the legal façade. In these exceptional cases "the law either goes behind the corporate personality to the individual members, or ignores the separate personality of each company in favour of the economic entity constituted by a group of associated companies."[99]

Instances of the veil being lifted may be classified into those expressly provided by statute and those under judicial interpretation.[1]

One example of a case where "the veil is lifted" by statute is where a company carries on business for more than six months with less than the statutory minimum of members (two), in which event every person who is a member during any part of the time that business is so carried on after the end of the six-month period and who knows that business is being so carried on, is jointly and severally liable for all the company's debts contracted during such time and may be severally sued therefor (s.31, intended to ensure that the number of members does not fall below the statutory minimum). This is exceptional because the general rule is that the company's debts cannot be enforced against the members.

Another example occurs in section 154[2] where the way in which a company's shares are held is relevant in determining whether it is a subsidiary of another company. Thus if more than half of the ordinary shares of a company are held by another company the first will normally be a subsidiary of the second.

Again, where an officer of a company signs, on behalf of the

---

[99] Gower, *Modern Company Law*, 4th ed., 1979, p. 112.

[1] See also Ruthven, *Lifting the Veil of Incorporation in Scotland*, 1969 Juridical Review, p. 1.

[2] *Post*, p. 52.

company, a bill of exchange, promissory note, cheque or order for money or goods in which the company's name is not mentioned, the officer is personally liable to the holder of the bill of exchange, etc., for the amount thereof unless it is paid by the company (s.108(4)).[3]

At common law, a company registered in England is an alien enemy if its agents or the persons in *de facto* control of its affairs are alien enemies, and in determining whether alien enemies have such control, the number of alien enemy shareholders and the value of their holdings are material.[4]

Another example is that in cases such as *Re Express Engineering Works Ltd.*[5] and the other cases dealt with on pages 306, 307, the decision of all the shareholders was held to be the decision of the company, *e.g.* something less formal than a resolution, even a special resolution, duly passed at a general meeting was regarded as the act of the company.

It was held in *Re Bugle Press Ltd.*[6] that if A Ltd. makes an offer for the shares in B Ltd. and in substance A Ltd. is the same as the majority shareholding in B Ltd., A Ltd. will not be able to invoke section 209[7] and compel the minority shareholders in B Ltd. to sell their shares to A Ltd. In these circumstances the law goes behind the corporate personality of A Ltd. to the individual members. The court will not allow the section to be invoked for an improper purpose.

Lord Denning M.R. was prepared to lift the veil in *Wallersteiner* v. *Moir*[8]—he said that in that case the plaintiff was also in breach of what is now section 49 of the 1980 Act (which in general prohibits a company making a loan to a director) because the company of which he was a director made a loan to another company which was his puppet, so that the loan should be treated as made to him.

The case of *Gilford Motor Co. Ltd.* v. *Horne*[9] shows that the courts will not allow a company to be used as a device to mask the carrying on of a business by a former employee of another person and to enable the former employee to break a valid covenant in restraint of trade con-

[3] *Post*, p. 63.
[4] *Daimler Co. Ltd.* v. *Continental Tyre, etc., Ltd.* [1916] 2 A.C. 307.
[5] [1920] 1 Ch. 466 (C.A.), *post*, p. 306.
[6] [1961] Ch. 270 (C.A.), *post*, p. 728.
[7] *Post*, p. 726.
[8] [1974] 1 W.L.R. 991 (C.A.).
[9] [1933] Ch. 935 (C.A.).

tained in the contract under which he was formerly employed. In that case the employee covenanted that after the termination of the employment he would not solicit his employer's customers. Soon after the termination of his employment he formed a company of which the two directors and shareholders were his wife and one other person and which sent out circulars to customers of his former employer. An injunction was granted against the ex-employee and the company. The *Gilford* case was followed in *Jones* v. *Lipman*[10] where, having agreed to sell land to the plaintiff, the defendant sold and transferred the land to a company controlled by him. It was held that the company was the creature of the defendant, a mask to avoid recognition by the eye of equity, and therefore specific performance could not be resisted by the defendant. Specific performance was also granted against the company.

Although in *Salomon's* case, *ante*, it was held that the company was not a mere agent for Salomon, in *Smith, Stone & Knight Ltd.* v. *Birmingham Corporation*[11] a subsidiary company which was carrying on the parent company's business was held to be the agent of the parent shareholder. Conversely, in *Wm. Cory & Son Ltd.* v. *Dorman Long & Co. Ltd.*[12] the parent company was held to be the agent of the subsidiary. In two recent cases the question has arisen whether a subsidiary could be regarded as a single entity with its parent company in order to enable the group to claim compensation for disturbance on a compulsory purchase. In *D.H.N. Food Distributors Ltd.* v. *Tower Hamlets London Borough Council*[13] the Court of Appeal in England allowed the claim on the basis that D.H.N. was in a position to control its subsidiaries in every respect. The House of Lords in the Scottish case of *Woolfson* v. *Strathclyde Regional Council*[14] distinguished the *D.H.N.* case on its facts but also doubted whether it was a correct application of the general principle that the veil should only be pierced where special circumstances exist indicating that it is a mere façade concealing the true facts.

The veil is lifted whenever the Act recognises the relationship of holding company and subsidiary.[15] An example is that, except in

---

[10] [1962] 1 W.L.R. 832.
[11] [1939] 4 All E.R. 116.
[12] [1936] 2 All E.R. 386 (C.A.).
[13] [1976] 1 W.L.R. 852 (C.A.).
[14] 1978 S.C. (H.L.) 90; 1977 S.C. 84.   [15] *Post*, p. 52.

certain specified cases, group accounts must be laid before the holding company in general meeting (s.150).[16] The power of an inspector of a company, under sections 166 and 172,[17] to investigate a related company, is also an example of the veil being lifted.

Other instances of the lifting of the veil of incorporation will be found in the field of taxation, *e.g.* the residence of a company, which is relevant in the ascertainment of the company's liability to U.K. corporation tax,[18] is determined by the location of the central management and control of the company. Another instance occurs when a close company makes inadequate distributions: "relevant income" is apportioned among the shareholders under the Finance Act 1972, s.94 and Sched. 16.[19]

If, in the event of fraudulent trading, an order is made under section 332[20] that parties thereto be personally responsible without limitation of liability for the company's debts, this is better regarded simply as a case where the privilege of limited liability is lost than one where the veil is lifted—creditors of the company have no direct right against those against whom an order is made.[21]

MANAGEMENT OF REGISTERED COMPANIES

We have seen that registered companies, although legal persons, are artificial persons and must act by human agents, the directors and other officers empowered by the articles to act on the company's behalf. In the case of a private company the shareholders and directors are usually the same persons but that is not so in the case of a public company, where the directors may have few shares in the company,[22] so that management is divorced from ownership of the company. This is important because, as is explained later,[23] under an article like Table

---

[16] *Post*, p. 494.

[17] *Post*, pp. 421, 425.

[18] See *Inland Revenue* v. *Lithgows Ltd.*, 1960 S.C. 405—two companies controlled by two different trusts were held not to be controlled by the same person, although one individual, the first named trustee in each trust, was entitled to cast the trustees' votes in each company.

[19] *Pinson, op. cit.*, paras. 15–28 *et seq*.

[20] *Post*, p. 643.

[21] Palmer's *Company Law*, 23rd ed., p. 201.

[22] *Post*, p. 334.

[23] *Post*, p. 350.

A, article 80, *infra*, the company in general meeting, *i.e.* the members or shareholders in general meeting, cannot control the exercise of the directors' powers.

Directors' powers are contained in the articles, *e.g.* Table A, article 80, states that the business of the company shall be managed by the directors who may exercise all the powers of the company except those which are, by the Act or the articles, required to be exercised by the company in general meeting. Thus when section 10[24] provides that a company may alter its articles by special resolution the alteration is required to be effected by the company in general meeting and cannot be effected by the directors.

Directors cannot delegate their powers except so far as the articles allow but, *e.g.* Table A, article 107, empowers the directors to appoint a managing director and article 109 empowers them to delegate any of their powers to him.

It should also be remembered that the directors must exercise their powers for the purposes for which they were granted and bona fide for the benefit of the company as a whole, *i.e.* the members as a body.[25]

A REGISTERED COMPANY'S SECURITIES

Two ways in which a registered company with a share capital may raise money to carry on its business are (1) by issuing shares, (2) by borrowing, *e.g.* of debentures or debenture stock.[26]

Shares

Preference shares and ordinary shares

A registered company's shares may be divided into different classes with different rights, *e.g.* preference shares[27] and ordinary shares. Preference shares give the holders priority in the payment of a dividend at a fixed rate, *e.g.* if a company with ordinary shares and 10 per cent. preference shares distributes profits, the preference shareholders are entitled to a dividend of 10 per cent. before the ordinary shareholders

[24] *Post*, p. 108.
[25] *Post*, p. 367.
[26] A company may borrow without issuing debentures or creating debenture stock.
[27] *Post*, p. 210.

receive anything. Another difference between ordinary shares and preference shares is that the former usually confer a right of voting at general meetings whereas the latter often deny a right to vote except in certain events.[28] It should be noted that for tax purposes a company may not deduct dividends paid to shareholders from its taxable profits.

Shares and stock

Paid-up shares may be converted into stock under section 61,[29] although there is no advantage in adopting such a course today. The procedure laid down in the section must be followed. It will be seen that the section provides that in the case of a limited company with a share capital, where there is authority in the articles, paid-up shares may be converted into stock by the company in general meeting, *i.e.* by an ordinary resolution which usually requires a bare majority of the votes of the members entitled to vote at a general meeting of which due notice has been given.[30] For example, a company which has 10,000 paid-up £1 shares may convert them into ten thousand pounds worth of stock. If shares are converted into stock the value of the holder's stake in the company remains the same although it is expressed in different terms, *e.g.* a person who formerly held 100 shares of a nominal amount of £1 each (market value £1·50 each) will now hold a nominal amount of one hundred pounds worth of stock (market value £150) and, in the case of ordinary stock, he will normally have a full right of voting at general meetings. Further, if profits are made, he may receive dividends. In the Acts "share" usually includes stock: 1948 Act, s.455; 1967 Act, s.56; 1976 Act, s.44; 1980 Act, s.87; 1981 Act, s.118.

Certificates and warrants

A shareholder is usually issued with a *share certificate*[31] in which case, subject to any restrictions contained in the articles, he may transfer the shares, *e.g.* by executing an instrument of transfer which is registered by the company.[32] Similarly, a stockholder is usually issued

---

[28] *Post*, p. 214.
[29] *Post*, p. 224.
[30] *Post*, p. 322.
[31] *Post*, p. 261.
[32] *Post*, p. 271.

with a *stock certificate,* in which case the stock can be transferred in the same way.

Occasionally, a shareholder may be issued with a *share warrant,* [33] in which case the shares may be transferred by simple delivery of the warrant to the transferee. Similarly, a stockholder may be issued with a *stock warrant,* in which case the stock is transferable by delivery of the warrant to the transferee.

Debentures

Debentures and debenture stock

A company limited by shares usually has power to borrow money and to give security for the loan.[34] Lenders may be issued with debentures to show that they have lent money to the company, in which event each debenture evidences a distinct debt, *e.g.* for £100. The debentures may give the debenture holders a mortgage[35] or charge on the company's property to secure the loan, in which case, if the company should fail to repay the loan, the debenture holders will have the usual remedies of a mortgagee[35] against the property. There may be a trust deed—as will be seen, there are advantages in having a trust deed.[36]

Debenture stock[37] is borrowed money consolidated into one mass for the sake of convenience. This is done by a trust deed which acknowledges one debt of the amount advanced by the lenders and owing from the company to the trustees. The deed may give the trustees a charge on the company's property as security. Each lender will be given a simple debenture stock certificate evidencing his share of the debt. In the Acts, "debenture" includes debenture stock: 1948 Act, s.455.

Thus a person who lends £100 to a company may be a debenture holder with a debenture for £100 or a debenture stockholder with a debenture stock certificate for one hundred pounds worth of debenture stock. In either event, unlike a shareholder, he is not a member of

[33] *Post,* p. 299.
[34] *Post,* p. 84.
[35] In Scots law the terms "security" and "security-holder" should be substituted for "mortgage" and "mortgagee" respectively.
[36] *Post,* p. 551.
[37] *Post,* p. 549.

the company and has no right to attend and vote at general meetings of the company. He is a creditor of the company and is entitled to interest at the specified rate on his loan. Unlike a dividend, interest paid on a debenture is a charge on income and so deductible from a company's taxable profits for corporation tax purposes.

Registered debentures and bearer debentures

A debenture is usually a registered debenture,[38] in which case the debt may be transferred by an instrument of transfer which is registered by the company. If a debenture is a bearer debenture[39] the debt may be transferred by delivery of the debenture to the transferee.

Debenture stock certificates and debenture stock warrants

If, as is usual, a debenture stock certificate is issued to a debenture stockholder, the debenture stock may be transferred by an instrument of transfer which is registered by the company. If he is issued with a debenture stock warrant the debenture stock may be transferred by delivery of the warrant.

REGISTERED COMPANIES AND PARTNERSHIPS CONTRASTED

Advantages of a registered company

A registered company has many advantages over a partnership, which is defined in the Partnership Act 1890[40] as the relationship which subsists between persons carrying on a business in common with a view of profit, and which is not, *e.g.* the relation between members of a company registered under the Companies Acts or incorporated by or in pursuance of any other Act of Parliament or Royal Charter. A registered company has the same advantages over an individual trader. These advantages include the following:

(1) A registered company is a corporation,[41] *i.e.* a separate legal person distinct from the members, whereas an English partnership is merely the aggregate of the partners (although a Scottish

---

[38] *Post,* p. 554.

[39] *Post,* p. 558.

[40] s.1. See generally on partnerships Burgess and Morse, *Partnership Law in England and Scotland* (Sweet & Maxwell, 1980).

[41] s.13(2); *Salomon* v. *Salomon & Co. Ltd.* [1897] A.C. 22, *ante,* p. 22.

partnership has one of the attributes of a corporation in that it is "a legal person distinct from the partners of whom it is composed").[42] Consequently:

(*a*) The debts and contracts of a registered company are those of the company and not those of the members, whereas in the case of an English firm every partner is jointly liable with the other partners for all the firm's debts and obligations incurred while he is a partner.[43] (In Scotland the firm's debts are those of the firm but, if the firm fails to pay, each individual partner may be made liable. Further, there is several as well as joint liability. Again, the firm's contracts are those of the firm but the individual partners may be made liable for them.)

(*b*) Unless it is wound up a registered company continues in existence[44] so that it is not affected by the death, bankruptcy, mental disorder or retirement of any of its members. For example, when a shareholder dies or retires the company is not dissolved and no drain is made on its resources or, usually, on the resources of its other members. In the case of a partnership, on the other hand, on the death or bankruptcy of a partner, subject to any agreement between the partners the partnership is dissolved as regards all the partners.[45] In practice the share of a partner who dies or retires has to be found out of the business or provided by the other partners, and this may cause serious financial embarrassment to the firm.

(*c*) The property of a registered company belongs to and is vested in the company, so that there is no change in the ownership of, or in the formal title to, the property on a change in the ownership of shares in the company. In an English partnership, the property belongs to the partners and is vested in them. In the case of land, it is vested in the partners or, where they exceed four in number, in up to four of them on trust for all.[46] Consequently there are changes in the ownership of, and

---

[42] Partnership Act 1890, s.4(2).

[43] *Ibid.* s.9.

[44] See *ante*, p. 21.

[45] Partnership Act 1890, s.33(1). As to dissolution by the court in the event of the mental disorder of a partner, see 1890 Act, s.35, and Mental Health Act 1959, s.103 (the latter not applicable to Scotland). As to dissolution by notice by a retiring partner, see 1890 Act, s.32.

[46] See Law of Property Act 1925, s.34; Trustee Act 1925, s.34.

in the formal title to, the firm's property from time to time on the death or retirement of a partner or trustee. (In a Scottish partnership, while the partnership property belongs to the firm as a separate *persona,* the formal title to that property may be, and in the case of heritable property must be, in the names of the partners or of other persons in trust for the firm.)

(*d*) A registered company can contract with its members and can sue and be sued on such contracts. In England a partner cannot contract with the firm. (In Scotland, by virtue of the firm's separate personality, a partner can contract with the firm and can sue and be sued on such contracts.)

(*e*) Each partner is normally an agent for the firm for the purpose of the business of the partnership[47] and, subject to any agreement to the contrary between the parties, may take part in the management of the partnership business.[48] The members of a registered company as such are not its agents and have no power to manage its affairs—the directors are agents, *i.e.* they have the powers given to them by the articles.[49]

(*f*) Subject to any restrictions in the articles, which there may be in the articles of a private company,[50] shares in a registered company can be transferred or mortgaged[51] without the consent of the other shareholders. Subject to any agreement to the contrary, a person cannot be introduced as a partner without the consent of all the existing partners[52] and if in England a partner charges his share of the partnership for his separate debt the other partners normally have the option to dissolve the partnership.[53]

(*g*) For tax purposes a partnership's profits are the profits of the partners and are apportioned between them. Thus income tax on a graduated scale is applicable. A company pays a flat rate on its profits, although with small companies, known as *close* companies, profits retained in the company may be apportioned to the members for income tax purposes.

[47] Partnership Act 1890, s.5.
[48] *Ibid.* s.24(5).
[49] *Ante,* p. 28.
[50] Following the 1980 Act these are no longer compulsory for private companies.
[51] In Scots law "transferred in security."
[52] Partnership Act 1890, s.24(7).
[53] *Ibid.* s.33(2) (not applicable to Scotland: see s.23(5)).

(2) The liability of a member of a registered company to contribute to its assets may be, and usually is, limited, *e.g.* limited, in the case of a company limited by shares, to the amount unpaid on his shares[54] (although the person controlling a private company may have to give a personal guarantee of the company's bank overdraft) but the members of a partnership are jointly (and in Scotland severally also) liable for all the debts of the firm.[55] This advantage can be secured in a partnership by a person's being a limited partner in a limited partnership formed under the Limited Partnerships Act 1907, but few such partnerships have been formed, owing to the superior advantages of the limited company.

(3) There is no limit to the number of members of a company, but, except in the case of, *e.g.*, certain partnerships of practising professional men such as solicitors, accountants within section 161(1)(*a*) or (*b*),[56] stockbrokers who are members of a recognised stock exchange,[57] certain patent agents, surveyors, auctioneers and estate agents, building designers, actuaries and consulting engineers, a partnership with more than 20 members for the purpose of carrying on any business which has for its object the acquisition of gain is prohibited.[58] As the Jenkins Report[59] said, the purpose of the prohibition is to protect the public from the hazards of dealing with large and fluctuating partnerships. The original restriction to 20 members[60] caused difficulty for large professional firms which cannot by law or professional practice be incorporated, and since the partners in such firms belong to professional organisations which exercise effective control over their members it was not necessary for the protection of the public to maintain the restrictions in their case. One result of the limit on the number of partners is that it

---

[54] s.1.

[55] Partnership Act 1890, s.9, *ante.*

[56] *Post*, p. 517.

[57] *i.e.* recognised for the purposes of the Prevention of Fraud (Investments) Act 1958.

[58] Companies Act 1948, s.434; Companies Act 1967, s.120; Partnerships (Unrestricted Size) Regulations: No. 1: S.I. 1968 No. 1222; No. 2: S.I. 1970 No. 835; No. 3: S.I. 1970 No. 992; No. 4: S.I. 1970 No. 1319.

[59] Paras. 76, 77.

[60] In s.434.

is generally impossible for a partnership to raise large sums of capital.

(4) A registered company has greater facilities for borrowing than a partnership, *e.g.* the company may borrow on debentures.[61]

(5) Floating charges can be created by a registered company but not by a partnership.[62]

Advantages of a partnership

A partnership or an individual trader has certain advantages over a registered company (although these are normally outweighed by the advantages of the latter over the former):

(1) There are fewer formalities to be observed, and therefore there is less publicity and less expense involved in forming a partnership, *e.g.* there is no need to be registered, or to file a memorandum and articles, with the Registrar, and therefore there are no registration fees, and stamp duty and legal costs are less. A partnership agreement may be oral or even inferred from conduct.

(2) There are fewer formalities and therefore less publicity and less expense in running a partnership, *e.g.* returns do not have to be delivered to a Registrar.

(3) A partnership's accounts are never open to public inspection. Except in the case of certain unlimited[63] and small companies,[64] those of a registered company are, as are the other documents which any registered company must lodge with the Registrar.[65]

(4) The *ultra vires* doctrine,[66] by which a registered company can only do the things authorised by its memorandum, does not apply to a partnership, which can do anything lawful that all the partners agree to do.

---

[61] *Ante*, p. 30.
[62] *Post*, p. 564.
[63] *Post*, p. 40.
[64] *Post*, p. 50.
[65] s.426.
[66] *Post*, p. 73.

(5) A partnership is not subject to the rules in connection with raising and maintenance of share capital, to which a registered company which is not an unlimited company is subject.[67]

(6) A partnership can make any arrangement with creditors that the partners think fit. A registered company can make only those authorised by the Act.[68]

---

[67] *Post*, pp. 222, 227.
[68] ss.206, 245, 303, 306.

Chapter 2

CLASSIFICATION OF REGISTERED COMPANIES

This chapter deals with the three main classifications of registered companies. The first classifies registered companies as being limited by shares, limited by guarantee or unlimited. The second classifies them as being either public companies or private companies. (Any limited company with a share capital may be either a public or a private company.) The third classifies private companies into small, medium-sized and large companies, a new classification relevant to the public disclosure of accounts. Finally something is said of holding companies and subsidiary companies.

Companies Limited by Shares, Companies Limited by Guarantee and Unlimited Companies

A registered company may be—

(1) a company limited by shares, in which case the liability of a member to contribute to the company's assets is limited to the amount, if any, unpaid on his shares; or

(2) a company limited by guarantee, in which case the liability of a member is limited to the amount which he has undertaken to contribute *in the event of its being wound up*; or

(3) an unlimited company, in which case the liability of a member is unlimited: section 1(2).

The vast majority of registered companies are companies limited by shares. Such companies must have a share capital, whereas unlimited companies may or may not have a share capital. Companies limited by guarantee may no longer be formed with a share capital and are often supported by subscriptions or fees paid by the members: 1980 Act, s.1(2).

Companies limited by guarantee

A company limited by guarantee is a registered company, public or private, in which the liability of members is limited to such amount as they respectively undertake to contribute to the assets of the company in the event of its being wound up: section 1. The members are not required to contribute whilst the company is a going concern. The memorandum of a company limited by guarantee, in addition to containing the clauses normally contained in a memorandum,[1] must state that each member undertakes to contribute to the assets of the company in the event of its being wound up while he is a member, or within one year after he ceases to be a member, for payment of its debts contracted before he ceases to be a member, and of the costs of winding up, and for adjustment of the rights of the contributories, such sum as may be required, not exceeding a specified amount: section 2(3). The sum specified in Table C, *post,* is £10. Whatever the amount of the guarantee specified in the memorandum, it cannot be increased or reduced.

The amounts which the members have agreed to contribute in a winding up cannot be mortgaged or charged by the company whilst it is a going concern.[2] They are not assets of the company whilst it is a going concern.

Prior to the 1980 Act a company limited by guarantee could be formed either with or without a share capital, but was usually formed without a share capital, in which event money to acquire such things as premises had to be raised by loans from the members. Since the 1980 Act no such company can be formed with, or acquire, a share capital: 1980 Act, s.1(2). For this purpose any provision in the memorandum or articles, or in any resolution, purporting to divide the undertaking of the company into shares or interests is treated as a provision for share capital even though the nominal amount or number of the shares or interests are not specified: 1980 Act, s.1(3).[3] The majority of companies limited by guarantee are formed to incorporate professional, trade and research associations, or clubs supported by annual subscriptions. Many will be able to take advantage of section 25 of the 1981 Act[4] and omit the word "Limited" from their names.

Every company limited by guarantee is obliged to register articles of association with the memorandum: section 6. If the company has no

---

[1] *Post,* p. 55.

[2] *Re Irish Club* [1906] W.N. 127; *Robertson* v. *British Linen Co.* (1890) 18 R. 1225 (O.H.), *approved obiter* in *Lloyds Bank Ltd.* v. *Morrison & Son*, 1927 S.C. 571.

[3] This prohibition was recommended in 1962 by the Jenkins Committee, para. 78.

[4] *Post,* p. 62.

share capital, the memorandum and articles must be in the form set out in Table C, or as near thereto as circumstances admit: section 11. Table C is a model form of memorandum and articles for such a company and is set out in the First Schedule to the Act.

An article of a company limited by guarantee with no share capital is not invalid just because it is not contained in Table C. Section 11 is concerned with the form of the articles of such a company and the word "form" here does not embrace contents. Provided that the draftsman of such articles follows the general form of Table C he is free to add, subtract or vary as the needs of the case suggest.[5]

The articles of a company limited by guarantee must state the number of members with which the company proposes to be registered: section 7. This is to give persons dealing with the company some idea of the value of the guaranteee.

Table C, article 2, provides: "The number of members with which the company proposes to be registered is 500, but the directors may from time to time register an increase of members."

Notice of any increase beyond the registered number must be given to the Registrar within 15 days: section 7.

Section 37 of the Companies Act 1976 empowers the Secretary of State to prescribe the fees to be paid to the Registrar upon the registration of a company limited by guarantee.

Every provision in the memorandum or articles of a company limited by guarantee and not having a share capital, or in any resolution of the company, purporting to give any person a right to participate in the divisible profits of the company otherwise than as a member is void, and every provision in the memorandum or articles, or in any resolution, purporting to divide the undertaking of the company into shares or interests is treated as a provision for share capital notwithstanding that the nominal amount or number of the shares or interests is not specified: section 21. The object of this section is to prevent the registration of companies with shares of no par value.[6]

Because of the strict régime applied to public companies few companies limited by guarantee can exist as such companies. In practice they will be private companies.[7]

---

[5] *Gaiman* v. *National Association for Mental Health* [1971] Ch. 317.
[6] Companies of the kind involved in *Malleson* v. *General Mineral Patents Syndicate Ltd.* [1894] 3 Ch. 538.
[7] *Post*, p. 45.

If a company limited by guarantee has a share capital it must make the annual return required by section 124.[8] If it has no share capital, it must make an annual return stating:

(1) The address of the registered office.
(2) If the register of members is not kept at the registered office, the address of the place where it is kept.
(3) If the register of debenture holders is not kept at the registered office, the address of the place where it is kept.
(4) The particulars of the directors and the secretary which are required to be contained in the register of directors and secretaries.[9]

Particulars of the total amount of the company's indebtedness in respect of all mortgages and charges required to be registered with the Registrar[10] must be annexed: section 125.

If the company has no share capital, an extraordinary general meeting of the company can be requisitioned by the members having at least one-tenth of the voting rights. If the company has a share capital, members holding at least one-tenth of the paid-up capital carrying the right to vote can requisition a meeting: section 132.

Apart from what has been said in this chapter, most of what is said elsewhere in this work applies to companies limited by guarantee as it does to companies limited by shares.

Unlimited companies

A company may be registered as an unlimited company, in which case there is no limit on the members' liability to contribute to the assets: section 1. In the years immediately preceding 1967 comparatively few such companies were formed, although they are the oldest class of registered company, but the exemption from publication of accounts[11] given by section 47 of the 1967 Act (as to which see now section 1 of the Companies Act 1976, *post*), made them more popular. Similar exemptions are now applicable to small private companies[12]

---

[8] *Post*, p. 204.
[9] *Post*, p. 336.
[10] *Post*, p. 573.
[11] *Post*, p. 41.
[12] *Post*, p. 50.

and this may have a contrary effect on the popularity of unlimited companies.

The memorandum and articles of an unlimited company with a share capital must be in the form set out in Table E, or as near thereto as circumstances admit: section 11. Table E is a model form of memorandum and articles in the First Schedule to the Act. The company is obliged to register articles with the memorandum: section 6. The articles must state the number of members with which the company proposes to be registered and, if the company is to have a share capital, the amount of the share capital: section 7. There is no requirement that the division of the share capital into shares of a fixed amount be stated. The name will not, of course, include the word "Limited," and there will be no limitation of liability clause in the memorandum.

Section 37 of the Companies Act 1976 empowers the Secretary of State to prescribe the registration fees to be paid to the Registrar. No capital duty is payable.[13]

Since the 1980 Act unlimited companies cannot be public companies: 1980 Act, s.1(1).

If the company has a share capital it must make the annual return required by section 124.[14] In certain cases an unlimited company is exempted from the requirements of section 1 of the Companies Act 1976 (delivery of accounts to Registrar).[15] If the company has no share capital, the provisions of sections 125 and 132, *ante,* apply to it. No return of allotments need be filed by an unlimited company: see section 52, *post.*

An unlimited company is exceptional in that its members may be associated on the terms that they may withdraw in the mode pointed out by the memorandum and articles, so as to be free from liability in the event of a winding up,[16] and it seems that such a company may validly provide by its memorandum and articles for a return of capital to its members, *i.e.* without the consent of the court. Similarly an unlimited company may purchase its own shares if its constituent documents authorise it to do so.[17]

---

[13] *Ante*, p. 19.
[14] See note 8 above.
[15] *Post*, p. 459.
[16] *Re Borough Commercial and Building Socy.* [1893] 2 Ch. 242.
[17] See, *e.g. Nelson Mitchell* v. *City of Glasgow Bank* (1879) 6 R. (H.L.) 66; (1878) 6 R. 420. Since the 1981 Act all companies may take this power.

Re-registration of unlimited company as a limited private company

Section 44 of the 1967 Act provides that an unlimited company (not registered by virtue of section 43, *post*) may be re-registered as a private company limited either by shares or by guarantee if a special resolution to that effect and complying with the requirements set out below is passed, and the application for re-registration is in the prescribed form, signed by a director or the secretary and lodged with the Registrar, together with certain documents, not earlier than the day on which the copy of the resolution filed under section 143 of the 1948 Act is received by him.

The resolution—

(1) must state the manner in which the liability of members is to be limited and the share capital if the company is to be limited by shares;

(2) must provide for the appropriate alterations in and additions to the memorandum and articles according to whether the company is to be limited by shares or by guarantee and so with or without a share capital.

The documents which must also be lodged are printed copies of the memorandum and articles as altered.

Section 37 of the Companies Act 1976 empowers the Secretary of State to prescribe re-registration fees. Capital duty is payable on a Statement of Capital (Form PUC6).[18]

The Registrar must issue an appropriate certificate of incorporation, whereupon the status of the company is changed and the alterations in and additions to the memorandum and articles take effect. Such a certificate is conclusive evidence of compliance with the requirements of the section with respect to re-registration and of re-registration.

Section 64 of the 1948 Act (power of unlimited company with a share capital to provide for reserve liability on re-registration as limited) applies to a re-registration under section 44.

In the winding up of a company re-registered under section 44—

(1) notwithstanding section 212(1)(*a*)[19] of the 1948 Act, a past member who was a member at the time of re-registration is,

---

[18] *Ante*, p. 19.
[19] *Post*, p. 651.

where the winding up commences within three years after the re-registration, liable to contribute to the assets of the company in respect of its debts and liabilities contracted before re-registration;

(2) where no persons who were members at the time of re-registration are existing members, a person who was then a present or past member is, subject to section 212(1)(*a*) of the 1948 Act and (1), *ante,* but notwithstanding section 212(1)(*c*),[20] liable to contribute as above even though the existing members have satisfied the contributions required of them;

(3) notwithstanding section 212(1)(*d*)[21] and (*e*) of the 1948 Act, there is no limit on the amount which a person who, at the time of re-registration, was a past or present member is liable to contribute as above.

Re-registration of unlimited company as a public company

No unlimited company can be a public company: 1980 Act, s.1(1). Since such a company is therefore a private company, conversion of an unlimited company to a public company requires two steps. First, the acquisition of limited liability and a share capital, and secondly, the acquisition of public company status. Both steps may be achieved in one process under sections 5 to 7 of the 1980 Act. The procedure for re-registration of a private company as a public company[22] is modified to include the appropriate requirements for the acquisition of limited liability; *i.e.* a special resolution similar to that required by section 44 of the 1967 Act: 1980 Act, s.7(2).

The Registrar must issue a certificate stating that the company has been incorporated as a company limited by shares and is a public company. Such a certificate is conclusive evidence of the fact that it is a public company: 1980 Act, ss.5(6), 7(3).

Section 64 of the 1948 Act and the winding-up provisions applicable to unlimited companies re-registered as private companies under section 44 of the 1967 Act,[23] apply equally to such companies re-registered as public companies: 1980 Act, s.7(4).

[20] *Post,* p. 653.
[21] *Post,* p. 652.
[22] *Post,* p. 48.
[23] *Ante,* p. 42.

Re-registration of limited company as unlimited

Section 43 of the Companies Act 1967 enables a limited private company (not registered in pursuance of section 44, *ante*) to be re-registered as unlimited with the unanimous consent of its members. The application for re-registration must be in the prescribed form, signed by a director or the secretary and lodged with the Registrar together with certain documents. A public company cannot be re-registered as an unlimited company—it must attain private company status first: 1980 Act, Sched. 3, para. 43.

The application must set out the appropriate alterations in and additions to the memorandum and, if articles have been registered,[24] the articles, according to whether or not the company is to have a share capital. If articles have not been registered the application must have annexed to it, and request the registration of, appropriate printed articles.

The following documents must be lodged with the application—

(1) the prescribed form of assent to the company's being registered as unlimited *subscribed by or on behalf of all the members* (a subscription by the personal representative of a dead member is deemed to be by him and the trustee in bankruptcy of a member is deemed a member to the exclusion of the member himself);

(2) a statutory declaration by the directors that the subscribers constitute the whole membership and, if any member has not subscribed himself, that they have taken all reasonable steps to satisfy themselves that the person who subscribed on his behalf was lawfully empowered to do so;

(3) a printed copy of the memorandum incorporating the alterations therein;

(4) if articles have been registered, a printed copy thereof incorporating the alterations to them.

Section 37 of the Companies Act 1976 empowers the Secretary of State to prescribe re-registration fees. No capital duty is payable.

The Registrar must issue an appropriate certificate of incorporation, which will be conclusive evidence of proper re-registration.

Quite a number of former limited companies, such as property and

[24] *Post*, p. 103.

finance companies, took advantage of section 43 and re-registered as unlimited in order to preserve secrecy about their affairs. Under the 1981 Act such secrecy is also possible for small private companies.

In a winding up a person who, when the application for re-registration was lodged, was a past member and did not thereafter again become a member is not liable to contribute more than he would have been liable to contribute had there been no re-registration: 1967 Act, section 43(6).

PUBLIC AND PRIVATE COMPANIES

A registered limited company may be a public company or a private company.

By section 1 of the 1980 Act a public company is a limited company with a share capital which has a memorandum stating that it is a public company and which has been registered or re-registered as such.

A company which is not a public company is a private company. Thus the private company is the residual class of companies, without any special requirements. This is a complete reversal of the position prior to the 1980 Act whereby all companies were public companies unless their articles contained three restrictions: as to the transferability of shares; the number of members; and invitations to the public to invest in the company: 1948 Act, s.28, repealed by the 1980 Act, Schedule 4. The reason for this change was the necessity to define more clearly the public company category so that the United Kingdom's obligations under the Second EEC Directive (control of the finances of public companies) could be applied only to such companies.

There are three requirements for the registration of a company as a public company:

(1) It must state that it is a public company both in its memorandum and by its name. There must be a clause to that effect in the memorandum[25] and its name must end with the word "public limited company" (frequently abbreviated to "plc").[26] A private company will continue to use the familiar "Limited" or "Ltd." at the end of its name;

[25] 1980 Act, s.3.
[26] *Post*, p. 59.

    (2) The memorandum must be in the form specified in Schedule 1 to the 1980 Act rather than in the forms applicable to private companies in Tables B and D of the 1948 Act;

    (3) The company must have an authorised capital figure (the amount of shares it may issue to the public) of at least the *authorised minimum,* currently £50,000[27]: 1980 Act, ss.2 and 3.

Following the 1980 and 1981 Acts there are substantial differences in the capital requirements as applied to public and private companies. In particular a public company cannot commence business or exercise any borrowing powers unless it has actually allotted shares up to the authorised minimum and has received at least one quarter of that amount: 1980 Act, ss.4 and 22.[28]

Private companies are no longer required to restrict the transferability of their shares, although they are perfectly at liberty to do so, *e.g.* to preserve family control of a company; nor need they limit their membership to 50. It is a criminal offence however for a private company to offer any of its securities to the public, either directly or indirectly (*i.e.* through an intermediary). Curiously enough however the actual sale remains valid: 1980 Act, s.15. To use the capital markets, *e.g.* the Stock Exchange, a company must be a public company.

The minimum number of members for both public and private companies is two but a public company must still have at least two directors whereas a private company need only have one director: section 176. Thus one recommendation of the Jenkins Committee has been implemented whilst another in the same paragraph (para. 31, Cmnd 1749) has not. A private company needs no minimum capital either for registration or the commencement of business.

Disadvantages of a private company

The effective embargo on access to the capital markets preserved by section 15 of the 1980 Act may be regarded as the only disadvantage of a private company as compared with a public company.

---

[27] 1980 Act, s.85.
[28] *Post,* p. 183.

Advantages of a private company

A private company has a number of advantages over a public company. These advantages include the following:

(1) A private company need not issue subsequent issues of shares by way of a rights issue: 1980 Act, s.17.[29]

(2) A private company does not need an authorised minimum capital either for registration or to commence business under sections 3 and 4 of the 1980 Act. It may commence business (and make binding contracts and exercise its borrowing powers) immediately on incorporation.[30]

(3) A private company is not subject to the majority of the provisions relating to the payment for shares. This enables a private company to issue shares in return for assets other than cash without lengthy and complex valuations: 1980 Act, ss.22–31.[31]

(4) A private company need not convene an extraordinary general meeting in the event of a serious loss of capital: 1980 Act, s.34.[32]

(5) A private company may give itself wider charges on its own shares to recover debts owed to it by its members. Public companies are restricted in this respect: 1980 Act, s.38.[33]

(6) A private company need not make provision for unrealised capital losses when distributing a dividend: 1980 Act, s.40.[34]

(7) Directors of private companies are much less restricted in their financial dealings with their company and need disclose far less information about such arrangements in the accounts: 1980 Act, ss.49–58.[35]

(8) The company secretary does not need to be specially qualified or experienced: 1980 Act, s.79.[36]

---

[29] *Post*, p. 166.
[30] *Post*, p. 183.
[31] *Post*, p. 169.
[32] *Post*, p. 241.
[33] *Post*, pp. 291, 295.
[34] *Post*, p. 535.
[35] *Post*, p. 360.
[36] *Post*, p. 387.

(9) Private companies may be excused from publication of some or all of their accounts, depending on their size: 1981 Act, ss.5–10.[37]

(10) Private companies may provide financial assistance for the purchase of their own shares by following the statutory procedure: 1981 Act, s.43.[38]

(11) Private companies may purchase or redeem their own shares out of capital: 1981 Act, ss.54–58.[39]

(12) There is no obligation to disclose the true ownership of private company shares, however substantial the holding: 1981 Act, ss.63–73.[40]

Other differences between a private company and a public company are:

(1) At a general meeting of a private company a motion for the appointment of two or more directors may be made by a single resolution: section 183(1).[41]

(2) A proxy can speak at a meeting of a private company: section 136.[42]

Re-registration of a private company as a public company

A private company may be re-registered as a public company if it complies with the three conditions set out in the 1980 Act, ss.5 and 6:

(1) It must pass a special resolution that it be so re-registered and that its memorandum and articles be amended accordingly (*e.g.* to provide for a change of name).

(2) It must send an application in the prescribed form signed by a director or secretary of the company to the Registrar together with a printed copy of the amended memorandum and articles, a copy of the latest balance sheet and an unqualified report by the auditors on that balance sheet, a copy of another report by the auditors that the company's net assets are not less than its capital as stated in that balance sheet, and a declaration of compliance by a director or secre-

[37] *Post*, p. 50.
[38] *Post*, p. 259.
[39] *Post*, p. 249.
[40] *Post*, p. 199.
[41] *Post*, p. 328.
[42] *Post*, p. 318.

tary and that the company's position *vis-à-vis* its net assets is unchanged since the last balance sheet.

(3) It must comply with the necessary financial criteria both for a public company to be able to commence business[43] and as to the payment for shares in public companies.[44] This applies equally to shares issued since the last balance sheet and before the application; in particular it must have the *authorised minimum* capital.

If the Registrar is satisfied he must issue a certificate of incorporation stating that the company is a public company. This is conclusive evidence that the company is a public company and that all the procedures as to re-registration have been complied with.

Re-registration of a public company as a private company

A public company may be re-registered as a private company if it complies with the conditions in the 1980 Act, sections 10 and 11:

(1) It must pass a special resolution that it be so re-registered and that its memorandum and articles be amended accordingly (*e.g.* to remove the statement in the memorandum that it is a public company).

(2) It must send an application in the prescribed form signed by a director or secretary of the company to the Registrar together with a printed copy of the amended memorandum and articles.

(3) 28 days must have elapsed from the passing of the resolution and, either no application has been brought under section 11 of the 1980 Act to have the resolution set aside, or the court has confirmed the resolution despite such an application. A minority action may be brought for the cancellation of the resolution to re-register by, either the holders of five per cent. or more of the issued share capital or any class of capital, or not less than 50 members, within 28 days of the passing of the resolution. No-one who voted for the resolution can make such an application. The court has extensive powers on hearing such an application, including confirming or cancelling the resolution, adjourning the proceedings for an arrangement to be made, altering the memorandum and articles, and, if neces-

[43] *Post*, p. 183.
[44] *Post*, p. 169.

sary, providing for the purchase by the company of the shares of the dissentient members. This is one of several minority protection sections which occur throughout the Act.

If the Registrar is satisfied he must issue a certificate of incorporation "appropriate to a company that is not a public company." This is conclusive evidence that the requirements as to re-registration have been complied with and that the company is a private company.

Re-registration of public companies by law

If a public company reduces its capital under section 66 of the 1948 Act[45] so that its allotted share capital is less than the *authorised minimum* the court is empowered to order that the company be re-registered as a private company and that its memorandum and articles be amended accordingly. In such a case no special resolution is necessary and no application by a minority is possible: 1980 Act, s.12.

SMALL AND MEDIUM-SIZED COMPANIES

The 1981 Act introduced a new classification of private companies for the purpose of certain accounting exemptions allowed by that Act. The directors of a *small* or *medium-sized* company may deliver to the Registrar copies of a modified and less detailed version of its accounts rather than the full version required of other companies.[46] Such companies are however still required to prepare the full accounts for their own members. The advantage thus is purely one of secrecy rather than a saving of labour or expense: 1981 Act, s.6.

Companies excluded from the classification

A company cannot qualify as a small or medium-sized company if it is a public company, or a banking, insurance or shipping company, or a member of a group which contains such a company; 1981 Act, s.5.

The classification—small companies

A company is a small company if for the past two years, including the one in which the classification is made, it has satisfied at least two

---

[45] *Post*, p. 229.   [46] *Post*, p. 459.

out of the following three criteria laid down by section 8(2) of the 1981 Act:

(1) the amount of its turnover must not exceed £1,400,000;
(2) its balance sheet total (*i.e.* its assets) must not exceed £700,000; and
(3) its average number of employees, determined on a weekly basis, must not exceed 50.

Any company which has so qualified will not lose its status if it ceases to fulfil the requirements for just one year, but once it has lost its status it will take two years compliance to re-acquire it. Any newly formed company will qualify if it fulfils two of the three criteria in its first financial year.

To claim small company status the directors must certify that their company satisfies the conditions and this must be backed by an auditors' report to that effect.[47]

The classification—medium-sized companies

A company is a medium-sized company if for the past two years, including the one in which the classification is made, it has satisfied at least two out of the following three criteria laid down by section 8(3) of the 1981 Act:

(1) the amount of its turnover must not exceed £5,750,000;
(2) its balance sheet total (*i.e.* its assets) must not exceed £2,800,000;
(3) its average number of employees, determined on a weekly basis, must not exceed 250.

The acquisition and loss of the status is governed by the same rules as in the case of small companies.

Groups of companies and the classification

A holding company[48] can itself only file modified accounts[49] if that company and its subsidiaries taken together fulfil the appropriate criteria as a small or medium-sized company: 1981 Act, ss.9 and 10.

[47] 1981 Act, s.7.
[48] *Post*, p. 52.
[49] These may be individual or group accounts: *post*, Chap. 22.

The details of the exemptions obtained by the small and medium-sized companies are set out in Chapter 22.

HOLDING AND SUBSIDIARY COMPANIES

It is sometimes important to know whether a registered company is a subsidiary or a holding company. One reason is that section 27[50] generally prevents a subsidiary from being a member of its holding company. The meaning of the terms "subsidiary" and "holding company" is given in section 154 and it is convenient to deal with that section here.

The effect of section 154 is that a company (which we shall call "X") is a subsidiary of another company ("Y") and Y is X's holding company if—

(1) Y is a member of X and controls the composition of X's board of directors; or

(2) Y holds more than half of X's equity share capital; or

(3) X is a subsidiary of a third company ("Z") which is itself a subsidiary of Y.

As to (1), Y must be a member of X—holding one share will suffice—*and* must control the composition of X's board. Section 154(2) provides that Y is deemed to control the composition of X's board only if Y, by the exercise of a power exercisable by it without the consent of any other person, can appoint or remove all or the majority of the directors. Further, that Y is deemed to have power to appoint a director of X if—

(*a*) a person cannot be appointed as a director of X unless Y exercises a power exercisable without the consent of any other person; or

(*b*) a person's appointment as a director of X follows necessarily from his being a director of Y; or

(*c*) Y itself or another subsidiary of Y is a director of X.

Y might have a power to appoint a director of X, which power it can exercise without the consent of any other person, *e.g.* by virtue of a provision in a contract between X and Y or of the shares in X held by Y.

---

[50] *Post,* p. 190.

As regards (2) above, subsection (5) provides that the "equity share capital" of a company means its issued share capital excluding any part which, neither as respects dividends nor as respects capital, carries any right to participate beyond a specified amount in a distribution. As will be seen, this will normally exclude preference shares so that in effect the equity share capital is the company's issued ordinary shares. It should be noted that in practice one company is in control of another if it holds less than half the other's equity share capital, *e.g.* if the first holds 30 per cent. of the second's ordinary shares. The Jenkins Report[51] recommended that section 154 be amended so that the definition of a subsidiary is based solely on membership and control, *i.e.* that (2) above be repealed.

As to (3), X is a subsidiary of Z and Z is a subsidiary of Y because in each case either the second company is a member of the first and controls its board or the second holds more than half of the first's equity share capital. The result of (3) is that X is also a subsidiary of Y.

As one would expect, in (1), (2) and (3) any shares held or power exercisable by a nominee for Y, or by, or by a nominee for, another subsidiary of Y, are treated as held or exercisable by Y (s.154(3)).

On the other hand, subsection (3) also provides that:

(i) Any shares held or power exercisable by Y in a fiduciary capacity are treated as not held or exercisable by it. This would be so where Y is a trustee company which holds shares in X on trust for some beneficiary.

(ii) Any shares held or power exercisable by any person by virtue of the provisions of any debentures of X, or of a trust deed for securing any such debentures, are disregarded. This provision might apply where Y is a member of X and has lent money to it and taken a debenture which gives Y power to appoint the majority of X's directors.

(iii) Any shares held or power exercisable by, or by a nominee for, Y or another subsidiary of Y are treated as not held or exercisable by Y if the ordinary business of Y or the other subsidiary includes the lending of money and the shares are held or the power is exercisable by way of security only for the purposes of a transaction entered into in the ordinary course of such business. This would be so where Y is a

[51] Para. 156.

money-lending company which has lent money to a shareholder in X who, in order to secure the loan, has transferred his shares to Y by way of mortgage.

Lastly, it should be noted that section 154(5) also provides that in the section the expression "company" includes any body corporate and that section 455(3) provides that a reference in the Act to a body corporate is to be construed as including a company incorporated outside Great Britain but as not including a Scottish firm. Thus many companies registered in Great Britain either have subsidiaries registered abroad or are themselves subsidiaries of an overseas parent company. These are part of the so-called multinational companies. In one case an employee of a British subsidiary was refused permission to sue the foreign parent company in America. The fact that greater damages are available in that country makes an action there very desirable from the injured person's point of view.[52]

[52] *Smith, Kline & French Laboratories Ltd.* v. *Bloch, The Times,* December 3, 1981.

Chapter 3

MEMORANDUM OF ASSOCIATION

EVERY registered company must have a memorandum of association, which is the registered company's charter.[1] This memorandum regulates the company's external affairs, whilst the articles regulate its internal affairs.[1] The purpose of the memorandum is to enable persons who invest in or deal with the company to ascertain what its name is, whether it is a public company, whether it is an English or a Scottish company, what its objects, and hence its powers, are, whether the liability of its members is limited and what share capital it is authorised to issue. The memorandum may contain other matters apart from those just referred to. It must contain an association clause and it must be properly subscribed. The provisions of the memorandum can be altered in certain specified cases.

Section 2 of the 1948 Act, as amended by section 30(1) and (3) of the 1976 Act, provides that the memorandum of every private company must state:

(1) The name of the company, with "Limited" as the last word of the name of a company limited by shares or by guarantee or, where the memorandum states that the registered office is to be in Wales, with "Cyfyngedig" as the last word of the name. The abbreviations "Ltd" or "cyf" may be used instead.[2]

(2) Whether the registered office of the company is to be situated in England and Wales, Wales or Scotland.

(3) The objects of the company.

(4) That the liability of the members is limited, if the company is limited by shares or by guarantee.

(5) In the case of a limited company having a share capital, the amount of share capital with which the company proposes to be registered and the division thereof into shares of a fixed amount.

---

[1] See, *per* Lord Cairns L.C., in *Ashbury Railway Carriage Co. Ltd.* v. *Riche* (1875) L.R. 7 H.L. 653, at pp. 667, 668.

[2] 1980 Act, s.78.

Section 2 of the 1980 Act provides that the memorandum of a public company must state, in addition to the information supplied by a private company memorandum, the fact that the company is a public company. The name of a public company must end with "public limited company," or where the registered office is to be in Wales with "cwmni cyfyngedig cyhoeddus." The abbreviations "p.l.c." or "c.c.c." may be used instead.[2]

In the case of a company limited by guarantee the memorandum must also state that each member undertakes to contribute to the assets of the company in the event of its being wound up while he is a member, or within one year after he ceases to be a member, such amount as may be required, not exceeding a specified amount.

The memorandum must state the desire of the subscribers to be formed into a company and the agreement of each to take a specified number of shares in the company.

Two or more persons, must subscribe their names to the memorandum: section 1(1).

The form of a memorandum of association of a private company must be that set out in Table B in the First Schedule to the Act, or as near thereto as circumstances admit: section 11.

TABLE B

Form of Memorandum of Association of a Private Company Limited by Shares

1st. The name of the company is "The Eastern Steam Packet Company, Limited."

2nd. The registered office of the company will be situate in England.

3rd. The objects for which the company is established are, "the conveyance of passengers and goods in ships or boats between such places as the company may from time to time determine, and the doing all such other things as are incidental or conducive to the attainment of the above object."

4th. The liability of the members is limited.

5th. The share capital of the company is two hundred thousand pounds, divided into one thousand shares of two hundred pounds each.

WE, the several persons whose names and addresses are subscribed, are desirous of being formed into a company, in pursuance of this memorandum of association, and we respectively agree to take the number of shares in the capital of the company set opposite our respective names.

Names, addresses, and descriptions of subscribers	Number of shares taken by each subscriber
1. John Jones, of , in the county of , merchant	200
2. John Smith, of , in the county of , merchant	25
3. Thomas Green, of , in the county of , merchant	30
4. John Thompson, of , in the county of , merchant	40
5. Caleb White, of , in the county of , merchant	15
6. Andrew Brown, of , in the county of , merchant	5
7. Caesar White, of , in the county of , merchant	10
Total shares taken	325

Dated the   day of   , 19   .

Witness to the above signatures,
A.B., No. 13, Hute Street, Clerkenwell, London.

The form of a memorandum of a public company must be in accordance with the form set out in Part I of Schedule 1 to the 1980 Act, or as near thereto as circumstances admit: 1980 Act, s.2(4).

SCHEDULE 1

FORMS OF MEMORANDUM OF ASSOCIATION OF A PUBLIC COMPANY

PART I

A PUBLIC COMPANY LIMITED BY SHARES

1. The name of the company is "The Western Steam Packet, public limited company."

2. The company is to be a public company.

3. The registered office of the company will be situated in England and Wales.

4. The objects for which the company is established are, "the conveyance of passengers and goods in ships or boats between such places as the company may from time to time determine, and the doing of all such things as are incidental or conducive to the attainment of the above object."

5. The liability of the members is limited.

6. The share capital of the company is £50,000 divided into 50,000 shares of £1 each.

We, the several persons whose names and addresses are subscribed are desirous of being formed into a company, in pursuance of this memorandum of association, and we respectively agree to take the number of shares in the capital of the company set opposite our respective names.

Names, Addresses and Descriptions of Subscribers			*Number of shares taken by each Subscriber*
"1. Thomas Jones	in the county of	merchant	1
2. Andrew Smith	in the county of	merchant	1
Total shares taken			2"

Dated   day of   19 .

Witness to the above
signatures
A.B., 13, Hute Street,
Clerkenwell, London.

No subscriber may take less than one share and each subscriber must write opposite to his name the number of shares he takes: section 2. Each subscriber must sign the memorandum in the presence of at least one witness, who must attest the signature: section 3.

Where the memorandum states that the registered office is to be in Wales, the memorandum and the articles may be in Welsh but, if they are, they must be accompanied by a certified translation into English (1976 Act, s.30(6)).

However, Table B was taken from the Companies Act 1862 and is very out of date so that, as will be seen, in practice considerable modifications are made to the form set out in it. Even the 1980 form for public companies is simply an amendment of the 1862 form and requires substantial amendments in practice. A specimen memorandum of association is set out at the end of this chapter.

The Name

The memorandum must state the name of the company: section 2. The general rule is that any name may be selected. However, a company cannot be registered by a name which is prohibited, either absolutely or conditionally: 1981 Act, s.22.[3] Further, the last word of the name of a private limited company must be the word "Limited" (s.2), unless the company can comply with the criteria in section 25 of the 1981 Act and dispenses with the word. The last words of a public company's name must be "public limited company" (1980 Act, s.2).[4] Where the memorandum of a limited company states that its registered office is to be in Wales, the last word of the name of the company may be "Cyfyngedig" (s.30(3) of the 1976 Act), if the company is a private company, or "Cwmni cyfyngedig cyhoeddus" if it is a public company. In all cases the appropriate abbreviations may be used: 1980 Act, s.78. In selecting a name, it is not necessary to use the word "Company," and the modern tendency is to omit it. A short name is an obvious practical convenience.

The word "Limited" is a misnomer. The company's liability for its own debts is not limited, and the members of the company are not liable for the company's debts (except to the limited extent provided by section 31),[5] because the company is a legal entity separate and distinct from its shareholders. The important thing about the name is that it should show to others that the company is a body corporate, and not a mere unincorporated partnership. It is too late now to reserve the word "Company" for the exclusive use of incorporated companies, because it is in common use by persons who are not incorporated, *e.g.* by partnerships. The American term "Incorporated" expresses the true idea, and that or some synonymous word is to be preferred to "Limited."

The use of the word "Limited" or "Cyfyngedig," or any contraction or imitation of it, as the last word of the name under which any person carries on business without being incorporated with limited liability, is prohibited: section 439. It has been held that a solicitor who enters an appearance for such a person, and uses the word "Limited" as describ-

[3] *Post*, p. 60
[4] *Post*, p. 60
[5] *Ante*, p. 24.

ing his client, will be personally liable for the costs.[6] Similarly the use of the words "public limited company" or its Welsh equivalent or any abbreviation of it by any person who is not a public limited company is an offence: 1980 Act, s.76.

Prohibited and controlled names

Section 22(1) of the 1981 Act provides five grounds upon which the registration of a name or change of name is absolutely prohibited.

(1) A name including "limited," "unlimited" or "public limited company," or their Welsh equivalents otherwise than at the end of the name;

(2) A name including any abbreviation of those words otherwise than at the end of the name;

(3) A name which is *the same as* a name appearing in the index of registered names kept by the Registrar;

(4) A name, the use of which would, in the opinion of the Secretary of State, constitute a criminal offence;

(5) A name which in the opinion of the Secretary of State is offensive.

The important prohibition is (3)—a name which is *the same as* one already on the index of registered names kept by the Registrar under section 23 of the 1981 Act. This includes the names of all registered companies, limited partnerships and industrial and provident societies, and so registration of a company name confers a monopoly of the use of that name. The onus of checking the index is on those who wish to register the name. There is no control on registration of names similar to, or "too like," those already on the index but such a name may be compulsorily altered within one year of registration under section 24 of the 1981 Act—so called "post-registration control."[7] When deciding whether one name is *the same as* another for this purpose minor differences are to be disregarded under section 22(3) of the 1981 Act. Accents, type and case of letters, the word "the" if it is the first word of the name, are examples of such minor differences.

Section 22(2) of the 1981 Act provides for the controlled use of certain words and expressions either on the registration of a company

---

[6] *Simmons* v. *Liberal Opinion Ltd.* [1911] 1 K.B. 966 (C.A.).

[7] *Post,* p. 65

or a change of name. The use of any name which in the opinion of the Secretary of State would be likely to give the impression that the company is connected in any way with Her Majesty's Government or with any local authority or includes any name or expression specified in the appropriate regulations cannot be registered without his consent. The appropriate regulations are The Company and Business Names Regulations 1981,[8] issued under sections 31 and 32 of the 1981 Act. These regulations specify 79 separate words or expressions which require consent before use. These include "Abortion," "Building Society," "Chamber of Commerce," "Duke," "English," "Health Visitor," "Insurance," "National," "Royal," "Stock Exchange," "Trade Union," "Trust," and "Windsor."

When a company wishes to use such an expression it must request the "relevant body," if one is specified, to indicate whether (and if so why) it has any objections to the proposal. Relevant bodies include the Home Office and the Scottish Home and Health Department. The reply of the relevant body must be sent to the Registrar by the applicant when registration or the change of name is applied for; 1981 Act, s.31. The Secretary of State will then make his decision.

Since similar names can now be registered there could be more passing-off actions brought against registered companies, even though such names can be compulsorily changed within one year of registration.[9] Under the general law, the court has jurisdiction to grant an injunction[10] to restrain a company from using a trade name colourably resembling that of the plaintiff if the defendant's trade name, though innocently adopted, is calculated, *i.e.* likely,[11] to deceive, either by diverting customers from the plaintiff to the defendant or by occasioning confusion between the two businesses, *e.g.* by suggesting that the defendant's business is in some way connected with that of the plaintiff.

In *Ewing* v. *Buttercup Margarine Co. Ltd.*,[12] the plaintiff, who carried on business under the trade name of the Buttercup Dairy Company, was held entitled to restrain a newly registered company from carrying on business under the name of the Buttercup Margarine Company Ltd. on the ground that

---

[8] S.I. 1981/1685. See also the Company and Business Names (Amendment) Regulations 1982 (S.I. 1982 No. 1653).

[9] *Post*, p. 66

[10] The Scottish equivalent is interdict.

[11] *Per* Earl of Halsbury L.C. in *The N. Cheshire and Manchester Brewery Co. Ltd.* v. *The Manchester Brewery Co. Ltd.* [1899] A.C. 83 at p. 84.

[12] [1917] 2 Ch. 1 (C.A.).

the public might reasonably think that the registered company was connected with his business.

However, if the company's business is or will be different from that of the complaining party, confusion is not likely to arise, and an injunction will not be granted.[13]

A company having a word in ordinary use as part of its name cannot prevent another company from using the same word.

So, Aerators Ltd. were unable to prevent the registration of Automatic Aerators Patents, Ltd. because the word "aerator" was a word in common use in the English language and Aerators Ltd. had no monopoly of it: *Aerators Ltd.* v. *Tollitt* [1902] 2 Ch. 319.

Exemption from using the word "Limited"

Prior to the 1981 Act private companies could obtain a licence from the Department of Trade to dispense with the word "Limited" on proof of compliance with certain criteria. Such licenses could be issued and revoked by the Department as it thought fit; section 19. This procedure was repealed and replaced by the 1981 Act. Section 25 of that Act applies, however, only to private guarantee companies and those private companies limited by shares previously licensed under section 19. Only guarantee companies may thus obtain exemption in the future. The major change is that under the new section there is a *right* to exemption from the use of the word "Limited" if certain criteria are met and certified, whereas each dispensation under the 1948 Act had to be negotiated individually.

The present criteria are that the company is to be formed for the promotion of commerce, art, science, education, religion, charity or any profession and anything incidental or conducive to any of those objects; that by its memorandum or articles it must apply its income solely for the promotion of those objects, prohibit the payment of dividends to its members, and require all its surplus assets on a winding up to be transferred to a similar body rather than to its members.[14] A statutory declaration either by the solicitor engaged in the formation,

[13] *Dunlop Pneumatic Tyre Co. Ltd.* v. *Dunlop Motor Co. Ltd.* 1907 S.C. (H.L.) 15, where the respondents carried on a motor-repairing company; similarly an interdict was refused in *The Scottish Union and National Insurance Co.* v. *The Scottish National Insurance Co. Ltd.*, 1909 S.C. 318.

[14] This requirement was always insisted on by the Department under the previous system.

or a director or secretary of the company, that the company is one to which the section applies will suffice to obtain the exemption; 1981 Act, s.25(4).

There is an absolute ban on any alterations of such a company's memorandum or articles so as to breach the criteria—there are fines in default: 1981 Act, s.25(5), (9). Any purported alteration will thus be void. If there is a breach of any of the criteria without any such change the Secretary of State can require the addition of the word "Limited" to the company's name and a resolution of the directors to that effect will suffice for the change of name: 1981 Act, s.25(6). Such a company cannot again acquire the exemption without the express approval of the Secretary of State: 1981 Act, s.25(7).

Any company which obtains exemption under section 25 of the 1981 Act, is relieved of the necessity of (1) having "Limited" as part of its name, (2) publishing its name,[15] and (3) sending lists of members to the Registrar,[16] although the European Communities Act, s.9(7), requires the fact that it is a limited company to be mentioned in its business letters and order forms.

Associations taking advantage of this exemption are typically chambers of commerce, schools and colleges, research associations, learned societies, professional qualifying bodies and charitable bodies doing social work.

Publication of name by company

Section 108 provides that every company must:

(1) Paint or affix its name on the outside of every office or place in which its business is carried on, in a conspicuous position, in letters easily legible.

(2) Engrave its name in legible characters on its seal.

(3) Mention its name in legible characters in all business letters of the company and in all notices and other official publications, and in all bills of exchange, promissory notes, endorsements, cheques and orders for money or goods, bills of parcels, invoices, receipts and letters of credit.

[15] Under s.108, *post.*
[16] Under s.124, *post.*

An exception is that by section 25(3) of the 1981 Act, a company entitled to dispense with the word "Limited" as part of its name[17] is excepted from the provisions of the Act relating to the publishing of its name, although, as noted above, the European Communities Act, s.9(7), requires the fact that it is a limited company to be mentioned in legible characters in all its business letters and order forms.

Where the last word of the name of a limited company is "Cyfyngedig," or "Cwmni cyfyngedig cyhoeddus" the fact that the company is a limited company must be stated in English and in legible characters—

    (a) in all prospectuses, bill-heads, letter paper, notices and other official publications of the company;

    (b) in a notice conspicuously displayed in every place in which the company's business is carried on (s.30(5) of the 1976 Act; s.77 of the 1980 Act).

Fines are imposed on the company and its officers for non-compliance with the above requirements. Further, if an officer of the company or any person on its behalf, *inter alia* (*a*) uses or authorises the use of a seal purporting to be a seal of the company whereon its name is not engraved, or (*b*) signs or authorises to be signed on behalf of the company any bill of exchange, cheque, or order for money or goods in which the company's name is not mentioned, he is liable to a fine and, in addition, he is personally liable to the holder of the bill of exchange, cheque or order, for its amount, unless it is paid by the company. Such personal liability is a secondary liability, arising only if the company itself fails to pay, *e.g.* because of liquidation.

A bill was drawn on a limited company described on the bill as "The Saltash Watermen's Steam Packet Company, Saltash," and was accepted by the secretary, who wrote across it "Accepted. John Martyr, Secy. to the sd. Coy." *Held*, when the bill was not honoured, the secretary was personally liable, as the company's correct name was not mentioned in the bill: *Penrose* v. *Martyr* (1858) 120 E.R. 595.[18]

"The intention of the enactment plainly was to prevent persons from being deceived into the belief that they had a security with the unlimited liability of common law, when they had but the security of a Company limited": *per* Crompton J. at p. 597.

---

[17] *Ante*, p. 63.
[18] See also *British Airways Board* v. *Parish* [1979] 2 Lloyds Rep. 361 (C.A.).

In *Durham Fancy Goods Ltd.* v. *Michael Jackson* (*Fancy Goods*) *Ltd.*
[1968] 2 Q.B. 839, where the plaintiff had prepared the form of acceptance
which misdescribed the company's name as "M. Jackson (Fancy Goods)
Ltd.," the plaintiff was held estopped from enforcing the personal liability
under section 108 of the officer who signed the bill.[19] On the other hand, in
Barber & Nicholls v. *R & G Associates (London) Ltd.* (1982) 132 N.L.J. 1076,
where the plaintiffs had previously written to the company and cashed
cheques drawn by the company in the name of R & G Associates Ltd.,
omitting the word "London," they were not estopped from enforcing the
personal liability of the director who signed a cheque with that omission. The
Durham Fancy Goods case was distinguished on the basis that the plaintiffs in
this case had not prepared the cheque themselves.

In *Banque de l'Indochine et de Suez S.A.* v. *Euroseas Finance Co. Ltd.*
[1981] 3 All E.R. 198, the name of the company was used correctly on two
cheques except that the word "Company" was abbreviated to "Co." This was
held not to be a breach of s.108(1)(*c*) so that the persons who signed the
cheques were held not to be personally liable on them.

If the name of the company appears on the face of the bill it need not
appear on the acceptance.

A bill was drawn on "J. & T.H. Wallis Ltd.," and accepted "James Wallis,
Thomas Wallis, Henry Bowles, Secty." *Held*, (1) the correct name of the
company was mentioned in the bill as required by the Companies Act, (2) the
abbreviation "Ltd." might be used for the word "Limited," (3) the individuals
who had signed the acceptance were not liable on the bill: *Stacey & Co. Ltd.* v.
Wallis (1912) 28 T.L.R. 209.

Change of name

Companies may change their registered names voluntarily or under
compulsion. The latter gives the Department control over names
similar to those already registered even though they cannot prevent
registration of such names.[20]

(1) A company may change its name at any time by a special
resolution which takes effect from the issue of a new certificate of
incorporation by the Registrar: 1981 Act, s.24(1). Such a change of
name is subject to the same restrictions as are applicable to the choice
of name for a new company registering a name for the first time.[20] The
only exception to this freedom to change a name applies where it is

---

[19] Contrast *Scottish and Newcastle Breweries Ltd.* v. *Blair*, 1967 S.L.T. 72 (O.H.), in
which the defence of personal bar was unsuccessful.
[20] *Ante*, p. 60

proposed to remove the word "Limited" from a company's name if there has been a direction of the Secretary of State to the contrary.[21]

(2) If a name has been registered which is *the same as* one already on the index of registered names or one that ought to have appeared on the index at the time of registration, or is in the opinion of the Secretary of State *too like* any such name, the name must be changed on the direction of the Secretary of State: 1981 Act, s.24(2). Such a direction must be given within 12 months of the original registration and must be complied with within such period as is specified.

Names are *the same as* existing ones as defined by section 22(3) of the 1981 Act.[22] The Registrar has published notes for guidance as to what will be considered *too like* names, *e.g.* phonetically identical names or where two names have a distinctive element in common, or where because of a similarity of the name and operations of two companies there is likely to be some confusion. These are not conclusive criteria however.

(3) When a company has applied to have a controlled name or expression as part of its name it will furnish information to the relevant body and the Department in order to obtain permission under section 22(2) of the 1981 Act.[23] If misleading information has been given or undertakings or assurances have not been fulfilled the Secretary of State may by direction require the company to change its name: 1981 Act, s.24(3). Such a direction may be given up to five years from the original registration and must be complied with within such period as is specified.

(4) If the Department of Trade considers that a name gives a misleading indication of the nature of the company's activities so as to be likely to cause harm to the public, they may direct a change. A direction must normally be complied with within six weeks. Within three weeks the company may apply to the court to have the direction set aside: 1967 Act, s.46. Failure to comply with any direction renders the company liable to fines.

When a company changes its name a new certificate of incorporation will be issued by the Registrar (1981 Act, s.24(6); 1967 Act, s.46) and it has been decided under previous legislation that the company retains its old name until the new certificate is issued.[24]

[21] 1981 Act, s.25(7) See *ante*, p. 63
[22] See note 20 above.   [23] *Ante*, p. 60
[24] *Shackleford, Ford & Co. Ltd.* v. *Dangerfield* (1868) L.R. 3 C.P. 407.

A change of name does not affect any rights or obligations of the company or any legal proceedings by or against the company: 1981 Act, s.24(7); 1967 Act, s.46.

Business names

If a company which has a place of business in Great Britain, whether or not incorporated here, carries on business in Great Britain under a business name which does not consist of its corporate name without any addition other than one which indicates that the business is being carried on in succession to the former owner, it becomes subject to sections 28 to 30 of the 1981 Act which replaced the repealed Registration of Business Names Act 1916: 1981 Act, s.28(1).

The first consequence is that the name may not without permission of the Secretary of State include any of the words or expressions subject to control on registration of a corporate name; *i.e.* those within section 22(2) of the 1981 Act and its regulations[25]: 1981 Act, s.28(2). An identical procedure to obtain permission must be followed: 1981 Act, s.31(2). There is a 12 month period of grace where a business has been transferred to a company which then uses the previous permitted business name.

The second consequence is that a company using a business name distinct from its corporate name must disclose its corporate name and an address for the service of any document on all its business letters, written orders for goods or services, invoices and receipts, and written demands for payment arising in the course of the business, and display a statutory notice of such particulars in each of its business premises (to which either its customers or suppliers have access). Further it must supply such particulars to anyone who asks for them and with whom anything is done or discussed in the course of the business. This must be done by giving him notice "immediately" on request: 1981 Act, s.29.

In default of these obligations the company and its officers may be liable to fines. In addition, failure to comply with the disclosure provisions is subject to some civil consequences under section 30 of the 1981 Act. If a company seeks to enforce any action arising out of a contract made at a time when it was in breach of the disclosure obligations, the court must dismiss the action if the other party can

[25] *Ante,* p. 60

show that he either has a course of action against the company which he was unable to pursue because of the breach or has suffered some financial loss in respect of that contract by reason of the company's breach. The section however has no application either to proceedings brought by such a company on counter-claim or to the right of set-off if it is sued by the other party.

THE REGISTERED OFFICE

A company must at all times have a registered office to which communications and notices may be addressed: 1976 Act, s.23(1). The memorandum must state whether the registered office is to be in England, Wales or Scotland: section 2 of the 1948 Act, as amended by section 30(1) of the 1976 Act. The address of the registered office need not be set out in the memorandum, but notice of the address must be given to the Registrar in the statement which, under section 21 of the 1976 Act, *ante*,[26] must be delivered for registration with the memorandum.

Subject to the rule that the registered office cannot be changed from England to Scotland, or vice versa, the address can be changed. Notice of a change must be given to the Registrar within 14 days (1976 Act, s.23(3)).[27]

The statement as to the registered office in the memorandum fixes the company's nationality and domicile, *e.g.* if the memorandum states that the office is to be in England (so that the company is registered with the Registrar in Cardiff, as opposed to the Registrar in Edinburgh: section 12) the company is an English company with British nationality and an English domicile. A corporation is domiciled where it is incorporated and cannot change this domicile,[28] except by Act of Parliament, and the law of a corporation's domicile governs all questions of its status, *e.g.*, is it duly incorporated, what are its powers, has it been dissolved? The nationality of a corporation although seldom relevant in private international law also depends on the place of incorporation.

The reason for requiring a company to have a registered office is that, since the company has a legal existence but does not have a

---

[26] p. 17.
[27] The change, though resolved on by the directors, does not become effective until this notice has been given: *Ross* v. *Invergordon Distilleries Ltd.*, 1961 S.C. 286.
[28] *Gasque* v. *I.R.C.* [1940] 2 K.B. 80.

physical existence, it is necessary to know where the company can be found, where communications and notices may be addressed and where documents can be served on it. A company need not, and very frequently does not, carry on its business at its registered office. There is nothing, for example, to prevent a company with a registered office in England from carrying on its business abroad.

A document can be served on a company by leaving it at or sending it by post to the registered office of the company: section 437(1). It is not necessary to send it by registered post.[29]

If a company registered in Scotland carries on business in England, the process of any court in England can be served at the principal place of the company's business in England, a copy being posted at the same time to the registered office: section 437(2), (3).

Section 9(3) of the European Communities Act 1972, as amended by section 23(6) of the Companies Act 1976, provides that the Registrar must publish in the *Gazette* notice of the receipt by him of notice of a change in the situation of a company's registered office. And section 9(4) provides that a company cannot rely against other persons (as regards service of any document on the company) on any change in the situation of the company's registered office if it had not been officially notified (under s.9(3)) at the material time and is not shown by the company to have been known at that time to the person concerned, or if the material time is less than 16 days after official notification and it is shown that the person concerned was unavoidably prevented from knowing of the event at that time.

Section 9(7) of the 1972 Act requires every company to mention its place of registration and registered number, and the address of its registered office, in legible characters on all its business letters and order forms. A company which fails to comply with the sub-section, or an officer of a company or other person on its behalf who issues or authorises the issue of a letter or form which does not comply, is liable to a fine. The phrase "order forms" means forms which the company makes available for other persons to order goods or services from the company and includes, *e.g.* coupons in newspapers which the public fill in asking for goods to be supplied.[30]

---

[29] *T. O. Supplies (London) Ltd.* v. *Jerry Creighton Ltd.* [1952] 1 K.B. 42.

[30] Pamphlet "Company law provisions of the European Communities Act," published by the Department of Trade. And see the Departmental Notice published in Law Notes, December 1972, p. 323.

Items which must be kept at the registered office

The following must be kept at the registered office of a company:

(1) The register of members and, if the company has one, the index of members, unless the register is made up at another office of the company, when they may be kept at that office, or is made up by an agent, when they may be kept at the agent's office: sections 110, 111.

(2) The minute books of general meetings: section 146.

(3) The register of interests in the notifiable percentage (five per cent. at present) or more of the shares carrying unrestricted voting rights and, if there is one, the index of names, unless the register of directors' interests is not kept at the registered office, when it must be kept where the register of directors' interests is kept: 1981 Act, ss.73, 75.

(4) The register of directors and secretaries: section 200.

(5) The register of directors' interests in shares in, or debentures of, the company or associated companies, together with, if the company has one, the index of names in the register, unless the register of members is not kept at its registered office, when they may be kept where the register of members is kept: 1967 Act, ss.27–29, 31.

(6) A copy of each director's contract of service or a memorandum thereof, unless kept where the register of members is kept or kept at the company's principal place of business: 1967 Act, s.26.

(7) If the company has one, the register of debenture holders, unless the register is made up at another office, when it may be kept where it is made up, or is made up by an agent, when it may be kept at the agent's office: section 86.

(8) A copy of every instrument creating any charge requiring registration under Part III of the Act or, in Scotland, Part IIIA: ss.95, 97, 103 (England), 106A, 106C, 106H (Scotland).[31]

(9) The company's register of charges affecting property of the company: sections 104, 106I.[31]

---

[31] See Companies (Floating Charges and Receivers) (Scotland) Act 1972, s.6 and Sched.

(10) Any proposed contract or option for an off-market purchase by a company of its own shares, for 15 days prior to the resolution to approve it: 1981 Act, ss.47, 48.

(11) Any proposed release by a company of its rights under an off-market purchase contract or option to purchase its own shares: 1981 Act, s.50.

(12) Any contract for the purchase by a company of its own shares approved by the company must be kept at the registered office for 10 years from the purchase of the shares or the determination of the contract: 1981 Act, s.52.

(13) The requisite statutory declaration of solvency and auditors' report where a private company intends to purchase or redeem its own shares out of capital; 1981 Act, s.56.

In general these documents must be kept open to inspection by members without fee during business hours, subject to reasonable restrictions leaving not less than two hours a day for inspection. The minute books are open only to the inspection of members. The register of debenture holders is also open to the inspection of debenture holders without fee. Copies of instruments creating a charge and the register of charges are also open to the inspection of creditors without fee (ss.105, 106J). The register of members (s.113), the register of directors and secretaries, the register of directors' interests, the register of debenture holders (s.87), the register of charges, and, subject to exceptions, the register of interests in five per cent. of the shares, are open to the public on payment of a small fee. The register of directors' interests must also be produced at the annual general meeting and remain open and accessible during the meeting to any person attending.

THE OBJECTS

The memorandum must state the objects of the company: section 2. As Lord Parker of Waddington said in *Cotman* v. *Brougham*,[32] the statement of the objects in the memorandum serves a double purpose: (1) It protects the subscribers who learn from it the purposes to which

---

[32] [1918] A.C. 514, at p. 520. See also, *per* Lord Wrenbury at pp. 522, 523.

their money can be applied.[33] (2) It protects persons dealing with the company, who can discover from it,[34] the extent of the company's powers.

At common law, a corporation has the same legal capacity as a human being[35] but, in order to protect the shareholders and those who deal with the company, the courts evolved the *ultra vires* doctrine to the effect that since a registered company is an artificial person incorporated by Parliament for the objects stated in the memorandum, it has power only to carry out such objects together with anything incidental thereto. The doctrine has been modified by the European Communities Act, s.9, as will be explained later.

In practice it is, therefore, usual to set out at length in the memorandum all the objects which the company might require, and the short form of objects clause, in the model memorandum in Table B in the First Schedule to the Act, is seldom employed. Further, many powers, *e.g.* a power to borrow money for the purposes of the business, most of which would otherwise be implied, are set out expressly.

Lord Parker continued[36]:

"The narrower the objects expressed in the memorandum the less is the subscribers' risk, but the wider such objects the greater is the security of those who transact business with the company. Moreover, experience soon showed that persons who transact business with companies do not like having to depend on inference when the validity of a proposed transaction is in question. Even a power to borrow money could not always be safely inferred, much less such a power as that of underwriting shares in another company. Thus arose the practice of specifying powers as objects, a practice rendered possible by the fact that there is no statutory limit on the number of objects which may be specified. But even then, a person proposing to deal with a company could not be absolutely safe, for powers specified as objects might be read as ancillary to and exercisable only for the purpose of attaining what might be held to be the company's main or paramount object, and on this construction no-one could be quite certain whether the court would not hold any proposed transaction to be *ultra vires*. At any rate, all the surrounding circumstances would require investigation. Fresh clauses were framed to meet

---

[33] A member can require the company to send him a copy of the memorandum on payment of 5p.: s.24, *post*, p. 114.

[34] They can inspect the memorandum and the other documents kept by the Registrar: s.426, *post*, p. 114.

[35] *Case of Sutton's Hospital* (1612) 10 Co. Rep. 23a; Blackstone, Comm. 1, 593; *University of Glasgow* v. *Faculty of Physicians and Surgeons* (1834) 13 S. 9; (1835) 2 S. & M. 275; (1837) 15 S. 736; (1840) 1 Rob. 397.

[36] See note 32 above.

this difficulty, and the result is the modern memorandum of association, with its multifarious list of objects and powers specified as objects and its clauses designed to prevent any specified object being read as ancillary to some other object."[37]

The shareholders and persons dealing with the company were also protected by the rule that the stated objects could not be altered except by a special Act of Parliament or a reconstruction. Later, the objects could be altered for certain specified purposes with the consent of the court and now, as we shall see, they can be altered for certain specified purposes and the consent of the court is generally not required.[38]

Ultra vires doctrine

In order to protect the subscribers and persons dealing with the company the courts held that a company incorporated by registration under the Companies Acts is incorporated by Parliament for the objects stated in the memorandum of association so that it has power only to carry out such objects and anything else which is reasonably incidental thereto. If an act is performed or a transaction carried out which, though legal in itself, is not authorised by the objects clause in the memorandum or by statute, it is *ultra vires, i.e.* beyond the powers of, the company and void, so that it cannot be ratified even if all the members wish to ratify.

A registered company has power to carry out the objects set out in the memorandum and also everything which is reasonably necessary to enable it to carry out those objects. As Lord Selborne L.C. said in *Att.- Gen.* v. *Great Eastern Railway Co.*[39] the doctrine of *ultra vires* "ought to be reasonably, and not unreasonably, understood and applied, and . . . whatever may fairly be regarded as incidental to, or conse- quential upon, those things which the Legislature has authorised, ought not (unless expressly prohibited) to be held, by judicial construc- tion, to be *ultra vires.*" For example, a company formed "to buy, sell and deal in coal" may, *for the purpose of carrying out the stated objects*, employ labour, open shops, buy and hire lorries, purchase supplies, draw and accept bills of exchange, borrow and give security, have a

---

[37] For comparable Scottish comments see Lord Skerrington in *John Walker & Sons Ltd., Petitioners*, 1914 S.C. 280, at p. 289, and the reporter in *North of Scotland etc. Steam Navigation Co. Ltd., Petitioners*, 1920 S.C. 633, at p. 637.
[38] And a subsidiary company can be incorporated with other objects.
[39] (1880) 5 App.Cas. 473, at p. 478.

banking account, employ agents and pay bonuses and pensions to employees.[40]

In ascertaining whether a particular act is *intra* or *ultra vires* regard must be had to the nature of the transaction and not to the means of execution.[41]

A contract *ultra vires* a company is void and incapable of ratification even if every member wishes to ratify it.

A company was incorporated with the following objects: (1) to make, and sell, or lend on hire, railway carriages and wagons; (2) to carry on the business of mechanical engineers and general contractors; (3) to purchase, lease, work, and sell mines, minerals, land and buildings. The directors contracted to purchase a concession for making a railway in Belgium. *Held*, the contract was *ultra vires* the company and void so that not even the subsequent assent of the whole body of shareholders could ratify it: *Ashbury Railway Carriage Co. Ltd.* v. *Riche* (1875) L.R. 7 H.L. 653. Note that if this case were to occur again it would almost certainly be decided differently because of section 9(1) of the European Communities Act 1972, *post*.

The words "general contractors" referred to the words which went immediately before and indicated such contracts as mechanical engineers make for the purpose of carrying on their business: see *per* Lord Cairns L.C. at pp. 664, 665.

"This contract was entirely . . . beyond the objects in the memorandum of association. If so, it was thereby placed beyond the powers of the company to make the contract. If so . . . it is not a question whether the contract ever was ratified or was not ratified. If it was a contract void at its beginning, it was void because the company could not make the contract. If . . . every shareholder of the company had said, 'That is a contract which we desire to make . . . ,' the case would not have stood in any different position from that in which it stands now. The shareholders would thereby, by unanimous consent, have been attempting to do the very thing which, by the Act of Parliament, they were prohibited from doing": *per* Lord Cairns L.C. at p. 672.

A Scottish illustration of the operation of the *ultra vires* doctrine is *Life Association of Scotland* v. *Caledonian Heritable Security Co. Ltd. in Liquidation* (1886) 13 R. 750, in which an agreement entered into by a heritable security company with a prior bondholder for the purpose of preventing an immediate sale by the prior bondholder of the security subjects was held to be *ultra vires* since it was neither expressly authorised by the memorandum nor "incidental or conducive to the attainment" of the stated objects.

---

[40] Palmer's *Company Law*, 23rd ed., p. 116; *Cape Insulation Ltd.* v. *Braid Investments Ltd.*, 1979 S.L.T. (Sh. Ct.) 66.

[41] *Thompson* v. *J. Barke and Company (Caterers) Ltd.*, 1975 S.L.T. 67 (O.H.), *ante*, p. 23.

It will be seen that, as an exception to the rule in *Foss* v. *Harbottle* or in his own right, an individual member can bring proceedings for an injunction to restrain the company from doing an *ultra vires* act or entering into an *ultra vires* transaction.[42] An unsecured creditor of the company cannot sue to restrain it from acting *ultra vires*[43] but a secured creditor, at least one who has a specific (or fixed) charge[44] on its assets, can.[45]

Main object

As stated earlier,[46] it is usual to set out in the objects clause any object that the company might require, and to set out powers, many of which would otherwise be implied. Once this practice developed the rule that the objects must be stated in the memorandum and the *ultra vires* doctrine ceased to achieve their purpose and, in order to counter the practice, the courts evolved the "main objects" rule of construction by which one of the objects could be held to be the main object of the company and the remainder to be merely ancillary to the main object.

The "main objects" rule of construction is that "where a memorandum of association expresses the object of the company in a series of paragraphs, and one paragraph, or the first two or three paragraphs, appear to embody the 'main object' of the company, all the other paragraphs are treated as merely ancillary to this 'main object,' and as limited or controlled thereby": *per* Salmon J. in *Anglo-Overseas Agencies Ltd.* v. *Green* [1961] 1 Q.B. 1 at p. 8.

However, the "main objects" rule of construction can be excluded by an appropriate provision in the memorandum. In some cases, *e.g. Cotman* v. *Brougham* and *Anglo-Overseas Agencies Ltd.* v. *Green, infra*, a sub-clause declares in effect, that each of the objects is to be regarded as a main object.

An objects clause contained 30 sub-clauses enabling the company to carry on almost every kind of business. The first sub-clause authorised the company to acquire, take over, work, and develop any licences, concessions, estates, plantations and properties, and in particular four specified licenses to collect rubber, etc. The twelfth authorised the company to buy or otherwise acquire

[42] *Post*, p. 397.
[43] *Mills* v. *Northern Rlwy, of Buenos Ayres Co.* (1870) L.R. 5 Ch.App. 621; *Lawrence* v. *West Somerset Mineral Rlwy., Co.* [1918] 2 Ch. 250.
[44] *Post*, p. 561.
[45] *Per* Eve J. in *Lawrence's* case, *ante*, at p. 257.
[46] p. 72.

in any way and hold, sell or deal with or in any stocks or in any shares of any company. The objects clause concluded with a declaration that every sub-clause should be construed as a substantive clause and not limited or restricted by reference to or inference from any other sub-clause or by the name of the company, and that none of the sub-clauses or the objects or powers therein should be deemed subsidiary merely to the objects in the first sub-clause. The company underwrote and had allotted to it shares in an oil company. When the oil company was wound up the rubber company was placed on the list of contributories. *Held*, the underwriting was *intra vires* the rubber company: *Cotman* v. *Brougham* [1918] A.C. 514.[47]

The objects of a company were, *inter alia*, (A) to carry on business as importers and exporters of merchandise, (E) to acquire any concessions and contracts and to carry the same into effect. The objects clause concluded with a declaration that the objects specified in any paragraph should, except where otherwise expressed in such paragraph, be in no wise limited or restricted by reference to or inference from the terms of any other paragraph or the name of the company. *Inter alia*, the company claimed damages against an architect and a firm of estate agents for breach of an agreement to assist the company to obtain a building lease of a site in a shopping centre for a large store, shops and business development. The defence was that the acquisition of a building lease and the making of such an agreement was *ultra vires* the company. *Held*, the "main objects" rule was excluded and the acquisition of the building lease and the agreement were *intra vires*: *Anglo-Overseas Agencies Ltd.* v. *Green* [1961] 1 Q.B. 1.

A declaration like that in the above cases is not the only provision which will exclude the "main objects" rule.

In *Bell Houses Ltd.* v. *City Wall Properties Ltd.* [1966] 2 Q.B. 656 (C.A.), after stating the principal business of the company, which was that of developing housing estates, the objects clause provided that the company was formed "to carry on any other . . . business whatsoever which can, in the opinion of the board of directors, be advantageously carried on by the company in connection with or as ancillary to any of the above businesses or the general business of the company."[48] In one isolated transaction the company agreed, in consideration of the promise of payment of a procuration fee, to introduce to another company a financier prepared to provide a large amount of short-term credit for property development. It was held that since the directors were

---

[47] Compare the approval by the Scottish court of an "independent objects" clause in *London and Edinburgh Shipping Co. Ltd., Petitioners*, 1909 S.C. 1, and its rejection of such a clause in *Union Bank of Scotland Ltd., Petitioners*, 1918 S.C. 21, and in the *North of Scotland* Case, *ante*, p. 73.

[48] In the Australian High Court case of *H. A. Stephenson & Son Ltd.* v. *Gillanders, Arbuthnot & Co.* (1931) 45 C.L.R. 476, one of the objects for which the company was formed was "to carry on any other businesses . . . as the company may deem expedient."

honestly of the opinion that such an activity could be so advantageously carried on it was *intra vires* even though there was no declaration like that in the *Anglo-Overseas* case.[49]

Other objects were "to . . . turn to account . . . any of the property and assets . . . of the company for such consideration as the company may think fit" and "to do all such other things as are incidental or conducive to the above objects. . . ." The Court of Appeal also held that the contract regarding the procuration fee was authorised by the former clause and Salmon L.J. held that it was further authorised by the latter.

It may be mentioned here that when the main object of a company fails for any reason the substratum of the company is said to have gone and it is just and equitable that the company be wound up, and the "main objects" rule cannot be excluded. The reason is, as Lord Parker of Waddington said in *Cotman* v. *Brougham*,[50] that: "The question whether or not a company can be wound up for failure of substratum is a question of equity between a company and its shareholders. The question whether or not a transaction is *ultra vires* is a question of law between the company and a third party."[51]

The objects of the company included the following—(1) to acquire and use a German patent for manufacturing coffee from dates, (2) to acquire and use any other inventions for that or similar purposes, (3) to import and export all descriptions of produce for the purpose of food. The German patent was never granted, but the company acquired a Swedish patent for the same purpose and also made coffee from dates without a patent in Hamburg. The company was solvent, and the majority of the shareholders wished to continue the company. Two shareholders petitioned for a winding-up on the ground that its objects had entirely failed. *Held*, the substratum had failed as it was impossible to carry out the objects for which the company was formed, and it was just and equitable that the company should be wound up, although the petition was presented within a year after incorporation.[52] The real object was not just to make substitute coffee from dates but to work a particular German patent in Germany. Sub-clauses (2) and (3) were ancillary (subordinate) to that: *Re German Date Coffee Co.* (1882) 20 Ch.D. 169 (C.A.).

"Where on the face of the memorandum you see there is a distinct purpose which is the foundation of the company, then although the memorandum may contain other general words which include the doing of other objects, those general words must be read as being ancillary to that which the memorandum shews to be the main purpose, and if the main purpose fails and fails

[49] In the *Bell Houses* Case the test of what was *intra vires* was subjective.
[50] [1918] A.C. 514, at p. 520. See also, *per* Dixon J. in *Stephenson's* case, *supra*, at p. 487 and *Re Tivoli Freeholds* [1972] V.R. 445.
[51] Scots law does not distinguish between equity and law in this way.
[52] See p. 608, *post*.

altogether, then, . . . the substratum of the association fails": *per* Kay J. at p. 177.

However, the company will not be wound up if the substratum has not gone.

By the memorandum, the objects of K. Co. were to carry on the business of general engineering *and, inter alia*, to acquire a specified existing business. Having acquired the existing business K. Co. later sold it. K. Co. intended to continue with the business of general engineering and to buy another existing business. Certain shareholders petitioned for a winding up, alleging that the substratum of K. Co. had gone. *Held*, since the main object was to carry on an engineering business of a general nature, the substratum had *not* gone, and the company was not wound up: *Re Kitson & Co. Ltd.* [1946] 1 All E.R. 435 (C.A.), distinguishing *Re German Date Coffee Co., ante.* [In the latter case the main object was to acquire and work a *particular* patent.]

Further, a company can only be wound up on the ground that the substratum has gone on a shareholder's petition and no shareholder is *obliged* to petition to have the company wound up if he would prefer it to carry on some other business authorised by its memorandum.

Effect of ultra vires transactions—ultra vires in the "narrow" and "wider" sense

In *Mahony* v. *East Holyford Mining Co.*[53] Lord Hatherley said that persons dealing with the company, even if they do not have actual notice of the company's objects because they have not inspected the memorandum, have constructive notice of the powers, *i.e.* they are deemed to know them, because the memorandum, like most of the documents registered with the Registrar of Companies, is open to public inspection under section 426 and could have been inspected. Accordingly, if they make a contract which is to their knowledge, actual or constructive, *ultra vires* the company, and the company takes the point, they cannot enforce it, as is shown, *e.g.* by *Re Jon Beauforte Ltd.*, *infra*, although this is now subject to section 9(1) of the European Communities Act 1972, *post*. If they have supplied goods or performed services under such a contract they cannot obtain payment, and if they have lent money the general rule is that they cannot recover it.[54]

[53] (1875) L.R. 7 H.L. 869, at p. 893.
[54] *Sinclair* v. *Brougham* [1914] A.C. 398, *post*, p. 547.

A company, authorised by its memorandum to carry on business as costumiers and gown makers, started the business of making veneered panels. This was *ultra vires*. Builders were employed to build a factory, suppliers sold veneers, and coke merchants sold coke. Correspondence showed that the coke suppliers had actual notice that the business being carried on and for which the coke was required was that of veneered panel manufacturers, and they had constructive notice of the contents of the memorandum and hence that the transaction was *ultra vires* the company. *Held*, they could not prove for their debts in the company's liquidation, although this was without prejudice to the questions whether they were entitled to trace their money or other property into any particular asset or the proceeds of sale thereof and to participate in the distribution of surplus assets after the claims of creditors entitled to prove and winding-up costs had been provided for: *Re Jon Beauforte (London) Ltd.* [1953] Ch. 131.[55] [Note: If this case were to recur it would almost certainly be decided differently because of the European Communities Act, s.9(1).]

A similar case is *Introductions Ltd.* v. *National Provincial Bank Ltd.*[56]

In *Re Jon Beauforte Ltd., supra*, the contract would not have been void had the coke merchant not had clear notice of the veneered panel business. Coke may be used for other businesses, *e.g.* costumiers, and thus the merchant could not have discovered from the memorandum alone the *ultra vires* nature of the transaction. Thus if a person dealing with a company enters into a contract which could come within the objects clause, but in fact does not, he is only subject to the *ultra vires* rule if he knew that the goods supplied under the contract were not in fact being used for a purpose within that clause. Recently this type of *ultra vires* cases have been categorised as being *ultra vires* "in the wider sense": *Rolled Steel Ltd.* v. *British Steel Corpn.* [1982] 3 W.L.R. 715, 734. An obvious example of such a contract is one to supply basic office equipment which could be used in any business. Only if the supplier knows that the supply is in furtherance of a purpose which is not an authorised purpose of the company will the *ultra vires* doctrine apply. Such contacts are different from those which are *ultra vires* in "the narrow sense," *i.e.* those which are patently outside the objects clause; *e.g.* the supply of veneers to a theatrical costumier. The latter contracts are caught by the *ultra vires* doctrine even if the supplier has no actual

---

[55] In the *Jon Beauforte* case the test of what was *ultra vires* was subjective. See also the New South Wales case of *Hawkesbury Development Co. Ltd.* v. *Landmark Finance Pty, Ltd.* (1970) 92 W.N. (N.S.W.) 199.

[56] [1970] Ch. 199 (C.A.), *post*, p. 85.

knowledge, because he is bound by his constructive notice of the objects clause. This distinction between contracts which are *ultra vires* in the "narrow" and "wider" sense is now subject to section 9 of the European Communities Act 1972, *post.*

Money or other property which can be traced into any particular asset of the company or the proceeds of sale of that asset can be claimed, because the company is deemed to hold it as a trustee of the person from whom it was obtained, and, if tracing is impossible, he is entitled to share in the distribution of surplus assets after the creditors entitled to prove and winding-up costs have been provided for.[57] Accordingly, where an *ultra vires* issue of shares has been made, and the company is solvent, the subscribers are entitled to recover their money.[58] However, in *Re Jon Beauforte Ltd.* the creditor's right to trace was worthless since, *e.g.*, the coke had been consumed and so had lost its identity.

It seems that the company can protect its property acquired by an *ultra vires* expenditure.[59]

Subject as below, the company cannot recover its money or other property which it has spent or disposed of for an *ultra vires* purpose. But a director, who parts with the company's money or property for an *ultra vires* purpose, will be liable to the company for the loss it has sustained, even if he acted in good faith, because the company itself cannot legally authorise him to do an *ultra vires* act. The company can, however, in such a case, validly resolve not to sue him, and there is nothing *ultra vires* in its so doing. A guarantee by the directors that the company will perform an *ultra vires* contract to procure the repurchase of its own shares is binding on the directors[60] if the promise is to pay whether the company can lawfully be called upon to pay or not.[61]

In the *Bell Houses* case, *ante*, Mocatta J. held at first instance[62] that a defendant sued on a contract by a company could take the point that the contract was *ultra vires* the company, and it was immaterial

---

[57] See note 54 above.

[58] *Per* Lord Simonds in *Linz* v. *Electric Wire Co. of Palestine Ltd.* [1948] A.C. 371 (P.C.), at p. 377. If a shareholder has sold his shares he cannot then say they were unlawfully issued. A Scottish case is *Waverley Hydropathic Co. Ltd.* v. *Barrowman* (1895) 23 R. 136 (*ultra vires* issue of preference shares).

[59] *National Telephone Co. Ltd.* v. *The Constables of St. Peter Port* [1900] A.C. 317.

[60] *Garrard* v. *James* [1925] Ch. 616.

[61] *Per* Fisher J. in *Heald* v. *O'Connor* [1971] 1 W.L.R. 497, at p. 506.

[62] [1966] 1 Q.B. 207.

whether the contract was executory or executed by the company. In the Court of Appeal, Salmon L.J. said[63] that since the contract was *intra vires* the company it was unnecessary to consider the question whether, the plaintiff company having fully performed its part and the defendant having obtained all the benefits under the contract, the defendant could take the point that the contract was *ultra vires* the plaintiff company and so avoid payment, although he added that it seemed strange that the defendant could take advantage of a doctrine, manifestly for the protection of the shareholders, in order to deprive the company of money which in justice should be paid to it by him. However, in the *Anglo-Overseas Agencies* case, *ante*,[64] the defence was that the contract was *ultra vires* the plaintiff company. Again, in the *Charterbridge* case, *infra*, a third party, who was a purchaser of land from the company, took the point that the legal charge on the land which the company had given to a bank was *ultra vires* the company.

In *Charterbridge Corpn.* v. *Lloyds Bank Ltd.* [1970] Ch. 62, the plaintiff, who was a purchaser of land from a company, alleged that a legal charge on the land which the company had given to a bank, was created for purposes not for the benefit of the company—that the bank account of another company in the same group was overdrawn, the first company guaranteed the overdraft and then gave the bank the legal charge on its land to secure its indebtedness to the bank including that under the guarantee. The charge was *intra vires*—it was held that where, as was the case on the facts, a company is carrying out the purposes expressed in its memorandum, and does an act within the scope of a power expressed in it, that act is *intra vires* (the objects were, *inter alia*, to acquire lands for investment and to secure or guarantee by mortgages, charges or otherwise the performance and discharge of any contract, obligation or liability of the company or of any other person or corporation with whom or which it has dealings or having a business or undertaking in which the company is concerned or interested whether directly or indirectly); it would be contrary to the whole function of the memorandum if objects unequivocally set out in it should be subject to some implied limitation by reference to the state of mind of the parties; the state of mind of the officers of the company and the bank as to whether the transaction was intended to benefit the company was irrelevant on the issue of *ultra vires*. Further, it was held that if the intention was relevant, the directors as reasonable men might have concluded that the transaction would benefit the company.[65]

In *Rolled Steel Ltd.* v. *British Steel Corpn.* [1982] 3 W.L.R. 715, however,

---

[63] [1966] 2 Q.B. 656 at pp. 693–694.

[64] p. 76.

[65] And see *Reid Murray Holdings Ltd.* (*In Liq.*) v. *David Murray Holdings Pty. Ltd.* (1972) 5 S.A.S.R. 386.

Vinelott J. said that where such a power could be construed as only applying for the furtherance of the company's commercial objects, *e.g.* a power of guaranteeing loans, the exercise of such a power would be *ultra vires* if the intention was not the furtherance of such commercial objects.

European Communities Act 1972

When it became the practice to draft objects clauses widely and to set out powers in the objects clause,[66] the *ultra vires* doctrine ceased to protect shareholders and persons dealing with a company. Further, in the odd case where the objects were not drafted widely the doctrine was a trap for persons dealing with the company. Consequently, statutory modification of the doctrine so as to protect such persons was necessary and was recommended in the Jenkins Report.[67] Effect was more or less given to the recommendation when, in order to bring company law in the United Kingdom into line with that of the European Economic Community, the doctrine of *ultra vires* was modified by the European Economic Communities Act 1972, s.9.[68]

Section 9(1) provides that "in favour of a person dealing with a company in good faith, a transaction decided on by the directors shall be deemed one within the capacity of the company to enter into, . . . and a party to such a transaction shall not be bound to inquire as to the capacity of the company to enter into it . . . and shall be presumed to have acted in good faith unless the contrary is proved."

The above provision was intended to mean that if, *e.g.*, a person enters into a contract with a company which, although lawful, is *ultra vires* the company, and he does not actually know that it is *ultra vires*, provided that it has been decided on by the directors he can assume that it is *intra vires* and he will be able to enforce the contract against the company, *i.e.* the company will be unable to plead *ultra vires*. The section thus has no application where a director of the company has used company money for his own purposes and is thus in breach of trust. The recipient of such money cannot rely on section 9(1); it applies only to give relief where the *ultra vires* doctrine would have otherwise applied: *International Sales and Agencies Ltd*. v. *Marcus* [1982] 3 All E.R. 551, 559.

---

[66] *Ante*, p. 75.

[67] Para. 42.

[68] S.9 was intended to give effect to the First Directive of the Council of Ministers of the EEC (March 9, 1968, No. 68/151).

The wording of section 9(1) is however far from clear. First, it only applies in favour of a person dealing with a company *in good faith*. What, if anything, apart from actual knowledge will amount to bad faith? Does this really include the person who is aware that there might be an *ultra vires* element but refuses to investigate the matter? However, a party to a transaction decided on by the directors is not bound to inquire as to the capacity of the company to enter into the transaction (his omission to inquire is not bad faith) and he is presumed to have acted in good faith unless the contrary is proved (the burden of proving the contrary is on the company). In *International Sales and Agencies* v. *Marcus, supra*, Lawson J. thought that a company had to prove lack of good faith and could only do this by showing that the third party had "actual knowledge that the transaction was *ultra vires* the company or . . . could not in view of all the circumstances, have been unaware that he was a party to a transaction *ultra vires*."[69]

Secondly, the person relying on the section must have been *dealing with the company*. It is for that person and not the company to prove this element, there is no presumption in the section as there is in relation to good faith. In *International Sales and Agencies* v. *Marcus, supra*, Lawson J. thought that a person who received company money in satisfaction of a private debt could not be said to be dealing with the company but with the director concerned, even though payment was by cheques drawn on the company. If this is correct it is a severe limitation on the usefulness of the section.

Section 9(1), further, applies only to a transaction *decided on* by *the directors*. Presumably this includes, *e.g.*, a transaction decided upon by a managing director or sole effective director where the directors have properly delegated the appropriate powers to him. This was the opinion expressed in *International Sales and Agencies Ltd.* v. *Marcus* (*supra*). It follows that a person proposing to enter into a transaction with a company should, before entering into the transaction, satisfy himself that it has been decided upon by the directors or the managing director.

If section 9(1) operates, a transaction *ultra vires* a company is deemed *intra vires* for some purposes.

The provision does not change the position of the company, or that of the directors or managing director, where a transaction decided on by the directors is *ultra vires*—at least in so far as the company cannot

[69] [1982] 3 All E.R. 551, 559.

enforce an *ultra vires* contract against the other party and the directors and others involved in the breach with actual knowledge of it are in breach of duty in deciding that such a contract be made and are liable to the company accordingly: *International Sales and Agencies Ltd.* v. *Marcus (supra).* And a shareholder, *e.g.*, can still obtain an injunction to restrain the company from acting *ultra vires.*

The effect of section 9(1) is that if cases like *Ashbury Railway Carriage Co.* v. *Riche* and *Re Jon Beauforte, ante,*[70] and, perhaps, *Introductions Ltd.* v. *National Provincial Bank, post,*[71] were to occur again in England they would almost certainly be decided differently.

Powers

As stated earlier, in addition to the objects strictly so called, the memorandum usually sets out expressly a number of powers many of which are reasonably incidental to the attainment of the company's objects and would be implied if not set out. Powers frequently given are:

(1) Power to acquire similar businesses.
(2) Power to amalgamate or enter into profit-sharing agreements with other companies, and to borrow money jointly with other companies. (A general power to borrow does not authorise a joint borrowing.[72])
(3) Power to take shares in another company.[73]
(4) Power to borrow money for the purposes of its business. (This is implied in the case of a company formed for trading purposes[74]—but an express power removes any difficulty if there is a doubt as to whether the company answers that description.)

Since a loan must be for some purpose, borrowing money is not an independent activity even if the memorandum expressly provides that the company has, as an independent object, power to borrow money.

The main object of a company was to provide entertainments and services for overseas visitors. The objects clause also expressly empowered the company to borrow or raise money in such manner as the company should think fit and provided that each of the objects was an independent object. A bank, which was given a copy of the memorandum and which knew that the only

---

[70] pp. 74 and 79.   [71] p. 85.
[72] *Re Johnston Foreign Patents Co. Ltd.* [1904] 2 Ch. 234 (C.A.).
[73] *Re Barned's Banking Co.* (1867) L.R. Ch.App. 105, and *Re Lands Allotment Co.* [1894] 1 Ch. 616 (C.A.).
[74] *General Auction Estate etc. Co.* v. *Smith* [1891] 3 Ch. 432, *post*, p. 544.

business being carried on by the company was pig-breeding, lent money to the company and took debentures as security. *Held*, the loan was for a purpose known to be *ultra vires* and the debentures were void: *Introductions Ltd.* v. *National Provincial Bank Ltd.* [1970] Ch. 199 (C.A.).

A similar rule applies to a power to lend and advance money. It may only be used for the commercial purposes of the company: *Rolled Steel Ltd.* v. *British Steel Corporation* [1982] 3 W.L.R. 715.

(5) Power to issue bills of exchange.

(6) Power to sell or otherwise dispose of any part of the property of the company. (A colliery company with express power to acquire land has been held to have implied power to sell it from time to time in a proper way.[75])

(7) Power to sell the undertaking of the company for shares in another company or other consideration. (The Jenkins Report[76] recommended that, notwithstanding anything in the memorandum or articles, the directors should not be able, without the specific approval of the company in general meeting, to dispose of substantially the whole of the company's undertaking or assets.)

(8) Power to give gratuities and pay pensions to officers and employees and to their wives and other dependants.

(9) Power to make provision for its employees or former employees or those of its subsidiaries in connection with the cessation or transfer of its business, even if this would not necessarily be in the best interests of the company. Approval must be given either by an ordinary resolution or according to the memorandum and articles. Such provision must be made out of profits or surplus assets: 1980 Act, s.74 reversing *Parke* v. *The Daily News Ltd.* [1962] Ch. 927.

(10) Power to award directors' remuneration. This may even be paid out of capital if such payments are genuinely directors' remuneration as opposed to disguised gifts of capital. In the absence of fraud the court will not inquire into whether the sums so awarded are reasonable: *Re Halt Garage (1964) Ltd.* [1982] 3 All E.R. 1016.

A company has implied power to make other gifts which are: (a) reasonably incidental to the carrying on of the company's business; (b)

[75] *Re Kingsbury Collieries Ltd. and Moore's Contract* [1907] 2 Ch. 259.
[76] Para. 122.

bona fide transactions; (c) done for the benefit of and to promote the prosperity of the company.[77]

In *Re Lee, Behrens & Co. Ltd.*[78] Eve J. held that the above three conditions must also be fulfilled in the case of an express power to make gifts but Pennycuick J. disagreed in the *Charterbridge* case, *ante*[79] and it is thought that condition (a) need not be fulfilled in the case of a gift made under an express power. This view was also taken by Buckley L.J. in *Re Horsley & Weight Ltd.* [1982] 3 W.L.R. 431, 440.

There also seems some doubt as to the applicability of (c) in the case of an express power. In *Re Horsley & Weight, supra*, Buckley L.J. said (at p. 440): "Of course, if the memorandum of association expressly or by implication provides that an express object only extends to acts which benefit or promote the prosperity of the company, regard must be paid to that limitation; but where there is no such express or implied limitation, the question whether an act done within the terms of an express object of the company will benefit or promote the prosperity of the company or of its business is, in my view, irrelevant."

In *Rolled Steel Ltd.* v. *British Steel Corpn.* [1982] 3 W.L.R. 715, Vinelott J. drew a distinction between those powers which, on their construction, are not conferred for the furtherance of the company's commercial purposes, *e.g.* a power to pay a pension to a former director, and those which are so conferred. The question whether the exercise of the former is bona fide for the benefit of the company is relevant only to the possible abuse of the powers of the directors[80] and not to the question whether the transaction was *ultra vires*. Commercial powers, on the other hand, *e.g.* lending or borrowing money, must be exercised for the furtherance of the commercial interests of the company, and therefore the question of the benefit to the company is relevant both to the possible abuse of power by the directors and the question of *ultra vires*. The latter cannot be ratified even by all the shareholders. Of course, if a company with an implied power to make gifts makes one which is not so reasonably incidental, it is *ultra vires*. Section 9 of the European Communities Act, *ante*,[81] may prevent the

---

[77] *Hutton* v. *West Cork Rlwy. Co.* (1883) 23 Ch.D. 654 (C.A.); *Parke* v. *Daily News Ltd.* [1962] Ch. 927; *Gibson's Executor* v. *Gibson*, 1978 S.C. 197 (O.H.).

[78] [1932] 2 Ch. 46, applied by Plowman J. in *Re W. & M. Roith Ltd.* [1967] 1 W.L.R. 432.

[79] p. 81.

[80] *Post*, p. 371. See also *Re Halt Garage (1964) Ltd.* [1982] 3 All E.R. 1016.

[81] p. 82.

company from recovering the money from the donee, although there is some doubt as to whether a donee is a "person dealing with the company," within the meaning of that section. If such a gift is only proposed, a shareholder can bring an action to restrain it.[82]

In *Evans* v. *Brunner, Mond & Co. Ltd.* [1921] 1 Ch. 359, a donation for scientific education and research by a chemical manufacturing company was held to be *intra vires*. The objects clause included an express power to do "all such business and things as may be incidental or conducive to the attainment of the above objects, or any of them." Such a power, it was decided, only authorises the company to do that which is incidental or conducive to the main object of the company, but the gift in question was so incidental.

Without any express mention in its memorandum a registered company has power to hold land for the purpose of carrying out the objects set out in the memorandum.[83]

The Jenkins Report recommended[84] that the Act should be amended to provide that every company should have certain specified powers except to the extent that they are excluded, expressly or by implication, by its memorandum; such powers being those which any company would normally need in order to pursue its objects. This might result in memoranda of association being drafted in less prolix terms by the omission of many common form powers.

Alteration of objects

If a company wishes to do something *ultra vires* it can usually alter its objects so that the transaction will be *intra vires*.

By section 5 a company may, by special resolution, alter the provisions of its memorandum with respect to its objects to enable the company:

(1) To carry on its business more economically or efficiently.

The objects clause was in the short form set out in Table B. An alteration gave the company general powers likely to be useful to it in its business. *Held*, the alteration enabled the company to carry on business more economically and efficiently: *Re New Westminster Brewery Co. Ltd.* [1911] W.N. 247.[85]

---

[82] *Hutton* v. *West Cork Ry. Co.* (1883) 23 Ch.D. 654 (C.A.).

[83] The Mortmain and Charitable Uses Acts of 1888, 1891 and 1892, and the Companies Act 1948, ss.14 and 408, were repealed by the Charities Act 1960, s.38 and Sched. 7, Pt. IIA. The Mortmain Acts did not apply to Scotland. Nor did the Charities Act except so far as it repealed the Companies Act.   [84] Para. 54.

[85] A comparable Scottish case is *North of Scotland etc. Steam Navigation Co. Ltd., Petitioners*, 1920 S.C. 633. See also *J. & P. Coats Ltd., Petitioners* (1900) 2 F. 829.

(2) To attain its main purpose by new or improved means.

The word "purpose" is more restricted than the term "object" and consequently the alteration must be one to carry out the main purpose of the company rather than one of the objects of the company, although that object may be described in the memorandum as a main object.[86]

The memorandum of a company, promoted to manage licensed premises mainly with a view to minimising evils of the drink traffic, provided that surplus profits, after payment of a dividend of not more than four per cent. per annum, should be applied to "purposes of public utility." The court doubted whether the company could competently alter the memorandum by deleting the provision as to surplus profits, but confirmed an amended alteration which increased the maximum dividend to six per cent., as being, in view of the changed financial situation, an improved means of attaining the company's main purpose: *Kirkcaldy Café Co. Ltd., Petitioners*, 1921 S.C. 681.

(3) To enlarge or change the local area of its operations.[87]

An alteration of this nature may necessitate an alteration in the name of the company.

A company, the principal object of which was to acquire land in Egypt, desired to alter its memorandum so as to give power to acquire land in the Soudan. *Held*, the alteration could be made provided that the company inserted the words "and Soudan" after the word "Delta" in its name: *Re Egyptian Delta Land and Investment Co.* [1907] W.N. 16.[88]

(4) To carry on some business which under existing circumstances may conveniently or advantageously be combined with the business of the company.[89] In this connection also a change of name may be required.[90]

The additional business to be carried on may be wholly different from the existing business of the company, and yet be capable of being

---

[86] *Re Governments Stock Investment Co.* [1891] 1 Ch. 649.
[87] A Scottish case illustrating "enlarge or change the local area of its operations" is *Scottish Veterans' Garden City Association (Incorporated), Petitioners*, 1946 S.C. 416.
[88] Contrast *Kirkcaldy Steam Laundry Co. Ltd., Petitioners* (1904) 6 F. 778.
[89] Scottish cases illustrating this purpose are *Hugh Baird & Sons Ltd., Petitioners*, 1932 S.C. 455, *Dundee Aerated Water Mfg. Co. Ltd., Petitioners*, 1932 S.C. 473, and *King Line, Petitioners* (1902) 4 F. 504.
[90] *Scottish Accident Insce. Co. Ltd., Petitioners* (1896) 23 R. 586; *Scottish Employers' Liability etc. Assce. Co. Ltd., Petitioners* (1896) 23 R. 1016.

conveniently or advantageously combined with it. Whether one business can be conveniently combined with another is essentially a business question to be determined by the persons engaged in the business of the company, namely the directors and the shareholders.

The company's business consisted of holding large investments in two companies. A special resolution was passed to enable the company to carry on the business of bankers, financiers, underwriters, and dealers in securities, *and to buy, sell and deal in real and personal estate of every description.* It was conceded that the words italicised were too wide. *Held,* subject to the omission of the words italicised the alteration was valid even though the new business bore no relation to the existing business: *Re Parent Tyre Co. Ltd.* [1923] 2 Ch. 222.[91]

A company may even add some business which its original memorandum specifically forbids.

A company which had power to carry on any kind of insurance business except life insurance was allowed to add life insurance to its objects on condition that it included "and Life" in its name: *Mutual Property Insurance Co. Ltd., Petitioners*, 1934 S.C. 61.

The additional business must not, however, be destructive of or inconsistent with the existing business. It must leave the existing business substantially what it was before.

The company's business was to promote, assist and protect cyclists. It was desired to include among the persons to be assisted all tourists, including motorists. *Held*, it was impossible to combine the two businesses, as one of the objects of the company was to protect cyclists against motorists: *Re Cyclists' Touring Club* [1907] 1 Ch. 269.

The provision does not "authorise the company to commit suicide . . . in other words, to do something which is inconsistent with the purpose of its incorporation."[92]

(5) To restrict or abandon any of the objects specified in the memorandum.

This provision cannot be used to enable a company to make a fundamental change in its character by the substitution of a new main object.

---

[91] Scottish judges took a less liberal view: see *Western Ranches Ltd.* v. *Nelson's Trustees* (1899) 1 F. 812, and *Edinburgh Southern Cemetery Co. Ltd., Petitioners*, 1923 S.C. 867.

[92] *Per* Lord President Clyde in *Tayside Floorcloth Co. Ltd., Petitioners*, 1923 S.C. 590, at p. 592.

The original objects of a company were to build and let a public hall with shops and cellars. The building was destroyed by fire. The court refused to confirm an alteration to substitute for the original objects the erection and letting of shops and houses and warehouses: *Strathspey Public Assembly etc. Hall Co. Ltd.* v. *Anderson's Trustees*, 1934 S.C. 385.

An alteration of objects promoting a default beneficiary to the status of a primary object with regard to taking surplus assets on a winding up is not an alteration for purpose (5).

Clause 3(1)(*t*) of a memorandum provided that surplus assets on a winding up should go to any institution having objects similar to those of the company and in default to any charity. The clause was altered so as to provide that any balance on a winding up should go to one specified charity. *Held*, the alteration was not one to enable the company "to restrict or abandon" any of its objects and was ineffective: *Re Hampstead Garden Suburb Trust Ltd.* [1962] Ch. 806; compare the *Kirkcaldy Café* case, *supra*.

    (6) To sell or dispose of the whole or any part of the undertaking of the company.

    (7) To amalgamate with any other company or body of persons.

Section 5 is not restricted to alteration of the objects *clause*.[93]

The section goes on to provide that certain dissentients may, however, within 21 days after the passing of the special resolution, apply to the court for an alteration of objects to be cancelled, and then the alteration is of no effect unless it is confirmed by the court. The application for cancellation can be made by the holders of not less than 15 per cent. in nominal value of the company's issued share capital or any class thereof[94] or, if the company is not limited by shares, not less than 15 per cent. of the members or, when debentures entitle the holders to object to an alteration of objects, by the holders of not less than 15 per cent. of the company's debentures. An application cannot be made by a person who consented to or voted for the alteration. Debentures entitling the holders to object are those secured by a floating charge[95] which were issued before December 1, 1947. The holders of such debentures must be given the same notice of a special resolution altering the company's objects as the members. In the

---

[93] *Incorporated Glasgow Dental Hospital* v. *Lord Advocate*, 1927 S.C. 400; *Scottish Special Housing Association Ltd., Petitioners*, 1947 S.C. 17.

[94] In the *Hampstead* case, *supra*, the petition was by the holders of not less than 15 per cent. in nominal value of the deferred shares.

[95] *Post*, p. 562.

Hampstead case, *ante*, it was held that notice to trustees for the debenture holders is not enough, even if the trust deed makes the trustees general agents for the debenture holders to receive notices.[96]

The section also provides that on an application for cancellation the court may confirm the alteration of objects wholly or in part and on such terms as it thinks fit, and may adjourn the proceedings to enable an arrangement to be made for the purchase, other than by the company, of the interests of dissentient members. Alternatively the court may provide for the purchase of the dissentient members' shares by the company or make any alterations to the memorandum or articles of the company. Such alterations have the same effect as ones duly authorised by the company. If the court orders that no specified or general alterations be made to the memorandum or articles this overrides any power in the Acts to the contrary.[97]

Section 5 is thus a "minority section," *i.e.* a section designed to prevent the minority of the members of the company being oppressed by the majority.[98] Even though the special resolution altering the objects was passed by the appropriate majority, the alteration requires confirmation by the court if a dissentient minority of members applies to the court.

A company exempt from using the word "Limited" at the end of its name cannot alter its objects so as to take them outside the conditions for such exemption (1981 Act, s.25(5)).

When the objects are altered, a printed copy of the special resolution, or a copy in some other form approved by him, must be delivered to the Registrar within 15 days (1948 Act, s.143; 1967 Act, s.51)[99] and, if no application is made for cancellation of the alteration, a printed copy of the memorandum as altered must be delivered to the Registrar between 21 and 36 days after the date of the resolution.[1] If an application for cancellation is made to the court, the company must forthwith give notice in the prescribed form thereof to the Registrar and, on the alteration being cancelled or confirmed, an office copy of the court order must be delivered within 15 days. In the case of confirmation, a

---

[96] The lack of notice to the debenture holders was another reason for the court's refusal to confirm the alteration.

[97] *Post*, p. 95.

[98] *Post*, p. 406.

[99] *Post*, p. 325.

[1] Although the original memorandum need not have been printed.

printed copy of the memorandum as altered must also be delivered:
section 5(7).

The validity of an alteration of objects cannot be questioned on the
ground that it was not authorised by section 5 except in proceedings
taken (whether under section 5 or otherwise) within 21 days after the
date of the resolution: section 5(9). The result would seem to be that if,
within 21 days after an alteration of objects, an application for cancellation is made by a member or members, whether or not holding 15 per
cent. of the issued shares, on the ground that the alteration was not for
one of the seven purposes specified in section 5, the court must declare
the alteration invalid. If no such application is made, an alteration for a
purpose outside the seven specified purposes is valid.

The Jenkins Report recommended[2] that section 5 should be
amended by doing away with the list of authorised alterations and
substituting a general power of alteration. This amendment would
make it appropriate to repeal subsection (9). It was also recommended
that the dissentient shareholders or debenture holders who may apply
to the court to cancel an alteration of objects should be five per cent.
instead of 15 per cent. and the time within which they may apply should
be 28 days instead of 21 days. Further, that the court should be enabled
to authorise the application of the company's capital in the purchase of
the interests of dissentients.

The Limitation of Liability

Whether the liability of the members is limited by shares or by guarantee it is enough if the memorandum merely states that the liability of
the members is limited: section 2.

Even though a company is exempted under section 25 of the 1981
Act from using the word "Limited" as part of its name, the memorandum must contain a statement that the liability of the members is
limited.

We saw earlier that under section 31[3] members who know that the
company is carrying on business with less than the statutory minimum
of members may become severally liable for its debts and may be
severally sued therefor, *i.e.* not only do they lose the privilege of

---

[2] Para. 54.
[3] *Ante*, p. 24.

limited liability but the veil of incorporation is lifted and they can be sued by the creditors of the company.

It has been noted that a private limited company may be re-registered as unlimited (1967 Act, s.43) and an unlimited company may be re-registered as limited (1967 Act, s.44; 1980 Act, s.7).[4]

THE SHARE CAPITAL

In the case of a limited company with a share capital, section 2 provides that the memorandum must state the amount of share capital with which the company proposes to be registered and its division into shares of a fixed amount, *e.g.* one hundred thousand pounds divided into one hundred thousand shares of one pound each. This capital, called the "nominal capital" or the "authorised capital," is that which the company is authorised to raise by the issue of shares. The amount of such capital will be determined by business considerations, and for private companies there is no fixed legal minimum or maximum. If it is proposed to purchase some property for £30,000 and £10,000 is wanted for working capital, the founders might fix the nominal capital at £60,000. This capital merely represents the aggregate amount of shares which the company is authorised to issue without paying further duty. The actual or issued capital will depend on how many shares are issued. The stated amount of each share is called its nominal amount or par value. Today it is usual to have shares of a nominal amount of £1 or less each because shares of such a nominal amount are more marketable than shares of £200 each like those in Table B.[5]

A public company, however, cannot be registered unless its memorandum has an authorised capital figure of not less than the *authorised minimum*; 1980 Act, s.3(2). This is currently £50,000 (1980 Act, s.85), which is a low figure in practical terms. Other financial requirements must be met by public companies before they commence business.[6] The present requirement merely relates to the shares it *may* issue.

The shares into which the nominal capital is divided may be divided into classes, *e.g.* preference and ordinary shares, but it is usual to do this in the articles rather than in the memorandum.[7]

---

[4] *Ante*, pp. 42 *et seq.*
[5] *Ante*, p. 56.
[6] *Post*, p. 183.
[7] See *Andrews* v. *Gas Meter Co.* [1897] Ch. 361 (C.A.), *post*, p. 207.

The nominal capital may be increased, if the articles authorise it, by an ordinary resolution under section 61.[8] Again, if the articles authorise it, capital can be reduced by a special resolution and the confirmation of the court under section 66.[9] No special provision need be made for these purposes in the memorandum.

A change in description of a share from, say, 5s. to 25p. is not a change in the fixed amount of the share within section 2(4) and therefore is not an alteration of a condition of the memorandum so that no formalities are required by virtue of the Act.[10]

OTHER CLAUSES

The matters set out *supra must* be stated in the memorandum: section 2. The contents of the memorandum, however, are not restricted to these and may include any other provisions which the framers desire to insert. Sometimes the memorandum contains provisions dealing with the rights attaching to particular classes of shares such as preference shares, *e.g.* dividend and voting rights and the right to participate in the assets in a winding up. When this is so, the articles cannot be referred to for the purpose of ascertaining the rights of the shareholders, unless there is some ambiguity to be explained or some omission to be supplemented.

A company had ordinary and preference shares. The memorandum provided that the holders of the preference shares should have "a preferential right in the distribution of the assets of the company in the event of a winding up or otherwise." The articles provided that on a winding up the surplus assets after repayment of the whole of the paid-up capital should be divided between all the members in proportion to the capital paid up on their shares, both preference and ordinary. *Held*, (1) the rights conferred by the memorandum on the preference shareholders were exhaustive; (2) they were limited to a preference in the distribution of the assets, and gave no right to participate in the surplus assets in a winding up or otherwise; and (3) the articles could not be referred to for the purpose of construing the memorandum: *Re Duncan Gilmour & Co. Ltd.* [1952] 2 All E.R. 871.[11]

[8] *Post*, p. 223.
[9] *Post*, p. 229.
[10] *Re Harris & Sheldon Group Ltd.* [1971] 1 W.L.R. 899.
[11] *cf. Liquidator of the Milford Haven Fishing Co. Ltd.* v. *Jones* (1895) 22 R. 577. Contrast, however, the Scottish cases which are authority for reading the memorandum and articles together as contemporaneous documents: *Oban, etc., Distilleries Ltd., Petitioners* (1903) 5 F. 1140, followed in *Marshall, Fleming & Co. Ltd., Petitioners*, 1938 S.C. 873 (O.H.)

However, the rights of the holders of particular classes of shares are now usually contained in the articles.

The Association Clause and Subscription

The association clause is the clause by which the subscribers to the memorandum (at least two: section 1; 1980 Act, section 2) declare that they desire to be formed into a company in pursuance of the memorandum and agree to take the number of shares set opposite their respective names. The subscription contains their names, addresses and descriptions and the number of shares which each subscribes for. The subscribers must take at least one share each: section 2. Each subscriber must write opposite his name the number of shares he takes (s.2) and must sign in the presence of at least one witness (s.3). The signatures must be attested but one witness may attest all or both signatures: section 3. The Registrar requires the date of execution to be given.

It is usual for each subscriber to sign the memorandum for one share only. This is because the subscriber may by contract be bound to take up a definite number of shares in the company, and if he has signed the memorandum for that number he might be bound to take twice the number he intended, once under his contract, and again under the memorandum.

The subscribers need not be independent persons. They may be nominees, or one of two subscribers may be a trustee, of the one share for which he subscribes, for the other subscriber to whom all the rest of the shares issued are allotted,[12] *i.e.* a "one-man" company is legal.

A minor[13] may sign the memorandum because, the contract being voidable and not void, any subsequent avoidance by him will not invalidate the registration.[14]

Another, existing, company may sign the memorandum. So can a person who is a partner in a firm, but an English firm cannot.

Alteration of the Memorandum Generally

A company may alter its memorandum of association only in the cases, in the mode and to the extent for which express provision is made in the

---

[12] See *Salomon* v. *Salomon & Co. Ltd.* [1897] A.C. 22.
[13] *i.e.* a person under the age of 18: see *post*, p. 187.
[14] *Re Laxon & Co.* (*No.* 2) [1892] 3 Ch. 555. And see 1980 Act, s.3(4), *ante* p. 20.

Act: section 4. It has been seen that the name, objects and share capital clauses may be altered under section 24 of the 1981 Act and sections 5, 61 and 66 of the 1948 Act respectively, *ante*. In addition, by section 23, subject to the provisions of section 22 of the 1948 Act and section 75 of the 1980 Act, *infra*, any condition in the memorandum which could have been in the articles (*i.e.* not such things as the name, the objects or the share capital, which must be in the memorandum) can be altered by special resolution, unless the memorandum itself provides for or prohibits the alteration of the condition, or it relates to class rights, *i.e.* the special rights of any class of members.

The *Hampstead Garden Suburb* case,[15] *ante*,[16] shows that if a company elects to express a given function as an object, *e.g.* the distribution of surplus assets in a winding up, it must be contained in the memorandum by virtue of section 2 and cannot be altered under section 23. The modes in which class rights may be varied are explained later.[17] Since provisions concerning class rights are the only important provisions which may be in either the memorandum or the articles, and they cannot be altered under section 23 if they are in the memorandum, it follows that the section is unimportant in practice. Further, as was stated earlier, class rights are normally contained in the articles.

Section 23 contains the same provisions as to application to the court for cancellation of an alteration as section 5,[18] except that debenture holders cannot apply and there is no equivalent of section 5(9).

Section 22 provides that neither the memorandum nor the articles can be altered so as to require a member to take up more shares, or in any way increase his liability to contribute to the share capital or otherwise pay money to the company, unless he consents in writing. Section 22 is, therefore, a "minority section," *i.e.* a section intended to prevent the minority of the members being oppressed by the majority.[19] Under section 75 of the 1980 Act the court can make an order to relieve any part of the members who are being unfairly prejudiced and such an order may alter the memorandum or the articles, in which event the company cannot make a further alteration, inconsistent with the order, without the leave of the court (1980 Act, s.75(5)).[20]

Any document making or evidencing an alteration in the memoran-

---

[15] *Re Hampstead Garden Suburb Trust Ltd.* [1962] Ch. 806.
[16] p. 90.   [17] *Post*, p. 215.   [18] *Ante*, p. 89.
[19] *Post*, p. 406.   [20] *Post*, p. 413.

dum or articles, and any copy of the memorandum or articles as altered, must be in the same language as the memorandum and articles orginally registered[21]; and, if that language is Welsh, must be accompanied by a certified translation into English (1976 Act, s.30(7)).

Section 9(5) of the European Communities Act 1972 provides that where a company is required to send to the Registrar any document making or evidencing an alteration in the company's memorandum or articles (other than a special resolution under section 5) the company must send with it a printed copy of the memorandum or articles as altered. As to what is "printed," see the Pamphlet "Notes for the Guidance of Registered Companies" (C. 56a, 6th revise, October 1974).[22]

Section 9(3) of the 1972 Act requires the Registrar to publish in the *Gazette* notice of the receipt by him of any document making or evidencing an alteration in the memorandum or articles of a company. Section 9(4) provides that a company cannot rely against other persons on any alteration to the memorandum or articles if it had not been officially notified (under s.9(3)) at the material time and is not shown by the company to have been known at that time to the person concerned, or if the material time is less than 16 days after official notification and it is shown that the person concerned was unavoidably prevented from knowing of the event at that time.

SPECIMEN MEMORANDUM OF ASSOCIATION OF A PRIVATE COMPANY

The Companies Acts 1948 *to* 1981

———

COMPANY LIMITED BY SHARES

———

10995293/3

MEMORANDUM OF ASSOCIATION

OF

X.Y.Z. EUROPE LIMITED

1. The name of the Company is "X.Y.Z. EUROPE LIMITED."

2. The registered office of the Company will be situate in England and Wales.

3. The objects for which the Company is established are—

(A) To carry on the business of manufacturers and suppliers of and dealers in products or commodities of all kinds comprising or constituting components of or being associated with or for use in or in connection with, and suppliers of services in relation to, vehicles of all descriptions, including motor vehicles, aircraft and ships, engineering of whatsoever nature, electrical and electronic equipment, cables, chemicals, natural and synthetic rubber and foam, general rubber goods, hose, belting, fire protection, flooring, textiles, sports equipment, footwear, paper, plastics and products, commodities and services of whatever nature which can conveniently be manufacturered, supplied or dealt in by the Company, and to carry on any other business which can conveniently be carried on in connection with any of the Company's objects.

(B) To acquire and hold shares, stocks, debentures, debenture stock or other securities or obligations of any other company incorporated in or carrying on business in any part of the world.

(C) To carry on the business of planters, growers and cultivators of rubber, gutta percha and other produce of the soil, and to treat, process, prepare, render marketable, buy, sell and dispose of any such products either in their raw or manufactured state and any product or by-product derived therefrom.

(D) To carry on research and development work and experiments.

(E) To procure the Company to be registered or recognised in any country or place outside the United Kingdom.

(F) To amalgamate or enter into partnership or into any arrangement for sharing of profits, union of interests, co-operation, joint adventure reciprocal concession or otherwise with any person, firm or company carrying on or engaged in or about to carry on or engage in any business or transaction which the Company is authorised to carry on or engage in, or any business or transaction capable of being conducted so as directly or indirectly to benefit the Company.

(G) To carry on any other trade or business whatsoever which can, in the opinion of the Directors, be advantageously carried on by the Company in connection with or as auxiliary to the general business of the Company.

(H) To buy, sell, manufacture, repair, alter, improve, manipulate, prepare for market, let on hire, and generally deal in all kinds of plant, machinery, apparatus, tools, utensils, materials, produce, substances, articles and things for the purpose of any of the businesses specified herein, or likely to be required by customers or other persons having, or about to have, dealings with the Company.

(I) To enter into contracts, agreements and arrangements with any other company for the carrying out by such other company on behalf of the Company of any of the objects for which the Company is formed.

(J) To acquire, undertake and carry on the whole or any part of the business, property and liabilities of any person or company carrying on any business which the Company is authorised to carry on or possess, or which may seem to the Company capable of being conveniently carried on or calculated directly or indirectly to enhance the value of or render profitable any of the Company's property or rights, or any property suitable for the purposes of the Company.

(K) To enter into any arrangements with any government or authorities, supreme, municipal, local or otherwise that may seem conducive to the Company's objects or any of them, and to obtain from any such government or authority any rights, privileges and concessions which the Company may think it desirable to obtain, and to carry out, exercise and comply with any such arrangements, rights, privileges and concessions.

(L) To apply for, or join in applying for, purchase or by other means acquire and protect, prolong and renew, whether in the United Kingdom or elsewhere, any patents, patent rights, brêvets d'invention, licences, registered designs, protections and concessions, which may appear likely to be advantageous or useful to the Company, and to use, and turn to account and to manufacture under or grant licences or privileges in respect of the same, and to expend money in experimenting and testing and making researches, and in improving or seeking to improve any patents, inventions or rights which the Company may acquire or propose to acquire.

(M) To subsidise, assist and guarantee the payment of money by or the performance of any contract, engagement or obligation by any persons or companies and to act as agents for the collection, receipt or payment of money and generally to act as agents for and render services to customers and others.

(N) To promote any company for the purpose of acquiring all or any of the property and liabilities of this Company, or for any other purpose which may seem directly or indirectly calculated to benefit this Company.

(O) To pay out of the funds of the Company all expenses which the Company may lawfully pay of or incidental to the formation, registration and advertising of or raising money for the Company, and the issue of its capital, or for contributing to or assisting any company either issuing or purchasing with a view to issue all or any part of the Company's capital in connection with the advertising or offering the same for sale or subscription, including brokerage and commissions for obtaining applications for or taking, placing or underwriting or procuring the underwriting of shares, debentures or debenture stock.

(P) Generally to purchase, take on lease or exchange, hire, or otherwise acquire any real or personal property and any rights or privileges which the Company may think necessary or convenient for the purposes of its business.

(Q) To receive money on deposit upon such terms as the Company may approve.

(R) To invest and deal with the moneys of the Company in such manner as may from time to time be determined.

(S) To lend money with or without security, but not to carry on the business of a registered money lender.

(T) To borrow or raise or secure the payment of money in such manner as the Company shall think fit, and in particular by the issue of debentures or debenture stock, perpetual or otherwise, charged upon all or any of the Company's property (both present and future), including its uncalled capital, and to purchase, redeem or pay off any such securities.

(U) To remunerate any company for services rendered or to be rendered in placing or assisting to place or guaranteeing the placing or procuring the underwriting of any of the shares or debentures or other securities of the Company, or of any company in which this Company may be interested or propose to be interested, or in or about the conduct of the business of the Company, whether by cash payment or by the allotment of shares or securities of the Company credited as paid up in full or in part, or otherwise.

(V) To draw, make, accept, endorse, discount, execute and issue promissory notes, bills of exchange, bills of lading, warrants, debentures and other negotiable and transferable instruments.

(W) To sell, lease, exchange, let on hire or dispose of any real or personal property or the undertaking of the Company, or any part or parts thereof, for such consideration as the Company may think fit, and in particular for shares, whether fully or partly paid up, debentures or securities of any other company, whether or not having objects altogether or in part similar to those of the Company, and to hold and retain any shares, debentures or securities so acquired, and to improve, manage, develop, sell, exchange, lease, mortgage, dispose of or turn to account or otherwise deal with all or any part of the property or rights of the Company.

(X) To adopt such means of making known the products of the Company as may seem expedient, and in particular by advertising in the Press, by circulars, by purchase and exhibition of works of art or interest, by publication of books and periodicals, and by granting prizes, rewards and donations.

(Y) To support or subscribe to any charitable or public object and any institution, society or club which may be for the benefit of the Company or its Directors, officers or employees, or the directors, officers and employees of its predecessors in business, or of any subsidiary, allied or associated company, or may be connected with any town or place where the Company carries on business; to give pensions, gratuities or charitable aid to any person who may have served the

Company or its predecessors in business, or any subsidiary, allied or associated company, or to the wives, children or other relatives or dependants of such persons; to make payments towards insurance and to form and contribute to provident and benefit funds for the benefit of any Directors or officers of or persons employed by the Company, or of or by its predecessors in business, or of or by any subsidiary, allied or associated company, and to subsidise or assist any association of employers or employees, or any trade association.

(z) To obtain any Provisional Order or Act of Parliament for enabling the Company to carry any of its objects into effect or for effecting any modifications of the Company's constitution, or for any other purposes which may seem expedient, and to oppose any proceedings or applications which may seem calculated directly or indirectly to prejudice the Company's interests.

(AA) To establish, grant and take up agencies in any part of the world, and to do all such other things as the Company may deem conducive to the carrying on of the Company's business, either as principals, or agents, and to remunerate any persons in connection with the establishment or granting of such agencies upon such terms and conditions as the Company may think fit.

(BB) To do all or any of the above things in any part of the world, and as principals, agents, contractors, trustees or otherwise, and by or through trustees, agents or otherwise, and either alone or in conjunction with others.

(CC) To distribute any of the property of the Company in specie among the shareholders.

(DD) To do all such other things whatsoever, whether of the like or other sorts, which the Company considers to be in any way incidental to or conducive with any of the above objects, or conducive to the attainment thereof, or otherwise likely in any respect to be advantageous to the Company.

And it is hereby declared that the word "Company" in this clause shall be deemed to include any person or partnership or other body of persons, whether domiciled in the United Kingdom or elsewhere, and words denoting the singular number only shall include the plural number and vice versa, and that the objects specified in each paragraph of this clause shall, except where otherwise expressed in such paragraph, be regarded as independent objects and in nowise limited or restricted by reference to or inference from the terms of any other paragraph or the name of the Company.

4. The liability of the members is limited.

5. The share capital of the Company is £100, divided into 100 Ordinary Shares of £1 each.

WE, the several persons whose names and addresses are subscribed, are desirous of being formed into a Company in pursuance of this Memorandum of Association, and we respectively agree to take the number of shares in the capital of the Company set opposite our respective names.

NAMES, ADDRESSES AND DESCRIPTIONS OF SUBSCRIBERS	Number of Shares taken by each Subscriber
A.B.C. 100A Old Jewry, London EC2 Solicitor	One
D.E.F. 100A Old Jewry, London EC2 Solicitor	One

Dated this 17th day of November, 1982
Witness to the above Signatures—

G.H.I.
44 Old Jewry,
London E.C.2
Solicitor

CHAPTER 4

ARTICLES OF ASSOCIATION

WHEREAS the memorandum is the company's charter, indicating its nationality, the nature of its business and its capital, the articles of association are the regulations for the internal arrangements and the management of the company. The articles deal with the issue of shares, transfer of shares, alteration of share capital, general meetings, voting rights, directors (including their appointment and powers), managing director, secretary, dividends, accounts, audit of accounts, winding up and various other matters which will be referred to later.

Re Duncan Gilmour, ante,[1] shows that, as between the memorandum and the articles, the memorandum is the dominant instrument so that in so far as their provisions conflict the memorandum prevails, although, apart from matters which by statute must be in the memorandum, reference may be made to the articles to explain an ambiguity in the memorandum or to supplement it where it is silent.[2]

Section 6 provides that articles *may*, in the case of a company limited by shares, and *must* in the case of a company limited by guarantee[3] or an unlimited company,[3] be registered with the memorandum.

The articles may adopt all or any of the regulations in Table A: section 8(1). Table A in Schedule 1 to the Act is a model form of articles for a public company limited by shares. Any company limited by shares, however, may (1) adopt Table A in full, (2) adopt Table A subject to modifications, or (3) register its own articles and exclude Table A.

In the case of a company limited by shares, if articles are not registered, or, if articles are registered, in so far as they do not modify or exclude Table A, Table A will automatically be the company's articles: section 8(2).

A private company should register its own articles adopting all or any of the regulations in Table A as are appropriate. Since the 1980 Act[4] there are no minimum requirements for the articles of a private

---

[1] p. 94.
[2] In *Liquidator of The Humboldt Redwood Co. Ltd.* v. *Coats*, 1908 S.C. 751, the memorandum was silent on the point and so the articles governed.
[3] Chap. 2.   [4] s.28 of the 1948 Act was repealed by the 1980 Act.

company although it may still be thought desirable to indicate whether and how the transfer of shares is restricted.[5]

Articles must—

(1) be printed (typewriting is not admissible);
(2) be divided into paragraphs numbered consecutively;
(3) be signed by each subscriber to the memorandum of association in the presence of at least one witness, who must attest the signature. Such attestation is sufficient in Scotland as well as in England: sections 6, 9.[6]

Articles must be dated.

If the memorandum states that the registered office is to be situated in Wales, the memorandum and articles to be delivered for registration under section 12 of the 1948 Act may be in Welsh but, if they are, they must be accompanied by a certified translation into English: section 30(6) of the 1976 Act.

> The Registrar accepts the following processes as satisfying the printing stipulation:
> Letterpress, gravure, lithography.
> Stencil duplicating using waxed stencils and black ink, offset lithography, "office" type-set.
> Electrostatic photocopying.
> "Photostat" or similar processes properly washed.[7]

The articles (and the memorandum) form a contract between the company and each member and between the members. The articles can be altered by special resolution.

Effect of memorandum and articles

Subject to the provisions of the Act, the memorandum and articles, when registered, bind the company and the members as if they had been signed and sealed by each member, and contained covenants on the part of each member to observe their provisions: section 20. The result is:

(1) The articles (and the memorandum) form a contract binding the members to the company. Presumably the rule in *Foss* v.

---

[5] This was formerly one of the minimum requirements for forming a private company.

[6] As amended by Finance Act 1970, Sched. 7, para. 1, *ante*, p. 20.

[7] Notes for the Guidance of Registered Companies (C. 56a, 6th revise, Oct. 1974).

Harbottle, infra, applies, *i.e.* an action to enforce the contract must be brought in the name of the company, except where a personal right is infringed.

The articles provided for the reference of differences between the company and any of the members to arbitration. H., a shareholder, brought an action against the company in connection with a dispute as to his expulsion from the company, *i.e.* a dispute between the company and him in his capacity as a member. *Held,* the company was entitled to have the action stayed, as the articles constituted a contract between the company and its members in respect of their ordinary rights as members: *Hickman* v. *Kent or Romney Marsh Sheep-Breeders' Assocn.* [1915] 1 Ch. 881.[8]

". . . articles regulating the rights and obligations of the members generally as such do create rights and obligations between them and the company respectively": *per* Astbury J. at p. 900.

A dispute as to a director's right to inspect the company's books, and accounts, including minutes of board meetings, *i.e.* a dispute between the company and the director in his capacity as director, is not within the terms of articles like those in *Hickman's* case, *supra,* even though the director is also a member. The plaintiff sued for, *inter alia,* a declaration in a representative capacity as a shareholder. It was then claimed that a director had received remuneration to which he was not entitled. He asked for a stay but was refused it: *Beattie* v. *E. & F. Beattie Ltd.* [1938] Ch. 708 (C.A.).

(2) Although section 20 does *not* provide that the memorandum and articles shall bind the company and the members as if they had been signed and sealed *by the company*, and contained covenants *on the part of the company* to observe their provisions, the articles constitute a contract binding the company to members.

A company declared a dividend and passed a resolution to pay it by giving to the shareholders debenture bonds bearing interest and redeemable at par, by an annual drawing, over thirty years. The articles empowered the company to declare a dividend "to be paid" to the shareholders. *Held* the words "to be paid" meant paid in cash, and a shareholder could restrain the company from acting on the resolution on the ground that it contravened the articles: *Wood* v. *Odessa Waterworks Co.* (1889) 42 Ch.D. 636.

On the other hand the fact that the articles are not so executed by the

[8] An article prohibiting any member from taking legal proceedings against his company is contrary to the public policy and not binding: *St. Johnstone Football Club Ltd.* v. *Scottish Football Assocn. Ltd.* 1965 S.L.T. 171 (O.H.).

company limits the time for enforcing such a contract against the company to six years and not the twelve years allowed for contracts under seal: *Re Compania de Electricidad de la Provincia de Buenos Aires Ltd.* [1978] 3 All E.R. 668, *post*.

(3) Members are only bound by and entitled on the above mentioned contract *qua* members, *i.e.* in their capacity as members: *Beattie* v. *E. & F. Beattie Ltd., ante; Eley* v. *Positive Life Assurance Co. Ltd., post*.

(4) The articles (and the memorandum) constitute a contract between each individual member and every other member but in most cases the court will not enforce the contract as between individual members[9]; it is enforceable only through the company or, if the company is being wound up, the liquidator.

> "It is quite true that. . . there is no contract in terms between the individual members of the company; but the articles . . . regulate their rights *inter se*. Such rights can only be enforced by or against a member through the company, or through the liquidator representing the company; but . . . no member has, as between himself and another member, any right beyond that which the contract with the company gives": *per* Lord Herschell in *Welton* v. *Saffery* [1897] A.C. 299 at p. 315.

It seems that it is the rule in *Foss* v. *Harbottle*[10] which prevents an individual member enforcing the contract. However, the rule is irrelevant where the articles give a member a personal right. In such a case the contract is directly enforceable by one member against another *without* the aid of the company.

Articles of a private company provided that if a member intending to transfer his shares should inform the directors, the *directors* "will take the said shares equally between them at a fair value." *Held*, the articles bound the defendant directors to buy the plaintiff's shares and related to the relationship between the plaintiff as a member and the defendants, not as directors, but as members of the company,[11] and it was not necessary for the company to be a party to the action: *Rayfield* v. *Hands* [1960] Ch. 1.

(5) The provisions of the articles and the memorandum do not constitute a contract binding the company or any member to an

---

[9] *Per* Farwell L.J in *Salmon* v. *Quin and Axtens Ltd.* [1909] 1 Ch. 311 (C.A.) at p. 318.

[10] *Post*, p. 397.

[11] As is usual, the directors had shares in the company and so were members.

outsider,[12] *i.e.* a person who is not a member of the company,[13] or to a member in a capacity other than that of member, *e.g.* that of solicitor, promoter or director of the company.[14]

This is on the general principle that a person not a party to a contract has neither rights nor liabilities under it.

> The articles provided that E. should be the solicitor to the company. He was employed as such for a time but subsequently the company ceased to employ him. *Held*, E. was not entitled to damages for breach of contract against the company. The articles did not create a contract between E. and the company: *Eley* v. *Positive Life Assurance Co. Ltd.* (1876) 1 Ex.D. 88 (C.A.).[15]

However, if a director takes office on the footing of an article providing for remuneration for the director, although the article is not in itself a contract between the company and the director, its terms may be implied into the contract between the company and the director.

> An article provided that the remuneration of the directors should be the annual sum of £1,000. The directors were employed and accepted office on the footing of the article. For some time the directors, who were also members, acted as directors but were not paid. The company went into liquidation. *Held*, the article was embodied in the contract between the company and the directors and they were entitled to recover the arrears of remuneration: *Re New British Iron Co.* [1898] 1 Ch. 324.

(6) Because of the words "Subject to the provisions of this Act" in section 20, the contract constituted by the memorandum and articles can be varied to the extent that those documents can be altered in accordance with the provisions of the Act. The extent to which the memorandum may be altered has been dealt with already.[16] It will be seen shortly that, subject to a number of restrictions, the company may alter the articles by special resolution.

---

[12] See *per* Astbury J. in *Hickman's* case, *ante*, at p. 900.
[13] A Scots illustration is *National Bank of Scotland Glasgow Nominees Ltd.* v. *Adamson*, 1932 S.L.T. 492 (O.H.); see also *Scottish Fishermen's Organisation Ltd.* v. *McLean*, 1980 S.L.T. (Sh. Ct.) 76.
[14] See note 12 above.
[15] A comparable Scottish case is *Muirhead* v. *Forth etc. Steamboat Mutual Insce. Assocn.* (1893) 21 R. (H.L.) 1; (1893) 20 R. 442.
[16] *Ante*, p. 95.

Alteration of articles

Subject to the provisions of the Act and to the conditions in its memorandum, a company may by special resolution alter or add to its articles. An alteration or addition so made is as valid and can be altered in the same way as if originally contained in the articles: section 10. Thus a provision in the articles purporting to deprive the company of its power to alter them is void,[17] *e.g.* a provision that no alteration of articles shall be effective without the consent of X, or that on a proposed alteration only the shares of those opposed shall have a vote.[18]

(1) By section 10 the power to alter articles is subject to the provisions of the Act, *e.g.* section 22 of the 1948 Act and section 75 of the 1980 Act, *ante*,[19] and section 72 of the 1948 Act.[20]

If, as is common, special rights are attached to a class of shares by the articles and the articles contain a "modification of rights clause" such as Table A, article 4[21] (which provides for alteration of the class rights with the consent of a specified proportion or the sanction of a specified resolution of the shareholders of the class), then those class rights can only be altered with such consent or sanction.[22] Further, by section 72 dissentient holders of not less in aggregate than 15 per cent. of the issued shares of the class may, within 21 days after the consent was given, apply to the court to have the variation cancelled.[23]

(2) A company's power to alter its articles is subject to the conditions in the memorandum: section 10. Consequently an alteration of articles must not conflict with the memorandum.

(3) Under the general law the power to alter articles must be exercised bona fide for the benefit of the company as a whole.

Articles gave the company a lien on partly paid shares for all debts and liabilities of a member to the company. Z., on his death, owed money to the company (arrears of calls on partly paid shares), and was the only holder of

---

[17] *Malleson* v. *National Insurance Corporation* [1894] 1 Ch. 200.
[18] *Per* Russell L.J. in *Bushell* v. *Faith* [1969] 2 Ch. 438 (C.A.) at p. 448.
[19] p. 95.
[20] *Post*, p. 216.
[21] *Post*, p. 215.
[22] 1980 Act, s.32(4); *post*, p. 216.
[23] See note 20 above.

fully paid shares. The articles were altered so as to give the company a lien on fully paid shares. *Held*, the alteration was valid and, as from the date of the alteration, gave the company a lien on Z.'s fully paid shares in repect of the debts contracted before the date of the alteration: *Allen* v. *Gold Reefs of West Africa Ltd.* [1900] 1 Ch. 656 (C.A.).[24]

The power conferred on companies to alter articles "must, like all other powers, be exercised subject to those general principles of law and equity which are applicable to all powers conferred on majorities and enabling them to bind minorities. It must be exercised, not only in the manner required by law, but also bona fide for the benefit of the company as a whole, and it must not be exceeded. These conditions are always implied, and are seldom, if ever expressed": *Per* Lord Lindley M.R. at p. 671. "The fact that Zuccani's executors were the only persons practically affected at the time by the alterations made in the articles excites suspicion as to the bona fides of the company. But, although the executors were the only persons who were actually affected at the time, that was because Zuccani was the only holder of paid-up shares who at the time was in arrear of calls. The altered articles applied to all holders of fully paid shares, and made no distinction between them. The directors cannot be charged with bad faith": *Per* Lord Lindley M.R. at p. 675. "Further, I may say that the alteration of the articles giving the extended lien was, in my opinion, in no true sense retrospective. The lien given was not made to take effect before the date of the alteration. It operated only from and after that date": *Per* Romer L.J. at p. 682.

It is for the shareholders, and not for the court, to say whether an alteration of articles is for the benefit of the company, unless no reasonable man could so regard it.

The articles provided that S. and four others should be permanent directors of the company, unless they should become disqualified by any one of six specified events. None of the six events had occurred. S. on 22 occasions within 12 months failed to account for the company's money he had received, and the articles were accordingly altered by adding a seventh event disqualifying a director, namely, a request in writing signed by all the other directors that he should resign. Such a request was made to S., who was also a shareholder. *Held*, the contract, if any, between the plaintiff and the company contained in the original articles was subject to the statutory power of alteration, and the alteration was bona fide for the benefit of the company as a whole and valid: *Shuttleworth* v. *Cox Bros. & Co. (Maidenhead) Ltd.* [1927] 2 K.B.9 (C.A.).

"Then the first thing to be considered is whether, in formulating the test I have mentioned, Lindley M.R [in *Allen's* case, *supra*] had in mind two separate and distinct matters; first, bona fides, the state of mind of the persons whose act is complained of, and secondly, whether the alteration is for the

---

[24] *cf. Liquidator of W. & A. M'Arthur Ltd.* v. *Gulf Line Ltd.*, 1909 S.C. 732. For comments on *Allen's* case, see *Moir* v. *Thomas Duff & Co. Ltd.* (1900) 2 F. 1265.

benefit of the company, apart altogether from the state of mind of those who procured it. In my opinion this view of the test has been negatived by this Court in *Sidebottom's* case.[25] So the test is whether the alteration of the articles was in the opinion of the shareholders for the benefit of the company. By what criterion is the Court to ascertain the opinion of the shareholders upon this question? The alteration may be so oppressive as to cast suspicion on the honesty of the persons responsible for it, or so extravagant that no reasonable men could really consider it for the benefit of the company": *Per* Bankes L.J. at p. 18. See also *per* Scrutton L.J. at p. 23.

The expression "bona fide for the benefit of the company as a whole" means that the shareholder must proceed upon what, in his honest opinion, is for the benefit of the company as a whole. The phrase "the company as a whole" does not mean the company as a commercial entity, distinct from the corporators; it means the corporators as a general body. It may be asked whether what is proposed is, in the honest opinion of those who voted in its favour, for the benefit of an individual hypothetical member. Looking at the converse, an alteration of articles is liable to be impeached if its effect is to discriminate between the majority shareholders and the minority so as to give the former an advantage of which the latter are deprived. It is not necessary that persons voting for an alteration of articles should dissociate themselves altogether from their own prospects.[26]

The articles of a private company prohibited a transfer of shares to a non-member so long as another member was willing to buy them at a fair value. The holder of the majority of the shares wished to transfer them to a non-member, so the articles were altered so as to permit a transfer to any person with the sanction of an ordinary resolution. *Held*, the alteration was bona fide and valid, although thereby the minority lost their rights of pre-emption: *Greenhalgh* v. *Arderne Cinemas Ltd.* [1951] Ch. 286 (C.A.).[27]

It has been said that the phrase "corporators as a general body" means both present and future members of the company.[28]

If an alteration of articles is bona fide for the benefit of the company, it is immaterial that it prejudices a minority of the members.

A private company, in which the directors held a majority of the shares, altered its articles so as to give the directors power to require any shareholder

[25] *Infra.*
[26] *Per* Lord Evershed M.R. in *Greenhalgh* v. *Arderne Cinemas* [1951] Ch. 286 (C.A.) at p. 291.
[27] *cf. Crumpton* v. *Morrine Hall Pty. Ltd.* [1965] N.S.W.R. 240, *post*, p. 112.
[28] *Per* Megarry J. in *Gaiman* v. *National Association of Mental Health* [1971] 1 Ch. 317 at p. 330.

who competed with the company's business to transfer his shares, at their fair value to nominees of the directors. S., who had a minority of the shares and was in competition with the company, brought an action for a declaration that the special resolution was invalid. *Held*, (1) as a power to expel a shareholder by buying him out was valid in the case of original articles it could be introduced in altered articles, provided that the alteration was made bona fide for the benefit of the company as a whole; (2) the alteration was so made and was valid: *Sidebottom* v. *Kershaw, Leese & Co.* [1920] 1 Ch. 154 (C.A.).[29]

> "I think . . . that it is for the benefit of the company that they should not be obliged to have amongst them as members persons who are competing with them in business and who may get knowledge from their membership which would enable them to compete better": *Per* Lord Sterndale M.R. at p. 166.

The principles of natural justice are not applicable in this field.[30]

It has been held that the members of a company, acting in accordance with the Act and the constitution of the company, and subject to any necessary consent on the part of the class affected, can alter the relative voting powers attached by the articles to various classes of shares, provided that the special resolution is passed in good faith for the benefit of the company as a whole.

The issued capital of S. Ltd. comprised 400,000 management shares, which under the articles carried 8 votes each, and 3,600,000 ordinary shares. On the acquisition by S. Ltd. of the shares in B. Ltd. in consideration of the issue of 8,400,000 ordinary shares in S. Ltd., the articles were altered so as to double the votes carried by management shares in order to ensure continuity of management. The special resolution was passed by a large majority at an extraordinary general meeting of the company. The holders of management shares, directors of S. Ltd., did not vote in respect of these shares or their ordinary shares. Nor did they vote at a separate class meeting of the ordinary shareholders which sanctioned the special resolution. *Held*, the alteration was valid: *Rights and Issues Investment Trust Ltd.* v. *Stylo Shoes Ltd.* [1965] Ch. 250.[31]

However, it has been said, in an Australian case, that the benefit of the company as a whole is an impossible test where the question is simply one as to the relative rights of different classes of shareholders. In this event there must be no fraud or oppression of the minority.[32]

---

[29] See also *Crookston* v. *Lindsay, Crookston & Co. Ltd.*, 1922 S.L.T. 62 (O.H.).

[30] *Per* Megarry J. in *Gaiman's* case, *ante*, at p. 335.

[31] A comparable Scottish case is *Caledonian Insurance Co.* v. *Scottish American Invest. Co. Ltd.*, 1951 S.L.T. 23 (O.H.).

[32] *Peters' American Delicacy Co. Ltd.* v. *Heath* (1939) 61 C.L.R. 457 (High Court of Australia), *per* Latham C.J. at p. 481 and Rich J. at p. 495.

The onus of showing that the power to alter articles has not been properly exercised is on the party complaining.[33]

If, in a rare case, an alteration is not for the benefit of the company as a whole, or its effect is to discriminate between the majority of the shareholders and the minority shareholders, so as to give the former an advantage of which the latter are deprived, the court will restrain the company from making it or acting on it.

In the New South Wales case of *Australian Fixed Trusts Pty. Ltd.* v. *Clyde Industries Ltd.* (1959) S.R. (N.S.W.) 33 the A. Co. held, as trustee for the holders of units in a unit trust about 300,000 of the 2,000,000 ordinary shares issued by the C. Co. C. Co. proposed to alter its articles so as to provide that a member holding ordinary shares as trustee for the holders of units in a unit trust should not vote in respect of the shares without the direction of the majority of the holders of the units. *Held*, the alteration would be invalid. Its effect was to discriminate between the majority of the shareholders and the minority. No reasonable man could decide that it was for the benefit of the company as a whole.

In another New South Wales case, *Crumpton* v. *Morrine Hall Pty. Ltd.* [1965] N.S.W.R. 240, C. owned a group of shares in a home unit company the articles of which provided that holding a specified group of shares entitled the registered holder to the absolute and exclusive use of a specified unit. The articles also provided that the directors could lease the unit to the holder of the appropriate shares for such period as he was the holder at a rent equivalent to the appropriate share of money payable for such things as maintenance and repairs of the property, rates, and cleaning and furnishing of the hall and stairways. C. was granted a monthly tenancy of her unit which tenancy provided that it would not be determined except by the written consent of each shareholder, *i.e.* including C. Under the articles C. had rights of subletting and licensing others to use the premises. Finally, the articles contained a modification of rights clause in the usual form.

A general meeting passed a special resolution purporting to alter the articles so as to provide that, subject to the prior approval of the directors, the holder of any group of shares should have the right to let his unit for not more than 12 months in any period of 36 consecutive months but otherwise he could not lease, license or part with possession or occupation. C. sought and obtained an injunction restraining the company from acting on the resolution and a declaration that it was void.

Jacobs J. *held*:

(1) That the alteration of articles was a fraud or oppression on the minority. He said that the courts in each generation or decade set a line up to which shareholders are allowed to go in affecting the rights of other shareholders by alterations of articles of association, and that the decision turns on a value judgment formed in respect of the conduct of the majority. Jacobs J. also said

---

[33] *Per* Latham C.J. in *Peters'* case, *supra*, at p. 482.

that where there is an attempt to take particular rights away from the holders of particular shares then, although the act may appear in theory to be a decision or resolution applicable generally to all holders of shares, if it appears that it affects one or a minority in particular then it should appear that full regard has been had to the proprietary rights involved, and that he did not think it is sufficient merely to say that it is considered that the property of the company will benefit as a result of the alteration of the articles (*cf. Greenhalgh* v. *Arderne Cinemas, ante,* p. 111).

(2) That the share capital of the company was divided into different classes within the meaning of the modification of rights clause, the alteration was a variation of class rights, the modification of rights clause should have been complied with and had not been complied with. In this respect the earlier case of *Fischer* v. *Easthaven* [1964] N.S.W.R. 261 was not followed.

Jacobs J. did not follow *Fischer* v. *Easthaven* in another respect when he said that he did not think that the duty on the company could be expressed in terms of a contractual duty not to alter the articles. It was a duty which arose by the application of principles of equity developed in the cases dealing with the power of a company to alter its articles and its inability to alter them so as to commit a fraud on a minority.

In the absence of a prohibition in the memorandum the articles can be altered so as to authorise the issue of preference shares taking priority over existing shares although no power to issue preference shares is conferred by the memorandum or the original articles.[34]

(4) An alteration of articles in breach of a contract to which the company is a party is valid but the other party is entitled to damages. If a person enters into an arrangement which can only take effect by the continuance of an existing state of circumstances, he is under an obligation to do nothing to put an end to that state of circumstances.[35]

S., a director of B. Co., was properly appointed managing director for ten years by a contract outside the articles. The articles provided that the managing director, *subject to his contract with the company,* was subject to the same provisions as to removal as the other directors, and that if he ceased to be a director, he should *ipso facto* cease to be managing director. The articles also provided that the company could remove a director before the expiration of his period of office. Later, F. Co. acquired the shares in B. Co. and the articles were altered so as to empower F. Co. to remove any director of B. Co. Before the expiration of 10 years F. Co. removed S. from the board of directors of

---

[34] *Andrews* v. *Gas Meter Co.* [1897] 1 Ch. 361 (C.A.).
[35] *Per* Lords Atkin and Porter in the *Southern Foundries* case at pp. 717 and 741 respectively.

B. Co. and he thereby ceased to be managing director. *Held*, it was an implied term of the contract that B. Co. would not remove S. as director during the term of ten years and B. Co. was liable to S. for breach of contract:*Southern Foundries (1926) Ltd.* v. *Shirlaw* [1940] A.C.701.[36]

"A company cannot be precluded from altering its articles thereby giving itself power to act upon the provisions of the altered articles— but so to act may nevertheless be a breach of contract if it is contrary to a stipulation in a contract validly made before the alteration": *per* Lord Porter at p. 740.

Note what was said earlier of section 9(3), (4) and (5) of the European Communities Act 1972 and an alteration of the articles.[37]

Any document making or evidencing an alteration in the company's memorandum or articles and a copy of the memorandum or articles as altered must be in the same language as the memorandum and articles originally registered and, if that language is Welsh, must be accompanied by a certified translation into English: section 30(7) of the 1976 Act.

Inspection of articles

A company is required to furnish a copy of its memorandum (embodying any alterations) and of its articles to its members on request, on payment of not more than five new pence a copy: sections 24, 25.

Any person, whether a member of the company or not, may inspect a copy of the memorandum and articles of association of any company at the office of the Registrar of Companies. He may also have a copy or extract of them: section 426 of the 1948 Act; section 38(3) and Schedules 2 and 3 of the 1976 Act.

Rectification of articles

The court has no inherent jurisdiction to rectify the articles, even if it is proved that they were not in accordance with the intention of the original signatories.[38]

---

[36] See also *Shindler* v. *Northern Raincoat Co. Ltd.* [1960] 1 W.L.R. 1038, *post*, p. 364, and *Carrier Australasia Ltd.* v. *Hunt* (1939) 61 C.L.R. 534, *post*, p. 363.

[37] p. 97.

[38] *Scott* v. *Frank F. Scott (London) Ltd.* [1940] Ch. 794 (C.A.).

CHAPTER 5

PROMOTERS

BEFORE a company can be formed there must be some persons who have an intention to form a company, and who take the necessary steps to carry that intention into operation. Such persons are called "promoters." Promoters stand in a fiduciary position towards the company and, as a result, they owe certain duties.

MEANING OF TERM "PROMOTER"

Apart from the definition for the purposes of section 43,[1] the term "promoter" is not defined in the Act. However, a promoter has been described, for example, as "one who undertakes to form a company with reference to a given project and to set it going, and who takes the necessary steps to accomplish that purpose."[2]

A company may have several promoters and, as is shown by cases such as the *Leeds Theatres* case, *post*, one existing company may promote another new company.

Persons who give instructions for the preparation and registration of the memorandum and articles of association are promoters. So, too, are persons who obtain the directors (very often a promoter is himself a prospective director), issue a prospectus, negotiate underwriting contracts or a contract for the purchase of property by the company, or procure capital.

A person may become a promoter after the company is incorporated, *e.g.* by issuing a prospectus, or by procuring capital to enable the company to carry out a preliminary agreement. Whether a person is actually a promoter and, if so, the date when he became one and whether he is still one, are questions of fact.

A person who has taken no active part in the formation of a company and the raising of the necessary share capital but has left it to others to get up the company on the understanding that he will profit from the operation is a promoter.[3]

---

[1] s.43(5)(*a*), *post*, p. 154.
[2] *Per* Cockburn C.J. in *Twycross* v. *Grant* (1877) 2 C.P.D. 469 (C.A.), at p. 541.
[3] See *per* Lindley J. in *Emma Silver Mining Co. Ltd.* v. *Lewis* (1879) 4 C.P.D. 396 at p. 408, and *Tracy* v. *Mandalay Pty. Ltd.* (1952–53) 88 C.L.R. 215.

Anyone who acts merely as the servant or agent of a promoter is not himself a promoter. A solicitor, therefore, who merely does the legal work necessary to the formation of a company is not a promoter.[4]

At one time the business of a company promoter was almost a separate business in itself but this is not so today. Further, the increasingly strict provisions of successive Companies Acts in relation to the issue and contents of a prospectus have almost eliminated the fraudulent company promoter.

POSITION AND DUTIES OF PROMOTERS

A promoter is not an agent for the company which he is forming because a company cannot have an agent before it comes into existence.[5] Furthermore, he is usually not treated as a trustee for the future company.[6] However, from the moment he acts with the company in mind, a promoter stands in a fiduciary position[7] towards the company and therefore he must not make any secret profit out of the promotion, *e.g.* a profit on a sale of property to the company.

A promoter must disclose a profit which he is making out of the promotion to either—

(1) an *independent* board of directors[8]; or
(2) the existing and intended shareholders, *e.g.* by making disclosure in a prospectus.[9]

"I do not say that an owner of property may not promote and form a joint stock company, and then sell his property to it, but I do say that if he does he is bound to take care that he sells it to the company through the medium of a board of directors who can and do exercise an independent and intelligent judgment on the transaction."[10]

[4] *Re Great Wheal Polgooth Ltd.* (1883) 53 L.J.Ch. 42.
[5] *Kelner* v. *Baxter* (1866) L.R. 2 C.P. 174, *post,* p. 123, *Tinnevelly Sugar Refining Co. Ltd.* v. *Mirrlees, Watson & Yaryan Co. Ltd.* (1894) 21 R. 1009.
[6] *Omnium Electric Palaces Ltd.* v. *Baines* [1914] 1 Ch. 332, *post; Edinburgh Northern Tramways Co.* v. *Mann* (1896) 23 R. 1056, *post.*
[7] *Henderson* v. *The Huntington Copper etc. Co. Ltd.* (1877) 5 R. (H.L.) 1; (1877) 4 R. 294, *post*; the fiduciary relationship was regarded as arising from agency rather than from trust in *Edinburgh Northern Tramways Co.* v. *Mann* (1896) 23 R. 1056, *post.*
[8] *Erlanger* v. *New Sombrero Phosphate Co.* (1878) 3 App.Cas. 1218 (P.C.), *post*; *Tracy* v. *Mandalay Pty. Ltd., ante.*
[9] *Lagunas Nitrate Co.* v. *Lagunas Syndicate* [1899] 2 Ch. 392 (C.A.); *Scottish Pacific Coast Mining Co. Ltd.* v. *Falkner, Bell & Co.* (1888) 15 R. 290.
[10] *Per* Lord Cairns L.C. in *Erlanger's* case, above, at p. 1236.

The requirement of an independent board of directors is one which, in most cases, cannot be complied with, as the promoters, or some of them, are usually the first directors of the company. In the formation of a private company, the promoter usually sells his business to a company, of which he is managing director, and in which he is the largest shareholder, but, nevertheless, the transaction cannot be impeached on the ground that there is no independent board of directors.[11]

"After *Salomon's Case* I think it is impossible to hold that it is the duty of the promoters of a company to provide it with an independent board of directors, if the real truth is disclosed to those who are induced by the promoters to join the company."[12]

If there is no disclosure to an independent board, there must be *full* disclosure of the profit made by the promoters to the existing and intended shareholders, either in a prospectus or in some other way.

"'Disclosure' is not the most appropriate word to use when a person who plays many parts announces to himself in one character what he has done and is doing in another."[13]

If a person buys property with the intention of reselling it to a company which he is forming, he is not presumed to acquire that property as trustee for the company and if, as a matter of fact, he intends to acquire it as a promoter, it is quite legal for him to resell to the company at a profit, provided that he discloses the profit.[14] If he intends to acquire as a trustee, he will have to hand over the property to the company at the price paid by him.

Remedies for breach of duty

If a promoter fails to make full disclosure of a profit made by him out of the promotion the following remedies may be open to the company. Since the promoter's duties are owed to the company the rule in *Foss* v. *Harbottle*[15] is relevant to their enforcement.

(1) Where the promoter has, *e.g.*, sold his own property to the company, the company may rescind the contract and recover the purchase-money paid.

---

[11] *Salomon* v. *Salomon & Co. Ltd.* [1897] A.C. 22, *ante*, p. 22.
[12] *Per* Lindley M.R. in the *Lagunas* case, above, at p. 426.
[13] *Per* Lord Macnaghten in *Gluckstein* v. *Barnes* [1900] A.C. 240, *post*, at p. 249.
[14] *Omnium Electric Palaces Ltd.* v. *Baines* [1914] 1 Ch. 332 (C.A.).
[15] *Post*, p. 397.

A syndicate, of which E. was the head, purchased an island in the West Indies said to contain valuable mines of phosphates for £55,000. E. formed a company to buy this island, and a contract was made between X., a nominee of the syndicate, and the company for its purchase at £110,000. *Held*, as there had been no disclosure by the promoters of the profit they were making, the company was entitled to rescind the contract and recover the purchase-money from E. and the other members of the syndicate: *Erlanger* v. *New Sombrero Phosphate Co.* (1878) 3 App.Cas. 1218 (P.C.).

The right of rescission may be lost in a number of ways. For example, it will be lost if the parties cannot be restored to their original positions, as where the property has been worked so that its character has been altered.[16] However, even if restitution is strictly not possible, rescission may be allowed if restitution is substantially possible. The right to rescind will also be lost if third parties have acquired rights for value, by mortgage or otherwise, under the contract.[17]

(2) The company may compel the promoter to account for any profit he has made.

Intending to buy property and to form a company and resell the property to the company or another purchaser, a syndicate of four persons bought charges on the property at a discount. They afterwards bought the property for £140,000, formed a company of which they were the first directors and resold the property to the company for £180,000. As a result of this, they made a profit of £40,000 on the property and one of £20,000 on the charges which were paid off in full with the £140,000 received for the property. A prospectus was issued, disclosing the profit of £40,000 but not that of £20,000. It appears that rescission had become impossible. *Held*, the £20,000 was a secret profit made by the syndicate as promoters of the company and they were bound to pay it to the company: *Gluckstein* v. *Barnes* [1900] A.C. 240.

A prospectus stated that the company had been formed for the purchase of certain mines at the price of £125,000, and named H. as a director; it did not disclose that H. was receiving £10,000 of the price from the vendor of the mines in consideration, as H. alleged, of services rendered by H. to the company. *Held*, in an action by the company against H., that since H. stood in a fiduciary relation to the company from the date when he agreed to become a director, the company was entitled to recover the £10,000 from H., the true price of

---

[16] As in *Lagunas Nitrate Co.* v. *Lagunas Syndicate* [1899] 2 Ch. 392 (C.A.).
[17] As in *Re Leeds and Hanley Theatres of Varieties Ltd.* [1902] 2 Ch. 809, below, where the mortgagee of the property had sold it.

the mines being only £115,000: *Henderson* v. *The Huntington Copper and Sulphur Co. Ltd.* (1877) 5 R. (H.L.) 1; (1877) 4 R. 294.

(3) The company may sue the promoter for damages for breach of his fiduciary duty.

> The F. Co. contracted to purchase two music-halls for £24,000 and had the property conveyed to its nominee, R., intending to sell it to the T. Co. when formed. The F. Co. then promoted the T. Co. and agreed to sell the music-halls to it for £75,000 and directed R. to convey them. The board of directors of T. Co. was not an independent board. A prospectus was issued to the public by the T. Co., giving R. as the vendor, and not disclosing the interest of F. Co. or the profit it was making. *Held*, the prospectus should have disclosed that F. Co. was the real vendor and the amount of profit it was making. For breach of their fiduciary duty to those invited to take shares the promoters were liable in damages to the company and the measure of damages was the promoters' profit: *Re Leeds and Hanley Theatres of Varieties Ltd.* [1902] 2 Ch. 809 (C.A.).

Where promoters sell their own property to the company, the company cannot affirm the contract and at the same time ask for an account of profits or for damages as this would be, in effect, asking the court to vary the contract of sale and order the defendants to sell their assets at a lower price.[18]

Apart from the remedies mentioned above, if a promoter fails to disclose a profit made by him out of the promotion other remedies may be available to the company. The company may be able to recover damages for fraud against the promoter[19] or, perhaps, damages for negligent misrepresentation.[20] And note section 333, *post*.[21]

If a promoter, even though he has not sold property to the company, makes a secret profit out of the promotion of the company, he must account for that profit to the company.[22] He is, however, only bound

---

[18] *Re Cape Breton Co.* (1885) 29 Ch.D. 795 (C.A.); *Jacobus Marler Estates Ltd.* v. *Marler* (1913) 85 L.J.P.C. 167n., *per* Lord Parker; *Tracy* v. *Mandalay Pty. Ltd.* (1952–3) 88 C.L.R. 215, *per* the High Court of Australia at p. 239.

[19] *Per* Romer L.J. in the *Leeds* case, *supra*.

[20] Under the principle in *Hedley Byrne Ltd.* v. *Heller & Partners* [1964] A.C. 645, *Mutual Life and Citizens' Assurance Co. Ltd.* v. *Evatt* [1971] A.C. 793 (P.C.) and cases such as *Esso Petroleum Co. Ltd.* v. *Mardon* [1975] 2 W.L.R. 147 or under the Misrepresentation Act 1967, s.2(1), *post*, p. 146.

[21] p. 416.

[22] *Henderson* v. *The Huntington Copper etc. Co. Ltd.* (1877) 5 R. (H.L.) 1; (1877) 4 R. 294, *ante; Mann* v. *Edinburgh Northern Tramways Co.* (1892) 20 R. (H.L.) 7; (1891) 18 R. 1140.

to account for the profit he has made, that is, after deducting all legitimate expenses, *e.g.* surveyors' and solicitors' charges, and printing costs, incurred in the formation of the company.[23]

PAYMENT FOR PROMOTION SERVICES

A promoter has no right against the company to payment for his promotion services in the absence of an express contract with the company. In England such a contract will normally have to be under seal since the company cannot make a valid contract before incorporation and when the contract can be made the consideration by the promoter will normally be past. In the absence of such a contract he cannot even recover from the company payments he has made in connection with the formation of the company.

A syndicate promoted a company and paid £416 2s. in respect of registration fees and *ad valorem* stamp duty incidental to the formation of the company. The company shortly afterwards went into liquidation. *Held*, the syndicate were not entitled to prove for the payments they had made: *Clinton's Claim* [1908] 2 Ch. 515 (C.A.).

The rule that consideration must not be past is not part of Scots law, and the promoter of a Scottish company might be entitled to found on a suitably worded provision in the memorandum or articles to the effect of recovering from the company payments made by him in connection with the formation of the company.[24] The success of a promoter's claim against the company seems to depend on his establishing that the relevant provision creates a *jus quaesitum tertio* in his favour. Where such a right is established, a promoter is entitled to remuneration for professional services rendered.[25] If no such right is established, neither promoters nor experts employed by them have a right to remuneration from the new company; such experts have no claim except against the persons who employed them, namely the promoters.[26]

In both countries it is usual for the articles to give the directors power to pay the preliminary expenses out of the company's funds. By article 80 of Table A: "The directors . . . may pay all expenses incurred in

---

[23] *Lydney and Wigpool Iron Ore Co.* v. *Bird* (1886) 33 Ch.D. 85 (C.A.).

[24] *Scott* v. *Money Order Co. etc. Ltd.* (1870) 42 Sc. Jur. 212.

[25] See, *e.g. Edinburgh Northern Tramways Co.* v. *Mann* (1896) 23 R. 1056.

[26] *Per* Lord M'Laren in *J.M. & J.H. Robertson* v. *Beatson, M'Leod & Co. Ltd.*, 1908 S.C. 921, at p. 928.

promoting and registering the company." Such an article gives the promoters no right to bring an action against the company for the preliminary expenses, as it only confers a discretion on the directors.[27] However, the promoters are usually directors so that in practice the promoters will receive their expenses.

Any amount or benefit paid or given within the two preceding years, or intended to be paid or given, to a promoter must normally be disclosed in a prospectus.[28]

SUSPENSION OF PROMOTERS

A person who has been convicted on indictment of any offence in connection with the promotion or formation of a company may have an order made against him by the court that he shall not, without leave of the court, be a director, liquidator, receiver or take part in the management of a company for a period of up to five years: section 188.[29]

---

[27] *Melhado* v. *Porto Alegre Ry. Co.* (1874) L.R. 9 C.P. 503. The same interpretation might be adopted in Scotland, but see *Scott's* case, *ante*.

[28] s.38(1) and Sched. 4, *post*, p. 135.

[29] *Post*, p. 330.

Chapter 6

CONTRACTS

THIS chapter deals first, with contracts made on behalf of a company before it is formed, and secondly, with those made after the company has been formed.

CONTRACTS MADE BEFORE INCORPORATION OF COMPANY

Effect on company

If, before the formation of a company, some person purports to make a contract on its behalf, or as trustee for it, *e.g.* a contract for the sale of property to the company, the contract, or "preliminary agreement" as it is sometimes called, is not binding on the company when it is formed, even if the company takes the benefit of the contract. Before incorporation the company lacks capacity to make the contract, and an agent cannot contract on behalf of a principal who is not in existence.

Solicitors, on the instructions of persons who afterwards become directors of the company, prepared the memorandum and articles of association of the company, and paid the registration fees. *Held*, the company was not liable to pay their costs: *Re English and Colonial Produce Co. Ltd.* [1906] 2 Ch. 435 (C.A.).

"There is no binding authority for the proposition that a company, because it has taken the benefit of work done under a contract entered into before the formation of the company, can be made liable in equity under that contract": *per* Vaughan Williams L.J. at p. 442.[1]

Conversely, a company cannot, after incorporation, enforce a contract made in its name before incorporation, or sue for damages for breach of such a contract.

N. Co. agreed with a person acting on behalf of a future company, P. Co., that N. Co. would grant a mining lease to P. Co. P. Co. discovered coal, whereupon N. Co. refused to grant the lease. *Held*, P. Co. could not compel

---

[1] For Scots law, *cf.* Lord President Dunedin in *Welsh & Forbes* v. *Johnston* (1906) 8 F. 453, at p. 457, and Lord M'Laren in *J. M. & J. H. Robertson* v. *Beatson, M'Leod & Co. Ltd.*, 1908 S.C. 921, at p. 928, *ante*, p. 120. See also *F.J. Neale (Glasgow) Ltd.* v. *Vickery*, 1973 S.L.T. (Sh. Ct.) 88.

N. Co. to grant the lease: *Natal Land etc. Co. Ltd.* v. *Pauline Colliery Syndicate Ltd.* [1904] A.C. 120 (P.C.).[2]

D., acting on behalf of a future company, T. Co. entered into a contract with M. Co. for the supply by the latter of certain machinery for a refinery. When T. Co. was registered it alleged that the machinery supplied was defective. *Held*, T. Co. could not sue M. Co. for damages: *Tinnevelly Sugar Refining Co. Ltd.* v. *Mirrlees, Watson & Yaryan Co. Ltd.* (1894) 21 R. 1009.

Further, such a contract cannot be ratified by the company after it is incorporated—the company was not a principal with contractual capacity at the time when the contract was made—although, as is explained later, the contract may be novated.[3]

The Gravesend Royal Alexandra Hotel Company Ltd. was being formed to buy an hotel from K. At a time when all concerned knew that the company had not been formed, a written contract was made "on behalf of" the proposed company by A, B and C for the purchase of £900 worth of wine from K. The company was formed, and the wine handed over to it and consumed, but before payment was made the company went into liquidation. *Held*, A, B and C were personally liable on the contract, and no ratification could release them from their liability: *Kelner* v. *Baxter* (1866) L.R. 2 C.P. 174.

"Where a contract is signed by one who professes to be signing "as agent," but who has no principal existing at the time, and the contract would be altogether inoperative unless binding on the person who signed it, he is bound thereby: and a stranger cannot by a subsequent ratification relieve him from that responsibility": *per* Erle C.J. at p. 183.

The Jenkins Report recommended[4] that a company should be enabled unilaterally to adopt, *i.e.* to ratify, contracts which purport to be made on its behalf or in its name prior to incorporation; until the company does so adopt such contracts, the persons who purported to act for the company should be entitled to sue and be liable to be sued thereon.

It appears that unilateral adoption (ratification) of such contracts by the company is prevented by section 9(2) of the European Com-

---

[2] *Molleson and Grigor* v. *Fraser's Trustees* (1881) 8 R. 630 is a Scottish authority.
[3] *Kelner* v. *Baxter*, below; *Tinnevelly* case, above. See also *Cumming* v. *Quartzag Ltd.*, 1980 S.C. 276, in which, following the *Tinnevelly* case, the Court of Session held that an agreement made on behalf of a company to be incorporated could not give rise to a *jus quaesitum tertio* in favour of the company when incorporated; Hector L. MacQueen, *Promoters' Contracts, Agency and the Jus Quaesitum Tertio*, 1982 S.L.T. (News) 257.
[4] Para. 54.

munitions Act 1972,[5] *infra*, although a novation, *post*, is not. The question of individual liability however has been adopted by that section.

Effect on individuals

Under the general law, if an individual contracts as "agent"[6] or trustee for a future company, whether there is a contract between him and the other person involved depends upon what a reasonable man would think the parties intended. If they have expressed themselves in writing the question is one of construction of the written terms for the judge. If orally, the question is one of fact for the jury if there is one.[7]

In *Kelner* v. *Baxter*, above, it was intended that A, B and C should contract personally. In the *Newborne* case, the intention was that the future company should contract.

Tinned ham was sold to S. Ltd. The contract was "We have this day sold to you . . . (Signed) Leopold Newborne (London) Ltd." The signature was typed and underneath was written "Leopold Newborne." The market price of ham fell and S. Ltd. refused to take delivery. When an action was brought it was found that Leopold Newborne (London) Ltd. had not been incorporated at the time of the contract and Leopold Newborne tried to enforce the contract in his own name. *Held*, neither Leopold Newborne (London) Ltd. nor Leopold Newborne could enforce the contract. It was not a case of an agent undertaking to do certain things himself as agent for somebody else. It was a contract in which a company purported to sell. Leopold Newborne did not purport to contract as principal or agent—the contract purported to be made by Leopold Newborne (London) Ltd., on whose behalf it was signed by a future director. "This company was not in existence and . . . the signature on that document, and indeed, the document itself . . . is a complete nullity": *Newborne* v. *Sensolid (Great Britain)* Ltd. [1954] 1 Q.B. 45. [*Note*: The decision in this case would probably be different now by virtue of the European Communities Act 1972, s.9(2), *infra*.]

If, in a case like *Kelner*, *supra*, the individual is personally bound, the contract should contain a provision (a condition subsequent, also referred to as a "resolutive" condition in Scots law) that his liability shall cease if and when the company is incorporated and enters into a contract with the vendor on the terms of the preliminary agreement,

---

[5] p. 125. The suggestion was taken up in Singapore. See *Cosmic Insurance Corporation Ltd.* v. *Khoo Chiang Poh* (1981) 131 N.L.J. 286 (P.C.).

[6] Strictly, one cannot be agent for a principal not yet in existence.

[7] *Per* Fullagar J. in *Summergreene* v. *Parker* (1950) 80 C.L.R. 304, at p. 324.

i.e. there is a novation, and a provision that he may rescind if the company does not enter into such a contract by a specified date.

Section 9(2) of the European Communities Act 1972 provides that where a contract purports to be made by a company, or by a person as agent for a company, at a time when the company has not been formed, then subject to any agreement to the contrary the contract shall have effect as one entered into by the person purporting to act for the company or as agent for it and he shall be personally liable on it.

This means that in circumstances like those in *Newborne's* case, *ante*,[8] today, unless there is an agreement to the contrary, there will be a contract between the individual who acts for the company and the other person involved. Presumably such individual will be entitled to sue on the contract as well as being liable to be sued on it. The words "subject to any agreement to the contrary" allow for the case where there is a novation.

In *Phonogram Ltd.* v. *Lane* [1981] 3 All E.R. 182, the Court of Appeal considered the effect of section 9(2). They held that it rendered the individual "agent" liable even though the company was not at the time in the course of formation.[9] Further a contract can be "purported" to be made by a company even though both parties to the contract knew that the company had not then been formed.

They also considered that signing the contract as an agent, or as in the *Newborne* case, *ante*, would not amount to an agreement to the contrary so as to avoid personal liability. Lord Denning M.R. considered that only a clear exclusion of personal liability would suffice.[10]

New contract after incorporation

Of course, a company may, after incorporation, enter into a new contract with the other party to the same effect as a contract made on its behalf before incorporation, in which event there is a novation, *i.e.* the old contract is discharged and replaced by the new. Such a new contract may be inferred from the acts of the parties after incorporation.

---

[8] See above.

[9] This rejected argument was based on the French text of the Directive implemented by the 1972 Act.

[10] Thus probably overruling *Newborne's* case.

J. had agreed with W., acting on behalf of a company about to be formed, to sell certain property to the company. After the company's incorporation, the directors resolved to adopt the agreement, and to accept J.'s offer to take part of the purchase-money in debentures instead of cash. *Held*, a contract was entered into by the company with J. to the effect of the previous agreement as subsequently modified: *Howard* v. *Patent Ivory Mfg. Co.* (1888) 38 Ch. D. 156.[11]

However, such a new contract will not be inferred if the acts of the company after incorporation are due to the mistaken belief that it is bound by the contract made before incorporation.

A contract was made between W. and D., who was acting on behalf of an intended company, for the grant of a lease to the company. The company, on its formation, entered on the land the subject of the lease and began to erect buildings on it but did not make any fresh agreement with respect to the lease. *Held*, the agreement, being made before the formation of the company, was not binding on the company, and was incapable of ratification; and the acts of the company were done in the erroneous belief that the agreement was binding on the company and not evidence of a fresh agreement between W. and the company: *Re Northumberland Avenue Hotel Co.* (1886) 33 Ch.D. 16 (C.A.).

Modern practice

Agreements to sell property to a company about to be formed are not now, as a rule, made with a person expressed to be acting on behalf of or as trustee for the company, because of the liability incurred by such person, and the absence of liability incurred by the company unless there is a novation. Although the other party will not be bound before the company is formed, the modern practice is for the promoters[12] to have prepared, before the company is incorporated, a draft agreement to which the company is expressed to be a party, and for the agreement to be executed by the other party and on behalf of the company after incorporation, pursuant to a clause in the company's memorandum to that effect. If, as is common, a company is being formed to acquire the promoters' business,[13] it does not matter that the promoters are not bound.

---

[11] *cf. James Young & Sons Ltd. and Liquidator* v. *Gowans (James Young & Sons' Trustee)* (1902) 10 S.L.T. 85 (O.H.).

[12] *Ante*, p. 115.

[13] *Ante*, p. 3.

Contracts Made Prior to Commencement of Business

Any contract made by a public company after it is incorporated but before it is entitled to commence business is nevertheless valid, but in such cases if the company fails to comply with its obligations within 21 days of being asked to do so the directors are liable to compensate the other party for any loss or damage consequent on its inability to commence business: 1980 Act section 4(8).

Form of Contracts

The rules as to the form of a registered company's contracts are the same as those for contracts made between private persons. Thus a contract on behalf of a company is made (by any person acting under the company's authority) in writing if such a contract is required by law to be in writing when made between private persons, and orally if it may be made orally when made between private persons. If the contract is, according to English law, required to be under seal even if made between private persons, it may be made under the company's common seal. A deed is validly executed according to Scots law if it is sealed with the company's common seal and subscribed by two directors or by a director and the secretary; witnesses are not required: section 32.[14]

The seal

The company's seal is affixed in the manner laid down in the articles.

Table A, article 113, provides: "The directors shall provide for the safe custody of the seal, which shall only be used by the authority of the directors or of a committee of the directors authorised by the directors in that behalf, and every instrument to which the seal shall be affixed shall be signed by a director and shall be countersigned by the secretary or by a second director or by some other person appointed by the directors for the purpose."

A company whose objects comprise the transaction of business in foreign countries may, if authorised by its articles, have for use in any place outside the United Kingdom, an official seal. The official seal must be a facsimile of the company's common seal, with the addition on its face of the name of every place where it is to be used: section 35.

---

[14] The same rules now apply to other corporations: Corporate Bodies' Contracts Act 1960, which does not apply to Scotland.

A document requiring *authentication* by a company may be signed by a director, secretary or other authorised officer of the company, and need not be under its common seal: section 36.

Section 2(1) of the Stock Exchange (Completion of Bargains) Act 1976 allows a company to have an official seal for use for sealing securities issued by the company and for sealing documents creating or evidencing securities issued by the company. This official seal must be a facsimile of the common seal of the company with the addition on its face of the word "Securities."

Bills of exchange

Bills of exchange and promissory notes can be drawn, accepted or indorsed on behalf of a company by any person acting under the company's authority: section 33. Officers who sign their own names without making it clear that they are signing on behalf of the company may incur personal liability.[15]

ULTRA VIRES CONTRACTS

These were dealt with in Chapter 3.[16]

---

[15] *Brebner* v. *Henderson*, 1925 S.C. 643; contrast *McLean* v. *Stuart and Others*, 1970 S.L.T. (Notes) 77 (O.H.).

[16] *Ante*, p. 55.

CHAPTER 7

PROSPECTUSES

THIS chapter begins by dealing with the question: "What is a prospectus?" This is because it is important for several reasons to be able to tell whether a document is a prospectus. If a document is a prospectus, certain sections of the Companies Act 1948 require it to state certain matters and set out certain reports. This is for the benefit of potential investors. Again, if a document is a prospectus, a section of the Act provides that a copy must be delivered to the Registrar of Companies before the prospectus is issued. Further, if a document is a prospectus and it contains a misleading statement, a section provides that the directors or other persons responsible for the statement are prima facie liable to pay compensation to those members of the public who, *e.g.* subscribe for shares in the company on the faith of the prospectus. The object of all the sections referred to is to control statements in prospectuses. The various sections are dealt with later in the chapter under the headings "Contents of a Prospectus," "Registration of Prospectus" and "Misrepresentation and Omission."

WHAT IS A PROSPECTUS?

When the public is asked to subscribe for shares or debentures in a company, the invitation involves the issue of a document setting out the advantages to accrue from an investment in the company. This document is termed a prospectus. As will be explained later, it may be issued by the company or a promoter (in which case there is a direct invitation to the public), by an issuing house (in which case there is an offer for sale), or by a share broker (in which case there is said to be a placing).[1] If the existing shareholders are given an option to take further shares in the company there is said to be a rights issue.[2] It is only in the case of a *public* company that an invitation can be made to the public to subscribe for shares or debentures—a private company must raise its capital privately.[3]

---

[1] *Post*, p. 146.
[2] *Post*, p. 223.
[3] 1980 Act, s.15, *ante*, p. 46.

Section 455 provides that in the Act, unless the context otherwise requires, the expression "prospectus" means any prospectus, notice, circular, advertisement or other invitation, offering to the public for subscription or purchase any shares or debentures of a company. It is only if there is a prospectus as so defined that the provisions of the Act dealing with such things as the contents of a prospectus, registration of a copy of a prospectus and compensation for misrepresentation in a prospectus come into play.

The words "invitation" and "offering" in section 455 reflect the fact that sometimes a prospectus is only an invitation to treat and sometimes it is an offer. In the case of a direct invitation the prospectus is an invitation to treat after which the public makes offers for such shares or debentures, as the case may be, as are required.[4] In the case of a rights issue the prospectus (the letter to existing shareholders, giving them an option of taking further shares) is an offer.[5]

Whether an invitation or offer is made to the public is a question of fact but section 55(1) provides that in the Act, subject to any provision to the contrary therein, the term "public" is not restricted to the public at large but includes any section of the public, whether selected as members or debenture holders of the company or as clients of the person issuing the prospectus or in any other manner. There is an offer to the members of a company when a rights issue is made. There may be an offer to clients of the person issuing the prospectus when shares or debentures are placed.

Only 3,000 copies of a document which offered shares for subscription and which was headed "for private circulation only" were distributed to the shareholders of a number of gas companies. *Held*, there was an offer of shares to the public, *i.e.* a prospectus: *Re South of England Natural Gas Co. Ltd.* [1911] 1 Ch. 573.

However, by section 55(2), an offer or invitation is not treated as made to the public if it can be regarded as not calculated to result in the shares or debentures becoming available for subscription or purchase by persons who have not received the offer or invitation,[6] or if it is

---

[4] See further, *post*, p. 167.

[5] *Jackson* v. *Turquand* (1869) L.R. 4 H.L. 305.

[6] s.55(2)(*a*) provides that a provision in a company's articles prohibiting invitations to the public to subscribe for shares or debentures shall not be taken as prohibiting the making to members or debenture holders of an invitation which can be so regarded.

otherwise the domestic concern of the person making and receiving it (*e.g.* where a director of a private company invites only a few friends to take shares).[7]

For this purpose any offer by a private cmpany to existing members of the company or to existing employees under an employees' share scheme[8] is to be regarded as a domestic concern of the persons making and receiving the offer. This can be extended to include the families[9] of such members or employees and may even allow for the offer to be renounced in favour of another member of the class or scheme: section 55(3).

The word "subscription" in section 455 means acquisition for cash from the company, by issue and allotment by the company, of unissued shares or debentures in the company.[10] The word "purchase" means acquisition for cash, by transfer from a person to whom the company has allotted them, of already issued shares or debentures in the company.[11]

The Jenkins Report stated[12] that:

"It is generally accepted that" subscription or purchase "involves the payment of money and accordingly that a document containing an offer of securities for a consideration other than cash (*e.g.* shares) cannot be a prospectus although it may be a circular to which the Prevention of Fraud (Investments) Act applies."

British and Commonwealth Shipping Co. Ltd., in a circular accompanied by a "Form of Acceptance and Transfer," offered to acquire all the issued shares in Union-Castle Mail Steamship Co. Ltd. and Clan Line Steamers Ltd.

---

[7] *Sherwell* v. *Combined Incandescent Mantles Syndicate (Limited)* (1907) 23 T.L.R. 482; *Sleigh* v. *Glasgow and Transvaal Options Ltd.* (1904) 6 F. 420, in which another reason for the document not being a prospectus was that it did not contain an invitation to take shares and an accompanying letter simply advised the friends to take shares.

[8] See 1980 Act, s.87(1).

[9] 1948 Act, s.55(4).

[10] *Per* Kekewich J. at p. 357 in *Arnison* v. *Smith* (1889) 41 Ch.D. 348 (C.A.).

[11] *Governments Stock* case, *infra; Mutual Home Loans Fund of Australia Ltd.* v. *Att.-Gen. (N.S.W.)* (1973) 130 C.L.R. 103. The acquisition of shares in a company by application and allotment is not a "purchase" within section 42 of the 1981 Act, *post*: *Re V.G.M. Holdings Ltd.* [1942] Ch. 235 (C.A.).

"The difference between the issue of a share to a subscriber and the purchase of a share from an existing shareholder is the difference between the creation and the transfer of a chose in action": *per* Lord Greene M.R., at p. 241. The Scots law equivalent of "chose in action" is "incorporeal moveable."

[12] Para. 236.

in exchange for shares in British and Commonwealth. *Held*, the circular was not a prospectus. It offered shares neither for purchase (because the shares offered were unissued shares in British and Commonwealth), nor for subscription (because the shares offered were not to be taken for cash). Further, the offer was not made to the public (because the offer could be accepted only by Union-Castle and Clan Line shareholders, and such shareholders as accepted were to be issued with *non*-renounceable letters of allotment, so the case fell within section 55(2)). The consent of the Board of Trade was obtained under section 13 of the Prevention of Fraud (Investments) Act 1939 on the basis that the circular was not a prospectus. Finally, it was not a form of application for shares within section 38(3) *post*: *Governments Stock, etc., Investment Co. Ltd.* v. *Christopher* [1956] 1 W.L.R. 237.

Section 455 speaks only of an invitation offering shares or debentures to the public but defines "debenture" as including debenture stock, bonds and any other securities of a company whether or not constituting a charge on the company's assets. It is thought that the word "share" includes an option to take a share.[13]

The word "company" in the Act means a company formed and registered under the Act or an existing company. An existing company is a company formed and registered under one of the earlier Companies Acts. (s.455.)

The Jenkins Report[14] recommended that the definition of a prospectus should be extended to cover documents offering securities for a consideration other than cash. And, further, that the Board of Trade[15] be empowered to regulate advertisements offering securities by wireless, television or cinematograph.

Contents of a Prospectus

The object of the legislature is to compel the company to provide in a prospectus the necessary information to enable the would-be investor to decide whether or not to subscribe for the company's shares or debentures. The statutory requirements are designed mainly to provide information about:

(1) Who the directors are, and what benefit they will get from their directorships.

---

[13] *Mutual Home Loans* case, *ante*.
[14] Para. 252.
[15] Now the Department of Trade.

(2) What profit is being made by the promoters.

(3) The amount of capital required by the company to be subscribed, the amount actually received or to be received in cash, and the precise nature of the consideration given for the remaining capital.

(4) What the company's financial record has been in the past.

(5) What the company's obligations are under contracts which it has entered into, and for commission and preliminary expenses.

(6) What are the voting and dividend rights of each class of shares.

Fourth Schedule matters and reports

Section 38(1) provides that, subject to certain exceptions which will be dealt with later,[16] the general rule is that every prospectus issued by or on behalf of a company or promoter must state the matters specified in Part I of the Fourth Schedule and set out the reports specified in Part II of the Fourth Schedule, whether the prospectus is issued on the formation of the company or subsequently. The company cannot contract out of its obligation to comply with these requirements: section 38(2).

The Fourth Schedule matters are:

(1) The *number of founders or management or deferred*[17] *shares,* if any, and the nature and extent of the interest of the holders in the property and profits of the company.

(2) The number of shares, if any, fixed by the articles as the *qualification*[18] *of a director,* and any provision in the articles as to the *directors' remuneration.* The amount of the directors' remuneration need not be set out.

(3) The *names, descriptions and addresses of the directors.*

(4) Where *shares* are offered to the public for subscription, particulars of—

    (*a*) the *minimum subscription, i.e.* the minimum amount which, in the opinion of the directors, must be raised by the issue of such shares to provide for—

        (i) the purchase price of any property which is to be defrayed wholly or partly out of the proceeds of the issue;

        (ii) preliminary expenses payable by the company, and commission payable by it to persons who have agreed to subscribe or procure subscriptions for shares;

---

[16] Under ss.38(5), 39, *post,* pp. 138, 139.

[17] *Post,* p. 220.

[18] *Post,* p. 334.

(iii) the repayment of any moneys borrowed by the company in respect of items (i) and (ii);

(iv) working capital; and

(*b*) the amounts to be provided for (i) to (iv), *ante*, otherwise than out of the proceeds of the issue, and the sources from which they are to be provided.

It has been suggested[19] that the provisions relating to the minimum subscription are inadequate in that, *e.g.*, they do not apply to a debenture issue, and the matters enumerated for the purpose of determining the minimum subscription do not include such things as the carrying out of a specific purpose or project the cost of which is to be defrayed in whole or part from the proceeds of the issue and the discharge of any liability due or to beome due.

(5) The time of the *opening of the subscription lists*.

(6) The *amount payable on application and allotment* on each share, including the amount, if any, payable by way of premium,[20] and, in the case of a second or subsequent offer of shares, the amount offered for subscription on each previous allotment within the two preceding years, the amount actually allotted, and the amount paid on the shares so alloted, including the amount, if any, paid by way of premium.[20]

(7) The *number, description and amount of any shares or debentures for which any person has, or is entitled to be given, an option to subscribe,* the period during which it is exercisable, the price to be paid for the shares or debentures, the consideration given or to be given for the option, and the names and addresses of the persons to whom it was given, or, if given to existing shareholders or debenture holders as such, the relevant shares or debentures.

(8) The *number and amount of shares and debentures* which, within the two preceding years, have been *issued or agreed to be issued as fully or partly paid up otherwise than in cash,* the extent to which they are so paid up, and the consideration for their issue.

(9) The *names and addresses of the vendors of any property* purchased or to be purchased by the company, which is to be paid for, wholly or partly, out of the proceeds of the issue for subscription by the prospectus (other than property purchased or to be purchased in the ordinary course of the company's business), the amount payable in cash, shares or debentures to each vendor, and short particulars of any transaction relating to the property within the previous two years in which any vendor, director or promoter of the company had any interest.

---

[19] *Fifth Interim Report of the Australian Company Law Advisory Committee* (1970), paras. 67–69.

[20] This paragraph was amended by s.33 of the Companies Act 1976.

A vendor is defined[21] as a person who has entered into any contract for the sale or purchase, or for any option of purchase, of any property to be acquired by the company in any case where—

(a) the purchase-money is not fully paid at the date of the issue of the prospectus;

(b) the purchase-money is to be paid or satisfied wholly or partly out of the proceeds of the issue offered for subscription;

(c) the contract depends for its validity or fulfilment on the result of such issue.

Examples.—X buys property from Y for £100,000 and contracts to sell it to the company for £130,000. X completes the purchase on April 30, and on May 1 the prospectus is issued. X's name only need be given as vendor. The price he paid to Y must be disclosed.

R buys property from S for £100,000 and contracts to sell it to the company for £130,000. The purchase is not completed when the prospectus is issued. Both R and S must be given as vendors, and the price at which R is buying from S must be disclosed.

(10) The *amount paid* or payable in cash, shares or debentures *for such property*, specifying the amount payable for goodwill.

(11) The amount paid within the two preceding years, or payable, as *commission* for subscribing or procuring subscriptions for shares or debentures of the company, or the rate of commission.

This includes underwriting commission and brokerage, but not sub-underwriting commission.[22]

(12) The amount or estimated amount of the *preliminary expenses,* and of the expenses of the issue, and the persons by whom they have been respectively paid or are payable.

These include the legal expenses incidental to the formation of the company, registration fees and stamp duty, the cost of the prospectus and other out-of-pocket expenses incurred by the promoters in forming the company.

(13) The *amount paid* or benefit given within the two preceding years, or intended to be paid or given, *to any promoter,* and the consideration therefor.

(14) The dates of, parties to and general nature of *every material contract,* not being a contract entered into in the ordinary course of the company's business or made more than two years before the date of issue of the prospectus.

It seems that a material contract is a contract which, whether deterrent or not, an intending investor ought to have an opportunity of considering in order to decide whether to apply for shares or not.[23]

Among material contracts are those for the purchase of property or of a business by the company, for the employment of a promoter as manager, and underwriting contracts.

---

[21] Sched. 4, Pt. III.
[22] *Post*, p. 162.
[23] *Broome* v. *Speak* [1903] 1 Ch. 586 (C.A.).

(15) The names and addresses of *the auditors.*

(16) The nature and extent of *the interest of every director* in the promotion of the company or in the property to be acquired by the company, with a statement of all sums paid or to be paid to him by any person, in cash or shares or otherwise, to induce him to become, or to qualify him as, a director, or for services rendered by him in connection with the promotion or formation of the company.

(17) In a prospectus inviting the public to subscribe for shares the *voting rights* and the rights in respect of dividends and capital attached to the different classes of shares into which the share capital is divided.

(18) The *length of time during which the business of the company* or any business which is to be acquired by the company *has been carried on, if* either business has been carried on for *less than three years.*

Paragraphs (2), (3), (12) (so far as it relates to preliminary expenses) and (16) above do not apply in the case of a prospectus issued more than two years after the company is entitled to commence business.[24]

The Fourth Schedule reports are:

(1) A *report by the company's auditors,* dealing with the profits or losses in each of the five financial years immediately preceding the issue of the prospectus (or, if the company has been carrying on business for less than five years, the years for which its accounts have been made up) and giving the rates of dividends paid on each class of shares during the same period. The report must also deal with the assets and liabilities of the company at the last date to which the accounts of the company were made up.

If the company has subsidiaries[25] the report must deal separately with the company's profits or losses, and in addition deal either—

- (a) as a whole with the combined profits or losses of its subsidiaries, so far as they concern members of the company; or
- (b) individually with the profits or losses of each subsidiary, so far as they concern members of the company;

or, instead of dealing separately with the company's profits or losses, deal as a whole with the profits or losses of the company and, so far as they concern members of the company, with the combined profits or losses of its subsidiaries.

Again, if the company has subsidiaries, the report, in addition to dealing separately with the company's assets and liabilities, must deal either—

- (a) as a whole with the combined assets and liabilities of the subsidiaries, with or without the company's assets and liabilities; or
- (b) individually with the assets and liabilities of each subsidiary,

---

[24] See note 21 above.
[25] *Ante,* p. 52.

and must indicate as respects the assets and liabilities of the subsidiaries the allowance to be made for persons other than members of the company.

(2) If the proceeds of the issue of shares or debentures are to be applied in *the purchase of a business,* a report by named accountants (qualified for appointment as auditors of a company)[26] upon the profits or losses of the business in each of the five financial years before the issue of the prospectus, and the assets and liabilities of the business at the last date to which the accounts of the business were made up.

(3) If the proceeds of the issue are to be applied in *the acquisition of shares in another company* which will become a subsidiary of the company issuing the prospectus, a report by named accountants (qualified for appointment as auditors of a company)[26] upon the profits or losses of the other company in each of the five financial years before the issue of the prospectus and upon the assets and liabilities of that company at the last date to which the accounts were made up. The report must also deal with the profits or losses and the assets and liabilities of any subsidiaries of that company, and indicate how the profits or losses of that company would have concerned members of the acquiring company, and what allowance would have been made, in relation to assets and liabilities, for holders of other shares, if it had held the shares to be acquired at all material times.

Statement as to partial subscriptions

Section 16 of the 1980 Act provides that no public company may allot any shares offered for subscription unless either the capital is subscribed for in full or the offer states that if the capital is not so subscribed, the amount subscribed may be allotted in any event or in the event of the conditions specified in the offer being satisfied. Any allotment in breach will be an irregular allotment within the meaning of the 1948 Act.[27]

Expert's consent

Section 40 provides that if a prospectus includes a statement by an expert, he must have given (and not, before delivery of a copy of the prospectus to the Registrar for registration,[28] withdrawn) his written consent to the inclusion of the statement, and the prospectus must state that he has done so.

Contravention of the section renders the company and every person knowingly a party to the issue of the prospectus liable to a fine.

[26] Sched. 4, Pt. III, and see, *post,* p. 517.
[27] See p. 179, *post.*
[28] *Post,* p. 142.

The section defines the expression "expert" as including an engineer, valuer, accountant *or any other person whose profession gives authority to a statement made by him.*

Other requirements

Every prospectus issued by or on behalf of a company or in relation to an intended company must—

(1) be dated, and that date must, unless the contrary is proved, be taken as the date of publication of the prospectus (s.37);
(2) state on the face of it that a copy has been delivered to the Registrar;
(3) specify any documents required to be indorsed on or attached to such copy (s.41). Such documents include an expert's consent, above, and will be explained later.[28]

When prospectus need not contain Fourth Schedule matters and reports

Section 38(5) of the 1948 Act, as amended by Schedule 2 to the 1976 Act, provides two exceptions to section 38(1):

(1) Where the prospectus or form of application is issued to existing members or debenture holders of the company, whether or not an applicant will have the right to renounce in favour of other persons. In this case the issue will normally be a rights issue.[29]
(2) Where the prospectus or form of application relates to shares or debentures uniform with shares or debentures previously issued and for the time being listed on a prescribed stock exchange.

(The Stock Exchange is prescribed for the purposes of section 38(5)[30]—all stock exchanges in Great Britain and Northern Ireland and that in Dublin have been amalgamated.)

In these two cases, a prospectus issued by or on behalf of the company or a promoter need not contain the Fourth Schedule matters and reports and is called "an abridged prospectus." In the first case the

---

[29] *Post*, p. 223.
[30] Companies (Stock Exchange) Order 1973 (S.I. No. 482).

persons to whom the prospectus is issued explain the exception; in the second, the kind of shares or debentures being issued.

Forms of application for shares or debentures

By section 38(3), subject to certain exceptions[31] dealt with below, the general rule is that it is unlawful to issue any form of application for shares or debentures unless the form is accompanied by a prospectus containing the Fourth Schedule matters and reports.

When prospectus not required

There are exceptions to section 38(3). In these cases a form of application for shares or debentures can be issued *without* a prospectus complying with section 38.

Exceptions are where:

(1) The form of application is issued to existing members or debenture holders of the company: section 38(5), *ante.*
(2) The form relates to shares or debentures uniform with shares or debentures previously issued and for the time being listed on a prescribed stock exchange: section 38(5), *ante.*
(3) The form is issued in connection with an invitation to a person to agree to underwrite the shares or debentures: section 38(3).
(4) The form is issued in relation to shares or debentures which are not offered to the public: section 38(3).

A person who underwrites shares usually agrees, in return for a commission, to take up to a specified number of shares if the public fail to apply for them.[32] Such a person will have or will obtain, before he agrees to underwrite, all the information he needs about the company.

Certificate of exemption

Section 39 of the 1948 Act, as amended by Schedule 2 to the 1976 Act, provides that section 38, above, is excluded where a prescribed stock exchange grants a certificate of exemption from compliance with the Fourth Schedule requirements, which it can do if—

[31] Under ss.38(3), (5), 39.
[32] *Post*, p. 161.

(1) a prospectus is to be issued generally, *i.e.* to non-members or non-debenture holders of the company;

(2) compliance with such requirements would be unduly burdensome, because of the size and other circumstances of the issue, and any limitations on the number and class of persons to whom the offer is to be made; and

(3) application is made to such stock exchange for permission for the shares or debentures to be listed.

When the certificate is granted, the prospectus is deemed to comply with the Fourth Schedule requirements *provided* that it contains the particulars and information which the stock exchange requires to be published in connection with the application for permission ((3), *ante*). A prospectus containing such particulars and information is called "an abridged prospectus."

The Stock Exchange is prescribed for the purposes of section 39 in the same way as for section 38(5), *ante*.[33]

Contravention of section 38

If any person contravenes section 38(3), *i.e.* issues a form of application for shares or debentures without a prospectus complying with the Act, he is liable to a fine (s.38(3)), and if section 38(1) is contravened, *i.e.* a prospectus which does not comply with the Act is issued by or on behalf of a company or promoter, it seems that the directors and other persons responsible for the prospectus are liable in damages to a person who takes shares or debentures on the faith of the prospectus and suffers damage by reason of the contravention.

A prospectus was issued which did not disclose the amount offered for subscription and actually allotted on a former prospectus. *Held,* this omission did not entitle an applicant for shares to rescind the contract. The remedy of the allottee was in damages against those responsible for the prospectus: *Re South of England Natural Gas Co. Ltd.* [1911] 1 Ch. 573.[34]

Unlike certain other sections, section 38 does not expressly provide that the allottee may rescind his contract for non-compliance with the Act but it does contemplate a liability in damages on the part of the directors and other persons responsible for the prospectus, for subsection (4) exonerates them

---

[33] p. 138.

[34] Although Lords Sumner and Warrington said in *Nash* v. *Lynde* [1929] A.C. 158, *post*, p. 143, at pp. 169, 175, that the decision in *Re South of England Natural Gas Co. Ltd.* is open to review.

from liability if they can prove certain matters. "In my opinion the allottee is not entitled to rescind his contract because of any breach of the statutory requirements, which extend to such comparatively unimportant matters as the names and addresses of the company's auditors. His remedy is against the directors and other persons responsible for the prospectus": *per* Swinfen Eady J. at p. 577.

However, in the event of contravention of either section 38(1) or section 38(3), section 38(4) provides that a director or other person responsible for the prospectus is not liable if—

(1) as regards any matter not disclosed, he proves that he did not know of it; or
(2) he proves that the contravention arose from an honest mistake of fact on his part; or
(3) the contravention was in respect of matters which in the opinion of the court were immaterial, or was such as ought, in the opinion of the court, reasonably to be excused.

Stock Exchange listing

If a Stock Exchange listing is desired for the shares or debentures offered to the public by a prospectus, the requirements of The Stock Exchange must be complied with[35] and these are more stringent than those of the Act. For example, the auditors' report must deal with the profits or losses in each of the 10 financial years immediately preceding the issue of the prospectus or in each of the years since incorporation if this occurred less than 10 years prior to publication of the prospectus.[36]

The Jenkins Report[37] recommended that the Fourth Schedule be amended so that it requires information on the lines of that required by the London Stock Exchange[38] about such matters as paid-up capital. It should also require turnover to be disclosed.

A Stock Exchange listing for the shares of a public company[39] is advantageous because it makes the shares more marketable. Investors know that the stringent requirements of The Stock Exchange are

---

[35] Rules and Regulations of The Stock Exchange, London, Rule 159(2) and App. 34, Sched. II.
[36] Compare the corresponding requirement of the Act, *ante*, p. 136.
[37] Para. 252.
[38] Now The Stock Exchange.
[39] The shares of private companies are not dealt in on The Stock Exchange because of the prohibition on public subscription for such shares, *ante*, p. 46.

complied with and that the shares can easily be bought or sold on the Exchange.

REGISTRATION OF PROSPECTUS

By section 41 no prospectus may be issued by or on behalf of a company or in relation to an intended company unless, on or before the date of publication, a copy is delivered to the Registrar for registration. Any such copy must—

(1) be signed by every person named in it as a director or proposed director, or by his agent authorised in writing;

(2) have indorsed on or attached to it—

   (*a*) any consent to the issue required from an expert[40];

   (*b*) when the prospectus is issued generally[41]—

      (i) a copy of any material contract[42];

      (ii) when the persons making any report required to be set out in the prospectus[43] have made any adjustments as respects the figures of any profits or losses or assets and liabilities, a signed, written statement by them setting out the adjustments and giving the reasons therefor.

The Registrar requires two copies of the prospectus and of all supporting documents to be lodged.

The Registrar cannot register a prospectus unless it is dated and the above conditions are complied with. The issue of a prospectus before the requisite copy has been registered is punishable by a fine.

The result of section 41 is that a director cannot say that the prospectus was issued without his knowledge or that he was ignorant of the contents of the prospectus. A record is also available for the information of anyone interested in the prospectus, because all the documents kept by the Registrar may be inspected: section 426 of the 1948 Act, as amended by Schedule 3 to the 1976 Act.

---

[40] *Ante*, p. 137.
[41] *Ante*, p. 140.
[42] *Ante*, p. 136.
[43] *Ante*, p. 136.

Time of Issue of Prospectus

For the purposes of sections 38 and 41, above, it is important to know *when* a prospectus can be said to have been issued. For example, a director or other person responsible will not be liable just because a prospectus which should contain the matters and reports specified in the Fourth Schedule does not do so, provided that the prospectus has not been issued.

However, the point has not yet been settled. It may be that a prospectus is issued when it is shown to any person as a member of the public and as an invitation to that person to take some of the shares referred to in the prospectus on the terms set out therein. On the other hand, it may be that a prospectus is only issued when it is issued to the public, *i.e.* when there is a general distribution.[44] If this latter view is correct, whether there is a general distribution in any case appears to be a question of degree.

A prospectus was sent by N., the managing director of a company, to a co-director. The co-director sent it to a solicitor who sent it to a client. The client sent it to his brother-in-law, L. The object was to induce L. to become a director, which he did. L. also took some shares in the company. *Held*, the prospectus had *not* been issued: *Nash* v. *Lynde* [1929] A.C. 158.

In *R.* v. *Delmayne*,[45] it was held that an advertisement inviting the public to deposit money was issued within the meaning of the now repealed Protection of Depositors Act 1963, when it was issued to a member of a deposit and loan society.

Control of Borrowing

The Borrowing (Control and Guarantees) Act 1946 provides for the regulation of borrowing and raising of money, the issue of securities, and the circulation of offers of securities for subscription, sale or exchange. However, because of a General Consent given by the Treasury, the control of borrowing machinery is in general not in use now. The upper limit of the general exemption has been raised from £1 million to £3 million.[46]

---

[44] In *Nash* v. *Lynde* [1929] A.C. 158, Lord Sumner was in favour of the latter view (p. 168), whereas Lord Hailsham L.C. was in favour of the former view (p. 164).
[45] [1970] 2 Q.B. 170 (C.A.).
[46] Control of Borrowing (Amendment) Order 1972 (S.I. 1972/1218, Sept. 1, 1972).

Direct Invitations, Offers for Sale, Placings

Shares or debentures may be offered to the public by means of—

(1) a prospectus issued by or on behalf of a company or promoter (in which case there is a direct invitation to the public); or
(2) an offer for sale; or
(3) a "placing."

We shall see that placing securities directly with financial institutions is unfair in that it favours the big investor and deprives the small one of the opportunity to acquire securities at bargain prices (although it must be remembered that The Stock Exchange requires a substantial percentage of a placing to be offered to the market). An offer for sale to the public is fairer. On the other hand, placing is simpler, quicker and cheaper than an offer for sale. Underwriting is unnecessary, advertising is reduced to a minimum and a large number of prospectuses need not be printed.

Offers for sale

An offer for sale is the usual way in which shares or debentures are offered to the public. It occurs when an issuing house (either a specialised concern or a department of a merchant bank) subscribes for an issue of shares or debentures and then invites the public to purchase from it at a higher price. To save stamp duty the issuing house will renounce the allotment to it in favour of those members of the public who apply for shares or debentures.

The offer for sale is within the definition of a prospectus[47] but it is not a prospectus issued by or on behalf of a company or promoter, so that, were it not for section 45, sections 38 and 41, which are concerned with the contents and registration of a copy of a prospectus,[48] would not apply to it. Section 45 provides that where a company allots or agrees to allot shares or debentures of the company with a view to their being offered for sale to the public, the document by which the offer is made is deemed to be a prospectus issued by the company, and all enactments and rules of law as to contents of prospectuses and to

---

[47] See ss.455 and 55(1), *ante*, p. 130.
[48] *Ante*, pp. 133, 142.

liability in respect of misrepresentation in prospectuses, or otherwise relating to prospectuses, apply as if the offer had been to the public for subscription and as if persons accepting the offer were subscribers for shares or debentures.

Consequently, subject to sections 38(5) and 39, the offer must comply with sections 38 and 41. Section 45 goes on to provide that, in addition to the section 38 matters, the offer must state—

(1) the net amount of the consideration received or to be received by the company for the shares or debentures to which the offer relates;

(2) the place and time at which the contract for allotment can be inspected.

The copy registered with the Registrar under section 41 must be signed by the persons making the offer—at least half of the partners if the offer is made by a firm, and two of the directors if made by a company: section 45(4).

It is presumed, unless the contrary is proved, that an allotment of, or an agreement to allot, shares or debentures was made with a view to their offer for sale to the public if (a) the offer was made within six months after allotment or agreement, or (b) the whole consideration was not received by the company before the offer for sale: section 45(2).

The persons making the offer for sale are prima facie liable to pay compensation under section 43[49] for damage caused by misleading statements in the offer, as persons who have authorised the issue of a prospectus. The directors of the company at the time are under a similar liability. And by virtue of the provisions of section 45 persons accepting the offer may rescind as against the company.

Where it is difficult to fix the issue price of the shares or debentures being offered to the public, because it is uncertain what the public response to the offer will be, *an offer for sale by tender* may be made. In this event, a minimum price is fixed and the issue price is determined by the prices tendered in the applications. Thus, where 250,000 ordinary 25p. shares are offered, a minimum price of 80p. a share may be fixed. The prices tendered may range from 80p. to £2 and the shares may all be sold at 87½p. The object is to ensure that the company

[49] *Post*, p. 154.

receives what the shares are worth to the public, and to defeat stags who, by taking shares and then immediately selling them at a higher price, would otherwise receive the difference between the issue price of a share and its worth to the public. In 1982 the shares of Britoil plc were issued in this way by the then Government to avoid those very consequences which had occurred in previous flotations of nationalised industries.

Placings

An issue of shares or debentures may be placed in one of two ways.[50] An issuing house may subscribe for the issue and then invite its clients (*e.g.* insurance companies and pension funds) to purchase from it at a higher price. Although the invitation is a prospectus unless section 55(2) or (3), *ante,* applies[51] it is not issued by or on behalf of the company and so is not caught by sections 38 and 41. However, it is caught by section 45, *ante,* and by section 43.

Alternatively, an issuing house or stockbrokers or a bank may, without subscribing, act as agents for the company and invite their clients to take from the company. In this case the agents will be paid a commission called "brokerage" for their services. The invitation to the clients is a prospectus unless section 55(2) or (3)[51] applies and, if it is, it is issued on behalf of the company and so caught by sections 38 and 41, and by section 43.

MISREPRESENTATION AND OMISSION

Civil liability

Since a company is liable for the misrepresentations of its directors and other agents acting within the scope of their authority,[52] a person induced to subscribe for shares or debentures in a company by a misrepresentation, *e.g.* in a prospectus, may have a remedy against the company or the individuals responsible, *e.g.* promoters, directors or

[50] See Gower, *Modern Company Law*, 4th ed., p. 339.
[51] p. 130.
[52] See *per* Lord Hatherley in the *Houldsworth* case, *infra,* at 7 R. (H.L.) 60; 5 App.Cas. 331.

experts.[53] The remedy may be available under the general law or it may be statutory.

The main remedy against the *company* is rescission[54] of the contract of allotment, with or without an action for damages. A shareholder cannot recover damages for fraud against the company without rescission, because that would be inconsistent with the contract between him and the other shareholders.[55] The same is true of a claim to damages, *e.g.* for breach of contract, which a shareholder *qua* shareholder may seek to enforce against the company.[56] Damages in lieu of rescission may be recovered under the Misrepresentation Act 1967, s.2(2), which states that where a person has entered into a contract after a misrepresentation made to him *otherwise than fraudulently,* and he would be entitled to rescind, then if rescission is claimed the court may award damages in lieu of rescission, if of opinion that it would be equitable to do so. Damages for *negligent* misrepresentation may be recovered from the company under section 2(1) of the Misrepesentation Act, which provides that where a person has entered into a contract after a misrepresentation made to him by another party thereto and as a result has suffered loss, then the representor is liable in damages unless he proves that on reasonable grounds he believed up to the time when the contract was made that the representation was true. Whether a shareholder can recover damages under section 2(1) without rescission is not clear. Section 2 of the Misrepresentation Act does not apply to Scotland.

The main remedies against the *individuals* responsible are compensation for negligent misrepresentation under section 43[57] and damages for fraud.[58]

---

[53] As in *Frankenburg* v. *Great Horseless Carriage Co.* [1900] 1 Q.B. 504 (C.A.), *post*, p. 154.

[54] The representee may elect to repudiate the contract, and legal proceedings are not essential, in the event of misrepresentation. However, if, as is usual, he wishes to recover money or property transferred by him under the contract he may have to initiate proceedings for rescission.

[55] *Houldsworth* v. *City of Glasgow Bank* (1880) 7 R. (H.L.) 53; (1880) 5 App.Cas. 317, where it was too late to rescind since the company had gone into liquidation. See also *Western Bank* v. *Addie* (1867) 5 M. (H.L.) 80.

[56] *Re Dividend Fund Incorporated (In Liquidation)* [1974] V.R. 451, where an unlimited company failed to repurchase shares in accordance with the articles and the shareholder had to pay calls in a liquidation.

[57] *Post*, p. 154.

[58] *Post*, p. 152.

It may also be possible to claim damages for negligent mis-representation under the principle in *Hedley Byrne & Co. Ltd.* v. *Heller & Partners Ltd.,*[59] which is that a negligent, although honest, misrepresentation, spoken or written, may give rise to an action for damages for financial loss caused thereby. The law implies a duty of care where one party seeks information or advice from another party, trusts the other to exercise due care, it is reasonable for him to do so, the other knows or ought to know that reliance is being placed on his skill or judgment or ability to make careful inquiry and he does not expressly disclaim responsibility for his representation. In *Mutual Life and Citizens' Assurance Co. Ltd.* v. *Evatt*[60] the Privy Council advised that the party from whom information or advice is sought must carry on the business of giving advice or in some other way he must have let it be known that he claims to possess the necessary skill and competence to do so and is prepared to exercise the necessary diligence to give reliable advice. A duty of care may also arise where the advisor has a financial interest in the transaction.[61]

Rescission of the contract of allotment

In order to obtain rescission of a contract of allotment on the ground that it was induced by misrepresentation, the allottee must prove (1) a material false statement of fact, (2) which induced him to subscribe.

(1) There must be a material false statement of fact.

A prospectus stated: "a large number of gentlemen in the trade and others have become shareholders." When the register of members was made up there were 55 shareholders, of whom 10 or 12 were connected with the trade. *Held,* there was not a sufficiently material misrepresentation to entitle a person who had taken shares on the faith of the prospectus to have his name deleted from the register: *City of Edinburgh Brewery Co. Ltd.* v. *Gibson's Trustee* (1869) 7 M. 886.

A statement of fact must be distinguished from a statement of opinion.[62] A statement that the property of the company is worth a certain sum of money, or that the profits are expected to reach a certain figure, is only opinion and gives no right to rescission except where it

---

[59] [1964] A.C. 465.
[60] [1971] A.C. 793 (P.C.).
[61] See *Anderson & Sons* v. *Rhodes Ltd.* [1967] 2 All E.R. 850.
[62] *Liverpool Palace of Varieties Ltd.* v. *Miller* (1896) 4 S.L.T. 153 (O.H.).

can be shown that the maker of the statement did not hold the opinion. Statements, on the other hand, that "the surplus assets, as appear by the last balance sheet, amount to upwards of £10,000"[63] that £200,000 of share capital has been subscribed,[64] and that certain persons have agreed to be directors,[65] are all material statements of fact and, if false, will give rise to a right to rescission.

Where the facts are not equally well known to both sides a statement of opinion by one who should know the facts often implies a statement of fact, *i.e.* that there are reasonable grounds for his opinion, and if it can be proved that he could not as a reasonable man honestly have had the opinion, there is misrepresentation of fact.[66] Again, a statement of intention does not amount to a representation of fact unless it can be proved that the alleged intention never existed.[67]

If a prospectus refers to a report which contains inaccurate statements of fact, the contract can be rescinded if the company has vouched for the accuracy of the report, but otherwise it cannot. Thus, if the company employs an accountant to go through the books and make a report, and then sets out the report in a prospectus, it will not be liable for any inaccuracy in the report.[68] But if the company makes statements of it own, although they are expressed to be based upon a report, it will be liable for an inaccuracy unless in clear and unambiguous terms it has warned intending applicants that it does not vouch for the accuracy of the report, or of any statement based on it.

A company issued a prospectus inviting subscriptions for the purpose of buying a rubber estate in Peru. The prospectus contained extracts from the report of an expert on the spot, which gave the number of matured rubber trees on the estate, and other information. The report was false. *Held,* the accuracy of the report was prima facie the basis of the contract and, therefore, if the company did not intend to contract on that basis, it should have dissociated itself from the report in clear and unambiguous terms, and warned the public that it did not vouch for the accuracy of the report. As there was no

---

[63] *Re London and Staffordshire Fire Insurance Co.* (1883) 24 Ch.D. 149.
[64] *Arnison* v. *Smith* (1889) 41 Ch.D. 348 (C.A.), where the share capital had only been allotted *as* fully paid up. But see *Akerhielm* v. *De Mare* [1959] A.C. 789 (P.C.), *post,* p. 152.
[65] *Re Scottish Petroleum Co.* (1883) 23 Ch.D. 413 (C.A.); *Blakiston* v. *London and Scottish Banking etc. Corpn. Ltd.* (1894) 21 R. 417; contrast *Chambers* v. *Edinburgh etc. Aerated Bread Co. Ltd.* (1891) 18 R. 1039.
[66] *Per* Bowen L.J. in *Smith* v. *Land, etc., Corpn.* (1884) 28 Ch.D. 7 (C.A.), at p. 15.
[67] *Edgington* v. *Fitzmaurice* (1885) 29 Ch.D. 459 (C.A.).
[68] *Bentley & Co.* v. *Black* (1893) 9 T.L.R. 580 (C.A.).

such warning the contracts to take shares could be rescinded: *Re Pacaya Rubber and Produce Co. Ltd.* [1914] 1 Ch. 542.[69]

An *innocent* misrepresentation is a sufficient ground for rescission. It is not necessary to prove knowledge of the untruth of the statement.[70]

Non-disclosure of a material fact amounts to misrepresentation if the omission makes what is stated misleading. It has been said[71] that "It is not that the omission of material facts is an independent ground for rescission, but the omission must be of such a nature as to make the statement actually made misleading." In other words, at least in English law, a contract of allotment is not a true contract *uberrimae fidei*,[72] *i.e.* a contract in which all material facts must be disclosed, although, as has been seen, section 38 and the Fourth Schedule usually require a number of particulars to be disclosed in a prospectus.[73]

A prospectus described a piece of land as "eminently suitable" for greyhound racing. The land in question was, however, affected by a town planning resolution, with the result that, unless the local authority's consent was obtained before any buildings were erected, the company would not be entitled to any compensation in the event of the removal of the buildings under the town planning scheme. The local authority refused its consent. *Held,* the omission to disclose the facts set out above rendered the description of the land as "eminently suitable" misleading, and persons who had subscribed for shares on the strength of the prospectus were entitled to rescind their contracts:*Coles* v. *White City (Manchester) Greyhound Assn. Ltd.* (1929) 45 T.L.R. 230 (C.A.).

It will be remembered that the omission on the part of the company to set out in a prospectus the particulars required to be set out by section 38 does not, of itself, entitle a subscriber to rescind.[74]

(2) The allottee must have been induced to subscribe by the false statement.

---

[69] An earlier Scottish case which went to the House of Lords is *Mair* v. *Rio Grande Rubber Estates Ltd.*, 1913 S.C. (H.L.) 74.

[70] *Per* Lord Shaw of Dunfermline in *Mair* v. *Rio Grande Rubber Estates Ltd.,* 1913 S.C. (H.L.) 74 at p. 81.

[71] *Per* Rigby L.J. in *McKeown* v. *Boudard Peveril Gear Co. Ltd.* (1896) 74 L.T. 712, at p. 713.

[72] And see, *per* Lord Watson in *Aaron's Reefs Ltd.* v. *Twiss* [1896] A.C. 273, at p. 287. There is no definitive authority as to the common law of Scotland on the point and, in view of the statutory provisions, it is now unlikely that there will be.

[73] *Ante*, p. 133.

[74] *Re South of England Natural Gas Co. Ltd.* [1911] 1 Ch. 573, *ante*, p. 140.

Whether or not an allottee was induced to subscribe by reason of the misrepresentation is a question of fact depending on the circumstances of each case. It is not sufficient that the prospectus has been widely advertised in the locality if there is proof that the applicant relied, not on the prospectus, but on independent advice.[75] He is entitled to rely upon the prospectus, and is not bound to verify the statements it contains. Where, therefore, a prospectus simply gave the dates of and parties to contracts and stated where they could be inspected, without indicating that they were material contracts, the omission of the applicant to inspect them did not fix him with notice of their contents.[76]

The false statement need not have been the decisive inducing cause of the contract. It is enough that it was one of the contributory causes.[77]

A later purchaser of shares on the Stock Exchange will usually not be able, on the ground of misrepresentation in a prospectus, to rescind the contract under which he purchased the shares from the allottee, or the contract which arose between the company and the purchaser when his name was entered on the register of members.[78] A purchaser from an issuing house where an offer for sale contains a misrepresentation will be able to rescind as against the company—as stated earlier,[79] section 45 provides that the offer for sale is deemed to be a prospectus issued by the company.

Rescission enables the allottee to recover what he paid for the shares or debentures, plus interest.

The right to rescind is lost—

(1) If, after discovering the misrepresentation, the allottee does an act which shows that he elects to retain the shares and so affirms the contract; for example, he attends and votes at general meetings,[80] receives dividends,[81] or attempts to sell the shares.[82]

(2) If he fails to act within a reasonable time of discovering the true facts.

[75] *M'Morland's Trustees* v. *Fraser* (1896) 24 R. 65.
[76] *Aaron's Reefs Ltd.* v. *Twiss* [1896] A.C. 273.
[77] *Edgington* v. *Fitzmaurice* (1885) 29 Ch.D. 459 (C.A.).
[78] *Collins* v. *Associated Greyhound Racecourses Ltd.* [1930] 1 Ch. 1 (C.A.), *post*, p. 164.
[79] p. 147.
[80] *Sharpley* v. *Louth and East Coast Ry. Co.* (1876) 2 Ch.D. 663 (C.A.).
[81] *Scholey* v. *Central Ry. of Venezuela* (1868) L.R. 9 Eq. 266n.
[82] *Ex p. Briggs* (1866) L.R. 1 Eq. 483.

The right to rescind must be exercised promptly if the company is a going concern, and even a delay of a fortnight has been held to be too long in such a case.[83] When a shareholder was put on inquiry in June, but took no steps to make any investigation until November, his delay prevented him from rescinding the contract.[84]

(3) If restitution is impossible,[85] *e.g.* because he sells the shares.

(4) If the company goes into liquidation.[86]

Events leading up to liquidation may have the same effect, *e.g.* where an unlimited banking company stops payment,[87] or calls a meeting to consider winding up.[88]

Damages for fraud

Fraud is difficult to prove. Nevertheless, promoters, directors, experts or the persons making an offer for sale, are liable for fraud if it can be shown that they signed, or authorised the issue of, a prospectus containing a false statement which they did not honestly believe to be true,[89] with the intention that another person should act upon it, and that he acted on it to his detriment. The test is subjective, *i.e.* did they honestly believe the statement to be true according to its meaning as understood *by them,* albeit erroneously, when it was made?[90] If they cannot be proved to have made a false representation knowingly, or without belief in its truth, or recklessly, careless whether it be true or false, they may have to pay compensation under section 43, *post,* the predecessor of which[91] was first enacted as a result of the decision in *Derry* v. *Peek.*[92]

---

[83] See *Re Scottish Petroleum Co.* (1883) 23 Ch.D. 413 (C.A.).

[84] *Re Christineville Rubber Estates Ltd.* [1911] W.N. 216; *cf. Caledonian Debenture Co. Ltd.* v. *Bernard* (1898) 5 S.L.T. 392 (O.H.). See also Lord President Inglis in *City of Edinburgh Brewery Co. Ltd.* v. *Gibson's Trustee* (1869) 7 M. 886, at p. 891.

[85] *Western Bank* v. *Addie* (1867) 5 M. (H.L.) 80.

[86] *Oakes* v. *Turquand* (1867) L.R. 2 (H.L.) 325; *Western Bank* v. *Addie,* above; *Houldsworth* v. *City of Glasgow Bank* (1880) 7 R. (H.L.) 53; (1879) 6 R. 1164.

[87] *Myles* v. *City of Glasgow Bank* (1879) 6 R. 718.

[88] *Alexander Mitchell* v. *City of Glasgow Bank* (1879) 6 R. (H.L.) 60; (1878) 6 R. 439.

[89] *Per* Lord Herschell in *Derry* v. *Peek* (1889) 14 App.Cas. 337 at p. 374.

[90] *Akerhielm* v. *De Mare* [1959] A.C. 789 (P.C.), *post.*   [91] *Ante,* p. 8.

[92] The explanation of fraud given in that case was referred to with approval in the Scottish case of *Boyd & Forrest* v. *Glasgow etc. Rlwy. Co.,* 1912 S.C. (H.L.) 93. See also *Lees* v. *Tod* (1882) 9 R. 807.

A tramway company by a special Act had power to move trams by animal power and, with the consent of the Board of Trade, by steam power. A prospectus was issued by the directors stating that the company, under its special Act, had the right to use steam power instead of horses. P. subscribed for shares on the strength of this statement. The Board of Trade afterwards refused its consent, and the company was wound up. P. sued the directors for damages for fraud. *Held,* the directors were not liable, the statement as to steam power having been made in the honest belief that it was true: *Derry* v. *Peek* (1889) 14 App.Cas. 337.

In *Akerhielm* v. *De Mare* [1959] A.C. 789 (P.C.), the representation that capital had been "subscribed in Denmark" was inapt to include shares allotted as fully paid to Kenya residents for services rendered in Denmark in connection with the formation of the company. The representor was not liable for fraud because he honestly believed the representation to be true *in the sense in which he understood it.*

A prospectus may be fraudulent, although it is composed of statements which in themselves are perfectly true, if, by reason of omissions, it is calculated as a whole to give a false impression of the position of the company,[93] but mere concealment, even of a material fact, is not at common law a ground for an action for fraudulent misrepresentation against the directors who have issued the prospectus unless the withholding of what is not stated falsifies that which is stated.[94]

If a prospectus issued in order to induce people to subscribe direct from the company contains a false statement, a later purchaser of shares on the Stock Exchange is not one to whom the prospectus was addressed and cannot bring an action for deceit.[95] If, however, a prospectus is issued not only to induce applications for allotment of shares but also to induce purchases in the open market, its function is not exhausted when the company has gone to allotment and a purchaser on the strength of false statements in such a prospectus can sue those responsible for it for fraud.[96]

The company can be sued for damages for the fraudulent misrepresentation of its directors and agents acting within the scope of their authority.

---

[93] *Per* James L.J. in *Arkwright* v. *Newbold* (1881) 17 Ch.D. 301 at p. 318.
[94] *Honeyman* v. *Dickson* (1896) 4 S.L.T. 150 (O.H.).
[95] *Peek* v. *Gurney* (1873) L.R. 6 (H.L.) 377.
[96] *Andrews* v. *Mockford* [1896] 1 Q.B. 372 (C.A.), where the prospectus was later supplemented by false statements in a telegram published in a financial newspaper.

The measure of damages for fraud is prima facie the difference between the actual value of the shares at the time of allotment and the sum paid for them.[97] The plaintiff recovers for all the actual damage directly flowing from the fraudulent misrepresentation.[98] It is not an action for breach of contract and therefore no damages in respect of prospective gains can be recovered.

Compensation under section 43

Section 43 provides that a promoter, a director at the time or a person authorising the issue of a prospectus is prima facie liable to pay compensation to those who subscribe on the faith of the prospectus for the loss they sustain by reason of any untrue statement contained therein.

The expression "promoter" in the section means a promoter who was a party to the preparation of the relevant portion of the prospectus: section 43(5)(*a*). The company is not liable under section 43. However, the persons making an offer for sale may be liable, as stated earlier.[99] So may those who place shares.[1] Liability under the section arises only if a prospectus is issued.

It has been held that the measure of compensation is the same as the measure of damages for fraud.[2]

Only a person who subscribes for shares or debentures can claim under section 43. Persons accepting an offer for sale to the public are subscribers by section 45, *ante*.[3]

Section 46 provides that a statement in a prospectus is deemed to be untrue if it is misleading. Of course, an omission from a prospectus may make what is stated misleading. To obtain compensation it is not necessary to prove that the directors knew that a statement was untrue. Under section 43 damages may be recovered for negligent misrepresentation.

Although compensation cannot be obtained from the *company*, a claim against the company for rescission of a contract to take shares,

---

[97] *McConnel* v. *Wright* [1903] 1 Ch. 546 (C.A.); *Davidson* v. *Tulloch* (1860) 3 Macq. 783; 22 D.(H.L.) 7.
[98] *Doyle* v. *Olby (Ironmongers) Ltd.* [1969] 2 Q.B. 158 (C.A.).
[99] *Ante*, p. 145.
[1] *Ante*, p. 146.
[2] *Clark* v. *Urquhart* [1930] A.C. 28; *Davidson* v. *Hamilton* (1904) 12 S.L.T. 353 (O.H.). [3] p. 144.

together with a return of the money paid, on the ground of mis-representation in a prospectus may be joined with an action against the directors for compensation.[4]

No *person other than an expert* is liable to pay compensation under section 43 if he can prove—

(1) that he withdrew his consent to act as *director* before the issue of the prospectus and it was issued without his authority or consent; or

(2) that the prospectus was issued without his knowledge or consent, and on becoming aware of its issue he gave reasonable public notice that it was so issued; or

(3) that he became aware of the untrue statement in the prospectus after it had been issued and before any allotment was made, and he thereupon withdrew his consent and gave reasonable public notice of the withdrawal *and* of the reason for it; or

(4) as regards the *untrue statement*—

    (*a*) that he had reasonable ground to believe, and did up to the time of allotment believe, that the statement was true[5]; or

    (*b*) that the statement was a fair representation of a statement by an expert,[6] or was contained in a correct copy of or extract from a report or valuation of an expert, and he had reasonable ground to believe, and did up to the issue of the prospectus believe, that the expert was competent; further, that the expert had given the consent required by section 40, *ante,* and had not withdrawn such consent before registration of a copy of the prospectus or, to the defendant's[7] knowledge, before allotment; or

    (*c*) that the statement was a correct and fair representation of an official statement or of a copy of or extract from an official document: section 43(2).

An *expert* is only liable to pay compensation in respect of his own untrue statement (s.43(1)) and he will escape liability if he can prove—

---

[4] *Frankenburg* v. *Great Horseless Carriage Co.* [1900] 1 Q.B. 504 (C.A.).

[5] See, *e.g. Smith* v. *Moncrieff* (1894) 2 S.L.T. 140 (O.H.); contrast *Gray* v. *Central Finance Corporation Ltd.* (1903) 11 S.L.T. 309 (O.H.).

[6] *Ante*, p. 137.

[7] The Scots term for "defendant" is "defender." Similarly, the Scots term for "plaintiff" is "pursuer."

(1) that, having given his consent to the issue of the prospectus, he withdrew it in writing before delivery of a copy of the prospectus for registration; or

(2) that, after delivery of a copy of the prospectus for registration and before allotment, he, on becoming aware of the untrue statement, withdrew his consent in writing and gave reasonable public notice of the withdrawal and of the reason for it; or

(3) that he was competent to make the statement and had reasonable ground to believe, and did up to allotment believe, that the statement was true: section 43(3).

Criminal liability

Section 44 provides that where a prospectus is issued and it includes an untrue statement, *i.e.* by section 46 a misleading statement, any person (other than an expert who has merely given his consent to the inclusion of a statement by him in the prospectus) who authorised the issue of the prospectus is liable to a fine or imprisonment for two years or both unless he proves—

(*a*) that he had reasonable ground to believe and did, up to the time of issue of the prospectus, believe that the statement was true; or

(*b*) that the statement was immaterial.

An intent to defraud is not necessary under section 44.

The Larceny Act 1861, s.84, provided that a director, manager or public officer of a body corporate who made a written statement, which he knew to be false in any material particular, with intent to deceive or defraud any member, shareholder or creditor, or with intent to induce any person to become a shareholder, or to entrust or advance any property to the company, or to enter into any security for its benefit, was liable to seven years' imprisonment.

A statement was false within section 84 if in its context it conveyed a misleading impression although it was literally correct.

Section 84 did not apply to Scotland.

A prospectus contained a statement which was true, that the company had paid dividends every year between 1921 and 1927. The result was that the prospectus gave the impression that the company had made trading profits during the years in question. However, during each of those years the company had incurred substantial trading losses and was only able to pay the specified dividends by the introduction into the accounts of non-recurring items, earned in the abnormal war period, such as repayments of excess profits duty, adjustment of income tax reserves and the like. No disclosure was made of these trading losses. *Held,* the prospectus was false, because it put before intending investors figures which apparently disclosed the existing position of the company, but in fact hid it, and K., a director who knew that it was false, was guilty of an offence under the Larceny Act, s.84: *R.* v. *Kyslant* [1932] 1 K.B. 442 (C.C.A.).

Section 84 of the Larceny Act has been repealed and replaced by section 19 of the Theft Act 1968 but the wording of section 19 is different. It provides that an officer of a body corporate or unincorporated association (or a person purporting to act as such) who, with intent to deceive members or creditors about its affairs, publishes or concurs in publishing a written statement or account which to his knowledge is or may be misleading, false or deceptive in a material particular, is liable to seven years' imprisonment. A person who has entered into a security for the benefit of a body corporate is treated as a creditor of it. In particular, the words "or with intent to induce any person to become a shareholder" do not appear in section 19. This provision of the Theft Act does not apply to Scotland.

Fraudulently inducing a person to acquire securities gives rise to liability under the Prevention of Fraud (Investments) Act 1958, s.13,[8]

PREVENTION OF FRAUD (INVESTMENTS) ACT 1958

This Act[9] aims at preventing (1) "share-hawking," (2) the private offer of securities in companies which have not filed a prospectus and (3) fraud in connection with dealings in securities.

The expression "securities" includes shares, stock, debentures, debenture stock, bonds, and rights or interests (whether described as units or otherwise) in any shares, etc.: 1958 Act. s.26.

Dealing in securities is prohibited except in the case of persons licensed for that purpose by the Department of Trade (1958 Act, s.1), or persons who do not require a licence. No licence is required by—

(*a*) a member of any recognised stock exchange or recognised association of dealers in securities; or

---

[8] p. 158.
[9] Which repealed and consolidated, *inter alia,* the Prevention of Fraud (Investments) Act 1939 and the Companies Act 1947, s.117.

(*b*) the Bank of England, any statutory or municipal corporation or any exempted dealer; or

(*c*) any person acting in the capacity of manager or trustee under a unit trust scheme authorised by the Department of Trade (1958 Act, s.2).

Contravention of section 1 is punishable by up to two years' imprisonment or a £500 fine or both.

Section 14 of the 1958 Act provides that a person, other than those mentioned above, commits an offence (punishable by up to two years' imprisonment or a £500 fine or both) if he distributes or causes to be distributed circulars which, to his knowledge, invite persons to acquire, dispose of, subscribe or underwrite[10] securities, unless the circular is—

(*a*) a prospectus complying wth the Companies Act 1948; or

(*b*) in the case of a corporation incorporated in Great Britain which is not a registered company, a document containing the information required by section 417 of the Companies Act.[11]

A circular may be in the form of a newspaper, journal, magazine or other periodical publication.

No offence is committed if circulars are distributed (i) in connection with a bona fide invitation to enter into an underwriting agreement, or (ii) by or on behalf of a corporation to holders of securities, creditors or employees of the corporation or its subsidiary; or (iii) to a person whose business involves the acquisition and disposal, or the holding, of securites.

By section 13 of the 1958 Act, as amended by the Banking Act 1979, any person who, by any statement, promise or forecast which he knows to be misleading, false or deceptive, or by any dishonest concealment of material facts, or by the reckless making (dishonestly or otherwise) of any statement, promise or forecast which is misleading, false or deceptive, induces or attempts to induce another person to enter into or offer to enter into any agreement for acquiring, disposing of, subscribing for or underwriting securities is liable to seven years' imprisonment.[12]

[10] *Post,* p. 161.

[11] See the 11th ed. of this work, p. 654.

[12] As regards the insertion of "dishonestly or otherwise," *R.* v. *Russell* [1953] 1 W.L.R. 77 (C.C.A.), and *R.* v. *Grunwald* [1963] 1 Q.B. 935, were adopted contrary to the recommendations of the Jenkins Report, para. 254.

CHAPTER 8

COMMISSIONS AND DISCOUNTS

In order to procure capital a company frequently desires to pay a commission or discount to a person introducing capital.

Section 53(1) allows a company to pay a commission to a person in consideration of his subscribing or agreeing to subscribe, absolutely or conditionally, or procuring or agreeing to procure subscriptions, for *shares* in the company if—

(1) the payment is authorised by the articles (authority in the memorandum is insufficient[1]);

(2) the commission does not exceed either (*a*) 10 per cent. of the price at which the shares are issued, or (*b*) the amount or rate authorised by the articles, whichever is the less;

(3) the amount or rate is (*a*) in the case of shares offered to the public for subscription, disclosed in the prospectus; (*b*) in other cases, disclosed in a statement in the prescribed form signed by all the directors and delivered to the Registrar before payment of the commission;

(4) the number of shares which persons have agreed for a commission to subscribe absolutely is disclosed in the manner set out above.

This subsection applies as well to private as to public companies.[2] It enables a company to pay underwriting commission or brokerage, which commissions are dealt with in detail later.[3]

Section 53(2) provides that, except as allowed by subsection (1), no company shall apply any of its shares or capital money, either directly or indirectly, in payment of any commission, discount or allowance to any person in consideration of his subscribing or agreeing to subscribe, whether absolutely or conditionally, or procuring or agreeing to procure subscriptions, absolute or conditional, for any *shares* in the company, whether the shares or money be applied by being added to the purchase money of any property acquired by the company or to the

---

[1] *Re Republic of Bolivia Exploration Syndicate Ltd.* [1914] 1 Ch. 139.

[2] *Dominion of Canada General Trading Syndicate* v. *Brigstocke* [1911] 2 K.B. 648.

[3] pp. 161, 163.

contract price of any work to be done for the company, or the money be paid out of the nominal purchase money or contract price, or otherwise.

In the nineteenth century, and especially after the decision in *Ooregum Gold Mining Co. of India Ltd.* v. *Roper*[4] that shares may not be issued at a discount so as to relieve persons taking shares from liability to pay up their nominal amount in full, there was uncertainty as to whether companies could pay underwriting commission. This uncertainty was removed by the Companies Act 1900, the relevant provisions of which are now embodied in the present section 53. Subsection (1) is intended to allow companies to pay underwriting commission when shares are underwritten, subsection (2) to preclude the issue of shares at a discount. The *Ooregum* case, and section 53(2), lay down a general rule, intended to protect the creditors of the company, that the company's share capital must be raised, as will be explained later.[5]

An agreement to pay commission in contravention of section 53 is invalid.

The company agreed to pay A. a commission of 10 per cent. on any sum accepted by the company on A.'s introduction. No statement in prescribed form, as required by section 53, was registered with the Registrar. A. was the means of introducing £4,600 to the company, and was paid £200 on account. A. sued for £260, the balance of commission. *Held*, A. was not entitled to recover, as the commission was unlawful, but the company could not recover the £200 already paid to A.: *Andreae* v. *Zinc Mines of Great Britain Ltd.* [1918] 2 K.B. 454.

An agreement by a company to apply some of its shares partly for underwriting services and partly for other services is caught by section 53(2), *ante*, and the whole agreement is invalid.[6]

If shares are allotted at par to persons who are given an option to subscribe for further shares at par within a certain time, an allotment of such further shares at par is not subject to the provisions of section 53, even though the market value of the shares has risen to a premium, because it does not involve the payment of a commission or discount.[7]

---

[4] [1892] A.C. 125, *post*, p. 174. The corresponding Scots case is *Klenck* v. *East India Co. etc. Ltd.* (1888) 16 R. 271.

[5] *Post*, p. 222.

[6] *Banking Service Corporation Ltd.* v. *Toronto Finance Corporation Ltd.* [1928] A.C. 333 (P.C.).

[7] *Hilder* v. *Dexter* [1902] A.C. 474; *cf. Cameron* v. *Glenmorangie Distillery Co. Ltd.* (1896) 23 R. 1092.

Whenever a company has paid any sums by way of commission in respect of shares or debentures, or allowed discount in respect of shares or debentures, the commission or discount must not be shown as an asset in any balance sheet or profit and loss account: Schedule 8, paragraph 3(2). Further, the commission or discount must be stated in the annual return to the Registrar: Schedule 6, paragraph 3.

A share premium account may be applied by the company in writing off the commission paid on any issue of shares or debentures of the company: section 56.[8]

UNDERWRITING

Before an issue of shares is made to the public, it is usual to insure the success of the issue by having it underwritten. Underwriting means "agreeing to take so many shares, more or less in number, as are specified in the underwriting letter if the public do not subscribe for them."[9] Another definition is, an agreement "to take up by way of subscription in a new company or new issue a certain number of shares if and so far as not applied for by the public."[10] An underwriter does not guarantee that the public will take up the shares; he agrees with the company to subscribe for them himself on the happening of an event, *i.e.* the failure of the public to subscribe them fully. The underwriter may be, for example, a broker, a bank or an issuing house.

The consideration for underwriting usually takes the form of an underwriting commission which the underwriter receives whether or not the public take up all the shares underwritten. The commission may be in the form of shares or it may be a payment out of the money derived from the issue of shares underwritten. Again, it is thought that it may be a payment out of the company's profits, if the company has profits in hand and they have not been capitalised. In any case, section 53(1) above must be complied with.

An underwriting contract may take the form of an agreement expressed to be made between the underwriter and the company, not necessarily signed by the underwriter,[11] or an offer may be made by

---

[8] *Post*, p. 176.

[9] *Per* Lindley L.J. in *Re Licensed Victuallers' Mutual Trading Association* (1889) 42 Ch.D. 1 (C.A.), at p. 7.

[10] *Per* Lord Tomlin in *Australian Investment Trust Ltd.* v. *Strand and Pitt Street Properties Ltd.* [1932] A.C. 735 (P.C.), at p. 745.

[11] *Curror's Trustee* v. *Caledonian Heritable Security Co. Ltd.* (1880) 7 R. 479.

letter from the underwriter which requires an acceptance on the part of the company and notice of acceptance given to the underwriter to make it a contract.[12]

In underwriting contracts the underwriter usually irrevocably appoints some person—frequently a director—to apply in his name for the shares he may have to take up. In such a case the authority being, according to English law, coupled with an interest, cannot be revoked by the underwriter.[13]

The underwriting contract being made before the prospectus is issued, it is usual to enter into it on the basis of a draft prospectus, and to provide that the contract is to be binding notwithstanding any variations between the draft and the final prospectus. If, however, there is a material variation between the draft and the final prospectus, the underwriter will not be bound, in spite of such a clause.[14]

Liability on an underwriting contract passes to the executors of the underwriter, if he dies, as the contract is not one involving personal skill on the part of the underwriter.[15]

Sub-underwriting

It is a common practice for underwriters to relieve themselves from some of their risk by entering into sub-underwriting contracts. In such cases a sub-underwriter, in return for a commission, becomes bound to take and pay for his proportion of the shares sub-underwritten which are not allotted to the public, and "the difference between the commission paid by the company to the principal underwriters and the commission paid by them to the sub-underwriters is known as *overriding commission*."[16]

By the nature of a sub-underwriting contract the sub-underwriter authorises the underwriter to apply for shares on his behalf if the public do not apply for them and he cannot revoke the authority so given, whether or not the sub-underwriting letter contains a formal grant of

---

[12] *Re Consort Deep Level Gold Mines Ltd.* [1897] 1 Ch. 575 (C.A.).

[13] *Carmichael's Case* [1896] 2 Ch. 643 (C.A.); *cf. Premier Briquette Co. Ltd.* v. *Gray*, 1922 S.C. 329.

[14] *Warner International, etc., Co. Ltd.* v. *Kilburn, Brown & Co.* (1914) 84 L.J.K.B. 365 (C.A.).

[15] *Warner Engineering Co. Ltd.* v. *Brennan* (1913) 30 T.L.R. 191; *Curror's case, ante.*

[16] Palmer's *Company Law*, 23rd ed., p. 272.

authority to the underwriter. The authority is coupled with an interest.[17]

In a sub-underwriting contract the personality of the sub-underwriter is of importance, and therefore an undisclosed principal cannot sue on such a contract made on his behalf by an agent.

X underwrote shares in a company on the basis of a draft prospectus and Y sub-underwrote some of those shares on the same basis. Y was agent for C., but this was not disclosed to X or the company. The public response to the issue was insufficient and shares were allotted to Y, who renounced in favour of C., who was entered on the register. The prospectus contained misrepresentations and, on learning of this, C. applied for his name to be removed from the register and for repayment of his money. *Held*, C. was not entitled to rescission because (1) the contract between Y and the company was of such a class that Y must be treated as a principal and not as agent for C., and (2) the contract between the company and C. through the entry of C.'s name on the register was not entered into on the basis of the prospectus, the function of the prospectus having been fulfilled before that contract was made: *Collins* v. *Associated Greyhound Racecourses Ltd.* [1930] 1 Ch. 1 (C.A.).

Underwriting debentures

The provisions of section 53 do not apply to the underwriting of debentures, as there is nothing to prevent the issue of debentures at a discount.[18] When commission is paid for underwriting debentures, however, the Act requires:

(1) Particulars of the amount or rate paid to be filed with the Registrar within 21 days of the issue of the debentures: sections 95(9), 106A(8).

(2) The amount or rate to be disclosed in any prospectus issued within two years thereafter: Schedule 4.

BROKERAGE

Brokerage is a payment made to an issuing house or brokers in return for their placing shares or debentures without subscribing.[19] It differs from underwriting commission in that it is a payment made to a person for placing shares or debentures without involving him in any risk of

---

[17] *Re Olympic etc. Reinsurance Co. Ltd.* [1920] 2 Ch. 341 (C.A.); *cf. Premier Briquette Co. Ltd.* v. *Gray*, 1922 S.C. 329.

[18] *Post*, p. 175.

[19] *Ante*, p. 146.

having to take them. Section 53(3) provides that nothing in the section affects the power of any company to pay such brokerage as was previously lawful. It was previously held in *Metropolitan Coal Consumers' Association* v. *Scrimgeour*[20] that brokerage of a reasonable amount payable in the ordinary course of business was legal. In that case the brokerage was $2\frac{1}{2}$ per cent. but a usual brokerage is $\frac{1}{4}$ per cent. Authority to pay brokerage must be contained in the articles, and need not be given in the memorandum.[21] Table A, article 6, authorises the payment of "such brokerage as may be lawful" on any issue of shares.

A payment is brokerage only if it is paid to "stockbrokers, bankers and the like, who exhibit prospectuses and send them to their customers, and by whose mediation the customers are induced to subscribe."[22] The person to whom it is paid must be one who, in some way, carries on the business of a broker. A payment, therefore, to a lady of a percentage on the amount of capital which she induced third parties to subscribe for shares in a company—such a transaction being an isolated one, and not in the ordinary course of the lady's business—was held not to be brokerage.[23]

The amount or rate of brokerage paid or payable must be disclosed in any prospectus issued within two years thereafter: Schedule 4.

---

[20] [1895] 2 Q.B. 604 (C.A.).
[21] See *per* Lindley L.J. [1895] 2 Q.B. 604, at p. 607.
[22] *Per* Bailhache J. in *Andreae* v. *Zinc Mines of Great Britain Ltd.* [1918] 2 K.B. 454, at p. 458.
[23] *Andreae* v. *Zinc Mines of Great Britain Ltd.*, *ante*, p. 160.

CHAPTER 9

ALLOTMENT AND COMMENCEMENT OF BUSINESS

THIS chapter deals first with the powers of the directors and the company to allot shares, then with the contract of allotment under which shares are allotted by a company to a person who has applied for them, certain statutory restrictions on allotment by a public company, and the return which the company usually must deliver to the Registrar after it has allotted shares. Further, this is a convenient place in which to deal with the general question of the consideration for the allotment of shares and in particular issue of shares at a discount and the issue of shares at a premium, as well as with certain statutory restrictions on the commencement of business by a public company.

Power to allot shares

Prior to the 1980 Act directors generally had the power to issue shares up to the limit of the authorised capital.[1] This led to several abuses by directors issuing shares to their allies in order to forestall take-over bids.[2] Under section 14 of the 1980 Act, however, the directors of any company may not now issue shares, or any right to acquire shares, without express authority being given either in the articles or by a resolution in general meeting.

Such authority may be given for a specific allotment or generally and must state the maximum amount of the shares which may be issued. Even if the authority is given by the articles it cannot last for more than five years, and, in any case, it can be varied, revoked or renewed by an ordinary resolution. Thus the articles may actually be altered, on this one occasion, by an ordinary resolution.[3] A copy of any resolution either conferring, revoking, varying or renewing the authority must, however, be registered with the Registrar as if it were a special resolution, under section 143,[4] and notice of it must be put in the

---

[1] *Ante,* p. 93.
[2] See *e.g. Hogg* v. *Cramphorn* [1967] Ch. 254; *Bamford* v. *Bamford* [1970] Ch. 212; *post,* p. 371.
[3] *cf.* 1948 Act, s.10; *ante,* p. 108.
[4] *Post,* p. 325.

appropriate Gazette under section 9(3) of the European Communities Act 1972.[5]

Nothing in section 14 affects the validity of any allotment, but any director who knowingly and wilfully contravenes it may be prosecuted and fined. It has no application to employee share schemes.[6] In practice many companies will put the authority in their articles with five yearly renewals at the annual general meeting.

Pre-emption rights

The 1980 Act introduced further restrictions on the issue of ordinary, "equity," shares by companies for cash, other than those subject to employee share schemes.[6] This basic restriction is, however, subject to wide exemptions.

Under section 17 of the 1980 Act ordinary shares issued for cash must first be offered to existing,[7] ordinary shareholders in proportion to the nominal value of their existing holdings. The articles may go further and provide for such pre-emption rights to apply within each class of ordinary shares. Such rights are not given by the Act to the holders of preference shares or shares to be paid for, in whole or in part, otherwise than by cash. Any pre-emption offer must be open for 21 days and notified in accordance with the Table A provisions.[8] Any shares not taken up on the *pro rata* basis must then be offered to the ordinary shareholders generally.

Any contravention of the statutory or other pre-emption rights renders the company and any officer in default liable to compensate any existing shareholders who have suffered a loss as a result.

Private companies may exclude the effects of section 17 of the 1980 Act by a provision to that effect in their articles. In addition, both public and private companies may qualify or exclude pre-emption rights if their directors have the authority to issue shares under section 14 of that Act.[9] If the directors have a general authority to issue shares under that section the company, either by its articles, or by a special resolution, may vary or exclude section 17 altogether. On the other hand, if the directors only have authority to make a specific allotment,

---

[5] *Ante*, p. 97.
[6] *Post*, p. 221.
[7] Including those who held shares 28 days before the offer was made.
[8] Regs. 132–134.
[9] *Ante*, p. 165.

section 17 can only be modified or excluded by a special resolution recommended by the directors and supported by a circular, sent out with the notices of the meeting, setting out the directors' reasons for making the recommendation, the amount to be paid to the company on the allotment, and the directors' justification for that amount. Directors who issue a misleading, false or deceptive circular in support of such a resolution may be convicted and fined or imprisoned. The exclusion or modification of pre-emption rights in this way may be renewed or revoked by a special resolution: 1980 Act, s.18.

AGREEMENT FOR ALLOTMENT

The ordinary law of contract, which usually requires an offer and an acceptance if there is to be an agreement, applies to agreements to take shares in a company. Where a prospectus is issued by the company, otherwise than on a rights issue, the prospectus is not an offer—it is merely an invitation to the public to make offers. An offer is made by the applicant in sending a form of application for shares to the company and it is accepted by the allotment of shares to the applicant. Under normal articles the power to allot shares is vested in the board of directors.

An acceptance must be unconditional[10] and correspond with the terms of the offer. If, therefore, the application was for 100 shares and only 25 were allotted, the allotment would be a counter-offer and the applicant could refuse to take any shares. An issue may be over-subscribed, and the company unable to make an allotment in full to every applicant; in order to obviate this difficulty the form of the application invariably runs, "I agree to accept such shares or any smaller number that may be allotted to me."

To constitute a binding contract, an acceptance must be communicated to the offeror.[11] If the parties must have contemplated that the post might be used to communicate acceptance, the posting of a letter of allotment is sufficient communication to the applicant.

G. applied for shares in the H. company. A letter of allotment was posted, but never reached G. *Held*, G. was a shareholder in the company: *Household Fire Insurance Co.* v. *Grant* (1879) 4 Ex.D. 216 (C.A.).[12]

[10] *Liquidator of the Consolidated Copper Co. etc. Ltd.* v. *Peddie* (1877) 5 R. 393.
[11] See *Entores Ltd.* v. *Miles Far East Corporation* [1955] 2 Q.B. 327 (C.A.).
[12] Doubted in Scotland: *Mason* v. *Benhar Coal Co. Ltd.* (1882) 9 R. 883, *per* Lord Shand at p. 890.

Communication, however, may be made in any way which shows the applicant that the company has accepted his offer,[13] *e.g.* by a letter demanding payment of an instalment on the shares,[14] or by receipt of a notice calling a general meeting and notification given orally by the secretary that shares have been allotted.[15] The applicant must, however, have *agreed* to take shares and not merely have expressed a "willingness" to take them[16]; the sending to a person who has not so agreed of notices of meetings and of letters making calls on the shares does not of itself make the recipient a shareholder.[17]

An offer can be revoked at any time before acceptance is communicated.

H. applied for shares in a company. Shares were allotted to him, and the letter of allotment sent to the *company's* agent to deliver by hand to H. Before the letter was delivered, H. withdrew his application. *Held*, H. was not a shareholder in the company: *Re National Savings Bank Association* (1867) L.R. 4 Eq. 9.

The above rule is now subject to an exception when the application is made in pursuance of a prospectus issued generally, *i.e.* to persons other than members or debenture holders of the company.[18] In such a case the application cannot be revoked until after the expiration of the third day after the time of the opening of the subscription lists: section 50(5).[19] This is to prevent the inconvenience caused by "stags" revoking their applications before allotment when they think the issue has not been successful.

To be effective, revocation of an offer must be communicated to the offeree. Thus notice of the revocation of an application must reach the company before the letter of allotment is posted.[20] If the revocation is communicated by post it is not effective until the letter is received by the company.

---

[13] *Chapman* v. *Sulphite Pulp Co. Ltd.* (1892) 19 R. 837.

[14] *Forget* v. *Cement Products Co. of Canada* [1916] W.N. 259 (P.C.).

[15] *Chapman* v. *Sulphite Pulp Co. Ltd.* (1892) 19 R. 837; see also *Curror's Trustee* v. *Caledonian Heritable Security Co. Ltd.* (1880) 7 R. 479 and *Nelson* v. *Fraser* (1906) 14 S.L.T. 513 (O.H.).

[16] *Mason* v. *Benhar Coal Co. Ltd.* (1882) 9 R. 883.

[17] *Goldie* v. *Torrance* (1882) 10 R. 174; and see *Liquidator of the Florida etc. Co. Ltd.* v. *Bayley* (1890) 17 R. 525.

[18] *Ante*, p. 139.

[19] *Post*, p. 180.

[20] *Byrne* v. *Van Tienhoven* (1880) 5 C.P.D. 344; *Thomson* v. *James* (1855) 18 D. 1.

An offer lapses if it is not accepted within the time prescribed or, if none is prescribed, within a reasonable time. Thus an allotment must be made within a reasonable time after the application, otherwise the application will lapse and the applicant will be entitled to refuse to take the shares.

On June 8 M. offered to take shares in the R. company. He heard nothing until November 23, when he received a letter of acceptance. M. refused to take the shares. *Held*, M. was entitled to refuse, as his offer had lapsed: *Ramsgate Victoria Hotel Co. Ltd.* v. *Montefiore* (1866) L.R. 1 Ex. 109.

An offer is also terminated by the failure of a condition subject to which it was made. Thus if an application for shares is conditional, *e.g.* on the applicant having a contract to supply goods to the company,[21] or on all capital being subscribed,[22] and the condition is not fulfilled when shares are allotted to him, the applicant is under no liability to take the shares.

A conditional application must be distinguished from an application for shares coupled with a collateral agreement, *e.g.* where £10 shares are to be paid up to the extent of £1.50 in cash on allotment, that the balance is to be set-off against goods to be supplied to the company by the allottee. In the latter case, when shares are allotted the applicant becomes a shareholder with the right merely of suing the company on the collateral agreement.[23]

A letter of allotment need not now be stamped.[24]

Consideration for Allotment

The general rule has always been that an allottee must pay for his shares in full.[25] However, payment in full need not be made on allotment if the company does not require it, *i.e.* if the shares are allotted in consideration of payment of part of the nominal amount and of a promise of payment of the remainder as and when required by the

---

[21] *Shackelford's Case* (1866) L.R. 1 Ch.App. 567.

[22] *Swedish Match Co. Ltd.* v. *Seivwright* (1889) 16 R. 989.

[23] *Elkington's Case* (1867) L.R. 2 Ch.App. 511; *cf. Liquidator of the Pelican etc. Insurance Co. Ltd.* v. *Bruce* (1904) 11 S.L.T. 658 (O.H.), and see opinions in *National House etc. Investment Co. Ltd.* v. *Watson*, 1908 S.C. 888.

[24] Finance Act 1949, s.35 and Sched. VIII, Pt. I, para. 17.

[25] *Ooregum Gold Mining Co. of India Ltd.* v. *Roper* [1892] A.C. 125, *post*, p. 174; *Klenck* v. *East India Co. etc. Ltd.* (1888) 16 R. 271.

company. If the company does not require payment in full on allotment, the shares are partly paid shares.

Under section 20(1) of the 1980 Act shares are only treated as paid up to the extent that the company has received money or money's worth (including goodwill and know-how) in return for them. This does not apply to bonus shares.[26] Section 20(2) further prohibits a public company from accepting an undertaking by any person to do work or perform services in return for shares. Such an undertaking may nevertheless be enforced by the company (1980 Act, s.30(2)), and the holder of shares issued in return for such an undertaking becomes liable to pay any shortfall in the value paid for the shares (1980 Act, s.20(3)).

Any subsequent holder of shares not regarded as fully paid up, as a result of a breach of section 20 of the 1980 Act, may be liable for the amount due, unless he is either a bona fide purchaser of the shares without actual notice of the defect, or an immediate or subsequent transferee from such a person (1980 Act, s.20(4)). The court may grant relief in appropriate circumstances (1980 Act, s.28). Contravention of section 20 of the 1980 Act by a company and any officer in default is a criminal offence (1980 Act, s.30(1)).

Under section 22 of the 1980 Act public companies are further prevented from alloting shares unless at least one quarter of the nominal value and the whole of any premium has actually been paid. This is a restriction on allotment and is dealt with later in this chapter.

Shares taken by any subscriber to the memorandum of a public company in pursuance of an undertaking of his in the memorandum must be paid up in cash (1980 Act, s.29).

Payment of non-cash consideration—public companies

Section 23 of the 1980 Act prohibits a public company from accepting as consideration for shares any undertaking, *e.g.* to transfer property, which is to be or may be performed more than five years after the date of the allotment. Any variation of a valid undertaking (*i.e.* within five years) taking it outside the five year period is void. Any allotment in contravention of this requirement, or a failure by the purchaser to fulfil a valid undertaking within the contract period, renders the allottee liable to pay the company the amount owed on the

[26] *Post,* p. 543.

shares, together with interest. Any subsequent holder of the shares is also liable subject to the bona fide purchaser exemption noted above.[27]

Sections 24 and 25 of the 1980 Act provide that a public company may not allot shares for any non-cash consideration unless a report on the value of the consideration has been made by an independent person qualified to be an auditor of the company. His report must be sent to the company within six months prior to the allotment and to the proposed allottee. He may accept another's valuation if it is reasonable to do so, provided that that person is also independent and appears to be qualified and such facts are disclosed in the report. The company's auditor may be so used.

The report must state the amount payable on the shares, a description of the consideration and the valuation methods used, the date of valuation and the extent to which the shares are to be treated as paid up by the consideration and in cash. It must be filed with the Registrar.

In making his report the expert may require from the officers of the company such information and explanation as he thinks necessary to enable him to carry out the valuation or to make the report. False, misleading or deceptive statements made in this context constitute criminal offences.

There is a general exemption for shares issued generally to shareholders in another company on a take-over or merger with that other company. Such issues are, however, subject to the extra-statutory rules on take-overs: see Chapter 31, *post*.

In default the allottee will be liable to pay any amount owed on the shares if, either he did not receive a copy of the report or he knew or ought to have known of the breach. Subsequent holders may also be liable subject to the bona fide purchaser exemption.[28] Relief may again be given by the court (1980 Act, s.28). Contravention by the company and any officer in default is a criminal offence (1980 Act, s.30).

These provisions only apply if the shares are issued "otherwise than for cash." Issues for cash are defined in section 87(3) of the 1980 Act as to include payment by a cheque received by the company in good faith, or the release of liability of the company for a defined sum (*i.e.* a set-off)[29] or an undertaking to pay cash at a future date. This may be thought to cover a multitude of sins.

---

[27] *Ante,* p. 170.
[28] *Ante,* p. 170.
[29] Thus preserving the decision in *Spargo's Case* (1873) L.R. 8 Ch.App. 407.

It is convenient to note here that similar provisions apply, by virtue of sections 26 and 27 of the 1980 Act, to the acquisition by public companies of non-cash assets from any subscriber of the memorandum, within two years of the issue of the certificate of incorporation, if the consideration to be given by the company is not less than 10 per cent. of the nominal value of the company's issued capital at that time.[30]

Payment of non-cash consideration—private companies

Shares may, with the consent of the company, be paid for otherwise than in cash, *e.g.* by the transfer of property to the company or by the rendering of services to the company. Sections 23 to 27 of the 1980 Act do not apply to private companies, but where shares are allotted as fully or partly paid up otherwise than in cash, a contract constituting the title of the allottee to the allotment together with any contract of sale, or for services or other consideration for the allotment, or, if such a contract is not in writing, particulars of the contract, must, with the return as to allotments, be delivered to the Registrar, usually within a month after the allotment: 1948 Act, s.52.[31] Default renders the officers of the company liable to penalties but does not make the allotment void.

Registration under section 52 does not make a "contract" binding on the company if there is no consideration for it, and past consideration is no consideration.[32]

A private company decided to turn itself into a public company. Before doing so it resolved to allot £6,000 of fully paid shares to the existing directors and shareholders, and a contract was made agreeing to allot the shares in consideration of their past services and expenses in forming the company and establishing the business. The contract was registered and the shares were allotted. The company afterwards went into liquidation. *Held,* the directors and shareholders were liable to pay for the shares, as there was no consideration in money or money's worth for the allotment, past services being no consideration: *Re Eddystone Marine Insurance Co.* [1893] 3 Ch. 9 (C.A.).

An agreement by a private company to allot shares in consideration of services to be performed in the future also renders the allottee liable

---

[30] *Post,* p. 207.
[31] *Post,* p. 182.
[32] The doctrine of consideration is not part of Scots law. *cf.* however, *Liquidator of the Pelican etc. Insurance Co. Ltd.* v. *Bruce* (1904) 11 S.L.T. 658 (O.H.).

to pay for the shares.[33] "It is not open to a company to agree with the holder or proposed holder of its shares to replace the statutory liability by a special contract sounding in damages only."[34] However, a private company may agree to pay a fixed sum immediately for services to be performed in the future, *e.g.* for the erection of a building, and to satisfy that debt by the allotment of shares.[35]

If there is a contract for the acceptance by a private company of specified property or services of substantial value in payment for shares, the court will not, whilst the contract stands, inquire into the adequacy of the consideration, as it is for the parties to make their own bargain.

The goodwill, stock-in-trade and property of a business was sold to a company for £46,000, of which £20,000 was to be paid in fully paid shares. The stock-in-trade was shown in the company's books at a figure £11,000 less than the sum allocated to it in the agreement. On the company's going into liquidation, a misfeasance summons was taken out to obtain payment for the shares. *Held*, since the agreement could not be impeached, the adequacy of the consideration could not be gone into: *Re Wragg Ltd.* [1897] 1 Ch. 796 (C.A.).

"Where a company, in good faith, issues shares as fully paid-up in consideration of property transferred or services rendered, the Court will not inquire into the value of that which was accepted by the Company as an equivalent of money:" *per* Lord Stormonth Darling (Ordinary) in *Brownlie and ors, Petitioners* (1898) 6 S.L.T. 249 (O.H.), at p. 251.

Where the contract is fraudulent or shows on the face of it that the consideration is illusory, the allottee is liable to pay for the shares.

G. agreed to sell a concession to a company which agreed to allot him as fully paid 400 shares forthwith and also one-fifth of any future increase of capital. *Held*, the agreement was good so far as it obliged the company to allot one-fifth of any future increase of capital but void so far as it relieved G. from paying for the shares. It was apparent that the value of the concession bore no relation to the amount of the shares: *Hong Kong and China Gas Co. Ltd.* v. *Glen* [1914] 1 Ch. 527.

"If the agreement were that the property to be purchased should be valued, and that against this property shares should be issued as fully paid to an extent exceeding the amount of the valuation by one-third, the arrangement would . . . be bad as to this excess of one-third. It would to this extent be apparent on the face of the contract that the attempted discharge of a part of the liability was illusory:" *per* Sargant J., at p. 539.

---

[33] *National House etc. Investment Co. Ltd.* v. *Watson,* 1908 S.C. 888.
[34] *Per* Parker J. in *Gardner* v. *Iredale* [1912] 1 Ch. 700, at p. 716.
[35] *Gardner* v. *Iredale,* above.

When shares are issued in pursuance of a contract registered under section 52, and the allottee also subscribes the memorandum for the same number of shares, care should be taken to see that the agreement makes it clear that the shares for which the memorandum is signed are the same as those referred to in the agreement, otherwise both lots of shares will have to be paid for.[36] To prevent this from happening, it is usual for the allottee under the agreement not to subscribe the memorandum.

ISSUE OF SHARES AT A DISCOUNT

The general rule has always been that shares must *not* be issued at a discount, *i.e.* must not be issued as fully paid for a consideration less than the nominal amount. This is now expressly stated in section 21 of the 1980 Act. The shareholder must pay the full nominal value of his shares, whether he pays in cash or in kind, together with interest on the discount. Any subsequent holder of the shares may also be held liable for the discount unless he is a bona fide purchaser for value without actual notice of the discount issue or a subsequent transferee of the shares from such a person. The court may grant relief under section 28 of the 1980 Act. Contravention of section 21 of the 1980 Act is a criminal offence by the company and any officer in default (1980 Act, s.30(1)). This principle was first established in England by the House of Lords in 1892.

The market value of the £1 ordinary shares of a company was 2s. 6d. The company thereupon issued preference shares of £1 each with 15s. credited as paid, leaving a liability of only 5s. a share. A contract to this effect was registered under what is now s.52. *Held,* the issue was *ultra vires,* and the allottees were liable to pay for the shares in full: *Ooregum Gold Mining Co. of India Ltd.* v. *Roper* [1892] A.C. 125.[37]

"The dominant and cardinal principle of [the Companies] Acts is that the investor shall purchase immunity from liability beyond a certain limit, on the terms that there shall be and remain a liability up to that limit:" *per* Lord Macnaghten at p. 145.

The share capital of a company must be raised. This means that money or assets equal to the paid-up capital must be received by the

---

[36] *Fothergill's Case* (1873) L.R. 8 Ch.App. 270.

[37] An earlier Scottish case to the same effect is *Klenck* v. *East India Co. etc. Ltd.* (1888) 16 R. 271, where the memorandum contained a power to issue shares at a discount.

company or, in other words, that shares can be treated as paid up only to the extent of the amount actually received by the company in cash or in kind. The idea is to protect creditors of the company.[38]

There is no issue at a discount where shares are issued at par, *e.g.* after the exercise of an option to take them up at par, even though they could otherwise be issued at a premium,[39] or where shares are issued at a lesser premium than that at which they might have been paid.[40]

There is nothing to prevent debentures being issued at a discount. However, in the case of convertible debentures, if the debentures are issued at a discount, with a right to exchange them for fully paid shares equal in nominal amount to the par value of the debentures, the right has been held void as being a right to an issue of shares at a discount.[41] The right will be valid if it is to fully paid shares equal in nominal amount to the issue price of the debentures—the shares will then not be issued at a discount.

The general rule is subject to the following exceptions:

(1) There is in effect a discount when shares are issued by a private company for an overvalued non-monetary consideration, as in *Re Wragg Ltd., ante.*[42]

(2) Similarly where, under section 53(1), *ante,*[43] commission is paid to a person who agrees to subscribe, or to procure subscriptions, for shares in a company.

ISSUE OF SHARES AT A PREMIUM

Where a company's issued shares have a market value greater than the amount paid up on them, when further shares are being issued the company may require applicants to agree to pay more than the nominal amount of the new shares, *i.e.* to pay a premium.

A company may, without any special power in its articles, issue its shares at a premium, *i.e.* for a consideration in cash or in kind which exceeds the nominal amount of the shares, although there is no law which obliges a company to issue its shares above par because they are

---

[38] See further, *post,* p. 222.
[39] *Hilder* v. *Dexter* [1902] A.C. 474, *ante,* p. 160.
[40] *Cameron* v. *Glenmorangie Distillery Co. Ltd.* (1896) 23 R. 1092.
[41] *Mosely* v. *Koffyfontein Mines Ltd.* [1904] 2 Ch. 108 (C.A.).
[42] p. 173.
[43] p. 160.

saleable at a premium in the market.[44] However, by section 56, where shares are issued at a premium, whether for cash or otherwise, a sum equal to the aggregate amount or value of the premiums must be transferred to the "share premium account."

As will be seen later, section 56 extends the principle that the share capital of a company must be maintained[45] to a share premium account, because the section goes on to provide that the provisions of the Act relating to reduction of capital apply to this account, *i.e.* it cannot be reduced without leave of the court, except where it is applied in—

(1) paying up unissued shares of the company to be issued to members as fully paid bonus shares[46]; or

(2) writing off (*a*) the preliminary expenses, or (*b*) the expenses of, or the commission paid or discount allowed on, an issue of shares or debentures of the company; or

(3) providing for the premium payable by the company on the redemption of debentures.[47]

In addition, by virtue of section 54 of the 1981 Act the share premium account may be used by private companies to pay off any premium on a redemption or purchase by such companies of their own shares.[48]

The object of the provisions relating to the share premium account is to prevent dividends being paid out of premiums received on an issue of shares.[49] When, therefore, any part of the share premium account is otherwise distributed among the shareholders it is to be treated as if the company were reducing its capital by repaying paid-up share capital.[50] Although share premiums are regarded as capital, it is not capital belonging to any individual shareholder. The shareholder paying the premium has no dividend rights in respect of it and has no right to repayment of it in a winding up.

---

[44] *Per* Lord Davey in *Hilder* v. *Dexter* [1902] A.C. 474, at p. 480; *Cameron's* case, *ante.*

[45] *Re Moorgate Mercantile Holdings Ltd.* [1980] 1 All E.R. 40. *Post*, p. 231.

[46] Other ways in which bonus shares can be paid for are dealt with *post*, p. 543.

[47] *Post*, p. 559.   [48] *Post*, p. 249.

[49] As in *Drown* v. *Gaumont-British Picture Corporation Ltd.* [1937] Ch. 402, where there was a trading loss in one year but a dividend was paid out of the reserve fund, part of which consisted of premiums on issues of shares.

[50] *Re Duff's Settlements* [1951] Ch. 923 (C.A.).

The amount of the share premium account must be specified in the balance sheet: Schedule 8.

The issue of shares at a premium accentuates the unreality of the nominal or par value of a share. The capital in the share premium account is an anomalous form of capital because it is capital on which no dividend is paid, which is not attributable to the ownership of any class of shares, which is not part of the company's nominal capital, and which the ordinary investor does not realise is part of the company's actual capital.

SHARE PREMIUM ACCOUNT AND ISSUES OTHER THAN FOR CASH

Shares can be issued at a premium not only for cash but also for consideration other than cash. If, in the latter case, the value of the consideration received, *e.g.* of land, exceeds the nominal value of the shares issued there is an issue of shares at a premium and section 56 applies.

In two cases this principle was applied where a company acquired shares in another company by virtue of an exchange of shares, *e.g.* on a merger or take-over, and the value of the shares acquired exceeded the value of the shares issued. The excess had to be transferred to the share premium account, with the result that the pre-acquisition profits of the acquired company, reflected in the value of its shares, were frozen and could not be distributed as dividends by the acquiring company: *Shearer* v. *Bercain* [1980] 3 All E.R. 295; *Head (Henry) & Co. Ltd.* v. *Ropner Holdings Ltd.* [1952] Ch. 124. Until the 1980 decision, however, this principle was regarded as fallacious by many lawyers and accountants, with the result that few such transfers to share premium accounts had been made. Following the 1980 decision, the 1981 Act provides two forms of relief from the obligations of section 56 in certain defined circumstances of "merger accounting."[51] The basic rule, however, remains valid in other circumstances.

Merger relief

Where the issuing company acquires a 90 per cent. holding in another company by way of a share for share exchange no transfer to

---

[51] These reliefs can be extended or varied by subsequent regulations: 1981 Act, s.41. A general amnesty for pre-February 1981 mergers was also provided by s.39 of the 1981 Act.

the share premium account need be made; 1980 Act, s.37. In fact this is a wide relief as it applies whether or not the issuing company owned any shares in the other company, *e.g.*, it applies to a company owning 60 per cent. of the shares of a subsidiary acquiring another 30 per cent. There is no obligation in such cases to disclose any "premiums" in the balance sheet. It also applies if the consideration provided by the acquired company is a cancellation of its issued shares rather than an issue—a frequent practice in schemes of reconstruction.

Group reconstruction relief

Where a wholly-owned subsidiary acquires a shareholding (not necessarily 100 per cent.) in a fellow subsidiary (not necessarily wholly-owned) in return for an allotment of its own shares to its holding company or another of its wholly-owned subsidiaries relief from section 56 is available: 1981 Act, s.38. Only the lower of the cost or book value to the issuing company of the acquired shares need be taken into account.

Where both sections 37 and 38 of the 1981 Act could apply only the latter relief can be claimed.

RESTRICTIONS ON ALLOTMENT

Sections 47 to 51 and sections 16 and 22 of the 1980 Act contain restrictions on allotment by *public* companies.

No allotment unless minimum subscription applied for

Section 47 provides that where a prospectus is issued, a *first* allotment of *shares* offered to the public for subscription cannot be made until—

(1) shares payable *in cash* to the amount of the minimum subscription have been *applied for*;
(2) the money payable on application for such shares has been paid to and *received* by the company.

We have already seen[52] that the minimum subscription is the minimum amount which, in the opinion of the directors, must be raised

[52] *Ante*, p. 133.

by the issue of shares to provide for such things as the purchase price of any property which is to be defrayed out of the proceeds of the issue.

The object of section 47 is to prevent a company making a first allotment of shares where the public response to the prospectus has been poor. If, *e.g.* offers have been made for shares payable in cash to the amount of the minimum subscription such offers can be accepted by the company which will then receive the amount of cash required to be raised by the prospectus. The section is satisfied if shares payable in cash to the amount of the minimum subscription are underwritten.[53]

In addition section 16 of the 1980 Act provides that no allotment can be made unless either the capital is subscribed for in full or the prospectus states that if it is not so subscribed the allotment will nevertheless take place subject to any specified conditions.

If any of the above conditions are not satisfied within 40 days of the first issue of the prospectus, all money received must be forthwith returned to the applicants without interest. If it is not returned within 48 days of the issue of the prospectus, the directors are jointly and severally liable to repay it with interest at five per cent. per annum. A director is not liable, however, if he proves that the default in repayment was not due to any misconduct or negligence on his part.

A sum is, for the purposes of this section, deemed to have been paid to and received by the company if a cheque for the sum has been received in good faith by the company and the directors have no reason to suspect that it will not be paid.

Any condition requiring an applicant to waive compliance with any of these requirements is void.

No allotment unless minimum payment paid up

Under section 22 of the 1980 Act no share may be allotted unless one quarter of the nominal value and the whole of any premium on the share has been paid up. In breach the share will be regarded as having been so paid up but the allottee and any subsequent holder will be liable to pay that amount together with interest. A bona fide purchaser without actual notice of the breach is not liable nor any successor to such a person. In addition the court may grant relief under section 28 of the 1980 Act. Contravention by the company and any officer in default is a criminal offence; 1980 Act, s.30.

---

[53] *Ante*, p. 161.

Effect of irregular allotment

When an allotment is made which does not satisfy the provisions of section 47, *ante,* section 49 gives the applicant two remedies, one against the company and the other against the directors.

As against the *company,* the allotment is *voidable* by the allottee within one month after allotment, even if the company is being wound up. Legal proceedings need not be taken within a month. Notice of avoidance within the month, followed by prompt legal proceedings after the month, is sufficient.[54]

As against the *directors,* the allottee can sue such of them as have knowingly contravened or authorised the contravention of the provisions for any loss, damages or costs he may have sustained or incurred thereby. Any such proceedings against directors must be brought within two years after allotment. The company has a similar remedy against the directors for any loss, damages or costs sustained or incurred by it.

Time of allotment

By section 50, when a prospectus is issued generally, that is, to persons who are not existing members or debenture holders of the company,[55] no allotment or sale of the shares or debentures can be made until the third day after that on which the prospectus is first issued or such later time as is specified in the prospectus—such third day or later time being called "the time of the opening of the subscription lists." The *two*-day interval is to give the Press time to comment and to enable possible applicants to obtain expert advice before applying for securities. When the prospectus is first issued as a newspaper advertisement, the day on which the prospectus is first issued is the day on which the advertisement first appears.

Contravention of these provisions does not render the allotment void, but the company and every officer in default, and, in the case of an offer for sale, the persons making the offer who knowingly and wilfully authorise or permit the contravention, are liable to a fine.

An application for shares or debentures in pursuance of a prospectus issued generally is irrevocable until *after* the expiration of the third day

---

[54] *Re National Motor Mail-Coach Co. Ltd.* [1908] 2 Ch. 228.
[55] *Ante,* p. 138.

after the time of the opening of the subscription lists, or the giving before the expiration of such third day, by some person responsible under section 43 for the prospectus, of a public notice having the effect of limiting his responsibility: section 50(5). This is an exception to the general rule that an offer can be revoked at any time before it is accepted. The idea is to restrain "stags" who would otherwise revoke their applications if the shares or debentures cannot be quickly resold at a profit. The company has a *three*-day period in which to accept the "stags'" offers and so prevent them from revoking.

Saturdays, Sundays and bank holidays are not counted for the purposes of this section: section 50(6).

Section 50 does not apply to a prospectus in respect of which a certificate of exemption under section 39[56] has been obtained: section 50(7).

The Jenkins Report[57] recommended that applications made in pursuance of a prospectus issued generally should be irrevocable until the expiry of seven working days after the date on which the prospectus is first so issued—the present interval is not long enough—and that no allotment of securities offered to the public should be allowed after three months from the first issue of the prospectus, *i.e.* no allotment should be allowed on a stale prospectus.

Stock exchange quotation being sought

If a prospectus states that application has been or will be made for permission for the shares or debentures to be listed on any stock exchange, section 51 of the 1948 Act, as amended by Schedule 2 to the 1976 Act, provides that the money received from applicants must be paid into a separate bank account under penalty of a fine on the company and every officer in default. The permission must be applied for before the third day after the first issue of the prospectus (Saturdays, Sundays and bank holidays not being counted: section 50(6)) and if this is not done, or if permission is refused before the end of three weeks from the closing of the subscription lists or such longer period not exceeding six weeks as may be notified by the stock exchange, the allotment or sale is *void* and the money must be returned by the

---

[56] *Ante*, p. 139.
[57] Para. 252.

company or the persons making the offer. Subscription lists close when the issue of shares or debentures is fully subscribed or it is obvious that the issue is not going to be so subscribed. If the money is not returned within eight days, the directors are jointly and severally liable to repay it with interest at five per cent. per annum, except that a director is not liable if he proves that the default was not due to misconduct or negligence on his part. Failure to apply for or to obtain permission also renders an allotment under an underwriting contract void. When permission is granted, the money can be taken out of the separate bank account and used in the ordinary way.

If, before the money is returned, the debenture holders appoint a receiver of the company's property, it seems that the money in the separate bank account is not part of the company's property and cannot be claimed by the debenture holders but must be returned to the applicants.[58]

RETURN AS TO ALLOTMENTS

Section 52 of the 1948 Act, as amended by Schedule 2 to the 1976 Act, provides that whenever a limited company with a share capital makes any allotment of its *shares*, it must, within a month, deliver to the Registrar—

(1) A return of the allotments (on Form PUC 2), stating the number and nominal amount of the shares, the names, addresses and descriptions of the allottees and the amount paid or payable on each share, whether on account of the nominal value of the share or by way of premium.

(2) In the case of shares allotted *otherwise than for cash,* a contract constituting the title of the allottee to the allotment, together with any contract of sale or for services or other consideration for the allotment, and a return (on Form PUC 3) stating the number and nominal amount of shares so allotted, the extent to which they are to be treated as paid up, and the consideration for the allotment.

[58] *Per* Harman J., *obiter,* in *Re Nanwa Gold Mines Ltd.* [1955] 1 W.L.R. 1080, at p. 1085.

If such a contract is not in writing, the prescribed particulars of the contract must be filed on Form 52, stamped with the same stamp duty as a contract.

RESTRICTIONS ON COMMENCEMENT OF BUSINESS

A private company can commence business, exercise any borrowing power[59] which it has and make binding contracts immediately on incorporation.

By section 4 of the 1980 Act a public company should do none of these things until it has either obtained a certificate from the Registrar that it may do so or is re-registered as a private company.

To obtain a certificate under this section the company must make a declaration to the Registrar in the prescribed form signed by a director or secretary of the company:

(1) Stating that the nominal value of the company's *allotted* share capital is not less than the authorised minimum (£50,000)[60];

(2) Disclosing the amount of such allotted share capital actually paid up at that time (at least 25 per cent. of the nominal value and the whole of any premium is necessary)[61];

(3) Stating the amount, or estimated amount, of the preliminary expenses of the company and the persons by whom any of those expenses have been paid or are payable; and

(4) Detailing any amount or benefit paid or given or intended to be paid or given to any promoter of the company, and the consideration for the payment or benefit.

This declaration may be accepted by the Registrar as sufficient evidence of the matters stated therein.

If the Registrar issues a certificate under this section it is conclusive evidence that the company is entitled to do business and exercise any borrowing powers.

If a public company enters into a transaction without a certificate under section 4, the transaction remains valid, but if the company fails to comply with any obligations under it within 21 days of being called

[59] *Post,* p. 544.
[60] 1980 Act, s.85.
[61] *Ibid.* s.22, *Ante,* p. 169.

upon to do so, the directors are liable to indemnify the other party for any loss suffered as a result (1980 Act, s.4(8)). In addition, the company and any officer in default will be guilty of a criminal offence.

Finally, if more than a year after the incorporation of a public company it has not been issued with a section 4 certificate, the Secretary of State may petition the court for the company to be wound up under section 222 of the 1948 Act.[62]

---

[62] As amended by the 1980 Act.

CHAPTER 10

MEMBERSHIP

THIS chapter is concerned with the members of a company, *i.e.* in the case of a company limited by shares, the shareholders. In addition to the ways in which a person can become a member and the persons who can become members, the following topics are dealt with: the register of members which every company must keep, disclosure of substantial shareholdings, and the annual return which every company with a share capital must make to the Registrar.

WAYS OF BECOMING A MEMBER

The members of a company consist of:

(1) The subscribers of the memorandum.[1] These are deemed to have agreed to become members, and on the registration of the company they must be entered as members in its register of members: section 26.
(2) Directors who have signed and delivered to the Registrar an undertaking to take and pay for their qualification shares.[2]
(3) All other persons who have agreed to become members of the company *and* whose names are entered in the register of members: section 26.

In the case of a company limited by shares the shareholders are the members.

Subscribers of the memorandum

A subscriber of the memorandum becomes a member on registration of the company, and an entry in the register of members is not necessary to make him a member of the company. It is the duty of the directors to enter his name at once in the register, but their failure to do this will not enable him to escape liability for calls on the shares for which he has signed the memorandum.[3]

---

[1] *Ante,* pp. 56, 95.
[2] *Post,* p. 334.
[3] *Evans's Case* (1867) L.R. 2 Ch.App. 427.

The subscribers to the memorandum of a company limited by shares are liable, by virtue of their subscription, to pay up the full amount of their shares, in cash if it is a public company,[4] as and when called up. Until the commencement of winding up the times and amounts of payment depend, apart from express agreement between the company and the signatories, on the articles.[5]

A subscriber's obligation to take the shares for which he has subscribed is not satisfied by the (later) allotment of shares credited as fully paid and to which someone else is entitled.

M. signed the memorandum for five shares. The company had agreed to allot paid up shares to C., as the purchase price of property sold to the company, and C. directed the company to allot five of these shares to M. This was done and the company was afterwards wound up. *Held,* M. was liable to pay for the five shares for which he had signed the memorandum: *Migotti's Case* (1867) L.R. 4 Eq. 238.

If, however, the entire share capital has been allotted to others, the subscriber is under no liability to take shares.[6]

A subscriber of the memorandum cannot rescind the contract to take shares on the ground of a misrepresentation made by a promoter, because (*a*) the company could not appoint an agent before it came into existence and it is therefore not liable for the promoter's acts, and (*b*) by signing the memorandum the subscriber became bound, on the registration of the company, not only as between himself and the company, but also as between himself and the other persons who should become members on the footing that the contract existed.[7]

Non-cash assets supplied by a subscriber to a public company in return for consideration from the company may require a valuation report from an independent valuer.[8]

In Scotland, specific implement is available as a remedy to enforce an undertaking to subscribe for shares.[9]

Other members

A person, other than those mentioned above, who has agreed to become a member of the company does not actually become one until

[4] 1980 Act, s.29.
[5] *Per* Lindley M.R. in *Alexander* v. *Automatic Telephone Co.* [1900] 2 Ch. 56 (C.A.), at p. 63.
[6] *Mackley's Case* (1875) 1 Ch.D. 247.
[7] *Lord Lurgan's Case* [1902] 1 Ch. 707.　　　　　　[8] *Ante,* p. 172.
[9] *Beardmore & Co.* v. *Barry,* 1928 S.C. 101; affirmed 1928 S.C. (H.L.) 47.

his name is entered in the register of members. Section 26 "makes the placing of the name of a shareholder on the register a condition precedent to membership."[10]

Such a person may take an allotment of his shares direct from the company,[11] or may purchase shares from an existing member,[12] or he may succeed to shares on the death or bankruptcy of a member.[13]

WHO CAN BE MEMBERS

Minors

In English law a minor, *i.e.* a person under the age of 18,[14] may be a member unless this is forbidden by the articles. However, a minor's contract to take shares is voidable by him before or within a reasonable time after he attains the age of 18. If he avoids he cannot recover the money paid for the shares unless there has been a total failure of the consideration for which the money was paid.

S., an infant,[15] agreed to take 500 £1 shares from a company, and paid 10s. on each share. She received no dividend on the shares. While still an infant she repudiated the shares, and brought an action (a) for a declaration that she was entitled to avoid the contract, and (b) to recover the money she had paid. *Held,* (a) S. was entitled to rescind and so was not liable for future calls, but (b) there was no total failure of consideration and S. could not recover money already paid because she had got the thing for which the money was paid, a thing of value: *Steinberg* v. *Scala (Leeds) Ltd.* [1923] 2 Ch. 452 (C.A.).

If the company is wound up the minor member loses his right to avoid unless the liquidator agrees.[16]

Scots law divides persons who are under the age of majority[17] into pupils (boys under 14 and girls under 12) and minors (young persons over the age of pupillarity but under the age of majority). A pupil has no capacity to be a member himself but his "tutor" (father or mother[18]

[10] *Per* Fry L.J. in *Nicol's Case* (1885) 29 Ch.D. 421 (C.A.), at p. 447; *per* Lord Deas in *Macdonald* v. *City of Glasgow Bank* (1879) 6 R. 621, at p. 633.
[11] *Ante,* p. 167.
[12] *Post,* p. 265.
[13] *Post,* p. 282.
[14] Family Law Reform Act 1969, s.1.
[15] The age of majority was formerly 21 and persons under that age were called "infants."
[16] *Symons' Case* (1870) L.R. 5 Ch. 298.
[17] 18 since January 1, 1970: Age of Majority (Scotland) Act 1969.
[18] Guardianship Act 1973.

or other guardian) may be a member on the pupil's behalf.[19] A minor
may become a member, but only with the consent of his "curator"
(father or mother[18] or other guardian) if he has one; a minor who has
no curator may become a member on his own initiative. However,
whether a minor has a curator or not, his contract to take shares may be
"reduced" (set aside) up to the end of the *quadriennium utile* (*i.e.* the
four-year period after he attains majority) on proof of "lesion" (*i.e.*
considerable loss to the minor's estate, the contract not being a fair and
reasonable one at the time when it was entered into).[20] Lesion is more
easily proved in the case of a minor who has no curator than in the case
of a minor who transacted with his curator's consent.

Personal representatives

Ownership of the shares of a deceased member is transmitted to his
executors[21] or administrators. They must produce to the company the
grant of probate of the will, or of letters of administration of the estate,
or, in Scotland, of confirmation and, notwithstanding anything in the
articles, such document must be accepted by the company as sufficient
evidence of the grant: section 82. Production to the company does *not,*
however, make the representatives members of the company.[22] The
deceased member's estate is the member for some purposes, such as an
article providing that on an increase of capital the new shares are to be
divided among the existing members in proportion to their existing
shareholdings.[23] However, the deceased member is not a member
within the meaning of a section such as section 31,[24] which is concerned
with reduction of the number of members below the legal minimum.

The personal representatives are liable for calls[25] on partly paid
shares only to the extent of the deceased's assets in their hands, and if
in England the personal representatives make default in paying calls,
the company can obtain an order for administration of the estate of the
deceased member: section 215.

[19] See *Inland Revenue* v. *Wilson*, 1928 S.C. (H.L.) 42; 1927 S.C. 733.
[20] *Hill* v. *City of Glasgow Bank* (1879) 7 R. 68.
[21] In Scots law the term "executors" is used whether there is a will or not, and
"confirmation" is the equivalent of both probate and letters of administration.
[22] *Macdonald* v. *City of Glasgow Bank* (1879) 6 R. 621.
[23] *Per* Lord Herschell in *James* v. *Buena Ventura Nitrate Grounds Syndicate Ltd.*
[1896] 1 Ch. 456 (C.A.), at p. 464.
[24] *Ante,* p. 24. See *Re Bowling & Welby's Contract* [1895] 1 Ch. 663 (C.A.).
[25] *Post,* p. 287.

The personal representatives are entitled to transfer the shares without being registered as members (s.76),[26] and to receive all dividends, bonuses or other benefits from the shares, but the articles usually prevent them from voting at general meetings.

Table A, art. 32, provides: "A person becoming entitled to a share by reason of the death or bankruptcy of the holder shall be entitled to the same dividends and other advantages to which he would be entitled if he were the registered holder of the share, except that he shall not, before being registered as a member in respect of the share, be entitled in respect of it to exercise any right conferred by membership in relation to meetings of the company."

Personal representatives may, however, be entitled to be given notice of general meetings, even though they have no right to attend and vote at the meetings. Table A, article 134, gives them a right to be given notice of general meetings.

To prevent the disadvantage of personal representatives who are not members, the articles frequently contain provisions to compel the personal representatives to elect either to be registered in respect of the shares or to transfer them.

In Table A, the proviso to article 32 is: "The directors may at any time give notice requiring any such person to elect either to be registered himself or to transfer the share, and if the notice is not complied with within 90 days the directors may thereafter withhold payment of all dividends, bonuses or other moneys payable in respect of the share until the requirements of the notice have been complied with."

Personal representatives are entitled, if they so choose and there is no contrary provision in the articles, to be registered as members.[27] The articles may give the directors, as does Table A, article 30, the same power to decline to register personal representatives as members as the directors would have had in the case of a transfer by the deceased shareholder before his death.[28]

If personal representatives are registered as members, they become personally liable for calls,[26] although they have a right of indemnity against the deceased's estate.[29]

---

[26] See also *Buchan* v. *City of Glasgow Bank* (1879) 6 R. (H.L.) 44; (1879) 6 R. 567.

[27] *Edwards* v. *Ransomes and Rapier Ltd.* [1930] W.N. 180.

[28] See, *e.g. Shepherd's Trustees* v. *Shepherd*, 1950 S.C. (H.L.) 60. See also *post*, p. 266.

[29] *Per* Cotton L.J. in *Duff's Executors' Case* (1886) 32 Ch.D. 301 (C.A.), at p. 309.

Trustees in bankruptcy

A bankrupt may be a member of a company, although the beneficial interest in his shares will be vested in his trustee in bankruptcy as from the time when he is adjudged bankrupt.[30] Unless the articles provide to the contrary, a shareholder does not cease to be a member of the company on becoming bankrupt. Accordingly, as long as he is on the register he is entitled to exercise any vote conferred by his shares at the meetings of the company, even though the articles provide—as does article 134 of Table A—that notice of meetings is to be sent to the trustee in bankruptcy and not to the bankrupt.[31] The bankrupt must vote in accordance with the directions of the trustee.

A minority action[32] may be brought by a bankrupt shareholder who is on the register of members.[33]

The position of the trustee in bankruptcy is similar to that of personal representatives of a deceased member.[34]

Other companies

1. A company may, if authorised by its memorandum, take shares in and be a member of another company. It attends meetings of the other by a representative authorised by resolution of its directors: section 139.[35]

2. *A company may in certain circumstances purchase or acquire its own shares.* Following the 1980 and 1981 Acts companies may redeem or purchase their own shares but they must cancel the shares so acquired. It cannot be a member of itself as this would amount to a false statement of its capital. Companies may also forfeit or accept the surrender of their shares. This topic is covered in Chapter 12, *post.*

3. For the same reason that a company cannot be a member of itself, section 27 provides that, *subject to certain exceptions, a subsidiary company*[36] *cannot be a member of its holding company,*[36] and any

[30] Bankruptcy Act 1914, s.18.
[31] *Morgan* v. *Gray* [1953] Ch. 83.
[32] *Post,* p. 397.
[33] *Birch* v. *Sullivan* [1957] 1 W.L.R. 1247.
[34] Bankruptcy Act 1914, s.48; Table A, arts. 30–32, *ante,* p. 189. The 1914 Act does not apply to Scotland. In Scotland the act and warrant of confirmation in favour of the trustee vests the bankrupt's property in the trustee: Bankruptcy (Scotland) Act 1913, s.97.
[35] *Post,* p. 321. [36] *Ante,* p. 52.

allotment or transfer of shares in a holding company to its subsidiary is void.[37] This prohibition cannot be evaded by having a nominee for the subsidiary. Exceptions are where the subsidiary is concerned (a) as a personal representative, or (b) as a trustee, unless the holding company or a subsidiary of it is beneficially interested under the trust otherwise than by way of security for the purposes of a transaction entered into in the ordinary course of a business which includes the lending of money.

For example, as regards (a), Y, who holds shares in X Bank Ltd., appoints its subsidiary, X Bank (Executor & Trustee) Ltd., as his executor and on Y's death the subsidiary is registered in respect of the shares.

As to (b), Y transfers his shares to the subsidiary on trust for a beneficiary, Z, who borrows money from X Bank Ltd. and secures repayment by mortgaging his interest in the shares to X Bank Ltd.

Issuing houses and brokers

A person who has only agreed to place[38] shares does not agree to become a member of the company, and should not be put on the register of members. His failure to perform his contract may make him liable in damages, but he is not liable for calls.[39] If, however, a person agrees to take shares himself for the purpose of placing them by the execution of transfers, his name is properly put on the register.[40]

REGISTER OF MEMBERS

Section 110 provides that every company must keep a register of its members containing:

(1) The names and addresses of the members, and, if the company has a share capital, a statement of the shares held by each member, distinguishing each share by its number[41] so long as it has one and by its class if there is more than one class of shares,[42] and the amount paid or agreed to be considered as

---

[37] In Scotland this does not prevent a company from arresting its subsidiary's shares to found jurisdiction, at least where the shares are marketable: *Stenhouse London Ltd.* v. *Allwright*, 1972 S.L.T. 255.

[38] *Ante*, p. 146.

[39] *Gorrissen's Case* (1873) L.R. 8 Ch.App. 507.

[40] *Miln* v. *North British Fresh Fish etc. Co. Ltd.* (1887) 15 R. 21.

[41] *Post*, p. 261. [42] Added by 1981 Act, s.101.

paid on the shares of each member. If the company has converted shares into stock, the register must show the amount of
stock held by each member. In any other case where the
company has more than one class of members the register must
show the class to which each member belongs.[43]

(2) The date at which each person was entered in the register as a
member.

(3) The date at which any person ceased to be a member.

Default renders the company and every officer in default liable to a
default fine.

A guarantee company which does not have a share capital must
disclose the particulars of any class of membership not stated in its
memorandum, articles or by a special or extraordinary resolution, to
the Registrar.[44]

The register may be kept by making entries in a bound book or by
recording the required information in any other manner, including a
computer, so long as adequate precautions are taken to guard against
falsification: section 436; Stock Exchange (Completion of Bargains
Act) 1976, s.3. Any entry relating to a former member may be
removed from the register after 20 years from the date on which he
ceased to be a member: section 110(5).

A company with more than 50 members must, unless the register of
members constitutes an index, keep an index (which may be a card
index) of the names of it members, and must alter the index within 14
days after any alteration in the register. The index must be kept at the
same place as the register and must contain sufficient information to
enable the account of each member in the register to be readily found:
section 111.

The register of members is prima facie evidence of any matters
directed by the Act to be inserted in it: section 118.

Inspection of register

The register is to be kept at the company's registered office, but if
the register is made up at another office of the company, it may be kept

---

[43] This applies therefore to guarantee companies without a share capital. It was
added by 1981 Act, s.101 and reverses the decision in *Re Performing Right Society
Ltd.* [1978] 3 All E.R. 972 (C.A.).

[44] 1981 Act, s.102.

there, and if it is made up by an agent, it may be kept at his office. If the company is registered in England, the register must not be kept outside England, and if the company is registered in Scotland, the register must not be kept outside Scotland. When the register has not always been kept at the registered office, notice must be given to the Registrar of the place where it is kept: section 110.

The Jenkins Report[45] recommended that these flexible provisions in section 110 should apply to the other statutory books such as the minutes of general meetings, the register of directors, copies of instruments creating charges registrable under section 95 and the company's own register of charges.

During business hours the register and index are to be open to the inspection of any member without charge, and of any other person on payment of 5p., or less if the company so prescribes. Within ten days after being required to do so, the company is bound to furnish, either to a member or to any other person, a copy of any part of the register on payment of 10p. for every 100 words or part thereof: 1948 Act, s.113; 1967 Act, s.52(2). A person inspecting the register has no right to take extracts from or make copies of the register.[46] The right of inspection terminates on the company going into liquidation.[47] Where there is a winding up the court may allow creditors and contributories to inspect under sections 266 and 307.

There is no obligation on the company to disclose under section 113 anything other than what is on the register. It need not disclose a part of the register which can only be defined by reference to something which is not on the register, *e.g.* those members over a certain age.[48]

The company may, on giving notice by advertisement in some newspaper circulating in the district in which its registered office is situate, close the register for any time or times not exceeding 30 days in each year: section 115. This is to enable the company to prepare a list of members entitled to payment of a dividend.

Importance of register

The importance of the register as a public representation of who the members are and what their liability is has often been emphasised in

[45] Para. 470.
[46] *Re Balaghat Co.* [1901] 2 K.B. 665.
[47] *Re Kent Coalfields Syndicate Ltd.* [1898] 1 Q.B. 754 (C.A.).
[48] *Re Performing Right Society Ltd.* [1978] 3 All E.R. 972 (C.A.).

Scottish cases,[49] and a company has no power to create a right of pledge or lien over the register, since that would deprive the public of their statutory right of access and inspection.[50] The register and not the share certificate is the document of title to shares, the share certificate being merely an acknowledgment on the part of the company that the name of the person mentioned in it is duly recorded in the register.[51]

Any liability incurred by a company as the result of making or deleting an entry in its register, or failing to do either, cannot be enforced against it more than 20 years after the date of first default: section 110(6). This is a final limitation provision; earlier ones may well apply.

Power of court to rectify register

Section 116 gives the court a discretion to rectify the register of members in two cases, namely—

(1) if the name of any person is, without sufficient cause, entered in or omitted from the register;
(2) if default is made or unnecessary delay takes place in entering on the register the fact of any person having ceased to be a member.

Application to the court for rectification may be made by the person aggrieved, or any member of the company, or the company. The application is made in a summary way—by originating summons or originating motion in England: R.S.C., O.102, r.3, and by petition in Scotland: R.C. 190.

The court may order rectification of the register by deleting a reference to some only of the registered shareholder's shares. It need not delete his name entirely. Thus when an existing shareholder was registered as the holder of an additional number of shares issued in breach of the then Exchange Control Regulations the court deleted the reference to those shares only: *Re Transatlantic Life Assurance Co. Ltd.* [1979] 3 All E.R. 357.

---

[49] *e.g. per* Lord Curriehill in *Liquidator of the Garpel etc. Co. Ltd.* v. *Andrew* (1866) 4 M. 617, at p. 623.

[50] *Liquidator of the Garpel etc. Co. Ltd.* v. *Andrew* (1866) 4 M. 617.

[51] *Per* Lord Sands in *Inland Revenue* v. *Wilson,* 1928 S.C. (H.L.) 42; 1927 S.C. 733, at p. 737.

There is no *Foss* v. *Harbottle*[52] complication—even a single member may apply to the court.

The court may order not only rectification of the register but also payment by the company of any damages sustained by any party aggrieved.

If an order is made in the case of a company required to send a list of members to the Registrar[53] notice of the rectification must be given to the Registrar: section 116(4).

The period of two months specified in section 78 for giving a transferee of shares notice of the company's refusal to register the transfer is the outside limit after which there is normally unnecessary delay.[54]

An order for rectification may be made even if the company is being wound up.

B, a transferee of shares in a company, sent in his transfer for registration but, by mistake, registration of the transfer was omitted. The company then went into liquidation with a view to reconstruction and B, thinking that he was on the register of members, served the liquidator with notice of dissent to the scheme. The liquidator disregarded the notice on the ground that B was not a member. *Held*, there was such "default or unnecessary delay" in registration as entitled B to rectification of the register: *Re Sussex Brick Co.* [1904] 1 Ch. 598 (C.A.).[55]

Section 116 does not exhaust the court's power to order rectification and does not prevent the court from altering the register in cases other than those specified. Accordingly where shares were registered in the names of two joint holders, and under the articles the first alone could vote and if the first was ill or absent the second could not vote or be appointed a proxy, an order was made to have the holding split into two holdings with the names of the shareholders in different orders.[56]

In difficult cases the court will refuse to proceed under the section and an action must be brought.[57]

[52] *Post*, p. 397.
[53] See, *post*.
[54] *Re Swaledale Cleaners Ltd.* [1968] 1 W.L.R. 1710 (C.A.), *post*, p. 271.
[55] See also *Stocker* v. *Liqdrs. of the Coustonholm Paper Mills Co. Ltd.* (1891) 19 R. 17.
[56] *Burns* v. *Siemens Brothers Dynamo Works Ltd.* [1919] 1 Ch. 225.
[57] *e.g. Simpson's Case* (1869) L.R. 9 Eq. 91; *Blaikie* v. *Coats* (1893) 21 R. 150.

Trusts not to be entered on register in England

Section 117 provides that no notice of any trust shall be entered on the register, or be received by the Registrar, in the case of companies registered in England (which, for this purpose, includes Wales).[58] This means that, subject as below, the company is entitled to treat every person on the register of members as the beneficial owner of shares, even if in fact he holds them on trust for another, *i.e.* the company need not take notice of equitable interests in shares. If, therefore, the company registers a transfer of the shares held by a person as trustee, it is under no liability to the beneficiaries even if the sale was a breach of trust and in fraud of the beneficiaries.

X's shares were, on his death, registered in the name of his executors. They subsequently transferred the shares to Y in breach of the terms of X's will, and the transfer was registered by the company. The company had a copy of the will in its possession, and its president was one of X's executors. *Held,* the company did not act wrongfully, as it was only bound to satisfy itself from the will that the executors were executors, and was not concerned with the disposition by X of his property: *Simpson* v. *Molson's Bank* [1895] A.C. 270.

A further result is that the company is not a trustee for persons claiming the shares under equitable titles. For example, if A, the owner of shares, makes an equitable mortgage of his shares by depositing his share certificate and a blank transfer with B as security for a debt and afterwards makes another equitable mortgage of the same shares by depositing another blank transfer of them with C as security for another debt, saying that he has lost his share certificate, C cannot by giving notice to the company affect the company with notice of his interest in the shares or gain any priority over B.[59] As will be seen later,[60] the proper way to protect the interest of a beneficiary in shares is to serve a stop notice. As a rule, if a company receives notice of an equitable claim it should allow the person giving the notice to apply for a restraining order, if he makes a request to that effect, before registering a transfer to his prejudice.[61]

The articles frequently deal with notice of trusts, as does Table A, article 7:

"Except as required by law, no person shall be recognised . . . as holding any share upon any trust, and the company shall not be bound by or be

---

[58] Wales and Berwick Act 1746, s.3.
[59] *Société Générale de Paris* v. *Walker* (1885) 11 App.Cas. 20.   [60] *Post,* p. 285.
[61] *Per* Lindley L.J. in *Société Générale de Paris* v. *Tramways Union Co.* (1884) 14 Q.B.D. 424 (C.A.), at p. 453.

compelled in any way to recognise (even when having notice thereof) any equitable . . . interest in any share . . . or any other rights in respect of any share except an absolute right to the entirety thereof in the registered holder.''

It is doubtful whether this adds anything to the effect of section 117, although the section deals only with entries on the register while the article is not limited to entries on the register.[62]

A trustee of shares who is entered on the register is entitled to exercise any vote conferred by the shares although he may be bound to vote in accordance with the directions of the beneficiary. The trustee is personally liable to the company for any calls or other obligations attaching to the shares but is entitled to an indemnity from the beneficiary, not only out of the trust property but to the full extent of his indebtedness in respect of the shares.[63] The company cannot put the beneficiary on the list of contributories but it can, through the trustee, enforce the trustee's right to an indemnity.[64]

A purchase of shares in the name of a nominee, even if an infant or a man of straw, is legal. In such a case the company cannot go behind the nominee to the beneficial owner.

M. and G., a firm of stockbrokers, bought shares which were registered in the name of L., their clerk. L. was an infant. On the company's going into liquidation, the liquidator applied that M. and G.'s names might be substituted for that of L. in the register of members and the list of contributories. *Held*, the application failed, as there was no contractual relation between the company and M. and G.: *Re National Bank of Wales Ltd.* [1907] 1 Ch. 582.

If a person applies for shares in a fictitious name, or in the name of a person who has never agreed to accept the shares, rectification of the register can be obtained so as to place the name of the real owner upon the register.[65]

Trusts may be entered on register in Scotland

It has always been competent for companies registered in Scotland to enter notices of trusts on their registers.[66]

---

[62] See, *post*, p. 285.   [63] *Hardoon* v. *Belilios* [1901] A.C. 118 (P.C.).

[64] *Per* James L.J. in *Re European Society Arbitration Acts* (1878) 8 Ch.D. 679 (C.A.), at p. 708.

[65] *Pugh and Sharman's Case* (1872) L.R. 13 Eq. 566; *Richardson's Case* (1875) L.R. 19 Eq. 588.

[66] As to the purpose of such entry, see, *per* Cairns L.C. in *Muir* v. *City of Glasgow Bank* (1879) 6 R. (H.L.) 21, at p. 26.

Entry of a notice of trust does *not* have the effect of limiting the liability of the trustees to the amount of the trust estate in their hands.[66a]

The legal position of trustees is distinct from that of executors.[67]

On the assumption of a new trustee by deed of assumption his name may be entered on the register without any transfer being executed, and the trustee will then be a member and liable as such.[68] A trustee who duly resigns his office by minute registered in the Books of Council and Session, and intimated to his co-trustees and to the company, is entitled to have his name removed from the register; no deed of transfer is necessary.[69] When one of several trustees dies, shares registered in the names of the trustees vest in the surviving trustees, and the executors of the deceased trustee are not liable as members even though no intimation of the death has been given to the company.[70] The last surviving trustee, however, is in a different position from the other trustees in that his death does not automatically terminate his liability as a member.[71]

The liability of trustees to the company is *in solidum*, not *pro rata*, *i.e.* the company may hold any one of the several trustees liable for the full amount due on the shares.[72]

Trustees who have been made liable for calls in respect of shares forming part of the trust estate are entitled to full relief from the trust estate without reference to their own payments or ability to pay; the trust estate may be made liable beyond what the trustees can personally pay, and the company may by diligence compel the trustees to make the right of relief available to the company.[73]

The persons for whom shares are held in trust are *not* members of the company, although their names may appear on the register.[74]

[66a] *Muir* v. *City of Glasgow Bank* (1879) 6 R. (H.L.) 21; (1878) 6 R. 392, following *Lumsden* v. *Buchanan* (1865) 3 M. (H.L.) 89.

[67] *Per* Lord Selborne in *Buchan* v. *City of Glasgow Bank* (1879) 6 R. (H.L.) 44 at p. 50.

[68] Trusts (Scotland) Act 1921, s.21; *Bell* v. *City of Glasgow Bank* (1879) 6 R. (H.L.) 55; (1879) 6 R. 548.

[69] 1921 Act, s.19(1): *Dalgleish* v. *Land Feuing Co. Ltd.* (1885) 13 R. 223.

[70] *Oswald's Trustees* v. *City of Glasgow Bank* (1879) 6 R. 461.

[71] *Low's Executors* v. *City of Glasgow Bank* (1879) 6 R. 830.

[72] *Cuninghame* v. *City of Glasgow Bank* (1879) 6 R. (H.L.) 98; (1879) 6 R. 679.

[73] *Cuningham* v. *Montgomerie* (1879) 6 R. 1333; contrast *Brownlie* v. *Brownlie's Trustees* (1879) 6 R. 1233.

[74] *Gillespie & Paterson* v. *City of Glasgow Bank* (1879) 6 R. (H.L.) 104; (1879) 6 R. 714.

Dominion register

If the objects of a company having a share capital comprise the transaction of business in any part of Her Majesty's dominions outside Great Britain, the Channel Islands, the Isle of Man, or in Malaysia,[75] South Africa,[76] Pakistan,[77] Singapore[78] or Bangladesh,[79] the company may keep a branch register (called a "dominion register") of its members resident in that part. Notice of the situation of the office where the dominion register is kept must be given to the Registrar within 14 days of the opening of the office or of any change in its situation. The same notice must be given if the dominion register is discontinued: section 119.

A dominion register is deemed to be part of the company's register of members ("the principal register"), and it must be kept in the same manner. A copy of every entry in the dominion register must be transmitted to the company's registered office as soon as may be after it is made, and the company must enter it in a duplicate dominion register which it must keep at the same place as the principal register. The dominion register can be rectified on application to the court in the dominion in which it is kept: section 120.

DISCLOSURE OF SUBSTANTIAL SHAREHOLDINGS

Sections 63–83 of the Companies Act 1981 contain provisions for securing the disclosure and registration of substantial individual interests in share capital carrying unrestricted voting rights. The aim is to ensure that directors,[80] shareholders and employees of a public company may ascertain the identity of, for instance, any person who may be in the process of buying shares in the company to gain control of it or of any person who is in a position to veto a special resolution of the company, and they allow companies to carry out their own investigations into such matters without necessitating intervention by the Department of Trade under sections 172–173 of the 1948 Act.[81]

[75] Companies Registers (Malaysia) Order, 1964 (S.I. 1964 No. 911).
[76] South Africa Act 1962, s.2 and Sched. 2.
[77] Pakistan Act 1973, Sched. 3.
[78] Singapore Act 1966, Sched. 2.
[79] Bangladesh Act 1973, Sched.
[80] For the other provisions relating to directors' shareholdings see, *post,* p. 337.
[81] *Post,* p. 425.

Disclosure obligations

Section 63 of the 1981 Act requires any person who acquires a five per cent. interest in the voting shares of a public company or who disposes of such an interest, to inform the company of that and of any significant change in the number of shares in which he is interested above the five per cent. level. In totting up any individual's interest to ascertain whether he has passed the disclosure threshold, sections 67–69 of the 1981 Act provide for the attribution to individuals of interests in shares. These attributed interests are added to those already clearly held by any person to ascertain whether or not he is obliged to make disclosure of his interest in shares.

Under section 72 of the 1981 Act failure to comply with section 63 is made a criminal offence. The prosecution must prove that the defendant knew enough to be aware that he had an interest or interests of the relevant amount and failed to report them but any interest which he has or had and does not know about will be irrelevant and will not make him liable for failure to make disclosure.

Section 64 of the 1981 Act empowers the Secretary of State by regulation affirmed by Parliament to alter the current five per cent. level which triggers off the obligation to disclose under section 63.

Under section 63 any person so obliged must within five days make disclosure of his interest in writing specifying the share capital to which it relates. He must also state either the number of shares in that public company in which he knows he was interested immediately after the time his obligation to notify arose, or state that he no longer has a notifiable interest if that is the case.

Section 63(9) states that the time an obligation arises is either the time the event or change of circumstances occurred or the time when the person becomes aware of those facts. Section 65 provides that where a person makes a notification under section 63 of his interest in shares he must include details in writing to the company of the identity of registered holders of any shares to which the notification relates and the number of shares that each holds so far as known by the person making the notification at the date of notification. Any known changes in those particulars must be subsequently notified to the company.

Sections 66 and 70 aim to make subject to the disclosure provisions of the 1981 Act interests in shares which arise indirectly. Section 66 specifies various instances where a person is attributed with the interests which are ostensibly held by other persons and which are to be taken into account in ascertaining whether or not he is obliged to make notification under sections 63–65. Other persons' interests which come into this category include those of his spouse or any infant child or step child and those of any company which is accustomed to acting in accordance with his directions or in which he is entitled to control one-third or more of the voting power at general meetings; and, where that company which he "controls" itself has a one-third shareholding in another company, the interest in shares of that other company is also attributable to him. The notifiable interests in shares defined in section 70 include interests in shares on which a person has an option and section 66(4) provides for the attribution of interests held by a company to persons with options on or any future entitlement to vote-carrying shares if the option or entitlement would give him control of one-third or more of the voting power of that company.

Further important attributions of interests in shares are contained in sections 68 and 69 which deal with so called *concert parties*,[82] *i.e.* those with agreements for the purpose of acquiring interest in shares. The aim is to prevent control in concert, in other words avoidance of the disclosure provisions by groups of persons secretly agreeing that while each acquires openly less than the disclosure threshold level they will secretly use the combined interests to gain control or to ensure a takeover or a special resolution. Section 67 provides that each person involved in any such agreement is to be attributed with the interests of all the other parties to it even though some of those persons' interests may have been acquired before or outside of the so-called "concert party" agreement. The effect is that in ascertaining the obligation of each member of a concert party individually to notify his interests, the interests of all the other members are added to his interest or interests and if the total exceeds five per cent. he must make notification in accordance with section 63, and, in addition, under section 66(8) shall state that he is a party to such an agreement, the names and if known to him, the addresses of the other parties to the agreement and which, if any, of the shares to which the notification relates are shares in which he is interested by reason of attribution under section 66 and if that is the case he must also notify the number of those shares.

In addition to the obligation to notify the company, section 68 obliges all the persons involved in a *concert party* to keep each other

---

[82] *cf.* the City Code on Take-overs and Mergers, *post*, p. 718.

informed of facts relevant to their shareholding. This provision aims to give all members of a concert party the ability to know whether or not the interests attributed to him under section 67 (alone or together with any other interest he might have) are such as to necessitate his making a notification under section 63. To do this he must know all the interests attributable to him and any changes in those interests.

Therefore all the concert party members must inform every other member of their existing interests, acquisitions and disposals of shares in that company and this obligation comes into being with the first acquisition of shares in that company in pursuance with the "concert party" agreement. Each party to the agreement has five days within which to notify the other parties in writing of his interest and of his current address. Failure to meet these obligations is made a criminal offence by s.72(3)(*c*).

Section 70 defines for the purpose of the duty to disclose the interests to be notified. Most significant is that a person is deemed to have an interest in shares if he enters into a contract for their purchase or where, even though he is not the registered holder, he is entitled to exercise or control the exercise of any right conferred by holding those shares or (trust aside) he has a right to call for delivery of the shares to himself or his order or he has a right to acquire an interest in shares or is under an obligation to take an interest in shares whether or not in any case that right or obligation is conditional or absolute. Contingent agreements which otherwise might be used to conceal an interest requiring disclosure are exposed.

Section 71 lists various interests in shares which do not give rise to the disclosure obligation under sections 63–65, for example an interest in shares as a security is an exempt security interest if it is held by specified bodies which lend money in the course of business. Criminal liability for failure to meet the obligations imposed under this part of the Act is contained in section 72 which also makes it an offence to fail without reasonable excuse to ensure that any agent who acquires or disposes of interests in shares on someone's behalf, notifies him immediately of any transaction which will or may give rise to an obligation under section 63.

Register of substantial shareholders

By section 73 of the 1981 Act every public company must maintain a register of interests in shares notified to it in accordance with section 63 and both the company and every officer[83] in default is made criminally liable for either failing to keep the register or failing to keep it in the manner prescribed.

Company's power to require information

Under section 74 a company can require information from existing members about the capacity in which they hold their shares, and it is further empowered to make enquiries of any person who it has been informed is, or who its investigations reveal to be, interested in shares in the company. Members may be asked whether or not any voting rights on their shares are controlled by another person under some agreement and if that is the case, particulars of the parties and terms of the agreement may be required. Members and persons who also indicated that they were interested in shares during the three years prior to the date of notice under this section must disclose details of their present interests or any past interests in shares held within the previous three years or of any other past or present interest not referred to in the notice issued under this section. Such information, known to a member, must be disclosed to the company. Likewise the company may require similar information from any person named or revealed as a party to such an agreement and will enable it to cross check the information it receives concerning interests in shares.

The company, in turn, is obliged by section 75 to register the information received in response to an inquiry under section 74 including an indication of the fact and date of the requirement imposed by the company under section 74.

Furthermore the company may be compelled to investigate and report under the power given in section 74 on persons who hold the controlling interest in the company. This power of compulsion is provided by section 76 to a 10 per cent. minority of shareholders at the date of making the requisition provided they comply with the procedures laid down in the section, such as specifying the manner in which the company is to exercise its power and the giving of reasonable grounds for their request. There is, however, nothing to stop the members making the request, applying to the court if the company is slow in responding to a good request or to the Department of Trade in terms of sections 172–174 of the 1948 Act if it refused to act at all.[84]

---

[83] *Post,* p. 327.

[84] *Post,* p. 425.

Should any person validly requested by the company fail to provide the requisite information in terms of section 74 he becomes subject to the penalties imposed by section 77. Under this provision the company can ask the court to impose restrictions on dealings in those shares including putting a stop on dividend payments to or the exercise of voting rights by that person. But no offence justifying such an order would be committed if the person can prove that the notice seeking information is frivolous or vexatious.

The company is empowered by section 78 to remove out-of-date entries from the register of interests in shares which it is required to keep under section 73[85] if these entries are six years old and second that a person has ceased to be a member or it is that old and has been superseded by a later entry against the name of that person.

Section 78(2) imposes on the company the obligation to notify within 15 days any person whose name has been provided to it as a member and state what entries in consequence have been made against his name on the register of interests in shares and inform him of his right to apply to have that entry removed in accordance with the procedures in section 78. Any other deletion is a criminal offence in terms of section 79.

Both the new section 73 register of interests and the new section 76 report on investigation must by virtue of section 80 be kept available for inspection without charge to members and non-members during business hours, at the company's registered office. Again, failure to do so makes both company and any officer in default criminally liable.

ANNUAL RETURN

Every company having a share capital must, once in every year, make a return (called the "annual return") to the Registrar of Companies, except that no annual return need be made in the year of the company's incorporation or, if the company is not required by section 131[86] to hold an annual general meeting during the following year, in that year: section 124. The word "year" means calendar year, *i.e.* the period 1st January to 31st December.[87]

---

[85] *Ante*, p. 202.
[86] *Post*, p. 302.
[87] *Gibson* v. *Barton* (1875) L.R. 10 Q.B. 329.

The annual return must contain the matters, and be in the form specified in the Sixth Schedule.

The Sixth Schedule matters are:—

(1) The address of the registered office.
(2) (*a*) If the register of members is not kept at the registered office, the address where it is kept.
    (*b*) If the register of debenture holders is not kept at the registered office, the address where it is kept.
(3) A summary of share capital and debentures, distinguishing between shares issued for cash and shares issued as fully or partly paid up otherwise than in cash, specifying—
    (*a*) the amount of the share capital and the number of shares into which it is divided;
    (*b*) the number of shares taken up to the date of the return;
    (*c*) the amount called up on each share, the amount of calls received and the amount of calls unpaid;
    (*d*) the amount of commission paid in respect of shares or debentures;
    (*e*) the discount allowed on any shares issued at a discount, or so much as has not been written off;
    (*f*) the discount allowed in respect of any debentures since the date of the last return;
    (*g*) the number of shares forfeited;
    (*h*) the amount of shares for which share warrants are outstanding, the number of shares comprised in each warrant, and the amount of share warrants issued and surrendered since the last return.
(4) The amount of indebtedness of the company in respect of all mortgages and charges which are required to be registered with the Registrar.
(5) A list of present and past members—
    (*a*) containing the names and addresses of all persons who, on the fourteenth day after the annual general meeting, are members, and of persons who have ceased to be members since the date of the last return or, in the case of the first return, since incorporation;
    (*b*) stating the number of shares held by each member at the date of the return, specifying shares transferred since the date of the last return and the dates of registration of the transfers;
    (*c*) if the members' names are not arranged in alphabetical order, having an index annexed.
    If any shares have been converted into stock, the amount of stock held by each member must be given: section 124(1), proviso (*b*). A complete return of the members and their holdings need be made only every third year, and in the intervening two years only a list of changes in the membership need be given: section 124(1),

proviso (*c*). As stated earlier,[88] a company which is exempt from using the word limited at the end of its name is excepted from the provisions of the Act relating to sending lists of members to the Registrar: 1981 Act, s.25(3).

(6) The same particulars of the directors and secretary at the date of the return as are required to be in the register of directors and secretaries.[89]

The return made by a company with no share capital need contain only matters (1), (2), (4) and (6), *ante*: section 125.

The annual return must be completed within 42 days after the annual general meeting and a copy signed by a director and the secretary must be sent forthwith to the Registrar: section 126.

If the annual return is not forwarded, the company and every officer in default is liable to a default fine.

---

[88] p. 62.
[89] See s.200, *post*, p. 336.

Chapter 11

SHARE CAPITAL

THE more important topics dealt with in this chapter are preference shares, the variation of the special rights of a class of shareholders, the rules that share capital must be raised and, once raised, must be maintained, and the reduction of share capital. The associated topics of the purchase and redemption by a company of its own shares and the giving of financial assistance by a company for the acquisition of its own shares are dealt with in the following two chapters.

MEANING OF "CAPITAL"

The word "capital" used in connection with a company has several different meanings; thus it may mean the nominal or authorised share capital, the issued share capital, the paid-up share capital or the reserve share capital of the company.

The *nominal* or *authorised capital* is the amount of share capital which the company is authorised to issue. As we have seen,[1] in the case of a limited company the amount of share capital with which it proposes to be registered, and the division thereof into shares of a fixed amount, must be set out in the memorandum of association, but this amount may be increased or reduced as explained later.[2] The amount of the company's nominal capital depends on its business requirements, actual or potential. It must be remembered that public companies must have at least £50,000 authorised capital: 1980 Act s.3(2).

The *issued* or *allotted capital* is that part of the company's nominal capital which has been issued to the shareholders. The company is not bound to issue all its capital at once, although a public company must issue at least £50,000 nominal value of shares before it may commence business (1980 Act, s.4(2)), and frequently when the nominal capital is increased the extent of the increase is not limited to the company's requirements at the time but covers its probable requirements in the future. In such a case, further issues of capital are made as they are

---

[1] *Ante*, p. 93.
[2] *Post*, pp. 223, 229.

needed. Such issues are made by the directors if properly authorised under the 1980 Act.[3]

The *paid-up capital* is that part of the issued capital which has been paid up by the shareholders. The company may, for example, have a nominal capital of £500,000 divided into 500,000 shares of a nominal amount of £1 each, of which £400,000 is issued, *i.e.* 400,000 of the shares have been issued, and only £100,000 is paid up, *i.e.* the company has so far required only 25p. to be paid up on each share. The *uncalled capital* is the remainder of the issued capital and can be called up at any time by the company from the shareholders in accordance with the provisions of the articles. Uncalled capital is rare today. Since the disastrous experiences of many companies in the years between the wars, when shareholders were often unable to pay calls made in respect of their shares, shares have usually been fully paid up within a short time after issue. Further, at least in the case of the ordinary commercial company, partly paid-up shares are not popular with investors. The 1980 Act by section 22 requires public companies to call up at least one quarter of the nominal value of a share and all the premium on allotment. It follows that uncalled capital is rare today.

The *reserve capital*, or reserve liability, is that part of the uncalled capital which a limited company has by special resolution determined shall not be called up except in the event and for the purposes of the company's being wound up and which cannot otherwise be called up: section 60. This capital is not under the control of the directors and cannot be reconverted into ordinary uncalled capital, or charged by the company, *e.g.* as security for debentures.[4] It is available only for the creditors on the winding up of the company, although it will be seen that it can be reduced with the consent of the court under section 66.[5] Reserve capital must be distinguished from capital reserves, a capital redemption reserve, revenue reserves, and a reserve or a general reserve, all of which will be dealt with later.[6]

The European Communities Act 1972, s.9(7), provides that if, in the case of a company having a share capital, there is on the stationery used for any business letters, or on the order forms of the company, a

---

[3] *Ante*, p. 165.

[4] *Re Mayfair Property Co.* [1898] 2 Ch. 28 (C.A.).

[5] *Re Midland Rlwy. Carriage Co.* (1907) 23 T.L.R. 661.

[6] *Post*, pp. 223, 541.

reference to the amount of the share capital, the reference must be to paid-up share capital.

The paid-up capital includes the nominal value of the shares paid-up and any premium on such shares.[7] For example if 10,000 £1 shares are sold for £2 each the paid up capital will be £20,000. This will however be expressed as £10,000 share capital and £10,000 share premium account in the balance sheet.

CLASSES OF SHARE CAPITAL

A company is not bound to issue all its shares with the same rights but may confer different rights on different classes of shares. Such classes may be described as ordinary shares and preference shares but the name by which a class of shares is called gives only an indication of the rights attaching to it in any particular company, and to ascertain the rights reference must be made to the articles or the terms of issue of the shares.

Although the memorandum of association is required to set out the division of the nominal capital into shares of a fixed amount, it is not required to set out, and in practice it will not usually set out, the different classes of shares into which the capital is divided. However, the articles will normally give the company power to issue different classes of shares.

Table A, article 2, provides: "Without prejudice to any special rights previously conferred on the holders of any existing shares or class of shares, any share in the company may be issued with such preferred, deferred or other special rights or such restrictions, whether in regard to dividend, voting, return of capital or otherwise as the company may from time to time by ordinary resolution determine."

If there is no such provision in the articles, in the absence of a prohibition in the memorandum they may be altered by special resolution to give such a power.[8]

Where a company issues shares with rights which are not stated in its memorandum or articles or in any resolution or document to which section

---

[7] *Ante*, p. 175.

[8] *Andrews* v. *Gas Meter Co.* [1897] 1 Ch. 361 (C.A.), *ante*, p. 95: *cf. Liquidator of The Humboldt Redwood Co. Ltd.* v. *Coats*, 1908 S.C. 751, and *Crookston* v. *Lindsay, Crookston & Co. Ltd.*, 1922 S.L.T. 62 (O.H.).

143 applies, or varies the rights attached to shares otherwise than by amendment of its memorandum or articles or by resolution or document to which section 143 applies, section 33 of the Companies Act 1980 requires the company to deliver particulars to the Registrar unless the shares are uniform with shares previously issued.

Preference shares

Preference shares are shares the issue of which was authorised by the memorandum or the articles and which are entitled to some priority over the other shares in the company. They usually carry a right to preference in payment of dividend (if a dividend is declared) at a fixed rate, and a right to preference in the repayment of capital in a winding up. There may be several classes of perference shares, first, second and third, ranking one after the other.

The rights attached to preference shares are always a question of construction of the memorandum, the articles or the terms of issue of the shares. However, unless the articles, etc., otherwise provide, the rights which attach to preference shares are as described below. These prima facie rights differ according to whether the company is a going concern or in liquidation.

When the company is a going concern

1. When a right to a preferential dividend is given without more, it is a right to a *cumulative* dividend, *i.e.* if no preference dividend is declared in any year the arrears of dividend are carried forward and must be paid before a dividend is paid on the other shares.[9] If, however, the shares are declared to be non-cumulative preference shares, or the preferential dividend is to be paid out of the yearly profits,[10] or out of the net profits of each year,[11] the dividend will not be cumulative.

2. Preference shares are *non-participating*, *i.e.* they do not confer any right to a participation in the surplus profits of the company after payment of a specified rate of dividend on the ordinary shares, in the

---

[9] *Webb* v. *Earle* (1875) L.R. 20 Eq. 556; *Ferguson & Forrester Ltd.* v. *Buchanan*, 1920 S.C. 154. Interest is not payable on the arrears: *Partick etc. Gas Co. Ltd.* v. *Taylor* (1888) 15 R. 711.

[10] *Adair* v. *Old Bushmills Distillery* [1908] W.N. 24.

[11] *Staples* v. *Eastman Photographic Materials Co.* [1896] 2 Ch. 303 (C.A.); contrast *Miln* v. *Arizona Copper Co. Ltd.* (1899) 1 F. 935.

absence of anything to that effect in the articles, etc. Where a special resolution that the holders of preference shares were entitled to a cumulative preference dividend at the rate of 10 per cent. per annum and that such shares should rank, both as regards capital and dividend, in priority to the other shares, the holders were only entitled to a 10 per cent. dividend in the distribution of profits—the provision defined the whole terms of the bargain between the shareholders and the company.[12] Sometimes, however, cumulative and participating preference shares are created, conferring a right to participate in surplus profits up to a fixed percentage, *e.g.* a right to a preferential dividend of seven per cent. may be given, together with a further right, after seven per cent. has been paid on the ordinary shares, to participate in the surplus profits equally with the ordinary shares until an additional seven per cent. has been paid, but no more.

3. Unless the articles, etc., otherwise provide, preference shares carry the *same voting rights* at general meetings as the other shares.[13] However if, as is common, the preference shareholders are expressly given a right to vote in certain specified circumstances, *e.g.* when the preference dividend is in arrears or the rights attached to the preference shares are being varied, prima facie they have no right to vote in other circumstances.

The Jenkins Report[14] recommended that holders of voteless preference shares should receive notices of general meetings and a copy of any chairman's statement which is circulated with the accounts. The majority of the Committee thought that the case for abolition of voteless shares had not been made out and rejected the suggestion that holders of voteless shares should be given a statutory right to attend and speak at company meetings.

When the company is being wound up

1. *In the absence of a provision in the articles, etc., arrears of cumulative preference dividend are not payable out of the assets in a liquidation, unless the dividend has been declared.*[15] If, however, as is

---

[12] *Will* v. *United Lankat Plantations Co. Ltd.* [1914] A.C. 11.

[13] See s.134(*e*), *post*, p. 317.

[14] Para. 140.

[15] *Re Crichton's Oil Co.* [1902] 2 Ch. 86 (C.A.); *Re Catalinas Warehouses & Mole Co. Ltd.* [1947] 1 All E.R. 51; *Robertson-Durham* v. *Inches*, 1917, 1 S.L.T. 267 (O.H.).

usual, the articles provide for the payment of arrears, such arrears are payable out of the surplus assets after payment of the company's debts, whether or not any undistributed profits are included in the assets.[16] If the articles provide only for payment of all arrears "due" at the date of winding up, no arrears will be payable unless dividends have been declared, because a dividend is not due until it has been declared.[17]

A provision that preference shares shall be entitled to "a fixed cumulative preferential dividend at the rate of x per cent. per annum . . . and . . . shall rank both as regards dividends and capital in priority to the ordinary shares, but shall not confer the right to any further participation in profits or assets," entitles the preference shareholders to receive arrears of dividends, although not declared, in priority to the repayment of capital to the ordinary shareholders—the early part of the provision applies to the state of affairs when the company is a going concern and the words "shall rank . . . as regards dividends . . . in priority to the ordinary shares" obviously apply in a winding up.[18] A similar provision omitting the word "preferential" and any reference to further participation in profits or assets confers no right to undeclared arrears of preference dividend in a winding up—it is not necessary to treat the words "shall rank . . . as regards dividends" as conferring priority in respect of arrears of cumulative preference dividend in a winding up, because there is no prior statement that the preference shareholders are to have a preference dividend.[19] A provision including the word "preferential" and merely omitting any reference to further participation in profits or assets also gives a right to arrears of preference dividend in a winding up in priority to the ordinary shares.[20]

2. *Prima facie, preference shares have no priority in the repayment of capital in a winding up.* However, such a right may be, and usually is, given by the articles, and its effect is that after the company's debts and

---

[16] *Re Springbok Agricultural Estates Ltd.* [1920] 1 Ch. 563; *Re Wharfedale Brewery Co. Ltd.* [1952] Ch. 913. The rules as to the payment of dividends (*post*, p. 532) have no application to the surplus assets in a winding up.

[17] *Re Roberts and Cooper Ltd.* [1929] 2 Ch. 383.

[18] *Re Walter Symons Ltd.* [1934] Ch. 308; *Re F. de Jong & Co. Ltd.* [1946] Ch. 211 (C.A.).

[19] *Re Wood, Skinner & Co. Ltd.* [1944] Ch. 323; *Robertson-Durham* v. *Inches*, 1917, 1 S.L.T. 267 (O.H.). And see *Re William Bedford Ltd.* [1967] V.R. 490.

[20] *Re E. W. Savory Ltd.* [1951] 2 All E.R. 1036; *Re Wharfedale Brewery Co. Ltd.*, *ante*.

liabilities, and any arrears of preference dividend which are payable, have been paid, the preference shareholders are entitled to repayment of their capital in full before the ordinary shareholders are repaid their capital.[21]

3. *Where there are surplus assets available after the discharge of all the company's liabilities and the repayment of the capital to the shareholders, such surplus assets are divisible rateably among all classes of shareholders in the absence of any provision in the articles, etc., to the contrary.*[22] But, if, as is common, the articles set out the rights attached to a class of shares to participate in profits while the company is a going concern or to share in the property of the company in liquidation, prima facie those rights are exhaustive. Thus, articles giving preference shareholders priority in the repayment of capital in a liquidation but containing no reference to any further rights in the capital do not entitle the preference shareholders to participate in such surplus assets.[23]

The colliery assets of a coal mining company had been transferred to the National Coal Board under the Coal Industry Nationalisation Act 1946 and the company was to go into voluntary liquidation. Meanwhile the company proposed to reduce its capital by returning their capital to the holders of the preference stock. The articles provided that in the event of a winding up the preference stock ranked before the ordinary stock to the extent of repayment of the amounts called up and paid thereon. *Held*, the proposed reduction was not unfair or inequitable. Even without it, the preference shareholders would not be entitled in a winding up to share in the surplus assets or to receive more than a return of their paid up capital. Accordingly, they could not object to being paid, by means of the reduction, the amount which they would receive in the proposed liquidation: *Wilsons and Clyde Coal Co. Ltd.* v. *Scottish Insurance Corpn. Ltd.*, 1949 S.C. (H.L.) 90; [1949] A.C. 462.

If articles expressly give preference shareholders a right to share in surplus assets after the repayment of capital, they are entitled to share in accumulated profits in a liquidation even if the articles give the ordinary shareholders a right to exclusive enjoyment of accumulated

---

[21] The preference shares were by the articles given priority in the return of capital in the cases cited in notes 18, 19, 20, *ante*.

[22] *Monkland Iron etc. Co. Ltd.* v. *Henderson* (1883) 10 R. 494; *Liquidators of Williamson-Buchanan Steamers Ltd., Petitioners*, 1936 S.L.T. 106 (O.H.); *Town and Gown Assocn. Ltd. Liquidator, Petitioner*, 1948 S.L.T. (Notes) 71 (O.H.).

[23] *Wilsons and Clyde Coal Co. Ltd.* v. *Scottish Insurance Corpn. Ltd.* 1949 S.C. (H.L.) 90; 1948 S.C. 360; *Re The Isle of Thanet Electricity Supply Co. Ltd.* [1950] Ch. 161 (C.A.).

profits not required for the preference dividend—the right of the ordinary shareholders depends on the appropriate resolutions being passed before a winding up.[24]

Preference shares contrasted with ordinary shares

Preference shares are more like debentures than like ordinary shares in that, if profits are available and if a dividend is declared on preference shares, it will be at a fixed rate just as debentures carry a fixed rate of interest (whether profits are available or not), whereas the rate of dividend on ordinary shares varies according to the amount of profits available.

Further, in the case of preference shares the right of the holders to vote at general meetings is usually restricted[25] to when their special rights are being varied, or their dividend is in arrear,[26] and debentures normally confer no right to vote at general meetings, whereas ordinary shares usually confer a full right of voting.

The above may be said to be, at least in times of inflation when profits are high, the main disadvantages of preference shares. Another disadvantage is that in a prosperous business the preference shareholder is now regarded as a temporary member of the company, whose rights are limited to his preferential dividend and to priority in the return of capital on a winding up, and whose capital is liable to be returned to him whenever the company can raise the necessary money at a lower dividend rate.[27] The advantage of preference shares is that they are a safe investment. In particular, in a winding up, under normal articles the preference capital is repayable after payment of the company's debts and before the ordinary capital is returned.

A significant disadvantage from the company's point of view is that dividends on shares are not allowed as a deduction for the purposes of calculating the net profits on which corporation tax is paid whereas debenture interest is so allowed.[28]

---

[24] *Dimbula Valley (Ceylon) Tea Co. Ltd.* v. *Laurie* [1961] Ch. 353.
[25] The Stock Exchange requires restricted voting shares to be designated as such: Admission of Securities to Listing, p. 164.
[26] *Ante*, p. 211.
[27] *Post*, p. 233.
[28] See *Pinson, op. cit.*, Chap. 16.

Variation of class rights

1. Where a company's shares are divided into classes, "class rights" are special rights of a class of shares, *e.g.* a preferential right as to dividend attached to preference shares where a company's shares are divided into preference shares and ordinary shares.

It has been said that the term "class" must be confined to those persons whose rights are not so dissimilar as to make it impossible for them to consult together with a view to their common interest.[29] Section 32 of the 1980 Act, which applies to alterations, governs the rights attaching to any class of shares in a company whose share capital is divided into shares of different classes.[30]

Class rights are usually given to preference shareholders and if articles give the *ordinary* shareholders a right to the distributed profits after payment of a dividend on the preference shares, and a right to surplus assets on a liquidation, these are *not* class rights—they are no more than would be implied if the articles did not refer to them[31] However, it seems that the original 2s. ordinary shares in *Greenhalgh* v. *Arderne Cinemas*,[32] *post*, formed a class of shares within the meaning of an article providing for variation of the rights attached to a class of shares. Again, in *Lord St. David's* v. *Union-Castle Mail Steamship Co. Ltd.*,[33] where under the articles the large number of preference shares carried a right to vote when the preference dividend was in arrears and, such dividend being in arrears, the preference shareholders proposed to alter the articles so as to give themselves a right to vote on all resolutions, it was held that the proposed resolution would affect the rights of the small number of ordinary shareholders unless the ordinary shareholders approved in accordance with an article providing for variation of class rights, *i.e.* class rights were attached to the ordinary shares.[34]

---

[29] *Per* Bowen L.J. in *Sovereign Life Assurance Co.* v. *Dodd* [1892] 2 Q.B. 573 (C.A.) at p. 583. (This case concerned the forerunner of s.206, *post*, p. 709. An arrangement was made between a company in course of being wound up and its creditors. Insured persons whose policies had matured formed a distinct class of creditors from those whose policies had not.) See also *Re Hellenic and General Trust Ltd.* [1976] 1 W.L.R. 123.

[30] See below.

[31] *Hodge* v. *James Howell & Co.*, *The Times*, December 13, 1958 (C.A.).

[32] [1946] 1 All E.R. 512 (C.A.).   [33] *The Times*, November 24, 1934.

[34] See, too, *Rights and Issues Investment Trust Ltd.* v. *Stylo Shoes Ltd.* [1965] Ch. 250, *ante*, p. 111.

Class rights may be attached to a class of shares by the memorandum or the articles of the company, or by the terms of issue of the shares, or by a special resolution of the company in general meeting as in *Re Old Silkstone Collieries Ltd.*[35] They are usually concerned with voting, dividend, and the distribution of assets in the event of the company's being wound up.

2. *If class rights are set out in the memorandum,* or incorporated therein by reference to the articles,[36] they are only alterable if all the members of the company agree[37] unless the memorandum itself provides a method of alteration which must be complied with, or a method of alteration is provided by articles which were included at the time of the original incorporation of the company,[38] or the consent of the court is obtained to a scheme of arrangement under section 206.[39]

An alteration by a method provided by the memorandum will probably be subject to section 72, *post.* If the proposed variation relates to the authority to issue shares[40] or a reduction of capital,[41] the specified majority will be three quarters whatever the procedure provided by the memorandum or articles might say: 1980 Act, s.32(3).

Any meeting held to vary the class rights must comply with the 1948 Act as to notice and conduct of meetings with a minimum quorum of the holders of at least one third of the nominal value of the class being at least two in number: 1980 Act, s.32(6).

Under section 206 a company may make a binding compromise or arrangement with a class of members. Application must be made to the court to order a meeting of the class. Then the compromise or arrangement must be approved at the meeting by a simple majority in number representing three-fourths in value of those voting in person or by proxy. Finally, the court must approve it.

The power to alter the memorandum conferred by section 23[42] does not authorise any variation or abrogation of the special rights of any class of members.

---

[35] [1954] Ch. 169, *post,* p. 235.
[36] *Dimbula Valley (Ceylon) Tea Co. Ltd.* v. *Laurie* [1961] Ch. 353.
[37] 1980 Act, s.32(5).
[38] *Ibid.* s.32(4).
[39] *Post,* p. 709.
[40] *Ante,* p. 165.
[41] *Post,* p. 229.
[42] *Ante,* p. 95.

3. *The rights of different classes of shares are usually set out in the articles and it is usual for the articles to provide for the variation of class rights.*

Table A, article 4, provides: "If at any time the share capital is divided into different classes of shares, the rights attached to any class may, whether or not the company is being wound up, be varied with the consent in writing of the holders of three-fourths of the issued shares of that class, or with the sanction of an extraordinary resolution passed at a separate general meeting of the holders of the shares of the class."

If articles attach class rights to a class of shares and contain a "modification of rights clause" like Table A, article 4, above, the class rights may in general be varied, with the consent of the specified proportion or resolution of the holders of shares of the class, by a valid alteration of the articles by a special resolution of the company in general meeting.[43] In two cases, *viz.* a variation relating to the directors' powers to issue shares[44] and one connected with a reduction of capital,[45] the required majority is three quarters whatever the articles may say: 1980 Act, s.32(3).

Such modification of rights clauses must be complied with: 1980 Act, s.32(4). Any meeting held must comply with the 1948 Act as to the notice and conduct of meetings with a minimum quorum of the holders of at least one third in nominal value of the class being at least two in number: 1980 Act, s.32(6).

There is no effectual sanction to a modification of class rights unless those holding a sufficient majority of the shares of the class vote in favour of the modification in the bona fide belief that they are acting in the interests of the general body of members of the class, *i.e.* at the class meeting the majority shareholders must consider what is best for the shareholders as a class, not what is best in their own interests.

A reduction of capital was to be effected by cancelling the five per cent. £1 cumulative preference shares and allotting the holders an equivalent amount of six per cent. unsecured loan stock repayable 1985/90. The majority of the preference shareholders, who supported the reduction, were also holders of 52 per cent. of the company's ordinary stock and non-voting ordinary shares. Minority preference shareholders opposed the reduction. The court refused to confirm it. The majority preference shareholders had considered what was

---

[43] *Ante*, p. 108.
[44] *Ante*, p. 165.
[45] *Post*, p. 229.

best in their own interests, based on their large equity shareholding, without considering what was best for preference shareholders as a class. Further, the reduction was unfair[46]—the advantages of the exchange into unsecured stock did not compensate for the disadvantages: *Re Holders Investment Trust Ltd.* [1971] 1 W.L.R. 582.

4. *Where there is in the articles (or the memorandum) a power to vary class rights, the exercise of the power is subject to section 72.* This section provides that if, in the case of a company with a share capital divided into different classes of shares, provision is made by the articles (or memorandum) for the variation or abrogation of the rights attached to any class of shares, subject to the consent of a specified proportion of the holders of the shares of the class or the sanction of a resolution passed at a separate meeting of the holders of such shares, and in pursuance of such provision the rights attached to any such class of shares are varied, an application can be made to the court to have the variation cancelled, whereupon it has no effect unless and until it is confirmed by the court.

Those who can apply are the holders of not less in the aggregate than 15 per cent. of the issued shares of the class who did not consent to or vote for the variation. The application must be made within 21 days after the giving of the consent or the passing of the resolution. In England it is made by petition by one or more of the dissenting shareholders authorised in writing by the 15 per cent.: R.S.C., Ord. 102, r.5. For Scotland, see R.C. 190.

The court may disallow the variation if, after hearing the various parties interested, it is satisfied that the variation would unfairly prejudice the shareholders of the class in question. If the court is not so satisfied it must confirm the variation.

The company must, within 15 days, send a copy of the order made by the court to the Registrar of Companies: section 72(5).

The object of the section is to protect shareholders from being prejudiced by the voting of other shareholders who hold shares of another class in addition to those of the class affected by the variation.

For example, if a variation reduces the dividend on preference shares from seven per cent. to six per cent. per annum, and 80 per cent. of the preference shareholders are also ordinary shareholders, the requisite consent of the preference shareholders is likely to be obtained, since the variation will leave more profits for a dividend on the ordinary shares. This would be unfair to the

---

[46] *Post,* p. 232.

20 per cent. of the preference shareholders who are not ordinary shareholders and they could apply under section 72.

A variation of class rights includes an abrogation of those rights: 1980 Act, s.32(9).[47] However it has been held that class rights are *not* "varied" by the subdivision of other shares, under a power in the articles, which results in the holders of the shares with the class rights being outvoted by the holders of the other shares.

2s. ordinary shares, as regards voting, ranked *pari passu* with the 10s. ordinary shares. Each 10s. share was sub-divided into 5 2s. ordinary shares. *Held,* the voting rights of the original 2s. shares had not been varied. The only voting right attached to that class was one vote per share, and that right remained: *Greenhalgh* v. *Arderne Cinemas Ltd.* [1946] 1 All E.R. 512 (C.A.).[48]

Again, class rights are *not* "affected" by the creation or issue of new shares of the class ranking equally with the old.

Capital was being increased by the issue of 660,000 £1 preference shares ranking *pari passu* with the existing 600,000 £1 preference stock, and 2,640,000 ordinary shares of 10s. each ranking *pari passu* with the existing £3,300,000 ordinary stock. The new shares were to be issued to the ordinary stockholders and paid for out of the reserve fund. *Held,* the proposed issue of new capital did not "affect" the rights of the existing preference shareholders. Only the enjoyment of the rights was affected, the rights themselves were not: *White* v. *Bristol Aeroplane Co. Ltd.* [1953] Ch. 65 (C.A.).[49]

Table A, article 5, states that, unless otherwise expressly provided by the terms of issue of a class of shares, the creation or issue of further shares ranking *pari passu* with the shares of the class is *not* a variation of the class rights.

A modification of rights clause in the articles cannot be altered by special resolution without the appropriate consent of shareholders of the class—a class right, that special rights of the class of shares will only be varied in accordance with the clause, is attached to the shares in question: 1980 Act, s.32(7).

If, in a rare case, class rights are set out in the articles but the articles do not contain a modification of rights clause, the rights can be varied either by the written consent of the holders of three quarters of the

---

[47] In accordance with the decision of the Court of Session in *Frazer Brothers Ltd., Petitioners,* 1963 S.C. 139.

[48] And see the *Dimbula* case, *ante,* p. 216.

[49] And see *Re John Smith's Tadcaster Brewery Co. Ltd.* [1953] Ch. 308.

issued shares of that class or by an extraordinary resolution to that effect passed at a separate meeting of that class: 1980 Act, s.32(2). The 1948 Act rules as to meetings apply and there must be a quorum of two people holding at least one third of the issued shares of that class: 1980 Act, s.32(6). Section 72 applies to such variations as if a specific modification of rights clause had been incorporated into the articles: 1980 Act, s.32(8). This implied variation procedure adopts a recommendation of the Jenkins Committee.[50]

Deferred shares

Deferred shares, which are sometimes called founders or management shares, are usually of small nominal amount with a right to take the whole or a proportion of the profits after a fixed dividend has been paid on the ordinary shares. The rights of the holders of deferred shares depend on the articles or the terms of issue.

The number of founders or management or deferred shares, and the nature and extent of the interest of the holders in the property and profits of the company, must be set out in a prospectus: Schedule 4.

Deferred shares are rarely issued now and the modern tendency is to convert existing deferred shares into ordinary shares.

Non-voting ordinary shares

In recent years a few companies have issued non-voting ordinary shares. The purpose of such issues was to enable the companies concerned to raise money and at the same time enable those with the majority of the existing voting shares to retain control. However, with the idea of ensuring that the public is not misled, The Stock Exchange requires non-voting shares to be designated as such.[51] This is usually done by describing the shares as A Ordinary shares, etc.

The Jenkins Report[52] recommended that holders of voteless equity[53] shares should receive notices of general meetings and a copy of any chairman's statement which is circulated with the accounts.

---

[50] Para. 198.
[51] Admission of Securities to Listing, p. 164.
[52] Para. 140.
[53] *Ante*, p. 52.

No par value shares

The memorandum of a limited company with a share capital must state the amount of share capital with which the company proposes to be registered and its division into shares of a fixed amount (s.2), and any provision in the memorandum or articles, or in any resolution, of a company limited by guarantee purporting to divide the undertaking into shares or interests is treated as a provision for a share capital, notwithstanding that the nominal amount or number of the shares or interests is not specified thereby (s.21). The requirement that the nominal share capital must be divided into shares of a fixed amount means that *shares of no par value cannot be issued.*

Such shares would not give rise to the misleading impression which is often created by the nominal or par value of shares. After a company has been in existence for any length of time, the nominal value of the shares rarely bears any relation to the real value, and so gives no assistance to investors or creditors. For example, after some years, a share of a nominal amount of £1 issued at a price of £1 may be worth £2. Further, if dividends are expressed as a percentage of the nominal value of such share, where the real return is, say, six per cent. on the market value of the share, the dividend will be expressed as 12 per cent. of the nominal value, and this may give rise to the mistaken impression that the dividend is excessive.

The Report of the majority of the Gedge Committee[54] recommended that companies should be able to issue ordinary shares of no par value if they wished, and the Jenkins Report[55] recommended[56] the amendment of the Companies Act to allow the issue of preference and ordinary shares of no par value, but, as yet, effect has not been given to these recommendations. Shares of no par value can be issued in a number of countries, including America.

Employees' shares

Some companies issue special shares to their employees. Modern tax legislation, however, only provides tax incentives for companies

[54] (1954) Cmd. 9112.
[55] (1962) Cmnd. 1749.
[56] Para. 34.

who provide their employees with ordinary shares, *i.e.* those not
specifically available only to employees.[57]

The issued share capital of a company is the fund to which creditors of
the company can look for payment of their debts and so, to protect the
creditors, it has been held that that share capital must be raised. This
means that shares can be treated as paid up only to the extent of the
amount actually received by the company in cash or in kind, and must
not be issued at a discount, *i.e.* must not be issued as fully paid for a
consideration less than payment or the promise of payment of the
nominal amount of each share,[58] although the company may not
require payment in full of the nominal amount on allotment. The rule
that the share capital must be raised is intended to ensure that money
or assets equal in amount or value to the paid-up capital on paper is or
are received by the company. Certain sections of the Act, *e.g.* section
53(2), which generally prohibits the payment of commissions and
discounts out of a company's shares or capital money,[59] and section 27,
which provides that a subsidiary company generally may not be a
member of its holding company,[60] also have the effect of ensuring that
the capital is raised. The provisions in the 1980 Act relating to payment
for share capital were intended to strengthen this rule.[61] It will be seen,
however, that the sections 42–44 of the 1981 Act[62] allow companies
considerable scope to assist in the acquisition of their own shares and
may prove to be a negative factor in ensuring the raising of capital. Of
course, the rule is no protection to creditors where a company does not
make a substantial issue of share capital.

There are certain exceptions to the rule that the share capital must
be raised. These exceptions have been explained already and are,
briefly:

[57] *Pinson, op. cit.*, para. 3–20A.
[58] *Ooregum Gold Mining Co.* v. *Roper* [1892] A.C. 125, codified by 1980 Act, s.21,
    ante, p. 169.
[59] *Ante*, p. 159.
[60] *Ante*, p. 190.
[61] *Ante*, p. 169.
[62] *Post*, Chap. 13.

(1) where shares are issued by a private company for an over-valued non-monetary consideration, as in *Re Wragg Ltd.*[63];

(2) where a company pays a commission under section 53(1) to a person who agrees to subscribe, or to procure subscriptions, for shares in the company.[64]

The rule does not apply to an unlimited company.[65]

ALTERATION OF SHARE CAPITAL

Section 61 provides that a limited company with a share capital, if so authorised by its articles, may alter the conditions of its memorandum by—

(1) increasing its share capital by new shares; or

(2) consolidating and dividing all or any of its share capital into shares of larger amount than its existing shares; or

(3) converting all or any of its paid-up shares into stock, or reconverting stock into paid-up shares of any denomination; or

(4) subdividing all or any of its shares into shares of smaller amount than is fixed by the memorandum; or

(5) cancelling shares which have not been taken or agreed to be taken by any person. (This is called "diminution of capital" and it should not be confused with reduction of capital which will be explained later.[66])

All these powers require for their exercise a resolution of the company in general meeting.

It was noted in Chapter 3[67] that a change in the description of a share from, say, 5s. to 25p. is not an alteration of a condition in the memorandum so that no formalities are required by the Act.

Increase of capital

Every increase of capital, *i.e.* nominal capital, must be effected by the company in general meeting: section 61. If the articles authorise the

---

[63] [1897] 1 Ch. 796 (C.A.), *ante*, p. 173. *cf. Waterhouse* v. *Jamieson* (1870) 8 M. (H.L.) 88 and *Penang Foundry Co. Ltd.* v. *Gardiner*, 1913 S.C. 1203 (O.H.).

[64] *Ante*, p. 159.

[65] See *Nelson Mitchell* v. *City of Glasgow Bank* (1879) 6 R. (H.L.) 66; (1878) 6 R. 420, *ante*, p. 40.

[66] *Post*, p. 229.   [67] *Ante*, p. 94.

increase of capital, whether an ordinary or a special resolution is required depends on the articles.

Table A, article 44, provides: "The company may from time to time by *ordinary* resolution increase the share capital by such sum, to be divided into shares of such amount, as the resolution shall prescribe."

If the articles do not give authority to increase capital, the articles must be altered by special resolution so that they do give authority but the one special resolution can both authorise and effect an increase.[68]

The notice convening the meeting must specify the amount of the proposed increase.[69] Within 15 days after the passing of the resolution effecting the increase, a notice in the prescribed form of the amount of the increase must be filed with the Registrar (s.63). A printed copy of the resolution effecting the increase, or a copy in some other form approved by him, must also be filed with the Registrar (1948 Act, s.63; 1967 Act, s.51). The processes which the Registrar is prepared to regard as satisfying the printing requirement have been noted already.[70]

The conditions on which the new shares are held are set out in the terms of issue. The articles usually provide that they shall be subject to the same provisions with reference to the payment of calls, lien, transfer, transmission, forfeiture, and otherwise as the shares in the original share capital.

Consolidation of shares

This takes place when several shares are consolidated into one, *e.g.* when 20 5p. shares are consolidated into one £1 share. Consolidation is effected in the same way as an increase of capital (s.61), *i.e.* if the articles authorise consolidation, the resolution specified in the articles must be passed. If the articles are silent, a special resolution to give authority and to effect the consolidation is necessary. Table A, article 45, requires an ordinary resolution. Notice must be given to the Registrar within a month of the consolidation (s.62).

Conversion of shares into stock

The difference between stock and shares was described by Lord Hatherley as follows: "Shares in a company, as shares, cannot be

---

[68] *Campbell's Case* (1873) l.R. 9 Ch.App. 1.
[69] *MacConnell* v. *E. Prill & Co. Ltd.* [1916] 2 Ch. 57. [70] p. 104.

bought in small fractions of any amount, fractions of less than a pound,[71] but the consolidated stock of a company can be bought just in the same way as the stock of the public debt can be bought, split up into as many portions as you like, and subdivided into as small fractions as you please." He also referred to stock as "simply a set of shares put together in a bundle."[72]

A company *cannot issue stock directly* but can only convert shares into stock under section 61, although there seems to be no reason for this rule today. The conversion can only be made if the shares are fully paid (s.61).

A company had fully paid-up ordinary and preference shares. It then (1) converted its ordinary and preference shares into stock; (2) gave the holders of preference stock carrying a lower rate of dividend extra bonus stock to maintain their former dividends; (3) made a direct issue of new fully paid-up ordinary and preference stock for cash, and (4) issued new partly paid-up ordinary and preference stock. Many years after these issues were made, the company went into liquidation and, after the creditors were paid, there was a surplus to distribute among the members. *Held*, (a) that the bonus stock was *ultra vires* and void, and no distribution could be made in respect of it; (b) that the direct issue of new stock was irregular, but having regard to the lapse of time the irregularity had to be treated as waived, and the holders were entitled to rank for distribution in respect of it; (c) that the partly paid-up stock was *ultra vires* and void and in the same position as the bonus stock; and (d) that the owners of the bonus and the partly paid-up stock were not liable for any calls: *Re Home and Foreign Investment, etc., Co. Ltd.* [1912] 1 Ch. 72.

The conversion of shares into stock (or a reconversion of stock into shares) is effected in the same way as an increase of capital (s.61). Table A, article 40, provides that the conversion of shares into stock and the reconversion of stock into shares shall be effected by ordinary resolution. Notice must be given to the Registrar within a month (s.62).

Although in theory stock can be transferred in fractional amounts, in practice the articles usually confer on the directors power to fix the minimum amount transferable. Table A, article 41, gives the directors this power, and provides that such minimum is not to exceed the nominal amount of the shares from which the stock arose. Thus, if the

---

[71] This only refers to the shares of the particular company under discussion. The nominal value of shares may be less than a pound.
[72] In *Morrice* v. *Aylmer* (1875) L.R. 7 H.L. 717 at pp. 724, 725.

shares were £1 shares, the minimum amount of stock transferable must not exceed £1's worth.

The method of transferring stock is laid down in the articles. Table A, article 41, provides that stock may be transferred in the same manner and subject to the same regulations as the shares from which the stock arose might previously to conversion have been transferred. Article 42 provides that stockholers shall, according to the amount of their stock, have the same rights, privileges and advantages as regards dividends, voting at meetings of the company and other matters as if the conversion had not taken place.

When shares are converted into stock the register of members must show the amount of stock held by each member: section 110. Stock certificates similar in form to share certificates must be issued except that stock warrants transferable by delivery may be issued if the articles so provide.[73]

When shares have been converted into stock the annual return must state the amount of stock held by each member: section 124.

The advantage of converting shares into stock was that the work caused by the fact that each share had a separate number was obviated. However, this advantage is now minimised by the proviso to section 74, under which shares need not have a distinguishing number.[74]

The distinctions between shares and stock can be summarised as follows:

(1) Shares are in units, whereas stock is in a lump holding.
(2) Shares can be issued directly; stock cannot be issued directly.
(3) Shares need not be fully paid; stock must be fully paid.
(4) Shares may be numbered; stock is never numbered.
(5) Shares cannot be transferred in fractional amounts; stock can be so transferred (although there may be a minimum fractional amount of stock which can be transferred).

Subdivision of shares

This is the division of shares into shares of smaller amount, *e.g.* the division of one £1 share into 20 5p. shares, and it is often resorted to for

[73] *Pilkington* v. *United Railways of The Havana etc. Warehouses Ltd.* [1930] 2 Ch. 108.
[74] *Post*, p. 261.

the purpose of improving the marketability of expensive shares. Subdivision is effected in the same way as an increase of capital: section 61. Table A, article 45, requires an ordinary resolution. If the shares are not fully paid up, the proportion between the amount paid and the amount unpaid on each reduced share must be the same as it was in the case of the share from which the reduced share is derived (s.61). The subdivision of shares must be registered with the Registrar within a month (s.62).

Cancellation of unissued shares

A company can cancel shares which have not been taken or agreed to be taken by any person, and *diminish* the amount of its nominal share capital by the amount of the shares so cancelled. This is not to be deemed a reduction of share capital[75] (s.61(3)). Cancellation is effected in the same way as an increase of capital: section 61. Table A, article 45, requires an ordinary resolution. Notice of cancellation must be registered with the Registrar within a month (s.62).

MAINTENANCE OF SHARE CAPITAL

It is a fundamental principle of company law that the share capital must be maintained. It has been said that "the whole of the subscribed capital of a company with limited liability, unless diminished by expenditure upon the company's objects (or, of course, by means sanctioned by statute) shall remain available for the discharge of its liabilities."[76] The term "subscribed capital" means "issued capital." Capital may be lost as a result of ordinary business risks and, as we shall see, it may be returned to the shareholders with the consent of the court under section 66, but otherwise, subject to the 1981 Act, it must be maintained since it is the fund to which creditors of the company look for payment of their debts.[77] Except under section 66 money or assets representing the paid-up share capital could not be returned to the

---

[75] *Post*, p. 239.

[76] *Per* Kitto J. in *Davis Investments Pty. Ltd.* v. *Commissioner of Stamp Duties (N.S.W.)* (1957–58) 100 C.L.R. 392, at p. 413. And see *per* Lord Herschell at p. 415, and Lord Watson at p. 423, in *Trevor* v. *Whitworth* (1887) 12 App. Cas. 409.

[77] See, *e.g.*, *Jenkins* v. *Harbour View Courts Ltd.* [1966] N.Z.L.R. 1 (C.A.), *post*, p. 240, and *Australasian Oil Exploration Ltd.* v. *Lachberg* (1958) 101 C.L.R. 119.

members, nor could the liability of the members in respect of any share capital not paid up be reduced. Of course, capital could be returned to the members when the company is being wound up, after its debts have been paid.[78] The 1981 Act provisions relating to the purchase and redemption by a company of its own shares have affected this general rule. These provisions are set out in Chapter 12 below.

The principle that the share capital of a company must be maintained boils down to this—paid up share capital must not be returned to the members and their liability in respect of capital not paid up on their shares must not be reduced.

The principle has the following consequences:—

(1) A company generally must not purchase its own shares unless it follows the strict procedures laid down by the 1981 Act. In any event it must not be a member of itself.[79]

(2) A subsidiary company generally must not be a member of its holding company and any allotment or transfer of shares in a holding company to its subsidiary is void: section 27.[80]

(3) It is generally unlawful for a company to give any kind of financial assistance for the acquisition of its own shares or those of its holding company, by any person. There are however wide exceptions to this rule: 1981 Act, sections 42–44.[81]

(4) Dividends must not be paid to the shareholders except out of distributable profits as defined by the 1980 Act.[82]

(5) Where a public company suffers a serious loss of capital, *i.e.* of more than half the subscribed capital, a meeting of the company must be called to discuss the issue.[83]

There are certain exceptions to the principle:—

(1) A company may reduce its share capital with the consent of the court under section 66, *post.*[84]

(2) A company may purchase or redeem its shares under Part III of the 1981 Act.[85]

---

[78] *Post*, p. 668.
[79] *Post*, p. 245.
[80] *Ante*, p. 190.
[81] *Post*, Chap. 13.
[82] *Post*, p. 532.
[83] *Post*, p. 241.
[84] p. 229.
[85] *Post*, p. 244.

(3) A company may purchase its own shares under a court order made either under section 75 of the 1980 Act to relieve an unfairly prejudiced minority[86] or section 11 of that Act to relieve a minority on the conversion of a public company to a private company.

(4) Capital may be returned to the members, after the company's debts have been paid, in a winding up.[78]

Other exceptions are forfeiture of shares and surrender to avoid a forfeiture, although here the amount paid on the shares remains with the company when the shareholder unable to pay a call is relieved of liability for future calls, and the shares revert to the company, bear no dividend and must either be re-issued or cancelled.[87]

Finally, the principle as to maintenance of share capital has been extended:—

(1) By section 53 of the 1981 Act, to a capital redemption reserve set up when redeemable shares are redeemed or other shares purchased by the company out of profits.[88]

(2) By section 56, to a share premium account.[89]

A company limited by guarantee and not having a share capital is subject to the principle of raising and maintenance of capital as far as the guarantee fund is concerned. The principle as applied to such a company is stricter than as applied to the company limited by shares, since in the latter type of company the principle does not prevent the creation of security over called or uncalled capital.[90]

The principle does not apply to an unlimited company.[91]

REDUCTION OF CAPITAL

The share capital of the company must be subscribed in money or money's worth. This capital may be lost or diminished according to the

[86] *Post*, p. 413.
[87] *Per* Lord Herschell at p. 417, and Lord Watson at p. 424, in *Trevor* v. *Whitworth*, *supra*.
[88] *Post*, p. 248.
[89] *Ante*, p. 176.
[90] *Robertson* v. *British Linen Co.* (1890) 18 R. 1225 (O.H.); approved *obiter* in *Lloyds Bank Ltd.* v. *Morrison & Son*, 1927 S.C. 571.
[91] *Nelson Mitchell* v. *City of Glasgow Bank* (1879) 6 R. (H.L.) 66; (1878) 6 R. 420.

fluctuations of the business, but otherwise, subject to the 1981 Act, it generally cannot be reduced without the sanction of the court. The object of requiring this sanction is threefold—(1) to protect persons dealing with the company, so that the fund available for satisfying their claims shall not be diminished except by ordinary business risks; (2) to ensure that the reduction is equitable as between the various classes of shareholders in the company; (3) to protect the interests of the public.[92]

Reduction procedure

Section 66 provides that, subject to confirmation by the court, a limited company with a share capital may, if authorised by its articles, by *special* resolution, reduce its share capital and, if and so far as is necessary, alter its memorandum by reducing the amount of its share capital and of its shares.

"The court," in relation to a company, means the court with jurisdiction to wind up the company: section 455. The courts with jurisdiction to wind up a company are set out in sections 218 and 220 and will be dealt with later.[93] The application for confirmation is by petition: R.S.C., O. 102, r.5 (England); R.C., 190 (Scotland).[94]

Power to reduce must be given in the articles; power in the memorandum is not effective.[95] The power must be a specific power to reduce.[96]

Table A, article 46, provides: "The company may by special resolution reduce its share capital, any capital redemption reserve fund or any share premium account in any manner and with, and subject to, any incident authorised, and consent required, by law."

---

[92] *Per* Lord Watson in *Trevor* v. *Whitworth* (1887) 12 App.Cas. 409, at p. 423; *per* Lord Macnaghten in *British and American Finance Corporation Ltd.* v. *Couper* [1894] A.C. 399 at p. 411.

[93] *Post*, p. 605.

[94] In Scotland the petition is presented to the Inner House of the Court of Session and, as a rule, a remit is made by the court to a "reporter" (a man of business, usually a solicitor of standing) who scrutinises the proposed reduction and draws the attention of the court to any doubtful points; the court may dispense with a remit to a "reporter," as in *Fowlers (Aberdeen) Ltd., Petitioners*, 1928 S.C. 186, and *Scottish Stamping etc. Co. Ltd., Petitioners*, 1928 S.C. 484, but only on sufficient cause being shown for departure from the ordinary practice: *J. Hay & Sons Ltd., Petitioners*, 1928 S.C. 622.

[95] *Re Dexine Rubber Co.* [1903] W.N. 82.

[96] *John Avery & Co. Ltd., Petitioners* (1890) 17 R. 1101.

If the articles do not authorise the reduction of capital, *two* special resolutions—one to alter the articles so as to give authority and the other to effect the reduction—will be necessary, in addition to the consent of the court.[97]

The court cannot condone a reduction which has been carried out without its prior approval.[98] The resolution must be in the correct form and comply with the requirements of section 141 as to notice.[99]

Stock[1] may be reduced without being first converted into shares.[2] Reserve liability, *i.e.* capital which can only be called up on a winding up of the company, may also be reduced.[3]

Cases of reduction

The power to reduce capital given by section 66 is general, *i.e.* if the proper procedure is adopted a company can reduce its share capital in any case. However, the section specifies three particular cases of reduction—

(1) the extinction or reduction of the liability on shares in respect of capital not paid up;

(2) with or without the extinction or reduction of liability on shares, the cancellation of paid-up share capital which is lost or unrepresented by available assets;

(3) with or without the extinction or reduction of liability on shares, the payment off of any paid-up share capital which is in excess of the wants of the company.

For example, if a company has more than enough capital, it may reduce the nominal amount of shares by repaying paid-up capital, as where fully paid shares of a nominal amount of £5 each are reduced to £2 fully paid shares and £3 is paid back on each share. This would reduce the company's nominal, issued and paid-up capital and, so far as the nominal capital and the nominal amount of the shares are

---

[97] *Re Patent Invert Sugar Co.* (1885) 31 Ch.D. 166 (C.A.); *Oregon Mortgage Co. Ltd., Petitioners,* 1910 S.C. 964.

[98] *Alexander Henderson Ltd., Petitioners,* 1967 S.L.T. (Notes) 17.

[99] *Re Moorgate Mercantile Holdings Ltd.* [1980] 1 All E.R. 40.

[1] *Ante,* p. 224.

[2] *Re House Property and Investment Co.* [1912] W.N. 10; *cf. Doloi Tea Co. Ltd., Petitioners,* 1961 S.L.T. 168.

[3] *Re Midland Rlwy. Carriage Co.* (1907) 23 T.L.R. 661.

concerned, alter the memorandum. In one case 10 per cent. of the capital was returned on the footing that the amount returned could be called up again.[4]

A return of capital to shareholders may, in some cases, be taxed as a dividend[5]; however it will normally rank as a disposal or part disposal for the purpose of Capital Gains tax, by the shareholder of his shares.

A return of capital may be at a premium.

A reduction of capital involved repaying the capital paid-up on each of the company's preference shares of 10s. each plus a premium of 5s. per share. The court confirmed the reduction: *Re Saltdean Estate Co. Ltd.* [1968] 1 W.L.R. 1844.

A reduction may involve the company paying off part of its share capital not with money but by transferring to the shareholders shares of another company.[6]

Moneys withdrawn from the capital and set free by the reduction can be employed in the purchase of the company's own shares which it is intended to extinguish.[7]

The reduction procedure cannot be used as a device to raise new capital to replace capital which has disappeared, *e.g.* by the conversion of £1 fully paid shares into £1 shares with only 75p. paid, thus imposing an additional liability on shareholders.[8]

Questions for the court on reduction

Subject to the discretion conferred on the court by section 66 and the statutory provisions for the protection of creditors, *post,* whether there should be a reduction of capital and, if so, how it should be effected, is a domestic question for the prescribed majority of the shareholders to decide.[9] The court should sanction a reduction unless what is proposed

---

[4] *Scottish Vulcanite Co. Ltd., Petitioners* (1894) 21 R. 752. *cf. William Brown Sons & Co. Ltd., Petitioners*, 1931 S.C. 701, and *Stevensons, Anderson & Co. Ltd., Petitioners*, 1951 S.C. 346.

[5] See *Pinson, op. cit.*, para. 14–40.

[6] *Westburn Sugar Refineries Ltd., Petitioners*, 1951 S.C. (H.L.) 57; [1951] A.C. 625.

[7] *Per* Lord Macnaghten in *British and American Finance Corporation* v. *Couper* [1894] A.C. 399, at p. 414.

[8] See s.22, and also *W. Morrison & Co. Ltd., Petitioners* (1892) 19 R. 1049.

[9] *British and American Finance Corpn.* v. *Couper* [1894] A.C. 399. See Lord President Inglis in *Hoggan* v. *Tharsis Sulphur etc. Co. Ltd.* (1882) 9 R. 1191, at p. 1212.

to be done is unfair or inequitable in the interests of (1) the creditors, (2) the shareholders and (3) the public who may have dealings with the company or may invest in its securities.[10] When creditors are not concerned (because the reduction does not involve the diminution of any liability in respect of unpaid capital or the payment to any shareholder of any paid-up capital) the questions to be considered by the court are:

(1) Ought the court to refuse its sanction to the reduction out of regard to the interests of those members of the public who may be induced to take shares in the company?

(2) Is the reduction fair and equitable as between the different classes of shareholders?[11]

In considering what is fair as between different classes of shareholders, the court proceeds upon the basis that a reduction is a sort of anticipation to a limited extent of what would take place in a winding up, *i.e.* the various classes of shareholders have the rights which they would have in a liquidation. Accordingly, if capital is lost, the loss should, prima facie, fall upon all the shareholders equally if their rights in respect of capital are equal. If, therefore, preference shareholders are only preferential as to dividend and not as to capital, a reduction of capital should be borne rateably by the preference and the ordinary shareholders.[12] On the other hand, if on a winding up the preference shareholders are entitled to preference as to capital, the ordinary shares should normally bear the loss first.[13]

If, under the memorandum and articles, preference shareholders have no priority as to capital and no voting power but are merely entitled to a fixed cumulative preference dividend on the amount paid up on their shares, a rateable reduction on all the shares, preference and ordinary, cancelling lost paid-up capital, though diminishing the preference dividend, is not an alteration of the rights of the preference shareholders so as to require their sanction under an ordinary modification of rights clause: *Re Mackenzie & Co. Ltd.* [1916] 2 Ch. 450.

---

[10] *Westburn Sugar Refineries Ltd., Petitioners,* 1951 S.C. (H.L.) 57; [1951] A.C. 625.
[11] *Poole* v. *National Bank of China Ltd.* [1907] A.C. 229. See Lord Parker of Waddington in *Caldwell & Co. Ltd.* v. *Caldwell,* 1916 S.C. (H.L.) 120, at p. 121.
[12] *Bannatyne* v. *Direct Spanish Telegraph Co.* (1886) 34 Ch.D. 287 (C.A.).
[13] *Re Floating Dock Co. of St. Thomas Ltd.* [1895] 1 Ch. 691. For exceptional circumstances where a different scheme of reduction was held just and equitable see *Balmenach-Glenlivet Distillery Ltd.* v. *Croall* (1906) 8 F. 1135.

When liability on shares is being extinguished or reduced, the proper capital to reduce in the first instance, is the unpaid capital (if any).[13a]

When capital is being returned as surplus to the company's requirements, it should normally[14] be returned first to the class of shareholders with priority as to capital in a winding up,[15] at any rate where preference shares are not entitled to participate in surplus assets.[16]

A coal company with a capital of £400,000, half of which was in ordinary shares and half in 6 per cent. preference shares, had a surplus of capital as a result of nationalisation. A special resolution was passed reducing the capital by paying off the preference shares. By the articles, the preference shareholders in the event of a winding up had a right to priority of repayment of capital *but no further right to participate in the surplus assets. Held*, the reduction should be confirmed as fair and equitable, the preference shareholders having no right to a continuance of their rate of dividend during the life of the company if the company desired and had the means to pay them off. The preference shareholders were being treated in accordance with their rights and it was immaterial that the elimination of their shares extinguished any hopes which they had of obtaining some additional advantage as a result of regulations to be made under the Coal Industry Nationalisation Act 1946, s.25: *Prudential Assurance Co. Ltd.* v. *Chatterley-Whitfield Collieries Ltd.* [1949] A.C. 512.

It is not necessary for the company to show by how much its capital is surplus to its requirements. "Public policy" is not a ground for the court's refusing to confirm a reduction which is otherwise unobjectionable, *e.g.* reduction may be confirmed although the motive for it may have been avoidance of the consequences of possible future nationalisation,[17] or minimisation of tax liability.[18]

A modification of rights clause in the articles has no application to a cancellation of shares on a reduction of capital which is in accord with the rights attached to the shares.[19]

[13a] *Per* Lord President Inglis in *Hoggan* v. *Tharsis Sulphur etc. Co. Ltd.* (1882) 9 R. 1191, at p. 1211.

[14] But not always: see *William Dixon Ltd., Petitioners*, 1948 S.C. 511.

[15] *Wilsons and Clyde Coal Co. Ltd.* v. *Scottish Insurance Corporation Ltd.*, 1949 S.C. (H.L.) 90; 1948 S.C. 360; *Prudential Assurance Co. Ltd.* v. *Chatterley-Whitfield Collieries Ltd.* [1949] A.C. 512.

[16] *Per* Lord Greene M.R. in the *Prudential* case, *supra*, in the Court of Appeal [1948] 2 All E.R. 593, at pp. 596, 600.

[17] See note 10, above.

[18] *David Bell Ltd., Petitioners*, 1954 S.C. 33.

[19] *Re Saltdean Estate Co. Ltd.* [1968] 1 W.L.R. 1844, *ante*, p. 232.

If a modification of rights clause in the articles provides that the special rights of the holders of any class of shares can be modified with the sanction of a specified majority of the shareholders of that class, a reduction modifying such rights which is so sanctioned will be approved unless it is unfair or has been sanctioned by the influence of some improper or extraneous consideration.[20] The burden of proving that the reduction is unfair lies on those who oppose it.[21] (If the proper sanction is not obtained the burden of proving that the reduction is fair lies on those in favour.)[21]

A company had an authorised capital of £95,000,000 divided into £1 ordinary, £1 preference and 10s. deferred shares. It was proposed to reduce the capital to £89,565,859 by cancelling half the amount of each of the 10s. deferred shares and then converting and consolidating each four deferred shares into one £1 ordinary share. The articles required any alteration of the rights of any class of shareholder to be approved by a meeting of the members of that class. Notices were sent out summoning an extraordinary general meeting of the shareholders, a class meeting of the ordinary shareholders and a class meeting of the deferred shareholders, at the same time and place. The resolutions sanctioning the proposed reduction were passed at each of the meetings. At the deferred shareholders' meeting the ordinary shareholders were present but neither spoke nor voted at the meeting and no objection was made to their presence. *Held*, (1) the objection which might have been taken by the deferred shareholders to the presence of the ordinary shareholders at their meeting had been waived, (2) as the reduction was approved by the deferred shareholders at their meeting they could not complain that it was unfair in the absence of proof that their interests were unfairly overridden by persons with other and conflicting interests (such as persons who held both ordinary and deferred shares), (3) on the evidence, the deferred shareholders were not unfairly treated for the benefit of the ordinary shareholders, and therefore (4) the reduction should be confirmed: *Carruth* v. *I.C.I. Ltd.* [1937] A.C. 707.

However, if a reduction of capital involves a variation of class rights, and a modification of rights clause in the articles is not complied with, the court will refuse to confirm the reduction.

A colliery company was nationalised and its assets vested in the National Coal Board. A reduction of capital, by the repayment of part of the capital paid up on preference shares, expressly reserved any rights which the

---

[20] *Re Welsbach Incandescent Gas Light Co. Ltd.* [1904] 1 Ch. 87 (C.A.). A scheme of arrangement is not necessary: *Oban and Aultmore-Glenlivet Distilleries Ltd., Petitioners* (1903) 5 F. 1140, and *Marshall, Fleming & Co. Ltd., Petitioners*, 1938 S.C. 873 (O.H.).

[21] *Re Holders Investment Trust Ltd.* [1971] 1 W.L.R. 583, *ante*, p. 217.

preference shareholders might have as a result of regulations (for the adjustment of rights as between preference and ordinary shareholders) to be made under the Coal Industry Nationalisation Act 1946, s.25, until the amount of the compensation payable to the company had been determined. When the directors later formed the opinion that such rights had no monetary value the court refused to confirm a later reduction by the repayment of the rest of the capital paid up on the preference shares. The first reduction attached a special right to the preference shares and the sanction of the preference shareholders, necessary under the modification of rights clause in the articles, had not been obtained to the second reduction, which reduction would have had the effect of extinguishing the special right: *Re Old Silkstone Collieries Ltd.* [1954] Ch. 169 (C.A.).[22]

In one case, where there were special circumstances, a reduction involving a variation of class rights was confirmed although no class meeting of the class of shareholders (the preference shareholders) had been held—no one objected, there was no prospect of liquidation (when the preference shareholders had the right to participate in surplus assets after repayment of capital), and the preference shareholders received more than they would have received by selling.[23]

When one part of a class of equity shareholders is treated differently from another, the usual practice is to proceed by scheme of arrangement under section 206, under which the interests of the minority are better protected.[24]

In England, where reduction is sought on the ground that capital has been lost or is not represented by available assets, evidence of the loss or that the available assets do not represent the capital must be given.[25] A reduction may be confirmed where capital has been lost but it is still represented by available assets.

A company had built up a reserve fund. It had incurred a loss arising from the depreciation in the value of its public-houses below the amount stated in the balance sheet, and it proposed to reduce its capital by apportioning the loss between its capital account and the reserve. *Held*, the loss ought to be rateably apportioned between the capital account and the reserve, and the company was not bound to apply the whole of its reserve to wipe out the loss: *Re Hoare & Co. Ltd.* [1904] 2 Ch. 208 (C.A.).

[22] See also *Frazer Brothers Ltd., Petitioners,* 1963 S.C. 139.
[23] *Re William Jones & Sons Ltd.* [1969] 1 W.L.R. 146.
[24] *Re Robert Stephen Holdings Ltd.* [1968] 1 W.L.R. 522.
[25] *Per* Lord Parker of Waddington in *Caldwell & Co. Ltd.* v. *Caldwell,* 1916 S.C. (H.L.) 120 at p. 121. Scottish courts dispense with such evidence where there is no reason to suspect the bona fides of the parties: *Caldwell's* case.

Creditors' right to object to reduction

If a proposed reduction of share capital involves either (1) diminution of liability in respect of unpaid share capital, or (2) payment to any
shareholder of any paid-up capital,[26] and (3) in any other case where
the court so directs, creditors who, if the company were being wound
up, would be able to prove against it, are entitled to object to the
reduction. For this purpose the court must settle a list of creditors, with
the nature and amount of their claims, and may publish notices fixing a
day by which creditors not entered on the list are to claim to be
entered. Such of the creditors as do not consent to the reduction must
be paid off, or the company must secure payment of their claims by
appropriating such amount as the court directs: section 67. In special
circumstances the court may dispense with these requirements: section
67(3). The court might dispense with the requirements where the
company has sufficient cash, trustee securities and good sundry
debtors[27] to more than cover any capital to be returned to shareholders
and the company's debts, or if the discharge of the debts is guaranteed
to the court's satisfaction, or if a simultaneous increase in capital results
in the paid-up capital being the same as it was before the reduction.[28]

Before dispensing with a list of creditors under section 67(3) the
court must be satisfied that no creditor who might be entitled to object
to the reduction would be prejudiced by it.

A company had sufficient cash resources to cover paid-up capital being paid
to preference shareholders and its liabilities but not rents prospectively payable in respect of long leases during the residues of the terms or ten years,
whichever was less, and so a direction extending to the lessors could not be
given under section 67(3): *Re Lucania Temperance Billiard Halls (London)
Ltd.* [1966] Ch. 98.[29]

In cases not within (1) and (2) above, the creditors have, prima facie,
no right to object to the proposed reduction of capital, because no asset
out of which their claims could be satisfied is being given up or returned
to the shareholders.

---

[26] Replacement of preference shares with loan stock, which has recently become a
common practice for the purposes of reducing liability to corporation tax, counts
as such payment, although the loan stock does not fall to be repaid by the company
until a future date: *Lawrie & Symington Ltd., Petitioners,* 1969 S.L.T. 221.

[27] *Anderson, Brown & Co. Ltd., Petitioners,* 1965 S.C. 81.

[28] *New Duff House Sanitarium, Petitioners,* 1931 S.L.T. 337 (O.H.); *cf. Cadzow
Coal Co. Ltd., Petitioners,* 1931 S.C. 272.

[29] *cf. Palace Billiard Rooms Ltd.* v. *City etc. Trust Corpn.,* 1912 S.C. 5.

A company had a paid-up share capital of £1,000,000, and had also issued £1,000,000 debentures secured by a trust deed constituting a floating charge. In 1904 losses to the extent of £800,000 were incurred and no dividends had since been paid, any profits being applied in reduction of the deficiency. By 1917 the deficiency had been reduced to £640,000, and the company proposed to reduce its capital to £360,000 by writing off the lost capital. The latest balance sheet showed assets worth £1,500,000. The debenture holders objected. *Held*, as the reduction involved no diminution of unpaid capital or repayment to shareholders of paid-up capital, creditors were not entitled to object unless a strong case was made out, and the debenture holders had not made out any such case: *Re Meux's Brewery Co. Ltd.* [1919] 1 Ch. 28.

The object of reducing capital, where capital has been lost or is not represented by available assets, is to enable the accounts to present a realistic picture of the company's financial positon, which may permit the company to pay dividends. To safeguard the creditors in the case of an application by a company to write off capital not lost or unrepresented by available assets, thereby setting free capital which might be distributed among the shareholders, the court is empowered by section 67 to give effect to a creditor's objection "in any other case."

Order for reduction; Minute of reduction

Confirmation by the court must precede the actual reduction of capital.[30]

On making an order confirming the reduction, the court may direct:

(1) for special reasons, that the company add the words "and reduced" to its name for a specified time.

(2) that the reasons for reduction and the causes leading to the reduction be published, with a view to giving proper information to the public (s.68).

These powers are rarely used today and the Jenkins Report recommended their repeal.[31]

Section 69 provides that the order for reduction must be produced to the Registrar, and a copy of the order and a minute approved by the court showing the amount of the share capital, the number of shares into which it is divided, the amount of each share and the amount, if any, deemed to be paid up on each share, must be registered with him.

[30] *Alexander Henderson Ltd., Petitioners*, 1967 S.L.T. (Notes) 17.
[31] Paras. 159, 187.

The Registrar then grants a certificate of registration, which is conclusive evidence of the reduction and that all the requirements of the Act with respect to reduction have been complied with—even if it is afterwards discovered that the special resolution for a reduction was not properly passed,[32] or that there was no power in the articles to reduce capital.[33] The reduction takes effect as from the date of registration. By section 143,[34] a copy of the special resolution must be forwarded to the Registrar within 15 days.

Reduction without the consent of the court

There are a number of cases in which, despite section 66, capital can be reduced without the consent of the court. Three such cases are:

(1) where, under power in the articles, shares are forfeited by the company for non-payment of a call or an instalment[35]—and in this rare case, as was stated earlier,[36] the forfeited shares may be re-issued, in which event there is no permanent reduction.

(2) where, under power in the articles, shares are surrendered to the company to avoid a forfeiture—in this rare case, too, the shares may be re-issued.[37]

(3) where a private company redeems or purchases its own shares out of capital under section 54 of the 1981 Act. In this case however there are stringent requirements for the protection of creditors.[38]

There are, however, cases in which at first sight there appears to be a reduction without consent but there is no reduction for the purposes of the Act, *e.g.*—

(1) where shares are redeemed or purchased otherwise than out of capital under sections 45 and 46 of the 1981 Act[38]—there is no real reduction, whether the shares are redeemed out of profits (because of the provisions with regard to the capital redemp-

---

[32] *Ladies' Dress Association* v. *Pullbrook* [1900] 2 Q.B. 376 (C.A.).
[33] *Re Walker and Smith Ltd.* [1903] W.N. 82.
[34] *Post*, p. 325.
[35] *Post*, p. 295.
[36] p. 229.
[37] *Post*, p. 298.
[38] *Post*, p. 249.

tion reserve) or out of the proceeds of a fresh issue of shares (because the fresh capital will replace the redeemed capital);

(2) where unissued shares are cancelled under section 61[39]—there is no real reduction because the issued capital is not reduced.

An example of an improper reduction of capital is the New Zealand case of *Jenkins* v. *Harbour View Courts Ltd.*[40] where the articles provided that each A class share should confer on the holder a right to occupy a flat in a block owned by the company on the terms of a lease in the schedule. The aggregate annual rentals were not to exceed the sum necessary to provide for rates, insurance and other outgoings as well as management and maintenance of the block. The plaintiff took 3,580 ordinary shares of £1 each and one A class share for which he paid £3,580. Since substantially the block was to be made the subject of leases for 99 years to shareholders for no rent in the form of landlord's reward to the company, this was held to be just as much an illegal return of capital to shareholders as if, from a fund of money, a substantial part was distributed among them. It made no difference that the plantiff by a different transaction might for the same expenditure have purchased a valid lease of her flat if the agreement between the company and the shareholder had been for the "purchase" and allotment of one share followed by a purchase for £3,580 of the lease.[41]

As to the liability of the officers responsible and of the shareholders concerned in the event of an illegal reduction of capital, see what is said later[42] as to the effect of paying dividends out of non-distributable profits.

Reduction below authorised minimum capital

Where the court confirms a reduction of capital of a public company which has the effect of bringing the nominal value of the company's allotted share capital below the authorised minimum capital[43] this will only be registered (and so will only be effective) if the company is first re-registered as a private company: 1980 Act s.12.

To ease this process the court may authorise the company to re-register as a private company under section 10 of the 1980 Act[44]

---

[39] *Ante*, p. 227.
[40] [1966] N.Z.L.R. 1 (C.A.).
[41] Another example of improper reduction is the Australian case of *Australasian Oil Exploration Ltd.* v. *Lachberg* (1958) 101 C.L.R. 119.
[42] p. 538.
[43] £50,000: 1980 Act, s.85.
[44] *Ante*, p. 49.

without passing a special resolution and will also specify the necessary alterations to the company's memorandum and articles.

SERIOUS LOSS OF CAPITAL

Following the EEC Second Directive,[45] under section 34 of the 1980 Act the directors of a *public* company are obliged to call an extra-ordinary meeting of the company within 28 days from the earliest date on which any director knew that the company had suffered a serious loss of capital.

A serious loss of capital occurs where the net assets of the company are half or less of the amount of the company's called up share capital. In other words if it has lost half or more of its called up share capital.

The meeting must be fixed for a date not later than 56 days from when the obligation arose. It is to consider whether any, and if so what, measures should be taken to deal with the situation. Directors who knowingly and wilfully authorise or permit a failure to convene such a meeting are liable on conviction to a fine.

There is some ambiguity as to what may actually be discussed. Section 34(3) provides that the meeting may not be used to discuss anything "which could not have been considered at that meeting apart from this section." Does this include a resolution to dismiss or censure the directors? Such a resolution may fall within the ambit of the section.

---

[45] Art. 17.

CHAPTER 12

THE ACQUISITION AND REDEMPTION BY A COMPANY OF ITS OWN SHARES

TRADITIONALLY companies have not been able to acquire their own shares. To do so was said to be a reduction of capital and the creation of a possible false market in those shares.[1] This concept has now been radically altered by the 1980 and 1981 Acts. Companies were, however, able to issue redeemable preference shares under section 58 of the 1948 Act; *i.e.* preference shares which were expressly redeemable at a future date. The 1981 Act has replaced that narrow power with a general power to issue redeemable shares of any type.

This chapter is mainly concerned with the powers of purchase and redemption given by the 1981 Act; covering a company's ability to do so, the mechanisms involved, the funds available and the capital consequences of so doing. These powers were part of a "package" designed to assist small companies in finding outside investors who might wish to be able to withdraw such investment at will. To this end it will be seen that private companies may in some cases fund the acquisition or redemption out of capital. The effect is that subject to certain procedures and authority all shares are now potentially redeemable, either by the terms of their issue or by subsequent agreement.

ACQUISITIONS—THE GENERAL RULE

Section 35 of the 1980 Act forbids a company to acquire its own shares. However, this does not apply to the following cases:

   (i) gifts of shares to the company[2];
  (ii) acquisitions on a reduction of capital under section 66[3];
 (iii) the redemption or purchase of its shares under the 1981 Act[4];

[1] See *Trevor* v. *Whitworth* (1887) 12 App. Cas. 409; *General Property etc. Co. Ltd.* v. *Matheson's Trustees* (1888) 16 R. 282.
[2] Following *Re Castiglione's W.T.* [1958] Ch. 549; *cf. Gill* v. *Arizona Copper Co. Ltd.* (1900) 2 F. 843.
[3] *Ante*, p. 229.
[4] *Post*, p. 244.

(iv) purchases authorised by the court under sections 11[5] or 75[6] of the 1980 Act or section 5 of the 1948 Act[7];

(v) the forfeiture of shares, or acceptance of any shares surrendered in lieu, for failure to pay for them.[8]

Shares acquired under (ii) and (iv) must be cancelled at once on acquisition. Shares acquired under (iii) are dealt with below. In the case of (i) and (v) section 37 of the 1980 Act provides that the shares must be disposed of or cancelled within three years and that in the meantime the company may not vote with them.

Acquisitions by nominees

Section 36 of the 1980 Act provides that if a person subscribes for shares in a company or buys them for a third party partly-paid up, apparently in his own name, but in reality as a nominee for the company, he is to be regarded as the full owner of the shares to the exclusion of the company. He thus becomes personally liable for the amount owed on the shares. If he fails to pay within 21 days of being asked to do so the other subscribers, or the directors, whichever is appropriate, will be liable to pay, subject to a defence that they acted honestly and reasonably and ought fairly to be excused.

The company, however, retains the ownership of such shares in two cases:

(i) if a public company provides financial assistance for the purchase of such shares. This topic is dealt with in the following chapter. Here we are only concerned with assistance given to a nominee. Such shares must be cancelled or disposed of within one year under section 37 of the 1980 Act;

(ii) where the company is a trustee only of the shares and has no beneficial interest in them. Thus a company acting as a trustee may accept shares issued by itself in the name of a nominee on behalf of a trust fund.

Of course the company retains the beneficial ownership of shares to which section 36 does not apply—*e.g.* fully paid up shares acquired from a third party.

---

[5] *Ante*, p. 49.
[7] *Ante*, p. 87.

[6] *Post*, p. 413.
[8] *Post*, p. 295.

Consequences of an acquisition

Apart from purchases and redemptions under the 1981 Act, shares acquired by a company or its nominee must be treated as follows:

(i) Shares acquired by the company as gifts, or by forfeiture or surrender for non-payment of calls, shares acquired by a nominee without financial assistance from the company and in which the company has a beneficial interest (*e.g.* gifts of fully paid up shares to a company's nominee)—disposal or cancellation of the shares within three years: 1980 Act, s.37;

(ii) Shares acquired by a nominee of a public company with financial assistance from the company—disposal or cancellation of the shares within one year: 1980 Act, s.37. Cancellation may be achieved by a resolution of the directors reducing the capital by the nominal amount of the shares acquired without complying with section 66. If necessary a public company must apply to be re-registered as a private company.[9]

REDEMPTION AND PURCHASE OF SHARES

Redeemable shares

Section 45 of the 1981 Act allows companies to issue redeemable shares of any class, *i.e.* those specifically redeemable under the terms of their issue. This replaces the narrower authority to issue redeemable preference shares found in section 58 of the 1948 Act.

To issue redeemable shares a company must have power to do so by its articles. No company may issue only redeemable shares[10] but one non-redeemable share will technically be enough. Shares issued under section 45 of the 1981 Act may be issued either as redeemable at a fixed date or event, or as redeemable at the option of the company or the shareholder.

Any shares redeemed must be fully paid up at the date of redemption—there must be no incidental reduction of capital, and the terms of redemption must provide for payment on redemption. Otherwise the terms of the redemption may be as specified by the articles of the company.

---

[9] *i.e.* because it ceases to comply with the authorised minimum capital under s.85 of the 1980 Act.

[10] Nor can a company purchase its own shares if that would leave only redeemable shares in existence: 1981 Act, s.46(3). See below.

When redeemable shares are redeemed they must be cancelled at once and the issued share capital figure reduced accordingly. A company must not be a member of itself. There is no option, as in section 37 of the 1980 Act noted above, for their re-issue within a limited time.

Replacement issues of shares can be made prior to the redemption without any increase in the authorised capital figure being necessary, so that if the new issue would take the nominal capital above the authorised figure section 61 will not apply.[11] If the replacement issue is made within one month prior to the redemption or subsequent to it no stamp duty is payable on the new issue unless the actual value of the new issue exceeds the value of the redeemed shares at the date of redemption. In such a case the charge will be on that excess.

The redemption of certain private company shares are given tax concessions.[12]

The funds available for redemption of shares are dealt with below.

Purchase by a company of its own shares

Section 46 of the 1981 Act allows companies to purchase their own shares by following one of three procedures contained in sections 47 to 49 of the Act. This totally new power to purchase must be included in the articles—it can include the purchase of redeemable shares, *e.g.* if the date for redemption has been reached. There is nothing in the 1981 Act which either allows or prohibits the *compulsory* purchase by a company of it own shares. It is doubtful whether a majority of the shareholders can be given this power because of the doctrine of a fraud on the minority[13] but the point remains open *vis-à-vis* the company itself.

Subject to the rule that a company cannot buy itself out completely or leave only redeemable shares the power in the articles can be framed as desired.

Replacement issues for purchased shares are regulated in the same way as those for redeemed shares. The purchase of some private company shares receive tax concessions.[14]

---

[11] *Ante*, p. 223.
[12] See *Pinson, op. cit.*, paras. 14–76 *et seq.*
[13] *Brown* v. *British Abrasive Wheel Co.* [1919] 2 Ch. 290; *Dafen Tinplate Co. Ltd.* v. *Llanelly Steel Co.* [1920] 2 Ch. 124; *cf. Sidebottom* v. *Kershaw, Leese and Co.* [1920] 1 Ch. 154.   [14] See note 12 above.

The funds available to a company for the purchase of its own shares are dealt with below.[15] The power to purchase its own shares can only be implemented however by one of the following three procedures:

Off-market purchases. A purchase of unquoted shares,[16] *i.e.* in general, those of private companies, is governed by section 47 of the 1981 Act. Such a purchase requires a special resolution of the company authorising it to make the contract to purchase (*N.B.* not the purchase itself). In the unlikely event of a public company buying its own unquoted shares such approval must then be limited to a contract made within a period of no more than 18 months from the granting of approval.

Such authority to contract may be varied, renewed or revoked by a special resolution.

The proposed contract, or a memorandum of its terms, must be available for inspection for at least 15 days ending with the date of the meeting at the company's registered office and at the meeting itself. The name of the proposed vendor(s) must be made clear. That is because such vendors may not vote with the shares concerned on the resolution if such a vote would affect the result. In such circumstances failure to abstain with those votes will invalidate the resolution. The vendor(s) can however vote with any other shares owned and can demand a poll[17] to exercise them.

Any variation of the contract itself, as distinct from the authority to enter into it, must be authorised in the same way as the original contract except that both contracts must be available for inspection.

Contingent purchase contracts. Companies may purchase options to acquire their own shares under section 48 of the 1981 Act. The procedure involved is that for an off-market purchase, *i.e.* a special resolution authorising each such option. In this way public companies cannot purchase traded options to acquire their own listed shares so as to speculate against the value of their own shares. Companies will eventually acquire their shares by exercising the option.

Market purchases. Public companies may purchase their quoted shares

[15] *Post,* p. 247.
[16] *i.e.* shares which are traded on neither the Stock Exchange nor the Unlisted Securities Market.
[17] *Post,* p. 316.

under the procedure laid down by section 49 of the 1981 Act. In essence the company needs the prior approval of an ordinary resolution[18] for the purchase of a number of shares within a specified price band and within a specified time, not greater than 18 months. The maximum and minimum figures in the price band may be settled by reference to a formula.

The need for a general rather than a specific authority to purchase is dictated by the Stock Exchange rules on trading. It is difficult to see, however, why only an ordinary resolution should be required.

The Stock Exchange will amend its own rules to cover such purchases.

Disclosure of purchases

Under section 52 of the 1981 Act details of all purchases must be registered within 28 days. A purchase may be effected by a surrender of shares so that no transfer document will be necessary.

All contracts of purchase or options to purchase must also be kept at the company's registered office for ten years from the date of completion of the purchase or expiry of the options, as appropriate. These must be open to inspection. Option contracts need only be registered if activated.

Assignment and release of a company's rights to purchase

Under section 50 of the 1981 Act any assignment by a company of its rights under a contract to purchase its own shares is totally prohibited. Companies are not allowed to speculate against their own share prices by buying and selling rights to purchase.

Companies with rights under an off-market purchase or option, however, may release such rights either under an option or a contract to purchase unquoted shares if such a release is approved by a special resolution. The vendor shareholders are, however, prohibited from voting with those shares if it would affect the result.

Funds available for redemption or purchase

The rules relating to the funding of a redemption or purchase of a company's own shares are the same. They are set out in sections 45(5) and (6) of the 1981 Act.

---

[18] This resolution must, however, be registered as if it was a special resolution.

The nominal values of the redeemed or purchased shares may be paid for either out of the company's distributable profits[19] or the proceeds of a specific fresh issue of shares made for the purpose. In either event there will be no reduction of capital—in the latter case a fresh amount of capital will replace that used.

The premium on any such shares may, however, only be paid for out of distributable profits, unless the shares themselves were originally issued at a premium. In that case the proceeds of a fresh issue may be used up to the amount of the company's share premium account at the time. In effect the share premium account may be used to fund the purchase or redemption and then be replaced by a fresh issue of shares.

Under section 51 of the 1981 Act any payment to acquire an option to purchase shares, or to obtain any variation or release from a contract to purchase, as distinct from the purchase from itself, must be found from distributable profits.

In so far as the company uses distributable profits for such payments the funds available for dividends[20] are thereby reduced: 1981 Act, s.60. Further, in such a case an amount equal to the amount of profits used must be transferred on the company's balance sheet to a fund known as the *capital redemption reserve*: 1981 Act, s.53. This is a capital fund to which the rules relating to reduction of capital apply. The object of this section is to prevent the balance sheet showing a paper profit which might be distributed by way of dividend. The profit would otherwise arise through the current assets being reduced by the amount necessary to redeem or purchase the shares, and the share capital and the revenue reserves being reduced.

Failure by a company to redeem or purchase its own shares

If a company has issued redeemable shares under section 45 of the 1981 Act and fails to redeem them, or agrees to purchase its own shares and fails to honour that agreement, the shareholder has a right of action for breach of contract under section 59 of the 1981 Act.

However, the shareholder is prevented by that section from suing for damages for breach of contract, and specific performance will only be granted if the company is able to fulfil its obligations out of distributable profits.

[19] *Post,* p. 532.
[20] *Post,* p. 532.

If the company goes into liquidation after the obligation to redeem or purchase has arisen, the shares are regarded as being cancelled on the liquidation but the vendor/shareholder may prove (apply for) any loss suffered as a creditor in the liquidation unless the company could not have fulfilled its obligations out of distributable profits at any time between the date of redemption or purchase and the date of liquidation. Such a vendor/shareholder is a deferred creditor[21] and, as such, will be paid after all the other creditors but before the shareholders.

Redemption and Purchase of Shares out of Capital

Sections 54 to 58 of the 1981 Act allow private companies to purchase or redeem their own shares out of capital. These sections do not increase the powers of redemption or purchase themselves—sections 45 to 49 of the 1981 Act must be complied with[22]—but they extend the funds available beyond distributable profits and proceeds of a fresh issue of shares. In essence, if those funds prove to be insufficient, *private* companies may resort to "capital."

"Capital" in this context is any fund other than distributable profits and the proceeds of a fresh issue, whether or not it is technically capital for the rules relating to reduction of capital etc.[23] Thus undistributable profits[24] may be used. Section 54 of the 1981 Act, however, makes it clear that private companies must first utilise distributable profits before resorting to "capital."

To use the power a private company must have authority to do so in its articles. Secondly there must be a shortfall in the funds available to all companies (distributable profits and issue proceeds). In reality this means distributable profits as there is no obligation to make a special issue of shares to provide any proceeds: 1981 Act, s.54.

To ascertain whether there is a genuine shortfall the company must calculate its available distributable profits under section 39 of the 1980 Act[25] by reference to accounts drawn up at any date within the three months immediately preceding the date on which the directors make the required declaration of solvency, which initiates the procedure.[26]

---

[21] *Post*, p. 667.
[22] *Ante*, p. 244.
[23] *Ante*, p. 229.
[24] *e.g.* the revaluation reserve.
[25] *Post*, p. 532.

[26] *Post*, p. 250.

The accounts must enable a reasonable judgment to be made. The shortfall between available profits and the amount needed for purchase or redemption is known as the *permissible capital payment* (P.C.P.).

If the P.C.P. and the proceeds of any issue used for the redemption or purchase are together less than the nominal value of the shares redeemed or purchased the remainder must have come from distributable profits. In that case section 54 of the 1981 Act provides that an equivalent amount to those profits must be transferred to the *capital redemption reserve* as in the general power and for the same reasons.[27]

However, if the P.C.P. and the proceeds of any issue used for the redemption or purchase amount to more than the nominal value of the shares redeemed or purchased, part of those capital funds must have been used to cover the redemption or purchase of the premium of those shares. In such a case section 54 of the 1981 Act provides that that excess must be deducted either from the capital redemption reserve, the share premium account, share capital figure or unrealised profits of the company. If such profits are subsequently realised they cannot then be used for dividends.

Exercise of the power

Section 55 of the 1981 Act makes it unlawful for a company to use its *permissible capital payment* unless the procedure laid down in that section is followed. This procedure is in addition to that required for the approval of the purchase; it is to approve the redemption or purchase *out of capital*.

Just as a specific off-market purchase requires the prior authority of a special resolution so does the use of capital. However, in this case it must be preceded not by details of the contract but by a statutory declaration of solvency by the directors. This declaration must relate both to the company's immediate ability to pay its debts after raising its P.C.P. and its ability to do so for the following year, taking into account the company's resources and the directors' management intentions.[28] It must be accompanied by an auditors' report that the

[27] *Ante*, p. 249.
[28] A similar procedure applies to the rules allowing financial assistance to be given by private companies for the purchase by others of these shares. See Chap. 13, *post*.

P.C.P. has been properly ascertained and that the declaration itself is not unreasonable.

That declaration must be followed on the same day or within one week by the necessary special resolution. After it has been passed no payment can be made for five weeks. (This is to enable any objection to the payment to be made to the court—see below.) The resolution must then be implemented within two further weeks.

The proposed vendor will invalidate the resolution if he votes with the shares in question in such a way as to affect the result.

The requirement of a special resolution will put the shareholders on notice as to what is intended. But since this involves "capital" the company's creditors need to know. It will affect their guarantee fund. Accordingly section 56 of the 1981 Act requires the company to place a notice both in the London or Edinburgh Gazette, as appropriate,[29] and in a national newspaper.[30] The latter can be avoided by giving a notice to each creditor of the company.

The notice must state that the resolution has been passed and what its effect is. It must also specify the P.C.P. and the date of the resolution, and state first that the statutory declaration of solvency and auditors' report are available for inspection at the company's registered office and second that a creditor may apply to the court, within five weeks of the date of the resolution, to have the resolution set aside.

The declaration of solvency and the auditors' report must be available both for shareholders at the meeting, and subsequently, for either shareholders and creditors at the registered office during the five week holding period. Further they must be registered with the Registrar by the first notice date—*i.e.* the date of publication in the Gazette or the newspaper, whichever is earlier.

Objections by members and creditors

Under section 57 of the 1981 Act a single member who did not vote for the special resolution authorising the use of capital, or any creditor,[31] may petition the court to have the resolution set aside within five weeks of the date of the resolution. For a creditor the effective time

---

[29] Depending on the location of the company's registered office.
[30] In England and Wales, or Scotland, as appropriate.
[31] There appears to be no minimum debt required.

limit may be four weeks since the advertisements putting him on notice can be put in up to a week after the resolution.

On such a petition the court has all the powers available to it as on a petition to prevent a public company re-registering as a private company under section 11 of the 1980 Act.[32] Thus it may order a compulsory purchase of the shareholder's shares by the company (and should therefore not be undertaken lightly!), alter the company's constitution, cancel, amend or confirm the resolution or impose new time scales for its implementation.

If either there are no objections, or the court overrides them, the P.C.P. may be used by the company for the purchase or redemption as appropriate.

Liability of shareholders and directors

Where a private company, which has made a payment out of capital under section 54 of the 1981 Act for the purchase or redemption of its own shares, is wound up unable to pay its debts within one year of the payments being made, section 58 of the 1981 Act applies.

In such a case the recipient of the payment, known as the relevant payment, and any director who signed the statutory declaration of solvency without having reasonable grounds for doing so, are liable to repay the amount of the relevant payment up to the amount needed to cover the company's insolvency. This liability is linked to the amount of the relevant payments needed to cover the company's outstanding debts.

Liability is joint and several so that any of the recipients or directors may be sued for the whole amount leaving him to recover a contribution from the others.

By way of protection anyone who might be liable to make payment under this section may petition to wind-up the company on the grounds of its insolvency or on the just and equitable ground under section 222(*e*) or (*f*).[33]

---

[32] *Ante,* p. 49.
[33] *Post,* p. 608.

CHAPTER 13

FINANCIAL ASSISTANCE BY A COMPANY FOR THE PURCHASE OF ITS OWN SHARES

UNDER section 54 of the 1948 Act it was unlawful for a company to give any person financial assistance for the purchase of, or subscription for, its own shares or those of its holding company. The intention was to prevent avoidance of the rule prohibiting a company from being a member of itself and the creation of a false market in that company's shares—*i.e.* by artificially stimulating demand for the shares.

Sections 42 to 44 of the 1981 Act have replaced section 54. Section 42 re-enacts the basic prohibition of section 54 in a much modified form and applies to all companies. It also contains many exceptions. Private companies are, however, to be allowed to give such assistance, subject to safeguards for creditors and minority shareholders, under sections 43 and 44.

The basic prohibitions

Section 42 of the 1981 Act applies two basic prohibitions on the giving of financial assistance—one when the assistance precedes the acquisition and the other when it follows it. In both cases a breach is a criminal offence, both for the company and any officer in default, which can lead to a term of imprisonment, or a fine, or both.[1] There are differences from the original section 54 brought about by the apparently very wide scope of that section.

(1) *Financial assistance given before or at the time of the acquisition.* It is unlawful[2] for a company to give financial assistance[3] directly or indirectly for the purpose of an acquisition or proposed acquisition by any person of its own shares or those of its holding company, either before or at the same time as the acquisition took place: 1981 Act, s.42(1).

Thus assistance may be direct or indirect. It applies to all acquisitions of shares so that it includes all transfers of shares. The most important

---

[1] Originally under section 54 the only sanction was a £100 fine. For the civil consequences see below.
[2] Subject to the exception set out below.   [3] *Post,* p. 254.

phrase is assistance given *for the purpose* of an acquisition, etc. This is an attempt to narrow the scope of the section and is important to remember when the exceptions are considered below.

(2) *Financial assistance given after the acquisition.* It is also unlawful for a company to give financial assistance[3a] directly or indirectly for the purpose of reducing or discharging any liability incurred by any person for the purpose of an acquisition of that company's own shares or those of its holding company, provided that the acquisition took place prior to the assistance being given: 1981 Act, s.42(2).

Again the important phrases concern the word *purpose*. This liability must be incurred by the acquiror or another for the purpose of the acquisition, and the financial assistance given by the company to the person who has incurred that liability must be for the purpose of reducing or discharging that liability.

For this prohibition a person incurs a liability if he changes his financial position by making any agreement of any type: 1981, s.42(9). That liability is reduced or discharged by the company if the financial assistance is given wholly or partly *for the purpose of* restoring that person's financial position to what it was before the acquisition took place: 1981 Act, s.42(10).

Financial assistance for the purposes of both these prohibitions is very wide. It is defined in section 42(8) of the 1981 Act. It clearly includes direct financing by the company and the more common indirect financing whereby a take-over bidder purchases the shares of a cash filled company by means of a loan and then uses the assets of the company to repay the loan.[4] Guarantees, provision of security to cover a loan, gifts, any form of credit are also included—in fact anything which reduces the net assets of a company to a material extent.

The purpose exceptions

One of the reasons for the revision of the rule on financial assistance was the judgment of the Court of Appeal in *Belmont Finance Corporation* v. *Williams Furniture Ltd.* (*No.* 2).[5] The case was concerned with the situation whereby a company enters into a commercial transaction,

---

[3a] *Infra.*

[4] See *e.g. Selangor United Rubber Estates Ltd.* v. *Cradock* (*No.* 3) [1968] 1 W.L.R. 1555; *Wallersteiner* v. *Moir* [1974] 1 W.L.R. 991.

[5] [1980] 1 All E.R. 393.

e.g. buying goods from X, and, at the same time, X uses the proceeds of sale to buy shares in the company. Buckley L.J. said[6] that in such a case if the company genuinely needed those goods there might be no breach of section 54. On the other hand if the company made the purchases solely to provide X with the means to buy its shares then there was a breach, even if the company paid a fair price for the goods. More difficult is the middle case, *i.e* when the company enters into the transaction genuinely in its own commercial interests but it is done partly to put X in funds to buy shares in that company. The Court of Appeal left that point open.

It was also decided that financial assistance could be given in breach of section 54 if it was made not to the purchaser but to the vendor of the shares *e.g.* when the company made a payment to the owner of some of its shares which persuaded him to sell them to a purchaser, even when the purchaser then paid the full price for them.[7]

As a result of these and other cases two new exceptions were introduced by section 42 of the 1981 Act. They can be found in section 42(3) in relation to financial assistance given before or at the same time as the acquisition and section 42(4) for post-acquisition assistance. However both contain the same two exceptions based on the purpose for which the assistance was given.

(1) *Where the principal purpose of giving the financial assistance was not for the purpose of the acquisition*[8] *and was given in good faith in the interests of the company.* It has already been noted that the prohibition only applies if the assistance is given for the purpose of enabling someone to acquire the company's shares.[8] This exception narrows the prohibition even further. Assisting the relevant acquisition must be the principal purpose of the assistance. This is clearly an attempt to limit the possibilities discussed in the *Belmont* case, above. Only if the company buys the goods from X with the principal purpose of giving assistance will the new section still apply.

This exception is only available, however, when the company is acting in good faith. This is a vague concept as discussed earlier.[9]

The new exception is also designed to protect groups of companies with relevance to the post-acquisition assistance prohibition. For ex-

---

[6] [1980] 1 All E.R. 393, 402.
[7] *Armour Hick Northern Ltd.* v. *Whitehouse* [1980] 3 All E.R. 833.
[8] Or reducing a liability as appropriate.
[9] *Ante,* p. 82.

ample when, following the acquisition of a new subsidiary company, the acquiring company has to charge the assets of that subsidiary to comply with a prior debenture which requires all the assets of the group to be charged on security. In such a case the security would not be given for the principal purpose of reducing a liability incurred for the purpose of acquiring the subsidiary.

(2) *Where even if the principal purpose of giving the financial assistance was for the acquisition of shares it was an incidental part of some larger purpose and was given in good faith in the interests of the company.* If (1) does not apply this second one might. The concept of *larger purpose* is no clearer than *principal purpose*. Good faith is again required.

Again, this exception is best explained by reference to post-acquisition financial assistance within a group of companies. For example, when a subsidiary company provides funds to its parent company some years after it has been acquired to effect a more efficient deployment of assets within the group, the proviso may relieve the parent company of indebtedness incurred for the purpose of acquiring the subsidiary but if the larger purpose can be established it will be exempt.

Authorised transaction exceptions

Section 42(5) of the 1981 Act sets out nine specific transactions permitted under company law which are not to be subject to the prohibition. These are as follows:

(i) the distribution of lawful dividends.[10-11] The rules relating to the funds available for dividends are considered strong enough to protect companies. One of the old abuses was to extract unusually large dividends from a company to repay a loan used by the borrower to gain control of the company.

(ii) distributions made in the course of a winding-up[12];

(iii) the allotment of bonus shares[13];

(iv) anything done under a court order under section 206[14];

(v) anything done under an arrangement between a company and its creditors under section 306[15];

[10-11] *Post*, p. 532.
[12] *Post*, p. 604.
[13] *Ante*, p. 543.
[14] *Post*, p. 709.
[15] *Post*, p. 702.

(vi) anything done under an arrangement made in pursuance of section 287[16];

(vii) any reduction of capital confirmed by the court under section 68[17];

(viii) a redemption of shares under section 45 of the 1981 Act[18];

(ix) a purchase of its own shares by a company under sections 46–62 of the 1981 Act.[18]

Loans and employee share scheme exceptions

The following three exceptions were available in the former section 54. They are only available to public companies if the book value of the net assets is not reduced as a result, or, if it is, the assistance is paid out of distributable profits[19]: 1981 Act, s.42(7).

(1) *Lending as part of the ordinary course of business.* If the lending of the money is in the company's ordinary course of business *and* the loan itself is within the ordinary course of that business section 42 of the 1981 Act does not apply. Banks may use this exception but an unusual loan will not qualify for exception[20]: 1981 Act, s.42(6)(*a*).

(2) *Employee share schemes.* There is no prohibition on the provision of money to a company for the acquisition of fully-paid shares in the company in accordance with an employees' share scheme.[21] This may include directors. Such schemes receive tax concessions as well[22]: 1981 Act, s.42(6)(*b*).

(3) *Loans to employees to purchase shares.* A company may lend money to those employed in good faith by the company in order for them to purchase shares in that company or its holding company for their own benefit. It does not apply to directors: 1981 Act, s.42(6)(*c*).

Validity of the transaction

Section 42 of the 1981 Act, like its predecessor, creates a criminal offence. What then is the validity of a loan or the provision of any security given to cover a loan which is in breach of the section? The judges have provided an answer.

---

[16] *Post*, p. 706.
[17] *Ante*, p. 229.
[18] *Ante*, p. 244.
[19] *Post*, p. 532.
[20] *Steen* v. *Law* [1964] A.C. 287. A loan deliberately made by a bank with the purpose of an acquisition in mind is unlikely to be regarded as a usual loan.
[21] Defined in 1980 Act, s.87.
[22] See *Pinson, op. cit.* paras. 3–20A *et seq.*

Any security given to provide financial assistance is void.[23] It canno' be enforced by the lender. So is any guarantee supporting the invalid agreement.[24] In most of the cases the action simply sought to enforce the security but in two cases the wider issue as to the validity of the whole agreement to buy the shares has been considered.

In *South Western Mineral Water Co.* v. *Ashmore*[25] Cross J. suggested that the agreement might be saved if the parties proceed with the acquisition of the shares in a manner dissociating the purchase from the invalid security—*e.g.* by the seller/lender waiving his rights in the security or by the buyer paying the price at once. In the absence of this, however, the whole agreement was in his opinion void. In *Lawlor* v. *Gray*,[26] however, the controller of a company agreed to sell his shares. The agreement could have been carried out in many ways but the controller chose one which was in breach of the financial assistance rules. The court allowed the purchaser to enforce the agreement. It seems therefore that if the agreement does not itself involve a breach of the section it can be enforced.

Liability of those participating in the breach

It has been held that section 54 was passed to protect the company from having its assets misused and not merely to protect its creditors[27] and this must apply to section 42 of the 1981 Act. Thus any director who is knowingly a party to a breach of this section will be in breach of duty to the company and liable to repay the loss.[28]

In addition anyone who receives the funds of the company so misapplied is liable to it as a constructive trustee if he knew or ought to have known of the breach.[29] Anyone who assists in the breach is also liable but only if he actually knew of the breach or was deliberately blind to it.[29]

---

[23] *Selangor United Rubber Estates Ltd.* v. *Cradock* (No. 3) [1968] 1 W.L.R. 1555; *Heald* v. *O'Connor* [1971] 1 W.L.R. 497; *cf. Victor Battery Co. Ltd.* v. *Curry's Ltd.* [1946] Ch. 242.

[24] *Heald* v. *O'Connor* [1971] 1 W.L.R. 497.

[25] [1967] 1 W.L.R. 1110.

[26] (1980) 130 N.L.J. 317.

[27] *Wallersteiner* v. *Moir* [1974] 1 W.L.R. 991, 1014, *per* Lord Denning M.R.

[28] *Belmont Finance Corp.* v. *Williams Furniture Ltd.* (*No.* 2) [1980] 1 All E.R. 393; *Wallersteiner* v. *Moir, above; Karak Rubber Co.* v. *Burden* (*No.* 2) [1972] 1 W.L.R. 602.

[29] *Belmont Finance Corp.* v. *Williams Furniture Ltd.*, above.

It appears from the *Belmont*[29] case that the company may also recover in the tort of conspiracy if it can prove: (1) that the conspirators combined to participate in a common agreement with a common purpose; (2) that the combination was to carry out an unlawful purpose; *i.e.* the provision of financial assistance contrary to section 42; (3) that the company suffered damage as a consequence. Damage must be proved.

General exemption for private companies

Private companies may obtain complete exemption from the prohibitions regarding the provision of financial assistance for the acquisition of their own shares provided that they comply with a set procedure and timetable under sections 43 and 44 of the 1981 Act. This general exemption is in addition to the exceptions already mentioned which are applicable to all companies. It is not available, however, for the acquisition of shares in a holding company unless that is itself a private company: 1981 Act s.43(3).

A general restriction on the use of the general assumption is that the assistance must either leave the book value net assets of the company untouched or be made out of distributable profits[30]: 1981 Act s.43(2). The idea is to protect creditors by ensuring that only funds available under section 39 of the 1980 Act for distribution as dividend are used.[30] That section, however, does not require companies to make provision for unrealised losses, so section 43(6) of the 1981 Act requires the directors to make a statutory declaration of the company's solvency prior to giving the assistance. If the shares to be acquired are in the company's holding company the directors of that company must also make a declaration.

Statutory declaration. Section 43(7) prescribes the form of the declaration. First, it must be set out the assistance to be given, the business of the company and the identity of the recipient. Second, the directors must state that *in their opinion* the company will be able to pay its debts both immediately after giving the assistance and as they fall due during the following year.[31]

---

[30] *Post*, p. 532. For the effect on profits available for dividend see s.60 of the 1981 Act, *ante*, p. 248.

[31] If it is intended to wind up the company during this time the declaration must state that the company will be able to pay its debts within 12 months of the winding up.

Attached to the declaration must be an auditors' report to the effect that they are not aware of anything to indicate that the opinion of the directors is unreasonable.

Special resolution. To protect shareholders rather than creditors the financial assistance must be approved by a special resolution of each of the companies (holding, subsidiary) involved: 1981 Act, s.43(4).

The statutory declaration and auditors' report must be available at the meeting at which the special resolution is passed. The meeting must take place on the same day as, or within one week of, the date on which the declaration is made. The declaration, auditors' report and resolution must be registered with the Registrar within 15 days of the passing of the resolution: 1981 Act, s.44.

After passing the resolution the company may not act upon it for four weeks unless all the members voted in favour. This allows a dissenting minority to petition the court to have the resolution set aside (see below). If more than one company is involved the period runs from the date of the last resolution to be passed.

Assuming that there are no minority shareholder objections the company must then implement the authority within eight weeks of the making of the declaration of solvency. In general therefore companies will have between three and four weeks to implement the authority after the four week delay, depending on how soon the resolution followed the declaration: 1981 Act, s.43(9).

Minority protection. Holders of at least 10 per cent. of the nominal share capital or any class, who did not vote for the authorising resolution, may apply to the court to have the resolution set aside. Such applications must be made within 28 days of the passing of the resolution—which corresponds to the waiting period for the company: 1981 Act, s.44(2).

The court has wide powers on such an application—those which are available to it on a petition under section 11 of the 1980 Act[32] to prevent the re-registration of a public company as a private one. One of these powers is to order that the minority be bought out. The court may otherwise cancel, confirm or vary the resolution. Whilst the petition is being considered the resolution cannot be implemented unless the court orders otherwise: 1981 Act, s.44.

[32] *Ante*, p. 49.

CHAPTER 14

SHARES

A SHARE has been defined as "the interest of a shareholder in the company measured by a sum of money, for the purpose of liability in the first place, and of interest in the second, but also consisting of a series of mutual covenants entered into by all the shareholders *inter se* in accordance with [the Companies Act 1948, s.20[1]]. The contract contained in the articles of association is one of the original incidents of the share."[2] The share is measured by a sum of money, namely, the nominal amount of the share, and also by the rights and obligations belonging to it as defined by the Companies Acts and by the memorandum and articles of the company. The undivided profits form an integral part of the shares to which they appertain.[2a]

Each share in a company must be distinguished by its appropriate number, provided that it need not have a number if all the issued shares, or all the issued shares of a particular class, are fully paid up and rank *pari passu* for all purposes: section 74. Numbers are often dispensed with today under the proviso to section 74.

A share certificate, which specifies the shares held by the member and which is prima facie evidence of his title to the shares (s.81), is usually issued to a shareholder.

Shares in a company are personal[3] estate, transferable in the manner provided by the articles of the company: section 73.

A shareholder may borrow money on the security of his shares, *i.e.* in England, he may give the lender a mortgage over the shares to secure the payment of interest and repayment of the principal sum.[3a]

SHARE CERTIFICATE

Every company must complete the share certificates and have them ready for delivery within two months[4] after the allotment of any of its

---

[1] *Ante*, p. 104.
[2] *Per* Farwell J. in *Borland's Trustee* v. *Steel Bros. & Co. Ltd.* [1901] 1 Ch. 279, at p. 288.
[2a] *Carron Co.* v. *Hunter* (1868) 6 M. (H.L.) 106.
[3] The Scottish equivalent of "personal" is "moveable": s.455.
[3a] For assignation of shares in security in Scots law, see *post*, p. 286.
[4] Fourteen days if the shares are quoted on a stock exchange: Rules of The Stock Exchange, App. 34, Sched. VIII.

shares or after the date on which a transfer of its shares is lodged for registration, unless the conditions of issue otherwise provide, under a penalty of a default fine: section 80. The form of the certificate is governed by the articles. Table A, article 8, gives the right to a certificate without payment and provides that it shall be under the seal of the company, or under the official seal kept by the company by virtue of section 2 of the Stock Exchange (Completion of Bargains) Act 1976, *ante*, and shall specify the shares to which it relates and the amount paid up thereon. If a quotation on the Stock Exchange is desired, the certificate must also have a footnote to the effect that no transfer will be registered without production of the share certificate and, in the case of preference shares, must state the conditions conferred thereon as to capital and dividends.[5]

If shares, debentures or debenture stock are or is allotted to a stock exchange nominee (SEPON Ltd.), or a transfer of shares, debentures or debenture stock to a Stock Exchange nominee is lodged with the company, the company is exempt from the obligation to prepare certificates under section 80: Stock Exchange (Completion of Bargains) Act 1976, ss.1, 7. This is to facilitate the Talisman system of transfers on the Stock Exchange.

The certificate is a formal statement by the company under its common seal, or its official seal under the Stock Exchange (Completion of Bargains) Act 1976, that the person named therein is the holder of the number of shares in the company specified in the certificate. It is prima facie evidence of the title of that person to the shares: section 81.[6] It is not a document of title (as the register of members is).[7] The object of the certificate is to facilitate dealings with the shares, whether by way of sale or security, and so make them more valuable to their owner. On the other hand, a share certificate is not a negotiable instrument, so that its accidental loss or destruction is not a matter of great moment. The articles usually make provision for the granting of a new certificate in such a case.

Table A, article 9, provides: "If a share certificate be defaced, lost or destroyed, it may be renewed on payment of a fee of 12½p. or such less sum and on such terms (if any) as to evidence and indemnity and the payment of

---

[5] Rules of The Stock Exchange, App. 34, Sched. IV. See *Rainford* v. *James Keith & Blackman Co. Ltd., post,* p. 284.
[6] See, *e.g. Woodhouse & Rawson Ltd.* v. *Hosack* (1894) 2 S.L.T. 279 (O.H.).
[7] *Ante,* p. 191.

out-of-pocket expenses of the company of investigating evidence as the directors think fit."

In England a share certificate is not a deed for the purposes of the Law of Property Act 1925, s.74,[8] *post.*[9]

Estoppel[10] as to statements in a certificate

The issue of a share certificate may give rise to an estoppel against the company. The company cannot deny the truth of the certificate as against a person who has relied on the certificate and in consequence has changed his position.

T., the registered holder of shares, left the share certificate with her broker. T.'s signature was forged to a transfer in favour of S., T. did not reply to notice of the transfer sent to him by the company and a new certificate in the name of S. was issued by the company. A. bought from S. and paid for the shares on delivery of the share certificate, and a new share certificate was issued to A. The fraud was subsequently discovered and T.'s name was restored to the register. *Held,* the company was liable to indemnify A. The giving of the certificate to S. amounted to a statement by the company, intended to be acted upon by purchasers of shares in the market, that S. was entitled to the shares, and A. having acted on the statement, the company was estopped from denying it. A. was entitled to recover from the company as damages the value of the shares at the time when the company first refused to recognise him as a shareholder, with interest: *Re Bahia and San Francisco Rlwy. Co.* (1868) L.R. 3 Q.B. 584.

There is no estoppel in favour of a person, such as S. in the above case, who procures the granting of a certificate on a forged transfer[11] or forged power of attorney,[12] even if he has acted in good faith. In fact the company may be able to claim an indemnity from such a person.[13]

The company may be estopped from denying the title to shares of the person to whom it has issued a share certificate.[14]

D. bought 30 shares through a broker, L., who was also secretary of the company, and paid L. She received and returned to L. a transfer of shares

---

[8] *Per* Clauson J. in *South London Greyhound Racecourses Ltd.* v. *Wake* [1931] 1 Ch. 496, at p. 503.
[9] p. 432.
[10] Personal bar is the Scottish equivalent of "estoppel." See Lord Kyllachy (Ordinary) in *Clavering, Son & Co.* v. *Goodwins, Jardine & Co. Ltd.* (1891) 18 R. 652, at p. 657.
[11] *Sheffield Corporation* v. *Barclay* [1905] A.C. 392, *post*, p. 282.
[12] *Starkey* v. *Bank of England* [1903] A.C. 114.   [13] *Post*, p. 281.
[14] *Balkis Consolidated Co. Ltd.* v. *Tomkinson* [1893] A.C. 396.

executed to L.'s direction by his clerk, P., who was never a man of substance and who did not hold any shares. The transfer, which did not specify the numbers of the shares, was put before the board by L. and passed without production of P.'s certificate being required, and a new certificate prepared by L. was issued to the effect that D. held 30 shares, numbers 115–144 inclusive. The chairman, who did not sign the certificate, did not notice that the shares were part of his holding (numbers 1–333). The board properly relied on the secretary to check transfers and certificates with the register. Two years later the board notified D. that P.'s transfer was invalid and declined to recognise her as a shareholder. L. was bankrupt by then and the company could not prove that he could not have reimbursed D. if, when the certificate was issued, the company had refused to issue it. *Held,* D. was entitled to damages: *Dixon* v. *Kennaway & Co.* [1900] 1 Ch. 833.

The company may be estopped from denying the amount stated to be paid up on shares.

B. lent money to a company on the security of fully paid shares in the company and was handed by the company share certificates for 10,000 shares of £1 each which the certificates stated to be fully paid up. No money had been paid on the shares, which had been issued direct by the company to B., but B. did not know this. On the company's going into liquidation, B. was placed on the list of contributories in respect of these shares. *Held,* the company was estopped by the certificate from denying that the shares were fully paid up and B. was entitled to have his name removed from the list of contributories: *Bloomenthal* v. *Ford* [1897] A.C 156.[15]

The company may be made liable in damages to the person who has relied on the statement in the share certificate.[16]

If B., in the last case, had known that the shares were not fully paid up, there would have been no estoppel—there is no estoppel in favour of a person who knows the untruth of statements in a share certificate.[17] An original allottee, therefore, will seldom be in a position to benefit from the principle.[17a]

The company is not estopped where[18] a certificate is a forgery.

---

[15] *cf. Waterhouse* v. *Jamieson* (1870) 8 M. (H.L.) 88, in which it was held that statements in the memorandum and articles, which also appeared in share certificates, as to the amount paid up on shares could not be contradicted by the liquidator.

[16] *Clavering, Son & Co.* v. *Goodwins, Jardine & Co. Ltd.* (1891) 18 R. 652.

[17] See *Crickmer's Case* (1875) L.R. 10. Ch.App. 614. In England, if the shares had been transferred to a purchaser without notice that they were not fully paid up he could give a good title to a purchaser from him with or without notice: *Barrow's Case* (1880) 14 Ch.D. 432 (C.A.).

[17a] *Liquidator of Scottish Heritages Co. Ltd.* (1898) 5 S.L.T. 336 (O.H.); contrast *Penang Foundry Co. Ltd.* v. *Gardiner,* 1913 S.C. 1203 (O.H.).

[18] See note 14 above.

R. lent money to the secretary of a company for his own purposes on the security of a share certificate issued to R. by the secretary and certifying that R. was registered as transferee of the shares. The secretary issued the share certificate without authority, affixed the common seal and forged the signatures of two directors, so that the certificate apparently complied with the articles. R. sued the company for damages for refusal to register him. *Held,* in the absence of evidence that the company had held out the secretary as having authority to do more than the mere ministerial act of delivering share certificates, when duly made, to those entitled to them, the company was not estopped from disputing the claim or responsible for the secretary's act: *Ruben* v. *Great Fingall Consolidated* [1906] A.C. 439.

TRANSFER OF SHARES

There is a distinction between a transfer of shares and a transmission of shares. A transfer is by the act of the member, while a transmission occurs by operation of law on the death or the bankruptcy of a member.[19]

Restrictions on transfer

Every shareholder has a right to transfer his shares to whom he likes, unless the articles provide to the contrary.[20]

By the Companies Acts "it is provided that the shares in a company under these Acts shall be capable of being transferred in manner provided by the regulations of the company. The regulations of the company may impose fetters upon the right of transfer. In the absence of restrictions in the articles the shareholder has by virtue of the statute the right to transfer his shares without the consent of anybody to any transferee, even though he be a man of straw, provided it is a bona fide transaction in the sense that it is an out-and-out disposal of the property without retaining any interest in the shares—that the transferor bona fide divests himself of all benefit. . . . In the absence of restrictions it is competent to a transferor, notwithstanding that the company is *in extremis*, to compel registration of a transfer to a transferee notwithstanding that the latter is a person not competent to meet the unpaid liability upon the shares. Even if the transfer be executed for the express purpose of relieving the transferor from liability, the directors cannot upon that ground

---

[19] *Post,* p. 282.
[20] *Weston's Case* (1868) L.R. 4 Ch.App. 20; *O'Meara* v. *The El Palmar Rubber Estates Ltd.*, 1913, 1 S.L.T. 383 (O.H.). It is otherwise, *e.g.* where the company is being wound up and a transfer is prevented by s.227, *post,* p. 623.

refuse to register it unless there is in the articles some provision so enabling them:" *per* Buckley L.J. in *Lindlar's Case* [1910] 1 Ch. 312 (C.A.) at p. 316.[21]

However, the directors must decline to register a transfer which is not properly stamped.[22]

An article providing that on the bankruptcy of a member he shall sell his shares to particular persons at a particular price, which is fixed for all persons alike and is not shown to be an unfair price, is valid.[23] So, too, is an article providing that on the death of a member his shares must be offered to "the other members" at par, even though there is only one surviving member.[24]

Table A, article 24, provides: "The directors may decline to register the transfer of a share (not being a fully paid share) to a person of whom they shall not approve, and they may also decline to register the transfer of a share on which the company has a lien."

In the case of a private company, the articles may, and usually do restrict the right to transfer its shares.[25] In the case of a public company, shares must normally be free from restrictions on the right of transfer if a stock exchange quotation is to be obtained.[26]

Any restrictions on the transfer of shares are a derogation from the common law right of free transfer. Any rights conferred by the articles will not be extended to situations not covered by them[27]; the procedure laid down in the articles for the exercise of the rights must be strictly followed[28]; and if the rights are not actively exercised the right of free transfer will revive.[29]

---

[21] For Scottish authority to the same effect, see, *e.g.* Lord Kincairney (Ordinary) in *Stewart* v. *James Keiller & Sons Ltd.* (1902) 4 F. 657, at p. 667.

[22] *Maynard* v. *Consolidated Kent Collieries Corpn.* [1903] 2 K.B. 121; Stamp Act, 1891, s.17.

[23] *Borland's Trustee* v. *Steel Bros. & Co. Ltd.* [1901] 1 Ch. 279.

[24] *Jarvis Motors (Harrow) Ltd.* v. *Carabott* [1964] 1 W.L.R. 1101, where one of the two members of a company, who each held half of the shares, died, and the executors of the deceased had to offer his shares at par to the surviving member.

[25] Until the 1980 Act such restrictions were obligatory: *ante,* p. 45. The restriction on the transfer of shares in a private company is one reason why such shares are not dealt in on stock exchanges.

[26] Rules of The Stock Exchange, App. 34, Sched. VII. The main advantage of a stock exchange quotation is that it makes the securities more marketable.

[27] *Furness & Co.* v. *Liquidators of "Cynthiana" Steamship Co. Ltd.* (1893) 21 R. 239.

[28] *Neilson* v. *Ayr Race Meetings Syndicate Ltd.,* 1918, 1 S.L.T. 63 (O.H.).

[29] *Shepherd's Trustees* v. *Shepherd,* 1950 S.C. (H.L.) 60 (application for registration granted, the two directors having failed to agree to refuse registration).

Pre-emption clauses

The articles of a private company usually contain a pre-emption clause, *e.g.* to the effect that no shares shall be transferred to any person not a member of the company so long as a member can be found to purchase them at a fair price to be determined in accordance with the articles.[30] Such a pre-emption clause does not entitle the company to refuse to register a transfer of shares from one member to another member of the company.[31] Where the value of shares for the purpose of such a clause falls to be fixed by the directors, the court will not review the directors' valuation provided that they have acted fairly and honestly.[32]

Sometimes the articles provide that a member desiring to sell any of his shares must inform the directors of the number of shares, the price and the name of the proposed transferee, and the directors must first offer the shares at that price to the other shareholders. In such a case, any member to whom the shares are offered cannot buy part only of the shares, and if none of the members is willing to buy all the shares the proposed transfer can be carried out.[33]

A member whose shares have been offered to other members under a pre-emption clause has been held entitled to withdraw his offer at any time before its acceptance.[34]

Articles provided that no transfer of shares should take place so long as any other shareholder was willing to purchase at a price to be ascertained by agreement between the intending transferor and the directors, or, failing agreement, at a price to be fixed by the auditors, and that any shareholder who was "desirous of transferring" his shares should inform the secretary of the number of shares which he desired to transfer. *Held,* shareholders who, on a take-over bid accepted an outside offer to buy their shares, received the price, gave the purchaser general proxies, and agreed to execute transfers and deliver up the share certificates when called upon to do so, were "desirous of transferring" their shares and had to comply with the pre-emption clause, unless they gave notice that they had changed their minds before the other shareholders exercised their pre-emption rights: *Lyle & Scott Ltd.* v. *Scott's Trustees,* 1959 S.C. (H.L.) 64; [1959] A.C. 763.

---

[30] *Post,* p. 530.
[31] *Delavenne* v. *Broadhurst* [1931] 1 Ch. 234.
[32] *Stewart* v. *James Keiller & Sons Ltd.* (1902) 4 F. 657.
[33] *The Ocean Coal Co. Ltd.* v. *The Powell Duffryn Steam Coal Co. Ltd.* [1932] 1 Ch. 654.
[34] *J. M. Smith Ltd.* v. *Colquhoun's Trustee* (1901) 3 F. 981.

Pre-emption clauses on the other hand do not prevent a shareholder declaring himself a trustee for a proposed transferee, or even on death allowing the executors to hold the shares on trust for a beneficiary. Unless the pre-emption clause expressly applies to such situations the other shareholders may not invoke it. There is no transfer upon which it can operate. It may be different if the shareholder also gives the beneficiary an irrevocable proxy to vote with the shares.[35]

If the provision in the articles relating to the offer of the shares to the existing shareholders before a transfer is made is disregarded, the transferee will not be entitled to be entered on the register. In England the same is true in the case of a sale, in disregard of the articles, by a mortgagee under his power of sale.[36] However, a transfer by a shareholder, in breach of the pre-emptive rights given by the articles, to a person who has paid for the shares operates as a transfer of the *beneficial interest* in the shares, so that the transferee takes priority over a judgment creditor who subsequently obtains a charging order[37] on the shares.[38]

Articles may provide that the other members are bound to buy the shares of a member who wishes to transfer them.[39]

It has also been held that a company enforcing a power of sale under a lien on its own shares must itself comply with the pre-emption clause in its articles in effecting that sale: *Champagne Perrier-Jouet S.A.* v. *H. H. Finch Ltd.*[39a]

Note what is said later as to the duty of care owed by an auditor who values shares in the knowledge that his valuation will determine the price to be paid under a contract.[40]

---

[35] *Safeguard Industrial Investments Ltd.* v. *National Westminster Bank Ltd.* [1982] 1 All E.R. 449 (C.A.).

[36] *Hunter* v. *Hunter* [1936] A.C. 222.

[37] *Post*, p. 285.

[38] *Hawks* v. *McArthur* [1951] 1 All E.R. 22.

Similarly, in Scotland, in a competition between a transferee and an arrester, the arrester was held not to be entitled to found on an alleged failure on the part of the company to observe the proper procedure relating to pre-emption and registration of transfers, with the result that the court declared that the shares had vested in the transferee: *National Bank of Scotland Glasgow Nominees Ltd.* v. *Adamson*, 1932 S.L.T. 492 (O.H.).

[39] *Rayfield* v. *Hands* [1960] Ch. 1, *ante*, p. 106.

[39a] [1982] 1 W.L.R. 1359.

[40] *Arenson* v. *Casson Beckman Rutley & Co.* [1975] 3 W.L.R. 815, (H.L.), *post*, p. 530.

Directors' power to refuse transfers

In addition to containing a pre-emption clause, the articles of a private company usually contain an article like the now repealed Table A, Part II, article 3, providing that the directors may, in their absolute discretion and without assigning any reason therefor, refuse to register any transfer of any share. In such a case, if the directors refuse to register a transfer the court will not interfere unless it can be shown that the directors are exercising their discretion improperly.[41]

When directors have power to decline to register a transfer, whether their power is absolute or limited to certain specified grounds, they need not disclose their reasons for refusing registration and if, having considered the questions, they refuse registration without giving any reasons, their refusal cannot be questioned unless there is evidence (which will be hard to come by) that they have not acted in good faith.[42]

The directors' discretionary power is a fiduciary power and must be exercised in good faith, *i.e.* legitimately for the purpose for which it is conferred. In exercising it the directors must act in good faith in the interest of the company and with due regard to the shareholder's right to transfer his shares, and they must fairly consider the question at a board meeting.[43]

Articles gave the directors "an absolute and uncontrolled discretion" to refuse to register any transfer of shares. The two directors each held 4,001 of the 8,002 ordinary shares. F. died and his son, as his executor, applied for the shares to be registered in his name. S. refused, but offered to register 2,001 shares if 2,000 were sold to him at a fixed price. F.'s son applied for rectification of the register but failed. There was nothing to show that the director's power was not exercised in the company's interest: *Re Smith and Fawcett Ltd.* [1942] Ch. 304 (C.A.).

There is a presumption that the directors have acted bona fide and reasonably.[44]

If the articles empower the directors to decline to register transfers

---

[41] See *Stewart* v. *James Keiller & Sons Ltd.* (1902) 4 F. 657.
[42] *Re Coalport China Co.* [1895] 2 Ch. 404; *Kennedy* v. *North British Wireless Schools Ltd.* 1916, 1 S.L.T. 407; 1915, 1 S.L.T. 196 (O.H.).
[43] *Per* Chitty J. in *Re Bell Bros. Ltd.* (1891) 65 L.T. 245 at p. 245; and see Lord Trayner in *Stewart* v. *James Keiller & Sons Ltd.* (1902) 4 F. 657, at p. 678.
[44] *Per* Lord Anderson (Ordinary) in *Kennedy* v. *North British Wireless Schools Ltd.*, 1916, 1 S.L.T. 407; 1915, 1 S.L.T. 196 (O.H.), at p. 198.

on certain grounds, *e.g.* on the ground that the transferor is indebted to the company, or that the transferee is a person of whom they do not approve, they can be interrogated as to the ground on which they have refused registration, although not as to the reasons for their refusal, unless the articles provide that they shall not be bound to specify the grounds for their refusal, in which case they cannot be interrogated at all.[45]

If the directors give reasons for their refusal, the court can decide whether they are sufficient to justify the refusal.

The articles empowered the directors to refuse to register a transfer if "in their opinion it is contrary to the interests of the company that the proposed transferee should be a member thereof." The directors declined to register transfers of single shares, stating that it was contrary to the interests of the company that shares should be transferred singly or in small amounts to outside persons with no interest in, or knowledge of, shipping. *Held,* this was a bad reason for refusing—refusal should have been on grounds personal to the transferee—and the transfers were directed to be registered: *Re Bede S.S. Co. Ltd.* [1917] 1 Ch. 123 (C.A.).

"A formal active exercise of the right of refusal to register is required before the company is authorised to refuse to register" shares in the names of the transferees. Where directors are equally divided and so come to no decision to decline to register, the transfer must be registered.[46]

Where the articles provided that no share should be transferred to a person not already a member of the company without the consent of the directors and, to prevent a particular transfer from being registered, a director purposely abstained from attending board meetings so that a quorum could not be obtained, it was held that the transferee was entitled to an order directing the company to register the transfer.[47]

In one case the board lost their right to veto a transfer because they were guilty of an unreasonable delay of four months in deciding whether or not to exercise the veto—the period of two months specified in section 78 for giving a transferee notice of the company's refusal to register a transfer is the outside limit after which there is

---

[45] *Berry and Stewart* v. *Tottenham Hotspur Football Co. Ltd.* [1935] Ch. 718.
[46] *Shepherd's Trustees* v. *Shepherd,* 1950 S.C. (H.L.) 60, *per* Lord Porter at p. 66; *Re Hackney Pavilion Ltd.* [1924] 1 Ch. 276.
[47] *Re Copal Varnish Co. Ltd.* [1917] 2 Ch. 349.

unnecessary delay, unless in an exceptional case it is impossible to constitute a board.[48]

In a rare case, the remedy of the transferee, or of the transferor, on a refusal to register a transfer is to apply to the court to rectify the register of members by substituting his name for that of the transferor under section 116. Unnecessary delay in registering a transfer does not in itself constitute a ground for rectification, and a transferor applying for rectification must be able to show that he has been prejudiced by the delay.[49] A winding-up petition is not the proper remedy for the transferor where registration of a transfer is refused.[50]

Form of transfer

Section 75, which was passed to make sure that there is an instrument which can be stamped with stamp duty, provides that it is unlawful for a company to register a transfer of shares unless a "proper instrument of transfer" has been delivered to the company. Consequently it is illegal to have an article that upon the death of a shareholder his shares shall be deemed to have passed to his widow, without any transfer.[51]

The form of the transfer may be that prescribed by the articles, but a "proper instrument" for the purposes of section 75 does not necessarily mean an instrument complying with the formalities prescribed by the articles—it means an instrument such as will attract stamp duty.[52] The articles may require transfers to be made in writing under seal.

Table A in the Companies Act 1948, as amended by the 1967 Act, contains the following provisions:

Article 22.—"The instrument of transfer of any share shall be executed by or on behalf of the transferor and transferee, and the transferor shall be deemed to remain a holder of the share until the name of the transferee is entered in the register of members in respect thereof."

Article 23.—"Subject to such of the restrictions of these regulations as may be applicable, any member may transfer all or any of his shares by instrument in writing in any usual or common form or any other form which the directors may approve."

---

[48] *Re Swaledale Cleaners Ltd.* [1968] 1 W.L.R. 1710 (C.A.).
[49] *Property Investment Co. of Scotland Ltd.* v. *Duncan* (1887) 14 R. 299.
[50] *Charles Forte Investments Ltd.* v. *Amanda* [1964] Ch. 240 (C.A.).
[51] *Re Greene* [1949] Ch. 333.
[52] *Re Paradise Motor Co. Ltd.* [1968] 1 W.L.R. 1125 (C.A.).

Formerly, the common form of transfer of shares had to be executed by the transferee as well as by the transferor and had to be attested.

Now, in the case of a company limited by shares, if shares are fully paid they may be transferred by a simplified form of transfer, namely a stock transfer under hand in the form set out in Schedule 1 to the Stock Transfer Act 1963.[53] Such a transfer need be executed only by the transferor and need not be attested: 1963 Act, s.1. Additional permitted forms were introduced for the computerised "Talisman" system of transfers on the stock exchange; *i.e.* where the transfer is to or from a stock exchange nominee under the Stock Exchange (Completion of Bargains) Act 1976.[54]

The 1963 Act applies to, *inter alia,* fully paid up registered securities issued by a company limited by shares, or by a statutory company or a chartered company (but not by a building society or an industrial and provident society), or, subject to exceptions, by the Government or by a local authority, or which are units of a unit trust scheme: section 1. The expression "registered securities" means transferable securities the holders of which are entered in a register, and "securities" includes shares, stock, debentures, debenture stock, loan stock, bonds and units of a unit trust scheme: section 4.

Where a stock transfer has been executed for the purpose of a stock exchange transaction, particulars of the consideration and of the transferee may be either inserted in such transfer or, where there are several transferees, supplied by brokers' transfers, *i.e.* separate instruments in the form set out in Schedule 2 to the 1963 Act, identifying the stock transfer and specifying the securities to which each relates. The transferor need not sign a brokers' transfer: section 1.

Procedure on transfer

If a shareholder has sold all his shares comprised in one share certificate[55] to one person,[56] the transfer is effected as follows:

(1) The transferor sends the transferee a "proper instrument of transfer" required by section 75 and complying with the articles

---

[53] As amended by the Stock Transfer (Amendment of Forms) Order 1974 (S.I. No. 1214).

[54] Introduced by the Stock Transfer (Addition of Forms) Order 1979 (S.I. No. 277).

[55] As to shares comprised in a share warrant, see, *post,* p. 299.

[56] As to the procedure when, *e.g.* part only of the holding is being sold, see Certification of transfers, *post.*

STOCK TRANSFER FORM [57]

		Certificate lodged with the Registrar
		(For completion by the Registrar/Stock Exchange)
Consideration Money	£	

Name of Undertaking.	
Description of security.	

	Words	Figures
Number or amount of Shares, Stock or other security and, in figures column only, number and denomination of units, if any.		(units of)

	in the name(s) of
Name(s) of registered holder(s) should be given in full: the address should be given where there is only one holder. If the transfer is not made by the registered holder(s) insert also the name(s) and capacity (e.g., Executor(s)), of the person(s) making the transfer.	

Delete words in italics except for stock exchange transactions. Bodies corporate should execute under their common seal.	I/We hereby transfer the above security out of the name(s) aforesaid to the person(s) named below *or to the several persons named in Parts 2 of Brokers Transfer Forms relating to the above security:*	Stamp of Selling Broker(s), or, for transactions which are not stock exchange transactions, of Agent(s), if any, acting for the Transferor(s).

Signature(s) of transferor(s)
1 .... 3 ....
2 .... 4 ....

Date ....

Full name(s), full postal address(es) (including County or, if applicable, Postal District number) of the person(s) to whom the security is transferred.	
Please state title, if any, or whether Mr., Mrs. or Miss. Please complete in typewriting or in Block Capitals.	

[57] This is the form used otherwise than under the stock exchange's Talisman system of transfers.

I/We request that such entries be made in the register as are necessary to give effect to this transfer.

Stamp of Buying Broker(s) (if any)	Stamp or name and address of person lodging this form (if other than the Buying Broker(s))

(Endorsement for use only in stock exchange transactions)
The security represented by the transfer overleaf has been sold as follows:

.... *Shares/Stock*   .... *Shares/Stock*
.... *Shares/Stock*   .... *Shares/Stock*
.... *Shares/Stock*   .... *Shares/Stock*
.... *Shares/Stock*   .... *Shares/Stock*
.... *Shares/Stock*   .... *Shares/Stock*
.... *Shares/Stock*   .... *Shares/Stock*
.... *Shares/Stock*   .... *Shares/Stock*

Balance (if any) due to Selling Broker(s)   ....

Amount of Certificate(s)

Brokers Transfer Forms for above amounts certified
Stamp of certifying Stock Exchange   *Stamp of Selling Broker(s)*

The only stock exchange now recognised for the purposes of the 1963 Act is The Stock Exchange.[58]

> or the Stock Transfer Act 1963, *ante,* and executed by the transferor, together with the share certificate relating to the shares comprised in the transfer.
>
> (2) The transferee then executes the transfer if it is in accordance with the articles, stamps it and forwards it, with the share certificate and the registration fee, to the company for registration.
>
> (3) Within two months[59] after the transfer is lodged the company must either issue a new share certificate to the transferee or, where the directors are exercising a power to refuse registration, send *him* notice of its refusal to register the transfer: sections 80, 78. In the case of transfers under the Talisman system of stock exchange transfers so that a stock exchange

---

[58] 1963 Act, s.4; Stock Transfer (Recognised Stock Exchanges) Order 1973 (S.I. No. 536).

[59] Fourteen days if the shares are quoted on a stock exchange: Rules of The Stock Exchange, App. 34, Sched. VIII, Pt. A.

nominee is the transferee the company is exempt from the obligation to prepare the new share certificate: Stock Exchange (Completion of Bargains) Act 1976, sections 1, 7.

The Jenkins Report[60] recommended that the period be five weeks and that notice of a refusal be given to the transferor too.

The penalty for non-compliance is a default fine on the company and every officer who knowingly authorises or permits the default: sections 78, 80.

Table A contains the following provisions as to transfers of shares:

Article 25.—"The directors may also decline to recognise any instrument of transfer unless:—

(a) a fee of 12½p. or such lesser sum as the directors may from time to time require is paid to the company in respect thereof[61];
(b) the instrument of transfer is accompanied by the certificate of the shares to which it relates, and such other evidence as the directors may reasonably require to show the right of the transferor to make the transfer; and
(c) the instrument of transfer is in respect of only one class of share."

Article 27.—"The registration of transfers may be suspended at such times and for such periods as the directors may from time to time determine, provided always that such registration shall not be suspended for more than thirty days in any year."

Directors must not register a transfer unless it is correctly stamped.[62] If the consideration expressed is substantially below the value of the shares, they should make inquiry as to the true consideration; even if the stamp duty is in accordance with the consideration expressed on the transfer, they are entitled to make inquiries as to the true consideration and to decline registration until the correct stamp duty is paid.[63]

The stamp duty on transfers is at the rate of £1 per cent. on the price.[64]

A transfer may also be registered, at the request of the transferor, in

---

[60] Para. 483.
[61] No fee is payable for registration of transfers if the shares are quoted on a stock exchange: Rules of The Stock Exchange, App. 34, Sched. VIII, Pt. A.
[62] Stamp Act 1891, s.17 (the penalty is a fine of £10).
[63] *Maynard* v. *Consolidated Kent Collieries* [1903] 2 K.B. 121.
[64] Stamp Act 1891, s.1, Sched. 1; Finance Act 1963, s.55, Sched. 2.

the same manner and subject to the same conditions as if registration were applied for by the transferee: section 77.

Certification of transfer

If a holder of shares sells some only of his shares comprised in a share certificate, *e.g.* 250 shares out of 1,000, it will be unsafe for him to deliver his share certificate for 1,000 shares to the purchaser. Similarly if he sells some of the shares to one person and the rest to another. The usual procedure in such cases, is, therefore:

(1) The transferor executes the transfer and sends it, with the share certificate, to the company.

(2) The secretary indorses on the transfer the words "certificate lodged" or similar words, and returns the transfer so certificated to the transferor.

(3) The transferor hands over this certificated transfer to the transferee against payment of the price.

(4) The transferee executes the transfer if it is in the form prescribed by the articles, has it stamped, and forwards it to the company for registration.

(5) Within two months[65] the company either issues new share certificates or, where a power to refuse registration is being exercised, informs the *transferee* of its refusal to register him: sections 78, 80, *ante.* This does not apply to transfers to a stock exchange nominee under the Talisman system, *ante.*

The certification of a transfer is a representation by the company to any person acting on the faith of the certification that there have been produced to the company such documents as show a prima facie title to the shares in the transferor, but it is not a representation that the transferor has any title: section 79(1). However, if a company *fraudulently or negligently* makes a false certification the company is liable in damages to a person who acts on the faith of it to his detriment: section 79(2).

Suppose that P transferred all his shares to X and his certificate was lodged by X with the company. Before registration was completed, P executed a transfer of some of the shares to Y, who sold them to B. Y's transfer to B was negligently certificated by the company and, on the strength of this, B paid Y.

---

[65] See note 59 above.

The company registered X and refused to register B. The company is liable in damages to B.

A certification is deemed to be made by the company if it is made by a person, such as the secretary, authorised to issue certificated transfers on the company's behalf and if it is signed by a person authorised to certificate transfers on the company's behalf: section 79(3).

When a transfer is certificated the company destroys the original certificate and issues new certificates. But if it *negligently* returns the original certificate with the certificated transfer to the transferor and the transferor then fraudulently deals with the original certificate so as to inflict loss on a third party, *e.g.* the transferor purports to transfer *all* the shares comprised in the original certificate to the third party, the company is not liable to the third party. The reason is that the share certificate is neither a negotiable instrument nor a warranty of title on the part of the company issuing it, and the company owes no duty to the public as to the custody of the certificate. Further, the company is not estopped from denying the validity of the transferor's title to the shares *previously* transferred, because the proximate cause of the third party's loss is the fraud of the transferor and not the negligence of the company.[66]

Rights as between vendor and purchaser

On a sale of shares the ordinary contract between the parties is that the vendor shall give to the purchaser a valid transfer and do all that is required to enable the purchaser to be registered as a member in respect of the shares, the purchaser's duty being to get himself registered.[67] The vendor's duty is not only to give a genuine transfer but also, where the vendor is not the transferor, one which is signed by a transferor willing that the transfer shall be registered.

Solicitors instructed stockbrokers to sell stock and enclosed the certificate and a blank transfer (*i.e.* a transfer in which the transferee's name had still to be inserted)[68] signed by the stockholder. The stockbrokers sold the stock but

[66] *Longman* v. *Bath Electric Tramways Ltd.* [1905] 1 Ch. 646. The Scottish equivalent of "estoppel" is personal bar, but, in the absence of Scottish authority on certification, it seems doubtful whether a company would be entitled to deny the validity of a share certificate in the circumstances mentioned: *cf. Clavering, Son & Co.* v. *Goodwins, Jardine & Co. Ltd.* (1891) 18 R. 652.

[67] *Skinner* v. *City of London Marine Insce. Corpn.* (1885) 14 Q.B.D. 882 (C.A.).

[68] Such a transfer may be invalid in Scots law: *post,* p. 286.

the stockholder repudiated the contract and the company, on her instructions, refused to register the transfer. The stockbrokers replaced the stock by a purchase on the Stock Exchange and sued the solicitors for an indemnity. *Held*, (1) the solicitors were principals of the stockbrokers as regards the sale, (2) it was the solicitor's duty to deliver a transfer executed by a transferor willing that it should be registered, and (3) the solicitors were liable: *Hichens, Harrison, Woolston & Co.* v. *Jackson & Sons* [1943] A.C. 266.

If the directors, in pursuance of a power in the articles, decline to register the transfer, the purchaser, unless he bought "with registration guaranteed," will be unable to sue the vendor for damages or rescind and recover the price from the vendor—there is no implied condition subsequent to such effect.[69] In such a case the vendor will be a trustee of the shares for the purchaser.[70] The vendor is, of course, under a duty to the purchaser not to prevent or delay the registration of the transfer.[71]

As from the time of the contract of sale, the equitable or beneficial interest in the shares passes to the purchaser, and the vendor holds the legal title as quasi-trustee for the purchaser.[72] The purchaser does not obtain the legal or complete title until his name is entered on the register of members.[73]

Until the transfer is registered, the vendor will receive any dividends or other benefits declared on the shares and, in the case of partly paid shares, calls may be made on him. As between the vendor and the purchaser the rights and liabilities depend on the terms of the contract. The shares may be bought "cum" or "ex" dividends or rights, or with a specified sum paid. In the absence of any such agreement, the purchaser is entitled to dividends or other benefits declared after the *date of the contract*.[74]

In September 1935, R. sold shares privately to W. In April, 1936, the company declared a dividend for the year ending December 31, 1935. *Held*, the sale being by private bargain and not governed by Stock Exchange rules,

---

[69] *London Founders Assocn. Ltd.* v. *Clarke* (1888) 20 Q.B.D. 576 (C.A.).

[70] *Stevenson* v. *Wilson*, 1907 S.C. 445; this quasi-trust would not, however, defeat a subsequent arrestment of the shares by a creditor of the transferor: *per* Lord Moncrieff (Ordinary) in *National Bank of Scotland Glasgow Nominees Ltd.* v. *Adamson*, 1932 S.L.T. 492 (O.H.), at p. 495.

[71] *Hooper* v. *Herts* [1906] 1 Ch. 549 (C.A.).

[72] See note 70 above.

[73] See, *per* Lord Gifford in *Morrison* v. *Harrison* (1876) 3 R. 406, at p.411; see also *Tennant's Trustees* v. *Tennant*, 1946 S.C. 420.

[74] *Black* v. *Homersham* (1878) 4 Ex.D. 24; *Re Kidner* [1929] 2 Ch. 121.

W. was entitled to the whole dividend and it was not apportionable between W. and R.: *Re Wimbush* [1940] Ch. 92.

Subject to contrary agreement, the purchaser must indemnify the vendor against calls made after the date of the contract.

X, owner of shares not fully paid up, sold to Y, giving him a blank transfer. Y, without being entered on the register, sold to Z, giving Z a blank transfer. Z was not entered on the register, and became bankrupt. The company made a call on X. *Held,* Y was bound to indemnify X, although Y had then no beneficial interest. The implied obligation arose out of the contract between them: *Spencer* v. *Ashworth, Partington & Co.* [1925] 1 K.B. 589 (C.A.).

Note: Z would have been liable to indemnify X only during the period of Z's beneficial ownership. The obligation would have arisen from the relationship of trustee and beneficiary between them.

Again, until the transfer is registered, the vendor is entitled to exercise any vote conferred by the shares but he must vote as directed by the purchaser.

An unpaid vendor of shares who remains on the register of members after the contract of sale retains *vis-à-vis* the purchaser the right to vote in respect of those shares unless the contract restricts such right.[75]

Priorities

In England, when the same shares are claimed by two innocent parties the general rules are:

(1) The party who is on the register of members and therefore has the legal title has priority.

(2) If neither party is on the register, the party whose equitable title is first in time has priority.

For example, if X, the registered owner, is trustee of the shares for Y and, in breach of trust sells the shares to Z, who buys without notice of the trust and becomes registered as owner before the company knows of the trust, Z will have priority over Y. A company, however, is entitled to a reasonable time for the consideration of every transfer before it registers the transfer,[76] and therefore if Y, in the example just given, had given notice of his claim to the company before Z was

---

[75] *Musselwhite* v. *C. H. Musselwhite & Son Ltd.* [1962] Ch. 964, where a contract for the sale of shares provided that the transfer and share certificate should be held by a third party until the price was paid by instalments over a period of years.

[76] *Re Ottos Kopje Diamond Mines Ltd.* [1893] 1 Ch. 618 (C.A.).

actually registered as owner, he would have been entitled to priority over Z, as his equitable title would have been first in time.[77]

C. assigned all his property to P. as trustee for C's creditors. The property included some shares. P. asked for the share certificates but was unable to obtain them from C.; he then gave notice of the assignment to the company. C., after the date of the assignment to P., sold the shares to X, who applied for registration. *Held,* P., having an equitable title which was prior in time, was entitled to registration: *Peat* v. *Clayton* [1906] 1 Ch. 659.

Entry on the register after notice of a prior equitable claim will not give priority.

In 1893 X transferred debentures of a private company to Y on trust for X for life with remainder to X's sons. The transfer was not registered. In 1894 one son sold his share of the debentures to Z. In 1911 X deposited the debentures with the bank as security for the company's overdraft. In 1914 the bank, on learning of the settlement and transfer to Y, took a transfer of the debentures from X, and were registered as owners. *Held,* Z was entitled to priority over the bank: *Coleman* v. *London County and Westminster Bank Ltd.* [1916] 2 Ch. 353.

It has been said[77] that even if a complete legal title has not been obtained, a person who has, as between himself and the company, a present, absolute, unconditional right to registration before the company learns of a better title, has the same priority as if he were actually registered. It is doubtful, however, whether anything short of registration will give priority, except perhaps in very special circumstances. Directors should refuse to register a transfer after receiving notice of an adverse equitable claim to the shares, unless the transfer has already been passed for registration.[78]

Delay in obtaining registration is dangerous to a transferee for two reasons: a later transferee may gain priority by obtaining registration first, or an earlier equity may come to light.

A husband mortgaged shares of which he was trustee for his wife. Before the mortgagee was registered the wife successfully claimed that her equitable title prevailed over that of the mortgagee: *Ireland* v. *Hart* [1902] 1 Ch. 522.

To protect himself such a transferee should issue a stop notice.[79]

In Scotland, if there are competing claims for membership of a

---

[77] *Per* Romer J. in *Moore* v. *North Western Bank* [1891] 2 Ch. 599, at pp. 602, 603.
[78] *Per* Joyce J. in *Ireland* v. *Hart* [1902] 1 Ch. 522, at p. 529.
[79] See, p. 285, *post.*

company, the person preferred is the one who first completes his title to the shares by having his name entered on the register; a mere assignation of shares, even though intimated to the company, does not make the assignee a member.[80]

Where a competition arises between a transferee and an arrester, the transferee is preferred to the arrester as soon as the transfer has been registered.[81] In a question between a transferee whose transfer has been duly intimated to the company but not registered and a subsequent arrester, the intimation of the transfer has been held to cut out the arrestment.[82]

Directors may delay registration where they suspect that a transfer is affected by fraud or dishonesty[83] but, if they receive intimation of a competing interest in the shares from some party other than the transferee, they are entitled to register the transfer unless the intimation is followed up by a legal measure such as interdict.[84] The company must be made a party to any such interdict process, and interdict has been refused where it was alleged that share transfers, bearing that the beneficial interest remained in the transferors, had been executed by a body of trustees to certain of their own number and another person in order to give the transferees a qualification to act as directors; the possibility that the shares had been transferred in breach of trust was not, the court held, a matter which concerned the company or which made the registration of the transferees invalid.[85]

Forged transfer

A forged transfer of shares is a nullity and cannot affect the title of the shareholder whose signature is forged. If the company, therefore, has registered the forged transfer and removed the true owner of the shares from the register, it can be compelled to replace him.[86] It can then claim an indemnity from the person who sent the forged transfer for registration if it has sustained loss through acting thereon. No

[80] *Morrison* v. *Harrison* (1876) 3 R. 406.
[81] *National Bank of Scotland Glasgow Nominees Ltd.* v. *Adamson*, 1932 S.L.T. 492 (O.H.).
[82] *Jackson* v. *Elphick* (1902) 10 S.L.T. 146 (O.H.).
[83] *Property Investment Co. of Scotland Ltd.* v. *Duncan* (1887) 14 R. 299.
[84] *Per* Lord M'Laren in *Shaw* v. *Caledonian Rlwy. Co.* (1890) 17 R. 466, at p. 482.
[85] *Elliot* v. *J. W. Mackie & Sons Ltd.*, 1935 S.C. 81.
[86] *Barton* v. *N. Staffordshire Rlwy. Co.* (1888) 38 Ch.D. 458.

estoppel in favour of such a person arises from a share certificate issued to him even though he knows nothing of the forgery—he has not relied on the act of the company in issuing the certificate.

B. sent to the corporation for registration a transfer of stock which stood in the names of T. and H. The transfer was a forgery, T. having forged H.'s signature to the transfer, but B. was ignorant of this. The corporation registered the transfer. B. transferred the stock to third parties to whom certificates were issued. The corporation was estopped from denying that those registered were the stockholders entitled. H. subsequently discovered the forgery and compelled the corporation to buy him an equivalent amount of stock and to pay him the missing dividends with interest. *Held,* B. was bound to indemnify the corporation upon an implied contract that the transfer was genuine: *Sheffield Corporation* v. *Barclay* [1905] A.C. 392.[87]

This right extends to an indemnity from a stockbroker who makes the application on behalf of the person with the forged transfer.[88] The company may not, however, be able to claim a complete indemnity if it is guilty of negligence in failing to spot the forgery. In such a situation it has been suggested that section 2(1) of the Civil Liability (Contribution) Act 1978 may prevent complete recovery.[88]

In an effort to prevent the registration of a forged transfer, companies usually, on a transfer being lodged for registration, write to the shareholder informing him of the transfer and of their intention to register it unless by return of post they hear that he objects. The neglect of the shareholder to reply to this communication does not estop him from proving that the transfer is a forgery.[89]

By the Forged Transfers Acts 1891 and 1892 companies are empowered to pay compensation for any loss sustained owing to forged transfers, even if they are under no legal obligation to pay it. The Acts provide for the formation of a fund, if the company thinks fit, to meet claims for compensation. Many companies insure against the risk of forged transfers.

TRANSMISSION OF SHARES

Section 75, *ante,*[90] provides that it does not prejudice any power of a company to register as shareholder any person to whom the right to

---

[87] *cf.* Lord Kyllachy (Ordinary) in *Clavering, Son & Co.* v. *Goodwins, Jardine & Co. Ltd.* (1891) 18 R. 652, at p. 657.
[88] *Yeung* v. *Hong Kong & Shanghai Bank Ltd.* [1980] 2 All E.R. 599 (P.C.).
[89] *Re Bahia and San Francisco Rlwy. Co.* (1868) L.R. 3 Q.B. 584, *ante,* p. 263; *Barton* v. *L. & N.W. Rlwy. Co.* (1890) 24 Q.B.D. 77 (C.A.).
[90] p. 271.

any shares in the company has been transmitted by operation of law. Transmission of shares occurs on the death or the bankruptcy of a member, or, if the member is a company, on its going into liquidation.

On the death of a sole shareholder the shares vest in his personal representative,[91] *i.e.* his executor or administrator.[92] The company is bound to accept production of the probate of the will or, in the case of an intestacy, letters of administration of the estate, or, in Scotland, the confirmation as executor, as sufficient evidence of the grant: section 82. Table A, article 28, provides that the company may charge a fee for the registration of any such instrument. Subject to any restrictions in the articles, the personal representative may be registered as a member or transfer the shares without himself becoming a member: section 76.[93]

Table A, article 30, provides: "Any person becoming entitled to a share in consequence of the death or bankruptcy of a member may, upon such evidence being produced as may from time to time properly be required by the directors and subject as hereinafter provided, elect either to be registered himself as holder of the share or to have some person nominated by him registered as the transferee thereof, but the directors shall, in either case, have the same right to decline or suspend registration as they would have had in the case of a transfer of the share by that member before his death or bankruptcy, as the case may be."

When shares are jointly held, the surviving holder becomes the sole holder. Under Table A, article 29, the estate of the deceased joint holder is not released from any liability in respect of the shares.

On the bankruptcy of a member, his shares vest in his trustee in bankruptcy who may,[94-95] subject to the articles, either be registered as a member himself or transfer the shares without being registered as a member.[96]

MORTGAGE OF SHARES (ENGLISH LAW)

In England, a shareholder who borrows money on the security of his shares may give the lender either a legal mortgage or an equitable mortgage over the shares.

---

[91] *Re Greene* [1949] Ch. 333.
[92] Executor in Scots law: see p. 188, *ante.*
[93] *Ante*, p. 189.
[94-95] Bankruptcy Act 1914, ss.18(1), 53(1), (2); Bankruptcy (Scotland) Act 1913, ss.70, 97 and Sched. D.
[96] *Ante*, p. 190.

Legal mortgage

A legal mortgage of shares is effected by transfer of the shares to the lender (the mortgagee) followed by registration of the transfer by the company. There should also be a document setting out the terms of the loan and containing an agreement to retransfer the shares on re-payment of the amount borrowed with interest. The document will empower the lender to sell the shares in the event of default by the borrower (the mortgagor).

This form of mortgage gives the lender complete security up to the value of the shares. He will be entitled to dividends and to exercise any voting rights in respect of the shares, unless it is agreed that the dividends shall be paid to the borrower and that he shall exercise the voting rights as the borrower directs.[97]

However, restrictions on the transfer of shares contained in the articles[98] may prevent this kind of mortgage being made. Further, it might not be advisable where the shares are not fully paid because the lender on the register would be personally liable for calls.

Equitable mortgage

1. An equitable mortgage of shares may be made by depositing the share certificate with the lender as security for a loan. In such a case the lender can enforce his security by applying to the court for a sale of the shares or for an order for transfer and foreclosure.[99]

2. A method more commonly adopted is for the borrower to deposit with the lender the share certificate together with a blank transfer, *i.e.* a transfer signed by the borrower with the transferee's name left blank. In such a case the lender has an *implied* power to sell the shares if default is made by the borrower in making repayment at the agreed time or, if no time for repayment is agreed, within a reasonable time after notice.[1] The implied power of sale includes power to insert the name of the buyer in the blank transfer if, as is usual, the articles provide for transfers to be in writing. The borrower is under an implied obligation not to delay registration of the transfer so filled up.[2]

3. If the articles require transfers to be by deed, the lender cannot fill up a blank transfer unless he is authorised by deed. In such a case an equitable mortgage may be made by deposit of the share certificate

---

[97] *Siemens Brothers & Co. Ltd.* v. *Burns* [1918] 2 Ch. 324.   [98] *Ante,* p. 265.
[99] *Harrold* v. *Plenty* [1901] 2 Ch. 314.   [1] *Hooper* v. *Herts* [1906] 1 Ch. 549.
[2] *Powell* v. *London and Provincial Bank* [1893] 2 Ch. 555 (C.A.).

plus a transfer by deed to the lender. If the borrower defaults, the lender can lodge the transfer for registration.

No equitable mortgage is in itself absolutely secure because the borrower remains on the register and may sell the shares and procure the registration of the purchaser with priority over the lender, who would have no remedy against the company.

C. deposited his share certificate and a blank transfer with R. as a security for a loan. Upon the certificate was printed: "Without the production of this certificate no transfer of the shares mentioned therein can be registered." C. sold the shares to Y. and induced the company to register Y. as owner of the shares without the production of the share certificate. R. sued the company for wrongfully registering the shares in Y's name. *Held,* the company was not liable as it owed no duty of care to R., and the statement on the certificate was only a warning to the owner of the shares to take care of the certificate and not a statement of fact giving rise to an estoppel: *Rainford* v. *James Keith & Blackman Co. Ltd.* [1905] 1 Ch. 296.[3]

However, the mortgagor must exercise any voting rights as directed by the mortgagee.[4]

Stop notice

To obtain complete protection, an equitable mortgagee of shares should serve a stop notice. This is done by filing an affidavit setting out the facts, and a notice in the prescribed form, in the Central Office of the Supreme Court or in a District Registry and serving an office copy of the affidavit and a duplicate notice on the company. The effect of the notice is that, whilst it continues in force, if the company receives any request to register a transfer of the shares in question it must give notice in writing to the person who has served the notice. Within eight days, such person must apply for an injunction restraining the transfer or the company will be at liberty to register the transfer.[5]

Charging order

A judgment creditor of the registered owner of shares may obtain an order charging the shares with payment of the judgment debt,[6] after

---

[3] Reversed on the facts [1905] 2 Ch. 147 (C.A.). On the facts the company was affected with notice of R's charge and he was able to recover the price of the shares which had been paid to the company in repayment of a loan made by the company to C.

[4] *Wise* v. *Lansdell* [1921] 1 Ch. 420.

[5] R.S.C., O.50, rr.11–15. See also the Charging Orders Act 1979.

[6] R.S.C., O.50, rr.2–7.

which, until the order is discharged, the company cannot permit a transfer except with the authority of the court. A charging order will not have priority over a mortgage created by deposit of the share certificate and a blank transfer before the date of the charging order, as the judgment creditor can be in no better position than the judgment debtor at the time when the order was made.

ASSIGNATION OF SHARES IN SECURITY (SCOTS LAW)

The only effective way of assigning shares in security is by the execution and registration of a transfer in favour of the lender. See the section headed "Legal mortgage," *ante*.[7]

No form of the equitable mortgage recognised by English law gives the lender any real security in competition with the general creditors of the borrower.[8] Accordingly, where a borrower delivers the share certificate to the lender and undertakes to transfer the shares to the lender when requested to do so, a transfer executed within six months before the borrower's notour bankruptcy is reducible as a fraudulent preference under the Bankruptcy Act 1696 (Scots Act 1696, c. 5) as amended by the Companies Act 1947, s.115,[9] and even intimation to the company of the lender's right to the shares will not avail the lender unless his right is completed by his actually becoming a shareholder.[10] Where, however, a completed transfer has been delivered to the lender along with the share certificate so that the lender is in a position to have himself registered as a member without further interposition of the borrower, registration of the transfer on the eve of the borrower's sequestration is not open to challenge as a fraudulent preference provided the delivery of the documents to the lender was made more than six months before the borrower's notour bankruptcy.[11] A blank transfer may be invalid under the Blank Bonds and Trusts Act 1696 (Scots Act 1696, c. 25) which declares null "bonds, assignations, dispositions or other deeds" subscribed blank in the name of the person or persons in whose favour they are conceived.

Stop notices and charging orders are not part of Scots law. When a

---

[7] p. 284.

[8] *Gourlay* v. *Mackie* (1887) 14 R. 403; *per* Lord Gifford in *Morrison* v. *Harrison* (1876) 3 R. 406, at p.411; *cf. Guild* v. *Young* (1884) 22 S.L.R. 520 (O.H.).

[9] *Gourlay* v. *Mackie* (1887) 14 R. 403.

[10] *Per* Lord Gifford in *Morrison* v. *Harrison* (1876) 3 R. 406, at p. 411.

[11] *Guild* v. *Young* (1884) 22 S.L.R. 520 (O.H.).

company called on to register a transfer receives intimation from some person other than the transferee that that other person has an interest in the shares, the company is entitled to proceed to register the transfer unless the intimation is followed up by an application for interdict or other legal measure.[12]

Shares are subject to arrestment at the instance of the creditors of the shareholder, whether the arrestment is in execution[13] or merely to found jurisdiction.[14] Where competition arises between a transferee and an arrester the transferee has the preferable right to the shares as soon as his transfer has been lodged, even although it is not registered before the lodging of the arrestment.

In January S. transferred 200 shares to M. and 1,000 shares to F., and the transfers were received by the secretary of the company on 19th January and 2nd February respectively. Because of an arrestment lodged the previous November against S. at the instance of a bank, the transfers were not registered. On 30th March arrestments were executed at the instance of D. against S. *Held,* the transfers to M. and F. were preferable to D.'s arrestments: *Harvey's Yoker Distillery Ltd.* v. *Singleton* (1901) 8 S.L.T. 369 (O.H.).

"An arrestment can only attach property belonging truly and in substance to the common debtor. Now these shares did not belong in substance to Singleton at the time of the arrestment, because he had by that time done all in his power to dispose of them by executing the transfers": *per* Lord Stormonth Darling (Ordinary) at p. 370.

An arrester is not entitled to found on any irregularity in the registration procedure to the effect of defeating the transferee's title.[15] Intimation to the company of a transfer, even without registration, has the effect, in a question between the transferee and a subsequent arrester, of cutting out the arrestment.[16]

CALLS ON SHARES

A call on shares is a demand by the directors that a member pay to the company money which is unpaid on his shares, whether on account of

---

[12] *Per* Lord M'Laren in *Shaw* v. *Caledonian Rlwy. Co.* (1890) 17 R. 466, at p. 482.
[13] *Sinclair* v. *Staples* (1860) 22 D. 600.
[14] *American Mortgage Co. of Scotland Ltd.* v. *Sidway,* 1908 S.C. 500.
[15] *National Bank of Scotland Glasgow Nominees Ltd.* v. *Adamson,* 1932 S.L.T. 492 (O.H.); for an arrestment made effective by the granting by the court of a warrant to sell the shares, see *Valentine* v. *Grangemouth Coal Co. Ltd.* (1897) 35 S.L.R. 12 (O.H.).
[16] *Jackson* v. *Elphick* (1902) 10 S.L.T. 146 (O.H.).

the nominal value of the shares or by way of premium.[16a] Since shares are now usually fully paid up, calls are uncommon today.[17] If, when shares are issued, the full amount of each share is not payable at once, the terms of issue will provide that part is payable on application, part on allotment and the remainder by instalments at fixed dates, in which case the instalments are not calls,[18] as the obligation of the shareholder to pay is not dependent on a call from the company. However, in a rare case, the company may not require all the nominal amount of a share, or the full amount of a premium on a share, to be paid at or soon after allotment but may leave part to be called up in accordance with the provisions of the articles as and when required by the company or, in the event of a winding up, by the liquidator. If so, a shareholder is bound to pay the whole or part of the balance unpaid on his shares "as and when called on," in accordance with the provisions of the articles. Calls must be made in the manner laid down in the articles.

Table A, article 15, provides: "The directors may from time to time make calls upon the members in respect of any moneys unpaid on their shares (whether on account of the nominal value of the shares or by way of premium) and not by the conditions of allotment thereof made payable at fixed times, provided that no call shall exceed one-fourth of the nominal value of the share or be payable at less than one month from the date fixed for the payment of the last preceding call, and each member shall (subject to receiving at least 14 days' notice specifying the time or times and place of payment) pay to the company at the time or times and place so specified the amount called on his shares. A call may be revoked or postponed as the directors may determine."

Table A, article 16, provides: "A call shall be deemed to have been made at the time when the resolution of the directors authorising the call was passed. . . ."

Where the articles require the time and place of payment and the amount of the call to be specified, a call is not properly made if the resolution of the directors authorising the call specifies the amount of the call but not the date of payment.[19] A verbal direction to the secretary fixing the date of payment is not enough.[20]

In England a call creates a specialty debt due from the shareholder

---

[16a] For Scots *dicta* on the nature of a call see Lord President M'Neill in *Wryght* v. *Lindsay* (1856) 19 D. 55, at p. 63; affd. (1860) 22 D. (H.L.) 5.

[17] *Ante*, p. 208.

[18] But articles may provide that they shall be *deemed* to be calls: see Table A, art. 19.

[19] *Re Cawley & Co.* (1889) 42 Ch.D. 209 (C.A.).

[20] *Per* James L.J. in *Johnson* v. *Lyttle's Iron Agency* (1877) 5 Ch.D. 687 (C.A.), at p. 694.

to the company (s.20(2)), and so the period within which an action can be brought for payment of it is 12 years.[21] In Scotland a call remains enforceable until the expiry of 20 years.[22] Table A, article 18, provides for payment of interest at the rate of five per cent. from the date fixed for payment until actual payment.

If authorised by the articles, a company may make arrangements on the issue of shares for a difference between the shareholders in the amounts and times of payment of calls: section 59(a). Table A, article 20, authorises such an arrangement. Such a power does not entitle directors to make calls on all the shareholders except themselves,[23] at any rate without the knowledge and sanction of the other shareholders—the directors' power to make calls must be exercised bona fide for the benefit of the company as a whole, and not so as to give themselves an advantage over other shareholders.[24]

Any arrangement made under section 59(a) must be made at the time of the issue of shares. If no such arrangement is made, the rule is that "prima facie it is entirely improper for the directors to make a call on some members of a class of shareholders who stand in the same relation to the company as the other members of the class without making a similar call on all the other members of that class."[25]

Table A, articles 33 to 39, provides for forfeiture for non-payment of a call or an instalment.[26]

In an action to enforce payment of a call it is no defence for the shareholder to say that he has repudiated the contract because of misrepresentations in the prospectus. To succeed he must show that he has taken steps to have his name removed from the register of members.[27]

Calls made by a liquidator in the course of a winding up are in some respects different from calls made by directors during the active existence of the company.[28]

---

[21] Limitation Act 1980, s.8(1).
[22] Prescription and Limitation (Scotland) Act 1973, s.7.
[23] *Alexander* v. *Automatic Telephone Co.* [1900] 2 Ch. 56 (C.A.).
[24] *Post*, p. 371.
[25] *Per* Sargant J. in *Galloway* v. *Hallé Concerts Society* [1915] 2 Ch. 233, at p. 239.
[26] *Post*, p. 295.
[27] *First National Reinsurance Co.* v. *Greenfield* [1921] 2 K.B. 260; *Scottish Amalgamated Silks Ltd.* v. *Macalister*, 1930 S.L.T. 593 (O.H.); see, however, *Liquidators of Mount Morgan (West) Gold Mine Ltd.* v. *M'Mahon* (1891) 18 R. 772.
[28] *Mitchell, Petitioner* (1863) 1 M. 1116; *Liquidators of Benhar Coal Co. Ltd., Petitioners* (1882) 9 R. 763.

Payment in advance of calls

If authorised by the articles, a company may accept payment from a member of the whole or a part of the amount remaining unpaid on his shares, although no part of this amount has been called up: section 59(*b*).

Table A, article 21, provides: "The directors may, if they think fit, receive from any member willing to advance the same, all or any part of the moneys uncalled and unpaid upon any shares held by him, and upon all or any of the moneys so advanced may (until the same would, but for such advance, become payable) pay interest at such rate not exceeding (unless the company in general meeting shall otherwise direct) 5 per cent. per annum, as may be agreed upon between the directors and the member paying such sum in advance."

When a payment in advance of calls has been made the consequences are:

(1) The shareholder's liability to the company is extinguished or reduced, as the case may be.

(2) He becomes a creditor to the extent of the payment in advance, so that interest on it can be paid out of capital,[29] *i.e.* whether profits are made by the company or not.

(3) The company cannot be compelled to repay the payment,[30] except in a winding up, *post.*

(4) The company cannot repay without the consent of the shareholder.[31]

(5) In a winding up he will rank after the other creditors but will be entitled to repayment of the advance with interest in priority to the other shareholders who have not paid in advance.[32]

The power of receiving payment in advance of calls is a fiduciary power and must be exercised by the directors bona fide for the benefit of the company as a whole, and not for the private ends of the directors. Accordingly, where directors, knowing the company to be insolvent, paid the amount remaining unpaid on their shares and on

---

[29] *Lock* v. *Queensland Investment and Land Mortgage Co.* [1896] A.C. 461; *Myles, Petitioner* (1893) 1 S.L.T. 90 (O.H.).

[30] *Per* Lindley and Kay L.JJ. in *Lock* v. *Queensland Investment etc. Co.* [1896] 1 Ch. 397 (C.A.), at pp. 405, 407.

[31] *London and Northern Steamship Co.* v. *Farmer* (1914) 111 L.T. 204.

[32] *Re Exchange Drapery Co.* (1888) 38 Ch.D. 171.

the same day appropriated the money in payment of their fees, it was held that they still remained liable on the shares.[33] However, although directors are trustees of their powers for the shareholders,[34] they are not trustees for the company's creditors, and where, the company being insolvent, they paid in advance the amount of their calls and applied the money in discharging the company's bank overdraft, which they had guaranteed, it was held that their shares were fully paid up.[35]

LIEN ON SHARES (ENGLISH LAW)

The articles of a private company may give the company a lien on the shares held by a member for his unpaid call or instalment, or for some other debt due from him to the company. Public companies, however, may only have a lien on such shares for an unpaid call or instalment on those shares: 1980 Act, s.38. By way of exception a money-lending or credit company may have a lien on any of its shares for non-payment of a debt owed by the shareholder in the ordinary course of the company's business.

Such a lien is an equitable charge upon the shares, and gives rise to the same rights as if the shares had been expressly charged by the member in favour of the company.[36]

Table A, article 11, provides: "The company shall have a first and paramount lien on every share (not being a fully paid share) for all moneys (whether presently payable or not) called or payable at a fixed time in respect of that share, but the directors may at any time declare any share to be wholly or in part exempt from the provisions of this regulation. The company's lien, if any, on a share shall extend to all dividends payable thereon."

The articles of a private company may extend article 11 to include any debt owed by a member to the company. Where a director had incurred a debt by virtue of the company paying bills on his behalf, the company was held to have a lien on his shares even though it was also, by virtue of another article, prohibited from making a loan to that director on security of its shares. The company had not made a loan to the director, he had simply become indebted to the company: *Champagne Perrier-Jouet S.A.* v. *H. H. Finch Ltd.* [1982] 1 W.L.R. 1359.

The articles may grant a lien on shares which are fully paid but in such a case an official quotation on The Stock Exchange cannot be

---

[33] *Sykes' Case* (1872) L.R. 13 Eq. 255.   [34] *Post*, p. 367.
[35] *Poole's Case* (1878) 9 Ch.D. 322 (C.A.).
[36] *Everitt* v. *Automatic Weighing Machine Co.* [1892] 3 Ch. 506.

obtained.[37] If the lien given by the articles extends only to shares not fully paid, the company can alter its articles so as to give a lien on all shares, even if only one member will be affected by the alteration.[38]

Table A, article 24, empowers the directors to decline to register the transfer of a share on which the company has a lien.

A shareholder against whom a lien is to be enforced can compel the company to assign its lien to his nominee who is willing to pay off the amount of the lien.[39]

How a lien is enforced

A lien is enforced, like any other equitable charge, by a sale. If the articles do not give the company power to sell the shares, an application for an order for sale may be necessary. It is probable that the company has the implied power of sale given by the Law of Property Act 1925, s.101, to a mortgagee whose mortgage is made by deed. However, since it is uncertain that the articles, which create the lien, are a deed for the purposes of section 101,[40] to avoid the necessity of an application to the court the articles usually give an express power of sale.

Table A provides: "12. The company may sell, in such manner as the directors think fit, any shares on which the company has a lien, but no sale shall be made unless a sum in respect of which the lien exists is presently payable, nor until the expiration of fourteen days after a notice in writing, stating and demanding payment of such part of the amount in respect of which the lien exists as is presently payable, has been given to the registered holder for the time being of the share, or the person entitled thereto by reason of his death or bankruptcy."

Further, articles usually give the company power to nominate someone to execute the transfer.

Table A provides: "13. To give effect to any such sale the directors may authorise some person to transfer the shares sold to the purchaser thereof. The purchaser shall be registered as the holder of the shares comprised in any such transfer, and he shall not be bound to see to the application of the purchase money, nor shall his title to the shares be affected by any irregularity or invalidity in the proceedings in reference to the sale."

[37] Rules of The Stock Exchange, App. 34, Sched. VII.
[38] *Allen* v. *Gold Reefs of West Africa Ltd.* [1900] 1 Ch. 656 (C.A.), *ante*, p. 109.
[39] See note 36 above.
[40] See s.20, *ante*, p. 108.

The first part of article 13 is necessitated by section 75, which requires a proper instrument of transfer to be produced before a transfer is registered.

Table A continues: "14. The proceeds of the sale shall be received by the company and applied in payment of such part of the amount in respect of which the lien exists as is presently payable, and the residue, if any, shall (subject to a like lien for sums not presently payable as existed upon the shares before the sale) be paid to the person entitled to the shares at the date of the sale."

However, the sale of the shares is subject to any restrictions on the transferability of those shares contained in the articles of a private company, *e.g.* a pre-emption clause requiring them to be offered to existing shareholders.[41]

A lien cannot be enforced by forfeiture even if power to forfeit is contained in the articles.

The articles of a company provided that the company should have a lien on shares for the debts of the shareholder, and also provided that the lien could be enforced by forfeiture. *Held,* (1) forfeiture for debts generally, as distinct from debts due from the shareholder as a contributory, amounted to an illegal reduction of capital; (2) power to forfeit on failure to redeem after notice amounted to a clog on the shareholder's equity of redemption, and was invalid and *ultra vires: Hopkinson* v. *Mortimer, Harley & Co. Ltd.* [1917] 1 Ch. 646.

Priority of lien

When a third party advances money on the security of shares, a question may arise as to whether the third party has priority over the company's lien. In such a case, if the third party gives notice of his security to the company before the company's lien arises, the third party will have priority, but otherwise not.

The articles of a company gave "a first and paramount lien and charge" on shares for debts due from the shareholder. A shareholder created an equitable mortgage of his shares by depositing the share certificate with a bank as security for an overdraft and the bank gave notice of the deposit to the company. The shareholder subsequently became indebted to the company whereupon a lien arose in favour of the company. *Held,* the bank had priority as the company's lien arose after notice of their equitable mortgage. The notice was not notice of a trust contrary to what is now section 117 but notice affecting the company, in its character of trader, with knowledge of the bank's interest: *Bradford Banking Co.* v. *Briggs & Co.* (1886) 12 App. Cas. 29.

---

[41] *Champagne Perrier-Jouet S.A.* v. *H. H. Finch Ltd.* [1982] 1 W.L.R. 1359.

It seems that the position may be different if the articles contain a clause like Table A, article 7,[42] relieving the company of the obligation to take notice of equities in relation to shares.[43]

Similarly, where the shareholder is a trustee, the company's lien will prevail over the claims of the beneficial owners unless the company is given notice, before the lien arises, that the shareholder is a trustee.

> Trustees held shares in a company, the articles of which gave the company a lien on shares standing either in a single name or in joint names for any debt due from any of the holders, either separately or jointly with any other person. There was also an article like Table A, article 7.[44] Long after the registration of the shares in the trustees' names, one of the trustees incurred a liability to the company. It was *not* alleged that the company had notice of the trust before the lien arose. *Held,* the company's lien prevailed over the title of the *cestuis que trust: New London and Brazilian Bank* v. *Brocklebank* (1882) 21 Ch.D. 302 (C.A.).

The title of the beneficial owners, however, will have priority if the company has notice, before the lien arises, that the shareholder is a trustee of the shares.[45]

The company has no lien on the shares registered in the name of a trustee for debts due to it from the beneficial owner.[46]

If a lien in favour of the company has arisen and the shareholder sells part only of his shares, the purchaser can require the company to discharge the lien primarily out of the shares not sold.[47]

A lien does not cease on the shareholder's death, but may be enforced against his executors.[48]

LIEN ON SHARES (SCOTS LAW)

A company has at common law and independently of any provision in its articles a lien on shares held by a member for debts due by the member to the company.[49] Articles, however, usually make express

[42] *Ante*, p. 196.
[43] *Champagne Perrier-Jouet S.A.* v. *H. H. Finch Ltd.* [1982] 3 All E.R. 713, 720–721.
[44] See note 42 above.
[45] *Mackereth* v. *Wigan Coal Co. Ltd.* [1916] 2 Ch. 293.
[46] *Re Perkins* (1890) 24 Q.B.D. 613 (C.A.).
[47] *Gray* v. *Stone* (1893) 69 L.T. 282.
[48] *Allen* v. *Gold Reefs of West Africa Ltd.* [1900] 1 Ch. 656 (C.A.), *ante,* p. 109.
[49] *Hotchkis* v. *Royal Bank* (1797) 3 Paton 618; (1797) M. 2673; *Burns* v. *Lawrie's Trustees* (1840) 2 D. 1348; *Bell's Trustee* v. *Coatbridge Tinplate Co. Ltd.* (1886) 14 R. 246.

provision to the same effect. The lien enables the company to refuse to register any transfer of the shares until the transferor's debt to the company has been satisfied.

A company whose articles expressly limit the lien to partly paid shares may alter the articles so as to extend the lien to all shares, but if such an alteration is not made until after a transfer of fully paid shares has been presented for registration the transferee's right to be registered is not affected by that alteration.[50]

A lien can be enforced by a sale only if the power of sale has been conferred by the articles, or a warrant is obtained from the court. A lien in respect of debts other than calls or instalments could not be enforced by forfeiture, since that would be an illegal reduction of capital.

Where X, a shareholder, has assigned his shares in security to Y who has completed his title to the shares by being registered as the holder of them, the company is no longer entitled to a lien on the shares in respect of debts due to it by X, since X is not the registered holder.[51]

For the provisions of section 38 of the 1980 Act and of Table A on lien, see "Lien (English Law)," above.

FORFEITURE OF SHARES

Although a forfeiture of a member's shares by the company is recognised by the Acts, the directors may forfeit shares only if expressly authorised to do so by the articles and only for non-payment of a call or an instalment: 1980 Act, s.35(4)(c).

Table A provides: "33. If a member fails to pay any call or instalment of a call on the day appointed for payment thereof, the directors may, at any time thereafter during such time as any part of the call or instalment remains unpaid, serve a notice on him requiring payment of so much of the call or instalment as is unpaid, together with any interest which may have accrued.

"34. The notice shall name a further day (not earlier than the expiration of fourteen days from the date of service of the notice) on or before which the payment required by the notice is to be made, and shall state that in the event of non-payment at or before the time appointed the shares in respect of which the call was made will be liable to be forfeited.

"35. If the requirements of any such notice as aforesaid are not complied with, any share in respect of which the notice has been given may at any time

---

[50] *Liquidator of W. & A. M'Arthur Ltd.* v. *Gulf Line Ltd.*, 1909 S.C. 732.
[51] *Paul's Trustee* v. *Thomas Justice & Sons Ltd.*, 1912 S.C. 1303.

thereafter, before the payment required by the notice has been made, be forfeited by a resolution of the directors to that effect."

Article 131, *post*,[52] deals with the way in which notice may be given to a member.

Forfeiture, being in the nature of a penal proceeding, is valid only if the provisions of the articles, *e.g.* as to notice, are strictly followed. Any irregularity will avoid the forfeiture.[53] To protect purchasers of the forfeited shares against possible irregularities in the forfeiture, the articles usually provide, as does Table A, article 38, that the title of the purchaser shall not be affected by any invalidity in the proceedings in reference to the forfeiture.

The power of the directors to forfeit shares must be exercised in good faith and not for the purpose of relieving shareholders with whom the directors are friendly from their liability.[54]

Table A, article 39, authorises forfeiture for non-payment of any sum which, by the terms of the issue of a share, is payable at a fixed time, including premiums. Forfeiture for non-payment of other debts due to the company is invalid.[55] Similarly, an article which authorises the forfeiture of shares held by a member who sues the company or the directors is invalid.[56]

An invalid forfeiture can be restrained by injunction.[57]

Forfeited shares may be sold or reissued by a private company according to the provisions of the articles.

Table A, article 36, provides: "A forfeited share may be sold or otherwise disposed of on such terms and in such manner as the directors think fit, and at any time before a sale or disposition the forfeiture may be cancelled on such terms as the directors think fit."

A public company, however, must cancel the forfeited shares unless they are disposed of within three years. In the interim period the company may not vote with the shares. If this cancellation takes the public company below the authorised minimum capital it must re-register as a private company: 1980 Act, s.37.

---

[52] p. 308.
[53] *Johnson* v. *Lyttle's Iron Agency* (1877) 5 Ch.D. 687 (C.A.).
[54] *Re Esparto Trading Co.* (1879) 12 Ch.D. 191; *Gower's Case* (1868) L.R. 6 Eq. 77.
[55] *Hopkinson* v. *Mortimer, Harley & Co.* [1917] 1 Ch. 646, *ante*, p. 293.
[56] *Hope* v. *International Financial Socy.* (1876) 4 Ch.D. 327 (C.A.).
[57] See note 53 above. The procedure in Scots law would be an interdict.

A forfeiture cannot be cancelled without the consent of the person whose shares have been forfeited.[58]

Forfeited shares can be reissued at less than the amount which has been paid on them.

A company had forfeited a number of shares of £5 5s. each, £2 5s. paid, and proposed to reissue them at the price of 30s. a share. *Held,* the company could do so, as it was not bound to treat the forfeited shares as if nothing had been paid upon them: *Morrison* v. *Trustees, etc., Corpn. Ltd.* (1898) 68 L.J.Ch. 11 (C.A.).

The purchaser of the reissued shares is liable for the payment of all future calls duly made, including one for the amount of the call which occasioned the forfeiture.[59] Consequently, there is no issue of shares at a discount, as the company has already received the amount paid up. The purchaser should be credited with any subsequent payments made by the ex-owner.[60]

The effect of the forfeiture on the former owner of the shares is to discharge him from his liability on the shares.[61] "The company on forfeiture gets its shares back, and the shareholder who has had his shares forfeited is wholly discharged from his liability."[62] To prevent this position from arising, the articles usually preserve the liability of the former owner.

Table A, article 37, provides: "A person whose shares have been forfeited shall cease to be a member in respect of the forfeited shares, but shall, notwithstanding, remain liable to pay to the company all moneys which, at the date of forfeiture, were payable by him to the company in respect of the shares, but his liability shall cease if and when the company shall have received payment in full of all such moneys in respect of the shares."

Such an article makes the person whose shares have been forfeited for non-payment of calls liable as a debtor to the company, and not as a

---

[58] *Larkworthy's Case* [1903] 1 Ch. 711.
[59] *New Balkis Eersteling Ltd.* v. *Randt Gold Mining Co.* [1904] A.C. 165, where the purchaser was to hold the shares "discharged from all calls due prior to such purchase."
[60] *Re Randt Gold Mining Co.* [1904] 2 Ch. 468. *Re Bolton*, below, shows that the converse is true.
[61] *Stocken's Case* (1868) L.R. 3 Ch.App. 412; in *Goldsmith* v. *Colonial Finance etc. Corpn. Ltd.* [1909] 8 C.L.R. 241, Griffith C.J., at p. 249, and Barton J., at p. 253, thought that what Lord Cairns L.J. said in *Stocken* was founded on the particular article there in question.
[62] *Per* Luxmoore J. in *Re Bolton* [1930] 2 Ch. 48, *post*, at p. 59.

contributory,[63] so that where, more than a year after the forfeiture, the company went into liquidation, it was held that the former owner of the shares was still liable.[64]

Even without the last part of Table A, article 37, the company cannot recover more than the difference between the calls due and the amount received on reissue.

> B. underwrote two blocks of shares in a company. The issue to the public was a failure and B. was consequently allotted (*inter alia*) 8,200 £1 shares in the company. He was unable to pay the calls on these shares, which were forfeited. They were then reissued so that the company received the balance of the calls in full, but to obtain the new allottees the company had to pay £1,018 by way of commission. B. became bankrupt. The articles provided that the holder of forfeited shares should remain liable for calls notwithstanding the forfeiture and the company attempted to prove for the balance of calls due from B. *Held*, the company could not receive payment of the calls twice over and could only prove for the actual loss sustained, *viz*. the £1,018 commission: *Re Bolton* [1930] 2 Ch. 48.

A surety for calls is released on forfeiture of the shares without his consent.[65]

SURRENDER OF SHARES

The Acts do not give a company any express power to accept a surrender of his shares by a member. A company's articles, however, frequently give power to the directors to accept a surrender of shares where they are in a position to forfeit such shares, *i.e.* for non-payment of calls or instalments on those shares: 1980 Act, s.35(4)(*c*).

A surrender of shares is lawful where it is accepted to save the company from going through the formalities of forfeiture.[66]

"These [surrenders of shares] have been admitted by the Courts upon the principle, as I understand it, that they have practically the same effect as forfeiture, the main difference being that the one is a proceeding *in invitum*,

---

[63] *Post*, p. 651.
[64] *Ladies' Dress Assocn. Ltd.* v. *Pulbrook* [1900] 2 Q.B. 376 (C.A.); *cf. Ferguson* v. *Central Halls Co. Ltd.* (1881) 8 R. 997, and *Liquidators of Mount Morgan (West) Gold Mine Ltd.* v. *M'Mahon* (1891) 18 R. 772.
[65] *Re Darwen and Pearce* [1927] 1 Ch. 176.
[66] *e.g. General Property Investment Co. Ltd. and Liquidator* v. *Craig* (1890) 18 R. 389.

and the other a proceeding taken with the assent of the shareholder, who is unable to retain and pay future calls on his shares."[67]

Surrender in these circumstances has been described as an "apparent exception" only to the principle of maintenance of capital,[68] since "the extinction of the obligation of a bankrupt shareholder can injure nobody."[69]

Following section 35 of the 1980 Act a company may only acquire its own shares in a few cases in addition to a surrender in lieu of forfeiture. These have been considered above.[70] It appears that in all those cases, *e.g.* a purchase by the company, a surrender of shares may be used as the method of acquisition. No other forms of surrender appear to be valid after the 1980 Act.

In particular, a surrender of partly paid shares, not liable to forfeiture, is unlawful, as it (*a*) releases the shareholder from further liability in respect of the shares, (*b*) amounts to a purchase by the company of its own shares, and (*c*) is a reduction of capital without the sanction of the court.

A company sustained a loss of £4,000 and the directors agreed to share the loss between themselves. They therefore surrendered shares to the amount of £4,000. The shares were £11 each, £10 paid, and the intention was that the directors should be released from the remaining £1 a share unpaid. The company subsequently became more prosperous and the directors took proceedings to have the surrender declared invalid. *Held*, the surrender was invalid as amounting to a purchase by the company of its own shares: *Bellerby v. Rowland & Marwood, Steamship Co. Ltd.* [1902] 2 Ch. 14 (C.A.).

Shares which have been validly surrendered can be reissued in the same way as forfeited shares, if the articles authorise their reissue.

SHARE WARRANT

A share warrant is a document issued by a company under its common seal stating that the bearer of the warrant is entitled to the shares specified therein: section 83.

Before share warrants can be issued the following conditions must be satisfied:

---

[67] *Per* Lord Watson in *Trevor* v. *Whitworth* (1887) 12 App.Cas. 409, at p. 429.
[68] *Ante*, p. 227.
[69] *Per* Lord M'Laren in *Gill* v. *Arizona Copper Co. Ltd.* (1900) 2 F. 843, at p. 860.
[70] *Ante*, p. 242.

(1) the company must be a company limited by shares.
(2) there must be authority in the articles. (Table A does not authorise the issue of share warrants.)
(3) the shares must be fully paid up: section 83.

A share warrant must be stamped with a duty of three per cent., three times the usual rate.[71]

When the issue of share warrants is authorised, the articles usually provide for such matters as the deposit of the share warrant with the company a certain number of days before any right is exercised, and for the giving of notices of meetings by advertisement.

On issuing a share warrant, the company must strike out of its register of members the name of the holder of the shares as if he had ceased to be a member and make the following entries in the register:

(1) the fact of the issue of the warrant;
(2) a statement of the shares included in the warrant, distinguishing each share by its number, so long as the share has a number;
(3) the date of issue of the warrant: section 112(1).

The bearer of a share warrant may, however, if the articles so provide, be deemed to be a member of the company either to the full extent or for any purposes defined in the articles: section 112(5).

A share warrant can, subject to the articles, be surrendered for cancellation, whereupon the holder is entitled to be entered in the register of members: section 112(2).

Stock warrants to bearer can be issued on the same terms as share warrants.[72]

When share warrants are issued, the annual return[73] must show:

(1) the total amount of shares for which share warrants are outstanding at the date of the return;
(2) the total amount of share warrants issued and surrendered respectively since the last return;
(3) the number of shares comprised in each warrant: Schedule 6, Part I, paragraph 3(*j*).

A share warrant differs from a share certificate[74] in the following respects:

[71] Stamp Act 1891, s.1, Sched. 1; Finance Act 1963, s.59.
[72] *Pilkington* v. *United Railways of Havana* [1930] 2 Ch. 108.
[73] *Ante,* p. 204.   [74] *Ante,* p. 272.

(1) the bearer of a warrant is not entered in a register: section 112.

(2) he is entitled to the shares specified in the warrant: section 83.

(3) the shares are transferable by delivery of the warrant: section 83.

(4) a warrant is a negotiable instrument and if it is stolen and afterwards gets into the hands of a bona fide purchaser for value without notice of the fraud, he can enforce against the company payment of coupons for dividends due in respect of such share warrant.[75]

(5) coupons for dividends may be attached to a warrant: section 83.

   Dividends are advertised, and then collected upon the handing over of the appropriate coupon. This procedure is necessary because the company does not know to whom to send the dividend.

(6) holding a share warrant is not enough where the articles require a director to hold a specified share qualification: section 182(2).[76]

Share warrants are not very common. This is because until recently, (1979), they could not be issued without Treasury consent and had to be deposited with an authorised depositary, because of the serious consequences of loss or theft, and also because of the heavy stamp duty. Another reason is that the company has to advertise in newspapers to get in touch with the shareholders. With the abolition of exchange controls in 1979 there are fewer restrictions on their use.

Section 85 makes special provision for certain offences in connection with share warrants in Scotland.

---

[75] *Webb, Hale & Co.* v. *Alexandria Water Co. Ltd.* (1905) 93 L.T. 339.
[76] *Post*, p. 335.

CHAPTER 15

GENERAL MEETINGS

THIS chapter is concerned with general meetings, *i.e.* meetings of the members or shareholders of a company and certain other persons (the auditors, the personal representatives of a deceased member and the trustee in bankruptcy of a bankrupt member). The various kinds of general meeting are dealt with first and it will be seen that the Act requires that certain meetings, *e.g.* an annual general meeting, are held and allows other meetings, called extraordinary general meetings, to be held, usually when the directors think fit. Then the notice that the members must be given of general meetings is explained. Thirdly, proceedings at general meetings are dealt with—how many members must be present to constitute a meeting and enable it to transact business, who takes the chair, how a vote is taken and so on. Finally, the various kinds of resolution that may be passed at a meeting are explained.

If a company has more than one class of shares, class meetings, *i.e.* meetings of the holders of the shares of a certain class, may be held. Some of the sections referred to below, *e.g.* section 133 with regard to the length of notice for calling meetings, also apply to meetings of any class of members of a company as they apply to general meetings of the company. Section 32(6) of the 1980 Act provides that the provisions of Table A relating to general meetings also apply to class meetings, except that a quorum shall be two persons at least holding or representing by proxy one-third of the issued shares of the class and that any holder of shares of the class present in person or by proxy may demand a poll.

KINDS OF GENERAL MEETING

Annual general meeting

By section 131 the general rule is that every company must hold an annual general meeting, specified as such in the notice calling it, every year, with an interval of not more than 15 months between one annual general meeting of the company and the next. The word "year" means calendar year, *i.e.* the period January 1 to December 31.[1] A limited exception is that as long as a company holds its first annual general meeting within 18 months of incorporation it need not hold it in the year of incorporation or, sometimes, in the following year, *e.g.* a company incorporated on October 1, 1984, might hold its first annual general meeting in March 1986.

The directors must call the annual general meeting (see Table A, article 80). The object of section 131 is to ensure that those members who wish to do so can meet together and confront the directors at least once a year. Table A, article 52, provides in effect that the business at an annual general meeting is—

(1) the declaration of a dividend, the consideration of the accounts, balance sheets and the reports of the directors and auditors, the election of directors in place of those retiring, and the appointment of, and the fixing of the remuneration of, the auditors;

(2) special business, *i.e.* any other business.

If default is made in holding an annual general meeting, the Department of Trade may, on the application of any member of the company, call or direct the calling of a meeting and give such ancillary directions as the Department thinks expedient, including a direction that one member present in person or by proxy shall be deemed to constitute the meeting: section 131.

The Jenkins Report[2] recommended that the Board of Trade[3] be empowered to extend the period within which a company is required to hold its annual general meeting. The idea is to assist companies endeavouring to avoid being in default, *e.g.* because no quorum is available.

Extraordinary general meetings

Any general meeting of a company, other than an annual general meeting, is an extraordinary general meeting. Table A, article 48, so provides and article 49 provides that the directors *may*, whenever they think fit, convene an extraordinary general meeting.

Further, by section 132, despite anything in the articles, the directors are *bound* to convene an extraordinary general meeting on the requisi-

[1] *Gibson* v. *Barton* (1875) L.R. 10 Q.B. 329.
[2] Para. 468.
[3] Now the Department of Trade.

tion of the holders of not less than one-tenth of the paid-up capital of the company carrying the right of voting at general meetings or, if the company has no share capital, of members representing not less than one-tenth of the total voting rights. The requisition must state the objects of the meeting and be signed by the requisitionists. If the directors do not, within 21 days of the deposit of the requisition at the registered office of the company, proceed to convene the meeting, the requisitionists, or the holders of more than half their voting rights, may convene it themselves so long as it is held within three months after such deposit.[4] The reasonable expenses of the requisitionists in convening the meeting must be repaid by the company, which must retain them out of any remuneration of the directors in default.

The business at an extraordinary general meeting is special business (Table A, article 52).

The Jenkins Report[5] recommended that section 132 be amended to enable the requisitionists to convene a meeting if the directors do not do so for a date not later than 28 days after the notice convening the meeting. At present directors may defeat the purposes of the section by calling an extraordinary requisition meeting for a date, say, six months ahead.

Section 34 of the 1980 Act requires the directors of a public company to call a general meeting in the event of a serious loss of capital. In such a case the meeting must be convened within 28 days for a date not later than 28 days after the notice convening the meeting.[6]

By section 135 of the 1948 Act, if for any reason it is impracticable to call a meeting in any manner in which meetings may be called, or to conduct a meeting in the manner prescribed by the articles or the Act, the court may, either of its own motion or on application by any director or any member entitled to vote at the meeting, order a meeting to be called, held and conducted in such manner as the court thinks fit, and may give such ancillary directions as it thinks expedient, including a direction that one member present in person or by proxy shall be deemed to constitute the meeting.

E. Ltd. had three members, A, B and C. A and B were directors and held five per cent. of the shares each. C, who was not a director, held 90 per cent. of

---

[4] This right may be abrogated if the requisionists are themselves directors who have, by failing to attend board meetings, been the cause of the directors' default: *Thyne* v. *Lauder*, 1925 S.N. 123 (O.H.).

[5] Para. 468.   [6] *Ante*, p. 241.

the shares. No general meetings were held. The articles provided that a quorum at a meeting should be two members. A and B frustrated C's efforts to call a meeting under section 132 by refusing to attend. C gave special notice of his intention to move ordinary resolutions to remove the directors at the next extraordinary general meeting, and asked the court to call a meeting under section 135 and to direct that one member should be a quorum. C's application was opposed by the directors. *Held,* the application should be granted because (1) otherwise C would be deprived of his right to remove the directors under section 184; (2) the directors were in breach of their statutory duty by not holding an annual general meeting: *Re El Sombrero Ltd.* [1958] Ch. 900.[7]

The Jenkins Report[8] recommended that section 135 should be amended so that personal representatives of deceased members should be treated, for the purposes of the section, as members of the company, *i.e.* able to apply under the section, and as having the same voting rights as the dead members would have had. This would enable the company to appoint directors when all directors and shareholders have died.

Notice of General Meetings

Length of notice for calling meetings

The effect of section 133 is that notwithstanding a provision in the articles providing for shorter notice:

(1) An annual general meeting must be called by not less than 21 days' written notice.

(2) Any other general meeting of a limited company must be called by not less than 14 days' written notice, unless a special resolution is to be proposed, in which case, by section 141, not less than 21 days' such notice is required.

Table A, article 50, provides that the notice shall be clear notice, *i.e.* exclusive of the day on which it is served or deemed to be served and of the day for which it is given.[9]

---

[7] For a Scottish instance, see *Edinburgh Workmen's Houses Improvement Co. Ltd., Petitioners,* 1935 S.C. 56.

[8] Para. 31.

[9] In Scotland articles may be so worded as not to require *clear* notice, *e.g.* a provision that "days shall be reckoned, excluding the first and including the last of such days," allows the day of the meeting to be counted: *The Aberdeen Comb Works Co. Ltd., Petitioners* (1902) 10 S.L.T. 210.

A meeting may be called by shorter notice than that specified above or in the articles if that is agreed to by—(1) all the members entitled to attend and vote in the case of an annual general meeting; (2) a majority in number of the members holding not less than 95 per cent. of the shares giving the right to attend and vote or, in the case of a company without a share capital, representing not less than 95 per cent. of the total voting rights, in the case of any other meeting: sections 133(3); 141(2). Such agreement is likely to be obtained only in the case of a company with few members.

Section 106 of the Companies Act 1981, however, requires a minimum notice of at least seven days' notice of a special resolution for voluntary winding up.

If a resolution is to be passed on short notice, it must be appreciated that the resolution is being so passed.[10]

Sections 133(3) and 141(2) are derived from cases like *Re Express Engineering Works Ltd.*[11] and *Re Oxted Motor Co. Ltd.*[12] which established that it is competent to all the shareholders to waive all formalities as regards notice of meetings, etc.

In the *Express Engineering* case five persons formed a private company in which they were the sole shareholders. They sold to the company for £15,000 a property which they had just bought for £7,000. The price was to be paid by the issue of debentures for £15,000 by the company. The transaction was carried out at a "board" meeting of the five individuals who appointed themselves the directors. The articles forbade a director to vote in respect of a contract in which he was interested. It was held that there was no fraud and the company was bound in the matter by the unanimous agreement of the members. Consequently the debentures were valid.

In the *Oxted Motor* case both the members of a company waived the normal length of notice of a meeting at which an extraordinary resolution for voluntary winding up was validly passed.

The *Express Engineering* case and the *Parker & Cooper* case, below, were applied in *Re Bailey, Hay & Co. Ltd.*[13] where short notice was given of a meeting to pass an extraordinary resolution for voluntary winding up but all five corporators attended and the resolution was passed by the votes of two shareholders, the other shareholders abstaining from voting. The resolution was deemed to have been passed with the unanimous agreement of all the corporators and those who abstained were treated as having acquiesced in the winding-up.

[10] *Re Pearce Duff & Co. Ltd.* [1960] 1 W.L.R. 1014.
[11] [1920] 1 Ch. 466 (C.A.), followed in the Victorian case of *E.H. Dey Pty. Ltd.* v. *Dey* [1966] V.R. 464.
[12] [1921] 3 K.B. 32.   [13] [1971] 1 W.L.R. 1357.

Cases such as *Parker & Cooper Ltd.* v. *Reading*[14] have gone further than the *Express Engineering* and *Oxted Motor* cases. It was decided in *Parker & Cooper* that if all the members assent to a transaction *intra vires* the company, although beyond the powers of the board, the company is bound and it is not necessary that they should hold a meeting in one room or one place to express that assent simultaneously.

In *Parker & Cooper* there was no actual meeting but the members individually and at different times informally ratified a debenture granted by the directors which, although *intra vires* the company, was beyond the powers of the directors because two directors had been invalidly appointed.

Parker & Cooper was applied in *Re Duomatic Ltd.*[15] in which it was held that when it can be shown that all shareholders who have a right to attend and vote at a general meeting of the company assent to some matter which a general meeting of the company could carry into effect, that assent is as binding as a resolution in general meeting. This principle was subsequently applied to such an assent to vary the articles of a company even though no formal special resolution to that effect had been passed. It was held to be a basic principle that all the shareholders acting together could do anything which was *intra vires* the company: *Cane* v. *Jones.*[16]

Further, Table A, article 73A, provides that, subject to the provisions of the Act, a written resolution signed by all the members entitled to attend and vote at general meetings shall be as valid and effective as if passed at a general meeting of the company duly convened and held. The Jenkins Report[17] recommended that the Act should expressly provide that in the case of any company such a resolution shall be equivalent to an ordinary or a special resolution duly passed at a general meeting but that seems to be the position now achieved by the courts.

Service of notice of meetings

Section 134 of the 1948 Act provides that, unless the articles provide to the contrary, notice of the meeting of a company is to be served on

---

[14] [1926] Ch. 975, doubted in the Victorian case of *Re Meyer Douglas Pty. Ltd.* [1965] V.R. 638.
[15] [1969] 2 Ch. 365.
[16] [1981] 1 All E.R. 533. See also *Re Horsley & Weight Ltd.* [1982] 3 W.L.R. 431.
[17] Para. 468.

every member of the company as required by Table A. Section 14 of the 1967 Act requires that notice of every general meeting be given to the auditors.

Table A provides in effect:

Article 131.—Notice may be given to any member either personally or by sending it by post to his registered address or, if he has no registered address within the United Kingdom, to the address within the United Kingdom supplied by him to the company for the giving of notice to him.

Where notice is sent by post, service is deemed to be effected by properly addressing, prepaying and posting a letter containing the notice, and to have been effected, in the case of notice of a meeting, at the expiration of 24 hours after posting, and, in other cases, at the time when the letter would be delivered in ordinary course of post.

Article 132.—Notice to joint holders of a share is given to the joint holder first named in the register of members.

Article 133.—On the death or bankruptcy of a member, notice is given to the personal representatives or the trustee in bankruptcy at the address within the United Kingdom supplied for the purpose.

Article 134.—Notice must be given to—

(1) every member except members who (having no registered address within the United Kingdom) have not supplied an address within the United Kingdom for the giving of notices to them;
(2) the personal representative or the trustee in bankruptcy of a member who, but for his death or bankruptcy, would be entitled to notice; and
(3) the auditor.

No other person is entitled to notice of a general meeting.

If notice of a meeting is not given to every person entitled to notice, any resolution passed at the meeting will be of no effect.

A committee of a club met and passed a resolution expelling Y from the club. X, a member of the committee, was not summoned to the meeting, as she had previously informed the chairman that she would be unable to attend meetings. *Held,* the omission to summon X invalidated the proceedings of the committee: *Young* v. *Ladies' Imperial Club Ltd.* [1920] 2 K.B. 523 (C.A.).

To obviate this result it is usually provided in the articles, as in Table A, article 51, that the accidental omission to give notice to, or the non-receipt of notice by, any person entitled to receive notice shall not invalidate the proceedings at that meeting.

In *Re West Canadian Collieries Ltd.* [1962] Ch. 370, the omission to give notice of a meeting to a few members, because the plates for these members were inadvertently kept out of the machine when the envelopes for the notices were being addressographed, was an accidental omission within an article like Table A, article 51.

However, in *Musselwhite* v. *C.H. Musselwhite & Son Ltd.* [1962] Ch. 964,[18] the omission to give notice of a general meeting to the unpaid vendors of shares who remained on the register of members, because the directors erroneously believed the vendors were no longer members, was due to an error of law and was not an accidental omission within such an article.

Nature of notice of meetings

The articles of a company will contain provisions dealing with the nature of the notice to be given of meetings. Table A, article 50, provides that the notice of a meeting shall state the place, date and hour of the meeting and, in the case of special business, the general nature of that business.

Notice of an annual general meeting was in common form and included in the business was "to elect directors." C., the retiring director, offered himself for re-election, but was not elected. A motion was proposed for the election of three new directors to fill up the places of the retiring director and two vacancies, but the chairman refused to accept it. *Held,* the refusal was wrong, as the notice sufficiently specified the general nature of the special business to bring it within the competence of the meeting to elect directors up to the number permitted by the articles: *Choppington Collieries Ltd.* v. *Johnson* [1944] 1 All E.R. 762 (C.A.).

Notice of special business must "state the resolution to be passed in such a way as fairly to state the purpose for which the meeting is convened, so that every shareholder may make up his mind whether he will or will not attend, with knowledge of the result of his act."[19]

Directors of a holding company had from 1907 to 1914 been receiving remuneration as directors of a subsidiary company without the knowledge of the shareholders of the holding company. Special resolutions, authorising the directors to retain the remuneration and altering the articles to allow the directors to receive remuneration as directors of subsidiary companies, were proposed and an extraordinary general meeting summoned to pass them. The notice did not specify the amount of the remuneration, which was £44,876. The resolution was passed. A shareholder brought an action on behalf of himself and all other shareholders of the company against the company and its directors claiming, *inter alia,* a declaration that the resolution was not binding upon the company. *Held,* the resolution was not binding as the notice was insufficient: *Baillie* v. *Oriental Telephone etc. Co. Ltd.* [1915] 1 Ch. 503 (C.A.).

[18] *Ante,* p. 279.
[19] Stiebel's *Company Law,* 3rd. ed., p. 335.

A notice convening a meeting stated that it was being held for receiving the directors' report, and the election of directors and auditors. The directors' report sent therewith stated that the meeting would be asked to confirm the appointment of R. as director. *Held,* the notice and the report together were sufficient notice of this special business: *Boschoek Proprietary Co. Ltd.* v. *Fuke* [1906] 1 Ch. 148.

The notice of a general meeting at which a special resolution or an extraordinary resolution is to be proposed must specify the intention to propose the resolution as a special resolution or an extraordinary resolution[20] as the case may be: section 141. There must be complete identity between the substance of the resolution as passed and the substance of the resolution set out in the notice. Thus in a resolution for a reduction of capital a change in the amount proposed to be reduced of £321, out of a total of £1,356,900 as shown in the notice, was held to invalidate the notice. Changes because of grammatical or clerical errors or the use of more formal language might, however, be allowed.[21]

Where a meeting has been requisitioned under section 132, *ante,*[22] it may competently deal with business additional to that specified in the requisition, provided adequate notice of the additional business has been duly given.[23]

Every notice calling a meeting of a company with a share capital must contain a statement, given reasonable prominence, that a member entitled to attend and vote may appoint a proxy to attend and vote instead of him, and that the proxy need not be a member of the company: section 136.

Notice of members' resolutions and statements

If some of the members of a company themselves wish to move a resolution at an *annual general meeting,* or to circulate to members a statement relating to any proposed resolution or the business to be dealt with at *any general meeting,* they can do so under section 140. The

---

[20] Strictly interpreted in *Rennie* v. *Crichton's (Strichen) Ltd.,* 1927 S.L.T. 459 (O.H.), in which a notice of a resolution for voluntary winding up was held invalid because it did not specify the intention to propose the resolution *as an extraordinary resolution;* for *obiter dicta* to the contrary see *North of Scotland etc. Steam Navigation Co. Ltd., Petitioners,* 1920 S.C. 94.

[21] *Re Moorgate Mercantile Holdings Ltd.* [1980] 1 All E.R. 40.   [22] p. 303.

[23] *Per* Lord Hill Watson (Ordinary), in *Ball* v. *Metal Industries Ltd.,* 1957 S.C. 315 (O.H.), at p. 316.

section provides that on the written requisition of members holding not less than one-twentieth of the voting rights of the members entitled to vote at the relevant meeting, or of one hundred members on whose shares there has been paid up an average sum of not less than £100 a member, the company must—

(1) give notice to every member entitled to receive notice of the annual general meeting of any resolution which may properly be moved and is intended to be moved at that meeting;
(2) circulate to every member entitled to receive notice of any general meeting any statement, of not more than 1,000 words, relating to any proposed resolution or the business to be dealt with at the meeting.

The notice of the resolution must be given, and any statement must be circulated, with the notice of the meeting or, if that is impracticable, as soon as possible afterwards. The company is not bound to circulate a *statement* if, on the application of the company or any aggrieved person, the court is satisfied that the rights given by the section are being abused to secure needless publicity for defamatory matter.

The requisition must be signed by the requisitionists and deposited at the registered office (1) at least six weeks before the meeting when notice of a resolution is required; and (2) at least one week before the meeting in any other case. A sum to cover the company's expenses must also be deposited (although at the meeting it may be resolved that the expenses shall be borne by the company, in which case the deposit will be returned).

If the directors call an annual general meeting for a date six weeks or less after deposit of the requisition, the requisition is deemed to have been properly deposited.

Special notice

Section 142 provides that where under the Act special notice is required of a resolution, notice of the intention to move it must be given *to the company* not less than 28 days before the meeting at which it is to be moved, *and* the company must give notice of the resolution *to the members* when it gives them notice of the meeting (or, if that is not practicable, either by advertisement in a newspaper having an appropriate circulation or in any other mode allowed by the articles, not less than 21 days before the meeting). To close a loophole which would otherwise allow directors to avoid the provision by claiming that the notice had not been given in time, the section also provides that if the directors call a meeting for a date 28 days or less after the notice has been given to the company, the notice is deemed to have been properly given. The notice to the company may be left at or sent by post to the registered office: section 437.[24]

Special notice is only required by sections 184 and 185 of the 1948 Act (removal of directors and appointment of a director who has attained the age of 70 respectively) and section 15 of the 1976 Act (appointment and removal of auditors).

Section 142 does not confer any rights on a shareholder to have a resolution to which it applies circulated if he cannot fulfil the requirements of section 140, above. It simply confers a right to receive notice in a special way if the resolution is being proposed in due form.[25]

PROCEEDINGS AT GENERAL MEETINGS

Quorum

Under Table A, Part I, article 53, no business is to be transacted at a general meeting unless a quorum of members is present when the meeting proceeds to business. In England this article has been held to be satisfied if the quorum is present at the beginning of the meeting,[26] but in Scotland there is authority to the contrary.[27]

The quorum must be an effective quorum, *i.e.* it must consist of members qualified to take part in and decide upon questions before the meeting,[28] and where articles require a quorum of members to be "present" (without any such addition as "personally or by proxy") that word means "present in person."[29]

By section 134, unless the articles otherwise provide, a quorum is two members present in person for any company. Table A, Part I, article 53, also fixes two members present in person or by proxy as a

---

[24] *Ante*, p. 68.

[25] *Pedley v. Inland Waterways Association Ltd.* [1977] 1 All E.R. 209.

[26] *Re Hartley Baird Ltd.* [1955] Ch. 143, distinguished in *Re London Flats Ltd.* [1969] 1 W.L.R. 711.

[27] *Henderson v. Louttit & Co. Ltd.* (1894) 21 R. 674.

[28] *Henderson's* case, above, *per* Lord President Robertson, at p. 676.

[29] *M. Harris Ltd. Petitioners*, 1956 S.C. 207, in which a member represented by an attorney was held not to be "present."

quorum in the case of any company. As to a quorum at a class meeting, see section 32(6) of the 1980 Act, *ante*.[30]

Strictly, since the word "meeting" prima facie means a coming together of more than one person, one person cannot constitute a meeting,[31] even where he attends in more than one capacity or holds proxies for other persons.[32] However, in *East* v. *Bennett Bros. Ltd.*[33] it was held that one member, who held all the shares of a class, constituted a class meeting. Further, under sections 131[34] and 135,[35] the Department of Trade and the court, respectively, may direct that one member shall be deemed to constitute a meeting.

If a quorum is not present within half an hour of the time appointed for the meeting, Table A, article 54, provides that the meeting, if convened upon the requisition of members, shall be dissolved, but in any other case it shall stand adjourned to the same day in the next week at the same time and place, or to such other day and at such other time and place as the directors may determine, and if at the adjourned meeting a quorum is not present within half an hour, the members present shall form a quorum. It is thought that a single member can constitute a quorum at an adjourned meeting.[36]

Chairman

Section 134 provides that, unless the articles otherwise provide, the members present at a meeting may elect any member as a chairman. However, the articles usually provide who is to be chairman. Table A, article 55, states that the chairman of the board of directors shall

---

[30] p. 217.

[31] *Sharp* v. *Dawes* (1876) 2 Q.B.D. 26 (C.A.), applied in *Re London Flats*, above; *cf. Souter, Petitioner*, 1981 S.L.T. (Sh. Ct.) 89, in which a single creditor was held not to constitute a committee of inspection (1948 Act, ss.252, 253).

[32] *James Prain & Sons Ltd., Petitioners*, 1947 S.C. 325. This case was distinguished in *Neil M'Leod & Sons Ltd., Petitioners*, 1967 S.C. 16, in which the requisite quorum of three *members* personally present was held to be constituted by two individuals, one of whom attended in two capacities (*i.e.* as a member holding shares in his own right and as a member entitled to vote in respect of a trust holding).

[33] [1911] 1 Ch 163.

[34] *Ante*, p. 303.

[35] *Ante*, p. 305.

[36] See *Jarvis Motors (Harrow) Ltd.* v. *Carabott* [1964] 1 W.L.R. 1101, *ante*, p. 266, where it was held that the Interpretation Act 1889, s.1(1), applied to the articles so that words in the plural included words in the singular and "members" included sole surviving member.

preside at every general meeting of the company, or if there is no such chairman, or if he is not present within 15 minutes after the time appointed for the meeting or is unwilling to act, the directors present shall elect one of themselves to be chairman. Article 56 provides that if no director is willing to act as chairman or if no director is present within 15 minutes, the members present may elect one of their number to be chairman of the meeting.

It is the duty of the chairman:

(1) to preserve order;
(2) to see that the proceedings are regularly conducted;
(3) to take care that the sense of the meeting is properly ascertained with regard to any question properly before it[37];
(4) to decide incidental questions arising for decision during the meeting, *e.g.* whether proxies are valid[38];

He must allow the minority of the shareholders to have a reasonable time to put forward their arguments, but at the expiration of that time he is entitled, if he thinks fit, to put a motion to the meeting that the discussion be terminated.[39]

The chairman has no casting vote unless expressly given one by the articles.[40] Table A, article 60, gives him a casting vote.

Adjournment

A chairman cannot adjourn a meeting at his own will, except in case of disorder. If, in any other case, he purports to do so, the meeting may elect another chairman and proceed with the business.[41]

The chairman is not bound to adjourn a meeting, even if the majority desire him to do so,[42] unless the articles otherwise provide.

Table A, article 57, provides: "The chairman may, with the consent of any meeting at which a quorum is present (and shall if so directed by the meeting), adjourn the meeting from time to time and from place to place, but no business shall be transacted at any adjourned meeting other than the business left unfinished at the meeting from which the adjournment took place. When

---

[37] *National Dwellings Society* v. *Sykes* [1894] 3 Ch. 159.
[38] *Post,* p. 320.
[39] *Wall* v. *London and Northern Assets Corporation* [1898] 2 Ch. 469 (C.A.).
[40] *Nell* v. *Longbottom* [1894] 1 Q.B. 767.
[41] See footnote 37.
[42] *Salisbury Gold Mining Co. Ltd.* v. *Hathorn* [1897] A.C. 268.

a meeting is adjourned for thirty days or more, notice of the adjourned meeting shall be given as in the case of an original meeting. Save as aforesaid it shall not be necessary to give any notice of an adjournment or of the business to be transacted at an adjourned meeting."

Conduct of a meeting

Subject to the provisions of the Companies Acts and the articles, the way in which the business at a meeting is to be conducted is decided by the meeting itself.

"There are many matters relating to the conduct of a meeting which lie entirely in the hands of those persons who are present and constitute the meeting. Thus it rests with the meeting to decide whether notices, resolutions, minutes, accounts, and such like shall be read to the meeting or be taken as read; whether representatives of the Press, or any other persons not qualified to be summoned to the meeting, shall be permitted to be present, or if present shall be permitted to remain; whether and when discussion shall be terminated and a vote taken; whether the meeting shall be adjourned. In all these matters, and they are only instances, the meeting decides, and if necessary a vote must be taken to ascertain the wishes of the majority. If no objection is taken by any constituent of the meeting, the meeting must be taken to be assenting to the course adopted": *per* Lord Russell of Killowen in *Carruth* v. *I.C.I. Ltd.* [1937] A.C. 707,[43] at p. 761.

Voting

1. *A show of hands*

The common law rule is that, unless the articles otherwise provide, a resolution put to a meeting is normally decided in the first instance by a show of hands.[44] Further, on a show of hands each member entitled to vote and present in person has one vote only, *i.e.* proxies[45] are not counted. In practice articles do not provide otherwise, *e.g.* Table A, article 58, below, provides that a vote shall be by a show of hands unless a poll is demanded, and article 62 provides that subject to any rights or restrictions attached to any class of shares,[46] every member present in person shall have one vote on a show of hands, *i.e.* proxies cannot vote.

---

[43] *Ante*, p. 235.
[44] *Re Horbury Bridge Coal Co.* (1879) 11 Ch.D. 109 (C.A.).
[45] *Post*, p. 318.
[46] *Ante*, p. 209.

Table A further provides, in effect:

Article 63.—In the case of joint holders, the vote of the holder whose name appears first in the register of members shall be accepted to the exclusion of the others.

Article 65.—No member shall be entitled to vote at any general meeting unless all calls or other sums presently payable by him in respect of shares in the company have been paid.

Article 66.—Objections to the qualification of a voter can only be raised at the meeting at which the vote is tendered. Objections are to be referred to the chairman and his decision is to be final.

In *Marx v. Estates & General Investments Ltd.* [1976] 1 W.L.R. 380, Brightman J. said that there is much to be said for an article like article 66. In that case a proxy form, which was liable to stamp duty because it authorised a proxy to vote at more than one meeting but which was unstamped, was not void but a valid authority capable of being stamped, and since the company had accepted it without objection at the meeting the votes cast by the proxy were valid. Further, by virtue of article 66 the objection taken several days after the meeting was made too late.

A bankrupt shareholder may vote if he is still on the register.[47]

A shareholder, even if he is a director, can vote although he has an interest in the question to be voted on, provided that the majority of the members do not unfairly oppress the minority.[48]

"The shareholder's vote is a right of property, and prima facie may be exercised by a shareholder as he thinks fit in his own interest": *per* Lord Maugham in *Carruth* v. *I.C.I. Ltd.* [1937] A.C. 707, at p. 765.

Table A, article 58, provides that, unless a poll is demanded, a declaration by the chairman that a resolution has on a show of hands been carried, or carried by a particular majority, or lost, and an entry to that effect in the minutes, is conclusive evidence of the fact without proof of the number or proportion of the votes recorded for or against.[49] See also section 141(3), *post.*[50]

2. *A poll*

Although a show of hands can be taken quickly, it is not an accurate method of ascertaining the wishes of the members of a company

---

[47] *Morgan* v. *Gray* [1953] Ch. 83, *ante*, p. 190.   [48] *Post*, p. 399.

[49] Where a show of hands has been taken and the minutes record the passing of the resolution but omit any mention of the show of hands, further evidence may be required to establish the validity of the procedure: *Fraserburgh Commercial Co. Ltd., Petitioners*, 1946 S.C. 444.

[50] p. 324.

because the votes of those voting by proxy are not counted. Again, it does not pay due regard to the wishes of a member holding a large number of shares since he has only one vote on a show of hands. Consequently, although the right to demand a poll exists at common law,[51] section 141(3) and (4) give a statutory right to demand a poll in the case of a special resolution or an extraordinary resolution and articles always make provision for taking a poll. The effect of Table A, article 58, is that a poll may be demanded before, or on the declaration of the result of, a show of hands, *i.e.* it is not necessary to have a show of hands before a poll is taken.[52] A proper demand for a poll does away with the need for, or the result of, a show of hands.

The number of votes which a member has on a poll depends upon the articles. Section 134(*e*) states that unless the articles otherwise provide a member shall have one vote in respect of each share or each £10 of stock held by him, and articles 62 and 67 of Table A provide that, subject to any rights or restrictions attached to any class of shares, on a poll every member present in person or by proxy shall have one vote for each share of which he is the holder, *i.e.* proxies can be counted.

A poll is complete when the result is ascertained, not on an earlier day when the votes are cast.[53]

Section 137 provides that, on any question other than the election of the chairman or the adjournment of the meeting, any article is void in so far as it excludes the right to demand a poll or requires more persons to demand a poll than (*a*) five members entitled to vote at the meeting, or (*b*) members representing one-tenth of the voting rights, or (*c*) members holding one-tenth of the paid-up capital conferring a right to vote. Further, a proxy has the same right to demand a poll as the member he represents. If articles could require a considerable number of members to demand a poll the right would be worthless. It is essential that a proxy be able to demand a poll—he has no vote on a show of hands.

Table A, article 58, provides that in addition to the members in (*b*) or (*c*), *ante*, a poll may be demanded by the chairman or by two

---

[51] *R.* v. *Wimbledon Local Board* (1882) 8 Q.B.D. 459 (C.A.).
[52] *Per* Jenkins L.J. in *Holmes* v. *Keyes* [1959] Ch. 199 (C.A.), at p. 212, although see *per* Lord Blanesburgh in *Carruth's* case, *ante*, at p. 755.
[53] *Holmes* v. *Keyes*, *post*, p. 335.

members present in person or by proxy, and that the demand for a poll may be withdrawn.

The poll is taken as laid down in the articles. Table A, article 61, provides that a poll demanded on the election of a chairman or on a question of adjournment shall be taken forthwith. If demanded on any other question, it shall be taken at such time as the chairman directs. Where, under articles similar to Table A, a poll was demanded on a question of adjournment and taken, but the scrutineers informed the chairman that the result could not be announced within the time during which the meeting hall was available, it was held that the meeting subsequently convened to hear the result was a continuation of the original meeting, with the result that no proxies deposited between the date of the original meeting and the date of the continuation meeting were valid, as the articles required proxies to be deposited 48 hours before the meeting.[54]

On a poll, a member entitled to more than one vote need not cast all his votes or cast them all in the same way: section 138. This provision was introduced to meet the difficulties of a large trust corporation which might hold shares in a company on behalf of two or more different trusts, whose respective interests might well require different exercises of its votes.[55]

Proxies

Although there is no common law right to vote by proxy,[56] section 136 gives such a right.

The section contains the following provisions: Any member entitled to attend and vote at a company meeting may appoint another person, whether a member of the company or not, to attend and vote as his proxy, and if the company is a private company, to speak as his proxy—the Jenkins Report[57] recommended that a proxy be allowed to speak at a meeting of any company. Every notice calling a meeting must state this right of a member to appoint a proxy. Unless the articles

---

[54] *Jackson* v. *Hamlyn* [1953] Ch. 577, applying *Shaw* v. *Tati Concessions Ltd.* [1913] 1 Ch. 292.

[55] *Per* Walton J. in *Northern Counties Securities Ltd.* v. *Jackson & Steeple Ltd.* [1974] 1 W.L.R. 1133, at p. 1147.

[56] *Per* Lord Hanworth M.R. in *Cousins* v. *International Brick Co. Ltd.* [1931] 2 Ch. 90 (C.A.), at p. 100.

[57] Para. 468.

otherwise provide, a proxy can only vote on a poll, a member of a private company cannot appoint more than one proxy to attend on the same occasion, and a member of a company without a share capital cannot appoint a proxy. Articles cannot require the instrument appointing a proxy to be deposited with the company more than 48 hours before a meeting or an adjourned meeting. If articles could require the instrument to be deposited a considerable time before a meeting the right to appoint a proxy would be worthless.

A proxy is appointed by an instrument in writing in accordance with the articles. There are two forms of proxy in use—a general proxy appointing a person to vote as he thinks fit, having regard to what is said at the meeting, and a special proxy appointing a person to vote for or against a particular resolution. A special proxy is often called "a two-way proxy." The Stock Exchange requires two-way proxy forms to be sent to shareholders.[58]

The articles usually provide for the form and proof of proxies. Table A contains the following provisions:

Article 67.—"On a poll votes may be given either personally or by proxy."

Article 68.—The instrument appointing a proxy must be in writing signed by the appointer; the proxy need not be a member.

Article 69.—The instrument must be deposited at the registered office at least 48 hours before the holding of the meeting or adjourned meeting—24 hours in the case of a poll—otherwise it is invalid.

Article 70.—Prescribes the form of a general proxy.

Article 71.—Prescribes the form of a special proxy.

Article 72.—The instrument appointing a proxy is deemed to confer authority to demand a poll.

Article 73.—A vote by proxy is valid notwithstanding the previous death or insanity[59] of the principal or revocation of the proxy, as long as no intimation in writing of such death, etc., has been received by the company at the registered office before the commencement of the meeting or adjourned meeting.

It has been held that directors acting bona fide in the interests of the company are entitled to send out to the shareholders proxy papers in favour of named directors at the expense of the company.[60] However, section 136(4) provides that if invitations to appoint as a proxy a person or one of a number of persons specified in the invitations are issued at the company's expense to some only of the members entitled to vote at

[58] Admission of Securities to Listing, pp. 164, 171.
[59] The death or mental disorder of the principal revokes a proxy.
[60] *Peel* v. *L. & N.W. Rlwy. Co.* [1907] 1 Ch. 5 (C.A.).

a meeting, every officer of the company who knowingly and wilfully authorises or permits their issue is liable to a fine, although an officer is not liable by reason only of the issue to a member, at his written request, of a form of appointment naming the proxy or of a list of persons willing to act as proxy, if the form or list is available to every member entitled to vote. If this were not so the directors might send the proxy papers to friendly shareholders only. The Jenkins Report[61] recommended that proxy forms issued by a board of directors should permit the member to instruct his proxy to vote for or against (or to exercise his discretion in respect of) each resolution dealing with special business.

It is the duty of the chairman to decide on the validity of proxies. If the articles provide, as does Table A, article 66, that votes tendered at a meeting and not disallowed shall be deemed to be valid, the court will not review the chairman's decision, even if it is wrong, in the absence of fraud or bad faith on his part.[62] Where articles do not incorporate Table A a mere misprint or some quite palpable mistake on the face of a proxy form does not entitle the company to refuse to accept the proxy.[63]

Where proxy forms were sent out to all the stockholders in a company and the chairman was named as their proxy, it was held that he was bound to demand a poll in order to ascertain the sense of the meeting, and bound to exercise all the proxies in accordance with the instructions which they contained.[64]

A shareholder who has given a proxy is free to attend the meeting and vote in person, in which case the vote tendered by the proxy may properly be rejected.[65] He does not thereby revoke the proxy and the proxy may, *e.g.* vote on a second resolution on which the shareholder does not vote.[66]

[61] Para. 468.
[62] *Wall* v. *Exchange Investment Corporation* [1926] Ch. 143 (C.A.). And see *Marx* v. *Estates and General Investments Ltd.* [1976] 1 W.L.R. 380, *ante,* p. 316.
[63] *Oliver* v. *Dalgleish* [1963] 1 W.L.R. 1274, where the proxies referred to the "annual general meeting" instead of to the "extraordinary general meeting" and there was no other meeting which could be confused with that the date of which was stated in the proxies.
[64] *Second Consolidated Trust Ltd.* v. *Ceylon, etc., Rubber Estates Ltd.* [1943] 2 All E.R. 567.
[65] *Cousins* v. *International Brick Co. Ltd., ante,* where the proxy had not been revoked under Table A, art. 73, above.
[66] *Ansett* v. *Butler Air Transport Ltd.* (*No.* 2) (1958) 75 W.N. (N.S.W.) 306.

A corporation, whether a company within the meaning of the Act or not, may, if it is a member of another corporation which is such a company, by resolution of its directors or other governing body authorise such person as it thinks fit to act as its representative at any meeting of the company or of any class of members of the company. The representative is entitled to exercise on behalf of the corporation the powers which the corporation could exercise if it were an individual shareholder of the company: section 139. Such a representative is *not* a proxy and may vote on a show of hands as well as on a poll, and may address the meeting even if the company is not a private company.

In one case,[67] where no committee of inspection had been appointed and no directions had been received from the body of creditors or the court, the liquidator in a creditors' voluntary winding up was held to be within the phrase "or other governing body" in section 139, *ante,* and entitled to appoint himself as representative of the company at general meetings of subsidiary companies.

Minutes

Every company must keep minutes of all proceedings of general meetings. Such minutes, signed by the chairman of the meeting at which the proceedings were had or of the next succeeding meeting, are evidence of the proceedings: section 145. Unless the articles so provide, they are not conclusive evidence, and so, if a resolution has been passed, but is not entered in the minutes, other evidence to prove it will be admitted.[68] However, when the articles provide that the minutes, signed by the chairman, shall be "conclusive evidence without any further proof of the facts therein stated," as between those bound by the articles, namely the company and the members *qua* members,[69] evidence cannot be called to contradict the minutes unless they have been fraudulently written up.[70]

When minutes have been duly made, there is a presumption that all the proceedings were in order, and all appointments of directors, managers or liquidators are deemed to be valid: section 145.

The books containing minutes of general meetings are to be kept at

---

[67] *Hillman* v. *Crystal Bowl Amusements Ltd.* [1973] 1 W.L.R. 162 (C.A.).

[68] *Re Fireproof Doors* [1916] 2 Ch. 142; *cf. Fraserburgh Commercial Co. Ltd., Petitioners*, 1946 S.C. 444.

[69] *Ante,* p. 106.

[70] *Kerr* v. *Mottram* [1940] Ch. 657.

the registered office and open to the inspection of any member without charge for at least two hours a day. A member is entitled to be furnished, within seven days, with a copy on payment of not more than 2½p. per 100 words. If inspection is refused or copies are not sent, the court can compel immediate inspection of the books[71] or direct that copies be sent to those requiring them: section 146. The minute books may be bound, or loose-leaf provided that adequate precautions are taken for guarding against falsification: section 436. Section 3 of the Stock Exchange (Completion of Bargains) Act 1976, *ante,* enables the company to use a computer to keep the minutes.

RESOLUTIONS

Kinds of resolution

In the absence of a contrary provision in the Act or in the memorandum or the articles the company in general meeting acts by ordinary resolution. Sometimes, however, the Act or the memorandum or articles require a special resolution or, occasionally, an extraordinary resolution. The Jenkins Report[72] recommended that references to extraordinary resolutions be omitted from the Act and special resolutions required in their stead.

An *ordinary resolution,* which is not defined in the Act, is a resolution passed by a simple majority of the votes of the members entitled to vote[73] and voting in person or, where allowed, by proxy, at a meeting of which notice has been duly given. The length of the notice depends upon a number of factors including the kind of meeting at which the resolution is passed.[74]

Section 141 defines an *extraordinary resolution* as a resolution passed by at least a three-fourths' majority of [the votes of] the members entitled to vote[75] and voting, in person or, where allowed, by proxy, at a general meeting of which notice specifying the intention to propose the resolution as an extraordinary resolution has been duly

[71] By the member himself or by a named expert on his behalf: *M'Cusker* v. *M'Rae,* 1966 S.C. 253.
[72] Para. 468.
[73] *Ante,* p. 214.
[74] *Ante,* p. 305.
[75] See footnote 73.

given. Again the length of the notice depends upon a number of factors including the kind of meeting at which the resolution is passed.[76]

A *special resolution* is defined as a resolution passed by a majority of at least three-fourths of [the votes of] the members entitled to vote[77] and voting, in person or, where allowed, by proxy, at a general meeting of which at least 21 days' notice specifying the intention to propose the resolution as a special resolution has been given: section 141.

The words in brackets must be read into section 141 because voting may be on a show of hands, in which case each member will usually have one vote, or on a poll, in which case each member will usually have one vote for each of his shares.

Table A, article 50, provides that the notice must be *clear* notice, *i.e.* exclusive of the day on which it is served or deemed to be served and of the day for which it is given. In England a provision in the articles that the day of service is to be included in the number of days' notice to be given does not apply to notice of a special resolution, *i.e.* the period of not less than 21 days prescribed by section 141 is a period of not less than 21 clear days, exclusive of the day of service of the notice and of the day on which the meeting is to be held. Articles cannot curtail the length of time which Parliament has said must elapse between the date on which the notice is served and the date on which the meeting is held.[78] In Scotland the requisite notice under section 141(2) means a notice of not less than 21 days computed by excluding the day on which the notice is received by the shareholder but including the day on which the meeting is to be held.[79] We have seen[80] that less than 21 days' notice of a special resolution may be given if it is so agreed by a majority in number of the members holding not less than 95 per cent. of the shares giving the right to attend and vote at the meeting: section 141(2).

At a meeting at which a special resolution or an extraordinary resolution is submitted to be passed, a declaration of the chairman that the resolution is carried is, unless a poll is demanded, conclusive evidence of the fact without proof of the number or proportion of the

[76] See footnote 74.
[77] See footnote 73.
[78] *Re Hector Whaling Ltd.* [1936] Ch. 208, applied in *Thompson* v. *Stimpson* [1961] 1 Q.B. 195.
[79] *Neil M'Leod & Sons Ltd., Petitioners*, 1967 S.C. 16, *per* Lord President Clyde at p. 20.
[80] *Ante*, p. 306.

votes recorded in favour of or against the resolution: section 141(3). This provision prevents a resolution from being challenged on the ground, *e.g.* that certain shareholders were not qualified to vote.[81] If, however, the declaration of the chairman is fraudulent, or shows on the face of it that the proper majority has not been obtained, it is not conclusive.

A special resolution was put to the meeting. The chairman then said: "Those in favour 6; those against 23; but there are 200 voting by proxy,[82] and I declare the resolution carried." *Held,* the declaration was not conclusive, and the resolution was not passed: *Re Caratal (New) Mines Ltd.* [1902] 2 Ch. 498.[83]

Further, the chairman's declaration is not conclusive where the resolution has not been effectively submitted to the meeting, *e.g.* if a show of hands has not been taken as required by the articles.[84]

The chairman can put a resolution to the meeting without its being seconded, unless the articles prohibit it.

Amendments

If a positive amendment, pertinent to the subject-matter of the proposed resolution, is proposed, it must be voted upon first. If the chairman refuses to put a proper amendment to the meeting, the resolution, if passed, is not binding.[85]

An amendment cannot be moved if it goes beyond the notice convening the meeting. Because notice of special business must state the resolution to be passed in such a way as fairly to state the purpose for which the meeting is convened,[86] there is little scope for amendment where a resolution is special business. Where a notice of a meeting stated that it was to pass, with such amendments as should be determined, a resolution that three named persons be appointed directors, an amendment to elect two other directors as well was held valid.[87] Again, there is little scope for amendment of special and

---

[81] *Grahams' Morocco Co. Ltd., Petitioners,* 1932 S.C. 269.

[82] Those "voting" by proxy could not vote on a show of hands.

[83] A corresponding Scottish case is *Cowan* v. *Scottish Publishing Co. Ltd.* (1892) 19 R. 437.

[84] *Citizens Theatre Ltd., Petitioners,* 1946 S.C. 14; contrast *Fraserburgh Commercial Co. Ltd., Petitioners,* 1946 S.C. 444.

[85] *Henderson* v. *Bank of Australasia* (1890) 45 Ch.D. 330 (C.A.).

[86] *Ante,* p. 309.

[87] *Betts & Co. Ltd.* v. *Macnaghten* [1910] 1 Ch. 430.

extraordinary resolutions since, as we have seen, the notice of a special resolution or an extraordinary resolution must set out in substance the exact wording of the resolution. However, where a notice of a meeting stated that it was to pass special resolutions to wind up voluntarily and to appoint X as liquidator, and the second resolution was dropped and a new one to appoint Y as liquidator was passed, it was held that Y's appointment was valid because as soon as the resolution to wind up was passed a liquidator could be appointed, without notice, under the Act.[88]

Registration and copies of certain resolutions

A printed copy of certain resolutions and agreements, or a copy in some other form approved by him, must be forwarded to the Registrar within 15 days after they are passed or made and, where articles have been registered, a copy must be annexed to every copy of the articles issued subsequently: 1948 Act, s.143; 1967 Act, s.51.

Section 143 applies to, *inter alia,* special and extraordinary resolutions, resolutions agreed to by all the members which would otherwise not have been effective unless passed as special resolutions or extraordinary resolutions, and resolutions agreed to by all the members of a class of shareholders. This section also applies to certain ordinary resolutions, *e.g.* one to vary or revoke the authority of the directors to issue shares: 1980 Act, s.14(6).

A resolution passed at an adjourned meeting is treated as having been passed on the date on which it was in fact passed, and is not deemed to have been passed on the date of the original meeting: section 144.

It will be remembered that a printed copy of a resolution effecting an increase of capital, or a copy in some other form approved by the Registrar, must also be filed within 15 days: 1948 Act, s.63; 1967 Act, s.51.

The various processes which the Registrar is prepared to regard as satisfying the printing stipulation have been dealt with already.[89]

When various resolutions required

The company in general meeting acts by ordinary resolution unless another kind of resolution is required by the Act or by the memoran-

---

[88] *Re Trench Tubeless Tyre Co.* [1900] 1 Ch. 408 (C.A.).   [89] p. 104.

dum or the articles. Thus an ordinary resolution is enough under section 14 of the 1976 Act (appointment of auditors).[90] In practice an increase of capital is effected by an ordinary resolution.[91] An ordinary resolution is *expressly* provided for by section 184 of the 1948 Act (removal of a director) and section 14(6) of the 1976 Act (removal of an auditor).

An extraordinary resolution is required in a few cases, for example by section 278[92] (initiation of a creditors' voluntary winding up, when the company is insolvent), by section 303[93] (to sanction the exercise of certain of the powers of the liquidator in a members' voluntary winding up) and by section 306[94] (arrangement between a company being wound up voluntarily and its creditors).

A special resolution is required for the more important matters, for example by section 5 (alteration of objects), section 10 (alteration of articles), section 66 (reduction of capital), section 278[95] (initiation of a members' voluntary winding up), section 287[96] (authority for the liquidator in a members' voluntary winding up to sell the company's business to another company for cash or shares in the other company).

The Jenkins Committee did not support the view that the Act should be amended to provide generally for voting on the above mentioned resolutions by postal ballot. They thought that where there is a possibility of there being a difference of opinion between members about such matters there should be a meeting at which the matter in question may be discussed (although they saw no need for a meeting where all the members entitled to vote are unanimous).[97]

[90] *Post*, p. 515.
[91] *Ante*, p. 223.
[92] *Post*, p. 687.
[93] *Post*, p. 697.
[94] *Post*, p. 702.
[95] See footnote 92.
[96] *Post*, p. 706.
[97] Para. 460.

CHAPTER 16

DIRECTORS

THE management of a company is usually entrusted to a small body of persons called "directors," although they are sometimes called "governors," or, in the case of a private company, "governing directors." It will be seen later that the Act requires a public company to have at least two directors and a private company to have at least one. The exact name by which a person occupying the position of director is called is immaterial as, under section 455(1), in the Act the expression "director" includes any person occupying the position of director by whatever name called. Section 455(1) also provides that in the Act the expression "officer" in relation to a corporation includes a director or manager. Some of the statutory rules applicable to directors apply also to "shadow directors." Section 63 of the 1980 Act provides that these are persons in accordance with whose instructions the directors are accustomed to act.

Among other things, this chapter deals with the appointment, remuneration and vacation of office of directors. It also shows that the directors of a company act as a board, that normal articles (*e.g.* Table A, article 80) give the directors extensive powers to manage the company's business (and that so long as the directors act within their powers, the company in general meeting cannot overrule them), and that articles usually empower the directors to appoint a managing director and delegate any of their powers to him.

The most important topics dealt with in the chapter are the fiduciary duties and duties of care which a director owes to his company. Recent statutory developments have further restricted the powers of the directors and provide for disclosure by them of many transactions involving themselves and the company.

It should be noted that in a private company the directors are usually substantial shareholders. In a public company, the directors normally have few shares, their fees and other emoluments, rather than their dividends, being their main sources of profit from the company, with the result that management and ownership of the company are divorced.

Number and Appointment of Directors

Every public company registered on or after November 1, 1929, must have at least two directors. Companies registered before that date, and every private company, must have at least one director: section 176. The Jenkins Committee recommended that every company should have at least two directors.[1] Apart from section 176, the number of directors is regulated by the articles.

As to the *first directors,* section 21(5) of the Companies Act 1976 provides that the persons named in the statement of first directors and secretary, which must be delivered for registration with the memorandum, shall, on the incorporation of the company, be deemed to have been appointed as the first directors and secretary, and any appointment by any articles delivered with the memorandum shall be void unless the person concerned is named as a director or secretary in the statement.

Subsequent directors are appointed in the way laid down in the articles, *e.g.* by the company in annual general meeting.

Table A provides:
"89. At the first annual general meeting of the company all the directors shall retire from office, and at the annual general meeting in every subsequent year one-third of the directors for the time being, or, if their number is not three or a multiple of three, then the number nearest one-third, shall retire from office.

90. The directors to retire in every year shall be those who have been longest in office since their last election, but as between persons who became directors on the same day those to retire shall (unless they otherwise agree among themselves) be determined by lot.

91. A retiring director shall be eligible for re-election."

The articles also usually contain clauses, as does Table A in articles 94 and 95, providing that the company may by ordinary resolution increase or reduce the number of directors, and that casual vacancies, *i.e.* vacancies occurring between two annual general meetings, may be filled by the directors. Article 95 also provides that the directors may appoint additional directors to hold office until the next annual general meeting but so that the total number of directors fixed in accordance with the articles is not exceeded. Where there are articles similar to articles 94 and 95 the power of appointing additional directors has not

---

[1] *Ante,* p. 46.

been delegated to the directors so as to exclude the inherent power of the company in general meeting to appoint directors.[2]

The appointment of directors at a general meeting, except in the case of a private company, must be voted on individually unless a resolution to the contrary has first been agreed to by the meeting without any vote being given against it. A motion for the appointment of two or more persons as directors of a public company by a single resolution is otherwise void (although the operation of section 180,[3] by which the acts of the "directors" are valid, is not excluded and no provision in the articles for the automatic reappointment of retiring directors in default of another appointment applies): section 183.

Table A, article 92, provides that the company at the meeting at which a director retires by rotation may elect a director to fill the vacancy and that the retiring director, if offering himself for re-election, is deemed to have been re-elected unless (*a*) another person is elected, (*b*) a resolution not to fill the vacancy is passed, or (*c*) a resolution for his re-election is lost. In the absence of a provision like (*c*), a retiring director will be deemed to be re-elected even though a resolution that he be re-elected is lost.[4] It is also provided, by article 93, that no person, other than the retiring director or a person recommended by the directors, is eligible for election as a director unless notice of intention to propose him, signed by a member entitled to vote, is left at the registered office not less than three nor more than 21 days before the meeting, together with a signed notice of his willingness to act.

The articles may appoint a named person a permanent director of the company, so that no re-election is necessary in his case. This was common in the case of the former exempt private companies.[5] The appointment of such a director, when the only contract he has is that contained in the articles, can be terminated by an alteration of the articles, or by his removal under section 184,[6] or by the company's going into liquidation.

The articles appointed F. governing director of the company for his life, or until he should resign or be removed by a special resolution of the company, at

---

[2] *Worcester Corsetry Ltd.* v. *Witting* [1936] Ch. 640.
[3] *Post,* p. 440.
[4] *Grundt* v. *Great Boulder Proprietary Mines Ltd.* [1948] Ch. 145 (C.A.).
[5] *Ante,* p. 10.
[6] *Post,* p. 346.

a salary of £300 a year. F. acted for 16 years, when the company went into voluntary liquidation. *Held,* F.'s employment was conditional on the continued existence of the company and ceased automatically when it was wound up, so that F. could not claim damages for breach of contract: *Re T. N. Farrer Ltd.* [1937] Ch. 352.

Power may be given to a particular person or company to nominate one or more directors; this is often done in the case of subsidiary companies.

Assignment of office by directors

If the articles or any agreement contains power for a director to assign his office to another person, an assignment is of no effect unless and until it is approved by a special resolution of the company: section 204.

Alternate directors

Although the Act does not say so, section 204, above, does not prevent the appointment by a director, if authorised by the articles and subject thereto, of an alternate or substitute director to act for him in certain circumstances. Because of the wide definition of the word "director" in section 455 it seems that an alternate is a director for the purposes of the Act, so that particulars with respect to him must be shown in registers such as the register of directors, *post.*[7]

PERSONS WHO CANNOT BE DIRECTORS

Certain persons cannot be appointed or act as directors:

(1) A person who has reached the age of 70 cannot be *appointed* director *unless* the company is private and not the subsidiary of a public company, *or* the articles otherwise provide, *or* he is appointed or approved by a resolution of which special notice, stating his age, has been given: section 185. The exceptions are such as to make this section ineffective.

A person who is *first* appointed a director of a company, other than a private company which is not the subsidiary of a public company, after he has reached the age at which the directors retire under the Act[8] or the articles, must give notice of his age to the company: section 186.

---

[7] p. 336. And see the Jenkins Report, para. 83.
[8] See s.185, above.

(2) An undischarged bankrupt must not act as director of, or be concerned in the promotion, formation or management of, a company without the leave of the court by which he was adjudged bankrupt,[9] under penalty of two years' imprisonment or a fine or both: section 187.

In England, on an application for leave to act as director, notice must be given to the Official Receiver, who can oppose the application if he is of opinion that it is contrary to the public interest.

(3) A person cannot, without leave of the court, be a director of or be concerned in the management of a company if he has been convicted of an indictable offence in connection with the promotion, formation, management or liquidation of a company, or with the receivership or management of a company, or if in a winding up it has appeared that he has been guilty of fraudulent trading[10] or that he has been guilty, while an officer, of fraud or breach of duty in relation to the company, and the court has ordered that he shall not be a director or be concerned in management for up to 15 years: section 188, as amended by section 93 of the 1981 Act. Such an order would also now prevent such a person being a liquidator, receiver or manager of a company or being concerned in the promotion of a company.

The period of disqualification must date from conviction, not, *e.g.,* from the convicted person's release from prison.[11]

An application for such a disqualification order may be made by the Secretary of State, the official receiver, the liquidator or any past or present member or creditor of the company concerned. Ten days' notice must be given and the person concerned may appear and give evidence or call witnesses. If any person contravenes an order under section 188 he may in respect of each offence be liable—

(a) on conviction on indictment, to up to two years' imprisonment or a fine or to both; or

(b) on summary conviction, to imprisonment for up to six months or to a fine or both.

When making an application the Secretary of State, official receiver or liquidator may give evidence and call the attention of the court to any

[9] For Scotland, substitute "sequestration of his estates was awarded" for "he was adjudged bankrupt."
[10] *Post,* p. 643.
[11] *R.* v. *Bradley* [1961] 1 W.L.R. 398 (C.C.A.).

matters which seem to him to be relevant. In *Re Gilgate Properties Ltd.* (1981) 131 N.L.J. 579, this was held to include D.o.T. inspectors' reports and a report of the City Panel on Take-overs and Mergers (*post*). The ordinary rules of evidence did not apply.

The Jenkins Report[12] recommended that section 188 be extended to cover, *e.g.* persons who have been persistently in default in complying with the Act and that disqualification should continue for up to five years after a convicted person's release from prison. The Jenkins Report further recommended that corporate bodies and Scottish firms should be prohibited from being directors. Only the first of these recommendations was implemented by section 28 of the 1976 Act. That section was repealed by section 93 of the 1981 Act which also amended section 188 to provide two further grounds for granting a disqualification order under that section. Accordingly the current law resides in section 188.

A person may now be disqualified from being a director of or being concerned in the management of a company if he has been persistently in default in relation to any provision of the Companies Acts which requires any document to be delivered, or notice of any matter to be given, to the Registrar.[12a]

The fact that a person has been persistently in default in relation to any provision of the Companies Acts may be conclusively proved by showing that in the five years ending with the date of the application he has been adjudged guilty (whether or not on the same occasion) of three or more defaults. A person is to be treated as being adjudged guilty of a default if—

(*a*) he is convicted of any offence by virtue of any contravention of or failure to comply with any provision of the Companies Acts (whether on his own part or on the part of the company); or

(*b*) a default order is made against him under sections 337, 375 or 428 of the 1948 Act, *ante*, or section 5(1) of the 1976 Act, *post*.

An order made on this basis may only last for five and not fifteen years.

In *Re Civica Investments Ltd.*, *The Times*, June 9, 1982, the judge said that deciding the length of the disqualification was similar to the passing of a sentence in a criminal case. Elaborate reasoning was

---

[12] Para. 85.

[12a] This includes acting as a liquidator, promoter, receiver, etc. The conditions for application for, and breach of, an order are as set out above.

therefore unnecessary for, as more of the cases arose, it would be undesirable for the judge to be taken through the facts of previous cases. The five year period was a maximum and should be reserved for serious cases. In the case before him, since most of the defaults had been remedied the judge imposed a one year disqualification only.

Alternatively a disqualification order may be made under section 188 if a person is convicted of any offence by virtue of or failure to comply with any provision of the Companies Acts and in the five year period up to that conviction he has been convicted of other such offences or received default orders (see above), totalling three in number. In this case the court making the conviction can impose the disqualification order which may last for fifteen years.

A register of the names and particulars of persons against whom disqualification orders have been made is available for public inspection during the currency of those orders at the Companies Registration Office in Edinburgh and the Royal Courts of Justice in London: Home Office Circular No. 52 of 1982, *post.*

(4) A person cannot, without leave of the court, be a director of, or be concerned directly or indirectly in the promotion, formation or management of, a company if, on an application by one of the persons mentioned below, it appeared to the court that—

(a) he was or had been a director of a company which had at any time gone into liquidation (while he was a director or subsequently) and he was insolvent at that time; and

(b) he was or had been a director of another company which had gone into liquidation within five years of the date on which the first company went into liquidation; and

(c) his conduct as a director of any of those companies made him unfit to be concerned in the management of a company,

and the court ordered that he must not, without its leave, be a director of or in any way be concerned or take part in the management of a company for such period beginning with the date of the order and not exceeding five years as was specified: Insolvency Act 1976, s.9. Such an order also relates to acting as a promoter, liquidator, receiver or manager of a company: Companies Act 1981, s.94.

If a company is being wound up by the court, an application must be made by the Official Receiver or, in Scotland, the Secretary of State, and the power to make a disqualifying order is exercisable by the court by which the company is being wound up. In any other case, an application must be made by the Secretary of State and the power to make an order is exercisable by the High Court or, in Scotland, the Court of Session.

The word "director" in section 9 includes any person in accordance with whose directions or instructions the directors of the company have been accustomed to act and, for the purposes of the section, a company goes into liquidation, if it is wound up by the court, on the date of the winding-up order and, in any other case, on the date of the passing of the resolution for voluntary winding-up.

Contravention of an order made under section 9 is an offence punishable, on conviction on indictment, by imprisonment for up to two years or a fine or both or, on summary conviction, by imprisonment for up to six months or a fine or both.

Register of disqualification orders

Section 29 of the 1976 Act provides that the prescribed officer of any court which makes an order that a person shall not, without the leave of the court, be a director of or be concerned in the management of a company for a specified period, or grants leave in relation to such an order, must furnish the Secretary of State with particulars of the order or the grant of leave whether the order is made under section 188 of the Companies Act 1948, *ante,* section 9 of the Insolvency Act 1976.

The Secretary of State must maintain a register of such orders and grants of leave, which register is open to inspection on payment of such fee as may be specified by the Secretary of State in regulations made by statutory instrument.

Share Qualification of Directors

A share qualification is a specified number of shares which a person must hold in the company to qualify him for appointment as a director of it. There is no share qualification unless the articles otherwise provide, as they sometimes do. The Rules of The Stock Exchange, London, do not require a qualification, nor does Table A provide for one.

Article 77 of Table A merely provides: "The shareholding qualification for directors may be fixed by the company in general meeting, and unless and until so fixed no qualification shall be required."

It should be remembered that in the case of a private company a director will in any event usually be a substantial shareholder.

When a qualification is imposed, a director not already qualified must obtain his qualification within two months of his appointment or the shorter time fixed by the articles: section 182. Where he is appointed by a resolution decided on a poll (on which each member usually has one vote for each of his shares) the two months' period, within which his name must be entered in the register of members, runs from midnight on the day on which the votes are counted and the result of the poll ascertained, not from midnight on an earlier date on which the votes are cast.[13]

If a director fails to obtain his qualification within the appropriate period, or if he thereafter ceases to hold it, his office is vacated and he is liable to a fine until he ceases to act as director: section 182.

A provision in the articles that "no person shall be eligible to, or shall continue in, the office of director" unless he holds a specified number of shares does not apply to persons who are expressly and unconditionally named as directors in the articles.[14]

Qualification shares need not be obtained from the company; the director may obtain them by transfer from a member,[15] but he should not obtain them by way of gift from a promoter.[16]

Where articles provide that a first director is to "be deemed to have agreed to take" his qualifying shares from the company, a person who has accepted office as one of the first directors and has acted as such is bound to accept an allotment of shares made in accordance with that provision.[17]

Shares held jointly with another person are a sufficient qualification, unless the articles otherwise provide.[18]

The holding of a share warrant does not constitute the holding of qualification shares (s.182(2)), as the shares can be transferred at any time by delivery of the warrant.

Sometimes the articles provide that the director must hold his qualification shares "in his own right." This does not mean that he

---

[13] *Holmes* v. *Keyes* [1959] Ch. 199 (C.A.).

[14] *Liquidator of the Consolidated Copper Co. etc. Ltd.* v. *Peddie* (1877) 5 R. 393.

[15] *Brown's Case* (1874) L.R. 9 Ch. 102.

[16] *Eden* v. *Ridsdales Railway Lamp Co. Ltd.* (1899) 23 Q.B.D. 368, *post*, p. 378.

[17] *The Kingsburgh Motor Construction Co. Ltd.* v. *Scott* (1902) 10 S.L.T. 424 (O.H.).

[18] *Grundy* v. *Briggs* [1910] 1 Ch. 444.

must be the beneficial owner of them.[19] It means "holding in his own right as distinguished from holding in the right of somebody else. . . . It means that a person shall hold shares in such a way that the company can safely deal with him in respect of his shares whatever his interest may be in the shares."[20] It is sufficient if the director holds the shares as trustee.[21]

A person described in the register as the liquidator of another company does not hold shares in his own right.[22] Nor does a bankrupt director whose trustee in bankruptcy has given the company notice that he is claiming the shares.[23]

REGISTER OF DIRECTORS AND SECRETARIES

Section 200 of the 1948 Act as amended by section 22(1) of the 1976 Act and section 95 of the 1981 Act provides that a company must keep at its registered office a register of its directors and secretaries. In the case of an individual director the register must contain his name and any former name, address, nationality and business occupation, together with particulars of any other present or past directorships held by him (except directorships of companies of which the company is the wholly owned subsidiary, or which are wholly owned subsidiaries either of the company or of another company of which the company is the wholly owned subsidiary) and the date of his birth (except in the case of a private company which is not a subsidiary of a public company). The obligation relating to past directorships only relates to the previous five years and does not apply to dormant companies, *post.* The register is open to inspection by members without fee and by others on payment of 5p.

Within 14 days of any change in the directors or secretary or in the particulars contained in the register, the company must notify the Registrar of the change and the date when it occurred. A notification

---

[19] *Howard* v. *Sadler* [1893] 1 Q.B. 1; *The Galloway Saloon Steam Packet Co.* v. *Wallace* (1891) 19 R. 330.

[20] *Per* Lindley L.J. in *Bainbridge* v. *Smith* (1889) 41 Ch.D. 462 (C.A.), at p. 475.

[21] *Pulbrook* v. *Richmond etc. Mining Co.* (1878) 9 Ch.D. 610, where the director was held entitled to an order restraining his co-directors from excluding him from the board. See further on this point *Hayes* v. *Bristol Plant Hire Ltd.* [1957] 1 W.L.R. 499 and *Elliot* v. *J. W. Mackie & Sons Ltd.*, 1935 S.C. 81.

[22] *Boschoek Proprietary Co. Ltd.* v. *Fuke* [1906] 1 Ch. 148.

[23] *Sutton* v. *English and Colonial Produce Co.* [1902] 2 Ch. 502.

of a person having become a director or secretary must contain his signed consent to act as such.

Section 9(3) of the European Communities Act 1972 as amended by section 22(3) of the Companies Act 1976 requires the Registrar to publish in the *Gazette* notice of the receipt by him of any notification of a change among the directors of a company. And subsection (4) provides that a company cannot rely against other persons on any change among its directors if it had not been officially notified at the material time and is not shown by the company to have been known at that time to the person concerned, or if the material time is less than 16 days after official notification and it is shown that the person concerned was unavoidably prevented from knowing of the event at that time.

Particulars of Directors on Business Letters

No company may state, in any form, the name of any of its directors in a business letter, unless in the text or as a signatory, unless it states in legible characters the Christian name, or initials, and surname of every director of the company: section 201, as amended by Schedule 3 to the 1981 Act.

Prior to the amendment this requirement applied to trade catalogues, circulars etc.[24]

Disclosure of Directors' Shareholdings, etc.

Obligation of director to notify company of his interests in shares in, or debentures of, it or associated companies

Subject to any exceptions made by the Department of Trade, a person who becomes a director when he is interested in shares in or debentures of the company or its subsidiary, holding company or co-subsidiary, must, within five days[25] (or, if he does not know of the interest, within five days after it comes to his knowledge), give the company written notice of his interests and of the number of shares of each class in, and the amount of debentures of each class of, the company and each of the associated companies: Companies Act 1967, s.27(1)(*a*) as amended by Companies Act 1976, s.24(1).

---

[24] The Jenkins Report recommended that section 201 be repealed (para. 456).
[25] Excluding Saturdays, Sundays and bank holidays.

A person in accordance with whose directions the directors are accustomed to act is deemed to be a director of the company.

A director must (within five days, if he knows of the event and that its occurrence gives rise to the obligation; otherwise within five days after he becomes aware that the occurrence of the event gives rise to the obligation) give the company written notice if, while he is a director—

    (i) an event occurs in consequence of which he becomes or ceases to be interested in shares in or debentures of the company or an associated company; or

    (ii) he contracts to sell any such shares or debentures; or

    (iii) he assigns a right given to him by the company to subscribe for shares in or debentures of the company; or

    (iv) he is granted by an associated company a right to subscribe for shares in or debentures of that other company, or he exercises or assigns such a right;

stating the number or amount, and class, of shares or debentures involved: section 27(1)(*b*) of the 1967 Act as amended by section 24(1) of the 1976 Act. Certain other matters such as the price or other form of consideration must be stated too.

Contravention of section 27(1), or making to the company a statement known to be false or recklessly making a false statement, gives rise to liability to two years' imprisonment or a fine or both. Proceedings can, in England or Wales, be instituted only by or with the consent of the Department of Trade or the Director of Public Prosecutions.

If it appears that section 27 has been contravened the Department of Trade may order an investigation: section 32.[26]

Rules for giving effect to obligation to disclose

Section 28 of the Companies Act 1967 as amended by Schedule 3 to the 1981 Act, contains the following rules for giving effect to section 27(1), *ante:*

(1) An interest in shares or debentures includes any form of interest in such shares or debentures even if the exercise of a right conferred by ownership is or may be made subject to restraint or restriction.

(2) An interest under a trust whereof the property comprises shares

[26] *Post,* p. 428.

or debentures is deemed an interest in the shares or debentures if it would otherwise not be so.

(3) A person is deemed interested in shares or debentures if a company is interested in them and—

(*a*) it or its directors are accustomed to act in accordance with his directions; or

(*b*) he is entitled to exercise or control the exercise of one-third or more of its voting power at any general meeting; or he is so entitled to exercise the votes of one company which in turn can exercise any voting power at the general meeting of another company, he is deemed interested in the relevant shares of that second company.

(4) A person is deemed interested in shares or debentures if—

(*a*) he enters into a contract for the purchase of them whether for cash or other consideration; or

(*b*) he has a right, otherwise than by virtue of having an interest under a trust, to call for delivery of them or to acquire an interest in them or is under an obligation to take an interest in them; or

(*c*) not being a registered holder, he is entitled (otherwise than by virtue of having been appointed a proxy or as representative of a corporation) to exercise any right conferred by the holding thereof.

(5) Each person with a joint interest is deemed to have an interest.

(6) It is immaterial that the shares or debentures are unidentifiable.

(7) Interests in reversion or remainder, or (as regards Scotland) in fee, are disregarded so long as a person is entitled to receive, during the lifetime of himself or another, income from trust property comprising shares or debentures.

(8) An interest in England and Wales as bare trustee or as custodian trustee, or in Scotland as simple trustee, is disregarded.

(9) An interest subsisting by virtue of, *inter alia,* an authorised unit trust scheme[27] is disregarded.

(10) An interest of the Church of Scotland General Trustees or of the Church of Scotland Trust is disregarded.

---

[27] *Ante*, p. 157.

(11) Delivery to a person's order of shares or debentures in fulfilment of a contract to purchase by him or in satisfaction of his right to call for delivery thereof, or failure to deliver to him in accordance with such a contract or right, or the lapse of his right to call for delivery, is deemed an event in consequence of which he ceases to be interested in them.[28]

Extension of obligation to disclose to interests of spouses and children

For the purposes of section 27 of the Companies Act 1967, *ante,* an interest of the spouse of, or of a child under the age of majority of, a director (not being himself or herself a director) in shares or debentures is treated as the director's interest, and a contract, assignment or right of subscription entered into, exercised or made by, or a grant made to, such a spouse or child is treated as that of the director: section 31(1).

Within five days after the event in question comes to his knowledge, a director must notify the company in writing if, while he or she is a director—

(*a*) the company grants the director's spouse or child a right to subscribe for shares in or debentures of the company; or

(*b*) such spouse or child exercises such a right.

In each case the like information as is required by section 27, *ante,* must be stated: section 31(2) of the 1967 Act as amended by section 24(1) of the 1976 Act. If section 31(2) appears to have been contravened the Department of Trade may order an investigation: section 32.[29]

In section 31, "son" includes step-son and adopted son, and "daughter" includes step-daughter and adopted daughter.

Register of directors' shareholdings, etc.

The Companies Act 1967, s.29, contains provisions for securing that information furnished under section 27,[30] and certain other information about directors' interests, is recorded and made available.

---

[28] The necessity for s.28(11) was questioned in the Second Interim Report of the Australian Company Law Advisory Committee, February 1969, at p. 5. It was also said that if the sub-section is to be included in Australian legislation it should be redrafted to express more clearly what is intended.

[29] *Post*, p. 428.

[30] *Ante*, p. 337.

Every company must keep a register for the purposes of section 27 and whenever it receives information from a director in consequence of that section, within three days[25] thereafter it must inscribe in the register, against his name, the information and the date of inscription.

When a company grants a director a right to subscribe for shares or debentures it must, within a similar time, inscribe against his name the date of the grant, the period during or time at which it is exercisable, the consideration for the grant, the description of the shares or debentures and the number or amount thereof, and the price to be paid. When such a right is exercised there must be inscribed that fact (identifying the right), the number or amount of shares or debentures involved, the fact that they were registered in his name or the names of the persons in whose names they were registered, together with the number or amount registered in the name of each person.

The entries against the names in the register must appear in chronological order. If a director requires it, the nature and extent of his interest in shares or debentures must also be recorded.

The company is not, by virtue of anything done for the purposes of section 29, affected with notice of, or put upon inquiry as to, the rights of any person in relation to shares or debentures.

Inspection of register

The register must be kept at the registered office or where the register of members is kept[31] and must be open during business hours for at least two hours each day to the inspection of members without charge and other persons on payment of 5p. per inspection. Except where it has always been kept at the registered office the company must notify the Registrar of the place where the register is kept. Any person may require a copy of the register or part thereof on payment of 10p. per 100 words or fractional part thereof. Any copy must be sent by the company within ten days after the requirement is received. The register must also be produced at the commencement of the annual general meeting and remain open and accessible during the meeting to any person attending.[32]

---

[31] *Ante*, p. 192.
[32] *Ante*, p. 302.

Index of names

Unless the register is in the form of an index the company must also keep an index of the names inscribed therein. The index must give a sufficient indication to enable the information against each name to be readily found and must be altered within 14 days after the date on which a name is entered in the register.

Contravention of section 29

There are default fines[33] and other fines for contravention of section 29, and the court is empowered to order inspection of the register and delivery of a copy.

Duty of company to notify stock exchange of acquisition of its securities by director

Section 25 of the 1976 Act provides that when a company whose shares or debentures are listed on a recognised stock exchange is notified of any matter by a director under section 27 or section 31 of the 1967 Act, *ante*, and that matter relates to shares or debentures listed on a stock exchange, the company must notify that stock exchange of the matter before the end of the following day (Saturdays, Sundays and bank holidays in any part of Great Britain being disregarded).

If there is default in complying with the section the company and every officer in default is guilty of an offence and liable on summary conviction to a fine and further to a default fine, although proceedings in England and Wales cannot be instituted except by, or with the consent of, the Secretary of State or the Director of Public Prosecutions.

DIRECTORS' SERVICE CONTRACTS

Section 26 of the Companies Act 1967, as amended by Schedule 1 to the 1976 Act and s.61 of the 1980 Act, provides that, subject as below, every company must keep a copy of each director's contract of service[34] or of any variation thereof, or a memorandum thereof setting

---

[33] *Ante*, p. 192.
[34] This applies also to "shadow directors," *post*, p. 360.

out its terms if it is not in writing, at one place. This obligation extends to the directors of its subsidiary companies, if any. The place may be—

(1) the company's registered office; or
(2) the other place where the register of members is kept; or
(3) its principal place of business in England, if the company is registered in England, or in Scotland if the company is registered in Scotland.

The documents must be kept open to the inspection of members without charge during business hours for at least two hours a day.

Notice of such place and of any changes in it must be given to the Registrar except where the documents have always been kept at the registered office.

Contracts requiring a director to work wholly or mainly outside the United Kingdom are excluded although a memorandum of the duration of the contract, and, if appropriate, the name and place of incorporation of the subsidiary company, must be kept. Also excluded are those where the unexpired term of the contract is less than 12 months or the contract can be terminated by the company without payment of compensation within 12 months.

There are default fines[35] and other fines for contravention of section 26 and the court is empowered to order an inspection.

To prevent possible abuse by directors granting themselves long-term service contracts in order to obtain large compensation payments in the event of a dismissal, section 47 of the 1980 Act limits the length of such contracts without the approval of the general meeting. Any term in such a contract which entitles a director to employment with the company for longer than five years must be approved by the company in general meeting.

Any term in breach of this section is void and replaced by one which enables the company to terminate the contract at any time, subject to reasonable notice. This requirement cannot be avoided by negotiating several consecutive five year agreements, since no second contract may succeed the first if that contract has more than six months left to run.

In addition to the disclosure rules noted above such contracts are to be set out in the company's accounts (*post*).

---

[35] See note 33 above.

Dealing by Directors in Certain Options

The Jenkins Report[36] stated that a director should not deal in options, in securities of his company or of the group to which the company belongs—a director who speculates in such a way with special inside information is clearly acting improperly. However, it was said that the prohibition should not extend to options to subscribe for securities given to directors by the company or another member of the group—the terms of such options are a matter for the company.

Accordingly, the Companies Act 1967, ss.25 and 30, penalise the dealing by directors, their spouses or children, in options to buy or sell quoted shares in, or quoted debentures of, the company or associated companies.

A director who buys a right to call for delivery, or a right to make delivery, or, at his election, a right either to call for or to make delivery, at a specified price and within a specified time of a specified number of relevant shares or a specified amount of relevant debentures, is liable to two years' imprisonment or a fine or both: section 25.

"Relevant shares" and "relevant debentures" mean, respectively, shares in, or debentures of, the company or its subsidiary, holding company or co-subsidiary, as respects which a stock exchange listing has been granted in Great Britain or elsewhere. A person in accordance with whose directions the directors are accustomed to act is deemed a director of the company, (although section 56(3) provides that a person is not to be deemed one in accordance with whose directions the directors are accustomed to act by reason only that they act on advice given by him in a professional capacity).

Buying a right to subscribe for shares or debentures is not penalised, nor is buying debentures which carry a right to subscribe for or convert into shares.

Section 30 extends section 25 to the spouse of, or child under the age of majority of, a director, not being herself or himself a director of the company, except that it is a defence for such a spouse or child, charged with an offence under section 25, to prove that he had no reason to believe that his spouse or parent was a director of the company in question. "Child" includes step-child and adopted child.

If it appears that section 25 has been contravened the Department of Trade may order an investigation: section 32.[37]

---

[36] Para. 90.

[37] *Post*, p. 428.

VACATION OF OFFICE BY DIRECTORS

A director may cease to be such for various reasons, *e.g.* death, dissolution of the company, retirement by rotation under articles like Table A, articles 89–92, *ante*,[38] or retirement under an age limit, disqualification, or removal under section 184.

Retirement of directors under age limit

A director must retire at the end of the first annual general meeting after he reaches 70 *unless*—

(1) the company is a private company which is not the subsidiary of a public company; or
(2) the articles otherwise provide; or
(3) he was appointed or approved by the company in general meeting by a resolution, *i.e.* an ordinary resolution, of which special notice, stating his age, was given: section 185.

If a director should have to retire under this section he may be reappointed by an ordinary resolution of which special notice,[39] stating his age, has been given. The result is that the section is a weak one and unimportant in practice. In particular, the articles may alter the age limit or provide that directors shall not be obliged to retire on reaching any age. The Jenkins Report[40] recommended that the section be strengthened, simplified and made to apply to all companies.

Disqualification of directors

The articles usually provide for the vacation of office by directors on the happening of certain events, *e.g.* bankruptcy or resignation.

Table A, article 88, provides: "The office of director shall be vacated if the director—

(a) ceases to be a director by virtue of section 182[41] or 185[42] of the Act; or
(b) becomes bankrupt or makes any arrangement or composition with his creditors generally; or

---

[38] p. 328.
[39] *Ante*, p. 311.
[40] Para. 85.
[41] *Ante*, p. 335.
[42] *Ante*.

    (c) becomes prohibited from being a director by reason of any order made under section 188[43] of the 1948 Act or section 9 of the Insolvency Act 1976; or

    (d) becomes of unsound mind; or

    (e) resigns his office by notice in writing to the company; or

    (f) shall for more than six months have been absent without permission of the directors from meetings of the directors held during that period."

When the articles provide that a director shall vacate his office if he absents himself from board meetings for a certain time, the office will not be vacated if the absence is involuntary, as where the director is ill and unable to travel.[44] On the other hand, if the director is absent because his doctor has advised that his health will be benefited by going abroad, the office will be vacated.[45]

On the happening of any of the events mentioned in the articles, the vacation of office is automatic and the board of directors has no power to waive the offence or condone the act.[46] Similarly, on the resignation of a director the office is automatically vacated, so that the resignation cannot be withdrawn without the consent of the company.[47]

Removal of directors

By section 184 a company may by ordinary resolution[48] remove a director (other than, in the case of a private company, a director holding office for life on July 18, 1945) before the expiration of his period of office, *notwithstanding* anything in the articles or in any agreement between him and the company. Special notice[48a] must be given of any resolution to remove a director or to appoint another person in place of a removed director at the meeting at which he is removed. On receipt of notice of an intended resolution to remove a director the company must send a copy to the director concerned, who is entitled to have his representations in writing of a reasonable length sent to the members of the company or read out at the meeting and also to be heard on the resolution at the meeting. The director may be

---

[43] *Ante*, p. 331.
[44] *Mack's Claim* [1900] W.N. 114.
[45] *McConnell's Claim* [1901] 1 Ch. 728.
[46] *Re The Bodega Co. Ltd.* [1904] 1 Ch. 276.
[47] *Glossop* v. *Glossop* [1907] 2 Ch. 370.
[48] This is the only case where the Act *expressly* provides for an ordinary resolution. But see now 1976 Act s.14(6)—a company may by ordinary resolution remove an auditor; *post*, p. 518.
[48a] See note 39, *ante*.

deprived of the former right if the court is satisfied that it is being abused to secure needless publicity for defamatory matter.

It has been held that nothing in the Act prevents the articles giving a director's shares special voting rights, *e.g.* three votes per share on a poll, on a resolution to remove him.[49]

Subsection (6) provides that nothing in section 184 deprives a removed director of any compensation or damages payable to him in respect of the termination of his appointment as director or of any appointment, *e.g.* as managing director, terminating with that as director; and nothing in the section derogates from any power of removal which may exist apart from the section, *e.g.* a power of removal given by the articles of the company. For example, as will be explained later,[50] he will be entitled to damages if he has a contract of service, outside the articles, appointing him managing director for a specified period which has not yet expired, and his removal is inconsistent with such contract. The Companies Act 1967, s.26, *ante,*[51] enables members to inspect the service contract and ascertain how much it will cost to remove a director.

A director suing for damages must, of course, try to mitigate his loss by obtaining suitable alternative employment. And in calculating the damages, as to £25,000 of the amount claimed, the court will deduct the tax which the removed director would have paid had he not been removed, *i.e.* he will be awarded a net sum. As to the excess over £25,000, the director will have to pay tax to the Revenue.[52] If compensation, *i.e.* liquidated damages or damages for breach of contract where the amount of damages is agreed in the contract, is paid, it is chargeable to tax in the recipient's hands in so far as it exceeds £25,000.[53]

A director validly removed from office may, if he is a member, in appropriate circumstances, be entitled to an order under section 75 of the 1980 Act where the affairs of the company have been conducted in an unfairly prejudicial manner,[54] or an order that the company be

[49] *Bushell* v. *Faith* [1970] A.C. 1099.
[50] p. 363.
[51] p. 342.
[52] *Parsons* v. *B.N.M. Laboratories Ltd.* [1964] 1 Q.B. 95 (C.A.); *Bold* v. *Brough, Nicholson & Hall* [1964] 1 W.L.R. 201.
[53] Income and Corporation Taxes Act 1970, ss.187–188 as amended. See *Pinson, op. cit.*
[54] *Post,* p. 413.

wound up by the court on the ground that winding up is just and equitable.[55]

It has been held that the New South Wales section 120, which corresponds to, although it differs in some respects from, section 184, *ante,* empowers a public company to remove not only particular directors but the board of directors as a whole by a single resolution.[56]

PROCEEDINGS OF DIRECTORS

Unless the articles otherwise provide, the directors must act as a board. Table A, article 98, provides that they "may meet together for the despatch of business, adjourn, and otherwise regulate their meetings, as they think fit."

Article 98 further provides that a director may, and the secretary on the requisition of a director must, at any time summon a board meeting.

Every director is entitled to have reasonable notice of a meeting except that article 98, *ante,* provides that notice need not be given to a director who is absent from the United Kingdom. What is reasonable notice depends on the practice of the company, but if a director wishes to complain of the shortness of the notice he should act promptly, otherwise the court will not interfere.[57]

If notice is not properly given, the proceedings at the meeting are void.

Application was invited for 106,000 shares, and the directors resolved not to allot until 14,000 shares were applied for. A subsequent meeting was held at which two directors, a quorum, were present, when a resolution was passed to allot the shares applied for, about 3,000. The meeting was held at a few hours' notice at 2 o'clock. This was much shorter notice than had ever been given before. One director did not receive notice until next day, and another gave notice that he could not attend until 3 o'clock. *Held,* the allotment was void: *Re Homer District Gold Mines* (1888) 39 Ch.D. 546.

A quorum is that number of directors which must be present to make the proceedings of the board valid. The articles usually fix a quorum. Table A, article 99, provides: "The quorum necessary for the

---

[55] *Re Westbourne Galleries Ltd.* [1973] A.C. 360, *post,* p. 407.
[56] *Taylor* v. *McNamara* [1974] 1 N.S.W. L.R. 164.
[57] See *Browne* v. *La Trinidad* (1887) 37 Ch.D. 1 (C.A.).

transaction of the business of the directors may be fixed by the directors, and unless so fixed shall be two."

If the number of directors sinks below the quorum, the directors cannot act unless the articles provide, as they usually do, that the continuing directors can act.

Table A, article 100, provides that if and so long as the number of directors is reduced below the number constituting a quorum, "the continuing directors or director may act for the purpose of increasing the number of directors to that number, or of summoning a general meeting of the company, but for no other purpose."

In ascertaining whether a quorum is present, those directors who are incompetent to vote on the matter under discussion must not be counted,[58] as is now provided by Table A, article 84, *post.*[59] Directors, however, can attend the meeting even if they are unable to vote.[60] One transaction cannot be split up into two resolutions so as to qualify directors to vote.

Y. and D., two directors of a company, had made advances to the company in consideration of receiving debentures. The company had four directors, three of whom were a quorum. A resolution was passed granting a debenture to Y. Y. did not vote on this resolution. Another resolution was then passed granting a debenture to D., on which D. did not vote. The two debentures ranked equally among themselves. *Held,* the issue of the two debentures formed one transaction in which Y. and D. were equally interested and that the two resolutions were invalid for want of a quorum: *Re North Eastern Insurance Co. Ltd.* [1919] 1 Ch. 198.

If an allotment is invalid owing to some informality in the constitution of the board it will in most cases be binding on the company, either because of the rule in *Royal British Bank* v. *Turquand* or section 180, *post,*[61] or because of subsequent ratification by a properly constituted board.[62]

The articles deal with the election of a chairman. By Table A, article 101, the directors may elect a chairman of their meetings and determine the period for which he is to hold office. Article 98 provides that questions arising at a board meeting shall be decided by a majority of

---

[58] *Re Greymouth Point Elizabeth Ry. etc. Co. Ltd.* [1904] 1 Ch. 32.
[59] p. 379.
[60] *Grimwade* v. *B.P.S. Syndicate Ltd.* (1915) 31 T.L.R. 531.
[61] pp. 433, 440.
[62] *Re Portuguese Consolidated Copper Mines Ltd.* (1890) 45 Ch.D. 16 (C.A.).

votes, and that in case of an equality of votes the chairman shall have a second or casting vote. (The chairman has no casting vote at common law.[63])

Table A, article 106, provides that a resolution in writing, signed by all the directors entitled to receive notice of a meeting of the directors, shall be as valid as if it had been passed at a board meeting duly convened and held. (The position is the same at common law.[64])

Section 145 provides that minutes of proceedings at directors' meetings must be entered in books kept for the purpose, and such minutes signed by the chairman of the meeting at which the proceedings were had, or by the chairman of the next succeeding meeting, are evidence of the proceedings. Where minutes have been duly made there is a presumption that the meeting was duly held and convened, that all proceedings were duly had and that all appointments of directors and managers were valid.

By section 436 the minutes may be kept in a bound book, or in a loose-leaf book provided that adequate precautions are taken for guarding against falsification. Minutes may also be kept on a computer under section 3 of the Stock Exchange (Completion of Bargains) Act 1976.

If the minutes are incomplete, a resolution duly passed can be proved by other evidence.[65]

Although section 145 contains no provision for the inspection of the minutes, the Court of Session may, on the petition of a director presented to the *nobile officium,* ordain a company to make them available for inspection by the director and by a named accountant on his behalf.[66]

POWERS OF DIRECTORS

The powers of the directors depend on the articles since, apart from requiring that certain things, *e.g.* alterations to the articles (s.10) or the capital (ss.61, 66) or the delegating of authority to issue shares (1980 Act, s.14), shall be done by the members in general meeting, the Act leaves the distribution of powers between the general meeting and the board to the articles, which always give the directors extensive powers.

[63] *Wall* v. *London and Northern Assets Corpn.* [1898] 2 Ch. 469 (C.A.).
[64] *Re Bonelli's Telegraph Co.* (1871) L.R. 12 Eq. 246.
[65] *Re Fireproof Doors Ltd.* [1916] 2 Ch. 142.
[66] *M'Cusker* v. *M'Rae*, 1966 S.C. 253.

Table A, article 80, provides: "The business of the company shall be managed by the directors, who may pay all expenses incurred in promoting and registering the company, and may exercise all such powers of the company as are not, by the Act or by these regulations, required to be exercised by the company in general meeting, subject, nevertheless, to any of these regulations, to the provisions of the Act and to such regulations, being not inconsistent with the aforesaid regulations or provisions, as may be prescribed by the company in general meeting; but no regulation made by the company in general meeting shall invalidate any prior act of the directors which would have been valid if that regulation had not been made."

If they act within the powers given to them by such an article, directors are not bound to obey resolutions passed by the shareholders at a general meeting; such resolutions cannot override a decision of the directors or control the exercise of their powers in the future.[67] The directors' powers can be altered for the future by an alteration of the articles in the proper way,[68] but the articles cannot be altered with retrospective effect. And it may be that the directors can be removed from office in the proper way.[69]

"A company cannot by ordinary resolution dictate to or overrule the directors in respect of matters entrusted to them by the articles. To do that it is necessary to have a special resolution": *per* Plowman J. in *Bamford* v. *Bamford* [1970] Ch. 212, at p. 220.

The articles of a company contained an article like Table A, article 80, except that it was stated to be "subject to such regulations as might be made by the company by extraordinary resolution." The majority of the shareholders arranged a sale of the company's undertaking and requisitioned a meeting at which an ordinary resolution requiring the directors to seal the contract was passed. *Held*, the directors were not bound to obey the resolution: *Automatic Self-Cleansing Filter Syndicate Co. Ltd.* v. *Cuninghame* [1906] 2 Ch. 34 (C.A.).

The articles contained an article like Table A, article 80, and also provided that no resolution of the directors to acquire or dispose of premises was to be valid unless neither A nor B dissented. (A and B were the managing directors.) The directors resolved to acquire premises. B dissented. An ordinary resolution to the same effect as the board resolution was passed at an extraordinary general meeting of the company. *Held*, the ordinary resolution was inconsistent with the articles and the company was restrained from acting on it: *Salmon* v. *Quin & Axtens Ltd.* [1909] 1 Ch. 311 (C.A.); [1909] A.C. 442.

"This Court decided not long since, in [the *Automatic Self-Cleansing* case],

---

[67] *Automatic Self-Cleansing Filter Syndicate Co. Ltd.* v. *Cuninghame* [1906] 2 Ch. 34 (C.A.); *Salmon* v. *Quin Axtens Ltd.* [1909] 1 Ch. 311 (C.A.); [1909] A.C. 442.

[68] *Ante*, p. 108.

[69] *Ante*, p. 346.

that even a resolution of a numerical majority at a general meeting of the company cannot impose its will upon the directors when the articles have confided to them the control of the company's affairs": *per* Farwell L.J. in [1909] 1 Ch. 311, at p. 319, quoting Buckley L.J. in *Gramophone & Typewriter Ltd.* v. *Stanley* [1908] 2 K.B. 89 (C.A.).

In accordance with the principle set out above, a resolution passed by a company in general meeting that the directors should make an advance of money to the shareholders pending the declaration of a dividend was held to be inoperative.[70]

If directors are unable to exercise one of their powers because of deadlock on the board or because their number has fallen below the number required for a quorum, the company in general meeting may exercise the power.[71]

The position is similar if a company has no directors.[72] Where a company has no directors and two individuals, acting without the authority of the company, commence an action in the company's name, the company in general meeting or, if the company is being wound up, the liquidator can ratify the proceedings.[73]

If directors exceed or improperly exercise their powers, their action can be ratified by an ordinary resolution of the company in general meeting.[74]

By way of defence to a take-over bid directors allotted 500,000 shares at par for cash to a third company which was the principal distributor of the products of the company to be taken over. The articles provided that the unissued shares were to be at the directors' disposal. Two shareholders brought an action against the three directors, the third company, and the company, claiming a declaration that the allotment was invalid in that the directors had not acted bona fide in the interests of the company. *Held,* assuming that the allotment was *intra vires* the company and the directors but not bona fide in the interests of the company and therefore voidable, it could after full disclosure be ratified by an ordinary resolution at a general meeting: *Bamford* v. *Bamford* [1970] Ch. 212 (C.A.), approving *Hogg* v. *Cramphorn Ltd., post.*[75]

[70] *Scott* v. *Scott* [1943] 1 All E.R. 582.
[71] *Barron* v. *Potter* [1914] 1 Ch. 895, where the articles gave the board of directors power to appoint an additional director and, owing to differences between the directors, no board meeting could be held for the purpose. *Held,* the company retained power to appoint additional directors in general meeting.
[72] *Per* Lord Hailsham of St. Marylebone in *Alexander Ward & Co. Ltd.* v. *Samyang Navigation Co. Ltd.,* 1975 S.C. (H.L.) 26, at p. 47.
[73] *Alexander Ward* case, *ante.*
[74] *Grant* v. *United Kingdom Switchback Rlwys. Co.* (1888) 40 Ch.D. 135 (C.A.).
[75] p. 372.

If directors improperly refuse to exercise a power to initiate an action in the company's name, a minority shareholders' action may be brought by way of exception to the rule in *Foss* v. *Harbottle*.[76]

In one case where the directors directed the company to plead guilty to a charge of conspiracy to defraud, the court granted an injunction to prevent the company so pleading because the company's interests would thereby suffer, *e.g.* the loss of a potential civil action against an individual defrauder: *Re A Company: F.F.I. (U.K. Finance) Ltd.* v. *Lady Kagan* (1982) 132 N.L.J. 830.

Power to manage the business of the company does not give directors power to fix their own remuneration.[77] The articles, however, may empower them, as does Table A, article 87, to pay a gratuity or pension or allowance on retirement to a director who has held a salaried office with the company, or to his widow or dependants.

The directors cannot delegate their powers unless empowered to do so by the articles. It will be seen later[78] that the articles usually provide for delegation to a managing director. They usually also provide for delegation to a committee of directors.

Table A, article 102, provides: "The directors may delegate any of their powers to committees consisting of such member or members of their body as they think fit; any committee so formed shall in the exercise of the powers so delegated conform to any regulations that may be imposed on it by the directors."

REMUNERATION OF DIRECTORS

Directors as such are not servants of the company,[79] but managers or controllers of the company's affairs. Accordingly they have no claim to payment for their services unless, as is usual, there is a provision for payment in the articles.[80]

Table A, article 76, provides: "The remuneration of the directors shall from time to time be determined by the company in general meeting. Such remuneration shall be deemed to accrue from day to day. The directors may also be paid all travelling, hotel and other expenses properly incurred by them in attending and returning from meetings of the directors or any committee of the directors or general meetings of the company or in connection with the business of the company."

---

[76] *Cook* v. *Deeks* [1916] 1 A.C. 554, *post*, p. 397.
[77] *Foster* v. *Foster* [1916] 1 Ch. 532.
[78] p. 362.
[79] *Post*, p. 366.
[80] *Per* McCardie J. in *Moriarty* v. *Regent's Garage* [1921] 1 K.B. 423, at p. 446; *cf.* Lord President Inglis in *M'Naughtan* v. *Brunton* (1882) 10 R. 111, at p. 113.

It should be remembered that a director may hold some other position with the company, *e.g.* he may also be the managing director, in which case he will be a servant of the company as regards that other position and will receive a salary fixed by his contract of service or employment with the company.[81]

Where the company pays remuneration to its directors under an express power, such as article 76, the court will not inquire into the reasonableness of the remuneration even if it is paid out of capital, unless at the suit of a dissenting shareholder. The power of the *company* to pay such remuneration is not subject to any bona fide test: *Re Halt Garage (1964) Ltd.* [1982] 3 All E.R. 1016.

If remuneration is voted to the directors, it constitutes a debt due from the company and is consequently payable not only out of profits but also out of capital.[82] As was shown earlier,[83] a clause in the articles that directors shall receive a certain sum as remuneration, although it cannot be directly enforced against the company, is binding if the directors have accepted office on the footing of the articles.[84]

A director who is entitled to remuneration for his services is not entitled to his travelling and other expenses in attending board and other meetings unless the articles expressly so provide.

The articles, which were not like Table A, article 76, provided that each director should be paid £200 a year by way of remuneration for his services, and that the company should pay all costs and expenses which any officer of the company should incur in the discharge of his duties. Y. was appointed a director, and shortly afterwards the directors passed a resolution that all reasonable travelling expenses should be reimbursed to the directors. *Held,* the resolution was *ultra vires* the directors, and Y. must repay the travelling expenses received. His expenses of attending directors' meetings were covered by his remuneration: *Young* v. *Naval and Military Society* [1905] 1 K.B. 687.[85]

It is unlawful for a company to make tax-free payments to directors. A provision for payment to a director of remuneration tax free has effect as if it were for payment, as a gross sum subject to income tax and

---

[81] *Anderson* v. *James Sutherland (Peterhead) Ltd.*, 1941 S.C. 203, in which a managing director was held to be a person "employed by the company in any capacity" within an article which enabled the directors to remove such a person from membership when he was dismissed as managing director for misconduct (assaulting a co-director by the firing of a revolver at a directors' meeting).

[82] *Re Lundy Granite Co.* (1872) 26 L.T. 673. [83] p. 107.

[84] *Re New British Iron Co.* [1898] 1 Ch. 324.

[85] See also *Marmor Ltd.* v. *Alexander*, 1908 S.C. 78, and *Tomlinson* v. *Liquidators of Scottish Amalgamated Silks Ltd.*, 1935 S.C. (H.L.) 1; 1934 S.C. 85.

surtax, of the net sum for which it actually provides: section 189. For example, a provision for payment of £100 free of tax has effect as if it were for payment of £100 subject to tax.[86]

Unless authorised by the articles, directors cannot vote remuneration to one of themselves or appoint one of their number to a salaried position with the company. It has been said that "Directors have no right to be paid for their services, and cannot pay themselves or each other, or make presents to themselves out of the company's assets, unless authorised so to do by the instrument which regulates the company or by the shareholders at a properly convened meeting."[87]

The article governing directors' remuneration was the same as Table A, article 76.[88] The *directors* passed a resolution appointing K., one of the directors, "overseas director" at a salary of £1,800 a year. In pursuance of this appointment K. was obliged to go, and did go, to Australia. He sued for arrears of salary. *Held,* the appointment was *ultra vires* the board, so that K. could not recover the arrears of salary and was liable to refund salary already received: *Kerr* v. *Marine Products Ltd.* (1928) 44 T.L.R. 292.

However, where directors held a majority of the shares and in virtue thereof secured the passing of a resolution increasing their remuneration, the resolution was held not invalid unless fraud was proved or the resolution was *ultra vires* the company.[89]

A resolution of the directors to forgo fees to which they are entitled is binding on them and on the company if the company is a party to the agreement.[90] Otherwise the directors may rescind the resolution and claim for fees.[91]

On a liquidation, directors are not entitled to preferential payment of fees owing to them, since as directors they are not servants of the company.[92] It is otherwise with regard to salary owing to them where they hold some other position with the company.[93]

When a director ceases to be a director during a year of office, a question arises as to whether he is entitled to have his remuneration

---

[86] *Owens* v. *Multilux Ltd.,* 1974 S.L.T. 189 (N.I.R.C.) (provision in contract between company and managing director for a "salary of £2,500 per annum net of deductions" held to give the managing director a legal right to payment of a gross sum of £2,500 per annum subject to income tax).

[87] *Per* Lindley L.J. in *Re George Newman & Co.* [1895] 1 Ch. 674 (C.A.), at p. 686.

[88] *Ante,* p. 353.   [89] *Harris* v. *A. Harris Ltd.,* 1936 S.C. 183.

[90] *West Yorkshire Darracq Agency Ltd.* v. *Coleridge* [1911] 2 K.B. 326.

[91] *Re Consolidated Nickel Mines Ltd.* [1914] 1 Ch. 883.

[92] *Re Newspaper Proprietary Syndicate Ltd.* [1900] 2 Ch. 349.

[93] *Post,* p. 664.

apportioned. If, *e.g.* the articles say that he is to be paid "at the rate of" so much a year, he is entitled to be paid for the period during which he was a director.[94] On the other hand, if he is to be paid £100 a year, or in any way other than at the rate of so much a year, it has been held that he is entitled to be paid only for each complete year he serves, and not for any broken period.[95]

The Apportionment Act 1870, ss.2 and 5, provides that all salaries and other periodical payments in the nature of income shall be considered as accruing from day to day and apportionable in respect of time accordingly but, in *Moriarty* v. *Regent's Garage Co. Ltd.,*[96] although a Divisional Court held that, in the absence of agreement to the contrary, that Act applied to directors' remuneration, the decision was reversed in the Court of Appeal on other grounds.[97] Whether or not that Act applies to directors' remuneration is, therefore, an open question. It is submitted that it applies. Further, it will be remembered that Table A, article 76, provides that remuneration shall accrue from day to day, with the result that, in cases to which such an article applies, the remuneration is definitely apportionable.

Disclosure of directors' emoluments

Any provision in the articles as to the directors' remuneration must usually be disclosed in a prospectus issued by the company: Schedule 4.[98]

By section 196, as amended, a note to the accounts which must be laid before the company in general meeting must show certain particulars of directors' salaries, pensions, etc.

The particulars are:

(1) The aggregate amount of the directors' emoluments.
     These include fees and percentages, sums paid as expenses allowances which are charged to income tax,[99] contributions paid in respect of the directors under any pension scheme, and the estimated

---

[94] *Swabey* v. *Port Darwin Gold Mining Co.* (1889) 1 Meg. 385, although despite the report, the articles did not contain the words "at the rate of," as pointed out in *Inman's* case, *post.*

[95] *Salton* v. *New Beeston Cycle Co.* [1899] 1 Ch. 775; *Inman* v. *Ackroyd & Best Ltd.* [1901] 1 Q.B. 613 (C.A.), followed in *Liquidator of the Fife Linoleum etc. Co. Ltd.* v. *Lornie* (1905) 13 S.L.T. 670 (O.H.).

[96] [1921] 1 K.B. 423.

[97] [1921] 2 K.B. 766.

[98] *Ante,* p. 136.   [99] See Finance Act 1976, ss.60–72.

money value of any other benefits received otherwise than in cash. The accounts must distinguish between emoluments in respect of services as directors and other emoluments such as sums received by the directors as salaried employees of the company.

(2) The aggregate amount of directors' or past directors' pensions.

This does not include pensions paid under a pension scheme where the contributions are substantially adequate for the maintenance of the scheme, but does include a pension paid to a director's widow or other dependant.

(3) The aggregate amount of any compensation paid to directors or past directors for loss of office.

This includes sums paid on a director's retirement from office.

These amounts must include all relevant sums received from the company, the company's subsidiaries and any other person. The amount shown under (3), above, must distinguish between sums received from the company, the company's subsidiaries and other persons.

Further, sections 6 and 7 of the Companies Act 1967, as amended, provide that, subject as below, a note to the accounts must contain certain additional particulars of directors' emoluments.

The additional particulars are:

(4) With respect to each person who has been chairman of the directors' meetings during the year, his emoluments so far as attributable to his period of office (unless his duties were mainly discharged outside the United Kingdom).

(5) With respect to all the directors (other than any whose duties were mainly discharged abroad), the number whose several emoluments did not exceed £5,000, exceeded £5,000 but not £10,000,[1] and so on in bands of £5,000.

(6) If the emoluments of one or more directors exceed the chairman's or chairmen's emoluments, his emoluments or the greater or, as the case may be, the greatest emoluments.

Emoluments include all such amounts (other than contributions paid in respect of a person under a pension scheme) as are caught by (1) above.

(7) The number of directors who have waived rights to receive emoluments and the aggregate amount of such emoluments.

Sections 6 and 7 do not apply to a company which is neither a holding company nor a subsidiary as respects a financial year in which the aggregate amount of the directors' emoluments does not exceed £60,000.[1a]

If accounts do not comply with sections 6 and 7 the auditors must, so far as they reasonably can, include the required particulars in their report.

[1] Companies (Accounts) Regulations 1979 (S.I. 1979 No. 1618).
[1a] Companies (Accounts) Regulations 1982 (S.I. 1982 No. 1698).

Each director is under a duty to give notice to the company of such matters relating to himself as may be necessary to enable the above information to be shown in the accounts, under penalty of a fine: 1948 Act, s.198; 1967 Act, ss.6, 7.

Compensation to Directors for Loss of Office

It is unlawful for a company to make to a director any payment by way of compensation for loss of office, or as consideration for or in connection with retirement, unless particulars of the proposed payment, including the amount, are disclosed to the members and the proposal is approved by the company: section 191. It was held in *Re Duomatic Ltd.*[2] that disclosure must be made to *all* members, even those with no right to attend and vote at general meetings, whilst the payment is still a proposed payment, although in *Wallersteiner* v. *Moir*[3] Lord Denning M.R. said that he imagined that payment could be later approved by the company in general meeting.

The section does not apply to a payment to a *managing director as such*.[4] Nor does it apply to a payment to a director who does not retire.

It is unlawful for anyone to make to a director a payment by way of compensation for loss of office, etc., in connection with the transfer of the whole or part of the company's undertaking or property unless particulars are disclosed and approved. If such a payment is not disclosed the director holds it upon trust for the company: section 192.

When, in connection with a transfer of all or any of the shares in the company resulting from (*a*) an offer made to the general body of shareholders, (*b*) an offer made with a view to the company becoming the subsidiary of another, (*c*) an offer made with a view to an individual obtaining control of not less than one-third of the voting power at a general meeting, or (*d*) any other offer conditional on acceptance to a given extent, a payment is to be made to a director as compensation for loss of or retirement from office, he must take reasonable steps to see that particulars of the proposed payment, including the amount, are sent with any notice of the offer for their shares given to the shareholders. If this is not done, or the payment is not, before the

---

[2] [1969] 2 Ch. 365.
[3] [1974] 1 W.L.R. 991 (C.A.), at p. 1016.
[4] *Lincoln Mills* v. *Gough* [1964] V.R. 193.

transfer of the shares, approved by a meeting of the shareholders summoned for the purpose, the director holds the payment on trust for the persons who have sold their shares as a result of the offer: section 193.

Sections 192 and 193 cannot be avoided, *e.g.* by paying more than the market value for a director's shares, because section 194 provides that, in connection with sections 192 and 193, the price paid to a director for any of his shares in the company in excess of the price which could have been obtained by other shareholders, or the money value of any valuable consideration given to him, is deemed to have been a payment to him of compensation for loss of office. References in sections 191, 192 and 193 to payments of compensation for loss of office exclude bona fide payments of damages for breach of contract or of pensions in respect of past services. But these provisions have been held not to protect an *ex gratia* payment in lieu of pension made on the eve of liquidation in the case of a company whose directors had no power to make such payments.[4a]

In so far as the compensation for loss of office paid to a director exceeds £25,000, it is liable to tax in his hands.[5]

The provisions of sections 191 to 193 do not apply, however, to payments which the company is already bound to make, *e.g.* under a director's service contract.[6] Thus it is important that the length of such contracts are now controlled and must be disclosed, *ante*.

SUBSTANTIAL PROPERTY TRANSACTIONS INVOLVING DIRECTORS

Section 48 of the 1980 Act, as amended by section 110 of the 1981 Act, is intended to prevent directors abusing their position by stripping the company of its assets. The section provides that no contract may be made, without the approval of the general meeting, between a director and his company involving the transfer, either way,[7] of a non-cash asset, if its value exceeds £50,000 or 10 per cent. of the company's net assets, provided it is not less than £1,000.

[4a] *Gibson's Executor* v. *Gibson*, 1978 S.C. 197 (O.H.).
[5] Income and Corporation Taxes Act 1970, ss.187–188. See *Pinson, op. cit.*, para. 3–25.
[6] *Taupo Totara Timber Co. Ltd.* v. *Darey Kevin Rowe* [1977] 3 W.L.R. 466 (P.C.).
[7] Thus applying both to sales to the company by a director, *e.g. Pavlides* v. *Jensen* [1956] Ch. 565; and sales to a director by his company, *e.g. Daniels* v. *Daniels* [1978] 2 W.L.R. 73.

This section applies equally to "shadow directors"[8] and persons "connected with a director."[9]

Any arrangement entered into in breach of this section is voidable by the company (unless restitution of the status quo is impossible). Further, the director concerned and any director who authorised the transaction are liable to account to and indemnify the company for any loss.

The section does not apply if the director concerned received the assets solely by virtue of being a member (*e.g.* on a general reduction of capital), or the transaction was entered into during the course of the winding up of an insolvent company. Most transactions within a group of companies are also excluded.

Disclosure of such arrangements in the accounts is required by section 54 of the 1980 Act.

Directors are also under a general duty to disclose their interests in contracts to the board of directors: section 199, *post*. This now includes disclosure of the arrangements detailed in section 48 of the 1980 Act: s.60.

LOANS TO DIRECTORS

Following certain major scandals in the 1970s the rules relating to loans to directors were strengthened and now appear in sections 49 to 53 of the 1980 Act, as amended by section 111 of the 1981 Act. Section 190, the former section governing loans, was repealed.

Section 49 of the 1980 Act prohibits various categories of loans and other credit transactions between a company and its directors, "shadow directors"[10] and "persons connected with its directors."[11] A subsidiary is equally restrained as regards its holding company.[12]

All companies are prohibited from making loans to, guarantees for, and giving security for loans to their directors or "shadow directors." The strength of this provision appears, however, to be somewhat

---

[8] 1980 Act, s.63; *ante*, p. 342.

[9] 1980 Act, s.64. This includes his minor children, spouse, partners, or any company in which he and his other associates control one-fifth of the equity share capital or votes.

[10] See note 8 above.

[11] See note 9 above.

[12] This includes a wholly-owned subsidiary, unlike s.48, above.

weakened by the decision of Walton J. in *Champagne Perrier-Jouet S.A.* v. *H. H. Finch Ltd.* [1982] 3 All E.R. 713, that where a company paid a great many bills for one of its directors it had not made a loan to that director. "Money paid to B at the request of A is quite definitely not a loan" (p. 717). This would seem to be an obvious loophole in the general embargo on loans.

In addition, however, public companies, and companies forming part of a group which includes a public company, may not make loans, give guarantees or securities to persons connected with such directors. Further, public companies may not make "quasi-loans" to their directors etc. nor may they provide credit facilities for such persons. A "quasi-loan" is defined (1981 Act, s.65) to include the provision of credit card facilities, *e.g.* where the company is the cardholder and the card is used by the director. A credit transaction is one where goods or services are provided on the undertaking that payment will be made later.

These prohibitions cannot be avoided by directors assigning their liabilities to their company or by "back to back" deals, *i.e.* where two companies each make what appear to be separate provisions for each other's directors.

Section 50 of the 1980 Act provides certain exceptions to the prohibitions of section 49. The effect is to allow all loans up to a total of £2,500 outstanding for each director; to allow all credit transactions, if they are on normal commercial terms; to provide an exemption for loans to cover expenses incurred by a director for company purposes, provided the transaction has the prior approval of the general meeting or is ratified within six months, subject to a maximum of £10,000 for directors of public companies; to allow quasi-loans up to £10,000 outstanding at any one time if the terms require repayment within two months; and to allow credit transactions up to £5,000 outstanding at any one time per director.

In addition moneylending companies[13] may make loans and quasi-loans to directors on normal commercial terms subject to a maximum of £50,000 outstanding at any one time, apart from "recognised banks."[14] Directors of such companies may also be allowed to participate in subsidised house purchase schemes up to a limit of £50,000.

---

[13] 1980 Act, s.65(1).
[14] *Ibid.*

The various sums used in section 50, *i.e.* £2,000, £5,000 £10,000 and £50,000 are sums outstanding at any time and are calculated in accordance with section 51 of the 1980 Act.

Section 52 of the 1980 Act provides that the civil consequences of a breach of section 49 are the same as those for a breach of section 48 (substantial property transactions), *ante*.[15] In addition section 53 provides for a series of criminal offences for public companies and their directors who know or have reasonable cause to believe that section 49 has been breached.

Sections 54 to 59 of the 1980 Act require particulars of all loans etc., whether prohibited or not, to be disclosed in the accounts. This includes disclosure of the principal terms of the transaction and the true beneficiary. Recognised banks[16] are subject to special rules by virtue of sections 56 and 57 of the 1980 Act. Auditors must disclose any breach of the disclosure requirements in their report.

MANAGING DIRECTOR

Unless the directors are empowered to appoint a managing director[17] by the memorandum[18] or the articles the directors cannot appoint a managing director.[19] When the articles empower the directors to appoint a managing director, the company in general meeting cannot itself make such an appointment without first altering the articles.[20]

Table A, article 107, provides that the directors may appoint *one or more of their body* to the office of managing director for such period and on such terms as they think fit, and, *subject to the terms of any particular agreement,* may revoke such appointment; that a director so appointed shall not, whilst holding that office, retire by rotation,[21] but

---

[15] p. 359.

[16] See note 14 above.

[17] For a discussion of the general nature of the post of managing director, see *Anderson* v. *James Sutherland (Peterhead) Ltd.*, 1941 S.C. 203, *ante*, p. 354; also *Hindle* v. *John Cotton Ltd.* (1919) 56 S.L.R. 625 (H.L.) (managing director held to be an "employee" within the meaning of the articles) and opinions in *Kerr* v. *Walker*, 1933 S.C. 458.

[18] *Re Scottish Loan & Finance Co. Ltd.* (1944) 44 S.R. (N.S.W.) 461.

[19] *Per* Swinfen Eady J. in *Boschoek Proprietary Co. Ltd.* v. *Fuke* [1906] 1 Ch. 148, at p. 159.

[20] *Thomas Logan Ltd.* v. *Davis* (1911) 104 L.T. 914; 105 L.T. 419.

[21] *Ante*, p. 328.

that the appointment shall be automatically determined if he ceases to be a director.

A managing director has two functions and two capacities, those of director and managing director. As managing director he is usually a party to a contract of employment or service with the company.[22] In a family company, however, if there is no express contract of service the managing director may not be regarded as an employee.[23]

Subject to the articles, the powers and duties of a managing director depend upon his contract of service with the company.

Table A provides:

"109. The directors may entrust to and confer upon a managing director any of the powers exercisable by them upon such terms and conditions and with such restrictions as they may think fit, and either collaterally with or to the exclusion of their own powers and may from time to time revoke, withdraw, alter or vary all or any of such powers."

C. was appointed a managing director of H. Co. His service agreement provided that he should perform the duties and exercise the powers in relation to the business of H. Co. and the businesses of its existing subsidiary companies which might from time to time be assigned to or vested in him by the directors. Later the directors resolved that C. should confine his attention to a particular subsidiary company. C. sued for damages for breach of contract. C.'s action was dismissed: *Caddies* v. *Harold Holdsworth & Co. (Wakefield) Ltd.*, 1955 S.C. (H.L.) 27; [1955] 1 All E.R. 725 (H.L.).

As will be seen in Chapter 20, a managing director may have implied power to enter into certain agreements on behalf of the company even though there has been no express delegation of the power to him by the board.[24]

Where a managing director is appointed under an article like Table A, article 107, above, his appointment may be prematurely determined by his removal from his directorship,[25] *e.g.* under section

---

[22] *Per* Lord Normand in *Anderson* v. *James Sutherland (Peterhead) Ltd.*, 1941 S.C. 203, at p. 218; *per* Jenkins L.J. in *Goodwin* v. *Brewster* (1951) 32 T.C. 80, at p. 96.

[23] *Parsons* v. *Albert J. Parsons & Sons Ltd.* [1979] I.C.R. 271 (C.A.).

[24] *Allison* v. *Scotia Motor etc. Co. Ltd.* (1906) 14 S.L.T. 9 (O.H.) (implied power to engage a works manager for a period of five years).

[25] *Southern Foundries (1926) Ltd.* v. *Shirlaw* [1940] A.C. 701, *ante*, p. 114; *Nelson* v. *James Nelson & Sons Ltd.* [1914] 2 K.B. 770 (C.A.); *Carrier Australasia Ltd.* v. *Hunt* (1939) 61 C.L.R. 534. In the *Nelson* case the articles empowered the board to appoint a managing director and to revoke the appointment. The board appointed the plaintiff managing director, the agreement providing that he was to hold the office so long as, *inter alia*, he efficiently performed the duties. The board revoked his appointment whilst he was still fulfilling the conditions of the agreement and he was held entitled to damages for breach of contract. In the *Carrier*

184,[26] but the company will be liable in damages if this is in breach of his contract of service, as it usually will be. In fact the company will often have to pay a large sum by way of liquidated damages.

S. was appointed managing director of N. Ltd., a subsidiary of L. Co., for ten years. The articles of N. Ltd. included article 68 of Table A in the 1929 Act (which provided that a managing director's appointment should be automatically determined if he ceased to be a director or if the company in general meeting resolved to terminate his appointment). M. Co. bought the shares in L. Co., and, at a general meeting of N. Ltd., resolutions were passed removing S. from office as a director and terminating his service agreement. S. sued for damages for wrongful dismissal. *Held,* S. succeeded. It was an implied term of the service agreement that N. Ltd. would do nothing of its own motion to put an end to the state of circumstances which enabled S. to continue as managing director: *Shindler* v. *Northern Raincoat Co. Ltd.* [1960] 1 W.L.R. 1038, applying *Stirling* v. *Maitland* (1865) 34 L.J. Q.B. 1 and *Southern Foundries (1926) Ltd.* v. *Shirlaw* [1940] A.C. 701.[27]

Per Diplock J., quoting Cockburn C.J. in *Stirling* v. *Maitland, ante:* "If a party enters into an arrangement which can only take effect by the continuance of a certain existing set of circumstances, there is an implied engagement on his part that he shall do nothing of his own motion to put an end to that state of circumstances."

R. was appointed managing director at £7 a week, the duration of his appointment not being specified. Article 68 of Table A in the 1929 Act (corresponding to Article 107 of Table A in the 1948 Act, *ante*) was one of the articles. Later, the directors dismissed R. on a month's notice and their action was confirmed by the company in general meeting. R. sued for damages for wrongful dismissal on the ground that he was not given reasonable notice. *Held,* the claim failed, because R.'s contract incorporated article 68 which empowered the company to dismiss him without notice by a resolution in general meeting. In the absence of any contract independent of article 68 and the directors' resolution appointing him, there was no ground for implying a term as to reasonable notice: *Read* v. *Astoria Garage (Streatham) Ltd.* [1952] Ch. 637 (C.A.).

Where directors have a discretionary power to dismiss a managing director, this power must be exercised in good faith in the interests of the company and not for some ulterior purpose such as appropriation of the managing director's shares.[28]

Australasia case the articles empowered the company to remove a director, subject to the provisions of any agreement. The articles were altered so as to delete the words "subject to . . . any agreement" and then the managing director was removed from his directorship. He was held to be entitled to damages.

[26] *Ante,* p. 346.
[27] *Ante,* p. 114.
[28] *Hindle* v. *John Cotton Ltd.* (1919) 56 S.L.R. 625 (H.L.).

The articles usually provide for the remuneration of a managing director.

Table A provides: "108. A managing director shall receive such remuneration (whether by way of salary, commission or participation in profits, or partly in one way and partly in another) as the directors may determine."

Table A, article 108, is an independent article providing for the remuneration of a managing director whether appointed by the articles or by the board under Table A, article 107.[29]

In a case[29] where a member was appointed managing director by the articles which also incorporated Table A, article 108, it was said[30] that "The effect of . . . article 108 . . . coupled with the fact that the applicant was a member of the company . . . is that a contract exists between himself and the company for payment to him of remuneration as managing director, and that remuneration depends on article 108 . . . ."

In practice a managing director's remuneration will be specified in his contract of service which the directors will negotiate on behalf of the company.

If, where the appointment of a managing director is in fact void, he performs services which are accepted by the company, he is entitled to reasonable remuneration.

The articles authorised the directors to appoint one of their number managing director. By contract under the company's seal, C. was appointed managing director at a salary. The seal was affixed to the contract by a resolution of the board of directors but none of the directors had acquired his qualification shares. C. himself acted as managing director, but also failed to acquire his qualification shares. *Held,* C.'s contract was void and C. was not properly appointed managing director. His claim for remuneration in contract failed but the alternative claim in quasi-contract succeeded, *i.e.* he was entitled to payment on a *quantum meruit* basis arising from the performance of his services and their acceptance by the company: *Craven-Ellis* v. *Canons Ltd.* [1936] 2 K.B. 403 (C.A.).

A managing director has been held not to be a "servant" of the company so as to be entitled to preferential payment of his salary on a winding up,[31] and has been held to be an "officer" of the company for the purpose of the provision, now in section 258, empowering the court

---

[29] *Re Richmond Gate Property Co. Ltd.* [1965] 1 W.L.R. 335.
[30] *Per* Plowman J. at p. 337.
[31] *Re Newspaper Proprietary Syndicate Ltd.* [1900] 2 Ch. 349, *post,* p. 664.

to require any officer of the company to deliver property to the liquidator.[32]

Position of Directors

As a company has no physical but only a legal existence, the management of its affairs is entrusted to human instruments called "directors" whose exact position in relation to the company is rather hard to define. Directors as such are not servants of the company, but are rather managers who in some respects may be said to be (1) quasi-trustees, and (2) agents for the company. The result is that they owe fiduciary duties and certain duties of care to the company, *i.e.* the members as a body, as will be explained later.

"The Directors are a body to whom is delegated the duty of managing the general affairs of the Company. A corporate body can only act by agents, and it is of course the duty of those agents so to act as best to promote the interests of the corporation whose affairs they are conducting. Such agents have duties to discharge of a fiduciary nature towards their principal. And it is a rule of universal application, that no one, having such duties to discharge, shall be allowed to enter into engagements in which he has, or can have, a personal interest conflicting, or which possibly may conflict, with the interests of those whom he is bound to protect": *per* Lord Cranworth L.C. in *Aberdeen Rlwy. Co.* v. *Blaikie Bros.* (1854) 1 Macq. 461, at p. 471.

"The directors are the mere trustees or agents of the company—trustees of the company's money and property—agents in the transactions which they enter into on behalf of the company": *per* Lord Selborne L.C. in *Great Eastern Rlwy. Co.* v. *Turner* (1872) L.R. 8 Ch. 149, at p. 152.

"The director's functions are in one view those of an agent, and in another those of a trustee. But the former predominate over the latter": *per* Lord Johnston in *M'Lintock* v. *Campbell,* 1916 S.C. 966, at p. 980.

Not being in a fiduciary position towards the company *qua* shareholder, a director has the same right as any other shareholder to transfer his shares to a man of straw in order to avoid payment of a call,[33] and he may exercise his voting power at general meetings, even although the effect is to increase his own remuneration[34] or to prevent the calling up of a loan made by the company to himself.[35]

---

[32] *Dunlop* v. *Donald* (1893) 21 R. 125.
[33] *M'Lintock* v. *Campbell,* 1916 S.C. 966.
[34] *Harris* v. *A. Harris Ltd.,* 1936 S.C. 183.
[35] *Baird* v. *J. Baird & Co. (Falkirk) Ltd.,* 1949 S.L.T. 368 (O.H.).

Directors as trustees

Directors have been described as trustees (1) of the company's money and property,[36] and (2) of the powers entrusted to them. More properly they may be regarded as being in a fiduciary position to the company, *post*.

They hold the company's property in their hands or under their control as if they were trustees for the company. Such property must be applied for the specified purposes of the company and a misapplication of it is a breach of fiduciary duty.[37] Where a person has improperly profited from his fiduciary position the court has equitable jurisdiction to award interest on the judgment for damages for misfeasance or breach of duty as a director.[38]

In an action to recover moneys of the company misapplied by them, directors can in England rely on the Limitation Act 1980, s.21, as if they were trustees,[39] *i.e.* the action must be brought within six years except where they have been guilty of fraud, or where the property is still in their possession or has been previously converted to their own use.

Directors are trustees of their powers in the sense that, as will be explained later,[40] they must exercise them for the purposes for which they were conferred and bona fide for the benefit of the company as a whole.

Directors had power to issue the unissued shares of the company. The company was in no need of further capital, but the directors made a fresh issue to themselves and their supporters with the object of maintaining control of the company and resisting the election of three additional directors which would have made the two existing directors a minority on the board: *Held*, the allotment of the shares was invalid and void. Directors are not entitled to use their power of issuing shares merely for the purpose of maintaining their control or the control of themselves and their friends over the affairs of the company, or merely for the purpose of defeating the wishes of the existing

---

[36] *Per* Lord Selborne L.C. in *Great Eastern Rlwy. Co.* v. *Turner* (1872) L.R. 8 Ch. 149, at p. 152.

[37] *Selangor United Rubber Estates Ltd.* v. *Cradock (No. 3)* [1968] 1 W.L.R. 1555, *post*, p. 376.

[38] *Wallersteiner* v. *Moir (No. 2)* [1975] Q.B. 373 (C.A.), where the interest awarded was compound interest at one per cent. per annum above the official bank rate or minimum lending rate in operation at the time.

[39] *Re Lands Allotment Co.* [1894] 1 Ch. 616 (C.A.), *ante*, p. 84; *cf. John S. Boyle Ltd.* v. *Boyle's Trustees*, 1949 S.L.T. (Notes) 45 (O.H.).

[40] p. 371.

majority of shareholders. The power to issue shares is primarily given to directors for the purpose of enabling them to raise capital when required for the company: *Piercy* v. *S. Mills & Co. Ltd.* [1920] 1 Ch. 77.[41]

If a director, who is about to retire and sell his shares in the company, makes a bargain with his intended successor and the purchaser of the shares that, when the latter controls the company, he will procure it to make a present to the former out of its assets, the recipient of the proceeds is as guilty of misfeasance or breach of trust as the directors who have procured it, *i.e.* the principle of the law of constructive trusts, referred to in *Head* v. *Gould*,[42] applies.[43]

In a few cases the directors may be in a position of trust *vis-à-vis* the shareholders. In one case the directors of a family company were so treated because of the nature of the company, the dominant position of the directors, their inside knowledge and the methods used.[44]

Directors really quasi-trustees

Directors are really only quasi-trustees because (1) the company's money and property are not vested in them but in the company, (2) their functions are not the same as those of trustees, (3) their duties of care are not as onerous as those of trustees.[45]

"The distinction between a director and a trustee is an essential distinction founded on the very nature of things. A trustee is a man who is the owner of the property and deals with it as principal, as owner, and as master, subject only to an equitable obligation to account to some persons to whom he stands in the relation of trustee, and who are his *cestuis que trust* . . . The office of director is that of a paid servant of the company"[46]: *per* James L.J. in *Smith* v. *Anderson* (1880) 15 Ch.D. 247 (C.A.), at p. 275.

"It is sometimes said that directors are trustees. If this means no more than that directors in the performance of their duties stand in a fiduciary relationship to the company, the statement is true enough. But if the statement is meant to be an indication by way of analogy of what those duties are, it appears to me to be wholly misleading. I can see but little resemblance between the duties of a director and the duties of a trustee of a will or of a marriage settlement. It is indeed impossible to describe the duty of directors in

---

[41] *Cook* v. *Barry, Henry & Cook Ltd.*, 1923 S.L.T. 692 (O.H.). See now 1980 Act, s.14.

[42] [1898] 2 Ch. 250.

[43] *Curtis's Furnishing Stores Ltd.* v. *Freedman* [1966] 1 W.L.R. 1219.

[44] *Coleman* v. *Myers* [1977] 2 N.Z.L.R. 225.

[45] Directors' duties of care are explained *post*, p. 382.

[46] "Paid manager" would be more accurate.

general terms, whether by way of analogy or otherwise. The position of a director of a company carrying on a small retail business is very different from that of a director of a railway company. The duties of a bank director may differ widely from those of an insurance director, and the duties of a director of one insurance company may differ from those of another. . . . The larger the business carried on by the company the more numerous, and the more important, the matters that must of necessity be left to the managers, the accountants and the rest of the staff": *per* Romer J. in *Re City Equitable Fire Insce. Co. Ltd.* [1925] Ch. 407, at p. 426.[47]

Directors as agents

Directors are agents through whom a company acts[48] and it is largely because they are agents that they owe fiduciary duties and certain duties of care to the company.

"Directors of a company are fiduciary agents, and a power conferred upon them cannot be exercised in order to obtain some private advantage or for any purpose foreign to the power": *per* Dixon J. in *Mills* v. *Mills* (1938) 60 C.L.R. 150, at p. 186.

Like other agents, directors incur no personal liability on contracts made by them on behalf of the company, within the scope of their authority.[49]

E. contracted to supply goods to a company of which H. was chairman of directors, payment to be made by the issue of £600 of the company's debentures. The contract was made at a board meeting at which H. was chairman. E. constantly pressed for the debentures, but none was issued, and eventually the company was wound up. *Held,* H. was not liable to an action at the suit of E.: *Elkington & Co.* v. *Hürter* [1892] 2 Ch. 452.

If, however, directors exceed the powers given to them by the memorandum and articles they will be liable for breach of warranty of authority.[50] Their actions may be ratified by the company in general meeting if they act within the powers in the memorandum but outside the powers conferred on them by the articles.

Directors may be *specifically appointed* agents for the shareholders to negotiate a sale of the company's shares. If so, the shareholders are liable for their fraud.

[47] And see Lord Johnson in *M'Lintock* v. *Campbell,* 1916 S.C. 966, at p. 980.
[48] See, *e.g. per* Lord Selborne L.C. in *Great Eastern Rlwy. Co.* v. *Turner* (1872) L.R. 8 Ch. 149, at p. 152.
[49] Directors may be personally liable under s.108 (4), *ante,* p. 64.
[50] *Firbank's Exors.* v. *Humphreys* (1886) 18 Q.B.D. 54 (C.A.), *post,* p. 548.

R., managing director of N. Ltd., by frauds of which the other directors were ignorant, made N. Ltd. profitable, and negotiated with E. Ltd. for the sale of the shares in N. Ltd. without disclosing that the profits were based on dishonest trading. The negotiations were reported to the shareholders who, in ignorance of R.'s fraud, authorised R. to complete the sale on the basis of his negotiations. The fraud was subsequently discovered and the shareholders were sued for damages. *Held,* they were liable as R. was their agent to negotiate the sale of their shares, and they were liable for his fraud even though it preceded his appointment as agent: *Briess* v. *Woolley* [1954] A.C. 333.

Further, directors may *hold themselves out* to the shareholders as agents for the shareholders, in which case the directors must disclose any profit made by them to the shareholders.

Directors entered into negotiations for the amalgamation of the company with other companies. Before the negotiations were completed they induced a number of shareholders to give them options on their shares at par, representing that this was necessary to effect the amalgamation. The directors then exercised the option and thereby made a handsome profit. *Held,* they had to account for this profit to the shareholders: *Allen* v. *Hyatt* (1914) 30 T.L.R. 444, distinguishing *Percival* v. *Wright,* below.

DUTIES OF DIRECTORS

Under the general law directors (and other agents of the company) owe fiduciary duties[51] and certain duties of care[52] to the company, *i.e.* the members as a body, and, except in cases like *Allen* v. *Hyatt* and *Coleman* v. *Myers ante,* not to the individual shareholders.[53]

The directors of a company bought shares from X. They did not disclose to him that negotiations were being conducted for the sale of all the company's shares at a higher price than that asked by X. The negotiations proved abortive. X sued to have his sale set aside on the ground that the directors ought to have disclosed the negotiations. *Held,* the sale was binding, as the directors were under no obligation to disclose the negotiations to X: *Percival* v. *Wright* [1902] 2 Ch. 421.

---

[51] *Per* Lord Cranworth L.C. in *Aberdeen Rlwy. Co.* v. *Blaikie Bros.* (1854) 1 Macq. 461, at p. 471, *ante,* p. 366.

[52] *Per* Romer J. in *Re City Equitable Fire Insurance. Co. Ltd.* [1925] Ch. 407, at p. 428.

[53] Nor to applicants for shares: *Brown* v. *Stewart* (1898) 1 F. 316; *Wilson* v. *Dunlop, Bremner & Co. Ltd.,* 1921, 1 S.L.T. 35 (O.H.) and 354.

Section 46 of the 1980 Act provides that directors must also have regard to the interests of the employees as a whole. However, the employees have no collective right to enforce this. Since the duties of directors are owed to the company and not to the individual shareholders or employees, the enforcement of the duties may be a problem where the directors in breach of duty control the company, as will be explained later.[54]

Fiduciary duties

The fiduciary duties of directors are—

  (1) to exercise their powers for the purposes for which they were conferred and bona fide for the benefit of the company as a whole, as defined above;

  (2) not to put themselves in a position in which their duties to the company and their personal interests may conflict.[55]

As to duty (1), directors' discretionary power to refuse to register a transfer of shares is a fiduciary power.[56] The directors' power to issue shares is also a fiduciary power even though it is now subject to the controls of section 14 of the 1980 Act, *ante,* and the exercise of such a power is invalid if it is not exercised for the purpose for which it was granted, which is primarily to raise capital when required by the company. Thus an issue of shares is invalid if the directors are motivated by self-interest, *e.g.* a desire to preserve their control of the company.[57]

Directors, in an endeavour to secure control in order to forestall a take-over bid, issued unissued shares in the company to trustees to be held for the benefit of employees, the shares being paid for by the trustees out of an

---

[54] p. 397.
[55] *Per* Lord Cranworth L.C. in *Aberdeen Rlwy. Co. v. Blaikie Bros.* (1854) 1 Macq. 461, at p. 471, and *per* Viscount Finlay and Lord Shaw in *Hindle* v. *John Cotton Ltd.* (1919) 56 S.L.R. 625 (H.L.), at p. 631.
[56] See *Re Smith and Fawcett Ltd.* [1942] Ch. 304 (C.A.), *ante,* p. 269.
[57] *Piercy* v. *S. Mills & Co. Ltd.* [1920] 1 Ch. 77, *ante,* p. 368; *Hogg* v. *Cramphorn Ltd.* [1967] Ch. 254; *Bamford* v. *Bamford* [1970] Ch. 212 (C.A.), *ante,* p. 352; *Ngurli* v. *McCann* (1954) 90 C.L.R. 425, where there was no take-over bid, shares were issued to a shareholder to give him control of the company, the interests of the company as a whole were not considered, and an attempted ratification was a fraud on the minority and so ineffective.

interest-free loan from the company. *Held,* the issue exceeded the directors' fiduciary power, it being immaterial that it was made in the bona fide belief that it was in the interests of the company. Since the directors did not hold the majority of the shares before the new issue, the issue could be ratified by the company in general meeting, the votes carried by the shares issued to the trustees not being exercised: *Hogg* v. *Cramphorn Ltd.* [1967] Ch. 254.

Where the self-interest of the directors is involved, they are not permitted to assert that their action was bona fide thought to be, or was, in the interest of the company.[58] However, self-interest is only one instance of improper motive—in the recent Privy Council case of *Howard Smith Ltd.* v. *Ampol Petroleum Ltd.*[59] the directors were not motivated by any purpose of personal gain but an allotment was set aside because they issued the shares for the purpose of destroying the existing majority block of shares.

On the other hand, it is wrong to say that the only valid purpose for which shares can be issued is to raise capital for the company. In a High Court of Australia case[60] the company had no immediate need of fresh capital but it was held that the directors' purpose in allotting shares to another company was to ensure the financial stability of the first company and the allotment was valid.

The phrase "bona fide in the interest of the company as a whole," if it does anything more than restate the general principle applicable to fiduciary powers, at best serves, negatively, to invalidate issues where the directors are acting sectionally, or partially, *i.e.* improperly favouring one section of the shareholders against another. It has been said[61] of such cases that: "The question which arises is sometimes not a question of the interest of the company at all, but a question of what is fair between different classes of shareholders. Where such a case arises some other test than that of the 'interest of the company' must be applied." In other words, where the interests of two or more classes of shareholders are fundamentally different and opposed, and it is virtually impossible to determine the interests of the company as a whole,[62] the directors must act fairly between the different classes.

[58] *Hogg's* case, *ante.*
[59] [1974] A.C. 821 (P.C.). See also *Ashburton Oil N.L.* v. *Alpha Minerals N.L.* (1971) 45 A.L.J.R. 162.
[60] *Harlowe's Nominees Pty. Ltd.* v. *Woodside (Lakes Entrance) Oil Co. N.L.* (1969–70) 121 C.L.R. 483.
[61] *Per* Latham C.J. in *Mills* v. *Mills* (1938) 60 C.L.R. 150.
[62] *Woods* v. *Cann* (1963) 80 W.N. (N.S.W.) 1583 was such a case but the articles had been drafted to meet the impossibility.

If directors exercise a power for a proper purpose and in good faith, their judgment is not open to review by the courts.[63] However, although it would be wrong for the courts to question the correctness of the management's decision on a question of management, if bona fide arrived at, when the question is whether directors exercised a power for one purpose or another, the courts are entitled to look at the situation objectively in order to ascertain how substantial an alleged requirement may have been.[64]

Where a director is also a shareholder in the company he may promote his own interests so long as his dominant motive is to benefit the company.[65]

A nominee director, *e.g.* a director appointed by a shareholder, owes the same duties to the company as any other director.[66]

Because a director owes a fiduciary duty, where in England a company owes a statute-barred debt, a balance sheet signed by a director (whose signature was necessary to its validity) who is himself interested in the debt, cannot constitute an acknowledgment for the purposes of what is now the Limitation Act 1980, ss.29 and 30, and the time within which an action may be brought does not run afresh,[67] unless it is sanctioned by every member of the company, in which event it cannot be said that the directors are in breach of their fiduciary duty.[68]

The Jenkins Report merely recommended[69] (1) that the Companies Act should provide that a director must observe the utmost good faith

---

[63] See the *Howard Smith* case, *ante,* at p. 835 and *per* Barwick C.J., McTiernan J. and Kitto J. at p. 493 in *Harlowe's* case, quoted in the *Howard Smith* case at p. 836.

[64] *Howard Smith* case, *ante,* at p. 834.

[65] *Mills* v. *Mills* (1938) 60 C.L.R. 150 where the directors believed that the bonus issue was in the best interests of the company and it was immaterial that one director derived some benefit from the passing of the board resolution.

[66] *Per* Lord Denning in *Meyer* v. *Scottish C.W.S. Ltd.,* 1958 S.C. (H.L.) 40, at pp. 67, 68; [1959] A.C. 324 at pp. 366, 367, *post,* p. 414; *per* Ungoed-Thomas J. in *Selangor United Rubber Estates Ltd.* v. *Cradock (No.* 3) [1968] 1 W.L.R. 1555, at pp. 1613, 1614. *cf., e.g. per* Jacobs J. in *Re Broadcasting Station 2 GB Pty. Ltd.* [1964–65] N.S.W.R. 1648, at p. 1663, where he said that so long as the nominee directors believed that the interests of the shareholder who nominated them were identical with those of the company, they could follow the wishes of the shareholder without a close personal analysis of the issues.

[67] *Re Transplanters (Holding Company) Ltd.* [1958] 1 W.L.R. 822.

[68] *Re Gee & Co. (Woolwich) Ltd.* [1975] Ch. 52, applying *Re Duomatic Ltd.* [1969] 2 Ch. 365, *ante,* p. 307.

[69] Para. 99(a)(i), (iii) and (iv).

towards the company in any transaction with it or on its behalf and must act honestly in the exercise of his powers and the discharge of his office, (2) that a director who commits a breach of such statutory duty should be liable to the company for any profit made by him and for any damage suffered by the company as a result of the breach and (3) that such statutory duty should be in addition to and not in derogation of the general law duties of a director.

Relief of directors from liability for breach of duty

By a resolution in general meeting

Since directors' fiduciary duties are owed to the members as a body, the majority of the members in general meeting may, after full disclosure of all material circumstances, waive a breach of fiduciary duty by a director[70]; and, if he is a member, the director may vote in favour of waiver, provided that there is no fraud on the minority of the members.

The directors of a company contracted to buy a ship from a vendor who was a director. (This was a breach of duty by him since the articles contained no clause authorising a director to contract with the company. Further, there was at the time no section like the present section 199, *post.*) At a general meeting a resolution affirming the contract was carried, against the wishes of the minority shareholders, by reason of the fact that the vendor held the majority of the shares in the company. *Held,* the resolution was valid. As a shareholder, the vendor was merely using his voting power to his own advantage, and there was no question of a fraud on the minority—there was no unfairness or impropriety: *N.-W. Transportation Co.* v. *Beatty* (1887) 12 App.Cas. 589 (P.C.).

Two directors of a construction company negotiated for a construction contract in the usual way in which the company's business was carried on, and then took the contract in their own names. A meeting of the company was called, and by their votes as holders of three-quarters of the shares a resolution was passed declaring that the company had no interest in the contract. *Held,* the benefit of the contract belonged to the company and the directors must account to the company for it, and the purported ratification was a fraud on the minority and ineffective: *Cook* v. *Deeks* [1916] 1 A.C. 554 (P.C.).

The general meeting may give advance authority for an exercise of power by the directors which would otherwise involve a breach of their fiduciary duty.[71]

---

[70] *Bamford* v. *Bamford* [1970] Ch. 212 (C.A.), *ante*, p. 352.
[71] *Winthrop Investments Ltd.* v. *Winns Ltd.* [1975] 2 N.S.W. L.R. 666 (C.A.). But not, according to Samuels J.A., if to do so would be to usurp the directors' powers.

Not by a provision in the articles

Under the general law a director can be exempted from liability for breach of duty by a provision in the articles of the company. However, section 205, first introduced in 1929, states that, subject as below, any provision, whether in the articles or in any contract with the company or otherwise, for exempting a director or other officer or the auditor from liability for negligence, default, breach of duty or breach of trust in relation to the company, or indemnifying him against such liability, is void.

The section goes on to provide that the company may, in pursuance of a provision in the articles, etc., indemnify such a person against any liability, *i.e.* against any costs, incurred by him in defending any proceedings, civil or criminal, in which judgment is given in his favour or in which he is acquitted,[72] or in connection with any application under section 448 in which relief is granted to him by the court. Table A, article 136, contains such a provision.

By the court

Section 448 provides that if, in proceedings for negligence, default, breach of duty or breach of trust against a director or other officer or auditor of a company, it appears that he has acted honestly and reasonably, and that, having regard to all the circumstances, including those connected with his appointment, he ought fairly to be excused, the court may relieve him, wholly or partly, from liability on such terms as it thinks fit.

Relief can be given even when the director has done an act *ultra vires* the company, as where the company's money was applied for a purpose which was *ultra vires,* but which the director, acting on counsel's opinion, thought to be *intra vires.*[73]

A director does not act reasonably unless he does everything which a normal man would do in the conduct of his own affairs.

The notice convening the meeting must set out clearly the nature of the contemplated breach of the directors' duty, and state that the directors seek to be absolved from such breach and that the meeting will be asked to authorise the breach and waive its consequences.

[72] *cf. Tomlinson* v. *Liquidators of Scottish Amalgamated Silks Ltd.,* 1935 S.C. (H.L.) 1.

[73] *Re Claridge's Patent Asphalte Co.* [1921] 1 Ch. 543.

B. and G., two of the directors of a company were present at a finance committee in June at which it was resolved to sell £60,000 War Bonds and to reinvest the proceeds at B.'s discretion. In September, G. inquired about the reinvestment of the proceeds and was told that they had been temporarily invested on the Stock Exchange. B. misappropriated the proceeds of sale. *Held*, (1) G. was negligent in allowing the money to remain in B.'s hands longer than was reasonable and in not making inquiries as to its permanent investment, and (2) though G. had acted honestly, he had not acted reasonably and ought not to be granted relief: *Re City of London Insurance Co.* (1925) 41 T.L.R. 521.

In *Selangor United Rubber Estates Ltd.* v. *Cradock (No. 3)*[74] directors of a public company who disposed of virtually all its assets without regard for minority shareholders, and without consideration, but blindly at the behest of the majority shareholder who nominated them to the board, did not act reasonably and could not be relieved. In *Re Duomatic Ltd.*[75] a director dealing with payment to another director of compensation for loss of office, who did not seek legal advice but dealt with the matter himself without a proper exploration of what should be done on the company's behalf, did not act reasonably.

Similarly in *Gibson's Executor* v. *Gibson*, 1978 S.C. 197 (O.H.), Lord Dunpark held that directors of a moribund company who had made an *ex gratia* payment of £5,000 to one of their number in lieu of pension could not "fairly" be excused for their breach of duty.

Section 448 only applies to proceedings against a director by, on behalf of or for the benefit of the company as a whole[76] or penal proceedings against a director for breach of the Companies Acts. It does not apply to claims against a director by a third party to enforce a debt, *e.g.* arrears of general betting duty.[77]

Secret benefits of directors

Because a director is in a fiduciary position,[78] he must not make a secret profit by reason of that position. If he does, he must account for it to the company. It is immaterial that the company itself could not have obtained the profit. The company in general meeting may consent to such a profit being made or kept.

A. was a director of B. Co. and, on the company's behalf, contracted for the building of fishing smacks. Unknown to the company, he was paid a commis-

[74] [1968] 1 W.L.R. 1555.
[75] [1969] 2 Ch. 365.
[76] As defined above.
[77] *Customs and Excise Commissioners* v. *Hedon Alpha* [1981] 2 All E.R. 697 (C.A.).
[78] p. 367.

sion on the contract by the shipbuilders. A. was also a shareholder in an ice company which, in addition to dividends, paid bonuses to shareholders who were owners of fishing smacks and who employed the ice company in supplying ice to the fishing smacks. A. employed the ice company in respect of B. Co.'s fishing smacks and received the bonus. *Held*, A. must account to B. Co. for both the commission and the bonus, although the bonus could never have been received by B. Co. as it was not a shareholder in the ice company: *Boston Deep Sea Fishing Co.* v. *Ansell* (1888) 39 Ch.D. 339 (C.A.).

R. Ltd. owned one cinema and wanted to buy two others with a view to selling the three together. R. Ltd. formed a subsidiary company to buy the two cinemas, but was unable to provide all the capital required, so all the directors of R. Ltd. except one subscribed for some of the shares in the subsidiary themselves. The cinemas were acquired and the shares in R. Ltd. and the subsidiary sold at a profit. *Held*, the former directors who subscribed for shares in the subsidiary themselves must account to R. Ltd. for the profit they made, because it was only through the knowledge and opportunity they gained as directors of R. Ltd. that they were able to obtain the shares. The one former director who did not himself subscribe but merely found someone else to do so was under no liability nor was a solicitor who was invited to subscribe by the directors: *Regal (Hastings) Ltd.* v. *Gulliver* [1967] 2 A.C. 134 (Note).[79]

In the *Regal* case the directors could have protected themselves by a resolution (either antecedent or subsequent) of the Regal shareholders in general meeting,[80] and the case was distinguished in *Lindgren* v. *L. & P. Estates Ltd.*[81] where the directors were released from liability by the company retaining them on the board, after it had knowledge of the facts (the alleged breach of duty was that the directors had merely "rubber-stamped" the decisions of other persons).

"The rule of equity which insists on those, who by use of a fiduciary position make a profit, being liable to account for that profit, in no way depends on fraud, or absence of bona fides; or upon such questions or considerations as whether the profit would or should otherwise have gone to the plaintiff [*i.e.* the company], or whether the profiteer was under a duty to obtain the source of the profit for the plaintiff, or whether he took a risk or acted as he did for the benefit of the plaintiff, or whether the plaintiff has in fact been damaged or benefited by his action. The liability arises from the mere fact of a profit having, in the stated circumstances, been made. The profiteer, however honest and well-intentioned, cannot escape the risk of being called upon to account:" *per* Lord Russell of Killowen in the *Regal* case at p. 144.

In a case before the Privy Council the managing director of a company obtained licences for the company to develop a mine but it was unable to

[79] [1967] 2 A.C. 134 (Note), applied in *Phipps* v. *Boardman* [1967] 2 A.C. 46. See also *Industrial Development Consultants Ltd.* v. *Cooley* [1972] 1 W.L.R. 443.

[80] *Per* Lord Russell of Killowen at p. 150.

[81] [1968] Ch. 572 (C.A.), in which it was also held that prospective directors of a company owe no duty to it and that directors of a parent company owe no duty to, and are not debarred from contracting with, a subsidiary with an independent board.

proceed due to financial problems. He resigned and, with the knowledge of the directors, he developed the mine himself. The Privy Council held that he was not liable to account for his profits since the rejection by the company and the knowledge of the board excused him: *Queensland Mines Ltd.* v. *Hudson* (1978) 18 A.L.R. 1 (P.C.). This decision also has some Canadian support,[82] but seems to be out of line with the established U.K. position as established by the *Regal* case.[82a]

Another example of the principle that a director must not make a secret profit out of his position is that a director must not, without the consent of the company, accept from a promoter any gift, *e.g.* of shares or money, either while any negotiations between the promoter and the company are still going on or after they have been completed.[83]

The Jenkins Committee recommended[84] (1) that the Companies Act should provide that a director of a company must not make use of any money or other property of the company, or of any information acquired by virtue of his position as a director or officer of the company, to gain directly or indirectly an improper advantage for himself at the expense of the company, (2) that a director who commits a breach of such statutory duty be liable to the company for any profit made by him and for any damage suffered by the company as a result of the breach and (3) that such statutory duty be in addition to the general law duties of a director.

Contracts of directors with their company

A consequence of the general duty of a director towards the company not to allow conflict between duty and interest,[85] is that even if he makes no profit, a director must not be interested in a contract or proposed contract with the company unless the articles permit it, as they usually do, *e.g.* Table A, article 84. If this rule is broken the contract is prima facie voidable by the company.

---

[82] *Peso Silver Mines Ltd.* v. *Cropper* (1966) 58 D.L.R. (2d) 1.

[82a] For Scotland see Lord Young in *Great North of Scotland Railway Co.* v. *Urquhart* (1884) 21 S.L.R. 377, 382, and *Laughland* v. *Millar, Laughland & Co.* (1904) 6 F. 413 (contract for indirect secret benefit of director held unenforceable).

[83] *Eden* v. *Ridsdales Railway Lamp Co. Ltd.* (1889) 23 Q.B.D. 368 (C.A.); *Archer's Case* [1892] 1 Ch. 322 (C.A.); *Henderson* v. *The Huntington Copper, etc., Co. Ltd.* (1877) 5 R. (H.L.) 1; *Scottish Pacific Coast Mining Co. Ltd.* v. *Falkner, Bell & Co.* (1888) 15 R. 290.

[84] Para. 99(a)(ii), (iii) and (iv).

[85] *Ante*, p. 371.

This is so even if his interest is only that of a shareholder in another company which contracts with the company of which he is a director.

T. Co. bought some shares in L. Co. from N.B. Co. H. was a shareholder in both T. Co. and N.B. Co. and also a director of T. Co. As such director he voted for the purchase and N.B. Co. had notice of it. H. did not disclose the nature of his interest (his shareholding in N.B. Co.) as required by the articles of T. Co., which also provided that a director was not to vote in respect of any contract in which he was concerned. *Held,* the contract was voidable at the option of T. Co.: *Transvaal Lands Co.* v. *New Belgium (Transvaal) Land, etc., Co.* [1914] 2 Ch. 488 (C.A.).

"Where a director of a company has an interest as shareholder in another company or is in a fiduciary position towards and owes a duty to another company which is proposing to enter into engagements with the company of which he is a director, he is in our opinion within this rule. He has a personal interest within this rule or owes a duty which conflicts with his duty to the company of which he is a director. It is immaterial whether this conflicting interest belongs to him beneficially or as trustee for others": *per* Swinfen Eady L.J., reading the judgment of the court, at p. 503.

His interest may be that of a partner in a firm which contracts with his company.[86]

It is usual to provide in the articles that a director who is interested in a contract with the company must declare his interest as required by section 199, *post,* that he shall not vote on any such contract, and that if he does vote his vote shall not be counted. The effect of this is to allow the director to contract with the company, on disclosing his interest, and to keep any profit he may make.[87]

Table A, article 84, provides: "(1) A director who is in any way, whether directly or indirectly, interested in a contract or proposed contract with the company shall declare the nature of his interest at a meeting of the directors in accordance with section 199 . . . ."

"(2) A director shall not vote in respect of any contract or arrangement in which he is interested, and if he shall do so his vote shall not be counted, nor shall he be counted in the quorum present at the meeting, but neither of these prohibitions shall apply to—

(a) any arrangement for giving any director any security or indemnity in respect of money lent by him to or obligations undertaken by him for the benefit of the company; or

(b) any arrangement for the giving by the company of any security to a third party in respect of a debt or obligation of the company for which

---

[86] *Aberdeen Rlwy. Co.* v. *Blaikie Bros.* (1854) 1 Macq. 461.
[87] *Costa Rica Ry.* v. *Forwood* [1901] 1 Ch. 746 (C.A.).

the director himself has assumed responsibility in whole or in part under a guarantee or indemnity or by the deposit of a security; or

(c) any contract by a director to subscribe for or underwrite shares or debentures of the company; or

(d) any contract or arrangement with any other company in which he is interested only as an officer of the company or as a holder of shares or other securities;

and these prohibitions may at any time be suspended or relaxed to any extent, and either generally or in respect of any particular contract, arrangement or transaction, by the company in general meeting."

(3) [A director may hold any other office of profit under the company (other than that of auditor) with the consent of the directors and may contract with the company.]

(4) [A director may be counted in the quorum present at a meeting at which he is appointed to hold any other office of profit under the company.]

"(5) Any director may act by himself or his firm in a professional capacity for the company, and he or his firm shall be entitled to remuneration for professional services as if he were not a director; provided that nothing herein contained shall authorise a director or his firm to act as auditor to the company."

Section 199, as amended by the 1980 Act, provides that a director who is any way interested in a contract or proposed contract with the company must declare the nature of his interest at a board meeting. Under section 60 of the 1980 Act this includes any arrangement or transaction whether or not it is a contract, and a director is deemed to have such an interest in any loan etc. controlled by section 49 of that Act.[88] Where a director is interested in a proposed contract, the declaration must be made at the meeting of the directors at which the question of entering into the contract is first considered. Otherwise, the declaration must be made at the first meeting after the director becomes interested in the contract or proposed contract. However, a general notice by a director that he, or a person connected with him, is a member of a specified company or firm and is to be regarded as interested in all contracts made with that company or firm is a sufficient declaration of interest if it is given at a meeting of the directors or the director takes reasonable steps to secure that it is brought up and read at the next meeting of the directors after it is given. Compliance with this statutory duty is enforced by a fine.

[88] *Ante*, p. 360.

It should be noted that only the nature of the interest need be declared, that the declaration of interest need not be to the company in general meeting and that a general declaration of interest is sufficient.

The section also provides that it does not prejudice the operation of any rule of law restricting directors from having an interest in contracts with the company. This means that the section does not imply in the articles a provision allowing a director to contract with the company.

If the articles do not contain such a provision and a director is interested in a contract with the company, the contract may be affirmed by the company in general meeting and, if the director is a member of the company, he can cast the votes conferred by his shares in favour of the resolution, so long as it is not a fraud on the minority of the shareholders.[89]

If a director does not disclose his interest in a contract with his company in accordance with section 199, the contract is prima facie voidable by the company[90] and the director must account to it for any secret profit which he has made out of the contract.[91]

Section 205, *ante*,[92] is qualified by section 199, which is a statutory extension of the general law in that, *e.g.* it imposes a penalty for a breach of the section.

The Jenkins Report[93] recommended that section 199 be amended so as to require a director to disclose only material interests in contracts, including contracts which do not come before the board.

One specific aspect of directors' duties relates to insider trading. This is dealt with in Chapter 21, *post.*

Directors competing with company

Under the general law, apart from the case where a director has a service agreement with the company which requires him to serve only the company, there is authority to the effect that he may become a director of a rival company, *i.e.* that in this way he may compete with the first company, provided that he does not disclose to the second company any confidential information obtained by him as a director of

---

[89] *N.-W. Transportation Co.* v. *Beatty* (1887) 12 App.Cas. 589 (P.C.), *ante*, p. 374.
[90] *Hely-Hutchinson* v. *Brayhead Ltd.* [1968] 1 Q.B. 549 (C.A.), *post*, p. 436, where it was too late to avoid because *restitutio* was impossible.
[91] *Per* Lord Cairns L.C. in *Parker* v. *McKenna* (1874) L.R. 10 Ch.App. 96, at p. 118.
[92] p. 374.
[93] Para. 99.

the first company, and that what he may do for a rival company he may do for himself[94] or a rival firm. However, it has been said that he must not subordinate the interests of the first company to those of the second and that if he does so it is at the risk of an application under section 75 of the 1980 Act[95] (Remedy in case of unfairly prejudicial conduct).[96]

Duties of care

Directors' duties of care towards the company cannot be said to be unduly burdensome, as will be seen from the three propositions laid down by Romer J. in *Re City Equitable Fire Insurance Co. Ltd.*[97] These were:

(1) A director need not exhibit in the performance of his duties (*i.e.* his functions) a greater degree of skill than may reasonably be expected from a person of his knowledge and experience (*i.e.* the particular director's own knowledge and experience). A director of a life insurance company, for instance, does not guarantee that he has the skill of an actuary or of a physician. It is perhaps only another way of stating the same proposition to say that directors are not liable for mere errors of judgment.

(2) A director is not bound to give continuous attention to the affairs of his company. His duties are of an intermittent nature to be performed at periodical board meetings. He is not, however, bound to attend all such meetings, though he ought to attend whenever, in the circumstances, he is reasonably able to do so.

(3) In respect of all duties that, having regard to the exigencies of business, and the articles of association, may properly be left to some other official, a director is, in the absence of grounds for suspicion, justified in trusting that official to perform such duties honestly.

---

[94] *London & Mashonaland Exploration Co.* v. *New Mashonaland Exploration Co.* [1891] W.N. 165; *per* Lord Blanesburgh in *Bell* v. *Lever Bros. Ltd.* [1932] A.C. 161 at p. 195.

[95] *Post*, p. 413.

[96] *Per* Lord Denning in *Meyer* v. *Scottish C.W.S. Ltd.*, 1958 S.C. (H.L.) 40, at p. 68; [1959] A.C. 324, at p. 368.

[97] [1925] Ch. 407, at p. 428. The *City Equitable* case was applied in *Huckerby* v. *Elliott* [1970] 1 All E.R. 189. For a similar description of a director's duties, see Lord Justice-Clerk Moncreiff in *Western Bank* v. *Baird's Trustees* (1872) 11 M. 96, at p. 112, and on the extent to which directors are entitled to rely on other officials, see *Western Bank* v. *Addie* (1867) 5 M. (H.L.) 80; (1865) 3 M. 899, and *Lees* v. *Tod* (1882) 9 R. 807.

As to (1) *ante,* a greater degree of skill than that indicated by Romer J. must be shown, *e.g.* by an executive director, such as a finance or legal director—it is an implied term of his contract of service that he will use reasonable skill in the performance of the duties of his office, *i.e.* the degree of skill which may reasonably be expected of a person in such a position.[98]

Further, the duties of directors vary according to the nature of the company and of its business, *e.g.* the responsibilities of directors of small private companies consisting of only two members differ from the responsibilities of directors of a large public company.[99]

As to (2), greater diligence than that indicated is required of, *e.g.* an executive director, such as a managing director, whose contract of service requires him to work full time for the company.

The directors of an insurance company left the management of the company's affairs almost entirely to B., the managing director. Owing to B.'s fraud a large amount of the company's assets disappeared. Items appeared in the balance sheet under the headings of "loans at call or at short notice" and "cash at bank or in hand," but the directors never inquired how these items were made up. Had they done so, they would have discovered that the loans were chiefly to B. and to the company's general manager, and that the "cash at bank or in hand" included £73,000 in the hands of a firm of stockbrokers in which B. was a partner. *Held,* the directors were negligent: *Re City Equitable Fire Insurance. Co.* [1925] Ch. 407. [In this case the articles protected the directors from liability except in case of wilful neglect or default, and consequently the directors were held not liable. Section 205, *ante*[1]; now makes any such article void.][1a]

What was said earlier[1] as to the relief of directors from liability for breach of duty in connection with their fiduciary duties applies also to their duties of care. As to relief by a resolution of the company in general meeting, it was held in *Pavlides* v. *Jensen*[2] that if the directors by their negligence had sold the company's mine at an undervalue, it was open to the company by a vote of the majority to decide that proceedings should not be taken against them.

Part II of the Supply of Goods and Services Act 1982 implies certain terms into a contract for the supply of services, including those of

[98] *Lister* v. *Romford Ice and Cold Storage Co. Ltd.* [1957] A.C. 555.
[99] *Per* Lord Johnson in *Brenes & Co.* v. *Downie,* 1914 S.C. 97, at p. 104.
[1] p. 375.
[1a] *cf. Liquidator of the Caledonian Heritable Security Co. Ltd.* v. *Curror's Trustee* (1882) 9 R. 1115.
[2] [1956] Ch. 565, *post,* p. 399.

directors. However, the main term, as to the exercise of reasonable care and skill, has been excluded, by statutory instrument, from directors' contracts. Another term, as to supply of services within a reasonable time, will, however, be implied by the Act into directors' contracts.

Liability for acts of co-directors

A director is not liable for the acts of his co-directors of which he has no knowledge and in which he has taken no part,[3] as his fellow directors are not his servants or agents to impose liability on him.[4] Moreover, if an *ultra vires* investment is made at a directors' meeting, a director who was not present at the meeting is not liable for the investment merely because he was present at a meeting at which the minutes of the meeting authorising the investment were confirmed.[5]

If a director is fraudulent, his co-directors are not liable for not discovering his fraud in the absence of circumstances to arouse their suspicions.

A bank sustained heavy losses by advances to customers made improperly. The irregular nature of the advances was concealed by means of fraudulent balance sheets, the work of the general manager and the chairman. *Held*, a co-director was not liable for not having discovered the frauds, as he was not, in the absence of circumstances of suspicion, bound to examine entries in the company's books to see that the balance sheets were correct: *Dovey* v. *Cory* [1901] A.C. 477.

Non-attendance at board meetings has been held not to impose liability on a director for the acts of the board.[6]

Where more than one director is alleged to have neglected his duties of care, both or all are jointly and severally liable, with the result that if an action is brought by the company against only one of them he is not entitled to plead that all parties interested have not been called.[7] However, the director sued is entitled to contribution from the other directors.

---

[3] *Perry's Case* (1876) 34 L.T. 716.
[4] *Cullerne* v. *London and Suburban Bldg. Socy.* (1890) 25 Q.B.D. 485 (C.A.).
[5] *Re Lands Allotment Co.* [1894] 1 Ch. 616 (C.A.), *ante*, p. 84.
[6] *Re Denham & Co.* (1884) 25 Ch.D. 752.
[7] *Liquidators of Western Bank* v. *Douglas* (1860) 22 D. 447, the reason being that the action is based on delict and not on contract: *per* Lord Justice-Clerk Inglis at p. 476.

Contribution between directors

When directors have misapplied the company's funds, as by paying dividends out of capital or advancing money for an unauthorised purpose, a director who has been sued for the misapplication is entitled to contribution from the other directors who were parties to it.[8] If, however, the money misappropriated has been applied for the sole benefit of one of the directors, that director is not entitled to obtain contribution.[9]

DIRECTORS' POWERS AND SHAREHOLDERS' CONTROL

We have seen that in modern public companies the directors have usually only a small shareholding, their salaries and other emoluments, rather than their dividends, being their main sources of profit from the company, with the result that management and ownership of the company have become divorced.[10]

We have also seen that the articles commonly delegate extensive powers to the directors, although there can be no delegation of powers which are required by the Act to be exercised by the company in general meeting, *e.g.* those of altering the articles (s.10), or the capital (ss.61, 66).[11] The Jenkins Committee[12] thought that wide delegation is necessary if the directors are to manage the company efficiently and that members are persistently reluctant to concern themselves with management.

The Committee[13] also thought that as a general rule directors exercise their powers in what they conceive to be the best interests of the company. Again, the Act provides shareholders with theoretically powerful weapons if they choose to use them, *e.g.* the powers of requisitioning meetings and of requiring the giving of notice of members' resolutions to be proposed at meetings (ss.132 and 140[14]), and

---

[8] *Ramskill* v. *Edwards* (1886) 31 Ch.D. 100; see also (for England) Civil Liability (Contribution) Act 1978, and (for Scotland) Law Reform (Miscellaneous Provisions) (Scotland) Act 1940, s.3.

[9] *Walsh* v. *Bardsley* (1931) 47 T.L.R. 564.

[10] *Ante*, p. 327.

[11] *Ante*, p. 350.

[12] Paras. 104 and 109 of the Report.

[13] Para. 110 of the Report.

[14] *Ante*, pp. 303, 310.

there are various sources of information available to members, *e.g.* the balance sheet and profit and loss account (s.158[15]), and, even if practical considerations (the large number of shareholders in the company, the lack of interest normally shown by the general body of shareholders, the difficulty of rallying support) make such weapons difficult for the small investor to wield, the institutional investors (such as insurance companies) are not always willing to submit to any major abuse of power by the directors. In fact in many cases they have established unofficial, but powerful, Investor Protection Committees, to safeguard their interests. Further, where quoted companies are concerned, the Stock Exchange requirements and the sanction for them in the shape of a suspension of quotation provide some protection.[16]

However, there are cases where directors abuse their power[17] and the Committee made certain recommendations[18] designed to protect the vital interests of shareholders without hampering directors in their conduct of the day-to-day business of the company. There are remedies available for such a breach and these are set out in Chapter 19, *post.*

---

[15] *Post,* Chap. 22.
[16] Jenkins Report, para. 106.
[17] *Ibid.* para. 111.
[18] *Ibid.* para. 122.

CHAPTER 17

THE SECRETARY

EVERY company must have a secretary and a sole director cannot also be secretary: section 177. The secretary may be an individual or a Scottish firm or a corporation, but a corporation cannot be the secretary if its sole director is also the sole director of the company: section 178. A company may have joint secretaries: see section 200(3).

Section 79 of the 1980 Act requires the directors of a public company to secure that the secretary is a person who appears to them to have the requisite knowledge and experience to be a secretary. In addition a public company secretary must have either been a public company secretary for 3 out of the 5 years before his present appointment, or be a barrister, advocate or solicitor, or a member of one of the professional accountancy bodies or of the Institute of Chartered Secretaries and Administrators, or be someone who, because of his position or qualifications, appears to the directors to be capable of discharging the duties of a public company secretary. A private company secretary need have no qualifications.

The secretary is usually appointed by the directors, but sometimes he is named in the articles.[1]

Table A, article 110, of the 1948 Act, as amended by Schedule 2 to the 1976 Act, provides: "Subject to section 21(5) of the Companies Act 1976, the secretary shall be appointed by the directors for such term, at such remuneration and upon such conditions as they may think fit; and any secretary so appointed may be removed by them."

The position of a company secretary has changed a great deal in the last 100 years. In 1887 it was said that: "a secretary is a mere servant; his position is that he is to do what he is told, and no person can assume that he has any authority to represent anything at all; nor can anyone assume that statements made by him are necessarily to be accepted as trustworthy without further inquiry."[2] Even in 1902 his duties were

---

[1] As to which see *Eley* v. *Positive Life Assurance Co. Ltd.* (1876) 1 Ex.D. 88 (C.A.), *ante*, p. 107.
[2] *Per* Lord Esher M.R. in *Barnett, Hoares & Co.* v. *South London Tramways Co.* (1887) 18 Q.B.D. 815 (C.A.), at p. 817.

described as "of a limited and of a somewhat humble character."[3]
Accordingly, it has been held that a company is not liable for the acts of
its secretary in fraudulently making representations to induce persons
to take shares in the company,[4] or in issuing a forged share certificate.[5]
The secretary is, however, the proper official to issue share certificates,
and so the company is estopped or barred from denying the truth of
genuine share certificates issued by him without the authority of the
company.[6]

It has also been held that the secretary has no independent authority
to bind the company by contract.[7]

> L., a director of N. Co., without any authority from the company, made a
> contract with H. The contract was confirmed by a letter written by the
> secretary on behalf of the company. *Held,* the secretary, as such, had no
> power to bind the company, and N. Co. was not liable on the contract:
> *Houghton & Co.* v. *Nothard, Lowe & Wills Ltd.* [1928] A.C. 1, *post.*[8]

Similarly, it has been held that he cannot borrow money on behalf of
the company.

> At the request of the secretary, a director, C., lent £17,353 to the company
> to discharge debts guaranteed by the company. The loans were confirmed by a
> meeting of the directors at which C. and one other director were present. The
> articles provided that two directors were a quorum, but that a director could
> not vote in respect of a contract in which he was interested. The company went
> into liquidation. *Held,* C. was not entitled to recover the money advanced.
> The secretary had no power to borrow on behalf of the company and his
> request was not made or confirmed at a properly constituted meeting of the
> directors: *Re Cleadon Trust Ltd.* [1939] Ch. 286 (C.A.).

Also, without the authority of the company, he cannot issue a writ in
the company's name[9] or lodge defences in the company's name,[10] and
it is not his duty as secretary to instruct the company as to its legal
rights.[11]

---

[3] *Per* Lord Macnaghten in *George Whitechurch Ltd.* v. *Cavanagh* [1902] A.C. 117,
at p. 124.

[4] *Barnett, Hoares & Co.* v. *South London Tramways Co., ante.*

[5] *Ruben* v. *Great Fingall Consolidated* [1906] A.C. 439, *ante*, p. 265.

[6] *Clavering, Son & Co.* v. *Goodwins, Jardine & Co. Ltd.* (1891) 18 R. 652.

[7] *Williams* v. *The Chester and Holyhead Ry. Co.* (1851) 15 Jur. 828.

[8] p. 437.

[9] *Daimler Co. Ltd.* v. *Continental Tyre, etc., Co. Ltd.* [1916] 2 A.C. 307.

[10] *Edington* v. *Dumbar Steam Laundry Co.* (1903) 11 S.L.T. 117 (O.H.).

[11] *Niven* v. *Collins Patent Lever Gear Co. Ltd.* (1900) 7 S.L.T. 476 (O.H.).

The secretary of a company is not "an official who *virtute officii* can manage all its affairs with or without the help of servants, in the absence of a regular directorate:" *per* Lord Parker in *Daimler Co. Ltd.* v. *Continental Tyre Co. Ltd.* [1916] 2 A.C. 307 at p. 337.

Again, the secretary cannot register a transfer until he is authorised to do so by the directors[12]; he cannot, without such authority, strike a name off the register of shareholders[13]; and he cannot summon a general meeting on his own authority.[14]

However, in a modern case[15] it was said[16] that a company secretary is a much more important person now than he was in 1887. He is the chief administrative officer of the company with extensive duties and responsibilities. This appears not only in the modern Companies Acts but in the role which he plays in the day-to-day business of the company. He is no longer a mere clerk. He regularly makes representations on behalf of the company and enters into contracts on its behalf which come within the day-to-day running of its business. So much so that he may be regarded as held out as having authority to do such things on behalf of the company. He is certainly entitled to sign contracts connected with the administrative side of a company's affairs, such as employing staff and ordering cars. All such matters come within the ostensible authority of a company's secretary.

The secretary, purportedly on behalf of the company, fraudulently hired cars, ostensibly for the purpose of meeting customers, and used the cars for his own private purposes. *Held*, the secretary had ostensible authority to enter into contracts for the hire of cars on behalf of the company and the company was liable to pay the hire charges: *Panorama Developments (Guildford) Ltd.* v. *Fidelis Furnishing Fabrics Ltd.* [1971] 2 Q.B. 711 (C.A.).

This new status of the company secretary was recognised by the introduction in the 1980 Act of a qualification standard for public company secretaries: 1980 Act, s.79, *ante*.

The duties of the secretary depend on the size and nature of the company, and on the arrangement made with him. In any case he will

---

[12] *Chida Mines Ltd.* v. *Anderson* (1905) 22 T.L.R. 27.
[13] *Re Indo-China Steam Navigation Co.* [1917] 2 Ch. 100.
[14] *Re State of Wyoming Syndicate* [1901] 2 Ch. 431.
[15] *Panorama Developments (Guildford) Ltd.* v. *Fidelis Furnishing Fabrics Ltd.* [1971] 2 Q.B. 711 (C.A.).
[16] *Per* Lord Denning M.R. and Salmon L.J., at pp. 716, 717.

be present at all meetings of the company, and of the directors, and will make proper minutes of the proceedings. He will issue, under the direction of the board, all notices to members and others. In practice he will usually countersign every instrument to which the seal of the company is affixed.[16a] He or his department will conduct all correspondence with shareholders in regard to transfers and otherwise, will certify transfers, and will keep the books of the company, or such of them as relate to the internal business of the company, *e.g.* the register of members, the share ledger, the transfer book, the register of charges, etc. He will also make all necessary returns to the Registrar, *e.g.* the annual return, return of allotments, notice of increase of capital, etc.

If a provision requires or authorises a thing to be done by or to a director and the secretary it is not satisfied by the thing being done by or to the same person acting both as director and as secretary: section 179.

If a person is secretary of two companies, a fact which comes to his knowledge as secretary of one company is not notice to him as secretary of another company, unless it was his duty to the first company to communicate his knowledge to the second company.

H. was secretary of two companies, A. Co. and B. Co. B. Co. drew a bill on a third company, C. Co., and indorsed it in favour of A. Co. The bill was dishonoured by C. Co. and no notice of dishonour was given to B. Co. It was claimed that as H., in his capacity of secretary, knew of the dishonour, no notice was necessary. *Held,* notice to H., as secretary of A. Co., was not notice to B. Co.: *Re Fenwick, Stobart & Co.* [1902] 1 Ch. 507.

In England a full-time secretary is a "clerk or servant" so as to be entitled to preferential payment of his salary on a winding up but a part-time secretary is not.[17]

The secretary is an officer of the company: section 455. In some instances therefore he is in the same position as a director so that a provision in the articles or in any contract for relieving him from liability is void: section 205.[18] Again, the court can relieve him from

[16a] His signature may not be essential for validity; see, *e.g. Clydesdale Bank (Moore Place) Nominees Ltd.* v. *Snodgrass*, 1939 S.C. 805.

[17] *Cairney* v. *Back* [1906] 2 K.B. 746, *post*, p. 664. Scottish cases in which a secretary was held not to be a "clerk or servant" for this purpose are *Scottish Poultry Journal Co.* (1896) 4 S.L.T. 167 (O.H.), *Clyde Football etc. Co. Ltd.* (1900) 8 S.L.T. 328 (O.H.) and *Laing* v. *Gowans* (1902) 10 S.L.T. 461 (O.H.).

[18] *Ante*, p. 375.

liability in certain cases: section 448.[19] His present Christian name and surname, any former Christian name and surname and his address must be set out in the register of directors and secretaries: section 200.[20] The disclosure in the accounts of loans, etc., to the secretary is less stringent than that for directors.[21] Under section 56 of the 1980 Act only the aggregate amounts outstanding need to be disclosed together with the number of officers involved.

A secretary has been held to have no lien over the books of the company coming into his possession in the course of his duties.[22]

The appointment of the secretary may be terminated by giving the agreed notice or, if no notice is agreed, by giving reasonable notice.[23] It may be terminated without any notice if the secretary makes a secret profit.[24]

If the secretary is an employee he is entitled to the minimum period of notice applicable to him under section 49 of the Employment Protection (Consolidation) Act 1978.

The appointment in England of a receiver and manager in a debenture-holders' action,[25] and the making of an order for the compulsory winding up of the company,[26] both operate as a dismissal of the secretary. The passing of a resolution for a voluntary winding up usually has this effect too.[27]

---

[19] *Ante*, p. 375.
[20] *Ante*, p. 336.
[21] *Ante*, p. 360.
[22] *Gladstone* v. *M'Callum* (1896) 23 R. 783 (minute book); *Barnton Hotel Co. Ltd.* v. *Cook* (1899) 1 F. 1190 (register of members and other books and documents at secretary's own premises).
[23] *Creen* v. *Wright* (1876) 1 C.P.D. 591.
[24] *McKay's Case* (1875) 2 Ch.D. 1.
[25] *Reid* v. *Explosives Co.* (1887) 19 Q.B.D. 264 (C.A.), *post*, p. 586.
[26] *Chapman's Case* (1866) L.R. 1 Eq. 346, *post*, p. 627; *Laing* v. *Gowans* (1902) 10 S.L.T. 461 (O.H.), *ante*, p. 390.
[27] *Reigate* v. *Union Manufacturing Co. (Ramsbottom) Ltd.* [1918] 1 K.B. 592 (C.A.); *per* Lord Stormonth Darling (Ordinary) in *Day* v. *Tait* (1900) 8 S.L.T. 40 (O.H.), at p. 41. And see, *post*, p. 694.

CHAPTER 18

CONTROLLING MEMBERS' DUTIES

IN this chapter the term "controlling members" means those members of a company who between them possess sufficient voting power to pass the appropriate resolution in general meeting, usually an ordinary resolution.

We have seen that the company in general meeting may waive a breach of fiduciary duty by a director who contracts with the company as in the *N.-W. Transportation* case,[1] or by one who makes a secret profit out of his position, as in *Regal (Hastings) Ltd.* v. *Gulliver,*[2] or may waive a breach of a director's duty of care, as in *Pavlides* v. *Jensen.*[3] In general therefore the majority of the company may exercise their votes to control the company provided that they comply with the Companies Acts. It has often been stated that although the directors of a company owe a fiduciary duty[4] to the company, as such, shareholders do not: "When voting, a shareholder may consult his own interests."[5]

Until recently it has thus been accepted that a share is a piece of property which is to be enjoyed and exercised for the owner's personal advantage.[6] Thus a shareholder may bind himself by contract to vote in a particular way, whereas a director may not.

"When a director votes as a director for or against any particular resolution in a directors' meeting he is voting as a person under a fiduciary duty to the company for the proposition that the company should take a certain course of action. When a shareholder is voting for or against a particular resolution he is voting as a person owing no fiduciary duty to the company and who is exercising his own right of property, to vote as he thinks fit. The fact that the result of the voting at the meeting (or at a subsequent poll) will bind the company cannot affect the position that, in voting, he is voting simply in exercise of his own property rights . . . a director is an agent, who casts his vote to decide in what manner his principal shall act through the collective

[1] (1887) 12 App.Cas. 589 (P.C.), *ante*, p. 375.
[2] [1942] 1 All E.R. 378 (H.L.), *ante*, p. 377.
[3] [1956] Ch. 565, *post*, p. 399.
[4] *Ante*, p. 371.
[5] *Per* Megarry V.-C. in *Estmanco (Kilner House)* v. *G.L.C.* [1982] 1 All E.R. 437, 444.
[6] See, *e.g. N.W. Transportation Co.* v. *Beatty*, above.

agency of the board of directors; a shareholder who casts his vote in general meeting is not casting it as an agent of the company in any shape or form. His act therefore, in voting as he pleases, cannot in any way be regarded as an act of the company": *per* Walton J. in *Northern Counties Securities Ltd.* v. *Jackson & Steeple Ltd.* [1974] 1 W.L.R. 1133, at p. 1144.

In *Greenwell* v. *Porter*,[7] where executors and trustees of a will who held shares agreed to sell some to G., who stipulated that he should nominate X as a director and that the executors should, when X retired by rotation, vote for his re-election, it was held that the executors were bound by the agreement. It may be mentioned that there was a voting agreement in *Greenhalgh* v. *Mallard*[8] but it was held that the shareholders who agreed to vote in a certain way were under no obligation to retain their shares and there was no continuing obligation running with the shares.

This right to vote has, however, always been subject to the doctrine of the fraud on the minority, so that the majority cannot waive a breach of a director's fiduciary duty by approving a misappropriation by him of the company's property which would be a fraud on the minority. That is what the majority tried to do in *Cook* v. *Deeks*.[9]

The same is true where there is an attempted confirmation of a share issue made by a director in order to give him control of the company and benefit the majority to the detriment of the minority, *i.e.* the general meeting cannot then waive the director's breach of duty.[10]

Members cannot, by resolution in general meeting, expropriate the company's property.

The shareholders in E. Co., which was formed with the object of constructing a submarine telegraph, were H. Co. with 3,000 shares, M. with 2,000 and thirteen other persons with 325 between them. H. Co. was to make and lay cables for E. Co. The directors of E. Co., who were nominees of H. Co., and H. Co., decided not to pursue an action in which E. Co. was claiming a concession to construct the telegraph, procured the passing of a resolution in general meeting to put E. Co. into voluntary winding up and concealed the fact that they had agreed to end the agreement between E. Co. and H. Co. so that H. Co. could sell the cable to a third company. M. brought an action on behalf of himself and the other shareholders, except those who were defendants, in which he joined E. Co. as a defendant. He claimed, *inter alia*, a declaration that H. Co. was a trustee of the resulting profit for M. and the other shareholders in E. Co. *Held,* M. succeeded. The majority shareholder had obtained certain advantages by dealing with something which was the

[7] [1902] 1 Ch. 530. See also *Puddephatt* v. *Leith* [1916] 1 Ch. 200.
[8] [1943] 2 All E.R. 234 (C.A.).
[9] [1916] 1 A.C. 554, *ante*, p. 375.
[10] *Ngurli* v. *McCann* (1954) 90 C.L.R. 425.

property of the whole company: *Menier* v. *Hooper's Telegraph Works* (1874) L.R. 9 Ch.App. 350.

As regards the property of other members of the company, we saw in Chapter 4 that, on the authority of *Sidebottom* v. *Kershaw, Leese & Co.*,[11] an alteration of the articles by special resolution in general meeting in order to enable some members to acquire the shares of other members must be bona fide for the benefit of the company as a whole.

Further, we saw that cases such as *Greenhalgh* v. *Arderne Cinemas Ltd.*,[12] *Shuttleworth* v. *Cox Bros. Ltd.*,[13] *Australian Fixed Trusts Pty. Ltd.* v. *Clyde Industries*[14] and *Peters' American Delicacy Co. Ltd.* v. *Heath*[15] established the rule that in making any alteration to the articles the general meeting must act bona fide for the benefit of the company as a whole. Similarly, a class meeting of preference shareholders sanctioning a modification of the special rights of the preference shares must act bona fide for the benefit of the class as a whole.[16]

It was said in a Scots case[17] that: "Prima facie, the shareholders are the best judges of their own affairs, and it is only where it appears that some sinister motive has operated, or that interests other than the interest of the company have plainly prevailed, that the Court will entertain a complaint. The test always is—Is the thing complained of a thing done in the interest of the company?—or, to put it perhaps more accurately, Is the action of the majority irreconcilable with their having proceeded upon any reasonable view of the company's interest?" In the case in question a resolution of a general meeting to issue unissued shares to the managing director at a lower premium than would have been obtained on the market was valid. In another Scots case it was said[18] that "The question . . . is whether the resolution complained of . . . can be held to be so oppressive and extravagant that no reasonable man could consider it to be for the benefit of the Company."

Thus controlling members do owe a duty to the company, *i.e.* the corporators as a body, to act bona fide for the benefit of the company as a whole and not to commit a fraud on the minority.

---

[11] [1920] 1 Ch. 154 (C.A.), *ante*, p. 111.
[12] [1951] Ch. 286 (C.A.), *ante*, p. 110.
[13] [1927] 2 K.B. 9 (C.A.).
[14] (1959) S.R. (N.S.W.) 33.
[15] (1939) 61 C.L.R. 457.
[16] *Re Holders Investment Trust Ltd.* [1971] 1 W.L.R. 583, *ante*, p. 217.
[17] *Per* Lord Kyllachy (Ordinary) in *Cameron* v. *Glenmorangie Distillery Co. Ltd.* (1896) 23 R. 1092, at p. 1095.
[18] *Per* Lord Wark (Ordinary) in *Harris* v. *A. Harris Ltd.*, 1936 S.C. 183, at p. 192.

It seems, however, that the controlling members may in fact be subject to more stringent controls than the accepted doctrine of a fraud on the minority, although not being subject to the full fiduciary duties of a director.

In *Clemens* v. *Clemens Bros. Ltd.*[19] the defendant owned 55 per cent of the issued shares of a family company. She was one of five directors and proposed to give the other directors shares and to set up a trust for long-service employees. The plaintiff, who was the defendant's niece, held 40 per cent. of the shares and was not a director. The defendant proposed resolutions to increase the capital so that the plaintiff's shares would fall below 25 per cent. of the total and her right to veto special resolutions would be lost. It was also clear that she would never now obtain control of the company. The judge held that the defendant was not entitled to exercise her majority votes as an ordinary shareholder in any way she pleased. That right was subject to equitable considerations which could make it unjust to exercise them in a particular way. In this case such considerations applied and the resolutions would be set aside.

The importance of this case is that it shows that the majority do not have unrestricted voting rights if it is "unjust" in the particular circumstances.

In *Estmanco (Kilner House) Ltd.* v. *Greater London Council*[20] Megarry V.-C., however, accepted the general proposition that the shareholders do not owe any fiduciary duties but affirmed that in altering the articles they are subject to the doctrine of fraud on the minority, *i.e.* they must act in what they believe to be in the best interests of the company as a whole. In that case the majority shareholder wished to deprive the company of a right of action under a contract and proposed, and carried, a resolution to that effect. A minority shareholder sought to bring an action on behalf of the company[21] to prevent this. Megarry V.-C. considered the situation thus:[22]

"Plainly there must be some limit to the power of the majority to pass resolutions which they believe to be in the best interests of the company and yet remain immune from interference by the courts. It

---

[19] [1976] 2 All E.R. 268.
[20] [1982] 1 All E.R. 437.
[21] *Post*, p. 400.
[22] [1982] 1 All E.R. 437, 444.

may be in the best interests of the company to deprive the minority of some of their rights or some of their property, yet I do not think that this gives the majority an unrestricted right to do this, however unjust it may be, and however much it may harm shareholders whose rights as a class differ from those of the majority."

CHAPTER 19

ENFORCEMENT OF DIRECTORS' AND CONTROLLING MEMBERS' DUTIES

THIS chapter attempts to present in a coherent form a number of matters, some of which have been explained already and others of which have been referred to.

One of the matters which has been referred to on more than one occasion is the rule in *Foss* v. *Harbottle* to the effect that the company is usually the proper plaintiff in an action to enforce the duties of directors and controlling members.

Majority rule and its counter balance, minority protection, are dealt with—under the general law the wishes of the majority of the members normally prevail over those of the minority but the majority must not perpetrate a fraud on the minority.

Statutory protection of the minority against the majority is explained, for example, under sections 222 and 224 of the 1948 Act even a single member can have the company wound up by the court if that is just and equitable and under section 75 of the 1980 Act a single member can obtain other relief from the court where the company's affairs are being conducted in an unfairly prejudicial manner.

Finally the protection afforded by Department of Trade investigations is set out. The rules relating to insider dealing—a particular abuse of directors' and others' duties—are explained in Chapter 21.

THE RULE IN FOSS *v.* HARBOTTLE[1]

The rule is that, as one would expect, the proper plaintiff[2] in an action to redress an alleged wrong to a company on the part of anyone, whether director, member or outsider, or to recover money or damages alleged to be due to it, is prima facie the company and, where the alleged wrong is any irregularity which might be made binding on

---

[1] The account which follows is largely based on the judgment of Jenkins L.J. in *Edwards* v. *Halliwell* [1950] 2 All E.R. 1064 (C.A.), at p. 1066 *et seq.*

[2] The Scots term is "pursuer."

the company by a simple majority of members, no individual member can bring an action in respect of it.[3]

In other words, the company is normally the proper plaintiff in an action to enforce a duty owed to the company by directors or controlling members, and where the breach of duty can be condoned by an ordinary resolution of the members in general meeting, no individual member or minority of members may sue. A general meeting may be held so that the members may by ordinary resolution decide whether to sue or not. It is for this reason that the employees of a company, to whom the directors now owe a duty, following section 46 of the 1980 Act,[4] may find it impossible to enforce such a right. Only the members have the right to enforce it.

It has been said[5] that there are two branches of the rule and these have been described[6] as—

(1) the proper plaintiff principle,
(2) the internal management principle.

Two members took proceedings on behalf of themselves and all other members except those who were defendants against the directors of a company to compel them to make good losses sustained by the company owing to the directors buying their own land for the company's use and paying themselves a price greater than its value. *Held*, as there was nothing to prevent the company from taking the proceedings, if it thought fit to do so, the action failed: *Foss* v. *Harbottle* (1843) 2 Ha. 461; 67 E.R. 189.[7]

A minority shareholder sought to bring an action on behalf of himself and all other shareholders, save three who were directors, against those directors

---

[3] See *per* Lord Davey delivering the judgment of the court in *Burland* v. *Earle* [1902] A.C. 82 (P.C.), at pp. 93, 94.

[4] *Ante*, p. 371.

[5] *Per* Jordan C.J. in *Australian Coal etc. Employees' Fedn.* v. *Smith* (1937) 38 S.R. (N.S.W.) 48.

[6] *Per* Street J. in *Hawkesbury Development Co. Ltd.* v. *Landmark Finance Pty. Ltd.* (1970) 92 W.N. (N.S.W.) 199.

[7] Applied in the *Hawkesbury* case, *ante*.

In a corresponding Scottish case, *Orr* v. *Glasgow etc. Rlwy. Co.* (1860) 3 Macqueen 799, "the ground of action . . . was that the directors were also directors of a rival company, and that they had acted in the interests of this latter company to the prejudice of the shareholders of the first. The action was dismissed on the ground that although the transaction complained of was beyond the powers of the directors, it was competent for the shareholders to sanction it, and therefore that a single shareholder, or a minority, had no title to sue": *per* Lord Kinnear (Ordinary) in *Rixon* v. *Edinburgh Northern Tramways Co.* (1889) 16 R. 653, at p. 656.

and the company for damages, alleging that the directors had been negligent in selling an asset of the company for less than its market value. Most of the shares in the company were held by another company the directors of which were also directors of the first company. *Held,* since the sale of the mine was *intra vires* the company, and there was no allegation of fraud by the directors or appropriation of assets of the company by the majority shareholders in fraud of the minority, the action was not maintainable. It was open to the company, on the resolution of a majority of the shareholders, to sell the mine at a price decided by the company in that manner, and it was open to the company by a vote of the majority to decide that, if the directors by their negligence had sold the mine at an undervalue, proceedings should not be taken by the company against the directors. *Semble,* it is sometimes admissible to go behind the apparent ownership of shares to discover whether a company is in fact controlled by wrongdoers, *e.g.* where the shares are held by nominees: *Pavlides* v. *Jensen* [1956] Ch. 565.[8]

The rule avoids multiplicity of suits. The reason for the last part of the rule is that litigation at the suit of a minority of the members is futile if the majority do not wish it.

"If the thing complained of is a thing which in substance the majority of the company are entitled to do, or if something has been done irregularly which the majority of the company are entitled to do regularly, or if something has been done illegally which the majority of the company are entitled to do legally, there can be no use in having litigation about it, the ultimate end of which is only that a meeting has to be called, and then ultimately the majority gets its wishes": *per* Mellish L.J. in *MacDougall* v. *Gardiner* (1875) 1 Ch.D. 13 (C.A.) at p. 25.[8a]

Under this rule, the court will not interfere with irregularities at meetings at the instance of a shareholder.

The articles empowered the chairman, with the consent of the meeting, to adjourn a meeting, and also provided for taking a poll if demanded by five shareholders. The adjournment was moved, and declared by the chairman to be carried; a poll was then demanded and refused by the chairman. A shareholder suing on behalf of himself and all other shareholders except those

[8] Scottish illustrations are *Lee* v. *Crawford* (1890) 17 R. 1094 (action against director for payment to the company of funds alleged to have been illegally lent to officials of the company), *Cameron* v. *Glenmorangie Distillery Co. Ltd.* (1896) 23 R. 1092 (directors carrying out shareholders' resolution to allot to managing director unissued shares at a premium considered by a shareholder to be inadequate) and *Brown* v. *Stewart* (1898) 1 F. 316 (claim for damages against directors on ground that they had acted recklessly in commencing business when so few shares had been applied for).

[8a] *cf.* Lord Hunter in *Harris* v. *A. Harris Ltd.*, 1936 S.C. 183, at p. 198.

who were directors brought an action against the directors and the company for a declaration that the chairman's conduct was illegal and an injunction to restrain the directors from carrying out certain arrangements without the shareholders' approval. *Held,* the action could not be brought by a shareholder; if the chairman was wrong, the company alone could sue: *MacDougall* v. *Gardiner* (1875) 1 Ch.D. 13 (C.A.).

Nor will the court grant a declaration that the accounts are not in the correct form at the instance of a shareholder: *Devlin* v. *Slough Estates Ltd.*, *The Times*, June 16, 1982.

The rule is subject to a number of exceptions, in which cases a minority of shareholders, or even an individual shareholder, may bring a minority shareholders' action, usually under R.S.C., O. 15, r.12,[8b] *i.e.* the minority shareholders sue on behalf of themselves and all other shareholders except those who are defendants, and may join the company as a defendant. The directors are usually defendants. This action is brought instead of an action in the name of the company.

"The form of the action is always 'A.B. (a minority shareholder) on behalf of himself and all other shareholders of the company' against the wrongdoing directors and the company": *per* Lord Denning M.R. in *Wallersteiner* v. *Moir* (*No.* 2) [1975] Q.B. 373 (C.A.) at p. 390.

This type of action is a *derivative action, i.e.* the right to sue derives from that of the company. The shareholders as such have no such right. If their own personal rights are being infringed they should bring a *representative* action, *post.*

The exceptions are:—

(1) Where the wrong complained of is a fraud by the majority of the members on the minority and the wrongdoers are in control of the company in general meeting, *i.e.* they control the majority of the shares in the company, and they will not permit an action to be brought in the name of the company. If the aggrieved minority could not bring a minority shareholders' action in this case their grievance would never reach the courts. Where an action is brought under this exception the wrongdoers are usually both directors and controlling shareholders.

[8b] Not applicable to Scotland. There is no special form for a "derivative action" in Scots law: the minority shareholder would require to proceed in his own name.

In *Cook* v. *Deeks*[9] a shareholder brought a minority shareholders' action to compel the directors to account to the company for the profits made out of the construction contract which they took in their own names.[10]

In Scotland it has been held that the minority must have first made a definite attempt to obtain the company's co-operation: it is not sufficient for them to plead that the majority had the power to outvote them; *per* Lord Kyllachy (Ordinary) in *Lee* v. *Crawford* (1890) 17 R. 1094 at p. 1096; *Brown* v. *Stewart* (1898) 1 F. 316.

Recent cases have widened this exception to the rule in two ways. First as to the meaning of "fraud" in this context:

In *Daniels* v. *Daniels*[11] the minority shareholders of a company were allowed to bring an action where the directors had authorised the sale of company land to one of them at a price alleged to be well below its market value. The directors objected that since fraud had not been alleged the action should not be allowed.

Templeman J. laid down a wider definition of "fraud" for this purpose: "If minority shareholders can sue if there is fraud, I see no reason why they cannot sue where the action of the majority and the directors, though without fraud, confers some benefit on those directors and majority shareholders themselves."[12]

The judge distinguished *Pavlides* v. *Jensen*, above, on the grounds that the directors had not benefited by this "negligence." The essence of this decision is that since fraud is often impossible to prove it may be presumed from such obvious facts.

In *Estmanco (Kilner House) Ltd.* v. *Greater London Council*[13] the majority shareholder proposed to alter a contract it had with the company in order to deprive the minority shareholders of certain rights. The majority shareholder then proposed a resolution whereby the company should not sue for breach of contract. When a minority shareholder sought to sue on the company's behalf the majority shareholder argued that since it had acted bona fide for the benefit of the company there was no fraud on the minority to allow such an action.

Megarry V.-C. refused to accept that test of fraud on the minority as applicable for the purposes of bringing an action. It only related to the

---

[9] [1916] 1 A.C. 554, *ante*, p. 374.
[10] See also *Menier* v. *Hooper's Telegraph Works* (1874) L.R. 9 Ch.App. 350, *ante*, p. 394. For Scotland see also *Rixon* v. *Edinburgh Northern Tramways* (1889) 16 R. 653 and *Hannay* v. *Muir* (1898) 1 F. 306.
[11] [1978] 2 All E.R. 89.
[12] *Ibid*. p. 96.
[13] [1982] 1 All E.R. 437.

alteration of the company's articles.[14] In this case the action of the majority shareholder injured one category of shareholder to the benefit of another. Fraud in this sense is abuse of a power.

Further in *Re A Company: FFI (U.K. Finance) Ltd.* v. *Lady Kagan* (1982) 132 N.L.J. 830, the judge granted an injunction, at the request of a shareholder, to prevent the company pleading guilty to a charge of conspiracy to defraud at the instigation of the directors, on the basis that this would damage the company's potential civil claims against others. Improper influence appeared to have been used.

The second development concerns the requisite element of "control" by the majority. It has always been accepted, as stated above, that this means actual voting control. But in *Prudential Assurance Co. Ltd.* v. *Newman Industries Ltd. (No. 2)*[15] Vinelott J. was prepared to extend the exception when the alleged fraud was committed by directors who did not exercise actual voting control but who exercised control *in practice*. Large public companies, such as *Newman*, are in fact controlled by less than 50 per cent. of the votes. The Court of Appeal in that case did not express any opinion on this point.

(2) Where the act is one which is illegal, or *ultra vires* the company.[16] Such an act cannot be condoned by the majority of the members.

(3) Where the matter is one which can be validly done or sanctioned, not by a simple majority, but only by some special majority, *e.g.* a special resolution, which has not been obtained. If an action could not be brought in this case the company could, in breach of the articles, do *de facto* by ordinary resolution that which according to its regulations can only be done by a special resolution.

Thus in *Baillie* v. *Oriental Telephone Co. Ltd.*,[17] a shareholder was able to bring a minority shareholders' action to restrain the company from acting on a special resolution of which insufficient notice had been given.[18]

It was assumed, although not decided, in *Heyting* v. *Dupont*[19] that there may be a further exception to the rule in *Foss* v. *Harbottle*—

[14] *Ante*, p. 108.   [15] [1982] 1 All E.R. 354 (C.A.); [1980] 2 All E.R. 841.
[16] *Flitcroft's Case* (1882) 21 Ch.D. 519 (C.A.). And see the *Hawkesbury* case, referred to in footnote 6.
[17] [1915] 1 Ch. 503 (C.A.), *ante*, p. 309.
[18] And see *Dunn* v. *Banknock Coal Co. Ltd.* (1901) 9 S.L.T. 51 (O.H.).
[19] [1964] 1 W.L.R. 843 (C.A.), *per* Russell and Harman L.JJ., at pp. 851, 854.

namely where justice demands that an action be brought, *e.g.* where all that is alleged is damage to the company arising from a director's misfeasance in withholding an asset of the company without fraud or *ultra vires*. The company was to exploit an invention of the defendant's consisting of a machine for making plastic pipes and the defendant withheld the company's patent application. However, the company could not have exploited the invention because it was in a state of paralysis owing to discord, so there was no damage to the company and therefore justice did not require that exception be made. Again, there is some authority to the effect that justice may demand that exception be made where the directors are in breach of duty which the company in general meeting could but will not condone and although the directors are not controlling shareholders they prevent the company suing because an article like Table A, article 80, gives them most of the powers of the company.[20]

In the *Prudential* case[21] Vinelott J. based his decision on the derivative action against the directors on the doctrine that a minority action could be allowed if "the interests of justice require that a minority action should be permitted."[21a] The Court of Appeal did not need to discuss the rule in *Foss* v. *Harbottle* because the company had actually adopted the case, but expressed the opinion that any exception based on the justice of the case was not a practical one.

The difficulty is that the question of whether a minority shareholder should be allowed to bring a derivative action ought to be a preliminary issue tried before the merits of the case, *e.g.* alleged fraud, are debated. If the justice exception is used it will in effect need a full trial of the issues to decide how justice will be best served. The Court of Appeal in the *Prudential* case thought that in such a preliminary action the minority shareholder should be required to establish at least a prima facie case that (a) the company is entitled to the relief claimed, and (b) the action falls within the proper boundaries of the rule restricting members' actions on behalf of the company.

On the other hand, the court may now authorise civil proceedings to be brought on behalf of the company by such persons and on such terms as it shall direct, as the result of a petition under section 75 of the 1980 Act, *post*.

---

[20] See *per* Hudson J. in *Kraus* v. *J. G. Lloyd Pty. Ltd.* [1965] V.R. 232, at pp. 236, 237.

[21] *Ante*, p. 402.   [21a] [1980] 2 All E.R. 841, at p. 877.

The minority shareholders' action is now called a derivative action[22] to indicate that the right being enforced is that of the company. The Legal Aid Act 1974 makes no provision for legal aid in a minority shareholders' action but it is open to the court in such an action to order the company to indemnify the plaintiff against the costs of the action. The minority shareholder should apply for the sanction of the court soon after issuing his writ. It would be unlawful as being contrary to public policy for a solicitor to accept a retainer for the plaintiff(s) to conduct the action on a contingency fee basis (*i.e.* he is paid the fee if he wins but not if he loses).[23]

Representative actions

In *Hogg* v. *Cramphorn*[24] the plaintiff was held to be justified in suing in a representative capacity in respect of the alleged wrongful disposition of the company's money by the directors which could be condoned by a resolution in general meeting, so that the action should have been dismissed unless it was not a *derivative* representative action but an individual rights *representative* action.

A member of a company may enjoy a right alone or in common with other members of the company and the rule in *Foss* v. *Harbottle* has no application where individual members sue, not in right of the company, but in their own right to protect their *individual* rights as members[25]—in such a case a member can bring an action in his own name and may sue on behalf of himself and other members, and the breach of duty owed to an individual shareholder cannot be ratified by a majority of shareholders. Thus in *Pender* v. *Lushington*,[26] a shareholder was able to enforce the article giving him a right to vote at meetings and compel the directors to record his vote.[27] Similarly,

---

[22] *Per* Lord Denning M.R., at p. 390 and Scarman L.J., at p. 406 in *Wallersteiner* v. *Moir* (*No.* 2) [1975] Q.B. 373 (C.A.). Scarman L.J. said that the American description of a minority shareholders' action, brought to obtain redress for the company, as a stockholders' derivative action, is apt.

[23] *Wallersteiner* case, *ante.*

[24] [1967] Ch. 254, *ante*, p. 372.

[25] *Per* Sir Geo. Jessel M.R. in *Pender* v. *Lushington* (1877) 6 Ch.D. 70, at pp. 80, 81.

[26] (1877) 6 Ch.D. 70.

[27] See also *Ngurli* v. *McCann* (1954) 90 C.L.R. 425, *ante*, p. 393 as explained in *Provident International Corpn.* v. *International Leasing Corpn. Ltd.* (1969) 89 W.N. (Pt. 1) (N.S.W.) 370.

actions for damages by shareholders in their own right do not come within the rule.[27a]

Circumstances in which an individual member can sue in his own name are:—

    (1) Where the company is acting illegally or *ultra vires.*[28]

    (2) Where a special majority is required and has not been obtained.[29]

    (3) Where the company is acting contrary to its articles.

It used to be thought that because the wrong complained of could be an invasion of the right of individual members as well as a breach of duty to the company, the individual members could sue for the damage to themselves as proper plaintiffs and so avoid the rule in *Foss* v. *Harbottle.* One member could thus sue on behalf of the others in a *representative* action. In the *Prudential* case[30] the minority shareholder used this form of action in addition to the derivative action. The claim was based on the loss suffered by the shareholders as a result of the directors' alleged fraud on the company. Because the company had lost money, the shareholders' profit expectations had been diminished. This argument failed in the Court of Appeal. The alleged loss to the shareholders was neither separate nor distinct from that suffered by the company. Only one loss had occurred and only one action could be allowed. Such actions would "subvert" the rule in *Foss* v. *Harbottle.* It seems therefore that personal actions of this type are in fact confined to the three instances set out above.

The rule does not apply where a shareholder relies on a statutory right, *e.g.* a right to have the register of members rectified under section 116.

Majority Rule and Minority Protection

Majority rule

The members of a company can express their wishes at general meetings by voting for or against the resolutions proposed. However,

---

[27a] *Lee* v. *Crawford* (1894) 17 R. 1094.

[28] *Per* Lord Campbell L.C. in *Simpson* v. *Westminster Palace Hotel* (1860) 8 H.L.C. 712, 11 E.R. 608, at p. 610; *Russell* v. *Wakefield Waterworks Co.* (1875) L.R. 20 Eq. 474, at p. 481.

[29] *Edwards* v. *Halliwell, ante.*   [30] *Ante,* p. 402.

the will of the majority of the members usually prevails and if the appropriate majority is obtained a resolution binds all the members, including those who voted against it. Sometimes the majority is a simple majority and sometimes it is a three-quarters majority—for example, an ordinary resolution is a resolution passed by a simple majority of the votes of the members entitled to vote and voting; a special resolution is a resolution passed by a three-quarters majority of the votes of such members.[31] This can be said to be the first example of what is called "majority rule."

Further, it should be remembered that, subject to a few restrictions, the articles of a company, which constitute a contract binding the company and the members, can be altered by special resolution.[32]

Another example of majority rule, as we have seen, is the rule in *Foss* v. *Harbottle,* by which, subject to certain exceptions, if a wrong to a company is alleged, or if there is an alleged irregularity in its internal management which is capable of confirmation by a simple majority of the members, the court will not interfere at the suit of a minority of the members.[33]

Minority protection

Both under the general law and under the Companies Acts there is some protection of the minority of the members against the acts of the majority. "A proper balance of the rights of majority and minority shareholders is essential for the smooth functioning of the company. Since the passing of the Joint Stock Companies Act 1856, most Acts have extended the protection of the minority. The Companies Acts 1948 to 1981, and the relevant case law, attempt to maintain that balance by admitting, on principle, the rule of the majority but limiting it, at the same time, by a number of well-defined minority rights."[34]

Examples of minority protection are:—

(1) Under the general law, the doctrine that the majority of the members must not commit a fraud on the minority but must act bona fide for the benefit of the company as a whole.[35] Thus, in *Cook* v.

---

[31] *Ante*, p. 323.
[32] *Ante*, p. 108.
[33] *Ante*, p. 397.
[34] Palmer's *Company Law* (23rd ed.), p. 597.
[35] *Ante*, p. 394.

Deeks[36] an individual shareholder was able, despite *Foss* v. *Harbottle*, to bring an action to recover the company's property from those who had taken it and who, by their voting power, prevented the company itself from suing. Again, an alteration of articles must not be in fraud of the minority.[37] As noted above the modern cases are tending towards a widening of these doctrines.

(2) The other exceptions to the rule in *Foss* v. *Harbottle*,[38] in which cases an individual member may bring a minority shareholders' action.

(3) The various sections of the Act intended to protect a minority of members. Under some minority sections even a single shareholder can defy the majority. Thus under sections 222 and 224[39] a member can petition the court to wind up the company on the ground that it is just and equitable that the company be wound up. And under section 75 of the 1980 Act[40] a member can petition the court for other relief where the company's affairs are being conducted in an unfairly prejudicial manner to some of the members, including himself. Other minority sections enable a number of shareholders to defy the majority. For example, under section 5, dissentient holders of 15 per cent. of the issued shares can apply to the court for cancellation of an alteration of objects.[41] Again, under section 72, where class rights are varied in pursuance of a clause in the articles, dissentient holders of 15 per cent. of the issued shares of the class can apply for cancellation of the variation.[42] Finally, under sections 164 and 172,[43] 200 members or the holders of one-tenth of the issued shares can apply to the Department of Trade for an investigation of the company's affairs or of the ownership of the company.

Some of these minority sections will now be examined in detail.

STATUTORY PROTECTION OF MINORITY SHAREHOLDERS

Winding up by the court on the "just and equitable" ground

Under sections 222 and 224 a contributory may petition that a company be wound up by the court and where the court is of opinion

---

[36] *Ante*, pp. 374, 401.
[38] *Ante*, p. 400.
[40] *Post*, p. 413.
[42] *Ante*, p. 218.

[37] *Ante*, p. 108.
[39] *Infra.*
[41] *Ante*, p. 87.
[43] *Post*, pp. 419, 425.

that it is just and equitable that the company should be wound up, the court may order winding up.

A member of a company is a contributory by sections 212 and 213, and it has been held that a holder of fully paid-up shares is a contributory.[44] Thus in appropriate circumstances even a single member can petition for a winding up. We shall see[45] that section 224 generally prevents a contributory from petitioning unless he has held his shares for at least six months.

In petitioning for a winding up on the just and equitable ground a member is not confined to such circumstances as affect him as a shareholder, *i.e.* he is not confined to cases where his position as a shareholder has been worsened by the action of which he complains; he is entitled to rely on any circumstances of justice or equity which affect him in his relations with the company or with the other shareholders,[46] although it is otherwise under section 75 of the 1980 Act.

The court will not, as a rule, order a winding up on a contributory's petition unless he alleges and proves, at least to the extent of a prima facie case, that there will be assets for distribution among the shareholders[47]; a purely private advantage will not suffice.[48] The reason is that unless there are such assets the contributory has no interest in a winding up. And a contributory's petition which is opposed by the majority of the contributories will usually not be granted except where the conduct of the majority is something of which the minority have a right to complain,[49] or the main object of the company has failed.[50] The petitioner need not establish that the other members have not acted bona fide in the interests of the company.[51]

---

[44] *Re National Savings Bank Assocn.* (1866) L.R. 1 Ch.App. 547; *Walker and Others, Petitioners* (1894) 2 S.L.T. 230 and 397 (O.H.).

[45] *Post*, p. 613.

[46] *Re Westbourne Galleries Ltd.* [1973] A.C. 360.

[47] *Re Rica Gold Washing Co.* (1879) 11 Ch.D. 36 (C.A.), distinguished in *Re W. R. Willcocks & Co. Ltd.* [1974] Ch.D. 163; *per* Lord Trayner in *Black* v. *United Collieries Ltd.* (1904) 7 F. 18. And see, *post*, p. 614.

[48] *Re Chesterfield Catering Co. Ltd.* [1976] 3 All E.R. 294.

[49] *Re Middlesbrough Assembly Rooms Co.* (1880) 14 Ch.D. 104 (C.A.), *post*, p. 607; *Re Tivoli Freeholds Ltd.* [1972] V.R. 445.

[50] *Re German Date Coffee Co.* (1882) 20 Ch.D. 169, *ante*, p. 78; *Pirie* v. *Stewart* (1904) 6 F. 847; contrast *Cox* v. *"Gosford" Ship Co. Ltd.* (1894) 21 R. 334 and *Galbraith* v. *Merito Shipping Co. Ltd.*, 1947 S.C. 446.

[51] See footnote 46.

Even where the minority is entitled to complain of the conduct of the majority a contributories' petition is uncommon. For one thing, winding up is a drastic remedy. For another, an alternative remedy may be available under section 75 of the 1980 Act, *post,* now.

An order for winding up will be made, *e.g.* in the following circumstances, some of which do not involve oppression of the minority:—

(1) Where the main object of the company has failed[52]—we saw in Chapter 3 that a clause excluding the "main objects" rule is irrelevant in this event—or the company is engaging in acts which are entirely outside what can fairly be regarded as having been within the general intention or common understanding of the members when they became members.[52]

A company was formed to acquire the English portion of the aircraft business of M. Blériot, a well-known airman. M. Blériot refused to carry out the contract. *Held,* the company should be wound up because its substratum had gone: *Re Blériot Aircraft Co.* (1916) 32 T.L.R. 253.

A company formed to purchase, charter and work ships and to carry on the business of shipowners lost its only vessel. Its remaining asset was a balance of £363 in the bank. A majority in number and value of shareholders petitioned for compulsory winding up, but a minority of shareholders desired to carry on the business as charterers. *Held,* it was just and equitable that the company should be wound up: *Pirie* v. *Stewart* (1904) 6 F. 847.

(2) If the company is a "bubble," *i.e.* there is no bona fide intent on the part of the directors to carry on business in a proper manner.[53]

The court will not order a solvent company to be wound up merely because it is making a loss or is deeply indebted if the majority of the shareholders are against a winding up,[54] or if no meeting of shareholders has been held to consider winding up.[55]

(3) Where the company was formed to carry out a fraud, or to carry on an illegal business.

---

[52] See footnote 50.

[53] *Re London and County Coal Co.* (1866) L.R. 3 Eq. 355.

[54] *Re Suburban Hotel Co.* (1867) L.R. 2 Ch.App. 737 (company making a loss), *Black* v. *United Collieries Ltd.* (1904) 7 F. 18 (company deeply indebted). See also *Galbraith* v. *Merito Shipping Co. Ltd.,* 1947 S.C. 446, *per* Lord Mackay, at p. 458.

[55] *Cox* v. *"Gosford" Ship Co. Ltd.* (1894) 21 R. 334; *Scobie* v. *Atlas Steel Works Ltd.* (1906) 8 F. 1052.

T. E. B. and his sons were relatives of, and had been employed by, persons who carried on the business of piano manufacturers under the name of J. B. & Sons. They left J. B. & Sons and formed a company called T. E. B. & Sons Ltd. for carrying on a similar business. A prospectus was issued which stated that the price paid for the business was £76,650, when it was really only £1,000 in cash together with £5,000 in shares in the company. Money was subscribed by the public and most of this money found its way into the hands of the persons who were the real, though not the ostensible, promoters. J. B & Sons obtained an injunction restraining the company from using the name B., and it was found that the company was formed to filch as much trade as possible from J. B. & Sons. Numerous actions were brought against the company for fraud in the prospectus. *Held,* the company should be wound up: *Re Thomas Edward Brinsmead & Sons* [1897] 1 Ch. 45; 406 (C.A.).

Fraudulent misrepresentation in the prospectus[56] or fraud in the course of business with the outside world[57] are not, by themselves, grounds for winding up the company, as the majority of the share-holders may waive the fraud, or there may be a change of manage-ment; but fraud in the real, though not the ostensible, object of the company will be such a ground.

A company formed to carry on an illegal business, *e.g.* one which infringes the Betting, Gaming and Lotteries Act 1963, will be wound up.[58]

(4) Where the mutual rights of the members are not exhaustively defined in the articles, *e.g.* where they entered into member-ship on the basis of a personal relationship involving mutual confidence or an understanding as to the extent to which each is to participate in the management of the company's business, and the right to transfer shares in the company is restricted, and the confidence is not maintained or the petitioner is excluded from the management.

From about 1945 E. and N. were partners in a carpet dealing business with an equal share in the management and profits. In 1958 they formed a private company to take the business over. E. and N. were the first directors and each held 500 £1 shares. The articles provided that shares could not be transferred without the directors' consent. Later, N.'s son, G., was appointed a director and E. and N. each transferred 100 shares to him. The company made good

---

[56] *Re Haven Gold Mining Co.* (1882) 20 Ch.D. 151 (C.A.).
[57] *Re Medical Battery Co.* [1894] 1 Ch. 444.
[58] *Re International Securities Corpn. (Ltd.)* (1908) 24 T.L.R. 837; 25 T.L.R. 31 (C.A.).

profits which were all distributed by way of directors' remuneration, *i.e.* no dividends were paid. After a disagreement between E. and N., with whom G. sided, N. and G. at a general meeting removed E. as director by ordinary resolution under section 184, and thereafter excluded him from the conduct of the company's business. E. petitioned for an order under section 222(*f*) that the company be wound up on the ground that it was just and equitable. *Held,* (by the House of Lords) that it was just and equitable that the company be wound up. After a long association in partnership, during which he had had an equal share in the management and profits, E. had joined in the formation of the company; the inference was indisputable that he and N. had done so on the basis that the character of the association would, as a matter of personal faith, remain the same; and E. had established that N. and G. were not entitled, in justice and equity, to make use of their legal powers of expulsion. Furthermore E. was unable to dispose of his interest in the company without the consent of N. and G.: *Re Westbourne Galleries Ltd.* [1973] A.C. 360.

Per Lord Wilberforce at pp. 374, 375: "... there has been a tendency to create categories or headings under which cases must be brought if the [just and equitable] clause is to apply. This is wrong. Illustrations may arise but general words should remain general and not be reduced to the sum of particular instances."

And at p. 379: "The words [just and equitable] are a recognition of the fact that a limited company is more than a mere legal entity, with a personality in law of its own: that there is room in company law for recognition of the fact that behind it, or amongst it, there are individuals, with rights, expectations and obligations inter se which are not necessarily submerged in the company structure. That structure is defined by the Companies Act and by the articles of association by which shareholders agree to be bound. In most companies and in most contexts, this definition is sufficient and exhaustive, equally so whether the company is large or small. The 'just and equitable' provision does not . . . entitle one party to disregard the obligation he assumes by entering a company, nor the court to dispense him from it. It does, as equity always does, enable the court to subject the exercise of legal rights to equitable considerations; considerations, that is, of a personal character arising between one individual and another, which may make it unjust, or inequitable, to insist on legal rights, or to exercise them in a particular way.

It would be impossible, and wholly undesirable, to define the circumstances in which these considerations may arise. Certainly the fact that the company is a small one, or a private company, is not enough. There are very many of these where the association is a purely commercial one, of which it can safely be said that the basis of association is adequately and exhaustively laid down in the articles. The superimposition of equitable considerations requires something more [than the fact that the company is a small one, or a private company], which typically may include one, or probably more, of the following elements: (i) an association formed or continued on the basis of a personal relationship, involving mutual confidence—this element will often be found where a pre-existing partnership has been converted into a limited company; (ii) an agreement, or understanding, that all, or some (for there may be 'sleeping members'), of the shareholders shall participate in the conduct of the business; (iii) restriction on the transfer of the members' interest in the company—so that if confidence is lost, or one member removed from management, he cannot take out his stake and go elsewhere."

Re Westbourne Galleries was applied in *Re A. & B.C. Chewing Gum Ltd.* [1975] 1 W.L.R. 579, where the petitioners held one-third of the company's shares on the basis that they should have equal control with the two individual respondents, who were brothers and directors of the company and owned the other two-thirds of the shares. To achieve equality of control, the articles were altered so as to provide, *inter alia,* that the petitioners could appoint and remove a director representing them, and that decisions at board meetings should be unanimous. The petitioners, the respondents and the company also signed and sealed a shareholders' agreement setting out the way in which the day to day business was to be conducted. The respondents refused to recognise the petitioner's removal of their director and the appointment of another in his place. This was not a case of one side making use of its legal rights to the prejudice of another—the petitioners were excluded from their legal and contractual rights. Their right to management participation was repudiated.

Weinberg and Rothman were the sole shareholders in and directors of a company, with equal rights of management and voting power. After a time they became bitterly hostile to one another and disagreed about the appointment of important servants of the company. All communications between them were made through the secretary. The company made large profits in spite of the disagreement. *Held,* mutual confidence had been lost between W. and R. and the company should be wound up: *Re Yenidje Tobacco Co. Ltd.* [1916] 2 Ch. 426 (C.A.).

A family company was formed to carry on a testator's business and to divide the profits among his family entitled under his will to share them. The managing director, who had a preponderating voting power, omitted to hold general meetings, submit accounts or recommend dividends, and laid himself open to the suspicion that his object in so doing was to acquire the minority's shares at an undervalue. *Held,* the company should be wound up. Confidence in the management was, justifiably, at an end: *Loch* v. *John Blackwood Ltd.* [1924] A.C. 783 (P.C.).[59]

Whether it is just and equitable to wind up a company depends on facts which exist at the time of the hearing and a petitioner is confined to heads of complaint set out in his petition.[60]

A shareholder is not entitled to a winding-up order on the "just and equitable" ground if his object is not a company purpose but the

---

[59] And see *Re Wondoflex Textiles Pty. Ltd.* [1951] V.L.R. 458. Scottish cases are *Symington* v. *Symingtons' Quarries Ltd.* (1905) 8 F. 121, *Thomson* v. *Drysdale,* 1925 S.C. 311, *Baird* v. *Lees,* 1924 S.C. 83 and *Lewis* v. *Haas,* 1971 S.L.T. 57 (O.H.).

[60] *Re Fildes Bros. Ltd.* [1970] 1 All E.R. 923.

securing for himself of an advantage in a question between himself and other shareholders.[61]

If, in the case of a contributories' petition, the court is of opinion that it is just and equitable that the company should be wound up and some other remedy, *e.g.* an injunction, or the removal from office of a director guilty of mismanagement, or an order under section 75 of the 1980 Act, *post,* is available to the petitioners, the court *must* make a winding-up order unless it is of the opinion that the petitioners are acting unreasonably in not pursuing the other remedy: section 225(2). The Jenkins Report[62] recommended that this provision be amended so as to remove the limitations on the court's discretion.

Alternative remedy for unfairly prejudicial conduct

Section 210 of the 1948 Act, now repealed and replaced by section 75 of the 1980 Act, provided that any member who complained that the affairs of the company were being conducted in a manner oppressive to some part of the members, including himself, could petition for an order under that section.

That section however suffered from several drawbacks. It required proof of oppression sufficient to justify putting the company into liquidation. This oppression had to be continuous.[63] The conduct had to be "a visible departure from the standards of fair dealing"[64] or "burdensome, harsh and wrongful."[65] Future oppression could not be anticipated.[66] In addition only one of three remedies could be sought and this had to be specified in advance, in the petition. Economic oppression and oppressive conduct of affairs were held to justify a petition:

An 88 years old controlling shareholder and his wife had the majority of the shares carrying a right to vote but the minority of a different class of shares carrying a right to share in the distributed profits of a private company. The majority of the latter class of shares were held by his sons, whose shares he had given to them. The controlling shareholder, who had founded the company and transferred his business to it, continued to regard the business as his own

---

[61] *Anglo-American Brush etc. Corpn. Ltd.* v. *Scottish Brush etc. Co. Ltd.* (1882) 9 R. 972.

[62] Para. 503(*i*).

[63] *Re Jermyn Street Turkish Baths Ltd.* [1971] 1 W.L.R. 1042 (C.A.).

[64] *Elder* v. *Elder and Watson*, 1952 S.C. 49, 55.

[65] *Meyer* v. *Scottish C.W.S. Ltd.*, 1958 S.C. (H.L.) 40, 47; [1959] A.C. 324, 342.

[66] *Re Five Minute Car Wash Service Ltd.* [1966] 1 W.L.R. 745.

and ignored the wishes of the other shareholders and of his co-directors, including the petitioners, his sons. Viscount Simonds' definition of "oppressive" as meaning "burdensome, harsh and wrongful" in *Meyer's* case[67] was adopted, and an order was made under section 210 that the controlling shareholder was not to interfere in the company's affairs except in accordance with board decisions: *Re H. R. Harmer Ltd.*[68]

A holding company, engaged in the same class of business as its subsidiary which had an independent minority of members, ruined the subsidiary in the interests of the holding company and its controllers by cutting off supplies. Three of the subsidiary's directors were nominated by, and were also directors of the holding company. These nominee directors actively supported the policy of the holding company. The minority shareholders of the subsidiary petitioned for an order that the holding company should purchase their £1 shares. At one time the shares had been worth £6 but by the time of the action they were practically worthless. *Held*, the conduct of the holding company through the nominee directors was conduct of the affairs of the subsidiary and was oppressive to the minority. The order made under section 210 was that the holding company buy the minority's shares at a fair price, namely £3 15s. per share: *Meyer* v. *Scottish C.W.S. Ltd.*[69]

"Whenever a subsidiary is formed . . . with an independent minority of shareholders, the parent company must, if it is engaged in the same class of business, accept . . . an obligation so to conduct what are in a sense its own affairs as to deal fairly with its subsidiary": *per* Viscount Simonds (p. 48) and Lord Keith (p. 63).

But allegations of negligence did not suffice.[70]

Above all the section was too closely allied to the rules regulating liquidation. Accordingly it was repealed[71] and replaced by section 75 of the 1980 Act.[72]

Under this new section any member[73] of the company can petition the court for an order under the section on the ground that the affairs of a company are being or have been conducted in a manner which is unfairly prejudicial to the interests of some part of the members (including at least himself) or that any actual or proposed act or omission of the company (including an act or omission on its behalf) is or would be so prejudicial.[74]

Thus the alleged conduct may be past, present or future. It may be by an act or omission and by an agent (*e.g.* the directors). There is no definition of what is "unfairly prejudicial" conduct. It is clearly wider

---

[67] At 1958 S.C. (H.L.) p. 47 [1959] A.C. 324 at p. 342.
[68] [1959] 1 W.L.R. 62 (C.A.). [69] [1959] A.C. 324.
[70] *Re Five Minute Car Wash, etc., ante.* [71] 1980 Act, s.75(11).
[72] For details of section 210, see previous editions of this work.
[73] A creditor cannot petition under section 75. [74] 1980 Act, s.75(1).

than oppression and is no longer allied to the rules for winding-up so that there is no compelling reason for the courts to insist that such conduct must be continuous.[75] It will not be enough to show that the conduct is prejudicial to the petitioner, it must be unfair as well. Perhaps the nearest guideline can be found in the court's approach to the doctrine of a fraud on the minority. As we have seen[76] in so far as the general law is concerned the majority are not liable if they injure a minority of shareholders provided that they are acting bona fide for the benefit of the company as a whole.[77] This has, however, been subject to doubt in other areas[78] and is suggested here only as one possible guide in the approach to section 75 of the 1980 Act as to the meaning of unfairly prejudicial. In *Re A Company* (*No.* 004475 *of* 1982) [1983] 2 W.L.R. 381, it was argued, but not decided, that unfairly prejudicial conduct would only found a petition if it could be said to have affected the value of the petitioner's shareholding.

In *Re Carrington Viyella plc, Financial Times*, February 16, 1983, Vinelott J. decided that the breach of an undertaking given by I.C.I. to the Government not to vote with more than 35 per cent. of the CV shares (they in fact owned over 49 per cent.) did not amount to unfairly prejudicial conduct, either because such undertakings did not form part of the inter-shareholder relationship, or there was no evidence of any other breach by I.C.I. He also rejected a claim that the non-reference of the chairman's contract to the general meeting of CV fell within the section. Although section 47 of the 1980 Act requires such approval, mere misfeasance did not amount to unfairly prejudicial conduct. This case shows a disturbing tendency to limit section 75 along the lines of its predecessor.

If the court is satisfied it may make such order as it thinks fit.[79] No specific request need be made in advance.[80] However, the section provides five possible orders which the court may make[81]:

(1) An order regulating the affairs of the company in the future[82];
(2) An order to restrain the doing or continuing of an act or to rectify an omission[83];

---

[75] *cf. ante*, p. 409. [76] *Ante*, p. 394.
[77] *Allen* v. *Gold Reefs of W. Africa Ltd.* [1900] 1 Ch. 656, *ante*, p. 109.
[78] *Estmanco* (*Kilner House*) *Ltd.* v. *G.L.C.* [1982] 1 All E.R. 437, *ante*, p. 395.
[79] 1980 Act, s.75(3).
[80] *cf. ante*, p. 413. [81] 1980 Act, s.75(4).
[82] This order could be made under s.210 and was in *Re H. R. Harmer Ltd.*, *ante*.
[83] This was new.

(3) An order authorising civil proceedings to be brought in the name and on behalf of the company by such persons and on such terms as the court may direct[84];

(4) An order providing for the majority to buy out the minority[85] or a purchase of the minority's shares by the company itself.[86] In the latter case it will arrange for the reduction of capital accordingly;

(5) An order altering the company's memorandum or articles. This will have automatic effect without any resolution of the company usually required for such alterations.[87] Such alterations may not be re-altered without the court's consent.[88]

In addition to petitions by members, the Secretary of State (for Trade) may bring a petition following an investigation[89] if he thinks that the criteria have been met.[90] Further, personal representatives and trustees in bankruptcy may petition under the section without being registered as members.[91] A copy of any order requiring a company to alter its memorandum or articles must be filed with the registrar within 14 days.[92] Much is expected of this new section. It still, however, requires a member to suffer in that capacity.

In the first case decided on section 75, the court refused to grant a petition to shareholders who were executors of a will for infant children, and who wished to sell the shares to release funds for the beneficiaries. The company was a private company with a power to refuse transfer of the shares given to the directors. The directors refused to allow the shares to be sold. *Held*, this omission of the directors did not affect the petitioners as shareholders but as executors. In effect therefore they were "locked in" the company: *Re A Company (No. 004475 of 1982)* [1983] 2 W.L.R. 381.

Misfeasance proceedings in a winding up

Section 333 provides that if in a winding up it appears that any promoter, past or present director, manager or liquidator, or any

---

[84] This was new and may alleviate the rule in *Foss* v. *Harbottle, ante.*

[85] As happened in *Meyer* v. *Scottish C.W.S. Ltd., ante.* It may be that the problem of fixing a valuation on the share will be re-opened now. Before, the value was that after the oppression.

[86] Following the 1981 Act provisions. This is an exception to s.35 of the 1980 Act, *ante*, p. 243.

[87] 1980 Act, s.75(6).   [88] *Ibid.* s.75(5).   [89] *Post*, p. 419.

[90] 1980 Act, s.75(2).   [91] *Ibid.* s.75(9).   [92] *Ibid.* s.75(7).

officer of the company, has misapplied or retained or become liable or accountable for any money or property of the company, or been guilty of any misfeasance or breach of trust in relation to the company, the court may, on the application of the Official Receiver,[92a] the liquidator or any creditor or contributory,[93] examine the conduct of such promoter, director, manager, liquidator or officer, and order him to repay or restore the money or property with interest, or to contribute to the assets of the company such sum as the court thinks just. Although "misfeasance" is not a Scots law term, the section does apply to Scotland.

The section is procedural only. It gives a summary remedy, not a new cause of action.[94] It has been said that it "does not create any new liability, any new right, but only provides a summary mode of enforcing rights which must otherwise have been enforced by the ordinary procedure of the Courts." Also, that the applicant "must shew something which would have been the ground of an action by the company if it had not been wound up." Further, that the word "misfeasance" in the section means "misfeasance in the nature of a breach of trust, that is to say, it refers to something which the officer . . . has done wrongly by misapplying or retaining in his own hands any moneys of the company, or by which the company's property has been wasted, or the company's credit improperly pledged. It must be some act resulting in some actual loss to the company."[95]

It follows that section 333 is not available in all cases in which the company has a right of action against an officer of the company. It is not available where a company has a right of action against an officer for common law negligence[96]—in this case an ordinary action must be brought.

A misfeasance summons[97] was taken out by the liquidator against the secretary of a company for sums overdrawn by him on account of his salary on

---

[92a] Not applicable to Scotland.   [93] *Ante*, p. 408.

[94] *Coventry and Dixon's Case* (1880) 14 Ch.D. 660 (C.A.). See Lord President Inglis in *Liquidators of City of Glasgow Bank* v. *Mackinnon* (1881) 9 R. 535, at p. 564, and Lord Guest (Ordinary) in *Lord Advocate* v. *Liquidators of Purvis Industries Ltd.*, 1958 S.C. 338 (O.H.), at p. 342.

[95] *Per* James L.J. in *Coventry and Dixon's Case*, at p. 670.

[96] *Re B. Johnson & Co. (Builders) Ltd.* [1955] Ch. 634 (C.A.); *per* Mason J. (Barwick C.J. concurring) in *Walker* v. *Wimborne* (1976) 50 A.L.J.R. 446.

[97] In Scotland the application to the court would take the form of a note in the petition process (compulsory winding up) or of a petition (voluntary winding up): R.C. 215.

the instructions of the managing director. *Held,* as this was a claim for repayment of an ordinary debt due from the secretary without any wrongful conduct on his part, no order on the summons ought to be made: *Re Etic Ltd.* [1928] Ch. 861.

Section 333 "is limited to cases where there has been something in the nature of a breach of duty by an officer of the company as such which has caused pecuniary loss to the company. Breach of duty of course would include a misfeasance or a breach of trust in the stricter sense, and the section will apply to a true case of misapplication of money or property of the company, or a case where there has been retention of money or property which the officer was bound to have paid or returned to the company": *per* Maugham J. at p. 875.

In England a receiver and manager appointed by a debenture holder has been held not to be a person whose conduct can be examined under the section.[98] He is not an "officer" of the company within section 455 because any work of management he might do is not done by virtue of any office which he holds in the company; nor is he a "manager" of the company because he is managing, not on behalf of the company, but on behalf of the debenture holders.

The Jenkins Report[99] recommended that section 333 be amended to deal with actionable negligence by directors and others, and to bring within its scope a receiver of any property of the company.

Instances of misfeasance are the improper receipt by a director of his qualification shares from a promoter,[1] or of an *ex gratia* payment in lieu of pension on the eve of liquidation,[1a] the certifying by an auditor of erroneous accounts whereby dividends were paid out of capital,[2] the receipt by the secretary of a secret profit from a person who sold a mine to the company,[3] the acts of a director in procuring the company to buy shares in another company from himself at an over-value, and making an unsecured loan to enable him and his co-directors to pay calls[4] and failure by a liquidator to make proper provision for the equal ranking and payment of all preferential claims.[5]

---

[98] See footnote 96.

[99] Para. 503.

[1] Which occurred in *Eden* v. *Ridsdales Railway Lamp Co. Ltd.* (1889) 23 Q.B.D. 368 (C.A.).

[1a] *Gibson's Executor* v. *Gibson,* 1978 S.C. 197 (O.H.).

[2] See *Re Kingston Cotton Mill Co.* (*No.* 2) [1896] 2 Ch. 279 (C.A.), *post,* p. 526.

[3] *McKay's Case* (1875) 2 Ch.D. 1 (C.A.).

[4] *Re V. G. M. Holdings Ltd.* [1942] Ch. 235 (C.A.).

[5] *Lord Advocate* v. *Liquidators of Purvis Industries Ltd.,* 1958 S.C. 338 (O.H.), *post,* p. 664.

No set-off is allowed to a claim for misfeasance.[6]

The court has a discretion as to the amount to be ordered to be paid on an application under section 333.

A liquidator negligently admitted a proof, which he should have disallowed, and as a result the company paid £38,000 to a creditor. An attempt to recover this failed, as there was no mistake of fact on the liquidator's part. *Held,* the liquidator was liable for misfeasance, but the court, in the exercise of its discretion, ordered him to pay only such a sum as would enable the creditors to be paid in full with interest at five per cent.: *Re Home and Colonial Insce. Co. Ltd.* [1930] 1 Ch. 102.

Further, the court's power under the section is not merely to specify a sum by way of compensation but to apportion it between co-defendants in such a way and with such priority of liability as the court thinks fit.[7]

Inspection

Statutory provision is made for a number of forms of inspection. These comprise investigation of a company's affairs, investigation of the ownership of a company, investigation of share dealings, and inspection of companies' books and papers.

Investigation of a Company's Affairs[8]

Appointment of inspectors

1. In the case of a company with a share capital, *on the application of not less than 200 members or of members holding not less than one-tenth of the shares issued, or on the application of the company,* the Department of Trade *may* appoint one or more inspectors to investigate the affairs of the company and to report on them. The application must be supported by evidence showing that the applicant or applicants have good reason for requiring the investigation. Security, not exceeding £5,000, for the costs of the inquiry, may be required by the Department of Trade: section 164, as amended by section 86 of the 1981 Act.

---

[6] *Ex p. Pelly* (1882) 21 Ch.D. 492 (C.A.).
[7] *Re Morecambe Bowling Ltd.* [1969] 1 W.L.R. 133.
[8] *e.g.* the investigation, by Mr. E. Milner Holland Q.C., of the affairs of the Savoy Hotel Limited, *post,* p. 427.

An inspector is usually a Queen's Counsel, a Chartered Accountant or an official of the Department of Trade.

2. The Department *must* appoint an inspector or inspectors *if the court by order,*[9] *declares that an investigation ought to be made:* section 165(*a*), as amended by section 86 of the 1981 Act.

In certain circumstances the transactions of a receiver and manager of the property of a company appointed by a debenture holder are affairs of the company within section 165(*a*).[10]

The Jenkins Report[11] recommended that section 164 be repealed and section 165(*a*) extended, *e.g.* so as to require the appointment of an inspector when over two hundred members or holders of one-quarter or more of the issued shares of any class request it, unless sufficient facts are known to the applicants to enable them to assert their rights on their own behalf. The 1981 Act amendments, however, made it more difficult for applicants to gain the appointment of inspectors.[12]

3. The Department *may, on their own initiative,* appoint inspectors if it appears—

(i) that a company's affairs are being or have been conducted with intent to defraud its creditors or the creditors of any other person or otherwise for a fraudulent or unlawful purpose or in a manner which is unfairly prejudicial to part of its members, or that any actual or proposed act or omission of the company is or would be so prejudicial or that it was formed for a fraudulent or unlawful purpose; or

(ii) that the promoters or the persons managing its affairs have been guilty of fraud, misfeasance or other misconduct towards the company or its members; or

(iii) that the members have not been given all the information as to the company's affairs which they might reasonably expect: section 165(*b*), as amended by 1981 Act, Sched. 3.

---

[9] The procedure in England is to apply to the Companies Court by originating motion under R.S.C., O. 102, r.4. For Scotland, see R.C. 190.

[10] *R.* v. *B.o.T., ex p. St. Martins Preserving Co. Ltd.* [1965] 1 Q.B. 603, where, since the company by special resolution had declared that such transactions ought to be investigated, the Board of Trade (now the Department of Trade) had to appoint an inspector.

[11] Para. 218.

[12] *e.g.* by increasing the security required.

If the Department appoints inspectors under these headings the company has no right to state its case before the inspectors are appointed. The only requirement is that the decision to appoint is made in good faith.[13]

Powers of inspectors

1. An inspector may, if he thinks it necessary, investigate any other body corporate which is or has been a related company, *i.e.* the company's subsidiary[14] or holding company[14] or a subsidiary of its holding company or a holding company of its subsidiary: section 166.

2. He may call for the production of documents by past or present officers and agents (including bankers, solicitors and auditors) of the company or related company, whose duty it is to produce to the inspector all books and documents of or relating to the company or related company which are in their custody or power, to attend before the inspector when required[15] and to give the inspector all reasonable assistance. This power extends to persons other than officers or agents if the inspectors consider that they are or may be in possession of any information concerning the company's affairs.

Further, if an inspector has reasonable grounds to believe that a director or past director has a bank account into which has been paid his undisclosed emoluments[16] or money used for a disclosable but undisclosed transaction between him and the company[17] or used in any way as part of the misconduct of that director, whether fraudulent or not, the inspector may require production of all documents under his control or in his possession in relation to that account: section 167, as amended by section 87 of the 1981 Act. If an officer or agent refuses to perform his duties under section 167, the court may punish him as if he were in contempt of court.

A solicitor or barrister need not disclose a privileged communication made to him, except as regards the name and address of his client, and a banker need not disclose the affairs of his customers other than the company: section 175, as amended by section 103 of the 1981 Act.

[13] *Norwest Holst Ltd.* v. *Department of Trade* [1978] 3 All E.R. 280.
[14] *Ante*, p. 52.
[15] Companies Act 1967, s.39.
[16] 1967 Act, s.6.
[17] 1980 Act, ss.54, 56 or 67.

3. The inspector may examine on oath any person from whom documents can be called in relation to the company's business: section 167, as amended by section 87 of the 1981 Act.

An answer given by a person to a question put under powers given by section 167 of the 1948 Act (or section 32 of the 1967 Act or rules made under section 365(1) of the 1948 Act) may be used in evidence against him (and a statement of the company's affairs, which by section 235 of the 1948 Act must be submitted to the Official Receiver in an English winding up, may be used in evidence against any person making or concurring in it): 1967 Act, s.50.

In general all evidence given to an inspector is admissible against him in both subsequent criminal and civil proceedings. This includes unsworn evidence. Section 50 of the 1967 Act is not limited to public interest proceedings brought by a public authority. Thus the section permits the evidence to be used in subsequent proceedings by the company or its liquidator to redress wrongs done to the company, *e.g.* against the company's auditors.[18]

4. The inspector may at any time during his investigation, without making an interim report, inform the Department of Trade of matters tending to show that an offence has been committed: 1967 Act, s.41.

It has been held that the inspectors' function is investigatory and not judicial but they must, in view of the consequences which may follow from their report, act fairly and, before they condemn or criticise a man, give him a fair opportunity to answer what is alleged against him.[19] It is sufficient for the inspectors to put to witnesses what has been said against them by other persons or in documents to enable them to deal with those criticisms in the course of the inquiry; it is not necessary for the inspectors to put their tentative conclusions to the witnesses in order to give them an opportunity to refute them.[20]

It has been said[21] that the considerations which are to be borne in mind in respect of an inquiry under the Companies Acts are:

[18] *London and County Securities Ltd.* v. *Nicholson* [1980] 3 All E.R. 861.
[19] *Re Pergamon Press Ltd.* [1971] Ch. 388 (C.A.), where the persons who were required to give evidence were not entitled to see the transcripts of evidence of witnesses. In *Testro Bros. Pty. Ltd.* v. *Tait* (1963) 109 C.L.R. 353, the majority of the High Court of Australia held that the inspector need not, before making a report on the company's affairs, give the company an opportunity of answering or explaining matters which, if unanswered or unexplained, might give rise to adverse findings or comment in the report.
[20] *Maxwell* v. *Department of Trade and Industry* [1974] 1 Q.B. 523 (C.A.).
[21] *Per* Lord Denning M.R. in *Maxwell's* case, *ante,* at p. 533.

(*a*) It is a very special kind of inquiry. It is not a trial. There is no accused, no prosecutor, no charge. It is simply an investigation.

(*b*) There is no one to present a case to the inspector. There is no "counsel for the Commission." The inspector has to do it all himself.

(*c*) The investigation is in private. This is necessary because witnesses may say something defamatory of someone else, and it would be quite wrong for it to be published without the party affected being able to challenge it.

(*d*) The inspectors have to make their report. They should state their findings on the evidence and their opinions on the matters referred to them. They should make it with courage and frankness, keeping nothing back. Before they condemn or criticise a man they must act fairly by him.

Inspectors' report

The inspectors may make interim reports, and on the conclusion of the investigation they must make a final report to the Department of Trade.

The Department of Trade may send a copy of a report to the company's registered office, and if the Department think fit, they may furnish a copy on request and on payment of the prescribed fee to any member of the company or other company dealt with in the report, or to any person whose conduct is referred to in the report, or to the auditors of the company, or to the applicants for the investigation, or to any other person whose financial interests appear to be affected by it, *e.g.* creditors. Where the appointment was under section 165 in pursuance of a court order, a copy *must* be furnished to the court: section 168, as amended by section 88 of the 1981 Act.

Proceedings on inspectors' report

Section 35 of the 1967 Act, as amended by Schedule 3 to the 1976 Act, provides that if it appears to the Department of Trade from the inspectors' report, or from any information or document obtained under Part III of the 1967 Act,[22] that it is expedient in the public interest that the company be wound up, the Department may present a

---

[22] *Post*, p. 428.

petition that it be wound up by the court if the court thinks it just and equitable that the company be wound up[23]: subsection (1). No evidence of fraud or misfeasance is necessary.

The affidavit verifying the petition should describe the position of the relevant officer in the Department, depose that he is entrusted with the section 35 power and explain that it appears to him to be expedient in the public interest that the company should be wound up.[24]

In addition a minority shareholder may use an inspector's report to support his own petition to wind up the company on the just and equitable ground under section 222(*f*).[25]

If from the report, etc., it appears that civil proceedings ought in the public interest to be brought by any company, section 37 of the 1967 Act empowers the Department to bring such proceedings in the name and on behalf of the company. The Department must indemnify the company against costs or expenses incurred by it in connection with any such proceedings. If civil proceedings are properly brought under this section and there is no evidence to show that the company will be able to pay the defendant's costs if the defence is successful, the defendant is fully protected by the indemnity provision in the section and security cannot be ordered under section 447 of the 1948 Act.[26]

Under section 75 of the 1980 Act the Department may bring a petition under that section consequent on a report.[27]

Expenses of investigation

The expenses of an investigation of a company's affairs are defrayed in the first instance by the Department of Trade but the following persons are liable to repay the Department:—

(1) Any person convicted on a prosecution instituted as a result of the investigation, or ordered to pay the costs of proceedings brought by virtue of section 37 of the 1967 Act, *ante,* may in the same proceedings be ordered to repay.

(2) Any company in whose name proceedings are brought is liable to repay to the extent of money or property recovered by it as a result of the proceedings.

[23] *Ante,* p. 384.
[24] *Re Golden Chemical Products Ltd.* [1976] Ch.D. 300.
[25] *Re St. Piran Ltd.* [1981] 3 All E.R. 270.
[26] *Selangor United Rubber Estates Ltd.* v. *Cradock* [1967] 1 W.L.R. 1168.
[27] *Ante,* p. 413.

(3) A company dealt with by the inspectors' report, where the inspectors were appointed otherwise than of the Department's own motion and except where it was the applicant, is liable except so far as the Department otherwise direct.

(4) The applicant for the investigation, where the inspector was appointed under section 164 of the 1948 Act, *ante,* is liable to such extent as the Department may direct: 1948 Act, s.170 as amended by 1967 Act, ss.36, 40, 1981 Act, Sched. 3.

Extension of Department of Trade's powers of investigation

Sections 165 to 171 and 175 of the 1948 Act now apply to all companies incorporated outside Great Britain which are carrying on business in Great Britain or have at any time carried on business therein, subject to any adaptations the Department of Trade may specify by statutory instrument: 1967 Act, s.42.

Investigation of the Ownership of a Company[28]

Appointment of inspectors

1. *Where they consider that there is good reason to do so,* the Department of Trade *may* appoint one or more inspectors to investigate and report on the membership of a company, for the purpose of determining the true persons who are, or have been, financially interested in the success or failure of the company, or able to control or materially influence its policy: section 172(1). The scope of the investigation may be defined either as to time or the matters to be investigated: section 172(2).

2. Unless the application is vexatious, the Department *must* appoint an inspector, *on the application,* with regard to particular shares or debentures, *of those members who can apply under section 164*[29] for an investigation of the company's affairs and the appointment shall not exclude from the scope of the investigation any matter stated by the applicants unless the Department are satisfied that it would be unreasonable to investigate it: section 172(3), as amended by 1981 Act, Sched. 3.

---

[28] *e.g.* the investigation, by Mr. J. B. Lindon Q.C., of the membership of the Savoy Hotel Limited, *post,* p. 427.

[29] *Ante,* p. 419.

Powers of inspectors. Inspectors' report

An inspector appointed under section 172, above, has the same power as an inspector appointed to investigate the affairs of a company has under sections 166 and 167 except for the provisions relating to directors' bank accounts; section 168 applies to the report of inspectors appointed under section 172.[30]

In addition, the sections apply in relation to all persons whom the inspector reasonably believes to be or to have been financially interested in the success or failure of the company or related company, or able to control or materially influence its policy. However, the Department of Trade may furnish the company or any person with an abbreviated copy of the report if they believe that there is good reason for not divulging part of it: section 172(5), as amended by section 89 of the 1981 Act.

Expenses of investigation

The expenses of an investigation under section 172 are defrayed by the Department of Trade out of money provided by Parliament: section 172(6).

Power to require information as to persons interested in shares, etc.

Where it appears that there is good reason to investigate the ownership of any shares or debentures of a company, and that it is unnecessary to appoint an inspector for the purpose, the Department of Trade may require any person whom they reasonably believe to have or to be able to obtain any information as to the present and past interests in the shares or debentures and the names and addresses of the persons interested therein and of any persons who act or have acted for them in relation to the shares or debentures to give them such information.

A person is deemed to have an interest in a share or debenture if he has a right to acquire or dispose of it or any interest therein, or to vote in respect thereof, or if his consent is necessary for the exercise of any right of other persons interested therein, or if such other persons can be required or are accustomed to exercise their rights in accordance with his instructions.

---

[30] *Ante*, pp. 421 *et seq.*

Failure to give information required under this section, or making a statement known to be false in a material particular, or recklessly making a statement false in a material particular, is punishable by six months' imprisonment or a fine or both: section 173, as amended by section 90 of the 1981 Act.

Power to impose restrictions on shares, etc.

If the Department of Trade have difficulty in finding out the relevant facts about any shares or debentures, they may direct that the shares or debentures shall be subject to restrictions. The restrictions prevent transfers and agreements to transfer, the exercise of voting rights, the issue of further shares or debentures in right of the shares or debentures or to the holder thereof, including an agreement to transfer such rights, and, except in a liquidation, payment, or agreement to transfer payment of any sums due from the company on the shares or debentures, whether in respect of capital or otherwise, *e.g.* payment of a dividend.[31]

If an order is made any person aggrieved may appeal to the court for the order to be lifted. The court may only lift an order if it is satisfied either that all the relevant facts about the shares have been disclosed and that no unfair advantage has accrued to anyone by the earlier failure to disclose or the shares are to be sold and the court approves the sale.

Where an order has been made either the Department or the company may apply to the court for a further order that the shares be compulsorily sold free from some or all of the restrictions. The proceeds of a compulsory sale are to be paid into a separate fund against which the owners can claim, subject to the payment of costs.

Contravention of such restrictions renders the person or company concerned liable to penalties, although a prosecution in England can be instituted only by or with the consent of the Department of Trade: section 174, as amended by section 91 of the 1981 Act.

The Savoy Hotel Investigations

In 1953 there was heavy buying of Savoy Hotel stock on the Stock Exchange. The real buyers were unknown since the buying was through nominees. The

---

[31] This includes payment on a take-over bid: *Re Ashbourne Investments Ltd.* [1978] 2 All E.R. 418.

object of the buyers was to obtain control of the Savoy Hotel Limited and develop its assets. 224 members of the company applied to the Board of Trade under sections 172 and 173 and Mr. J.B. Lindon Q.C. was appointed to investigate the ownership of the company. From the inspector's interim report,[32] it appeared that Land Securities Investment Trust Limited, of which Mr. Harold Samuel was chairman and principal shareholder, had bought Savoy stock carrying 20 per cent. of the votes on a poll at a general meeting of Savoy Hotel Limited, and Princes Investments Limited, controlled by Mr. Charles Clore, had bought stock carrying nine per cent. of the votes.

The Berkeley Hotel Company Limited was a subsidiary of the Savoy Company, with substantially the same directors, and it would have been possible to make a large immediate profit by turning the Berkeley Hotel into offices. To put the Berkeley Hotel out of the reach of anyone who might obtain control of the Savoy Company, the Savoy directors formed Worcester Buildings Company Limited and sold the Berkeley Hotel to the Worcester Company at a price satisfied by the issue to the Berkeley Company of fully paid preference shares in the Worcester Company. The Worcester Company gave the Berkeley Company a lease of the hotel for 50 years at a rent. The hotel could not be used otherwise than as a hotel without the consent of the Worcester Company. However, the Worcester Company was controlled by a number of ordinary shares of small nominal amount which were issued for cash to the trustees of the Savoy Company's benevolent fund. The cash was provided from the fund, which had been transferred to the trustees. The Board of Trade, under section 165(*b*), appointed Mr. E. Milner Holland Q.C. to investigate the affairs of the Savoy Company. His report[33] stated that, on the analogy of *Piercy* v. *Mills & Co.*,[34] the transaction was an invalid use of the powers of management of the Savoy directors, even though they thought they were acting for the benefit of the companies and their shareholders, and even though they had legal advice that they could act as they did. The purpose of the transaction was to deny to the majority holding voting control of the Savoy Company the power, by the exercise of that control, to cause the Berkeley Hotel to be used otherwise than as a hotel.

Investigation of Share Dealings

The 1967 Act, section 32, provides that if it appears to the Department of Trade that sections 25[35] or 27[36] or 31(2)[37] of the 1967 Act (these sections being concerned with penalisation of dealing in options by,

---

[32] Dated November 28, 1953, and published by H.M.S.O.
[33] Dated June 14, 1954, and published by H.M.S.O.
[34] [1920] 1 Ch. 77, *ante*, p. 368.
[35] *Ante*, p. 342.
[36] *Ante*, p. 337.
[37] *Ante*, p. 340.

and notification of interests of, directors or their spouses or children) may have been contravened, they may appoint one or more competent inspectors to investigate and report to them.

Section 167[38] of the 1948 Act, which imposes on officers and agents the duty to assist inspectors, applies with one or two modifications. Thus section 32 applies, *e.g.* to members of a recognised stock exchange or of an association of dealers in securities who are individuals and to officers (past and present) of members who are companies.

Section 175[39] of the 1948 Act (savings for lawyers and bankers) applies.

The expenses of an investigation under section 32 are defrayed by the Department of Trade.

Inspection of a Company's Books and Papers

This is dealt with in Part III (sections 109 to 118) of the 1967 Act as follows—

Power of Department of Trade to require production of documents

Section 109 of the 1967 Act provides that the Department of Trade may, if they think there is good reason to do so, require certain companies, including a company formed and registered under the 1948 Act and a company incorporated outside Great Britain which is carrying on or has carried on business in Great Britain, to produce such books or papers (including accounts, deeds, writings and documents: section 117) as may be specified.

This section gives effect to a recommendation of the Jenkins Committee and is intended to make it easier for the Department of Trade to decide when an inspection of a company's affairs is justified.[40] The Department will be less likely to be inhibited from appointing inspectors by fear of causing unnecessary damage to a company. Further, the Department can now test the complainants' Statement of Facts without necessarily revealing to the directors the case against them and without the delays sometimes involved in awaiting the directors' reply.[41]

---

[38] *Ante*, p. 421.
[39] *Ante*, p. 421.
[40] *Ante*, p. 419.
[41] Cmnd. 1749, paras. 215, 218.

Without prejudice to any lien he may have, production of documents may be required from any person who appears to be in possession of them. Copies or extracts may be taken, and explanations may be required from such person or from present or past officers or employees of the company. If the documents are not produced, the person required to produce may be required to state, to the best of his knowledge and belief, where they are: section 109.

Nothing in Part III compels a lawyer to produce a document containing a privileged communication made by or to him: section 116.

Non-compliance with a requirement to produce documents or provide an explanation or make a statement renders the company or person concerned liable to three months' imprisonment or a fine or both. Where a person is charged with failing to produce books it is a defence for him to prove that they were not in his possession or under his control and that it was not reasonably practicable for him to produce them: section 109.

If a person provides or makes an explanation or statement which he knows to be false, or recklessly provides or makes a false explanation or statement, he is liable to two years' imprisonment or a fine or both: section 114.

Entry and search of premises

If a justice of the peace, or in Scotland the sheriff or a magistrate, is satisfied, on information on oath laid by an officer of the Department of Trade, that there are reasonable grounds for suspecting that there are on any premises any books or papers of which production has been required under section 109, *ante,* and which have not been produced, he may issue a warrant authorising any constable to enter and search the premises and take possession of any books or papers appearing to be such.

Any documents of which possession is taken may be retained for three months or, if within that period there are commenced certain criminal proceedings mentioned in section 111, *post* (being proceedings to which the documents are relevant), until the conclusion of the proceedings.

Penalties are imposed for obstructing the exercise of a right of entry or search, or of a right to take possession of documents: 1967 Act, s.110.

Provision for security of information

No information or document obtained under section 109 or 110, *ante*, may, without the previous written consent of the company, be published or disclosed, except to a competent authority (normally the Department of Trade, an officer of the Department, an inspector appointed under the 1948 Act by the Department, the Lord Advocate, the Director of Public Prosecutions, any constable and any procurator fiscal, the Treasury or an officer thereof), unless the publication or disclosure is required, *e.g.*—

(1) with a view to the institution of, or for the purposes of, any criminal proceedings pursuant to certain Acts, including the Companies Act 1948, the Insurance Companies Act 1974, the Protection of Depositors Act 1963, and the Companies Acts 1967 and 1981, or any criminal proceedings for an offence entailing misconduct in connection with the management of the company or misapplication or wrongful retainer of its property; or

(2) for the purpose of the examination of any person by an inspector appointed under the 1948 or 1967 Acts in the course of his investigation; or

(3) for the purpose of enabling the Department to exercise its functions under the Companies Acts, the Prevention of Fraud (Investments) Act 1958, the Insurance Companies Act 1974 and the Insolvency Act 1976.

Publication or disclosure of any information or document in contravention of the section is punishable by up to two years' imprisonment or a fine or both: 1967 Act, s.111.

Penalisation of destruction, etc., of company documents

Section 113 of the 1967 Act provides that an officer of a company mentioned in section 109, *ante,* who destroys, mutilates or falsifies, or is privy to the destruction, etc., of a document affecting or relating to the property or affairs of the company is guilty of an offence unless he proves that he did not intend to conceal the state of affairs of the company or to defeat the law. Similarly if he fraudulently parts with, alters or makes an omission in, any such document. The penalty is up to two years' imprisonment or a fine or both.

Section 329 of the 1948 Act contains a similar provision with regard to an officer or contributory of a company being wound up.

CHAPTER 20

PROTECTION OF OUTSIDERS

THIS chapter is concerned with a number of rules, some of which are general law rules and others of which are statutory, for the protection of persons other than members, *i.e.* non-members who deal with the company and who are sometimes referred to as "outsiders."

If a person, *e.g.* a director, purports to act for a company without actual authority, the other person with whom he deals (the outsider) will be able to hold the company bound by the act if the rule in *Royal British Bank* v. *Turquand*, *post*, applies.

Where there is a defect in the appointment of a director who acts for the company, the outsider may be able to rely on section 180 (which provides that the acts of a director or manager are valid despite any defect in his appointment or qualification) and an article like Table A, article 105, *post*.[1]

The outsider may sometimes be able to rely on an article like Table A, article 79 (directors' borrowing power), *post*.[2]

In England he may be able to rely on the Law of Property Act 1925, s.74, where he is a purchaser and there is a defect in the sealing of a deed. Section 74 provides that in favour of a purchaser—by section 205, one who acquires an interest in property in good faith and for valuable consideration—a deed is deemed to have been duly executed by a corporation if it purports to have been sealed in the presence of and attested by a director and the secretary. For Scottish deeds, see Chapter 6.[3]

Again, the outsider may be able to rely on section 145 (minutes of meetings), *ante*,[4] as regards the onus of proof.

If, *e.g.* a director acts for a company without authority and the outsider has no actual or constructive knowledge of the lack of authority, the director is liable to the outsider in damages for breach of express or implied warranty of authority.[5]

---

[1] p. 440.
[2] p. 545.
[3] *Ante*, p. 122.
[4] p. 350.
[5] *Hely-Hutchinson* v. *Brayhead Ltd.* [1968] 1 Q.B. 549 (C.A.); *Firbank's Exors.* v. *Humphreys* (1886) 18 Q.B.D. 54 (C.A.), *post*, p. 548.

The rule in Royal British Bank v. Turquand

The so-called[6] rule in *Royal British Bank* v. *Turquand*[7] may protect a person dealing with a company (an "outsider") where there is some irregularity in its internal management, *e.g.* where the board of directors contract with him on behalf of the company without authority. (A person dealing with a company in good faith in a case like that given in such example is now protected by the European Communities Act 1972, s.9(1), *ante*.)[8]

A person dealing with a company, even if he does not have actual notice, has constructive notice of the contents of its public documents, such as the memorandum and articles, special resolutions, register of charges[9] and, presumably, list of directors, because they are open to public inspection at the Companies Registration Office,[10] but, where the persons entitled to manage its affairs do so in a manner apparently consistent with such documents, then, subject as below, he is not affected by an internal irregularity, *e.g.* the lack of an ordinary resolution required by the articles as authority for the directors to enter into the transaction. The maxim *omnia praesumuntur rite esse acta* (all things are presumed to have been done rightly) applies.

The reason is that since documents such as the memorandum and articles are registered, and accessible to all who care to consult them, persons dealing in good faith with the company are bound to see that externally everything is in order, but they are not concerned with the indoor management because they cannot check that the rules of internal management have been complied with. Thus the doctrine of constructive notice of the contents of such documents is qualified by the rule in *Turquand*'s case.

A company issued a bond under its common seal, signed by two directors. The registered deed of settlement (the equivalent of the modern memorandum and articles) provided that the directors might borrow on bond such sums as they should be authorised by an ordinary resolution of the company. No such resolution was passed. *Held*, the bond was binding on the company, as the lenders were entitled to assume that a resolution authorising the borrow-

---

[6] *Per* Lord Simonds in *Morris v Kanssen* [1946] A.C. 459, at p. 474.
[7] (1856) 6 El. & Bl. 327; 119 E.R. 886.
[8] p. 82.
[9] See, *per* Eve J. in *Wilson* v. *Kelland* [1910] 2 Ch. 306, at p. 313, *post*, p. 573.
[10] Under s.426, *ante*, p. 78.

ing had been passed: *Royal British Bank* v. *Turquand* (1856) 6 El. & Bl. 327; 119 E.R. 886.[11]

The maxim is also illustrated by the doctrine of ostensible or apparent authority in the law of agency.[12]

A company is bound by the acts of its agent within his actual authority, express or implied. As to express actual authority, an individual director may be specifically authorised by the board of directors to make a particular contract on behalf of the company.[13] As to implied actual authority, a director may, under a power in the articles, be appointed to an office, *e.g.* that of managing director, which carries with it authority to make a contract on behalf of the company.[14] However, the question of implication does not stop there and authority may be implied from the conduct of the parties and the circumstances of the case.[15] A person with actual authority to obtain quotations of prices has no implied actual authority to communicate acceptance of such quotes where no decision to purchase has been made by his principal—at most such a person may have an ostensible authority.[16]

A company is also bound by the acts of its agent within his apparent authority where he lacks actual authority (although actual authority and apparent authority are not mutually exclusive and generally co-exist).[17] Thus an outsider may be protected where an individual direc-

---

[11] Applied in *Albert Gardens (Manly) Pty. Ltd.* v. *Mercantile Credits Ltd.* (1973) 131 C.L.R. 60. For a full exposition of the rule in a Scottish case see the opinions of Lord President Inglis and Lord Shand in *Heiton* v. *Waverley Hydropathic Co. Ltd.* (1877) 4 R. 830. The rule was applied in Scotland in *Gillies* v. *Craigton Garage Co. Ltd.*, 1935 S.C. 423. See also *Scotmotors (Plant Hire) Ltd.* v. *Dundee Petrosea Ltd.*, 1982 S.L.T. 445.

[12] *Per* Lord Simonds in *Morris* v. *Kanssen* [1943] A.C. 459, at p. 475.

[13] Or a board of directors may pass a resolution authorising two of their number to sign cheques: *per* Lord Denning M.R. in *Hely-Hutchinson* v. *Brayhead Ltd.* [1968] 1 Q.B. 549 (C.A.), at p. 583.

[14] *Per* Willmer L.J. in *Freeman & Lockyer* v. *Buckhurst Park Properties (Mangal) Ltd.* [1964] 2 Q.B. 480 (C.A.), at pp. 488, 489. Diplock L.J. agreed. And see *Paterson's Trustees* v. *Caledonian Heritable Security Co. Ltd.* (1885) 13 R. 369 (manager borrowed money for purposes of company, and used money to purchase heritable property the title to which was taken in his own name).

[15] As in *Hely-Hutchinson's* case, *ante.*

[16] *Crabtree-Vickers Pty. Ltd.* v. *Australian Direct Mail Advertising etc. Co. Pty. Ltd.* (1976) 50 A.L.J.R. 203, following the *Freeman & Lockyer* case and *Turquand*'s case.

[17] *Panorama Developments (Guildford) Ltd.* v. *Fidelis Furnishing Fabrics Ltd.* [1971] 2 Q.B. 711 (C.A.), *ante*, p. 389, where the secretary had apparent authority to hire cars on behalf of the company.

tor acts on behalf of the company without actual authority but with apparent authority, which apparent authority may arise from a representation that he has authority made by the board of directors or such a representation contained in the company's public documents.

If a person acts on behalf of a company without actual authority the company, *i.e.* usually the board of directors, may ratify the contract, in which case the company will be bound by it.

Further, if in such a case the company does not ratify, then, subject as below, the company will still be bound if the other party can prove—

(1) that he was induced to make the contract by the agent being held out as occupying a certain position in the company;

(2) that the representation, which is usually by conduct, was made by the persons with actual authority to manage the company, generally or in respect of the matters to which the contract relates, who are usually the board of directors[18]; and

(3) that the contract was one which a person in the position which the agent was held out as occupying would usually have actual authority to make.

Condition (2), *ante,* is due to the fact that the principal, the company, is not a natural person. It follows from the condition that the outsider cannot as a rule[19] rely on the agent's own representation that he has authority.[20]

R., the chairman of the directors of the defendant company, B. Ltd., acted as its *de facto* managing director. The board knew of and acquiesced in that and the articles of B. Ltd. empowered the board to appoint a managing director. H. was the chairman and managing director of a public company, P. Ltd., which needed financial assistance. B. Ltd. was prepared to help and accordingly in January, 1965, B. Ltd. bought shares in P. Ltd. from H. for £100,000 and proposed to inject £150,000 into P. Ltd. H. became a director of B. Ltd. but never saw its memorandum and articles and did not attend board meetings until May 19, 1965. After that meeting R. and H. agreed that H. would put more money into P. Ltd. if B. Ltd. would secure his position. R., on behalf of B. Ltd., signed letters to H. in which B. Ltd. purported to indemnify H. against loss on his guarantee of a bank loan of £50,000 to P. Ltd. and to guarantee a loan by H. to P. Ltd. H. then advanced £45,000 to P. Ltd. When

---

[18] But occasionally the shareholders: *Mahony* v. *East Holyford Mining Co.* (1875) L.R. 7 H.L. 869, *post.*

[19] See the *Crabtree-Vickers* case, *ante.*

[20] *Per* Diplock L.J. in the *Freeman & Lockyer* case, *ante,* at p. 505 and Lord Pearson in the *Hely-Hutchinson* case, *ante,* at p. 593.

P. Ltd. went into liquidation H. had to honour his guarantee and he claimed the £50,000 and the £45,000 from B. Ltd. B. Ltd. denied liability and said that R. had no authority to sign the letters (and that the contracts were unenforceable for non-disclosure of H.'s interest in accordance with s.199). *Held,* that on the facts R. had actual authority implied from the conduct of the parties and the circumstances of the case to enter into the contracts with H. (and that it was too late to avoid them for non-disclosure of H.'s interest as required by the articles): *Hely-Hutchinson* v. *Brayhead Ltd.* [1968] 1 Q.B. 549 (C.A.),[21] applying the *Freeman & Lockyer* case, below.

The articles of a company formed to purchase and resell an estate empowered the directors to appoint one of their body managing director. K., a director, was never appointed managing director but, to the knowledge of the board, he acted as such. On behalf of the company he instructed architects to do certain work in connection with the estate. *Held,* the company was bound by the contract and liable for the architects' fees. K. had apparent authority because he had been held out by the board as managing director and, therefore, as having authority to do what a managing director would usually be authorised to do on behalf of the company, and his act was within the usual authority of a managing director. Accordingly, the plaintiffs could assume that he had been properly appointed: *Freeman & Lockyer* v. *Buckhurst Park Properties (Mangal) Ltd.* [1964] 2 Q.B. 480 (C.A.).[22]

"It must be shown:

(1) that a representation that the agent had authority to enter on behalf of the company into a contract of the kind sought to be enforced was made to the contractor;

(2) that such representation was made by a person or persons who had 'actual' authority to manage the business of the company either generally or in respect of those matters to which the contract relates;

(3) that he (the contractor) was induced by such representation to enter into the contract, that is, that he in fact relied upon it; and

(4) that under its memorandum or articles of association the company was not deprived of the capacity either to enter into a contract of the kind sought to be enforced or to delegate authority to enter into a contract of that kind to the agent": *per* Diplock L.J. at pp. 505, 506.

The persons who signed the articles of a company, and who under the articles were entitled to appoint directors, treated some of themselves as directors although there was no proper appointment. The articles provided that cheques should be signed as directed by the board. The person acting as secretary informed the company's bank that the "board" had resolved that cheques should be signed by two of three named directors and countersigned

---

[21] And see, *ante,* p. 381. A corresponding Scots case is *Allison* v. *Scotia Motor etc. Co. Ltd.* (1906) 14 S.L.T. 9 (O.H.), where a *de facto* managing director engaged a works manager of the company for a period of five years.

[22] Applying *Biggerstaff* v. *Rowatt's Wharf Ltd.* [1896] 2 Ch. 93 (C.A.) and *British Thomson-Houston Co.* v. *Federated European Bank Ltd.* [1932] 2 K.B. 176 (C.A.). See also *Clay Hill Brick Co. Ltd.* v. *Rawlings* [1938] 4 All E.R. 100.

by the secretary. The bank acted on the communication and honoured cheques so signed. *Held*, the bank was entitled to honour the cheques and was not liable to refund the money paid. The rule in *Turquand*'s case applied and there was an article like Table A, article 105: *Mahony* v. *East Holyford Mining Co.* (1875) L.R. 7 H.L. 869.

The requirement appears to be that the representation was made by a person with "actual" authority to manage the business. Thus if the representation is made by someone with no such authority the outsider cannot rely on it.

A sales representative, with the title of "unit manager," purported to bind his company to repay sums advanced by the bank to another company. He had no actual or apparent authority to do so. The bank sought confirmation from the company's "general manager" of its City branch. He confirmed the "unit manager's" authority, but he himself had no authority to make loans. *Held*, the bank could not rely on the general manager's statements as to the unit manager's authority: *British Bank of the Middle East* v. *Sun Life Assurance of Canada (U.K.) Ltd.* (1982) (C.A.); unreported February 19. See [1982] J.B.L. 496.

Where the outsider relies on a representation by the board of directors it is not necessary that he should actually have inspected the company's public documents but where he is seeking to rely on a representation in the public documents it is essential that he inspected them. A party seeking to set up an estoppel (or, in Scots law, a personal bar) must show that he relied on the representation which he alleges, be it a representation in words or a representation by conduct.

A director purported to make, on behalf of the company, an agreement whereby an outsider was to sell on commission goods imported by the company and to retain the proceeds as security for a debt due from another company. The outsider had not inspected the company's public documents and did not know of the power of delegation contained in the articles. Further, the agreement was so unusual as to put the outsider upon inquiry to ascertain whether the director had authority in fact. *Held*, the company was not bound: *Houghton & Co.* v. *Nothard, Lowe and Wills Ltd.* [1927] 1 K.B. 246 (C.A.); affirmed on other grounds [1928] A.C. 1.

R. Co., by their principal director, A., purported to enter into an oral contract with B., who was a director of and purported to act for P. Co. but had no actual authority. The alleged contract was that the two companies should finance the sale of a telephone directory holder produced by a third company. R. Co. claimed repayment of money paid by them to B. as agent for P. Co. in pursuance of the contract. R. Co. alleged that P. Co. were estopped from denying B.'s authority because the P. Co.'s articles provided that the directors could delegate their powers to a committee of one or more directors. However, A. had not inspected the articles until after the action began (and even if A. had inspected the articles a single director would not normally have authority to act for the company). *Held,* because A. had not inspected the articles when the contract was made, they could not be relied on as conferring ostensible or apparent authority on B., and the action failed: *Rama Corporation Ltd.* v. *Proved Tin, etc., Ltd.* [1952] 2 Q.B. 147.

Further, even in the case of a representation by the board of directors, the company is not bound where the public documents show that the contract is *ultra vires* the company—the outsider will have constructive notice of the fact—although, by the European Communities Act 1972, s.9(1), *ante,*[23] in favour of a person dealing with a company in good faith, the company is bound even if the public documents show that a contract is *ulta vires* the company, provided that the transaction is decided upon by the directors or the managing director where the directors have properly delegated the appropriate powers to him. Similarly, the company is not bound where the public documents show that authority to make the contract cannot be delegated to the particular agent.

The rule in *Turquand*'s case does not apply, *i.e.* the company is not bound and the outsider is not protected, in the following cases:—

(1) Where the outsider knows of the irregularity or lack of actual authority.

Under the articles the directors had power to borrow up to £1,000 on behalf of the company without the consent of a general meeting and to borrow further money with such consent. The directors themselves lent £3,500 to the company without such consent, and took debentures. *Held,* the company was liable, and the debentures were valid, only to the extent of £1,000: *Howard* v. *Patent Ivory Manufacturing Co.* (1888) 38 Ch.D. 156.

(2) Where the outsider purported to act as a director in the transaction, *i.e.* to act for and on behalf of the company in the transaction. On the other hand, if a director, acting in his private capacity, contracts with his company, acting by another director, the former director is not automatically to be treated as having constructive knowledge of any defect in the latter's authority, so as to exclude the rule.[24]

C., whose appointment as director had ceased, and S., who had never been appointed a director, purported to hold a board meeting and appoint M. a director. Then all three purported to allot shares to M. *Held,* the invalid

[23] p. 82.
[24] *Hely-Hutchinson* v. *Brayhead Ltd.* [1968] 1 Q.B. 549 (Roskill J.).

appointment of M. and allotment to him were not validated by what are now section 180 and Table A, article 105, *post*, because there was no appointment of C. and S. as directors after C.'s appointment had expired. Further, the rule in *Royal British Bank v.* Turquand did not apply to the allotment since M. purported to act as a director in the transaction: *Morris* v. *Kanssen* [1946] A.C. 459.

(3) Where there are suspicious circumstances putting the outsider on inquiry.

The sole director of and main shareholder in a company paid cheques, drawn in favour of the company, into his own account. *Held,* the bank was put upon inquiry and not entitled to rely on his ostensible authority, and could not rely on the rule: *A. L. Underwood Ltd.* v. *Bank of Liverpool & Martins* [1924] 1 K.B. 775 (C.A.).

The articles of a company carrying on business as forwarding agents empowered the directors to determine who should have authority to draw bills of exchange on the company's behalf. C., the company's Manchester manager, drew bills on the company's behalf in favour of K., who took them, believing C. to be authorised to draw them. C. had no such authority, and it was unusual for a branch manager to have such authority. *Held,* the company was not liable to the holders on the bills because (1) K. did not know of the power of delegation in the articles and therefore could not rely on its supposed exercise; (2) the bills were forgeries; (3) even if K. had known of the power of delegation, he was not entitled to assume that a branch manager had ostensible authority to draw bills on behalf of his company: *Kreditbank Cassel GmbH* v. *Schenkers Ltd.* [1927] 1 K.B. 826 (C.A.).

(4) Where a document is forged so as to purport to be the company's document, unless, perhaps, it is held out as genuine by an officer of the company acting within the scope of his authority.[25]

Prior to the European Communities Act 1972, s.9(1), *ante*, there was another exception to the rule in *Turquand*'s case where, *e.g.* a special resolution of the company in general meeting, required by the articles as authority for the transaction, had not been passed—the public documents of the company at the Companies Registration Office would not include a copy of the resolution[26] and the outsider would have constructive notice of the irregularity.[27] In favour of a person dealing with the company in good faith, at least in the case of a

[25] *Ruben v. Great Fingall Consolidated* [1906] A.C. 439, *ante*, p. 265, particularly *per* Lord Loreburn L.C. at p. 443.
[26] *Ante*, p. 325.
[27] *Irvine* v. *Union Bank of Australia* (1877) 2 App.Cas. 366 (P.C.), *post*, p. 548.

transaction decided on by the directors, the powers of the directors to bind the company are deemed free of any limitation under the memorandum or the articles today.

Validity of acts of directors

Where there is a defect in the appointment of a director who has acted for the company, the outsider may be protected by section 180 and an article like Table A, article 105. The section provides that the acts of a director or manager are valid notwithstanding any defect that may afterwards be discovered in his appointment or qualification. Table A, article 105, provides that all acts done by any meeting of the directors or of a committee of directors or by any person acting as a director shall, notwithstanding that it be afterwards discovered that there was some defect in the appointment of any such director or person acting as aforesaid, or that they or any of them were disqualified, be as valid as if every such person had been duly appointed and was qualified to be a director.[28]

The effect of these provisions is to validate the acts of a director who has not been validly appointed because there was some slip or irregularity in his appointment. Thus, an outsider dealing with the company, *or a member,* is entitled to assume that a person who appears to be a duly appointed and qualified director is so in fact.

The articles included an article like Table A, article 105. T., N. and S., *de facto* directors, made a call, payment of which was resisted by some shareholders on the ground that T., N. and S. were not *de jure* directors. For example, unknown to his co-directors, N. had vacated office by parting with his qualification shares, although he later acquired a share qualification and continued to act as a director. *Held,* the article operated not only as between the company and outsiders but also as between the company and its members, and covered the irregularities alleged, so that the call was valid: *Dawson* v. *African Consolidated Land etc. Co.* [1898] 1 Ch. 6 (C.A.).

It is immaterial that it is clear from the company's public documents that a director is not duly qualified to act.[29]

---

[28] The N.S.W. section corresponding to s.180 and the rule in *Turquand*'s case applied in *Albert Gardens (Manly) Pty. Ltd.* v. *Mercantile Credits Ltd.* (1973) 131 C.L.R. 60.

[29] *Per* Farwell J. in *British Asbestos Co. Ltd.* v. *Boyd* [1903] 2 Ch. 439, at p. 444. In this case a director vacated office on becoming secretary.

The provisions do not validate acts where there has been no appointment at all.[30]

Nor do they validate acts which could not have been done even by a properly qualified director. Thus, in *Craven-Ellis* v. *Canons Ltd.*,[31] what is now section 180 did not empower improperly qualified directors to do what properly qualified directors could not do, namely, appoint an improperly qualified director as managing director.

---

[30] *Morris* v. *Kanssen* [1946] A.C. 459, *ante*, p. 439, applied in *Grant* v. *John Grant & Sons Pty Ltd.* (1950) 82 C.L.R. 1.
[31] [1936] 2 K.B. 403 (C.A.), *ante*, p. 365.

CHAPTER 21

INSIDER TRADING

INTRODUCTION

THE Companies Act 1980, in sections 68 to 73, deals with certain forms of insider trading and makes them criminal offences. This attempt to regulate dealings in a company's shares came about because of widespread concern about the misuse of confidential information by officers of the company in particular[1] but also by their associates, their families and friends to whom information about the company had been relayed by them, or the misuse by others outside the company such as accountants, auditors and bankers who might equally have access to restricted information about the company which would affect the value of its shares on the market.

Insider trading occurs where an individual or organisation buys or sells securities while knowingly in possession of some piece of confidential information which is not generally available and which is likely, if made available to the general public, to materially affect the price of these securities. So, for example, there is insider trading where a company director knows that the company is in a bad financial state and sells his shares in it knowing that in a few days time this news will be made public together with an announcement of a cut in dividend payment. Likewise, the director would be insider trading if, on being informed, before it was generally known by the public, that the company has discovered oil on its own land, he bought more shares in the company in the not unrealistic expectation of an increase in their market value as a result of the subsequent public announcement.

Ethical and legal objections

The moral or ethical reasons for prohibiting such activities should be self-evident. The use of such inside information is clearly unfair to those who deal with the insider. It is a practice akin to, and as reprehensible as, cheating at cards because the insider possesses a

---

[1] See Companies Act 1948, ss.455 and 323(3) and see s.63(1) Companies Act 1980.

secret advantage which is certain to benefit him at the other party's expense.

From the point of view of company law, perhaps a more significant reason for attempting to regulate insider trading by law is that the insider with access to confidential information is thereby in a potential conflict-of-interest situation. For example he may be in such a position within the company as to be able to dictate or at least influence when the public disclosure of price-sensitive information is to be made. In that situation his decision and his own desire to trade advantageously in the company's shares may conflict; in other words the best interests of the company may wrongly take second place to his own self interest. Directors are duty bound, subject to the exception contained in section 74 of the Companies Act 1980, only to act bona fide in the best interests of the company as a whole.[2]

Furthermore, such unethical conduct is likely to bring not only the reputation of the company concerned but also of the securities market in this country into disrepute with the possible risk of a consequent adverse investment effect.

Methods of control

Given that it is recognised as wrong for a director or another to deal in a company's shares knowing of some development which will affect the price of the shares and to which other members or the public generally are not privy, then the question arises how to put an end to such unethical activity. The universal condemnation of this malpractice has produced differing solutions for its eradication.

In the United States of America, which has been in the forefront of the attack on insider trading, the solution adopted is to make the insider disgorge his ill-gotten gains either to the company itself or to the individual with whom he dealt.

In the United Kingdom on the other hand, the solution contained in the Companies Act 1980 is to prohibit, under pain of criminal penalty, an individual connected with a company from trading or dealing on a recognised stock exchange, or through an off-market dealer, in securities of that company. He is prohibited from such activity if he is in

---

[2] *Hutton* v. *W. Cork Ry.* (1883) 23 Ch.D 654 C.A., *Re Lee Behrens & Co.* [1932] Ch. 46; *Evans* v. *Brunner Mond & Co.* [1921] 1 Ch. 359; *Parke* v. *Daily News* [1962] Ch. 927, and *Re Roith* [1967] 1 W.L.R. 479.

possession of unpublished price-sensitive information concerning the company. Likewise, he is subject to a penalty if he attempts to have someone else dealing on his behalf and he must not communicate the information he possesses to any other person if he has reasonable cause to believe that that person might deal in the shares, taking unfair advantage of such confidential information.

Previous controls

Prior to the implementation of the 1980 Companies Act, the only statutory restrictions on insider trading by company officers were the prohibitions on option dealings by directors and the requirement that a register of their share dealings and the dealings of their spouses and children be maintained and available for inspection by any interested person.[3] These 1967 statutory provisions were ineffective because although they purported to create a legal duty or obligation to disclose share dealings, yet they provided no remedy for failure to comply with the Act's requirements.

Also by that time there were sanctions conceived and imposed by the Stock Exchange Authorities and the City Panel under the City Code on Take-overs and Mergers.[4] These, however, are only an extra-statutory form of self regulation and open to criticism because they have no legal backing.[5] Despite that, these bodies have devised strict rules, for example, relating to the disclosure of directors' personal interests in shares in relation to certain profitable transactions such as take-over bids, for absolute secrecy before any significant announcement is made, and for regulating dealings by insiders in the shares while negotiations continue.[6] In theory any breach of the rules, at the Panel's direction, will be investigated by it or the Stock Exchange Authority and improprieties chastised or corrected by appropriate action.

It must be reiterated that being self regulatory and devoid of legal force these rules and principles have not always been effective especially against those who are uninfluenced or unaffected by the withdrawal of access to the facilities of the City.

---

[3] See Companies Act 1967, ss.25, 27, 29 and 31.
[4] See Chapter 31 below.
[5] They rely on private reprimand, public censure or the withdrawal of access to the facilities of the securities market.
[6] The City Code on Take-overs and Mergers, Rules 10, 30, 31, 36 and 37, and Practice Notes Nos. 4–6.

At common law officers of a company had always been freely permitted to hold and deal in the shares of their company. The only sanction which the common law imposed was to make actionable the use of certain confidential information belonging to the company. Such information included industrial or trade secrets and details concerning customers.[7] The misuse of such information by directors, whether it occurred during the course of, or after the termination of, corporate office, was actionable.

The reason why the common law imposed no clear prohibition on the use of inside information in share dealings stems largely from the decision in *Percival* v. *Wright*.[8] In this case where directors had purchased a member's shares in the knowledge that there was a ready buyer for all the shares of the company at a higher price than they paid him, it was held that the transaction could not be set aside for the director's failure to disclose the negotiations which were already taking place at a higher price. There was said to be no duty to disclose because there was no fiduciary relationship between the directors and individual shareholders. The director's duty was owed to the company alone. Subsequently in the case of *Allen* v. *Hyatt*[9] the courts did recognise special but very limited circumstances in which a duty might be owed by directors to individual shareholders. In that particular case the directors had profited through share purchases from members and were held accountable to them because they had purported to act as agents for the members by inducing the latter to give them purchase options over each member's shares supposedly to facilitate a proposed amalgamation. Unless some special relationship of this type could be shown so as to establish a legal duty to disclose all relevant information, the officer retained his profit without adverse legal consequences.

Initiation of reform

The Cohen and the Jenkins Committee Reports and the more recent 1973 White Paper on company law declared their opposition to

---

[7] See *British Industrial Plastics* v. *Ferguson* [1938] 4 A.E.R., 504; *Cranleigh Precision Engineering Ltd.* v. *Bryant* [1965] 1 W.L.R. 1293; *Measure Bros.* v. *Measures* [1910] 1 Ch. 336, [1910] 2 Ch. 248; *Printers & Finishers Ltd.* v. *Holloway* [1965] 1 W.L.R. 1.

[8] [1902] 2 Ch. 421.

[9] (1914) 30 T.L.R. 444.

insider trading.[10] All recommended more mandatory disclosure and statutory restrictions to prevent the abuse of inside information. The Jenkins Comittee also recommended the provision of remedies similar to those in America to compensate parties injured by the insider's activities.[11] This latter recommendation has not been implemented specifically by the 1980 Companies Act or any other enactment,[12] despite the impression to the contrary given by a recent decision in Scotland.[13] The concern and aim of the 1980 legislation is not the compensating of any injured parties or the forcible disgorging of wrongfully acquired gains. The only intendment of the relevant part of this legislation was to make insider trading or dealing a criminal offence, in the hope that all who possess material corporate information will feel compelled (*in terrorem*) to refrain from dealing until that information has been properly made available to the general public.

THE 1980 COMPANIES ACT PROVISIONS

Sections 68–70 of the Companies Act 1980 prohibit insider trading. In detail, section 68 prohibits Stock Exchange dealings in shares by insiders and those who obtain information from them. Also it prohibits the procuring of such deals, the provision of information to make such deals possible, and dealing by persons who have made or withdrawn a take-over offer or dealing by persons who have access to any such information. Section 69 prohibits dealings by Crown servants who have or have had access to prescribed information. Section 70 prohibits dealing in advertised securities using an off-market dealer who is making a market in those securities.

Prescribed information

The information, the use of which is the concern of these provisions, is only what is termed "unpublished price-sensitive" information. This consists of information which relates to specific matters concerning the

[10] The Cohen Committee Report 1945 (Cmnd. 6659, para. 8b). The Jenkins Committee Report 1962 (Cmnd. 1749, paras. 98–100). The Company Law Reform White Paper (July 1973, Cmnd. 5391).

[11] 1962 Cmnd. 1749 at para. 98.

[12] See, however, Powers of Criminal Courts Act 1973, ss.35–38 and Criminal Justice (Scotland) Act 1980, ss.58–67, which enable compensation to be awarded.

[13] *P.F.* v. *Bryce*, August 21, 1981, Edinburgh Sheriff Court (unreported).

company in question, either directly or indirectly, and which is not generally known to those persons who are accustomed or likely to deal in those securities but which would, if generally known to them, be likely materially to affect the price of those securities.

Criminal law implications

Contravention of the prohibitions is made a criminal offence by section 72. Sections 68–70 make very clear that the prosecution, to secure a conviction, must prove both of the traditional pre-requisites of the criminal law. First the *actus reus*, the doing of something which is prohibited[14]—in this instance the act of dealing or trading in securities as an insider, or counselling, procuring or imparting of prescribed information to enable such dealings to take place. Secondly, the prosecution must prove *mens rea* or the requisite criminal intent or guilty state of mind. Depending on the nature of the offence and the precise wording of any statutory provision defining the offence, the *mens rea* element may be satisfied by proof of either intention, recklessness or negligence.

In relation to the principal offence of dealing in securities, section 68 specifies a number of factual and mental elements which are to be proved. The accused must be proved:

(a) to be "knowingly connected" with the company;
(b) to have information by virtue of that connection;
(c) to have been reasonably expected not to disclose the information by reason of that connection;
(d) to have known that the information is unpublished, price-sensitive information in relation to the securities of the company; and
(e) to have dealt in those securities on the Stock Exchange or, if they are advertised securities, through an off-market dealer.

In relation to the other offences of counselling or procuring dealing or communicating information, the prosecution must prove in addition to the other alleged facts, that the accused "knew or had reasonable cause to believe" that dealing would occur on a Stock Exchange or outside Great Britain. An accused with knowledge that the dealing would be either on a recognised Exchange or an unrecognised or off-

[14] In limited circumstances an *actus reus* may result from an omission to act, *e.g. R.* v. *Dytham* [1979] 3 W.L.R. 467.

market Exchange but who does not know or care which, will be caught by the section.

Technically the words "knowingly" or "to know" indicate the traditional requirement of *mens rea* or intent as to all the elements of the *actus reus* or offence.[15] This means that the prosecution will only satisfy the necessary *mens rea* element if it can prove intention as opposed to either recklessness or negligence. This may be achieved by showing that the defendant voluntarily did the *actus reus* intending the forbidden consequence to occur or the forbidden circumstance to be produced, or by showing foresight on his part that a particular consequence or circumstance would follow inevitably from the doing of that *actus reus* even though that "more than highly probable" consequence or circumstance was not necessarily desired as an end in itself.[16] Generally words like "knowingly" will include the state of mind of a person who suspects the truth but deliberately avoids finding out, "shutting his eyes to an obvious means of knowledge" or "deliberately refraining from making enquiries the results of which he might not care to have. 'Connivance,' as this attitude of mind is sometimes called, is closely akin to recklessness."[17] Recklessness consists of either being aware of a risk and unjustifiably taking it or failing to consider that there is a risk in circumstances in which the risk should have been evident.[18] Clearly there is a degree of overlap between conscious disregard, which is the first limb of recklessness, and knowing conduct, which is intentional. At very least, evidence of conscious disregard may raise the implication that the defendant did act "knowingly."[19] Proof of "connivance" even more certainly would satisfy the requirement that the accused "knew" or was "knowingly connected."

Corporate connection

For the purposes of the principal offences specified in section 68, a person is connected with a company if he is a director of that company

---

[15] But it has not invariably been held to do so—see Smith and Hogan, *Criminal Law*, 4th ed., at p. 102.

[16] See *Hyam* v. *D.P.P.* [1975] A.C. 55; *Mohan* [1976] Q.B. 1; *Belfon* [1976] 1 W.L.R. 741, and *Cunningham* (1981) Cr.App.R. 253.

[17] Smith and Hogan, *Criminal Law*, 4th ed., at p. 103.

[18] cf. *R.* v. *Stephenson* [1979] Q.B. 695; *R.* v. *Caldwell* [1981] 1 All E.R. 961 and *R.* v. *Lawrence* [1981] 1 All E.R. 974.

[19] See *Derry* v. *Peek* (1889) 14 App.Cas. 337.

or a related company such as a subsidiary or he is an officer or employee of either or he is in a position involving a professional or business relationship between himself and that company or any related company.[20] In addition such a position must be reasonably expected to give him access to unpublished price-sensitive information about the securities of either company.

The ambit of this provision is such as to include a company's independent auditors, brokers and other financial or legal advisers. Any individual who is, or who at any time in the preceding six months has been, so knowingly connected may not deal in securities of that company if he had information which as stated above he gained by virtue of his position which is confidential and which he knows to be unpublished price-sensitive information.

Also, such a person may not deal in the securities of any other company if the confidential, connected information which he possesses is known similarly by him to be unpublished price-sensitive information relating to the securities of that other company and relates to any transaction, actual or contemplated, involving both the company with which he is connected and the other company, or involving one of them and the securities of the other, or relates to the fact that any such transaction is no longer contemplated.

Outsiders prohibited

Section 68(3) necessarily closes an otherwise convenient loophole by prohibiting persons who receive unpublished price-sensitive information from dealing in securities of the company to which it relates. Any persons, sometimes referred to as "tippees," who receive information, directly or indirectly, from another who is or was connected with the company within the period of six months prior to the receipt of the information is now caught by the dealing prohibition. The recipient or "tippee" must be shown either to know or to have reasonable cause to believe that the imparter of the information held it by virtue of being connected with the company and that because of the latter's position it would be reasonable to expect him not to disclose it.

Section 69 deems any Crown servant or ex-Crown servant to be connected with any company about which he received prescribed information in his capacity as a civil servant. Such persons may not deal

---

[20] Companies Act 1980, s.73(1).

in the securities to which that information relates until that confidential information has become general knowledge or ceases to be price-sensitive.

Statutory exceptions

Section 68(8)–(11) provides for certain exceptions or defences. A person may deal if he does so otherwise than with a view to profit or avoidance of a loss for himself or another. This would seem to cover the situation where circumstances compel the realisation of securities despite the knowledge of unpublished price-sensitive information and together with subsection (11) protects trustees who act on advice in certain circumstances. Other exemptions apply to liquidators, receivers and trustees in bankruptcy acting in good faith in performance of their duties and jobbers acting in good faith in the course of business and specified persons dealing in relation to an international bond issue.[21]

Statutory penalties

The penalties specified in section 72 for contravention of sections 68–70 are: (a) on conviction on indictment, a term of imprisonment not exceeding two years or a fine, or both and (b) on summary conviction, a term of imprisonment not exceeding six months or a fine not exceeding the statutory maximum, or both.[22] This section also provides that proceedings in England and Wales may only be instituted by the Secretary of State, or with the consent of the Director of Public Prosecutions. The aim of this provision is to prevent malicious private prosecutions and it also reflects the fact that most prosecutions will be the product of an investigation by the Department of Trade.[23]

Finally, section 72(3) states that although insider trading is illegal the transactions which do occur remain valid. This is a recognition of the difficulties that would be involved in any attempt by statute to put the parties fairly back into their original positions or the position they

---

[21] Companies Act 1980, s.71, and see s.112 of the Companies Act 1981.

[22] Currently set at £1,000 by section 87(1) of the 1980 Act in accordance with section 61 of the Criminal Law Act 1977 and section 289D of the Criminal Procedure (Scotland) Act 1975.

[23] See ss.164–165 of the Companies Act 1948, as amended by s.86 of the Companies Act 1981; see p. 419, *ante*.

would have been in but for the mischief of the insider with whom they dealt. Once bona fide purchasers or third parties have intervened that task becomes virtually impossible if injustice is to be avoided. Further, although this legislation makes no provision for compensating or indemnifying either any injured party with whom the insider dealt or the shareholders or company generally, for the profits wrongfully gained through the misuse of inside information, this does not preclude legal action in equity against such a director, in particular to recover the profits made by his insider trading in breach of his fiduciary duty[24] and the criminal courts themselves do have the power to award compensation in any criminal proceedings to individuals who have actually suffered loss as a result of the convicted person's criminal activity.[25]

---

[24] *Phipps* v. *Boardman* [1967] 2 A.C. 46. See, however, the difficulty that arises in this connection because of the rule in *Foss* v. *Harbottle* (1843) 2 Ha. 461.
[25] See, Powers of Criminal Courts Act 1973, ss.35 and 38, and Criminal Justice (Scotland) Act 1980, ss.58–67.

CHAPTER 22

ACCOUNTS

INTRODUCTION

WHEN the original legislation was passed in the 1850s enabling limited
liability companies to be set up merely by registration, the intention
was primarily to provide a minimum framework which would facilitate
economic development in a manner consistent with *laissez-faire*
capitalism.[1] The view which implicitly seems to have been taken was
that companies would find it in their own interests to disclose a certain
amount of reliable information, so reducing uncertainty in the minds of
creditors, shareholders and other interested parties, and to the extent
that they might be reluctant to do this it would be up to both the
individuals dealing with a company, its officers and agents, and to its
members to protect their interests by making appropriate contracts
with the parties concerned. The justification for intervention in this
process could only exist if it were perceived that the benefits to society
that might be expected to result would more than offset the costs of
complying with any regulations imposed.

Against this background it is hardly surprising that in the latter half
of the nineteenth century disclosure requirements were minimal, the
view in particular being taken that record-keeping and the preparation
of financial statements for a company were really a domestic matter, of
concern only to the directors and shareholders, unless the rights of
third parties were directly affected.[2] As a result the only guidance in
accounting matters in the early legislation was to be found in the model
articles given in Table A.[3] At the same time the non-interventionist

[1] See T. Hadden, *Company Law and Capitalism* (2nd ed.), 1977, Wiedenfield and
Nicolson, London, Chap. 1 and *passim*. The idea has been given a new lease of life
recently with the development of the economic theory of agency: see, for instance,
W. H. Beaver, *Financial Reporting: An Accounting Revolution*, 1981, Prentice
Hall, Englewood Cliffs, N.J., Chap. 2 and *passim*.

[2] See *In re Spanish Prospecting Co. Ltd.* [1911] 1 Ch. 92; *Edwards* v. *Saunton Hotel
Co. Ltd.* [1943] 1 All E.R. 176; *Young* v. *Brownlee and Co. Ltd.* 1911 S.C. 677.

[3] See H. C. Edey and Prot Panitpakdi, *British Company Accounting and the Law
1844–1900*, in *Studies in the History of Accounting*, ed. A. C. Littleton and B. S.
Yamey, 1956, Sweet and Maxwell, London (pp. 356–379). (In fact, under the
original 1856 Act what became Schedule A from 1862 onwards was designated as
Schedule B.)

philosophy was reflected in a number of decisions concerning the payment of dividends by companies, the overall view apparently being that the courts should not in general interfere in the business decision-making process unless there were good grounds for believing that the rights of certain interested parties were being prejudiced—a laudable policy given the fact that from an economic viewpoint there is no necessary connection between profit, however calculated, and the distribution decision.[4]

Towards the end of the nineteenth century views about mandatory disclosure gradually began to change. The formal accounts were beginning to be used for purposes (such as a basis for assessing income tax liabilities) which were different from those apparently originally intended. Moreover, specific examples of inequality of information and manipulation of data arose, and at a time when a third of new companies failed within a short space of time[5] the view that unsecured creditors had insufficient information on which to base their decisions gained a certain currency. The result was that the statutory audit was introduced in 1900, and in 1908 the 10,000 businesses in the newly created "public" class of company were required to file their balance sheets. However, the 30,000 or so "private" concerns were still exempted from this provision.

By 1925 the number of companies registered had risen to around 95,000 (of which some 85,000 were private), but the 1929 Companies Act nevertheless did not extend the duty to file accounts to private companies, nor did it substantially expand the disclosure requirements for company financial statements. However, the climate of opinion began to change in the 1930s, it being increasingly recognised that the affairs of the modern corporation are often of interest to a much wider constituency than just the existing body of shareholders.[6] The gradual shift in opinion was given added impetus by the Royal Mail debacle[7] and the creation of the Securities and Exchange Commission in the

---

[4] See E. A. French, *The Evolution of the Dividend Law of England*, in *Studies in Accounting* (3rd ed.), 1977, ed. W. T. Baxter and S. Davidson, Institute of Chartered Accountants in England and Wales, London (pp. 306–331); and R. C. Morris, *Distribution Policy: An Economic Rationale*, *Accountancy*, October 1982 (pp. 80–82).

[5] See H. A. Shannon, *The Listed Companies of 1866–1883*, in *Essays in Economic History*, Vol. 1, ed. E. M. Carus-Wilson, 1954, Edward Arnold, London.

[6] See Hadden, *op. cit., passim.*

[7] *R. v. Kylsant* [1932], 1 K.B. 442; see above, p. 157.

United States, events which forced lawyers and accountants in Great Britain to question the accepted wisdom in relation to the disclosure of a company's financial affairs. The result was that the Cohen Committee[8] on company law reform of 1945 was charged with considering the needs of the public as well as shareholders and creditors. It recommended that so-called reserve accounting should be outlawed; that the preparation of group accounts (where appropriate) should be mandatory; and that for the first time companies should be required to prepare an income statement worthy of the name. By that time there were some 200,000 registered companies, of which over 90 per cent. enjoyed private status, but the 1948 Companies Act only required public and a small proportion of (non-exempt) private companies to file their annual accounts.

The Jenkins Committee[9] on company law reform, reporting in 1962, favoured further compulsory disclosure, and it proposed that exempt private companies (which comprised some 75 per cent. of the 400,000 or so companies then registered) should be required to file their financial statements, the purpose being to benefit unsecured creditors. A requirement to this effect was included in the 1967 Companies Act, and this led to a rapid increase in the number of company searches, which rose from 600,000 in 1960 and 1.3 million in 1969 to 2.6 million in 1980. The Act also greatly extended the disclosures which had to be made in the income statement and in notes to the accounts and the directors' reports (*e.g.* turnover, hire charges, movements in fixed assets and segmental analysis of activities).

The 1970s witnessed an upsurge in activity aimed at regulating the ways in which companies report their financial affairs, most of it of a quasi-legal nature. Successive governments between 1965 and 1979 attempted to monitor and control price increases, first through the National Board for Prices and Incomes (1965–1971) and later through the Price Commission (1973–1979), and these bodies (like the Monopolies Commission and the Restrictive Trade Practices Court before them) relied heavily on accounting information, which for the Price Commission had to be prepared following certain specified rules. Meanwhile companies had had for many years to keep detailed records to ensure PAYE, national insurance contributions and excise duties

---

[8] (1945) Cmnd. 6659.
[9] (1962) Cmnd. 1749.

were properly accounted for, and the introduction of value added tax in 1973 made this even more necessary. In addition, powers were taken in the Industry Act 1975 which meant that certain companies might be required to disclose supplementary information to ministers and to trade unions. On the accounting front, the leading accountancy bodies set up the Accounting Standards Committee (ASC) in 1969, and it has issued a number of mandatory statements concerning the preparation and publication of companies' annual accounts, two of the most important relating to the preparation of supplementary flow of funds and current cost accounting statements, the latter following the publication of a lengthy government report on the matter.[10] The ASC's efforts have been backed up by the statements of the International Accounting Standards Committee (IASC), set up in 1973, and the Stock Exchange Listing Agreement, published in 1972, the latter applying to the 3,000 or so British quoted companies. Elsewhere, the OECD and the United Nations have both published disclosure guidelines concerning the activities of international concerns.

Another major factor, of more direct relevance to changes introduced in the Companies Acts 1980 and 1981, has been the EEC's attempts to harmonise accounting regulations within the Common Market countries, the avowed aim being to encourage the efficient allocation of capital within the Community. These two Acts have incorporated most of the accounting and disclosure proposals contained in the Commission's Second and Fourth Directives, but those in the draft Seventh Directive,[11] concerning the preparation of group accounts, have yet to be agreed by the Council and be enacted.

What is perhaps surprising about recent developments has been the lack of debate in a succession of discussion documents[12] about the economic rationale for requiring greater disclosure by companies, particularly as further regulation seems to imply an increasing degree of market failure. Yet it should be remembered that the data contained in a set of published accounts are only part of a much wider information set available to decision makers, be they shareholders, potential investors, creditors or employees, and there is an impressive amount of empirical evidence suggesting that financial and other markets are

---

[10] (1975) Cmnd. 6225.
[11] Draft Seventh Directive on Company Law Harmonization, O.J. 1979 C14/2.
[12] *e.g.* (1973) Cmnd. 5391; (1979) Cmnd. 7654.

efficient in obtaining and processing information perceived to be relevant.[13] Now that the law of negligence has gradually been extended through *Hedley Byrne* v. *Heller*[14] and subsequent cases to offer some protection to third parties, there is even more reason to question the validity of extending disclosure requirements, particularly since the costs of complying with the regulations are far from negligible, but this is a matter which rather surprisingly does not seem up till now to have greatly concerned lawyers and accountants, though businessmen are at last beginning to question the wisdom of the policies being pursued. It is therefore against this background that the current legislative rules should be viewed.

In what follows, this chapter deals, first, with the accounting records which must be kept by a company; secondly, with the reference period for which accounts must be prepared; thirdly, with the regulations for laying them before the company in general meeting and filing copies with the Registrar of Companies; fourthly, with the form and content of the annual accounts and the accounting principles which must be applied in their preparation; fifthly, with the regulations concerning group accounts; sixthly, with the directors' report; seventhly, with the auditors' report; eighthly, with a note on special requirements for certain classes of company; ninthly, with some brief details of other accounting and disclosure regulations; and finally with the question of whether the inclusion of a debt in a signed balance sheet amounts to an acknowledgment of its existence by the company.

Previous editions of this book have included a detailed specimen set of accounts, but in view of the fact that Schedule 1 to the Companies Act 1981 now requires companies to prepare their accounts according to a prescribed format this precedent has not been followed here. However, interested readers may well find it useful to examine closely the annual accounts of major British companies, such as Marks and Spencer, or (for group accounts) ICI, and so familiarise themselves with common practice. Comprehensive pro-forma sets of accounts are also given in Coopers and Lybrand's *Form and Content of Company Accounts* (Financial Training Publications Ltd: London, 1982), pp. 123–180.

---

[13] See, for instance, Beaver, *op. cit.*, especially Chaps. 5–6.
[14] [1964] A.C. 465. For a discussion of this and later cases, see pp. 556–559.

ACCOUNTING RECORDS

Section 12 of the Companies Act 1976 requires every company to ensure that adequate accounting records are kept, sufficient to show and explain its transactions. Moreover, they must be such as to disclose with reasonable accuracy at any time the financial position of the company, and also enable a balance sheet and profit and loss account to be prepared so as to give a true and fair view of the company's financial position and profit or loss.

In particular, the accounting records must contain (a) entries from day to day of all monies received and expended, with details of transactions, and (b) a record of assets and liabilities. In addition, a company dealing in goods must keep statements of stock held at the end of each financial year and of stocktakings from which the year end statements are made up, as well as records of all goods sold and purchased (other than in ordinary retail trade transactions), showing goods, buyers and sellers so as to allow identification. However, there is no requirement to keep statements of work in progress.

The accounting records must be open for inspection by the officers of the company at all times, but there is no express statutory provision authorising the court to compel inspection. However, it was held in *M'Cusker* v. *M'Rae*[15] that the Court of Session may, on the petition of a director presented to the *nobile officium*, ordain a company to make the accounting records available for inspection by the director and by a named accountant on his behalf.

If the accounting records are kept outside Great Britain, such accounts and returns must be kept in Britain as will disclose the position of the business at intervals not exceeding six months and will enable the directors to ensure that any balance sheet or profit and loss account prepared by them gives a true and fair view of the company's financial position and profit or loss.

The accounting records must normally be kept for a minimum period of three years for a private company, or six years for a public company.

Failure to keep accounting records as required is an offence for which officers of the company are liable, the penalty being a maximum of two years' imprisonment and/or a fine.

[15] 1966 S.C. 253.

A shareholder has no right to inspect the books of account of the company unless one is given to him by the articles. In this regard Table A, article 125, provides: "The directors shall from time to time determine whether and to what extent and at what times and places and under what conditions or regulations the accounts and books of the company or any of them shall be open to the inspection of members not being directors, and no member (not being a director) shall have any right of inspecting any account or book or document of the company except as conferred by statute or authorised by the directors or by the company in general meeting."[16]

ACCOUNTING REFERENCE PERIODS

Section 1 of the Companies Act 1976 provides that the directors of a company must prepare accounts based on an *accounting reference period*. This commences on the day after the date to which the last accounts were prepared and ends on the last day of the company's normal financial year. However, the directors may at their discretion move such reference date to up to seven days before or after the last day of the company's normal financial year.

Section 3 of the 1976 Act makes provision for alteration of the accounting reference period. Under its terms notice may be given to the Registrar in prescribed form at any time during an accounting reference period specifying a new accounting reference date altering the current and subsequent accounting reference periods of the company. This may be done after the end of a reference period so as to change the date by which the accounts would normally be laid and filed only if the company is a holding or subsidiary company and the change is made in order that the accounting reference dates of the companies may coincide. However, the change cannot be made in any case if the period allowed for laying and delivering accounts in relation to the previous accounting reference period has expired.

Notice under section 3 must state whether the new period is to be shorter or longer than the current reference period, and in any case

---

[16] Counsel's opinion, as taken by the Auditing Practices Committee, interprets books of account and accounting records in this context as comprising information organised and labelled so as to be capable of retrieval, which would include computerised records: *Accountancy,* March 1978, pp. 74–75. See also the Report of the Jenkins Committee (1962), Cmnd. 1749, para. 423.

extension is not possible if a current period plus the extension is more than 18 months in duration. Moreover, not more than one extension will generally be allowed within a period of five years except to bring the reference periods of holding and subsidiary companies into line.

A new company must notify an accounting reference date within six months of incorporation and the reference period must be not less than six nor more than 18 months, while the period covered by the profit and loss account must begin with the first day of that accounting reference period and end not more than seven days before or more than seven days after the reference period, as the directors may determine.

Laying the Accounts Before the Company in General Meeting and Filing Them With the Registrar

Under section 1 of the 1976 Act the financial statements, comprising the balance sheet, the profit and loss account and the notes to the financial statements (1948 Act, s.149(1), (8)(*a*)), together with the attached auditors' and directors' reports (1948 Act, ss.156–157), must be laid before the company in general meeting and, except for certain unlimited companies which are exempt from the disclosure requirements, be filed with the Registrar within seven months of the reference date (public companies) or 10 months (private companies). A three months' extension can be claimed where a company carries on business overseas. Moreover, if the profit and loss account, balance sheet, auditors' report or directors' report are in a language other than English, the directors must annex to the copy delivered to the Registrar a translation into English certified to be a correct translation (1976 Act, ss.1, 6).

Section 5(1) of the Companies Act 1981 offers concessions to small and medium sized companies, as defined in section 8 of the Act, permitting them to file "modified" financial statements with the Registrar of Companies (see below, pages 463–465), though it should be noted that these concessions do not affect the information that must be provided to members of the company. Unofficially it is estimated that some half a million registered companies will qualify as small companies under section 8.

Every balance sheet of a company and every copy of such a balance sheet which is laid before the company in general meeting or delivered to the Registrar must be signed by two directors or, if there is only one director (as there might be in the case of a private company), by that director (1948 Act, s.155, as amended by Sched. 2 to the 1976 Act). In the case of a modified set of accounts delivered to the Registrar, a statement must be included immediately above the signatures indicating that the directors have relied on the exemptions offered under section 6 of the 1981 Act and that the company is entitled to benefit from those exemptions (1981 Act, s.7).

Section 9(3) of the European Communities Act 1972, as amended by section 1 of the Companies Act 1976, provides that the Registrar must cause to be published in the *Gazette* notice of the receipt by him of any document delivered by a company in pursuance of section 1.

Non-compliance with the requirement to lay the financial statements and auditors' and directors' reports before a general meeting and to file them with the Registrar can result in conviction of the directors, the penalty being a fine (1976 Act, s.4; 1980 Act, Sched. 2). In addition, failure to comply with the requirement to file the relevant documents with the Registrar makes the company itself liable for penalties which are recoverable by the Department of Trade in civil proceedings. Moreover, a member, creditor or the Registrar may serve a notice on the directors requesting compliance, and if the documents are then not filed within 14 days they can apply for a court order to have the default remedied, the costs being borne by the directors (1976 Act, ss.4, 5).

The right to receive accounts

The general rule is that a copy of every balance sheet, including every document required by law to be annexed thereto, of which a copy is to be laid before the company in general meeting, together with a copy of the auditors' report, must be sent to every member, whether or not he is entitled to receive notices of general meetings, and also to every debenture holder, at least 21 days before the date of the meeting. If all the members entitled to attend and vote so agree, a shorter time will suffice. Any member or debenture holder, whether entitled to receive a copy or not, is entitled to a copy on demand without charge (1948 Act, s. 158, as amended by the 1976 Act, Sched. 2).

Section 24 of the 1967 Act gives a right to receive copies of the directors' report by providing that section 158 above shall have effect as if references to the auditors' report included references to the directors' report.

THE ANNUAL ACCOUNTS

Neither the law nor the accountancy profession has satisfactorily defined the role and purpose of the annual accounts of a company, though the traditional view is that they primarily represent "a stewardship record." Thus the Jenkins Committee expressed the opinion that "a profit and loss account is an historical record. It shows as the profit or loss the difference between the revenue for the period covered by the account and the expenditure chargeable in that period."[17]

Unfortunately the only objective historical record of a company's affairs is afforded by its cash account—any attempt to measure profit inevitably involves valuation, either of the business itself as a going concern, or (more usually) of the individual net assets it owns. Yet experience seems to suggest that what potential users want above all *is* a measure of profit, even though this must inevitably involve an element of subjectivity in its calculation. The traditional accounting approach, substantially influenced no doubt by the needs of the auditing side of the accountancy profession, has been to value the net assets according to a reasonably flexible set of conservatively biased rules, the overall effect of which is to delay the recognition of profit through time. However, when there is a significant systematic rise in prices over a given period the expenses (representing assets used up) that are matched against current revenues can give rise to a misleadingly inflated profit figure, thus defeating the accountants' aim to exercise prudence in determining the income figure. Another result is that the asset values in a balance sheet are even less likely to approximate to current market values (if indeed that is what is deemed desirable) than might be the case in a period when increases in the general price level are relatively small.

In practice most classes of user of financial statements are well aware of the shortcomings of conventional accounts, and certainly for listed companies they seem primarily to look upon published profit figures as one amongst several signals they receive concerning a company's

---

[17] (1962) Cmnd. 1749, para. 333.

relative performance and its likely future prospects. In such circumstances the main purpose of the profit calculation would therefore appear to be to enable users of the accounts to compare reported outcomes against what was expected, and this is even true for unquoted companies where alternative sources of information (except at the wider industry level) are rather more limited.

It is against this background, then, that the statutory disclosure requirements contained in the Companies Acts (and most recently in the Companies Act 1981, Sched. 1) should be seen. They establish a basic minimum of information which must be disclosed and be subjected to audit, thus increasing its credibility in the eyes of the reader and so hopefully reducing his uncertainty about future likely outcomes. Many companies will disclose more, either in the statutory accounts themselves and in supplementary statements demanded by the ASC (such as the flow of funds statement and current cost accounts) and by the Stock Exchange Listing Agreement (which *inter alia* requires quoted companies to publish half-yearly interim accounts); or, alternatively, by other means (*e.g.* for quoted companies through the chairman's report, press releases, or news leaked onto the market via stockbroker's reports; and for unquoted companies by disclosing relevant information directly to bank managers, other major creditors and employee representatives).

Basic principles

Section 1(1) of the Companies Act 1981 restates s.149 of the 1948 Act and thus re-establishes two basic principles with regard to a company's financial statements: first, that insofar as they are prepared under section 1 of the Companies Act 1976 they must comply as to their form and content with the provisions of the amended Schedule 8 to the 1948 Act (Sched. 1 to the 1981 Act); and, secondly, that the balance sheet and profit and loss account and notes thereto must give a true and fair view of the company's financial position and its profit or loss for a given period (1981 Act, s.1).

Where a company does not trade for profit, the financial statements will include an income and expenditure account instead of the profit and loss account, together with the balance sheet and notes to the accounts.

A company that has subsidiaries need not publish a separate profit and loss account if it prepares a consolidated profit and loss account which complies with the relevant requirements of the 1948 Act and this shows how much of the group profit or loss for the financial year is dealt with in the financial statements of the company itself. However, the fact that the company has taken advantage of this must be disclosed in the notes to the group financial statements (1948 Act, s.149; 1981 Act, s.1).

The requirement for the financial statements to give a true and fair view is an overriding one, so where information additional to the minimum specified in the Acts is necessary for the financial statements to give a true and fair view, such extra information must be included in those statements. Likewise, where the circumstances are such that strict compliance with a requirement of the Acts would not result in a true and fair view, the company must depart from that requirement, full particulars of the reasons for the departure and its effect being disclosed in the notes to the accounts (1981 Act, Sched. 1, para. 15).

Despite the fact that it is an overriding requirement that the financial statements should give "a true and fair view" of a company's financial affairs, the exact meaning of the phrase is unfortunately unclear, a matter which is now being highlighted by the presence of an alternative current cost set of accounts in the annual reports of most listed companies.

The figures included in the annual accounts have been given added significance recently as a result of sections 39–45 of the Companies Act 1980, which prescribe that distributable profit is generally the aggregate of accumulated realised net profits as reported in the latest audited (or, if relevant, interim) accounts. Moreover, a public company can only pay a dividend if the net assets (after payment of the dividend) at least equal its capital plus any reserves not available for distribution (see below, page 532). Apart from introducing the problem of deciding which profits are actually realised and which are not—a somewhat arbitrary distinction and a matter anyway of some dispute amongst accountants—such rules cannot ensure the protection of unsecured creditors, while at the same time they may possibly inhibit the efficient workings of the capital market.

Large, medium, and small sized companies

Under the 1967 Companies Act all limited companies were required to comply with the provisions of the eighth Schedule to the 1948 Act, as amended, except insofar as such requirements were modified by the Department of Trade: 1948 Act, s.149; 1967 Act s.9. Apart from exemptions for special classes of business (like banks and insurance and shipping companies), the only concessions were for companies below a certain size which were permitted not to disclose details of turnover and directors' remuneration, the criteria (set in terms of the size of the amounts involved) being altered from time-to-time by statutory instrument. Exemptions were also granted in relation to a turnover criterion permitting companies not to disclose in their directors' reports the value of exports, the average number of employees and their aggregate remuneration, and turnover and pre-tax profit or loss by each class of business. It was the view of the Bolton Committee of enquiry on small firms that these concessions did not seriously prejudice the work of credit agencies and the interests of unsecured creditors.[18]

Using a size criterion to determine the extent of disclosure in the accounts filed with the Registrar of Companies is a principle now established by section 5(1) of the Companies Act 1981. Briefly, while all limited companies (other than investment companies and companies engaged in banking, insurance and shipping—see below, page 508) must prepare and lay detailed accounts before their members in general meeting in accordance with one or other of a set of prescribed forms of financial statement given in Schedule 1 to the Act (s.1), medium and small sized non-public companies can avail themselves of concessions whereby they need only *file* "modified" accounts.

The 1981 Act in fact distinguishes between "full" and "abridged" accounts (s.11). The former, relating to either an individual company or a group, comprise both the financial statements laid before the company in general meeting and any modified accounts properly filed with the Registrar; whereas the abridged accounts are any abbreviated set of financial statements, such as preliminary announcements, or simplified accounts prepared for employees. The full accounts must be accompanied by the auditors' report. For the accounts as laid before the company in general meeting, this will be the audit report made under section 14 of the Companies Act 1967; but where the accounts are a modified set of financial statements it must in addition state

---

[18] (1972) Cmnd. 4811, Chap. 17.

whether, in the auditors' opinion, the requirements for exemption are satisfied (1981 Act, ss.11(1), (9); 7(4), (5)).

Where a company publishes[19] abridged financial statements, either for itself alone or for itself and its subsidiaries, it must indicate that (a) the statements are not the full statements; (b) whether the full statements have been delivered to the Registrar; (c) the fact that the company is exempt from filing by virtue of its being an unlimited company; (d) whether the auditors have reported on the full statements, and whether their report was unqualified (1981 Act, s.11(6)). Moreover, the auditors' report relating to the full accounts must not be published with a set of abridged accounts (s.11(7)).

The size criteria relating to the privilege of being able to file modified financial statements are basically that a small company is one that for the current and previous year meets two of the following three requirements: annual turnover less than £1·4 million; total assets valued below £700,000; and average number of employees under 50 (s.8(2)). A medium sized company is one which for the current and previous year meets two of three criteria: annual turnover less than £5·75 million; assets valued at less than £2·8 million; and average number of employees 250 or fewer (s.8(3)). All other companies are regarded as "large."

For new companies the criteria are assessed on the first year's figures, and where an accounting period is greater or less than a year the turnover figure has to be adjusted *pro rata*. A small or medium sized company may submit the appropriate modified statements in the first year in which it fails to meet the criteria, but if it still does not meet them in the subsequent year it then loses this privilege.

Form and content of accounts

1. *General rules*

The approach adopted in the EEC's Fourth Directive (on which the first Schedule to the 1981 Act is substantially based) was essentially prescriptive in nature, reflecting the influence of continental Europe. Thus Section A of Part I of the Schedule establishes the general rules in relation to the form and content of the accounts, indicating that one of

---

[19] Publication in this context is defined in s.21(3) of the 1981 Act.

the prescribed formats (four for the profit and loss account and two for the balance sheet) must be used (para. 1) and be adhered to year by year unless there are special reasons justifying a change (para. 2). However, some flexibility is allowed—where necessary, directors may give greater detail than prescribed (para. 3(1)) or adapt the formats to reflect the special nature of a company's business (para. 3(3)), and certain items (indicated in the model statements by Arabic numerals) can be combined if the combination facilitates an assessment of the company's performance or position (para. 3(4)). Comparative figures for the previous accounting period are also to be shown (para. 4), but individual items may not be set off against each other (para. 5).

2. *Balance sheet*

Section B of Part I of the first schedule to the Companies Act 1981 sets out two alternative formats of balance sheet, the contents of which are in fact identical. The first (reproduced below) equates net assets to the aggregate of share capital and reserves, and is thus not dissimilar to the vertical layout commonly used in the United Kingdom before the Act came into effect. The second format equates assets against claims, a method of presentation more commonly used in continental European countries.

Balance sheet—Format 1

A   Called up share capital not paid

B   Fixed assets
    I   Intangible assets
        1   Development costs
        2   Concessions, patents, licences, trade marks and similar rights and assets
        3   Goodwill
        4   Payments on account
    II Tangible assets
        1   Land and buildings
        2   Plant and machinery
        3   Fixtures, fittings, tools and equipment
        4   Payments on account and assets in course of construction
    III Investments
        1   Shares in group companies
        2   Loans to group companies

3 Shares in related companies
4 Loans to related companies
5 Other investments other than loans
6 Other loans
7 Own shares

C Current assets
  I Stocks
    1 Raw materials and consumables
    2 Work in progress
    3 Finished goods and goods for resale
    4 Payments on account
  II Debtors
    1 Trade debtors
    2 Amounts owed by group companies
    3 Amounts owed by related companies
    4 Other debtors
    5 Called up share capital not paid
    6 Prepayments and accrued income
  III Investments
    1 Shares in group companies
    2 Own shares
    3 Other investments
  IV Cash at bank and in hand

D Prepayments and accrued income

E Creditors: amounts falling due within one year
    1 Debenture loans
    2 Bank loans and overdrafts
    3 Payments received on account
    4 Trade creditors
    5 Bills of exchange payable
    6 Amounts owed to group companies
    7 Amounts owed to related companies
    8 Other creditors including taxation and social security
    9 Accruals and deferred income

F Net current assets (liabilities)

G Total assets less current liabilities

H Creditors: amounts falling due after more than one year
    1 Debenture loans
    2 Bank loans and overdrafts
    3 Payments received on account
    4 Trade creditors
    5 Bills of exchange payable
    6 Amounts owed to group companies

          7   Amounts owed to related companies
          8   Other creditors including taxation and social security
          9   Accruals and deferred income

I   Provisions for liabilities and charges
          1   Pensions and similar obligations
          2   Taxation, including deferred taxation
          3   Other provisions

J   Accruals and deferred income

K   Capital and reserves
     I   Called up share capital
     II   Share premium account
     III Revaluation reserve
     IV   Other reserves
          1   Capital redemption reserve
          2   Reserve for own shares
          3   Reserves provided for by the articles of association
          4   Other reserves
     V   Profit and loss account

Preliminary expenses, issuing expenses and commissions, and research expenditure are not permitted to be treated as assets in a company's balance sheet (Sched. 1, para. 3(2)). Intangible assets, such as patents and trade marks, can however be included if they were either acquired for valuable consideration or were created by the company itself. Similarly, only goodwill acquired for valuable consideration can be shown as an asset in a balance sheet, but its cost (except insofar as it relates to goodwill on consolidation: para. 66) must be written off systematically over a period which must not exceed its estimated useful economic life (para. 21). The amount of each item to be shown under the head "Debtors" must be split between those amounts receivable within one year of the balance sheet date and those receivable later than that; and in determining the amount to be shown under "Net current assets," amounts shown as "Prepayments and accrued income" have to be taken into account.

As regards claims, where there are debenture loans these have to be split between convertible and non-convertible loans; and the amounts of allotted and paid-up share capital have also to be shown separately. Payments received on account for orders must be shown under creditors unless disclosed as a deduction from stocks of finished goods.

A "related company" is effectively an associated company in which the investing company holds on a long term basis over 20 per cent. of the voting equity shares (Sched. 1, para. 91).

A provision is "any amount retained as reasonably necessary for the purpose of providing for any liability or loss which is either likely to be incurred, or certain to be incurred but uncertain as to amount or as to the date on which it will arise" (Sched. 1, para. 88).

A company will normally only hold its own shares where it has acquired them by forfeiture or surrender. Where it purchases or redeems its own shares they must be cancelled (1980 Act, s.37; 1981 Act, ss.45(8), 46(2)).

For the rules relating to share premium and capital redemption reserve accounts, see pages 176, 248.

Medium and large sized companies, as defined previously, have to file a full balance sheet, but small companies need only submit a modified statement that discloses only those items that are preceded by a letter or a Roman numeral. However, the aggregate amounts of debtors and creditors have to be divided between amounts receivable or payable within one year and those receivable or payable beyond that period. Details can be disclosed either in the balance sheet itself or in the notes to the accounts (1981 Act, s.6).

3. *Profit and loss account*

Of the four profit and loss account formats given in the first schedule to the 1981 Act, the first two (reproduced below) are presented in a vertical form (and are therefore probably the most likely to be used in the United Kingdom), while the third and fourth show expenses on the left and income on the right. Formats 1 and 3 classify expenses by function, whereas formats 2 and 4 classify them by type.

Profit and loss account—Format 1

1 Turnover
2 Cost of sales
3 Gross profit or loss
4 Distribution costs
5 Administrative expenses
6 Other operating income
7 Income from shares in group companies
8 Income from shares in related companies

9   Income from other fixed asset investments
10 Other interest receivable and similar income
11 Amounts written off investments
12 Interest payable and similar charges
13 Tax on profit or loss on ordinary activities
14 Profit or loss on ordinary activities after taxation
15 Extraordinary income
16 Extraordinary charges
17 Extraordinary profit or loss
18 Tax on extraordinary profit or loss
19 Other taxes not shown under the above items
20 Profit or loss for the financial year

Profit and loss account—Format 2

1   Turnover
2   Change in stocks of finished goods and in work in progress
3   Own work capitalised
4   Other operating income
5   (*a*) Raw materials and consumables
    (*b*) Other external charges
6   Staff costs:
    (*a*) wages and salaries
    (*b*) social security costs
    (*c*) other pension costs
7   (*a*) Depreciation and other amounts written off tangible and intangible fixed assets
    (*b*) Exceptional amounts written off current assets
8   Other operating charges
9   Income from shares in group companies
10 Income from shares in related companies
11 Income from other fixed asset investments
12 Other interest receivable and similar income
13 Amounts written off investments
14 Interest payable and similar charges
15 Tax on profit or loss on ordinary activities
16 Profit or loss on ordinary activities after taxation
17 Extraordinary income
18 Extraordinary charges
19 Extraordinary profit or loss
20 Tax on ordinary profit or loss
21 Other taxes not shown under the above items
22 Profit or loss for the financial year

Where the format classifies expenses by function (*i.e.* formats 1 and 3) the amounts to be shown under cost of sales, distribution costs and administrative expenses are to be net of depreciation charges and provisions for diminution in the value of assets. However, the amounts of any such charges or provisions for both tangible and intangible fixed assets must be disclosed separately in the notes to the financial statements. In addition, any interest or similar charges payable to group companies must be shown separately.

Apart from the above, whichever format is adopted the following items must be disclosed separately in the profit and loss account:

  (i) profit or loss on ordinary activities before taxation;
 (ii) the aggregate amount of any dividends paid or proposed; and
(iii) movements to or from reserves (Sched. 1, paras. 3(6), (7)).

Large sized companies have to choose one of the four profit and loss account formats and file the full version. However, medium sized companies are permitted to file a modified statement. Effectively the following items can be combined and be shown as one item, "gross profit or loss":

 (a) where expenses are classified by function—turnover, cost of sales, gross profit or loss and other operating income; and
 (b) where expenses are classified by type—turnover, change in stocks of finished goods and work in progress, own work capitalized, other operating income, raw materials and consumables, and other external charges (1981 Act, s.6).

The directors of a small company are exempted from having to file a profit and loss account (1981 Act, s.6).

Various Statements of Standard Accounting Practice (SSAPs) issued by the ASC affect the calculation and presentation of items in the profit and loss account, and they can be accommodated either in the notes or in the body of the statement as supplementary disclosures. The most important in this regard are probably the standards on earnings per share (SSAP 3), which requires listed companies to show this figure on the face of the statement itself; on associated companies (SSAP 1), which requires partial consolidation of associated companies' profits; on group accounts (SSAP 14), which deals with the methods of consolidation; on extraordinary items (SSAP 6), which indicates how and where such items should be disclosed; and on taxation (SSAPs 8 and 15), which indicate how current and deferred tax charges should be disclosed.

Notes to the financial statements

Much of the information previously required to be disclosed by the second schedule to the Companies Act 1967, but which cannot be accommodated in the model formats given in the first schedule to the 1981 Act, now has to be revealed in notes to the financial statements, which themselves form an integral part of the accounts. Moreover, such information can no longer be given in the directors' report as an alternative means of disclosure, as was the case under the 1948 and 1967 Acts (1981 Act, s.16(2)(*a*) (*b*)). The details are given in Part III of the Schedule, though items in the model statements which are preceded by Arabic numerals can also be relegated to a note if necessary (1981 Act, Sched. 1, para. 3(4)). Conversely, items required to be shown in notes may, where feasible, be shown on the face of the accounts (1981 Act, Sched. 1, paras. 3(1) and 35).

1. *General notes*

The accounting policies used by a company must be disclosed, in particular indicating the depreciation and foreign currency translation methods employed, a requirement which substantially meets the conditions of the ASC's Statement of Standard Accounting Practice (SSAP) No. 2 (1971). Other SSAPs relevant in this context are group accounts (No. 14, 1978), associated companies (No. 1, 1971), the treatment of government grants (No. 4, 1974), accounting for value added tax (No. 5, 1974), depreciation (No. 12, 1977), research and development (No. 13, 1977), stocks and work in progress (No. 9, 1975), taxation (No. 8, 1974; and No. 15, 1978), and four proposed statements (or Exposure Drafts, EDs): foreign currency translations (ED 27, 1980), accounting for leases (ED 29, 1981), accounting for goodwill (ED 30, 1982), and accounting for acquisitions and mergers (ED 31, 1982).

Corresponding amounts for the previous financial year (adjusted if necessary to make them comparable), have to be given for all items disclosed in the notes, except for movements on reserves, provisions, fixed asset and depreciation accounts; loans and other transactions with directors and officers of the company under sections 54 and 56 of the Companies Act 1980; and information on subsidiaries and significant shareholdings that has to be disclosed under sections 3–4 of the Companies Act 1967, as amended: *i.e.* Balance Sheet items (B), (C), (D)(ii)–(iv), and (I) below (1981 Act, Sched. 1, para. 58).

2. *Balance sheet*

The following details (which largely correspond to the old 1967 Act second schedule requirements) must be disclosed by way of notes:

(A) *Share capital and loan stock*

    (i) Authorised share capital and number and nominal value of each class of shares allotted (para. 38).

    (ii) Where redeemable shares (either preference or equity) have been allotted the notes must disclose the earliest and latest dates of redemption, whether the company is obliged to redeem them or merely has the option to do so, and whether any premium is payable on redemption, and if so the amount (para. 38).

    (iii) Where shares or debentures have been allotted during the year, the reasons for making the issue, the classes of securities involved and the amount/number issued or allotted, and the aggregate nominal value and the consideration received for each class. Moreover, in respect of debentures particulars must be disclosed of any redeemable debentures the company has power to re-issue, and the nominal amount and book value of any debentures held by a nominee or trustee of the company (paras. 39, 41).

    (iv) Where options or similar rights exist in relation to shares, the number, description and amount of the shares involved, the period during which the right is exercisable, and the price payable have to be disclosed (para. 40).

(B) *Reserves and provisions*

The aggregate amounts of each reserve and provision (including any material amount included in the category "other provisions") at the beginning and end of the financial year must be disclosed, together with details of movements to and from such reserves and provisions during the year (para. 46). In addition, the amount of any provision for taxation other than deferred taxation must be disclosed separately (para. 47); while under the terms of SSAP 15 the balance on the deferred tax account has to be shown separately. Other requirements in relation to the presentation of tax liabilities in the balance sheet and profit and loss account and accompanying notes are to be found in SSAP 8.

(C) *Fixed assets*

For each item under this heading, both tangible and intangible assets, and also for long-term investments, the notes must disclose in respect of cost or valuation the aggregate amounts at the beginning and end of the year, the amounts of any acquisitions, disposals and transfers, and the effect of applying the alternative accounting valuation rules (see below). In addition, details must be given of the cumulative amounts of provisions for depreciation or for the diminution in the value of assets at both the beginning and end of the financial year, and the amounts of any additions, reductions through asset disposals, and any other adjustments to such provisions made during the year (para. 42).

Where a fixed asset (other than listed investments) has been revalued, the notes must disclose the year in which the assets were severally valued and the several values; and in the years of each valuation the names or qualifications of the valuers and the bases of valuation (para. 43).

As under the second schedule to the 1967 Act, land and buildings must be divided among freeholds, long leaseholds (*i.e.* with more than 50 years of lease unexpired at the year end) and short leaseholds (1981 Act, Sched. 1, paras. 44, 82).

(D) *Investments*

Regardless of whether investments are shown as fixed or current assets the following details must be disclosed:

(i) The amount of listed investments, split between investments listed on a recognised stock exchange, together with their quoted value (and estimated market value where this is higher) if it (or they) differ from the value shown in the balance sheet; and unlisted investments. The latter category includes securities traded on the Unlisted Securities Market and the over-the-counter market, but there is no longer a requirement (as there was under para. 5A of the second schedule to the 1967 Act) to disclose either the directors' valuation of the unlisted securities or other information relating to them (paras. 45 and 83).

(ii) Under section 3 of the 1981 Act an investor company has to disclose the identity of an investee company (other than a subsidiary) in which shares are held which exceed $\frac{1}{10}$ of the nominal value of any class of equity shares or the total allotted share capital of the investee company. Similarly, the identity of such an investee company must be revealed where the amount invested as shown in the investor company's balance sheet exceeds $\frac{1}{10}$ of its assets. The details to be disclosed about such an investee company are its name, its country of registration and/or incorporation, and the identity and proportion of each class of share held. The Stock Exchange Listing Agreement in addition requires, for all investments in which there is a participation of 20 per cent. or more, details of the countries in which the investee operates to be disclosed.

(iii) Under section 3 of the Companies Act 1967 a holding company is required to disclose the identities, places of incorporation and particulars of shareholdings in subsidiary companies. Under section 4 of the 1981 Act further financial information relating to such subsidiaries and investee companies in which the investor company holds $\frac{1}{5}$ or more of the allotted nominal share capital has to be disclosed, unless the investor company is exempt from preparing group accounts, or does so (including using the equity partial consolidation method) in such a way as to include the relevant information (which will generally be the case in the United Kingdom), or the subsidiary or investee company is exempt from having to file its accounts with the Registrar. The additional financial information in question is the aggregate capital and reserves, and the profit or loss, of the subsidiary/investee company as shown in its last accounts.

(iv) Where information required to be disclosed in (ii) and (iii) above is immaterial and would involve preparing a statement of excessive length, the details can merely be annexed to the company's annual return (1981 Act, s.4(8)).

(E) *Creditors*

For each item under heading H in format 1 of the balance sheet (above) and its equivalent in format 2, the following must be disclosed:

(i) Amounts payable (other than by instalments) more than five years hence.

(ii) The aggregate amount of any instalments payable five or more years hence.

(iii) The terms of payment and any applicable rate of interest.

(iv) The aggregate figure for secured creditors and the nature of securities given.

(v) The amount and period of any arrears of fixed cumulative dividends (paras. 48, 49, 84).

(F) *Guarantees and financial commitments*

The following items must be disclosed, and be analysed as between (a) any holding company or fellow subsidiary, and (b) any subsidiary:

(i) The amount of third party liabilities secured by charges on the company's assets.

(ii) The amount, nature and security provided (if any) in relation to any contingent liability. (SSAP 18 requires additional disclosures for such items.)

(iii) The aggregate of capital expenditure (a) contracted for, and (b) authorised by the directors but not contracted for.

(iv) Pension commitments (a) provided for, and (b) not provided for. (However, there is no requirement to disclose the basis for estimating such commitments, though the ASC is studying the matter.)

(v) Any other commitments relevant to a proper understanding of the company's affairs (para. 50).

(G) *Dividends*

The aggregate amount of proposed dividends has to be disclosed (paras. 3 and 51).

(H) *Loans made for the purchase of a company's shares*

Details of any outstanding loan made for the purpose of acquiring the company's shares under sections 42–43 of the Companies Act 1981 must be disclosed in aggregate for each item in which they are included (para. 51).

(1) *Transactions with directors and officers of the company*

Under sections 54–56 of the Companies Act 1980 particulars must be disclosed in notes to the accounts of any material transaction or arrangement with a director, shadow director, connected person or officer other than a director. The information to be disclosed is, generally:

    (i) The fact that the transaction, loan, arrangement or agreement was made or existed during the financial year; and

    (ii) The name of the director and/or person concerned (1980 Act, s.55(1)).

With regard to transactions, the value has to be disclosed, as well as the nature of any material interest; while for loans and similar arrangements the following details must be given:

    (i) Principal and interest at the beginning and end of the financial year, the maximum amount of the liability during the year, interest due but not paid, and related bad debt provisions; and

    (ii) The liability of the company or its subsidiaries under guarantees or security and other similar arrangements at the beginning and end of the year, the maximum potential liability, and expenses or liabilities incurred in discharging the guarantee or security arrangement (1980 Act, ss.49–50, 55(1)).

Disclosure must also be made of loans and other equivalent arrangements with officers other than directors in terms of the aggregate amounts outstanding at the end of the year, together with the number of persons concerned, under the following headings:

    (i) Loans or security therefor and similar arrangements.

    (ii) Quasi-loans or security therefor and similar arrangements; and

    (iii) Credit transactions or security therefor and similar arrangements (1980 Act, ss.49, 56).

Exemptions from these disclosure requirements are permitted on a number of grounds, most notably in relation to service contracts and where the values of the items or interests are small (generally if they do not exceed £5,000 in aggregate at any time during the year) (1980 Act, s.58).

3. *Profit and loss account*
   (A) *Segmental analysis*

     (i) Where, in the opinion of the directors, a company has carried on two or more classes of business which differ substantially the notes must for each class show the turnover and the pre-tax profit or loss. Turnover in this context means revenues from ordinary activities net of trade discounts, VAT and other duties. (This treatment of VAT is consistent with the terms of SSAP 5.) In determining the source of turnover or of profit or loss the directors are to have regard to the way in which the company's activities are organised (paras. 55 and 94).

     (ii) Where, in the opinion of the directors, a company has supplied goods and services to two or more geographical *markets* the turnover must be disaggregated as between such markets (para. 55). By contrast the Stock Exchange Listing Agreement requires a geographical analysis of turnover and contribution to trading results of trading (*i.e.* manufacturing, etc.) *operations* abroad.

     (iii) Segmental information need not be disclosed if the directors are of the opinion that its publication would be detrimental to the company's best interests, but if this is the case the fact that such an analysis is being withheld must be stated (para. 55(5)).

(B) *Other sources of income*

Income from listed investments or net rents from land must be disclosed (para. 53). (Before the Companies Act 1981 there was also a requirement to disclose income from unquoted investments.)

(C) *Extraordinary items*

Particulars must be disclosed of prior year transactions included in the profit and lost account; extraordinary items (gross and net of associated tax); and exceptional items (*i.e.* those which arise as a result of the ordinary activities of the business but are abnormal by virtue of their size or incidence) (para. 57). (These requirements are substantially the same as the terms of SSAP 6, except that in relation to extraordinary items that standard only requires disclosure of the net amounts.)

(D) *Taxation*

The notes must disclose the amounts of the charges to both United Kingdom corporation and United Kingdom income taxes, together with a note of the gross amount of the former before any double taxation relief, and details of any overseas taxation borne. Moreover, the tax associated with any extraordinary item must also be shown separately. In addition, the basis of the United Kingdom corporation tax charge must be disclosed, together with details of any special circumstances that affect any liability to taxation (para. 54).

Further requirements concerning the calculation and disclosure of taxation are given in SSAPs 8 and 15.

(E) *Specific expenses*

Details of the following must be disclosed:

(i) Interest on loans outside the group, analysed between (a) bank loans, overdrafts and other loans repayable either in a lump sum within five years or by instalments with the last instalment payable within that period; and (b) any other loans (para. 53).

(ii) Hire charges for plant and machinery (para. 53). (ED 29 covers the treatment of leased assets.)

(iii) Auditors' remuneration (including expenses) (para. 53).

(iv) Amounts set aside for the redemption of (a) share capital; and (b) loans (para. 53).

(F) *Employees and their remuneration*

Details must be disclosed of the following:

(i) The average number of employees in the financial year, found by summing the number of employees (both full- and part-time) week-by-week and dividing by the number of weeks in the period. This figure is then broken down into such categories of employee as the directors select, having regard to the company's organisation (para. 56). (The data are to relate to all employees, not just to those working in the United Kingdom, as was the requirement under section 18 of the 1967 Act.)

(ii) Insofar as they are not disclosed in the profit and loss account, the aggregate amount of each of the following: (a) wages and salaries payable; (b) social security costs, including contributions to state run pension schemes; and (c) other pension costs incurred, comprising contributions to a private pension scheme by the company, any other sums set aside for that purpose, and any pension payments (paras. 56 and 93).

(iii) Under section 196 of the Companies Act 1948 (a) directors' emoluments (b) directors' pensions; and (c) compensation payments to directors for loss of office.

(iv) Under section 6 of the Companies Act 1967 (as amended by S.I. 1982 No. 1698), where the total emoluments of all the directors exceed £60,000 in the year in question, the emoluments of the chairman, the highest paid director (if other than the chairman), the number of directors who did not receive emoluments, and the number of directors who received emoluments in the following bands: £0 up to £5,000; over £5,000 and up to £10,000; over £10,000 and up to £15,000; and so on, the bands rising by increments of £5,000. (It is only necessary to show those bands for which there are entries.)

(v) Under section 7 of the 1967 Act the number of directors who have waived rights to receive emoluments and the aggregate amount of those emoluments.

(vi) Under section 8 of the 1967 Act (as amended) the numbers of employees (other than directors and employees working wholly or mainly outside the United Kingdom) who received emoluments in the following bands: £30,000 and up to £35,000; over £35,000 and up to £40,000; and so on, the bands rising by increments of £5,000. (Again, it is only necessary to show those bands for which there are entries.)

For the purposes of (iii)–(vi), above, "emoluments" includes fees and percentages, expenses allowances so far as charged to United

Kingdom income tax, and the estimated money value of any other benefits received otherwise than in cash (1967 Act, s.8). In addition, for directors of a company it includes any contribution paid in respect of him under any pension scheme (1948 Act, s.196). The amounts to be brought into account for a financial year are the sums receivable in respect of that year, whenever paid, or, in the case of sums not receivable in respect of a period, the sums paid during that year. With regard to remuneration, the details given in the parent company's accounts must relate to the emoluments, etc., of its directors or employees from all sources, including subsidiaries.

4. *Other notes*

Certain other information has to be disclosed in notes to the financial statements (or sometimes on the face of the accounts themselves) in order to comply with the provisions of the Companies Act 1981 on accounting principles and rules (discussed below), and provisions of various accounting standards and (for quoted companies) the Stock Exchange Listing Agreement.

In addition, under section 5 of the 1967 Act a subsidiary must state in a note to its accounts the name of the company regarded at the year end by the directors as being the company's ultimate holding company and its country of incorporation. However, such disclosure is not required of a company carrying on business outside the United Kingdom if it would be harmful to the business of the ultimate holding company or members of the group, the matter to be assessed by the directors and the Department of Trade.

5. *Modified financial statements*

Under section 6 of the 1981 Act the directors of a *medium sized* company may omit from the statements that they file with the Registrar of Companies detailed information concerning turnover and pre-tax profit by line of business and geographical market (*i.e.* profit and loss account note (A), above).

The concessions offered to *small sized* companies are more far reaching—of the items which may be disclosed in notes listed above, only the following have to be disclosed:

1. General notes: Accounting policies, including in particular the bases of foreign currency translations.

2. Balance sheet:	(A) Share capital and loan stock: items (i) and (ii), and in so far as it relates to shares (but not to loan stock) (iii). (E) Creditors, items (i), (ii) and (iv). (I) Transactions with directors and officers of the company.
3. Profit and loss account:	None
4. Other notes:	None of those required by Sched. 1 to the 1981 Act (*e.g.* relating to accounting principles and rules, except in so far as they can be interpreted as accounting policies).

Comparative amounts for previous years must still be given where appropriate for such items as are disclosed in notes.

Accounting principles and rules

Prior to 1981 successive Companies Acts gave little guidance as to what accounting principles and rules should be followed in preparing the annual accounts of companies. However, the view taken by the Cohen and Jenkins Committees on company law reform, reporting respectively in 1945 and 1962, was that in general the traditional historical cost convention used by accountants was appropriate, and it was largely left to the professional accountancy bodies themselves to formulate such rules as they deemed necessary.[20] The supposed inadequacy of such rules was highlighted in the late 1960s in a number of instances referred to the City Panel on Take-Overs and Mergers (see page 718), and this led to the creation of the Accounting Standards Committee in 1969, whose avowed aim was to codify the different practices and narrow the choice between them. In the decade since then the ASC has succeeded in deflecting much of the criticism formerly directed at the accountancy profession, and while it has provided a useful framework for codifying conventions and agreeing standard forms of presentation, it has not greatly changed the substance of accounting practice. Only in relation to current cost accounting, on which its hand was forced by the report of the government-appointed Sandilands Committee,[21] has it taken a new initiative.

---

[20] (1945) Cmnd. 6659, and (1962) Cmnd. 1749, respectively: the relevant paragraphs are 98 for Cohen and 333 for Jenkins.

[21] (1975) Cmnd. 6225.

In the meantime the EEC's Fourth Directive on company law harmonization included guidance on the so-called accounting principles which should be employed in preparing company accounts. For the most part these related to the historical cost convention, widely applied in a particularly conservative manner in most continental countries, largely to delay profit recognition for tax purposes. However, it was necessary to accommodate current (replacement) cost accounting, used for over 30 years by some major companies in the Netherlands, and also the practice whereby many major listed companies in the United Kingdom have in recent years taken to revaluing all or part of their fixed assets, partly it seems as a way of signalling to the public changes in managerial expectations. Moreover, it was also perceived necessary to provide a framework within which any new form of current price level or current cost system of accounting could be accommodated—a matter of some importance since there were moves afoot in the late 1970s to introduce such systems in various continental countries as well as in the United Kingdom.

The result is that Part II of the first schedule to the 1981 Act is divided into three sections: 1. accounting principles; 2. historical cost accounting rules; and 3. alternative accounting rules.

1. *Accounting principles and conventions*

Schedule 1 to the 1981 Act reiterates the four so-called principles or concepts contained in SSAP 2 which, so long as they are consistent with the statements presenting a true and fair view, are supposed to underlie the preparation of annual accounts: going concern concept, consistency concept, accruals concept, and prudence doctrine. The going concern concept implies that the net realisable values of fixed assets will not normally be the relevant values to use in the accounts—indeed, they will only be appropriate where liquidation is envisaged. Consistent application of accounting policies is necessary to try to ensure comparability from year to year and reduce opportunities to manipulate results. As a result the user should have a better chance of being able to identify the permanent (as opposed to transitory) element in profit, which should improve his forecasting ability. The accruals concept requires that revenues and expenses reported should relate to the financial year in question, regardless of when cash is actually received or spent. In practice, however, accountants rarely take the accruals principle to its logical conclusion, preferring to apply the prudence doctrine, which SSAP 2 (but not the 1981 Act) indicates should prevail where there is conflict between the two. Paragraph 12 of the schedule specifies two rules in relation to the prudence doctrine: (a) that only realised profits should be included in the income statement (though para. 90 defines such profits only in terms of best accounting practice at the time), and (b) that all liabilities and losses that have arisen and are likely to arise should be taken into account. Moreover, they must be included even when they only become apparent after the end of the accounting year, which is consistent with the terms of SSAP 17 on accounting for post balance sheet events.

Paragraph 14 of the Schedule indicates that each asset and liability must be valued separately. Since an asset is undefined this might technically cause problems—for instance, where a machine is owned, is it the machine itself or its component parts that constitute(s) the asset(s)? However, the main purpose of the requirement seems to be to try to ensure that assets which may reasonably be regarded as separate (such as different lines of stock) are valued on an individual rather than a group basis. In fact, the standard on stock valuation, SSAP 9, requires use of the individual item valuation basis, though for tax purposes the group basis remains acceptable.[22]

Paragraph 15 of the Schedule permits directors to depart from any of the principles referred to above if their application is inconsistent with the presentation of a true and fair view. However, particulars of such a departure, the reasons and the effect must be disclosed.

2. *Historical cost accounting rules*
(A) *Fixed assets*

Paragraph 75 of the schedule defines fixed assets as those assets intended for use on a continuing basis, and the basic rule is that they should be shown at either the purchase price or production cost (the meaning of which terms is discussed below), net of any depreciation or diminution in value (para. 17). The latter apply where a fixed asset is wasting in nature and has a limited useful economic life, cost (net of estimated scrap value) being written off "systematically" over such life. Additional depreciation *may* be provided for fixed asset investments in respect of a decline in value (para. 19(1)), and *must*

---

[22] *IRC* v. *Cook, Russell and Co.* [1949] 29 T.C. 387.

be for any fixed asset (including a fixed asset investment) where such decline in value is expected to be permanent (which is consistent with the terms of SSAP 12) (para. 19(2)). The basis of such valuation is not defined, but under the going concern concept it will presumably normally be current value in use. Charges for additional depreciation, and amounts written back if such provisions are deemed no longer necessary, must be separately disclosed in the profit and loss account itself or in the notes thereto. Moreover, as regards the former a distinction must be drawn between charges made under para. 19(1) and those under para. 19(2).

(B) *Intangible fixed assets*

(i) The original amount at which acquired goodwill (other than that arising on consolidation: para. 66) is shown in the accounts must be written off "systematically" over a period chosen by the directors which must not exceed its useful economic life. The period of, and the reasons for choosing such period, must be disclosed in a note.

The proposed accounting standard on goodwill, ED 30, would permit purchased goodwill either to be written off immediately against reserves representing realised profits, or to be amortised through the profit and loss account over its estimated useful economic life, which should not exceed 20 years. The amount attributed to purchased goodwill is to be the difference between the fair value of the consideration given and the fair value of the separable net assets acquired.

Under the 1981 Act, the amount written off goodwill year by year has to be disclosed in the profit and loss account, but where it is written off immediately against reserves on acquisition (a not uncommon practice in the United Kingdom) such disclosure would not appear to be necessary. However, ED 30 requires that the amount of goodwill recognised as a result of any acquisitions during the year should be shown separately for each acquisition where material, even where it is written off immediately to reserves.

(ii) Paragraph 20 permits development (but not research) costs to be "capitalised" (a term defined in para. 78) and be shown in the balance sheet, and then only in "special circumstances." Where this is done notes must disclose the reasons for capitalising such development costs and the period over which they are being written off. Development expenditure is defined in SSAP 13 (though not in the Act)—it is essentially identifiable expenditure related to a specific project which can reasonably be expected to be recovered in the future, and upon capitalisation is to be amortised on a systematic basis. Where such expenditure is capitalised a further note to the accounts will generally be required by section 84 of the 1981 Act to indicate that such unamortised expenditure is not being treated as a realised loss in calculating distributable profits and the justification for such treatment (which under para. 90 of the first schedule to the 1981 Act is likely to be that it is consistent with accepted accounting principles and practice).

(C) *Current assets*

    (i) Such assets are defined in para. 75 of the first Schedule to the 1981 Act as any assets not intended for use on a continuing basis in the company's activities. In general they are to be valued at the lower of, on the one hand, purchase price or production cost (the meaning of which is discussed below); and, on the other, net realisable value (paras. 22–23). This is slightly more restrictive than previous accounting practice, where the rule was the lower of original cost and market value at the balance sheet date, the latter in some circumstances being capable of interpretation for stocks, both for tax and financial reporting purposes, as replacement cost rather than net realisable value.[23]

    Accounting practice in showing debtors net of a bad debts provision is consistent with this rule. Small companies may well determine such provisions in relation to specific debts, as is required for calculating the company's liability to corporation tax.[24] However, larger companies

---

[23] *B.S.C. Footwear Ltd.* v. *Ridgway* [1971] T.R. 121; SSAP. 9.
[24] Income and Corporation Taxes Act 1970, s.130(1).

may well prefer to use general bad debt provisions for financial reporting purposes.

Where the going concern assumption is reasonable, accounting practice is generally to value work-in-progress at cost since net realisable value (which would usually be far lower) is irrelevant in such circumstances. Moreover, it is also common practice, in line with the terms of SSAP 9, for profits to be recognised gradually over the period of long-term contracts.

Paragraph 23 of the schedule indicates that where an asset has been written down to net realisable value, but such value has subsequently risen, even if not fully up to cost again, the amount of the provision so made and no longer required must be written back.

(ii) Under para. 27 of the Schedule, the purchase price or production cost of each class of stocks and similar fungible items (that is, assets where individual units—such as shares held—are indistinguishable from each other), may be determined using the most appropriate of any one of four methods: first in first out (FIFO), last in first out (LIFO), weighted average cost, and any similar method. In addition, para. 25 of the schedule (referred to below) effectively permits use of the base stock method for stocks of raw materials and consumables. LIFO and base stock methods are not acceptable for tax purposes in the United Kingdom[25] and in such circumstances, because of the need to keep a second set of stock records, it is generally impractical to use the former for financial reporting purposes. Moreover, SSAP 9 suggests that neither LIFO nor base stock methods provide reasonable approximations to the cost of stocks. Nevertheless, some companies (notably in the sugar and base metal industries) continue to use the base stock method, and overseas subsidiaries of many British companies often use LIFO to obtain certain tax advantages, thus securing nominal qualification in the

---

[25] The relevant cases are, respectively: *Minister of National Revenue* v. *Anaconda American Brass Ltd.* [1956] A.C. 85; and *Patrick* v. *Broadstone Mills* [1953] 33 T.C. 44.

auditors' report on the group accounts as they do not technically comply with the terms of SSAP 9.

(iii) As discussed below, where stocks and work-in-progress are valued at production cost, the latter *may* include a reasonable proportion of manufacturing overheads. Presumably these can comprise either just variable or both variable and fixed overhead costs. Tax law is fairly flexible on this matter,[26] but SSAP 9 in fact *requires* that for financial reporting purposes a reasonable proportion of overheads (including a proportion of fixed costs) should be included in the valuation of stocks and work-in-progress.

(iv) Whatever method of stock valuation is used, any *material difference* between the purchase price or production cost and the "relevant alternative amount" must be shown in a note to the accounts. Such "relative alternative amount" will normally be replacement cost at the balance sheet date, but an acceptable approximation very often will be a value based on the most recent purchase price or production cost (paras. 27(3), (4), (5)).

(D) *Purchase price and production cost*

(i) Purchase price is defined in the first schedule to the 1981 Act as the actual price paid for an asset, including expenses incidental to its acquisition (paras. 26(1) and 89).

(ii) Producton cost is the sum of (a) the purchase price of raw materials and consumables used; and (b) direct production costs incurred (but, in the case of current assets, excluding distribution costs); plus (c) other costs that *may* be included, being a reasonable proportion of indirect costs in so far as they relate to the period of production. These latter may include interest on borrowed capital, where appropriate, but if this is the case, the fact and the amount involved must be disclosed in a note (para. 26).

(iii) Where there is no record for an asset of its original purchase price or production cost, or of related expenditure, the earliest value ascribed to it may be used instead,

---

[26] *Ostime* v. *Duple Motor Bodies* [1961] 39 T.C. 537.

but this fact must be disclosed in the accounts or the notes thereto (paras. 28 and 51(1)).

(iv) Paragraph 25 of the schedule permits tangible fixed assets and stocks of raw materials and consumables to be shown at a fixed quantity and fixed value where they are constantly being replaced and (a) their overall value is not material to the assessment of the company's state of affairs; and (b) their quantity, value and composition is not subject to material variation.

(v) Under para. 24, where an amount owed to a creditor is greater that the value of the asset received, the difference may be treated as an asset rather than an expense, analogous to acquired goodwill. However, it must be written off by "reasonable amounts" each year and must be completely written off before repayment of the debt. Any such asset in the balance sheet must be disclosed either in the statement or in the notes thereto. There is no reference to systematic amortisation in these provisions, as there is in relation to acquired goodwill, nor apparently is it necessary to indicate the period over which the asset is being written off.

3. *Alternative accounting rules*

If they so determine, companies may adopt any of the alternative accounting rules outlined in Section C of Part II of the first schedule to the 1981 Act. Such rules apply only to the main financial statements, which as a result can be prepared not only in terms of the historical cost convention, but can instead be modified to take into account selective revaluations or be completely re-stated in current cost terms.

SSAP 16 permits those companies to which it applies (generally listed companies and companies meeting two of three criteria: turnover over £5m per annum; total assets in the historical cost accounts in excess of £2·5m; and average number of employees over 250) to present current cost accounts either as supplementary statements (which appears to be usual practice) or as the main financial statements. Only in the latter case will the alternative accounting rules apply to the current cost accounts prepared so as to comply with SSAP 16.

The alternative rules (paras. 31–34) are as follows:

(i) Intangible assets, other than goodwill, may be shown at current cost.

(ii) Goodwill (for which current cost has no clear meaning) should be shown at its cost of acquisition, less amortisation, unless it is written off immediately.

(iii) Tangible fixed assets may be stated either at their market values on the dates they were last valued or at current cost. (The latter could either be the second-hand value or the current cost new less notional depreciation.)

(iv) Fixed asset investments may be stated either at their market values on the dates they were last valued or at a value determined on an appropriate basis given the company's circumstances, in which case the method and reasons for using it must be disclosed. (Such a basis might be the equity "net assets" basis appropriate for accounting for associated companies under SSAP 1.)

(v) Current asset investments and stocks may be stated at their current costs.

(vi) As regards wasting fixed assets, depreciation should be based on the revalued amounts, not the purchase price or production cost. The charge to the profit and loss account can either be that based on the current value or just be the historical cost charge. However, in the latter case the difference between the two must be disclosed either in the accounts or in the notes thereto. This would appear to allow such differences to be debited or credited direct to the revaluation reserve.

(vii) Accumulated unrealised holding gains arising from revaluations which result from application of the alternative accounting rules must be credited to a revaluation reserve, and this must be shown separately in the balance sheet. Amounts can only be transferred from the revaluation reserve to the profit and loss account where (a) the amount in question was previously charged to the profit and loss account; or (b) it represents a realised profit. Otherwise the balance of the reserve has to be reduced where there is no longer any justification for its existence (*e.g.* where there has been a subsequent decline in the value of an asset previously revalued upwards). An explanation of the tax effects of increases or reductions in the revaluation reserve (such as the tax that would be payable if the asset were sold at its revalued amount) must be disclosed in a note to the accounts.

(viii) Where alternative rules are applied the notes must state the items affected, the basis of valuation of each balance sheet item, and (with the exception of stocks) for each of the latter items, including provisions separately, either the corresponding amount under the historical cost convention or the differences between the two sets of figures. Alternatively the basis of valuation, and the corresponding amounts or differences, can be disclosed on the face of the balance sheet rather than in notes.

Powers of the Secretary of State for Trade

Under section 454 of the Companies Act 1948 and section 18 of the Companies Act 1981 the Secretary of State for Trade can alter, add to or otherwise modify by statutory instrument the requirements relating to the financial statements and annexed reports that have to be laid before the company in general meeting and/or have to be filed with the Registrar. Moreover, section 5 of the 1981 Act gives the Secretary of State power to alter the exemptions offered to small and medium sized companies in respect of the statements they file with the Registrar; and he also has powers to exempt individual groups from disclosing information about unconsolidated subsidiaries (1981 Act, Sched. 1, para. 69(6)) and overseas companies from certain requirements (1976 Act, s.9, as amended by 1981 Act, s.19).

Penalties for failure to comply with the requirements

It is the duty of a company's directors to ensure that the accounts and other documents laid before the company in general meeting or filed with the Registrar comply with the Companies Acts 1948 to 1981. Each director who fails in this duty, and in his duty to ensure the rules for publication are met, will be liable to a fine, unless he can show he took all reasonable steps to ensure that the requirements of the Acts were complied with (1948 Act, s.149(7); 1981 Act, ss.1(1), 11(10)).

Non statutory requirements

Amongst the more important additional disclosures required of companies by the Accounting Standards Committee are a flow of funds statement (SSAP 10) and a set of current cost financial statements (SSAP 16). The former applies to all companies with an annual turnover or gross income of more than £25,000. The statement, which should give a true and fair view of changes in the financial position of a company (or, where appropriate, group) should be capable of reconciliation with the profit and loss account and balance sheet, but may nevertheless include supplementary disclosures. As has been previously indicated on page 489, listed companies and companies meeting two of three size criteria (other than subsidiaries, insurance and property companies, and investment trusts) are required to publish (consolidated) current cost accounts. Basically, for the profit and loss account these show adjustments required to bring depreciation and cost of sales charges to their current cost equivalents and a working capital adjustment to offset the impact of inflation on the company's net investment in debtors. These adjustments are deducted from historical cost profit before charging interest and taxation to show current cost operating profit. An amount called the gearing adjustment is then added back, net of interest charged, to produce the pre-tax current cost profit figure.

Amongst the requirements imposed on quoted companies by the Stock Exchange Listing Agreement are provisions for the publication of half-year and preliminary profit statements, and disclosure in the annual report under para. 10 of the agreement of reasons for any significant departure from standard accounting practice; an explanation of a substantial difference between trading results and any profit forecast made by the company; details of loans repayable in less than a year, in periods between one and two years and between two and five years, and beyond five years; and a statement as to whether or not for tax purposes the company is a close company (*i.e.* is under the control of a limited number of people).

GROUP ACCOUNTS

Some users of accounting statements may only be interested in the financial affairs of the particular *legal entity* with which they are dealing, most obviously unsecured creditors. However, others (such as existing and potential shareholders) may instead be rather more interested in the affairs of an *economic entity,* since those are likely to be more relevant for their decision-making needs. Such an entity can extend as far as a colluding group of companies between which there are no formal legal links; or it may exist where companies are tied together economically in a joint venture arrangement or even sometimes by the existence of a long term contract. This latter notion of a group, where undertakings are managed on a central and unified basis, is essentially the view taken in Germany and adopted in the EEC Commission's draft Seventh Directive on company law harmonization.[27] The traditional British view is somewhat narrower, section 154 of the Companies Act 1948 determining the existence of a group where the holding company either controls the composition of the board of directors of a subsidiary, or holds more than half the nominal value of its equity share capital.

The advantage to a user of financial statements of having access to a set of group accounts, however the term "group" is defined, is that the statements can be prepared so as to eliminate the often sizeable internal, intra-group transactions and show a more complete picture of the group financial structure. However, the preparation of full consolidated accounts may of necessity mean some particularly interesting piece of information will be lost—for instance, the fact that one subsidiary has been operating at a loss may no longer be apparent. Nevertheless, the potential significance of group accounts has long been recognised, and many large public companies in the United Kingdom began publishing them on a voluntary basis in the 1920s, long before section 150 of the 1948 Companies Act made their preparation compulsory.[28] Moreover, it is interesting that several large economic entities, most notably Unilever and Royal Dutch-Shell, publish joint venture accounts as well as the strictly legal accounts for their British participant companies, and it is these supplementary statements which are accorded most prominence in the group annual reports and which are critically scrutinised by professional financial analysts.

[27] Draft Seventh Directive on Company Law Harmonization, O.J. 1979 C14/2. However, the Draft Directive is now being subjected to extensive revisions.
[28] See J. Kitchen, *The Accounts of British Holding Company Groups: Developments and Attitudes to Disclosure in the Early Years, Accounting and Business Research,* Spring 1972, pp. 114–136.

General requirements

By section 150 of the 1948 Act, as amended, the general rule is that where at the end of its financial year a company has subsidiaries, its directors must prepare for the appropriate accounting reference period a group profit and loss account and balance sheet which have to be laid before the company in general meeting. Moreover, where a holding company publishes its own full individual financial statements, it must also publish with them its group accounts (1981 Act, s.11(3)). Normally such group accounts will comprise a consolidated profit and loss account and balance sheet, though the directors may, if they feel it will be more appropriate in presenting a true and fair view of the affairs of the group, present the same or equivalent information in more than one set of consolidated accounts, each dealing with a sub-group of companies (in practice typically operating in separate, distinct activities), or in individual accounts for each unconsolidated subsidiary, or in supplementary statements annexed to the accounts giving equivalent information (1948 Act, s.151; 1981 Act, s.2 and Sched. 1, para. 68). However, the directors need not submit group accounts if a company is itself a wholly owned subsidiary of another company incorporated in Great Britain; or if they are of the opinion that (a) such accounts are impracticable, or in view of the insignificant amounts involved would be of no real value to members, or would involve expense or delay out of proportion to their value to members; or (b) the result would be misleading, or be harmful to the business of the group; or (c) the business of the holding company and that of the subsidiary are so different that they cannot be treated as a single undertaking. In case (c), and when they are said to be harmful, group accounts can only be dispensed with by approval of the Department of Trade (1948 Act, s.150), but normal practice where consolidated accounts would be misleading and/or where businesses are substantially different is for companies to use one of the alternative methods of presentation authorised in s.151 of the 1948 Act, referred to above.

The effect of the above provisions is that most groups in Great Britain publish fully consolidated profit and loss accounts and balance sheets, and these are published together with the individual balance sheet of the holding company, though its unconsolidated profit and loss account does not have to be presented (see above, page 462). The EEC's draft Seventh Directive would require that all groups should prepare consolidated accounts, but only the group profit and loss account and balance sheet, not the balance sheet of the holding company as well[29]; and it also provides for each company with subsidiaries to prepare sub-group consolidated statements.[30]

Under section 2 of the Companies Act 1981 group accounts must give a true and fair view of the state of affairs and profit and loss of the holding company and subsidiaries dealt with thereby as a whole, so far as concerns the members of the company. To enable this to be done properly the directors of the holding company, except where there are good reasons to the contrary, have to secure that the financial year of each subsidiary coincides with that of the holding company (1948 Act, s.153). Both para. 70 of the first Schedule to the Companies Act 1981 and article 6(2) of the draft Seventh Directive require that the reasons for any differences in accounting date should be fully disclosed in notes to the accounts; and para. 70 furthermore requires disclosure of the balance sheet dates of the subsidiaries involved or the earliest and latest of those dates.

Methods of consolidation

There are several different ways of preparing consolidated accounts, a matter apparently not fully appreciated by most lawyers and accountants in Britain. However, now that some of these alternatives are being recognised in legislation it may be helpful to examine them briefly with the help of some examples.

Let it therefore be assumed there are two companies, X and Y, whose summarised balance sheets at December 31, 1981, are as shown in Figure 1.

	X	Y
Net assets	£5,000,000	£2,000,000
Ordinary £1 shares	1,500,000	500,000
Distributable reserves	3,500,000	1,500,000
	£5,000,000	£2,000,000

Figure 1

[29] *Op. cit.*, article 9.
[30] *Op. cit.*, articles 6a and 6b.

First, let it be supposed that X acquires for cash the entire share capital of Y at December 31, 1981, the cash being part of its net assets of £5m. The going concern value of Y is agreed as £3m. The consolidated balance sheet would generally be shown as in Figure 2(a), though in practice the net assets would be added together line-by-line for each different asset and liability category identified. It can be seen that goodwill is created as an asset: it represents the difference between the going concern value at the date of acquisition and the book value of the net assets acquired. It can also be seen that the pre-acquisition profits of Y, the subsidiary, are no longer free for distribution. Only the post-acquisition profits of the subsidiary will be added in to the group's free reserves.

		X Group		X Group
Goodwill	(£3m−£2m)	1,000,000	(£3m−£2m)	1,000,000
Other net assets	(£5m−£3m;+£2m)	4,000,000	(£5m+£2m)	7,000,000
		£5,000,000		£8,000,000
Ordinary share capital (X only)		1,500,000	(£1·5m+£·75m)	2,250,000
Share premium		–	(£3m−£·75m)	2,250,000
Distributable reserves (X only at date of acquisition)		3,500,000		3,500,000
		£5,000,000		£8,000,000

Figure 2 (a) (b)

Now let it be supposed that the consideration given to acquire Y was not cash, but instead was new shares issued by X. It is now necessary to value the consideration given and received. If the shares of X and Y are both quoted this may be relatively easy to assess, though depending on the dates chosen there may be slight differences in the total values of the shares issued and acquired. However, where the companies are unquoted it will be necessary either to assess the value by appraisal or to use the nominal value of the shares given as consideration. The latter gives rise to a problem which will be discussed below. For the moment, let it be assumed here that 750,000 new shares are issued in X to acquire the entire share capital of Y, the one third stake in the new combined enterprise and its future earning power being regarded by both parties as acceptable consideration. Given a market share price in X of £4 per £1 nominal share unit, the consolidated balance sheet appears as in Figure 2(b).

The method of consolidation shown in Figure 2 is known as the *acquisition* (or, in the United States, the *purchase*) method, reflecting the "parent company approach" to group consolidation, and it is that most commonly used in the United Kingdom. Moreover, it can easily be adapted to allow for a situation where less than the entire equity in a subsidiary is acquired. Thus in the case of 2(b), above, let it now be assumed that only three quarters of the share capital in Y is acquired for an issue of 562,500 shares in X, the value of the transaction being assessed at £2·25m. The consolidated balance sheet is then as shown in Figure 3, the goodwill only relating to the majority stake acquired. The minority interest comprises the outside shareholders' stake in a subsidiary's share capital and both its pre- and post-acquisition reserves.

	X Group
Goodwill (£2·25m − ¾×£2m)	750,000
Net assets	7,000,000
	£7,750,000
Ordinary share capital (X only) (£1·5m+£·5625m)	2,062,500
Share premium (£2·25m−£·5625m)	1,687,500
Distributable reserves (X only at acquisition)	3,500,000
Minority interest (¼×£2m)	500,000
	£7,750,000

Figure 3

It would technically be possible, without altering the basic technique, to allow the accounts to reflect a wider entity concept than the parent company approach by showing a notional goodwill figure for the *whole* group (here presumably £750,000 × ⅓ = £1m) and crediting the appropriate share (here £250,000) to the minority interest, but this is never done in practice.

The above examples should have made it clear that the goodwill figure has little economic significance. It merely measures the *historic* difference between the going concern value of *part* of the group (typically the majority share in a subsidiary) and the corresponding book value at the date of purchase. Going concern values, even for parts of businesses, change from day-to-day as expectations of future likely outcomes alter; moreover, goodwill as such has no separate existence from the business as a whole, as do most other assets which appear in balance sheets.

A very different approach to consolidation, known as the *merger* (or, in the United States, the *pooling*) method avoids some of these problems and is probably more appropriate if it is deemed necessary to try to reflect a wider entity concept than the narrow parent company approach. Quite apart from avoiding the creation of goodwill on acquisition, it also has the advantage of bringing all or some of the pre-acquisition profits of the technical subsidiaries into the group balance sheet as distributable reserves. It is therefore particularly attractive where two companies of more or less equal size merge their activities.

To illustrate the technique, return to the facts used to derive the consolidated balance sheet in Figure 2(b). If it is argued that the value of the shares issued is their par value of £750,000, only £250,000 (the difference between the par values of shares issued and acquired by X) of the pre-acquisition profits of Y has to be regarded as non-distributable. The consolidated balance sheet would then appear as in Figure 4.

	X Group
Net assets (£5m+£2m)	£7,000,000
Ordinary share capital (X only) (£1·5m+£·75m)	2,250,000
Distributable reserves (£3·5m+(£1·5m−£·25m))	4,750,000
	£7,000,000

Figure 4

The merger method is apparently the normal method of consolidation for share exchanges in Germany, probably reflecting the fact that it offers a reasonable reflection of the economic entity group concept (though strangely the EEC's draft Seventh Directive seems to favour the parent company approach).[31] It is also popular in the United States, though it has been abused there, some companies using it to inflate reported group profits in the year of acquisition. However, empirical evidence suggests the investing public sees through such manoeuvres.[32] In Great Britain the method was used by a growing number of leading quoted companies in the late 1960s to account for mergers between large groups. A draft accounting standard was published on the subject in 1971, but doubts were expressed about the validity of the merger treatment in view of the decision in *Head (Henry) & Co. Ltd.* v. *Ropner Holdings Ltd.*,[33] concerning the need to establish a share premium account (see above, pp. 177–178). The decision in that case was confirmed in *Shearer* v. *Bercain, Ltd.*,[34] which was widely regarded by the accountancy profession as closing the door on the merger method of consolidation. However, sections 37–41 of the 1981 Act now provide relief from section 56 of the 1948 Act, thus making it legitimate to use the approach as long as the necessary conditions are met—the main one is that the acquiring company should secure at least 90 per cent. in nominal value of each class of the share capital of the company being taken over (see above, pp. 177, 178). Since the Act came into force a draft accounting standard has been issued by the ASC (ED 31, October 1982) indicating mutually exclusive conditions where merger and acquisition accounting methods should be used. The conditions are slightly more restrictive in relation to merger accounting than those contained in the 1981 Act.

A third approach to consolidation is the proprietary approach, which eliminates recognition of the outside interest in both the balance sheet and the profit and loss account and is usually applied where the ownership stake is 50 per cent. or less. The concept can be implemented in one of two ways: either (a) by proportional consolidation, where income, assets and liabilities are separately added in to the holding company's accounts on a *pro rata* basis item by item; or (b) by the equity method of consolidation, where an investment is shown in the group balance sheet *pro rata* to its current net asset value, the net

---

[31] *Op. cit.*, article 12.
[32] Hong, H., R. S. Kaplan and G. Mandelker, *Pooling v. Purchase: The Effects of Accounting for Mergers on Stock Prices, The Accounting Review,* January 1978, pp. 31–47.
[33] [1952] Ch. 124.
[34] [1980] 3 All E.R. 295.

changes each year usually being dealt with in the profit and loss account. Both methods are accommodated within the EEC's draft Seventh Directive,[35] though proportional consolidation, not uncommon on the Continent, is rarely practised by British companies. However, BP used it to account for its Abu Dhabi investments up until 1972. The equity method has long been used in the United States to account for joint ventures and for subsidiaries not fully consolidated, and since the early 1970s it has been employed in Britain to account for associated companies, an accounting standard on the subject being issued in 1971. Reference is also made to the equity method of accounting in Schedule 1, para. 65, of the 1981 Act. However, it should be noted that there is more than one way of showing the equity value of an investment in a consolidated balance sheet—the Seventh Directive implies that the goodwill (or premium) on acquisition should be shown separately, although this has only recently become standard British practice.[36]

Unrealised intra-group profits

One further point relating to consolidated accounts, which is of some relevance in relation to distributable profits as defined in sections 39–43 of the Companies Act 1980, concerns the treatment of unrealised inter-company profits. Briefly, if one member of a group sells goods to another, such goods as are in stock at the balance sheet date will potentially include an element of unrealised profit. This can logically be eliminated in one of two ways—either by adopting a "single entity" approach and treating the transactions as though they had never taken place: this means writing back the unrealised profit against the company which sold the goods, with the minority interest in the selling company bearing its appropriate share; or, alternatively, by adopting a "separate entity" approach, in which case any unrealised profit must be written back against the company which holds the goods, with the minority interest in that company (if any) again bearing its appropriate share. In practice, however, British companies tend either to write back the whole of the unrealised profit regardless against the majority's profits; or eliminate the majority's profit only against the company which sold the stock.[37]

---

[35] *Op. cit.*, articles 17–18.
[36] *Op. cit.*, article 17; *cf.* SSAP 1, as revised April 1982, paras. 8 and 26.
[37] See D. A. Egginton, *Unrealised Profit and Consolidated Accounts, Accountancy,* May 1965, pp. 410–415.

Disclosure requirements

Although the EEC's Fourth Directive applied only to the annual accounts of individual companies, the disclosure provisions of the 1981 Companies Act as outlined in its first schedule for the most part, and so far as is practicable, equally apply to group financial statements (1981 Act, s.2; Sched. 1, paras. 61–62). The most notable exception is goodwill on consolidation, which under para. 66 of the schedule does not have to be amortised over its economic life.[38] Moreover, investments in closely associated companies can be dealt with in the consolidated accounts using the equity method of accounting (para. 65).

In its own financial statements a holding or subsidiary company must disclose separately the aggregate amounts owed to or from, and any interests in, any holding company or fellow subsidiary; and to or from any subsidiary (Sched. 1, para. 59). A holding company must also disclose in notes to the accounts the number, description and amount of any of its shares or debentures which are held by its subsidiaries or their nominees, except where the subsidiary is concerned only as a personal representative or trustee (Sched. 1, para. 60). The same information required by paras. 59–60 must also be given in respect of any subsidiaries that are not consolidated (para. 67).

Where a holding company does not prepare group accounts, or prepares group accounts which do not deal with one or more of its subsidiaries, the reasons for such treatment must be disclosed in a note, together with an indication of any material qualification in the auditors' reports or reservation in the accounts of such subsidiaries, and the amount of the investment arrived at by applying the equity method of accounting. However, the latter information need not be disclosed if the company is itself the wholly owned subsidiary of another company incorporated in Great Britain and there is a note indicating that, in the directors' opinion, the aggregate value of shares in, and amounts owing from, such subsidiaries is not less than the aggregate of the amounts at which those assets are shown in the balance sheet (Sched. 1, para. 69).

The following provisions of the Companies Acts do not apply to consolidated financial statements:

(i) Section 196 of the 1948 Act, concerning disclosure of directors' emoluments, pensions, etc.

---

[38] However, under the terms of the proposed accounting standard on goodwill, ED 30, it would have to be so amortised if not written off immediately on acquisition.

(ii) Sections 6–7 of the 1967 Act, concerning disclosure of particulars of directors' emoluments and waived emoluments.

(iii) Sections 54 and 56 of the 1980 Act, concerning the disclosure of directors' loans, etc., to the extent that they apply to financial statements other than the group accounts.

(iv) Section 8 of the 1967 Act, concerning particulars of the remuneration of higher paid employees.

(v) Section 4 of the 1967 Act, concerning details of shareholdings in companies other than subsidiaries.

(vi) Section 4 of the 1981 Act, concerning disclosure of financial information in respect of subsidiaries and other companies in which shares are held (Sched. 1, para. 63).

Modified financial statements

The provisions relating to the delivery of modified financial statements to the Registrar equally apply to groups, so long as the group itself, on the basis of group accounts, qualifies for the relevant exemptions and the directors of the holding company take advantage of the exemptions in submitting its own accounts. However, where the group is large or medium sized, the holding company will be treated as being of the same size category, even if on the basis of its unconsolidated accounts it technically qualifies for a smaller size category (1981 Act, ss.9–10).

DIRECTORS' REPORT

Section 157 of the Companies Act 1948 requires that the directors' report should deal with the company's affairs generally and indicate the amount recommended as dividends and the amount proposed to be carried to reserves. However, section 163 of the Act further permitted any item otherwise required to be disclosed in the accounts or notes thereto to be shown instead in the directors' report, though corresponding figures for the previous year had to be given and the item was still subject to audit. Sections 16–23 of the 1967 Act required certain additional matters to be dealt with in the report, but one of these (particulars of exports where annual turnover exceeded £50,000) is no longer required under the terms of the 1981 Act, and several others are now dealt with directly in notes to the accounts (contracts with the company (except service contracts) in which a director has an interest, new issues of shares and debentures and the reasons therefor, directors' options to subscribe for the company's securities, turnover and profit or loss before tax of different classes of activity, and the average weekly number of United Kingdom employees and their total remuneration for the year).

This shift in emphasis reflects the approach of the EEC's Fourth Directive towards the directors' report, where the intention was that it should merely supplement the financial details given in the accounts with certain narrative information about the company's activities and its future prospects. As a result, section 13(1) of the 1981 Act modifies the wording of section 157(1) of the 1948 Act to ensure that henceforward directors should include in their report "a fair review of the development of the business of the company and its subsidiaries during the financial year . . . and of their position at the end of it," but gives no guidance as to how this might be achieved. However, section 13(3) of the 1981 Act replaces a provision in the 1967 Act requiring disclosure of any matters required for an appreciation of a company's affairs by its members with a clause requiring information on any important post balance sheet events, together with an indication of future likely developments in the business and of activities in the field of research and development. Other changes in the 1981 Act included the repeal of section 163 of the 1948 Act (referred to above); and (under s.13(4)) a modification of section 16(1)(e) of the 1967 Act, enabling details of directors' interests at the beginning and end of each year in shares or debentures of the company or its group to be disclosed in notes to the accounts as an alternative to disclosure in the directors' report.

Consequently, the items requiring disclosure in the directors' report are as follows:

(i) A fair review of the development of the business of the company and its subsidiaries during the financial year ending with the balance sheet date and of their position at the end of it (1948 Act, s.157(1), as amended by s.13(1) of the 1981 Act).

(ii) An indication of future likely developments in the business of the company and of its subsidiaries (1981 Act, s.13(3)).

(iii) Amount recommended to be paid by way of dividend (1948 Act, s.157(1)).

(iv) Amount proposed to be carried to reserves (1948 Act, s.157(1)).

(v) Principal activities of the company and its subsidiaries and significant changes in those activities (1967 Act, s.16(1)).

(vi) Names of directors at any time during the year under review (1967 Act, s.16(1)).

(vii) Directors' interests at the beginning and end of each year in shares or debentures of the company or its group companies (1967 Act, s.16(1)(e)), if such information is not shown in a note to the accounts (1981 Act, s.13(4)).

(viii) Significant changes in the company's or its subsidiaries' fixed assets (1967 Act, s.16(1)(a)).

(ix) An indication of the difference between the book amount and the market values of land and buildings if, in the opinion of the directors, the difference is of such significance that it should be drawn to the attention of the members or debenture holders (1967 Act, s.16(1)(a)).

(x) Details for a company or group of its UK charitable and political contributions where in aggregate they exceed £200, as follows:

	£
U.K. charitable organisations	xxx
Political donations of over £200 each:	
UK political organisations (by party, etc.)	xxx
Individuals (by name)	xxx
Others under £200 each (Total)	xxx
	xxx

"Giving money for political purposes" is defined as giving a donation or subscription to—

(1) a political party in the United Kingdom; or

(2) a person who, to the company's knowledge, is carrying on, or proposing to carry on, activities which can at the time reasonably be regarded as likely to affect public support for such a political party.

Money given for charitable purposes to a person ordinarily resident outside the United Kingdom is ignored. "Charitable purposes" mean exclusively charitable purposes (1967 Act, s.19; S.I. 1980 No. 1055).

(xi) Particulars of any important events affecting the company which have occurred since the end of the year (1981 Act, s.13(3)). SSAP 17 additionally requires disclosure in the accounts and in the notes thereto of events which require adjustment to the accounting figures and those which do not.

(xii) An indication of the activities (if any) of the company and its subsidiaries in the field of research and development (1981 Act, s.13(3)). SSAP 13 requires disclosure in the accounts or notes thereto of deferred development expenditure at the beginning and end of the year, movements during the year, and the accounting policy adopted.

(xiii) In respect of purchases of its own shares during the year by the company, the number and nominal value of the shares; the percentage of called-up capital so purchased; aggregate consideration paid; and the reasons for such purchase. In respect of other acquisitions of its own shares, either directly by the company, or by persons with financial assistance from the company where the company has a beneficial interest in the shares, or where such shares are made subject to a charge: the maximum number and nominal value held at any time during the year, and percentage of called-up capital; the amount of any charge; the number and nominal value disposed of or cancelled during the year, and the percentage of called-up capital; and the consideration received in respect of disposals (1981 Act, s.14).

(xiv) A statement of the company's policy in respect of applications for employment from disabled persons; employees who have become disabled; training, career development and promotion of disabled persons (S.I. 1980 No. 1160).[39]

---

[39] Section 79 of the Health and Safety at Work, etc., Act 1974, amended section 16 of the Companies Act 1967, so that the Secretary of State for Trade may require any class of company to disclose specified information in the directors' report relating to the health, safety and welfare at work of employees (1967 Act, s.16(1)(g)). However, no orders have yet been made under this provision.

(xv) Where during the year a company has had on average more than 250 employees in the United Kingdom, a statement describing action taken to introduce, maintain or develop arrangements aimed at providing relevant information to those employees, consulting them or their representatives on a regular basis, encouraging their involvement in the business, and making them more aware of the financial and economic factors affecting its performance (Employment Act 1982, s.1).

Under section 15 of the 1981 Act the auditor has a statutory duty to carry out such investigations as are necessary for him to form an opinion as to whether or not the information contained in the directors' report is consistent with the financial statements. Moreover, he is required to draw attention in his report to any inconsistency between the two for the year in question.

The directors of a small company need not file a directors' report with the annual accounts delivered to the Registrar (1981 Act, s.6(6)).

AUDITORS' REPORT

Section 156 of the Companies Act 1948 requires that an auditors' report should be attached to the balance sheet (see below, page 521), and it should state whether, in the opinion of the auditors, the financial statements comply with the Companies Acts 1948 to 1981 and give a true and fair view of the state of the company's affairs at the balance sheet date and of its profit and loss account for the year ended on that date (1967 Act, s.14(3)(a)). The auditors must state the fact if in their opinion any of the following is the case:

(i) Proper accounting records have not been kept.

(ii) Proper returns have not been obtained from branches not visited by them.

(iii) The financial statements are not in agreement with the accounting records and returns.

(iv) Full information and explanations regarded as necessary for the audit have not been obtained.

(v) The information relating to the year given in the directors' report is not consistent with the financial statements (1967 Act, s.14(4), (6); 1981 Act, s.15).

Where the audit report is qualified and the company proposes to pay a dividend, the auditors must indicate whether the qualification is material in determining whether the distribution can lawfully be made (1980 Act, s.43). Moreover, where particulars of emoluments of directors and of higher paid employees and transactions with directors and officers of the company are not disclosed in the notes to the accounts as required by the Companies Acts, the auditors must so far as they are reasonably able to do so give such information in their report. Auditors belonging to the main professional accountancy bodies in the United Kingdom (which under section 13 of the 1976 Act is the vast majority—see below, page 517) are also required by those bodies to refer in their reports to any breaches of accounting standards. This has meant that in recent years audit qualifications for listed companies have become more common, though empirical research seems to suggest that the investing public is able to distinguish between material and merely technical qualifications.[40] Moreover, although professionally qualified accountants tend to follow a pattern of recognised procedures in carrying out company audits, the professional accountancy bodies are also now attempting to codify auditing practices through a series of Auditing Standards and Guidelines published by the Auditing Practices Committee, which largely reflect the methods employed by the leading practising firms of accountants which audit the accounts of most large and medium sized limited companies.

In addition to the general requirements stated above, where a company's directors propose to rely on exemptions for individual accounts in delivering any documents to the Registrar (*e.g.* enabling them to file modified accounts) the auditors must provide them with a report that states whether, in their opinion, the necessary conditions for such a privilege have been met (1981 Act, s.7(6)). Moreover, where advantage is taken of such exemptions, a "special" auditors' report must be attached to the filed statements, stating that in their opinion the requirements for exemption have been met and reproducing the text of the auditors' report relating to the accounts laid before the shareholders in general meeting (1981 Act, s.7(4)). However, the auditors' report, in either its original or its special form, must not be published with a set of abridged financial statements (1981 Act, s.11(7)).

[40] M. Firth, *Qualified Audit Reports: Their Impact on Investment Decisions, The Accounting Review*, July 1978, pp. 642–650.

Special Classes of Company

Dormant companies

Under section 12 of the 1981 Act a dormant company, which is one in which no significant accounting transaction occurred during the period in question, need not have appointed auditors and hence need not file an auditors' report with the accounts. Instead, the directors must include a statement immediately above their signatures on the balance sheet to the effect that the company was dormant throughout the relevant period. To qualify for such exemption the company must meet the following three conditions: (i) it was not a holding company during the preceding period; (ii) it was classed as a small company during the preceding period; and (iii) it has been dormant since the end of the last period.

Investment companies

Companies qualify for special treatment if they are investment companies within the meaning of section 41(3) of the Companies Act 1980 (which effectively applies to investment trust companies) and was not during the year prohibited from making a distribution under s.41(5) of that Act (1981 Act, Sched. 1, para. 73). The provisions of the 1981 Act are adapted in four ways for such companies: (i) there are limitations of the provisions concerning consolidated accounts; (ii) revaluations of investments need not be credited or debited to the revaluation reserve; (iii) where the value of fixed asset investments is written down, such a debit need not be passed through the profit and loss account if it is either charged against a reserve to which investment revaluations have been credited, or is shown as a separate item under "other reserves"; (iv) disclosure must be made in a note of any distribution reducing the company's net assets to less than the aggregate of its called-up capital and undistributable reserves (which can arise if it chooses to apply the asset ratio test for distribution rather than the capital maintenance criterion: 1980 Act, s.40) (1981 Act, Sched. 1, paras. 71–72, 74).

Banking, insurance and shipping companies

Under the Companies Act 1948 the financial statements of banking, insurance and shipping companies have not had to be prepared and published in the full form required of other limited companies (Part III of the Eighth Schedule of that Act, as amended). Moreover, the EEC's Fourth Directive was not intended to apply to banking and insurance companies, the reporting of whose financial affairs is the subject of other directives at present only at the draft stage. As for shipping companies, the Fourth Directive permitted the application of its disclosure provisions to such concerns to be deferred for eight years.[41] As a result, in framing the Companies Act 1981 the United Kingdom government took advantage of these concessions, and under section 17 qualifying companies are permitted to continue to prepare their financial statements under the old provisions, renumbered as sections 149A and 152A and Schedule 8A to the 1948 Act, subject to some very minor modifications contained in Schedule 2 to the 1981 Act (for instance, relating to the disclosure of any of its own shares which a company has acquired, or loans made in respect of the purchase of its shares). Companies taking advantage of these concessions cannot submit modified accounts, and the financial statements must contain a statement that they have been prepared in accordance with sections 149A or 152A and Schedule 8A to the Companies Act 1948.

The broad effect of the concessions is to enable qualifying companies to conceal movements on reserve and fixed asset accounts, and for banks and insurance companies at least this is normally justified on the grounds that it is desirable not to undermine public confidence in such financial institutions. Yet the very fact that members of the public, as depositors or policy holders, have a direct interest in the financial affairs of such concerns has led successive governments to develop alternative means of monitoring their financial viability. In the case of banks and discount houses, the control machinery is informally operated and modified as the need arises by the Bank of England,[42] though since 1970 the major clearing banks have developed their own more liberal code concerning disclosure in their published accounts. Insurance companies are subject to the Insurance Companies Act 1982, and the Department of Trade also requires certain very detailed returns to be made.[43] For long term business (mainly life assurance)

---

[41] Moreover, the Jenkins Committee ((1962) Cmnd. 1749, para. 416) recommended that the exemption should be revoked.

[42] See *Bank of England Quarterly Bulletin*, June 1975, pp. 188–194.

[43] Most recently governed by S.I. 1980 No. 6: The Insurance Companies (Accounts and Statements) Regulations 1980.

the conventional profit and loss account has relatively little significance, and more attention has to be paid to the actuarial report,[44]
balance sheet, and other supplementary statements than to the income
(*i.e.* fund) account. For short term business (*i.e.* for one year contracts
concerning fire, theft, motor and similar insurance) the rules are
slightly different and have been tightened up in recent years following
the collapse of Fire, Auto and Marine in 1966[45] and Vehicle and
General in 1971,[46] though again detailed returns have to be filed.[47]

Other Accounting and Disclosure Regulations

In recent years, beyond the conventional limits of company law, there
has been lengthy debate, on the one hand about the extent of
disclosure relating to such matters as the state of a company's industrial
relations, the impact of its activities on society, and its dealings with
national governments; and on the other how best to ensure proper
disclosure to various groups of interested parties other than existing
shareholders, most obviously employees and the government and its
agencies. Many of these issues were examined in general terms in the
ASC's 1975 discussion paper, *The Corporate Report*, and since its
publication many large companies have responded by including in
their annual reports some of the supplementary information it proposed in Value Added Statements, Employment Reports, Statements
of Money Exchanges with Government and Transactions in Foreign
Currency, and (less commonly) Statements of Corporate Objectives
and Future Prospects. In the meantime various pieces of legislation
(most notably the Industry Act 1975 and the Employment Protection
Act 1975) have imposed new disclosure requirements on companies.

As regards the extent of disclosure, the argument in relation to the
state of industrial relations is fairly straightforward. Clearly investors
and other interested parties may well be interested in learning some-

---

[44] The significance of the actuarial valuation is in fact recognised in section 42 of the
Companies Act 1980, which recognises actuarial surpluses or deficits as the
appropriate measure of realised profits or losses available for distribution.

[45] Part II of the Companies Act 1967.

[46] *Report of the Tribunal on the Vehicle and General Insurance Co. Ltd.*, February
18, 1972, H.C. 133.

[47] Insurance Companies Acts 1974 and 1982, and various Statutory Instruments,
including S.I. 1980 No. 6.

thing about such matters since this can potentially be at least as important in colouring their expectations about future likely outcomes as knowledge of a company's policy on research and development. Indeed, it is quite possible (and not unknown) for managers to seek short term advantage and higher immediate reported profits by neglecting training programmes and pressurising the work-force, but at the expense of long-term profitability. Various methods of human resource accounting have been proposed and experimented with to try to deal with these aspects of a company's affairs, but they are probably better dealt with in a narrative report. The same can generally be said of the impact of a company's activities on society, though some companies in the United States now publish narrative social balance sheets, listing the benefits they afford the community (*e.g.* through their general research and development programmes and their support of educational institutions, hospitals, etc.) as well as the costs (*e.g.* pollution).

As regards specific interest groups, the government most obviously requires accounting information from companies to assess their corporation tax liabilities. Briefly, a company's conventional annual accounts are used by the Inland Revenue as a starting point from which to calculate income subject to tax. The income itself has to be disaggregated by type into its schedular components, the most important source for most companies being Schedule D Case I income, relating to trading profits. Adjustments have to be made to the reported figures for disallowable expenses (*e.g.* expenditure not wholly and exclusively incurred for the purpose of the trade, appropriations of profit, capital expenditure, depreciation, taxation, charges on income, etc.), and for stock relief and capital allowances, before the liability to corporation tax can be assessed.

Another important piece of legislaton concerning disclosure of financial and other information by companies to the government is the Industry Act 1975, which greatly extended the provisions of the Industry Act 1972. One of the aims of the legislation was to encourage companies to establish voluntary planning agreements with the authorities on an annual basis. The government would provide grants and loans, support export programmes, help find skilled workers, and make available its economic forecasts in return for information from the company concerning its long-term plans and specific aspects of its budgets concerning United Kingdom sales, exports, investment, productivity, employment and training. However, the Act further empowers ministers in certain circumstances to require companies to disclose past or budgeted information relating to specific matters for individual manufacturing establishments. The circumstances are defined in section 28 of the Act as being where such information is in the opinion of the relevant minister needed either to form or further national economic policies, or is needed for consultations between government, employers or workers on the outlook for a particular sector of manufacturing industry. Where the circumstances are met the minister can make out an order requiring the company to furnish him within a specified reasonable time with matters relating to the business in the United Kingdom of the undertaking concerning persons employed, capital expenditure, fixed capital assets, productive capacity and capacity utilisation, output and productivity, sales and exports of products, and certain details of research and development activity. After receiving the information specified in the order the minister may require the company to furnish the whole or part of the information to an authorised representative of each trade union recognised by the company within a reasonable period.

Employee representatives are also empowered to receive financial information under section 17 of the Employment Protection Act 1975 (which effectively embodies sections 56–57 of the Industrial Relations Act 1971, repealed in 1974). If certain grounds for exemption do not apply, an employer is obliged by this section to disclose to trade union representatives material information relevant to collective bargaining procedures, and indeed any information relevant to collective bargaining which would be "in accordance with good industrial relations pratice." The Advisory Conciliation and Arbitration Service (ACAS) has published a draft code to try to establish what constitutes such good practice, and its suggests relevant data should include work schedules, orders, market share, productivity figures, relevant cost structures, transfer prices, government financial assistance, intra-group loans and interest charged.

In several continental countries legislation has established alternative means through which relevant information can be communicated to employee representatives, the most obvious being through works councils. Such committees have their informal counterparts in many British companies, but these latter do not enjoy the same legal status. However, it appears to be Common Market policy to encourage the creation of such councils throughout the Community, and the draft European company statute makes provision for their existence.[48] Another way of trying to ensure employee representatives are fully informed about a company's financial affairs is to give them board representation. This is the practice in West Germany where such representatives by law sit on supervisory boards which oversee the actions of executive directors. Yet although the EEC's draft Fifth Directive on company law harmonisation[49] and the draft European company statute[50] contain provisions which would make this regular practice throughout the Community, little enthusiasm has been shown for the two-tier board structure in the United Kingdom, but in practice many large British companies appoint non-executive directors to fulfil a similar supervisory function. Moreover, proposals by the Bullock Committee[51] that employee representatives should be appointed as directors have found little support either amongst management or trade unions.

ACKNOWLEDGMENT OF DEBTS

Finally, there is the question of whether or not the inclusion of a debt in the balance sheet amounts to an acknowledgment of that debt by the company.

In *Jones* v. *Bellgrove Properties Ltd.*[52] it was held that a statement in a balance sheet "To sundry creditors £7,638," the balance sheet being signed by the company's agents, a firm of chartered accountants, was an acknowledgment, within the meaning of section 24(2) of the Limitation Act 1939[53] (see now the Limitation Act 1980) of a debt of £1,807 owed to a shareholder and included in the £7,638. Consequently[53] the right of action to recover the debt was by section 23(4) of the 1939 Act deemed to have accrued on the date of the acknowledgment and the

---

[48] European Company Statute, J.O. 1970 C124/1.
[49] Draft Fifth Directive on Company Law Harmonization, J.O. 1972 C131/49. However, in 1982 the EEC Commission agreed to drop the idea of making the two-tier board compulsory. A revised Draft Directive to this end is due to be published early in 1983. See J.O. 1982 C149/22.
[50] European Company Statute, J.O. 1970 C124/1.
[51] (1977) Cmnd. 6706.
[52] [1949] 2 K.B. 700 (C.A.).
[53] Not applicable to Scotland; any similar question arising in Scotland would be governed by the Prescription and Limitation (Scotland) Act 1973.

action was not barred by the six-year limitation period fixed by section 2(1) of the 1939 Act. The *Jones* case was distinguished in *Re Transplanters (Holding Co.) Ltd.*[54] (where the directors had made the acknowledgment in favour of one of themselves) and considered in *Good* v. *Parry,*[55] but in *Consolidated Agencies Ltd.* v. *Bertram Ltd.,*[56] where a section of the Indian Limitation Act 1908, which was similar to but not identical with section 23(4) of the 1939 Act, was construed, it was held that the word "acknowledgment" meant acknowledgment of a debt existing at the date of signature and, since the balance sheet was signed many months after the year to which it related, it was not an acknowledgment of such an existing debt but an acknowledgment of a past debt as at the date when the balance sheet was made up. It was said that the *Jones* case was rightly decided on its facts (no question arose there as to the date to which the acknowledgment related although it was taken to be the date of the annual general meeting) and that it is questionable whether a signature on a balance sheet, which must of necessity be made some time after the date to which the balance sheet has been made up, can amount to an acknowledgment of an existing debt. However, in *Re Gee & Co. (Woolwich) Ltd.,*[57] the *Consolidated Agencies* case was distinguished and it was held that a balance sheet, duly signed by the directors, is capable of being an effective acknowledgment of the state of the company's indebtedness as at the date of the balance sheet, so that the cause of action should, in an appropriate case, be deemed to have accrued at that date, being the date to which the signature of the directors relates. On the facts of the *Gee* case, the acknowledgment was effective even though it was made by the directors in favour of one of themselves, because it was sanctioned by every member of the company.

---

[54] [1958] 1 W.L.R. 822.

[55] [1963] 2 Q.B. 418 (C.A.) (for there to be an acknowledgment the debt must be quantified in figures or it must be liquidated in the sense that it is capable of ascertainment by calculation or by extrinsic evidence without further agreement of the parties).

[56] [1965] A.C. 470 (P.C.).

[57] [1975] Ch. 52.

Chapter 23

AUDITORS

THE position of the auditor has become a very important one. As we shall see,[1] he is given wide powers by section 14 of the Companies Act 1967, and can enforce them by qualifying his report and, in an extreme case, by refusing to certify the accounts.

The most important matters dealt with in this chapter are the way in which auditors are appointed, their qualifications (in effect they must be qualified accountants who are not, *e.g.* officers or servants of the company), and their powers and duties, including their duty to make a report to the members of the company.

Appointment of Auditors

1. The first auditors of a company may be appointed by the directors at any time before the first general meeting at which the directors lay before the company a copy of every document required to be comprised in the accounts in respect of the relevant accounting reference period, in which case they hold office until the end of that meeting. If the directors do not appoint the first auditors, the company in general meeting may do so: Companies Act 1976, s.14(3), (4).

2. Every company must, at each general meeting at which the directors lay before the company a copy of every document comprised in the accounts, appoint an auditor or auditors to hold office from the end of that meeting until the end of the next such general meeting: 1976 Act, s.14(1).

This obligation may be excluded in the case of *dormant companies* by a special resolution passed at a general meeting. A *dormant company* is a small company for accounting purposes[2] which has not made a significant accounting transaction in the preceding year or since incorporation. This means that it must not have made any transaction which is required to be entered in the accounts, other than one relating to the issue of its shares to the subscribers to the memorandum. Once a

---

[1] *Post*, p. 516.
[2] *Ante*, p. 463.

significant accounting transaction is made the directors or the members must appoint auditors under section 14 of the 1976 Act: 1981 Act, s.12.

If no auditor is appointed or reappointed at a general meeting, the company must give the Secretary of State notice of the vacancy within one week, whereupon he may appoint an auditor: 1976 Act, s.14(2). If the company fails to give due notice, the company and every officer in default is guilty of an offence and liable, on summary conviction, to a default fine: 1976 Act, s.14(7).

3. Any casual vacancy in the office of auditor may be filled by the directors or the company in general meeting, but while the vacancy continues the surviving or continuing auditor or auditors, if any, may act: 1976 Act, s.14(5).

Special notice[3] must be given of a resolution—

(*a*) appointing as auditor a person other than a retiring auditor, or
(*b*) filling a casual vacancy in the office, or
(*c*) re-appointing a retiring auditor appointed by the directors to fill a casual vacancy, or
(*d*) removing an auditor before the expiration of his term of office[4]: 1976 Act, s.15(1).

On receipt of such notice the company must forthwith send a copy—

(*a*) to the person to be appointed or removed;
(*b*) where some other person is to be appointed, to the retiring auditor;
(*c*) where a casual vacancy was caused by a resignation, to the auditor who resigned: 1976 Act, s.15(2).

Where notice is given of a resolution to appoint as auditor someone other than a retiring auditor or to remove an auditor, the retiring auditor or the auditor to be removed may make written representations of a reasonable length whereupon the position is the same as that where a director is being removed under section 184 of the 1948 Act, *ante*[5]: 1976 Act, s.15(3), (4), (5).

---

[3] *Ante*, p. 311.
[4] Removal of an auditor is dealt with *post*, p. 518.
[5] p. 346

QUALIFICATIONS OF AUDITORS

No person can be appointed auditor unless—

(1) he is a member of a body of accountants established in the United Kingdom and recognised for the purpose by the Department of Trade; or

(2) he is authorised by the Department of Trade to be appointed because—

   (*a*) he has similar qualifications obtained outside the United Kingdom, or

   (*b*) he has obtained adequate knowledge and experience in the course of his employment by a member of a body of accountants recognised as above and was authorised before April 19, 1978 (1976 Act, s.13(4) and S.I. 1977 No. 529), or

   (*c*) he practised in Great Britain as an accountant before August 6, 1947, and he applied to the then Board of Trade to be authorised before January 27, 1968: 1948 Act, s.161(1) 1967 Act, ss.2, 13(4); 1976 Act, s.13(4).

The following bodies are recognised by the Secretary of State for the purposes of (1), *ante:* The Institute of Chartered Accountants in England and Wales; The Institute of Chartered Accountants of Scotland; The Association of Certified Accountants; The Institute of Chartered Accountants in Ireland: 1976 Act, s.13(1). The Secretary of State may alter the above list of bodies by the procedure laid down in section 13(2).

None of the following persons can be appointed auditor:

(1) An officer or servant of the company.

(2) A partner or employee of an officer or servant of the company. This does not prevent a person employed by the auditor from being an officer or servant of the company. "Officer" includes a director, manager or secretary (s.455).

(3) A body corporate. This prevents a limited company from being an auditor.

(4) A person who, by reason of (1) or (2), *ante,* cannot be appointed auditor of the company's holding company or subsidiary or co-subsidiary: 1948 Act, s.161(2), (3); 1967 Act, s.2.

No person must act as auditor of a company when he knows that he is disqualified for appointment, and if an auditor to his knowledge becomes disqualified during his term of office he must thereupon vacate office and give written notice thereof to the company: 1976 Act, s.13(5). Any person who acts as auditor in contravention of subsection (5), *ante,* or fails without reasonable excuse to give notice of vacating his office, is guilty of an offence and liable, on conviction on indictment, to a fine, and on summary conviction, to a fine: 1976 Act, s.13(6).

A Scottish firm may be appointed auditor if, but only if, all the partners are qualified for appointment as auditor of the company in question: 1948 Act, s.161(4).

VACATION OF OFFICE BY AUDITORS

Removal of auditors

A company may, by ordinary resolution, remove an auditor before the expiration of his period of office, notwithstanding anything in any agreement between it and him (1976 Act, s.14(6)), although nothing in that subsection is to be taken as depriving a removed auditor of compensation or damages payable to him in respect of the termination of his appointment as auditor or of any appointment terminating with that as auditor: 1976 Act, s.14(10).

Special notice[6] of the resolution is required: 1976 Act, s.15. This has been explained already.[7]

A removed auditor is entitled to attend the general meeting at which his term of office would otherwise have expired, and any general meeting at which it is proposed to fill the vacancy, to receive all notices of, and other communications relating to, any such meeting which any member of the company is entitled to receive, and to be heard at any such meeting which he attends on any part of the business which concerns him as former auditor of the company: 1976 Act, s.15(6).

Within 14 days after a resolution removing an auditor is passed at a general meeting the company must give notice thereof to the Registrar (1976 Act, s.14(6)), and if the company fails to give notice, the company and every officer in default is guilty of an offence and liable, on summary conviction, to a default fine: 1976 Act, s.14(7).

[6] *Ante,* p. 311.   [7] *Ante,* p. 516.

Resignation of auditors

An auditor of a company may resign by depositing a notice of resignation at the company's registered office and his term of office will end on the date of deposit or any later date specified in the notice, provided that the notice contains either a statement that there are no circumstances connected with his resignation which he considers should be brought to the attention of the members or creditors of the company or a statement of any such circumstances: 1976 Act, s.16(1), (2).

Within 14 days after the deposit of a notice of resignation the company must send a copy to the Registrar and, if it contains a statement of circumstances which should be brought to the attention of the members or creditors, to every member, whether or not he is entitled to receive notices of general meetings, and to every debenture holder: 1976 Act, s.16(3).

Within 14 days after the receipt of a notice containing a statement of circumstances which the auditor considers should be brought to the attention of the members or creditors, the company or any aggrieved person may apply to the court for an order that copies need not be sent out and that the auditor pay the whole or part of the company's costs on the application. The court may make such an order if the auditor is using the notice to secure needless publicity for defamatory matter: 1976 Act, s.16(4), (5).

Within 14 days of a court order being made the company must send a statement of the effect of the order to the members and creditors. If no order is made, a copy of the statement of circumstances must be sent: 1976 Act, s.16(6).

If section 16(3) or (6) of the 1976 Act is not complied with, the company and every officer in default is guilty of an offence and liable, on conviction, to a fine: 1976 Act, s.16(7). Further, section 428 of the 1948 Act[8] applies: 1976 Act, s.16(8).

Right of auditor who resigns to requisition meeting of company

When an auditor's notice of resignation contains a statement of circumstances which he considers should be brought to the attention of the members or creditors, he may deposit with it a signed requisition

---

[8] *Ante.*

that the directors forthwith duly convene an extraordinary general meeting of the company to receive and consider an explanation of the circumstances connected with his resignation. Further, in such a case he may require the company to circulate to the members a written statement of a reasonable length of such circumstances before the general meeting at which his term of office would otherwise have expired or before the general meeting at which the vacancy is to be filled or one convened on his requisition: 1976 Act, s.17.

The auditor is entitled to attend such meeting, to receive notices of, and other communications relating to, the meeting and to be heard thereat on any part of the business which concerns him as former auditor to the company.

If the directors do not within 21 days of the deposit of the requisition proceed duly to convene a meeting on not more than 28 days' notice, every director who failed to take all reasonable steps to see that it was convened is guilty of an offence and liable, on conviction, to a fine. If the written statement is not sent out as required, the auditor may have it read out at the meeting.

The written statement need not be sent out or read out if the court considers that the auditor is abusing his rights to secure needless publicity for defamatory matter.

POSITION OF AUDITORS

The auditor is not a person included in the definition of "officer" in section 455, *ante*. Nor is he an officer for the purposes of section 161(2), *ante*. However, he is an officer of the company for the purpose of a misfeasance summons under section 333,[9] and for the purpose of offences under sections 328 and 330 of the Companies Act 1948 (which sections also are concerned with offences by officers of companies in liquidation). An auditor is presumably an officer for the purpose of the Theft Act 1968,[10] section 19, *ante*,[11] which is concerned with false statements by an officer of a body corporate, but an auditor appointed ad hoc for a limited purpose, *e.g.* appointed by the directors for a private audit, is not an officer.[12]

[9] *Re London and General Bank* [1895] 2 Ch. 166 (C.A.). S. 333 is dealt with *ante*, p. 416.
[10] Not applicable to Scotland.
[11] *Ante*, p. 157.   [12] *R. v. Shacter* [1960] 2 Q.B. 252 (C.C.A.).

An auditor is an agent of the company for the purposes of section 167, dealing with investigations[13] and may be examined on oath by an inspector. Otherwise the auditor is not (in the absence of special contract) an agent of the company, and his normal certificate as to the correctness of the balance sheet, under section 14 of the Companies Act 1967, cannot constitute an acknowledgment by an agent for the purposes of the Limitation Act 1980.[14]

An auditor is treated in the same way as an officer by sections 205 (provisions relieving officers and auditors from liability) and 448 (relief of officers and auditors).[15]

There is no provision in the Companies Acts or in Table A to the effect that an auditor shall cease to hold office on becoming bankrupt or insane. His position in these respects should be compared with that of a director.

REMUNERATION OF AUDITORS

The remuneration of the auditor of a company appointed by the directors or by the Secretary of State, is fixed by the directors or by the Secretary of State, as the case may be. In any other case it is fixed by the company in general meeting or as the company in general meeting may determine. "Remuneration" includes sums paid by the company in respect of his expenses: 1976 Act, s.14(8).

The auditor's remuneration (including expenses paid by the company) must be shown under a separate heading in the profit and loss account: Schedule 8, introduced by 1981 Act, Sched. 1.

AUDITORS' REPORT

The auditors must report *to the members*[16] on the accounts examined by them, including interim and initial accounts used for the calculation

---

[13] *Ante*, p. 419.

[14] *Re Transplanters (Holding Co.) Ltd.* [1958] 1 W.L.R. 822, *ante*, p. 514.

[15] *Ante*, pp. 374, 375.

[16] The 1974 Labour Party Green Paper on Reform of Company Law said, at p. 31, "In law, the auditors derive their position and authority from the shareholders to whom they report on [the] company's affairs; in practice, auditors work closely with the company's Directors and senior executives and their relationship with shareholders particularly in non-director-controlled companies is frequently very tenuous indeed."

of distributable profits,[17] and on every balance sheet, every profit and loss account and all group accounts prepared under section 1 of the Companies Act 1976, of which, in accordance with section 1(6) of the 1976 Act, a copy is laid before the company in general meeting during their tenure of office: 1967 Act, s.14(1), as amended by 1976 Act, Sched. 2. The auditors' report must be read before the company in general meeting and be open to inspection by any member: section 14(2).

The report must state (except in the case of a company entitled to the benefit of Part III of Schedule 8A[18])—

(*a*) whether in the auditors' opinion the balance sheet and profit and loss account and (in the case of a holding company submitting group accounts) group accounts have been properly prepared in accordance with the provisions of the Companies Acts 1948 to 1981; and, without prejudice to (*a*),

(*b*) whether in their opinion a true and fair view is given—
   (i) in the case of the balance sheet, of the state of the company's affairs at the end of its financial year;
   (ii) in the case of the profit and loss account (if not framed as a consolidated profit and loss account), of the company's profit or loss for its financial year;
   (iii) in the case of group accounts, of the state of affairs and profit or loss of the company and its subsidiaries dealt with thereby, so far as concerns members of the company: section 14(3).

In the excepted cases,[18] the report must state whether in the auditors' opinion the balance sheet and profit and loss account and, if applicable, group accounts, have been properly prepared in accordance with the provisions of the Acts: section 14(3).

If the company wishes to take advantage of the accounting exemptions,[19] the auditors must prepare a special report which is their usual report together with a statement that the company fulfils the exemption requirements: 1981 Act section 7(5).

If the auditors think that proper accounting records or returns have not been kept or received, or that the balance sheet and (unless framed

---

[17] *Post*, p. 532.
[18] *i.e.* a banking, insurance or shipping company.
[19] *Ante*, p. 463.

as a consolidated profit and loss account) profit and loss account are not in agreement with the accounting records and returns, they must state that fact in the report: 1967 Act, s. 14(4), as amended by 1976 Act, Sched. 2.

Further, if auditors fail to obtain all the information and explanations which, to the best of their knowledge and belief, are necessary for their audit, they must state that fact in the report: section 14(6).

If the accounts do not contain particulars of the directors' emoluments, the auditors' report must normally include the required particulars; 1967 Act, ss.6 and 7.[20]

In preparing their report the auditors must carry out certain investigations, namely those which will enable them to form an opinion as to—

(*a*) whether proper accounting records have been kept by the company and proper returns adequate for their audit have been received from branches not visited by them;

(*b*) whether the balance sheet and (unless framed as a consolidated profit and loss account) profit and loss account are in agreement with the records and returns: 1967 Act, s.14(4), as amended by 1976 Act, Sched. 2.

They must also, in preparing their report, consider whether the information given in the directors' report relating to the financial year in question is consistent with the accounts. If there is an inconsistency they must state that fact in their report: 1967 Act, s.23A.

The auditors perform their duty to the members by forwarding their report to the secretary. They are not responsible if the report is not put before the members.[21] However, an Australian case has held that they must pay due regard to the possibility of fraud and must warn the appropriate level of management promptly and without waiting for the general meeting to report to the shareholders.[22]

The articles cannot preclude the auditors from availing themselves of all the information to which they are entitled as material for their report.[23]

---

[20] *Ante*, p. 357.
[21] *Re Allen, Craig & Co. (London) Ltd.* [1934] Ch. 483.
[22] *Pacific Acceptance Corpn. Ltd.* v. *Forsyth* (1970) 92 W.N. (N.S.W.) 29.
[23] *Newton* v. *Birmingham Small Arms Co. Ltd.* [1906] 2 Ch. 378.

POWERS OF AUDITORS

The auditors have a right of access at all times to the books and accounts and vouchers of the company, and are entitled to require from the officers of the company such information and explanation as they think necessary for the performance of their duties as auditors: 1967 Act, s.14(5). This power is necessary to enable them to obtain particulars of the directors' emoluments, including expenses charged to tax and benefits in kind[24] which may not be ascertainable from an examination of the books.

The auditors cannot require the information to be furnished in any particular form or that it should be certified in some way, as by the board of directors. There is no power to require the information to be supplied in writing but auditors can reasonably say that they are not in a position to perform their duties without making further inquiries if they are asked to act on unrecorded oral statements. If proper information is not given, the auditors' remedy is to qualify their report.

If an officer of the company makes a statement to the auditors which purports to convey any information or explanation which they are entitled to require, and it is misleading, false or deceptive in a material particular, he is guilty of an offence and liable, on conviction on indictment, to imprisonment for up to two years or a fine or both, or, on summary conviction, to imprisonment for up to six months or a fine or both: 1976 Act, s.19.

Auditors also have the right to attend any general meeting of the company and to receive the same notices of general meetings as the members, and to be heard at any general meeting on any part of the business which concerns them as auditors: 1967 Act, s.14(7).

Powers in relation to subsidiaries

If a subsidiary company is incorporated in Great Britain, the subsidiary and its auditors must give the auditors of the holding company such information and explanation as they may reasonably require for the purposes of their duties. In any other case, the holding company, if required by its auditors to do so, must take such steps as are reasonably open to it to obtain from the subsidiary such information and explanation: 1976 Act, s.18.

[24] *Ante,* p. 356.

If a subsidiary or holding company fails to comply with section 18, it and every officer in default is guilty of an offence. Similarly with an auditor of a subsidiary who fails to comply.

DUTIES OF AUDITORS

The duties of auditors depend on the terms of the articles as well as on the statutory provisions.

Table A, article 130, provides: Auditors shall be appointed and their duties regulated in accordance with section 161 of the 1948 Act, sections 14 and 23A of the 1967 Act, sections 13 to 18 of the 1976 Act and sections 7 and 12 of the 1981 Act.[25]

Their duties may be summarised as follows—

(1) They must acquaint themselves with their duties under the articles and the Acts.[26]

(2) They must report to the members on the accounts examined by them, and on every sheet, every profit and loss account and all group accounts prepared under section 1 of the 1976 Act, of which, in accordance with section 1(6) of the 1976 Act, a copy is laid before the company in general meeting during their tenure of office: 1967 Act, s.14(1) as amended, *ante*.[27] The report must state the matters specified in sections 6, 7 and 14(3), (4) and (6) of the 1967 Act and section 7(5) of the 1981 Act, *ante*.[27] In preparing the report they must carry out the investigations specified in sections 14(4) and 23A, *ante*.[27]

They must ascertain and state the true financial position of the company by an examination of the books. This examination must be not merely to ascertain what the books show, but also to ascertain that the books show the true financial position.[28]

"The duty of the auditor" is "not to confine himself merely to the task of verifying the arithmetical accuracy of the balance sheet, but to inquire into its substantial accuracy, and to ascertain that it . . . was properly drawn up, so as to contain a true and correct representation

---

[25] 1976 Act, Sched. 2; 1981 Act, s.15 and Sched 3.

[26] *Re Republic of Bolivia Exploration Syndicate Ltd.* [1914] 1 Ch. 139.

[27] pp. 459 *et seq.*

[28] *Per* Lindley L.J. in *Re London and General Bank (No. 2)* [1895] 2 Ch. 673 (C.A.), at pp. 682 *et seq.*

of the state of the company's affairs": *per* Stirling J. in *Leeds Estate Co.* v. *Shepherd* (1887) 36 Ch.D. 787, at p. 802.

An auditor "is not to be written off as a professional 'adder-upper and subtractor.' His vital task is to take care to see that errors are not made, be they errors of computation, or errors of omission or commission, or downright untruths. To perform this task properly he must come to it with an inquiring mind—not suspicious of dishonesty, I agree—but suspecting that someone may have made a mistake somewhere and that a check must be made to ensure that there has been none": *per* Lord Denning in *Fomento (Sterling Area) Ltd.* v. *Selsdon Fountain Pen Co. Ltd.* [1958] 1 W.L.R. 45 (H.L.), at p. 61.

The statutory duty of an auditor, *e.g.* to state whether in his opinion a true and fair view is given by the balance sheet and the profit and loss account, is a personal one, and if he adopts the opinion of the company's accountant, and he is sued by the company for wrongly stating that a true and fair view is given, it has been held in Australia that he has no cause of action against the accountant.[29]

(3) They must act honestly, and with reasonable care and skill.

"An auditor is not bound to be a detective, or . . . to approach his work . . . with a foregone conclusion that there is something wrong. He is a watchdog, but not a bloodhound. He is justified in believing tried servants of the company in whom confidence is placed by the company. He is entitled to assume that they are honest, and to rely on their representations, provided he takes reasonable care. If there is anything calculated to excite suspicion he should probe it to the bottom; but in the absence of anything of that kind he is only bound to be reasonably cautious and careful": *per* Lopes L.J. in *Re Kingston Cotton Mill Co. (No.* 2) [1896] 2 Ch. 279 (C.A.), at p. 288.

"It is the duty of an auditor to bring to bear on the work he has to perform that skill, care and caution which a reasonably competent, careful, and cautious auditor would use. What is reasonable skill, care and caution must depend on the particular circumstances of each case. An auditor . . . is not bound to do more than exercise reasonable care and skill in making inquiries. . . . He is not an insurer; he does not guarantee that the books do correctly show the true position of the company's affairs; . . . he must be honest—*i.e.,* he must not certify what he does not believe to be true, and he must take reasonable care and skill before he believes that what he certifies is true. . . . Where there is nothing to excite suspicion very little inquiry will be

[29] *Dominion Freeholders Ltd* v. *Aird* [1966] 2 N.S.W.R. 293 (C.A.) distinguishing *Hedley Byrne & Co. Ltd.* v. *Heller & Partners Ltd.,* [1964] A.C. 465.

reasonably sufficient. . . . Where suspicion is aroused more care is obviously necessary; but, still, an auditor is not bound to exercise more than reasonable care and skill, even in a case of suspicion. . . .": *per* Lindley L.J. in *Re London and General Bank (No.* 2) [1895] 2 Ch. 673 (C.A.), at p. 683.

It may be that entries in or omissions from the books ought to make the auditors suspicious. In such a case they must make full investigations into the suspicious circumstances, but they are not liable for "not tracking out ingenious and carefully laid schemes of fraud when there is nothing to arouse their suspicion."[30]

B. was the managing director of the company and the senior partner of E. & Co., stockbrokers. E. & Co. owed £250,000 to the company but on February 27, just before the close of the financial year, E & Co. bought Treasury Bills for £200,000 and credited the company with them, thus reducing their debt to £50,000. The company's balance sheet accordingly showed an investment in Treasury Bills for £200,000, and a debt from E & Co. for £50,000. On March 3, after the close of the financial year, E & Co. sold the Treasury Bills and became debtors again for £250,000. This was done for three successive years. *Held,* although the transactions, when isolated, should have led the auditors to conclude that fraud had taken place, yet as they formed only one item in a large audit, there was no negligence on the part of the auditors: *Re City Equitable Fire Insurance Co. Ltd.* [1925] Ch. 407 (C.A.).

If payments are made or sums borrowed by the company, the auditors should see that they are authorised and made in accordance with the articles and the Acts.[31]

"When it is [shown] that audited balance sheets do not [show] the true financial condition of the company and that damage had resulted, the onus is on the auditors to show that this is not the result of any breach of duty on their part."[32]

They must satisfy themselves that the securities of the company in fact exist and are in safe custody. This duty is discharged by their making a personal inspection of the securities in question. If, however, the securities are in the possession of a person who in the ordinary course of his business keeps securities for his customers, *e.g.* a banker, and that person is regarded as trustworthy, the auditors may safely accept his certificate that the securities are in his custody.

[30] *Per* Lopes L.J. in *Re Kingston Cotton Mill Co. (No.* 2) [1896] 2 Ch. 279 (C.A.), at p. 290.
[31] See *Thomas* v. *Devonport Corpn.* [1900] 1 Q.B. 16 (C.A.).
[32] *Per* Astbury J. in *Re Republic of Bolivia Exploration Syndicate Ltd.* [1914] 1 Ch. 139, at p. 171.

The auditor accepted the certificate of the company's stockbrokers that they held securities on the company's behalf. In fact they did not hold the securities and the company suffered heavy loss. *Held*, by Romer J., the auditor was negligent, as he should have inspected the securities and either insisted on their being put in proper custody or reported the matter to the shareholders[33]: *Re City Equitable Fire Insurance Co. Ltd.* [1925] Ch. 407.

They must check the cash in hand and also the balance at the bank, by inspecting the pass book (or bank statement) or obtaining a certificate from the bank.[34]

Auditors are under no duty to take stock.[35] This is part of the wider question of the auditors' duty as to the value of the assets.

The duty of the auditors as to the value to be placed on the fixed assets is discussed in the previous chapter.[36] Apart from complying with the requirements of the new Eighth Schedule, if the auditors have formed an opinion that the assets are overvalued, they are bound to report it to the shareholders.

Auditors made a confidential report to the directors, calling their attention to the fact that the security for loans was insufficient, and that there was a difficulty in realisation. They also reported that in their opinion no dividend should be paid for the year. In their report to the shareholders, however, they merely said that the value of the assets was dependent upon realisation. A dividend of seven per cent. was declared out of capital. *Held*, the auditors were guilty of misfeasance and liable to make good the dividend paid: *Re London and General Bank* (*No.* 2) [1895] 2 Ch. 673 (C.A.).

As to current assets, they are entitled to take the values of stocks and work in progress from the manager or other responsible official of the company, unless they have any reason to suppose them inaccurate.

The auditors accepted the certificate of J., the manager, a person of acknowledged competence and high reputation, as to the value of the stock-in-trade. This was grossly exaggerated, as a result of which dividends were paid out of capital. Had the auditors compared the amount of stock at the beginning of the year with the purchases and sales during the year, they would have been put on inquiry, but they did not do so. *Held*, the auditors were not liable, as they were entitled to rely on J.'s certificate in the absence of anything to excite suspicion: *Re Kingston Cotton Mill Co.* (*No.* 2) [1896] 2 Ch. 279 (C.A.).

[33] The Court of Appeal expressed no concluded opinion on this point. In any event, the articles protected the auditors from liability. See, *ante*, p. 383.
[34] *Fox & Son* v. *Morrish, Grant & Co.* (1918) 35 T.L.R. 126.
[35] *Re Kingston Cotton Mill Co.* (*No.* 2), *ante*.
[36] *Ante*, p. 474.

The facts were similar to those in the *Kingston Cotton Mill* case except that on discovery of the invoices with altered dates (by which the managing director had caused the price payable on purchases of stock made shortly before the end of each period of account to be included in the outgoings of the succeeding period) the auditor accepted the explanation of the managing director, whom he believed to be of the highest integrity, when he should have examined the suppliers' statements and where necessary have communicated with the suppliers, and having ascertained the precise facts so far as possible he should have informed the board. By not taking these steps he failed in his duty and was liable for, *inter alia*, the amount of the dividends: *Re Thomas Gerrard & Son Ltd.* [1968] Ch. 455.

"The standards of reasonable care and skill are, upon the expert evidence, more exacting today than those which prevailed in 1896": *per* Pennycuick J., at p. 475.

If directors do not allow auditors time to conduct such investigations as are necessary in order to make the statements required to be contained in their report, the auditors must either refuse to make a report or make an appropriately qualified report: they are not justified in making a report containing a statement the truth of which they have not had an opportunity of ascertaining.[37]

Auditors are not concerned with the policy of the company or whether the company is well or ill managed.

"It is no part of an auditor's duty to give advice, either to directors or shareholders, as to what they ought to do. An auditor has nothing to do with the prudence or imprudence of making loans with or without security. It is nothing to him whether the business of a company is being conducted prudently or imprudently, profitably or unprofitably. It is nothing to him whether dividends are properly or improperly declared, provided he discharges his own duty to the shareholders. His business is to ascertain and state the true financial position of the company at the time of the audit": *per* Lindley L.J. in *Re London and General Bank (No. 2)* [1895] 2 Ch. 673 (C.A.), at p. 682.

Auditors cannot be relieved from liability for any breach of duty by any provision in the articles or any contract (s.205), but in certain circumstances they may obtain relief from the court (s.448).[38]

In England the auditors can plead the Limitation Act after six years.[39]

Apart from the auditor's contractual duty of care to the company he owes a duty of care to third persons with whom he is not in contractual

---

[37] *Per* Pennycuick J. in *Re Thomas Gerrard, ante,* at p. 477.
[38] *Ante,* pp. 374, 375.
[39] *Leeds Estate Co.* v. *Shepherd* (1887) 36 Ch.D. 787.

or fiduciary relationship if, as a reasonable man, he knows that he is being trusted or that his skill and judgment are being relied on and he does not make it clear that he accepts no responsibility for information or advice which he gives.[40] For breach of this duty an action for negligence lies if damage results from the negligence.

The scope of this duty was defined originally as follows:

". . . to whom do these professional people owe this duty? I will take accountants, but the same reasoning applies to . . . others. They owe the duty, of course, to their employer or client; and also I think to any third person to whom they themselves show the accounts, or to whom they know their employer is going to show the accounts, so as to induce him to invest money or take some other action on them": *per* Denning L.J. in *Candler* v. *Crane, Christmas & Co.* [1951] 2 K.B. 164 (C.A.), at p. 180.

This liability applies not only to persons to whom auditors show the accounts and those to whom they knew the company would show them but also to persons whom they ought reasonably to have foreseen at the time the accounts were prepared might rely on the accounts. Thus where the accountants knew at that time that outside finance was needed by the company they ought to have foreseen that the accounts would be used by someone providing such finance, *e.g.* in the form of a take-over offer, and owed a duty accordingly. However, they are only liable if reliance on the accounts caused the other person loss so that, *e.g.,* where the take-over offer would have been made anyway there is no liability: *JEB Fasteners Ltd.* v. *Marks, Bloom & Co.* [1981] 3 All E.R. 289, affd. [1983] 1 All E.R. 583.

VALUATION OF SHARES

Articles of private companies often provide that a member who wants to sell his shares must first offer them to the existing members at a price to be fixed by the auditors. Similar provisions are often applicable in the case of a member's death.[41] In valuing the shares for this purpose, the auditor is not obliged to explain the basis of his valuation or to give his reasons for it, and in such circumstances there can be no action to

---

[40] *Hedley Byrne & Co. Ltd* v. *Heller & Partners Ltd.* [1964] A.C. 465, disapproving *Candler* v. *Crane, Christmas & Co.* [1951] 2 K.B. 164 (C.A.). See also *Esso Petroleum Co. Ltd.* v. *Mardon* [1976] 2 All E.R. 5 (C.A.) and *Yionni* v. *Edwin Evans & Sons* [1981] 3 All E.R. 592.

[41] *Ante*, pp. 267 *et seq.*

have the valuation set aside by a party who is dissatisfied with it, if it is of the right property by the right man who is acting in good faith.[42] These are known as "non-speaking" certificates. If, however, he does give an explanation, *i.e.* by a "speaking" certificate, the court can inquire into it and, if satisfied that the valuation has been made on the wrong basis, can declare that it is not binding, *i.e.* the valuation can be impeached for[43] fraud, mistake or miscarriage, but on matters of opinion the court will not interfere.[44] In this respect it is irrelevant either that the transaction has been completed or that the auditors might be liable in negligence.[45]

An auditor may be so liable in negligence to either party, however, even though the valuation may not be liable to be set aside. To be liable in this way an auditor must be acting as a valuer and not as an arbitrator, *i.e.* settling a dispute between at least two parties which was sent to him to resolve in such a way that he had to exercise a judicial discretion.[46] An auditor of a private company who, on request, values its shares in the knowledge that this valuation will determine the price to be paid under a contract owes a duty of care to both the vendor and the purchaser. An agreement for valuation is not generally one for arbitration. The function of a valuer is usually to settle a price so that no differences arise between the parties. His function is not to make on award after a difference has arisen. Only in the latter case will no duty of care arise.[47]

[42] *Baber* v. *Kenwood Manufacturing Co. Ltd.* [1978] 1 Lloyd's Rep. 175.
[43] The Scottish equivalent of "impeached for" is "challenged on the ground of."
[44] *Dean* v. *Prince* [1954] Ch. 409 (C.A.). In this case the articles of a private company provided that a deceased director's shares should be purchased by the surviving directors at a price to be certified by an auditor as a fair value. The director who held a controlling interest died. The auditor stated that he had not regarded the company as a going concern but had valued on a "break-up" basis because in his opinion the shares had no value on any other basis because of losses made by the company *Held*, the auditor was right. See further *Jones (M.)* v. *Jones (R. R.)* [1971] 1 W.L.R. 840, where the valuation was not made by the stipulated expert.
[45] *Burgess* v. *Purchase and Sons (Farms) Ltd.* [1983] 2 W.L.R. 361.
[46] *Arenson* v. *Casson Beckman Rutley & Co.* [1975] 3 W.L.R. 815 (H.L.), applying *Sutcliffe* v. *Thackrah* [1974] A.C. 727.
[47] See *Leigh* v. *English Property Corporation* [1976] 2 Lloyd's Rep. 298.

CHAPTER 24

DIVIDENDS

A DIVIDEND is the share, received by a shareholder, of the company's profits legally available for dividend and divided among the members. Commercial companies are formed to earn profits for the shareholders out of which dividends can be paid,[1] and no express power to pay dividends is required in the memorandum or the articles. It has been held that dividends must only be paid out of profits and articles, *e.g.* Table A, articles 114–122, *post,* usually so provide and also deal with such things as interim dividends, the method of payment of dividends and the creation of reserve funds.

Dividend must be distinguished from interest. Interest is a debt which, like all debts, is payable out of the company's assets generally. A dividend, however, is not a debt until it has been declared by the company, and dividends cannot be declared out of the assets generally; they can be declared only out of the profits available for the purpose.

PROFITS AVAILABLE FOR DIVIDEND

Dividends must only be paid out of profits

We have seen that a fundamental principle of company law is that the issued share capital must be maintained.[2] Paid-up capital must not be paid to the shareholders except by leave of the court or under strictly defined circumstances. It must be spent only upon the objects defined in the memorandum. Any other expenditure is *ultra vires* and reduces the fund available for the company's creditors in satisfaction of their claims.[3]

W. guaranteed the preference dividends for three years and the company agreed to repay to W. on demand any sums paid by him under the guarantee. *Held,* the company's agreement was *ultra vires* and void, as it might involve capital being reduced otherwise than by expenditure on the company's objects: *Re Walters' Deed of Guarantee* [1933] Ch. 321.

---

[1] Under s.25 of the 1981 Act, a company may be prohibited from paying a dividend.
[2] *Ante,* pp. 227 *et seq.*
[3] See, *per* Jessel M.R. in *Flitcroft's Case* (1882) 21 Ch.D. 519 (C.A.), at p. 533.

The principle that share capital must be maintained requires that a dividend, in money or kind,[4] declared by a company, should not be paid except out of profits. Prior to the 1980 Act there were no statutory provisions governing the funds available for distribution to the shareholders as dividend. The courts evolved some basic rules as to the distinction between income which could be used and capital which could not. These rules proved to be difficult to interpret and the Jenkins Committee made several recommendations[5] for the provision of a statutory code. This is now contained in sections 39 to 45 of the 1980 Act.

The new rules apply to all *distributions* made by a company. A distribution is defined as any payment of a company's assets to members of the company except: (a) an issue of bonus shares[6]; (b) the redemption or purchase by a company of its own shares[7]; (c) an authorised reduction of capital under section 66[8]; and (d) distributions on a winding up: 1980 Act, s.45(2).

Such *distributions* may only be made out of the profits available for the purpose: 1980 Act, s.39(1). There are two tests to ascertain such profits. The first applies to all companies, the second only to public companies.

REALISED PROFITS TEST

A company's profits available for distribution are its accumulated realised profits (so far as not already distributed or capitalised[9]) less its accumulated realised losses (so far as not already written off by a proper reduction of capital): 1980 Act, s.39(2). There is no attempt to distinguish between income and capital profits or losses—the only criteria is whether they are *realised*. Unrealised profits, *e.g.* on a re-valuation upwards of an asset in the accounts which produces a paper gain, cannot be used. Now the gain must be realised; the asset sold. This confirms the previous case law in Scotland[10] but changes the law

---

[4] *Post*, p. 540.
[5] Para. 350.
[6] *Post*, p. 543.
[7] *Ante*, p. 244.
[8] *Ante*, p. 229.
[9] *Post*, p. 541.
[10] *Westburn Sugar Refineries Ltd.* v. *Inland Revenue*, 1960 S.L.T. 297.

in England.[11] Further, realised losses, *e.g.* previous trading losses, must be deducted before a dividend can be paid, again confirming the Scottish cases[12] but changing the English law.[13] Unrealised profits cannot be used to pay up debentures or any amounts unpaid on issued shares: 1980 Act, s.39(3).

Realised profits

Basically these are all the profits, capital or income, which have been realised, *i.e.* actually received by the company. The only unrealised profits are on the revaluation upwards of fixed assets (plant, machinery, land etc.), which simply produces a higher figure in the balance sheet.

However, if on such a revaluation giving rise to an unrealised profit it is found that less is needed to be set aside for depreciation of that asset, then the difference between what would have been required and what was actually set aside can be regarded as a realised profit: 1980 Act, s.39(5).

When a company makes a distribution of a non-cash asset, *e.g.* part of its undertaking on a de-merger, any element of unrealised profits (*e.g.* on a revaluation) represented by those assets may be regarded as a realised profit: 1980 Act, s.43A.

Realised losses

All losses are to be regarded as realised other than those in respect of any diminution in value of a fixed asset (*i.e.* a revaluation downwards) appearing on a revaluation of all the fixed assets[14]: 1980 Act, s.39(4).

For this purpose the directors may in fact revalue only one particular asset and, if appropriate, revalue it downwards so as to give rise to an unrealised loss even though no general revaluation has in fact been made, provided that the directors are satisfied that the aggregate value of all the fixed assets is not less than their value as stated in the company's accounts: 1980 Act, s.39(4A).

---

[11] *Dimbula Valley (Ceylon) Tea Co. Ltd.* v. *Laurie* [1961] Ch. 353, 373.
[12] *Niddrie etc. Coal Co. Ltd.* v. *Hurll* (1891) 18 R. 805.
[13] *Ammonia Soda Co. Ltd.* v. *Chamberlain* [1918] 1 Ch. 266 (C.A.).
[14] Development costs shown as an asset in the accounts must be regarded as a general rule as a realised loss: 1980 Act, s.42A.

In effect therefore the realised profits test does not require any account to be taken of the depreciation of fixed assets.

When there is no record of the original cost of an asset or it cannot be obtained without unreasonable expense or delay the calculations of any loss or gain in respect of that asset may be taken from the earliest available record of its value since acquisition by the company: 1980 Act, s.39(6).

NET ASSETS TEST

The realised profits test applies to all companies. As we have seen, however, it does not require the depreciation of fixed assets to be taken into account. For private companies that is the only test so that in this respect the law is the same as before the 1980 Act.[15]

Public companies, however, are subject to a second test. Even if it has profits available under the realised assets test a public company may only make a distribution if at the time the amount of its net assets is not less than the aggregate of its called-up share capital and its undistributable reserves, and the amount of the proposed distribution will not lower the amount of those assets to less than that aggregate: 1980 Act, s.40(1).

Public companies cannot therefore ignore depreciation of their assets. They must keep the value of their assets in line with the capital figures on the balance sheet.

Net assets

A public company's net assets for this purpose are the aggregate of its assets less the aggregate of its liabilities, including any provision for liabilities in the accounts: 1980 Act, s.87(4)(c). Uncalled share capital[16] may not, however, be used as an asset for this purpose: 1980 Act, s.40(5).

Called-up share capital and undistributable reserves

The net assets must be measured against the called-up share capital and undistributable reserves of the company.

---

[15] *Lee* v. *Neuchatel Asphalte Co.* (1889) 41 Ch.D. 1 (C.A.); *Verner* v. *General and Commercial Investment Trust* [1894] 2 Ch. 239.
[16] *Ante,* p. 208.

The called-up share capital is the aggregate amount of the calls made on its shares whether or not they have been paid, any amount paid without being called and any instalments due on the shares.[17] It is therefore more than the amount necessarily received by the company: 1980 Act, s.87(1).

The undistributable reserves are those set out in section 40(2) of the 1980 Act:

(*a*) the share premium account[18];
(*b*) the capital redemption reserve[19];
(*c*) the excess of its unrealised profits over its unrealised losses[20]; and
(*d*) any other fund which cannot be distributed, *e.g.* a capital reserve fund[21]; *i.e.* the quasi-capital funds.

INVESTMENT COMPANIES

Public companies certified by the Department of Trade as investment companies, *i.e.* companies investing in securities or land with the aim of spreading investment risk, are subject to the realised profits and net assets value tests but with modifications

The realised profits test only applies to revenue and not capital profits or losses. Capital profits are thus excluded from the funds available for distribution. The net assets value test applies but their value must be at least $1\frac{1}{2}$ times the aggregate of the company's liabilities: 1980 Act, s.41.

RELEVANT ACCOUNTS

In deciding whether a company has distributable profits reference must be made to its accounts. Section 43 of the 1980 Act provides which are the relevant accounts for this purpose. Any breach of section 43 is regarded as a breach of the relevant test: s.43(1). The general rule is that the relevant accounts are the company's *latest annual accounts*

---

[17] *Ante*, p. 208.
[18] *Ante*, p. 176.
[19] *Ante*, p. 248.
[20] As calculated according to s.39 of the 1980 Act, above: 1980 Act, s.40(4).
[21] *Ante*, p. 208.

prepared in respect of the last preceding accounting reference period.[22] However, in two cases other accounts may be used. First, such accounts as are necessary to enable a reasonable judgment to be made as to the amount of any relevant item—these are referred to as *interim accounts*. Second, if the distribution is proposed during the company's first year before any annual accounts are prepared, such accounts as are necessary for a reasonable judgment to be made. These are referred to as *initial accounts*: 1980 Act, s.43(2).

Last Annual Accounts

These must have been properly prepared for all companies in accordance with the Companies Acts in all material respects. The auditors must have prepared either an unqualified report[23] on the accounts or, if it is qualified, they must state in writing whether their qualification is relevant to the question of distributable profits. Finally a copy of any such statement must be laid before the company in general meeting: 1980 Act, s.43(3).

Interim accounts

A public company may only use interim accounts if they have been properly prepared in compliance with the format of accounts set out in sections 149 and 155[24] of the 1948 Act in all material respects. A copy must be sent to the Registrar with a certified English translation if appropriate. A private company may use any interim accounts: 1980 Act, s.43(5).

Initial accounts

A public company may only use initial accounts if they have been properly prepared in compliance with the format of accounts set out in sections 149 and 155[24] of the 1948 Act in all material respects. Further there must be an auditors' report that the accounts have been so prepared and which is either unqualified or, if qualified, accompanied by a statement that the qualification is irrelevant to the question of distributable profits. A copy of the accounts must be sent to the

[22] *Ante,* p. 458.
[23] *Ante,* p. 521.
[24] *Ante,* p. 465.

Registrar with a certified English translation if appropriate. A private company may use any initial accounts: 1980 Act, s.43(6).

Effect of paying dividends out of capital

It was established prior to the 1980 Act that directors who are knowingly parties to the payment of dividends out of capital (*e.g.* where debts known to be bad were entered as assets in reports and balance sheets, so that an apparent profit was shown, and the shareholders, relying on these documents, declared dividends) are jointly and severally liable to the company to replace the amount of dividends so paid, with interest, and ratification is impossible so as to bind the company.[25] In such a case they are entitled to be indemnified by each shareholder who received dividends, *knowing them to be paid out of capital,* to the extent of the dividends received.[26] A shareholder who has knowingly received a dividend paid out of capital cannot, individually or on behalf of the company, maintain an action against the directors to replace the dividends so paid, at any rate until he has repaid the money he has received.[27]

Section 44 of the 1980 Act further provides that any shareholder who receives a distribution which he knows, or has reasonable grounds to believe, has been paid in breach of the 1980 Act rules, must repay that amount to the company. This is expressly made an addition to the shareholders' existing liabilities set out above.

PAYMENT OF DIVIDENDS

Dividends are paid in the manner laid down in the articles.

Table A, article 114, provides:

"The company in general meeting may declare dividends, but no dividend shall exceed the amount recommended by the directors." This relates to the final dividend, declared at the annual general meeting. As to an interim dividend, which is a dividend paid on some date between two annual general meetings of the company,[28] article

---

[25] *Flitcroft's Case* (1882) 21 Ch.D. 519 (C.A.); *Liquidators of City of Glasgow Bank* v. *Mackinnon* (1881) 9 R. 535.

[26] *Moxham* v. Grant [1900]1 Q.B. 88 (C.A.).

[27] *Towers* v. *African Tug Co.* [1904] 1 Ch. 558 (C.A.); *Liquidators of City of Glasgow Bank* v. *Mackinnon* (1881) 9 R. 535.

[28] *Per* P. O. Lawrence J. in *Re Jowitt* [1922] 2 Ch. 442, at p. 447.

115 provides: "The directors may from time to time pay to the members such interim dividends as appear to the directors to be justified by the profits of the company."

Before recommending a dividend, directors should have a complete and detailed list of the company's assets and investments prepared for their information, and should not rely for their value merely on the opinion of the chairman or the auditors.[29]

In the absence of anything to the contrary in the articles,[30] a company cannot be compelled to declare a dividend, and no action can be brought for its recovery until it has been declared.[31] In England the declaration of a dividend creates a simple contract debt due from the company to the shareholder which will be barred in six years from the date of declaration.[32] In Scotland the period of prescription is 20 years.[33]

When preference shares entitle the holders to receive out of the profits of the company for each year a fixed dividend, the "profits of the company" are the profits available for dividend after setting aside such reserves as the directors think fit. If the whole of the profits are transferred to reserve the preference shareholders are not entitled to any dividend.[34]

When the articles, *e.g.* Table A, article 115, above, give the directors power to pay interim dividends, a resolution by the company in general meeting requiring the directors to declare an interim dividend is inoperative.[35]

In English law, unless the articles otherwise provide, dividends are payable to the shareholders in proportion to the nominal amounts of their shares, irrespective of the amounts paid up.[36] Section 59, how-

---

[29] *Per* Romer J. in *Re City Equitable Fire Insce. Co. Ltd.*[1925] Ch. 407 at pp. 471, 474.

[30] For articles which were interpreted as requiring the whole profits to be divided, see *Paterson* v. *R. Paterson & Sons Ltd.*, 1917 S.C. (H.L.) 13; 1916 S.C. 452.

[31] *Bond* v. *Barrow Haematite Steel Co.* [1902] 1 Ch. 353.

[32] *Re Compania de Electricidad de la Provincia de Buenos Aires Ltd.* [1978] 3 All E.R. 668.

[33] Prescription and Limitation (Scotland) Act 1973.

[34] *Re Buenos Aires Great Southern Ry. Co. Ltd.* [1947] Ch. 384; *cf.* the Scottish case *Wemyss Collieries Trust Ltd.* v. *Melville* (1905) 8 F. 143, in which transfer of a sum to reserve was, on an interpretation of the articles, held to be valid, although preference shareholders were thereby deprived of an additional non-cumulative dividend.

[35] *Scott* v. *Scott* [1943] 1 All E.R. 582.

[36] *Birch* v. *Cropper* (1889) 14 App. Cas. 525.

ever, permits a company, if so authorised by its articles, to pay dividend in proportion to the amount paid up on each share where a larger amount is paid up on some shares than on others. Table A, article 118, accordingly provides that "subject to the rights of persons, if any, entitled to shares with special rights as to dividend, all dividends shall be declared and paid according to the amounts paid or credited as paid on the shares."

In Scots law, if articles provide that "the directors may . . . declare a dividend to be paid to the members in proportion to their shares" and define "shares" as shares in the nominal capital, dividends fall to be declared according to the nominal amounts of the shares, irrespective of the amounts paid up[37]; where, however, there is no provision in the articles as to how dividends are to be paid, the common law principle applicable is that they are payable in proportion to the amounts paid up on the shares.[38]

The articles usually provide, as does Table A, article 121, that dividends payable in cash may be paid by cheque or warrant sent through the post to the registered address of the shareholder, or to such person and to such address as the shareholder may in writing direct. In the absence of such a provision in the articles, the company will have to issue a fresh dividend warrant to the shareholder should the warrant first sent be lost in the post.[39]

Unless power is given in the articles, dividends declared must be paid in cash, and a shareholder can restrain the company from paying them in any other way.

A company declared a dividend and passed a resolution to pay it by giving to the shareholders debenture bonds bearing interest and redeemable at par, by an annual drawing, over thirty years. The articles empowered the company to declare a dividend "to be paid" to the shareholders. *Held,* the words "to be paid" meant paid in cash, and a shareholder suing on behalf of himself and the other shareholders could restrain the company from acting on the resolution on the ground that it contravened the articles: *Wood* v. *Odessa Waterworks Co.* (1889) 42 Ch.D. 636.

Accordingly, if it is desired to have the power to pay dividends otherwise than in cash, the articles should give such power, as they usually do.

[37] *Oakbank Oil Co. Ltd.* v. *Crum* (1882) 10 R. (H.L.) 11; (1881) 9 R. 198.
[38] *Hoggan* v. *Tharsis Sulphur etc. Co. Ltd.* (1882) 9 R. 1191.
[39] See *Thairlwall* v. *Great Northern Ry.* [1910] 2 K.B. 509.

Table A, article 120, provides: "Any general meeting declaring a dividend or bonus may direct payment of such dividend or bonus wholly or partly by the distribution of specific assets and in particular of paid-up shares, debentures or debenture stock of any other company or in any one or more of such ways."

CREATION OF RESERVE

The articles often contain provisions dealing with the creation of a reserve fund.

Table A, article 117, states: "The directors may, before recommending any dividend, set aside out of the profits of the company such sums as they think proper as a reserve or reserves which shall, at the discretion of the directors, be applicable for any purpose to which the profits of the company may be properly applied, and pending such application may, at the like discretion, either be employed in the business of the company or be invested in such investments (other than shares of the company) as the directors may from time to time think fit. The directors may also without placing the same to reserve carry forward any profits which they may think prudent not to divide."

Even without such a power in the articles a company may create a reserve, as this is a business question for the decision of the company itself.[40] "The general practice of companies certainly is not to divide the total available profits, but to carry forward a part to make provision for meeting current liabilities."[41]

A reserve find may at any time be distributed as dividend or employed in any other way authorised by the articles.[42] The fact that it has been used in the business does not show that it has been capitalised so as not to be available for dividend.[43]

CAPITALISATION OF PROFITS

If the articles so provide, as they usually do, the realised profits may be used to issue members with bonus shares credited as fully paid.

[40] *Burland* v. *Earle* [1902] A.C. 83 (P.C.). Scottish cases decided on the interpretation of articles were *Cadell* v. *Scottish Investment Trust Co. Ltd.*(1901) 9 S.L.T. 299, affirming (1901) 8 S.L.T. 480 (O.H.) (power to carry forward profits to the next year instead of paying a larger dividend on deferred shares), and *Wemyss Collieries Trust Ltd.* v. *Melville* (1905) 8 F. 143 (transfer of profits to reserve fund instead of paying additional dividend on preference shares).
[41] *Per* Lord M'Laren in *Cadell* v. *Scottish Investment Trust Co. Ltd.* (1901) 9 S.L.T. 299, at p. 300.
[42] *e.g. Blyth's Trustees* v. *Milne* (1905) 7 F. 799.
[43] *Re Hoare & Co. Ltd.* [1904] 2 Ch. 208 (C.A.).

Table A, article 128, provides: "The company in general meeting may upon the recommendation of the directors resolve that it is desirable to capitalise any part of the amount for the time being standing to the credit of any of the company's reserve accounts or to the credit of the profit and loss account or otherwise available for distribution, and accordingly that such sum be set free for distribution amongst the members who would have been entitled thereto if distributed by way of dividend and in the same proportions on condition that the same be not paid in cash but be applied either in or towards paying up any amounts for the time being unpaid on any shares held by such members respectively or paying up in full unissued shares or debentures of the company to be allotted and distributed credited as fully paid up to and amongst such members in the proportion aforesaid, or partly in the one way and partly in the other, and the directors shall give effect to such resolution:

Provided that a share premium account and a capital redemption reserve fund may, for the purposes of this regulation, only be applied in the paying up of unissued shares to be allotted to members of the company as fully paid bonus shares."

Further, article 128A provides: "The company in general meeting may on the recommendation of the directors resolve that it is desirable to capitalise any part of the amount for the time being standing to the credit of any of the company's reserve accounts or to the credit of the profit and loss account which is not available for distribution by applying such sum in paying up in full unissued shares to be allotted as fully paid bonus shares to those members of the company who would have been entitled to that sum if it were distributed by way of dividend (and in the same proportions), and the directors shall give effect to such resolution.

When profits are capitalised, instead of the shareholders getting a dividend in cash, the profits available for dividend are retained by the company and unissued shares or debentures of the company, credited as fully paid up, are allotted to the shareholders, the shares or debentures being called "bonus shares" or "bonus debentures." In such cases there is said to be a "bonus issue" but the term "bonus" is misleading, because if the shareholder had not received, *e.g.* bonus shares, he might have received a dividend in cash. Consequently, the term "capitalisation issue" is preferable to "bonus issue." Alternatively, already issued partly paid shares may be credited with a further amount paid up. In any event, the appropriate sum will be transferred from profit and loss account or from reserve account to share capital account or loan capital account in the balance sheet.

A company which by its articles could, prior to the 1980 Act, use a reserve resulting from the revaluation of capital assets to pay for bonus shares, may continue to do so: 1980 Act, s.45(1). Such a reserve could arise on a revaluation in the value of fixed assets made in good faith by competent valuers and not likely to fluctuate in the short term.[44]

Bonus shares

As shown above, bonus shares can be paid for out of profits available for dividend, if the articles so provide. In addition, by section 56 of the 1948 Act[45] and section 53 of the 1981 Act,[46] a share premium account and a capital redemption reserve can be used to pay for unissued shares of the company to be allotted to members as fully paid bonus shares.

If bonus shares are to be issued:

(1) There must be authority in the company's articles.[47]
(2) Its nominal share capital must be sufficient.
(3) The members must resolve to capitalise profits, or to apply the share premium account or the capital redemption reserve fund, and to issue bonus shares.
(4) The shares must be allotted by the board in the proportions specified in the articles, usually the same proportions as those in which the members would have received a cash dividend.[48]
(5) A return of allotments and a contract between the members and the company (which may be signed on the members' behalf by the person authorised by the articles) must be delivered to the Registrar within one month after the allotment.[49] The Jenkins Report[50] recommended that it should be enough to file a copy of the resolution authorising the issue of the shares credited as fully paid up.

[44] *Dimbula Valley (Ceylon) Tea Co. Ltd.* v. *Laurie* [1961] Ch. 353.
[45] *Ante*, p. 176.
[46] *Ante*, p. 248.
[47] *Wood's case, ante*. See also Table A, article 128A, *ante*.
[48] See Table A, articles 128 and 128A, *ante*.
[49] s.52, *ante*, p. 182.
[50] Para. 495.

CHAPTER 25

DEBENTURES

THIS chapter is concerned with the borrowing of money by a company where the borrowing is on debentures or on debenture stock, and with fixed and floating charges which the company may create over its property in order to secure the principal sum borrowed and interest thereon until re-payment. Thus the chapter deals fully with a number of matters touched upon in Chapter 1, including registered debentures and trust deeds. As stated in that chapter references to sections of an Act are to be read as references to the 1948 Act unless the context indicates otherwise.

Ultra vires borrowing is also dealt with and it will be seen that here the general law has been modified by the European Communities Act 1972 s.9(1).

Perhaps the most important part of the chapter is that with regard to charges and the registration of charges, particularly registration with the Registrar of Companies under section 95. It will be seen that the former differences between English law and Scots law (under which it was formerly impossible to create floating charges) have been largely removed by statute, the present statute being the Companies (Floating Charges and Receivers) (Scotland) Act 1972.

Finally, receivers are dealt with and here it will be seen that the 1972 Act now enables a receiver to be appointed in Scotland.

A Company's Power to Borrow Money

As stated earlier,[1] the memorandum of association of a company usually contains an express power to borrow money, although a *trading* company, unless prohibited by its memorandum or articles, has implied power to borrow money for the purposes of its business, and to give security for the loan by creating a mortgage or charge over its property,[2] since such a power is incidental to the objects of a trading company. A non-trading company requires express power to borrow.

---

[1] p. 84.
[2] *General Auction Estate, etc. Co.* v. *Smith* [1891] 3 Ch. 432; *Paterson's Trustees* v. *Caledonian Heritable Security Co. Ltd.* (1885) 13 R. 369.

A *public* company cannot exercise a borrowing power until the requirements of section 4 of the 1980 Act, *ante*,[3] have been complied with. Sometimes the borrowing powers of a company are restricted by the memorandum and articles to, *e.g.* two-thirds of the paid-up capital of the company.

If there is nothing to the contrary in the memorandum and articles, a power to borrow by mortgage or otherwise includes the power to charge the uncalled capital of the company.[4] A power given by the memorandum to raise money upon any security of the company, etc., authorises a charge on the uncalled capital.[5] In Scots law an assignation of uncalled capital in security confers no preference on the assignee unless the assignation is validly intimated to the shareholders.[6] Capital which can only be called up in the event of winding up cannot be charged as security for a loan.[7]

A company's powers to borrow and issue debentures are usually exercised by the directors, as they are under article 79 of Table A.

Table A, article 79, provides: "The directors may exercise all the powers of the company to borrow money, and to mortgage or charge its undertaking, property and uncalled capital, or any part thereof, and, subject to section 14 of the 1980 Act,[8] to issue debentures, debenture stock, and other securities whether outright or as security for any debt, liability or obligation of the company or of any third party."

Sometimes a limit is placed upon the power of the directors to borrow on behalf of the company.

Table A, article 79, provides: ". . . the amount for the time being remaining undischarged of moneys borrowed or secured by the directors . . . (apart

---

[3] *Ante*, p. 183.
[4] *Re Pyle Works* (1890) 44 Ch.D. 534 (C.A.).
[5] *Newton* v. *Debenture-holders, etc. of Anglo-Australian Investment Co.* [1895] A.C. 244 (P.C.).
[6] *Liquidator of Union Club Ltd.* v. *Edinburgh Life Assce. Co.* (1906) 8 F. 1143; the reading out at a company meeting of a report that an assignation has been made is not a valid intimation, at least to shareholders not attending the meeting. For an instance of security validly created over uncalled capital, see *Liquidator of the Ballachulish Slate Quarries Co. Ltd.* v. *Malcolm* (1908) 15 S.L.T. 963 (O.H.).
[7] *Re Mayfair Property Co.* [1898] 2 Ch. 28 (C.A.) (reserve liability); *Robertson* v. *British Linen Co.* (1890) 18 R. 1225 (O.H.) (statutory guarantee fund in company limited by guarantee); contrast *Lloyds Bank Ltd.* v. *Morrison & Son*, 1927 S.C. 571 (assignation of additional independent guarantee fund held valid).
[8] That section restricts the power only in relation to convertible debentures. *Ante*, p. 165.

from temporary loans obtained from the company's bankers in the ordinary course of business) shall not at any time, without the previous sanction of the company in general meeting, exceed the nominal amount of the share capital of the company for the time being issued, but nevertheless no lender or other person dealing with the company shall be concerned to see or inquire whether this limit is observed."

Obtaining an overdraft from the company's bank is borrowing.[9]

Ultra vires borrowing

Under the general law

1. If there is borrowing beyond the powers of the company, *e.g.* for an *ultra vires* purpose, the position under the general law is that the borrowing and any security given for it, is void, and no ratification can render it valid. Such borrowing does not give rise to any indebtedness either at law or in equity[10] on the part of the company.[11] Consequently, no action can be brought on the contract, or in quasi-contract for money had and received. However, it will be seen later[12] that the general law rule has been modified by statute.

Even under the general law the lender has the following remedies:

    (*a*) If the money borrowed has been applied in paying off debts incurred by the company *intra vires*, he ranks as a creditor to the extent to which the money has been so applied and can recover from the company.[13]

Whether this is based on the ground that the contract of loan is validated to such extent because the *ultra vires* borrowing does not increase the indebtedness of the company, or on the principle that the *ultra vires* lenders are subrogated to the rights of the legitimate creditors who have been paid off, is doubtful.[13] If the contract is validated one would expect any security given to be validated too.[13]

However, it has been held that the lender is not, in such a case, entitled to any securities or priorities of the creditors who are paid by means of his money.

[9] *Brooks & Co.* v.*Blackburn Benefit Society* (1884) 9 App.Cas. 857.
[10] This distinction has no place in Scots law.
[11] *Baroness Wenlock* v. *River Dee Co.* (1885) 10 App.Cas. 354; *Sinclair* v. *Brougham* [1914] A.C. 398.
[12] p. 548.
[13] *Per* Lord Parker of Waddington in *Sinclair* v. *Brougham,* at p. 441.

A company had A, B and C debenture stock, and in issuing this stock had exhausted its borrowing powers. A bank advanced money to pay the interest on these three classes of debentures. A receiver was then appointed, who had funds in hand sufficient to pay the interest to the A stockholders, but not enough to pay the B and C stockholders in full. The bank claimed (i) that before any interest was paid to the stockholders they were entitled to be repaid their advance, (ii) alternatively that they were entitled to be repaid the sum lent by them to pay interest to the A stockholders before any payment was made to the B and C stockholders. *Held*, as the advance was not a valid one, they were not entitled to either of these claims: *Re Wrexham, etc., Rlwy. Co.* [1899] 1 Ch. 440 (C.A.).

On the other hand, the lender may retain any securities deposited with him as security for such part of the money lent as has been applied in paying the company's debts.[14]

(*b*) At law, if the lender can identify his money, or any property purchased with it, he is entitled to what is known as a tracing order,[15] and can recover.[16] If tracing is impossible at law, the lender may be able to obtain an equitable tracing order.[17]

A building society started an *ultra vires* banking business. The contracts of borrowing from depositors were therefore void. In the liquidation of the society the assets were insufficient to pay the shareholders and the depositors in full after outside creditors had been paid. The depositors claimed repayment in quasi-contract on the ground that the deposits were money had and received by the society to their use. This claim failed but it was held that the mixed mass of assets in the liquidator's hands was in part shareholders' money wrongfully employed in the banking business and in part depositors' money. Each class could follow their property into the assets by an equitable tracing order, *i.e.* the assets were divided proportionately between them: *Sinclair* v. *Brougham* [1914] A.C. 398

"A company or other statutory association cannot by itself or through an agent be party to an *ultra vires* act. If its directors or agents affecting to act on its behalf borrow money which it has no power to borrow, the money borrowed is in their hands the property of the lender. At law, therefore, the lender can recover the money, so long as he can identify it, and even if it has been employed in purchasing property, there may be cases in which, by ratifying the action of those who have so employed it, he may recover the property purchased. Equity, however, treated the matter from a different standpoint. It considered that the relationship between the directors or agents

---

[14] *Blackburn Bdg. Society* v. *Cunliffe, Brooks & Co.* (1882) 22 Ch.D. 61; 9 App.Cas. 857.

[15] See note 13, above.   [16] A term of English law.

[17] *Sinclair* v. *Brougham* [1914] A.C. 398; *Re Hallett's Estate* (1880) 13 Ch.D. 696; *Re Diplock* [1948] Ch. 465.

and the lenders was a fiduciary relationship, and that the money in their hands was for all practical purposes trust money. Starting from a personal equity, based on the consideration that it would be unconscionable for anyone who could not plead purchase for value without notice to retain an advantage derived from the misapplication of trust money, it ended . . . in creating what were in effect rights of property, though not recognised as such by the common law": *per* Lord Parker of Waddington in *Sinclair* v. *Brougham, ante,* at p. 441.

(c) The lender may recover damages from the directors, *e.g.* for breach of warranty of authority—unless the fact that the borrowing was *ultra vires* could have been discovered from the company's registered documents.

F. did work for the company. The company, being unable to pay cash, agreed to allot debenture stock to F. At the time, although F. was ignorant of it, all the debenture stock which the company had power to issue had already been issued. *Held*, the defendant directors were liable on an implied warranty that they had authority to issue valid debenture stock which would be a good security and in the circumstances F. was entitled to recover as damages against the directors the par value of the debenture stock he ought to have received. F. could not know that the company had issued all the debenture stock it was authorised to issue: *Firbank's Exors.* v. *Humphreys* (1886) 18 Q.B.D. 54 (C.A.), applying *Collen* v. *Wright* (1857) 8 El. & Bl. 647; 120 E.R. 241.

A guarantee by directors that the company will repay money borrowed *ultra vires* may be binding on the directors.[18]

2. If borrowing is in excess merely of the directors' powers and not of the powers of the company, it can be ratified and rendered valid by the company in general meeting.[19]

Where such borrowing is not so ratified, if the excess consists of noncompliance with some internal regulation of the company, the lender may be able to rely on the rule in *Royal British Bank* v. *Turquand*[20] and recover the amount of the loan from the company.

Under the European Communities Act 1972, s.9(1)

1. We have seen[21] that the *ultra vires* doctrine has been modified by the European Communities Act 1972, s.9(1). If a company borrows

---

[18] *Garrard* v. *James* [1925] Ch. 616; *cf. Heald* v. *O'Connor* [1971] 1 W.L.R. 497, *ante*, p. 80.

[19] *Irvine* v. *Union Bank of Australia* (1877) 2 App.Cas. 366 (P.C.).

[20] (1856) 6 El. & Bl. 327; 119 E.R. 886, *ante*, p. 433; *Gillies* v. *Craigton Garage Co. Ltd.*, 1935 S.C. 423.   [21] p. 82.

beyond its powers from a lender who does not actually know that the borrowing is *ultra vires*, he can enforce the contract provided that it is decided upon by the directors or the managing director, although they will be in breach of duty to the company and liable accordingly.

2. As to the case where directors merely exceed their borrowing powers, it will be recalled that section 9(1) provides, *inter alia*, that in favour of a person dealing with a company in good faith, the powers of the directors to bind the company shall be deemed free of any limitation under the memorandum or the articles, and a party to a transaction decided upon by the directors shall not be bound to inquire as to any such limitation on the powers of the directors, and shall be presumed to have acted in good faith unless the contrary is proved.

DEBENTURES AND DEBENTURE STOCK

A debenture is a document which creates or acknowledges a debt due from a company. Such document need not be, although it usually is, under seal, it need not give, although it usually does give, a charge on the assets of the company by way of security, and it may or may not be one of a series.[22] Thus debentures may be (1) secured, or (2) unsecured. A debenture is always for a specified sum, *e.g.* £100, which can only be transferred in its entirety. As will be seen, debentures may be collaterally secured by a trust deed.[23] Convertible debentures, *i.e.* debentures which the holder has the right to convert, at stated times, into shares in the company, have already been mentioned.[24]

It may be helpful to mention here that some of the differences between shares and debentures are:

(1) the holder of a debenture is a creditor, not a member, of the company; a shareholder is a member[25];

(2) debentures may be issued at a discount; shares, in general, may not be[26];

(3) a company may purchase its own debentures; it must not purchase its own shares except in accordance with specific procedures[27];

[22] See *Lemon v. Austin Friars Investment Trust Ltd.* [1926] Ch. 1 (C.A.).
[23] *Post*, p. 551.
[24] See *Mosely v. Koffyfontein Mines* [1904] 2 Ch. 108, *ante*, p. 175.
[25] *Ante*, p. 30.
[26] *Ante*, p. 174.   [27] *Ante*, p. 245.

(4) interest at the specified rate on debentures may be paid out of capital; dividends on shares must be paid only out of distributable profits.[28]

The Companies Act 1948, s.455, defines "debenture" as including debenture stock, bonds, and any other securities[29] of a company whether constituting a charge on the assets of the company or not. A mortgage of land by a company is a debenture.[30]

Debenture stock is borrowed money consolidated into one mass for the sake of convenience. This is normally done by a trust deed,[31] which may give the trustees a charge on the company's property. Where there is no charge, debenture stock is commonly called unsecured loan stock. The main advantage of debenture stock is that it is transferable in fractional amounts, although the trust deed may specify the minimum fractional amount which can be transferred. Again, the debenture stockholders will be given simple debenture stock certificates instead of debentures.

ISSUE OF DEBENTURES

As we saw earlier in this chapter,[32] debentures are issued in accordance with the provisions of the articles, usually by a resolution of the board of directors.

Debenture prospectuses and offers for sale were dealt with in Chapter 7.[33]

When debentures have been issued, the prospectus cannot be looked at to ascertain the contract, but if the contract was intended to be contained in the prospectus and the debenture together, or if the prospectus contains a collateral contract the consideration for which was the taking up of the debentures, the prospectus can be looked at.[34]

---

[28] *Ante*, p. 532.

[29] "Securities," as used in s.455, does not include shares.

[30] *Knightsbridge Estates Trust Ltd.* v. *Byrne* [1904] A.C. 613, *post*, p. 560.

[31] See note 23, above.

[32] p. 545.

[33] *Ante*, p. 129; for an action of damages by a debenture holder against a promoter on the ground that by false and fraudulent representations of the promoter he had been induced to advance money to the company, see *Dunnett* v. *Mitchell* (1885) 12 R. 400.

[34] *Jacobs* v. *Batavia and General Plantations Trust Ltd.* [1924] 2 Ch. 329 (C.A.).

Debentures or debenture stock certificates must be completed and ready for delivery within two months after allotment or after the lodging of a transfer, unless the conditions of issue otherwise provide: section 80. As with shares this obligation does not apply to allotments or transfers to SEPON on a stock exchange dealing.[35]

There is no objection to the issue of debentures at a discount[36] but when any commission, allowance or discount has been paid or made to any person in consideration of his subscribing or procuring subscriptions for debentures, particulars of the amount or rate of the commission or discount must be sent to the Registrar within 21 days. The omission to do this does not, however, affect the validity of the debentures. The deposit of debentures as security for a debt of the company does not, for this purpose, amount to the issue of debentures at a discount: sections 95(9) and 106A(8).

A contract to take up debentures may be enforced by specific performance: section 92. This section provides an exception to the rule, laid down in *South African Territories Ltd.* v. *Wallington*,[37] that specific performance will not be granted of a contract to lend money since damages are an adequate remedy for breach of such contract.

Apart from the section, an agreement to issue debentures made in consideration of an actual advance of money has the effect in English law of putting the lender in equity in the same position as if the debentures had actually been issued.

A syndicate agreed to sell goods to a company on the terms that, as part payment, £3,000 debentures charged upon all the company's assets were issued. On this agreement the syndicate allowed the company to remove the goods, which were subsequently taken in execution by F. *Held*, although no debentures were actually issued, the syndicate was in the same position as if they had been and so F. was entitled subject to the charge: *Simultaneous Colour Printing Syndicate* v. *Foweraker* [1901] 1 K.B. 771.

TRUST DEEDS

Debentures and debenture stock are usually secured by a trust deed.[38]

---

[35] Stock Exchange (Completion of Bargains) Act 1976, s.1.
[36] *Ante*, p. 174.
[37] [1898] A.C. 309.
[38] *Ante*, p. 549.

Contents of a trust deed

The main terms of a *debenture trust deed* are:

(1) A covenant by the company for payment to the debenture holders of the principal moneys and interest.

(2) Clauses giving the trustees a legal mortgage by demise of the company's freeholds and leaseholds, which are specified,[39] and a floating charge over the rest of the undertaking and property.

(3) A clause specifying the events on which the security is to become enforceable, *e.g.* default in the payment of interest or principal moneys, order made or resolution passed for winding up, appointment of a receiver, cessation of business, breach of covenant by the company.

(4) A clause giving the trustees power to take possession of the property charged when the security becomes enforceable, to carry on the business and to sell the property charged and to apply the net sale moneys in payment of the principal and interest and to pay the balance to the company.

(5) Power for the trustees to concur with the company in dealings with the property charged.

(6) Covenants by the company to keep a register of debenture holders, to insure and to keep in repair the property charged.

(7) Provision for meetings of debenture holders.

(8) Power for the trustees to appoint a receiver when the security becomes enforceable.

(9) Provision for serving notices on the debenture holders by post.

A *debenture stock trust deed*, in addition to containing the foregoing terms, constitutes the stock by acknowledging that the company is indebted to the trustees in a specified sum and provides for the issue of debenture stock certificates.

A trust deed usually contains a clause providing that the rights of the debenture holders against the company or any property charged by the deed may be modified or compromised by extraordinary resolution of the debenture holders

---

[39] In Scotland security over specified heritable property would be created by the execution of a standard security which would be referred to in the trust deed.

Advantages of a trust deed

The advantages of a trust deed are:

(1) The trustees will have a legal mortgage[40] over the company's land, so that persons who subsequently lend money to the company cannot gain priority over the debenture holders or debenture stockholders.

(2) Events are specified on the happening of which the principal moneys and interest become payable, *e.g.* non-payment of interest or non-performance of the covenants in the deed; the appointment of trustees, who are usually paid, ensures that there are definite persons whose duty it is to take action on the happening of these events.

(3) The company is given a number of powers over the mortgaged property which it can exercise with the consent of the trustees, *e.g.* powers of sale, exchange or leasing. This enables the company to use the property advantageously for the purposes of its business without prejudicing the interests of the debenture holders or debenture stockholders.

(4) Covenants are entered into by the company for insurance, repair and other matters, and can be enforced by the trustees.

(5) Power is given to the trustees to appoint a receiver or to enter into possession of the property and carry on the business of the company in case of urgency.

Liability of trustees

Trustees for debenture holders are in the same position towards their beneficiaries as any other trustees, and cannot purchase the debentures, the subject of the deed, without making full disclosure of all the information relating to them which is in their possession.[41] Any provision in a trust deed, or in a contract with the holders of debentures secured by a trust deed, for exempting the trustees from, or indemnifying them against, liability for breach of trust where they fail to show the degree of care and diligence required of them as trustees, is void, except that the trustees may be released from liability by a release given after the liability has arisen, and a provision in a trust deed for the

---

[40] In Scotland a fixed security.
[41] *Re Magadi Soda Co.* (1925) 41 T.L.R. 297.

giving of such a release by a majority of not less than three-fourths in value of the debenture holders present and voting in person or by proxy at a meeting summoned for the purpose is not void: section 88. (Contrast section 205, *ante*,[42] as regards officers and auditors.)

Section 448 (power of court to grant relief), *ante*,[43] does not apply to the trustees although the Trustee Act 1925, s.61, and the Trusts (Scotland) Act 1921, s.32, do, and so in an appropriate case the court may relieve the trustees from liability.

Right to copy of trust deed

A debenture holder is entitled to require a copy of the trust deed on payment of 20p. in the case of a printed trust deed or 10p. per 100 words or part thereof in other cases: 1948 Act, s.87(3); 1967 Act, s.52(1).

REGISTERED DEBENTURES

Debentures or debenture stock may be payable to either (1) the registered holder; or (2) the bearer.

Contents of a registered debenture

Where there is a trust deed, the usual form of debenture payable to the registered holder is a document issued under the seal of the company and containing two clauses. The clauses are as follows:

(*a*) The company, for valuable consideration, received covenants to pay the registered holder the principal sum on a specified day or on such earlier day as it becomes payable under the indorsed conditions, and in the meantime to pay interest by equal half-yearly payments on specified dates at a specified rate.

(*b*) The debenture is said to be issued subject to and with the benefit of the conditions indorsed thereon.

The indorsed conditions usually include the following:

(i) The debenture is said to be one of a series, each for securing a specified sum.

---

[42] p. 375.
[43] p. 375.

(ii) The registered holders of all the debentures of the issue are said to be entitled *pari passu* to the benefit and subject to the provisions of the trust deed, the date of execution of which and the parties to which are specified, and the charges conferred by the trust deed are recited.

This has the effect of putting all the debentures of the issue on an equal footing; in the absence of such a clause the debentures would rank according to the order in which they were executed.[44]

(iii) The company is empowered, at any time after a specified date, by giving not less than a specified number of months' notice, to pay off the principal moneys secured with interest to the date of payment.

(iv) Provision is made for keeping a register of debenture holders at the registered office. We shall see that this will comply with section 86 and that a right of inspection is given by section 87.[45]

(v) The company is not to be bound to recognise anyone as having any title to the debenture except the registered holder, or his personal representative, and is not to be bound to enter notice of any trust in the register.

Section 117 of the Act, which provides that trusts are not to be entered on the register of members, does not apply to the register of debenture holders, and consequently such a clause is necessary. If the company does receive notice of a trust, the clause relieves it from the obligation of entering it on the register, but if it deals with the debentures as a trader, *e.g.* by advancing money on them, after notice of a trust, it will be bound by that trust.[46]

(vi) Transfer of the debenture is provided for. Every transfer must be in writing, as will be explained later.

(vii) Equities or, in Scots law, rights of compensation, between the company and any person other than the registered holder are excluded. This will be explained later.[47]

---

[44] *Gartside* v. *Silkstone and Dodworth Coal etc. Co.* (1882) 21 Ch.D. 762.
[45] *Post,* p. 558.
[46] *Bradford Banking Co.* v. *Briggs & Co.* (1886) 12 App.Cas. 29; *Mackereth* v. *Wigan Coal Co. Ltd.* [1916] 2 Ch. 293.
[47] *Post,* p. 557.

(viii) The principal moneys and interest are made payable at the company's registered office or at its bankers.

If this clause is not inserted it is the company's duty to follow the usual rule and seek out its creditor and pay him.

F. held 18 £100 debentures repayable in June, 1913, in the M. Corporation. Before the date of redemption F. died, and her executors neglected to present the debentures to the company for payment. In June, 1916, the company was sued for principal and interest. *Held*, as the debentures contained no clause to the effect set out above, it was the company's duty to seek out the debenture holder and pay her; as this had not been done, the company was liable to pay the principal with interest until the date of actual payment: *Fowler* v. *Midland Electric Corpn.* [1917] 1 Ch. 656 (C.A.).

   (ix) The company is empowered to purchase any of the debentures of the issue at any time.
    (x) Interest is made payable by warrant on the company's bank payable to the order of the registered holder and sent by post to his registered address.
   (xi) The principal monies are made immediately payable if the company defaults in the payment of interest for a specified number of months, or if a winding-up order is made or resolution passed, or if the security constituted by the trust deed becomes enforceable and the trustees enforce it.

The debenture holder is entitled to repayment of his principal on the company's going into liquidation, whether or not the date fixed for repayment has arrived.[48]

Transfer of registered debentures

Registered debentures are transferred in the manner laid down in the indorsed conditions (which usually require a transfer to be in writing under the hand of the registered holder or of his personal representatives) or by a stock transfer under the Stock Transfer Act 1963. As in the case of a transfer of shares,[49] it is unlawful for a company to register a transfer of debentures unless a "proper instrument of transfer" has been delivered to the company: section 75.

The company must have the debenture or debenture stock certificate ready for delivery within two months of the lodging of the

---

[48] *Hodson* v. *Tea Co.* (1880) 14 Ch.D. 859.   [49] *Ante*, pp. 271 *et seq.*

instrument of transfer unless the conditions of issue otherwise provide or the transfer is to SEPON, *i.e.* on a transfer under the stock exchange procedure: section 80; Stock Exchange (Completion of Bargains) Act 1976, s.1. If registration of a transfer is refused, notice of refusal must be given to the transferee within two months: section 78.

Registered debentures are in England choses in action, and in Scotland incorporeal moveable property to the assignation of which the rule *assignatus utitur jure auctoris* ("the assignee acquires no higher right than his cedent had") applies. They are not negotiable instruments, and consequently a transferee takes them subject to all claims which the company may have against prior holders at the date of the transfer.

After a receiver had been appointed and a winding-up petition had been presented, P., a debenture stockholder, transferred £10,000 debenture stock to X, who was registered as the owner. P. was also a director of the company and a claim was made against him for money had and received by him while a director. *Held,* X was not entitled to payment until the amount due from P. to the company had been ascertained and deducted: *Re Rhodesia Goldfields Ltd.* [1910] 1 Ch. 239.

To avoid this result, the indorsed conditions usually provide that the principal and interest shall be paid to the registered holder without regard to any equities or rights of compensation existing between the company and any prior holder of the debenture. Such a clause amounts to a contract by the company that it will not rely on equities or rights of compensation, and its effect is to make the debentures more marketable.

A company was in liquidation. C., who had been a director of the company, transferred debentures to R. as security for a loan. The debentures contained a clause similar to that set out above. It was then discovered that C. had been guilty of misfeasance and he was ordered to pay a sum of money to the liquidator in respect thereof. The liquidator refused to register R.'s transfer. *Held,* the right to transfer and to have the transfer registered was not affected by the winding up, and R. was entitled to payment without regard to C.'s debt to the company: *Re Goy & Co. Ltd.* [1900] 2 Ch. 149.

A transferee cannot claim the benefit of such a clause unless and until he is registered.

B. held debentures containing a clause similar to that set out above. After a resolution for winding up had been passed he transferred them for value to C., who took without notice of any defect in B.'s title. Notice of transfer but no request for registration was given to the liquidator. C. claimed payment but the court found that B. had paid nothing for the debentures and had obtained them by misrepresentation. *Held*, notwithstanding the clause, C. took subject to the company's claim against B. *Re Goy & Co.*, *ante*, was distinguished on the ground that when the transfer in that case was sent for registration the company was not aware of and was not setting up any equities between itself and the transferor: *Re Palmer's Decoration and Furnishing Co.* [1904] 2 Ch. 743.

Section 79 (certification of transfers), *ante*,[50] applies to transfers of debentures as well as to transfers of shares.

Register of debenture holders

A company is not required to keep a register of debenture holders but there are provisions regulating those companies which do. A company registered in England must not keep its register of debenture holders in Scotland, and vice versa. The register must be kept at the registered office or at any other office of the company where it is made up or, if it is made up by an agent, it may be kept at the agent's office: section 86. Debenture holders and shareholders in the company may, without fee, inspect the register of debenture holders subject to such reasonable restrictions as the company may in general meeting impose, so that not less than two hours a day is allowed for inspection. Other persons may inspect the register on payment of a fee of 5p. The register may be closed for not more than 30 days in any year. A copy may be demanded on payment of 20p. for every 100 words or part thereof: 1948 Act, s.87; 1967 Act, s.52(1). A computer may be used to keep the register of debenture holders: Stock Exchange (Completion of Bargains) Act 1976, s.3.

The Jenkins Report[51] recommended that a company which issues a series of debentures ranking *pari passu* or debenture stock not transferable by delivery should be required to keep a register of the holders.

BEARER DEBENTURES

Debentures payable to bearer are in the same form as registered debentures except that they are expressed to be made payable to bearer and coupons for the interest are attached. The indorsed condi-

---

[50] p. 276.
[51] Para. 306.

tions are also in the same form with the necessary modifications for bearer, instead of registered, instruments.

Bearer debentures are negotiable instruments and consequently a transferee in good faith and for value takes them free from any defects in the title of a prior holder.

The B. Company owned some bearer debentures and kept them in a safe. The secretary fraudulently took them from the safe and deposited them with the bank, who took them in good faith and as security for advances to the secretary. *Held*, the debentures were negotiable instruments transferable by delivery and the bank was entitled to them as against the B. Company: *Bechuanaland Exploration Co.* v. *London Trading Bank* [1898] 2 Q.B. 658.

The courts take judicial notice of the fact that bearer debentures are negotiable instruments.[52]

Bearer debentures are transferable by delivery and no stamp duty is payable on transfer. Interest is payable by means of the coupons which are cut off and presented for payment to the company's bankers when the date of payment arrives.

Debentures to bearer issued in Scotland are expressly declared by section 93 of the 1948 Act to be valid and binding notwithstanding anything in the Blank Bonds and Trusts Act 1696 (Scots Act 1696, c.25).[53]

REDEEMABLE DEBENTURES

Debentures may be (1) redeemable at the option of the company, or (2) irredeemable or perpetual.

Sometimes debentures are issued on the terms that the company is bound to redeem a certain number each year by "drawings" (in which case, in effect, the numbers of the debentures to be redeemed are drawn out of a hat),[54] or that it may purchase, *e.g.* on the Stock Exchange, or that it is bound to set aside a sinking fund for redemption purposes on a specified date. When debentures have been so redeemed, section 90 empowers the company to reissue them or issue other debentures in their place, unless—

[52] *Edelstein* v. *Schuler* [1902] 2 K.B. 144.

[53] *Ante*, p. 286.

[54] For difficulties which may arise from the company's inability to trace the holders to whom repayment is due, see *United Collieries Ltd.* v. *Lord Advocate*, 1950 S.C. 458.

(*a*) the company, in its articles or otherwise, has contracted not to reissue them; or

(*b*) the company has shown an intention to cancel the debentures by passing a resolution to that effect, or by some other act.

Under the general law, once a debenture was transferred to the company the debt was absolutely gone and the security ceased to exist.[55]

On a reissue of redeemed debentures, the person entitled to them has the same priorities as if the debentures had never been redeemed: section 90. The date of redemption of the reissued debentures cannot be later than that of the original debentures.[56]

Particulars of any redeemed debentures which can be reissued must be included in the balance sheet: Schedule 8 (as introduced by 1981 Act, Sched. 1).

Reissued debentures are treated as new debentures for the purpose of stamp duty: section 90.

PERPETUAL DEBENTURES

Debentures are not invalid merely because they are made irredeemable, or redeemable on the happening of a contingency, however remote, *e.g.* the winding up of the company, or on the expiration of a period, however long, *e.g.* 100 years after the issue of the debentures, *i.e.* the legal or contractual date for redemption may be postponed, despite any rule of equity to the contrary: section 89.

A company mortgaged 75 houses and other properties to secure £310,000 repayable by instalments over 40 years. There was no right of redemption before the 40 years expired. *Held*, the mortgage was a debenture and valid under what is now section 89: *Knightsbridge Estates Trust Ltd.* v. *Byrne* [1940] A.C. 613.

The issue of perpetual debentures amounts to the granting of a perpetual annuity.[57] If the debentures are secured by a floating charge, the money secured will become payable on the company's going into liquidation and the security will be enforceable on the class of assets charged as it exists at that time.[58]

---

[55] *Re George Routledge & Sons Ltd.* [1904] 2 Ch. 474.
[56] *Re Antofagasta (Chile) and Bolivia Ry. Co.'s Trust Deed* [1939] Ch. 732.
[57] *Re The Southern Brazilian Rio Grande do Sul Ry. Co. Ltd.* [1905] 2 Ch. 78.
[58] *Hodson* v. *Tea Co.* (1880) 14 Ch.D. 859.

In English law, subject to section 89, *ante*, the equitable doctrine against clogging the equity of redemption applies to a floating charge securing debentures. The debentures may, however, provide for a collateral advantage for the debenture holder, to endure after the debentures have been paid off, provided it is not (a) unfair and unconscionable; or (b) in the nature of a penalty clogging the equity of redemption; or (c) inconsistent with the contractual or equitable right to redeem.[59]

By an agreement dated August 24, 1910, a firm of woolbrokers agreed to lend a company carrying on the business of meat preservers £10,000 with interest at six per cent. per annum. If interest was punctually paid the loan was not repayable until September 30, 1915, but the company might repay at any time on giving one month's notice. The loan was secured by a floating charge on the undertaking and property of the company. The agreement stipulated that for five years from the date thereof the company should not sell sheepskins to anyone other than the lenders so long as the lenders were willing to buy at the best price offered by anyone else. The loan was repaid in January 1913, whereupon the lenders claimed to exercise their option of pre-emption. *Held*, the stipulation for the option was a collateral advantage entered into as a condition of the company obtaining the loan; it was not a clog on the equity of redemption or repugnant to the right to redeem; and the lenders were entitled to an injunction restraining the company from selling sheepskins to anyone else: *Kreglinger* v. *New Patagonia Meat etc. Co. Ltd.*[1914] A.C. 25.

In Scotland, the Conveyancing and Feudal Reform (Scotland) Act 1970, ss.11 and 18, conferred on the debtor in a standard security the right, which could not be varied by agreement, to redeem the security on giving two months' notice. The Redemption of Standard Securities (Scotland) Act 1971, however, amended the 1970 Act on this point by providing that the condition relating to the debtor's right of redemption might be varied by agreement. The 1971 Act also, for the avoidance of doubt, declared that the provisions of the 1970 Act relating to the standard security do not affect the operation of section 89 of the 1948 Act.

CHARGES SECURING DEBENTURES

A charge on the assets of a company given by a debenture or a trust deed in order to secure money borrowed by the company may be either (1) a specific or fixed charge, or (2) a floating charge. If the

---

[59] *Kreglinger* v. *New Patagonia Meat etc. Co. Ltd.* [1914] A.C. 25.

debentures are issued in a series and give a specific charge on the company's property, *e.g.* its land, they are always secured by means of a trust deed. The trust deed usually gives a floating charge, *e.g.* on the rest of the company's property, in addition to the fixed charge.

Fixed charges (English law)

A fixed charge is a mortgage of ascertained and definite property, *e.g.* a legal or an equitable mortgage of a specified factory, and prevents the company from realising that property, *i.e.* disposing of it free from the charge, without the consent of the holders of the charge.

If the charge is on fixed assets it has been held in a New Zealand case that those are assets which are normally expected to be available to the company and remain permanently with the company for the purpose of carrying out its business. It is not limited to those assets physically attached to its premises.[60]

Floating charges (English law)

In *Re Yorkshire Woolcombers Association Ltd.*[61] Romer L.J. said that if a charge has the three characteristics set out below it is a floating charge:
   (1) it is a charge on a class of assets of a company, present and future;
   (2) which class is, in the ordinary course of the company's business, changing from time to time;
   (3) it is contemplated by the charge that, until the holders of the charge take steps to enforce it, the company may carry on business in the ordinary way as far as concerns the class of assets charged.

Thus a floating charge is an equitable charge on some or all of the present and future property of a company, *e.g.* the company's undertaking, *i.e.* all its property, present and future.[62] It is effective as to future property only when that property is acquired by the company. The company may, in the ordinary course of business, realise property which is subject to the charge. However, when the security is enforce-

---

[60] *Tudor Heights Ltd.* v. *United Dominions Corporation Finance Ltd.* [1977] 1 N.Z.L.R. 532.
[61] [1903] 2 Ch. 284 (C.A.), at p. 295.
[62] *Re Panama etc. Royal Mail Co.* (1870) L.R. 5 Ch.App. 318.

able, *i.e.* there is default with regard to payment of interest or repayment of the principal sum, and the debenture holders or the trustees enforce it, *e.g.* they appoint a receiver of the property charged,[63] the floating charge is said to "crystallise," *i.e.* it becomes a fixed charge on the assets in the class charged at the time of crystallisation or, where the floating charge so provides, assets which come to the company after crystallisation.[64] Crystallisation also occurs on the commencement of the winding up of the company, even if it is a voluntary winding up for the purpose of reconstruction,[65] or possibly when the company ceases business.

It is possible that the charging deed may provide for crystallisation on a certain event, *e.g.* an attempt by the company to create another charge over the assets in the class charged. There is no United Kingdom authority as to whether such clauses are enforceable. One has been allowed in a New Zealand case[66] but doubted in a Canadian one.[67] Such "automatic crystallisation" is therefore uncertain. One problem is that it would seem to prevent the company dealing with the assets charged and that it could happen without anyone else being aware. The established grounds of crystallisation all require an event, *e.g.* the appointment of a receiver.

The characteristics of a floating charge are therefore:

(1) It is an equitable charge on assets for the time being of the company.[68]

(2) It attaches to the class of assets charged in the varying condition in which they happen to be from time to time,[68] *i.e.* it does not fasten on any definite property but is a charge on property which is constantly changing.

(3) It remains dormant, subject to any possible automatic crystallisation, until the undertaking charged ceases to be a going concern, or until the person in whose favour it is created intervenes. His right to intervene may be suspended by agree-

---

[63] *Post,* p. 585.
[64] *N. W. Robbie & Co. Ltd.* v. *Whitney Warehouse Co. Ltd.* [1963] 1 W.L.R. 1324 (C.A.); *Ferrier* v. *Bottomer* (1972) 126 C.L.R. 597.
[65] *Re Crompton & Co.* [1914] 1 Ch. 954.
[66] *Re Manurewa Transport Ltd.* [1971] N.Z.L.R. 909.
[67] *R.* v. *Consolidated Churchill Copper Corpn. Ltd.* [1978] 5 W.W.R. 652.
[68] *Per* Lord Macnaghten in *Governments Stock Investment Co. Ltd.* v. *Manila Ry. Co. Ltd.* [1897] A.C. 81, at p. 86.

ment but if there is no agreement for suspension he may intervene whenever he pleases after default.[69] When this happens the charge is said to "crystallise" and becomes fixed.[70]

(4) Although it is an immediate and continuing charge, until it becomes fixed the company can, without consent, deal with the class of assets in the ordinary course of business, *e.g.* it has been held that a company can sell all or any of its business or property for shares or debentures of another company if the memorandum gives it power to do so, and the debenture holders cannot prevent such a sale if the company remains a going concern[71]; similarly, a company with three businesses may sell one of the three.[72]

Where, before crystallisation of a floating charge over all the company's assets and undertaking, the company contracted to sell goods to a buyer to whom it owed money under a previous contract, and the goods were delivered after crystallisation, the company's right to sue for the debt due to it was embraced, when it arose, by the floating charge, but the debenture holder could not be in a better position to assert the rights under the previous contract than the company.[73]

Recent attempts by suppliers of goods to companies to retain title to those goods until paid have been construed as floating charges on the goods supplied.[74]

The advantage of a floating charge from the *company's* point of view is that the company can give security for a loan to it by charging property which changes in the course of business and over which it is impracticable to create a fixed charge, *e.g.* the company's stock-in-trade. Further, until crystallisation the company can carry on business in the ordinary way.

A floating charge can be created by a registered company but not by a partnership or a sole trader. One reason is that such a charge created by a firm over chattels would be a bill of sale within the Bills of Sale

[69] See note 65 above.
[70] *Evans* v. *Rival Granite Quarries Ltd.* [1910] 2 K.B. 979 (C.A.).
[71] *Re Borax Co.* [1901] 1 Ch. 326.
[72] *Re H. H. Vivian & Co. Ltd.* [1900] 2 Ch. 654.
[73] *Rother Iron Works Ltd.* v. *Canterbury Precision Engines Ltd.* [1974] Q.B. 1 (C.A.) applied in *George Barker (Transport) Ltd.* v. *Eynon* [1974] 1 W.L.R. 462 (C.A.).
[74] *Re Bond Worth Ltd.* [1980] Ch. 228; *Borden (U.K.) Ltd.* v. *Scottish Timber Products Ltd.* [1980] Ch. 672 (C.A.).

Acts 1878 and 1882, and would have to be registered and, as a mortgage bill, would have to be in the statutory form and specify the chattels, which is impossible.

From the *chargee's* point of view, an important advantage is that, upon crystallisation of the floating charge, the chargee obtains priority in the payment of debts over unsecured creditors. However, there are a number of disadvantages attached to a floating charge. For example:

(1) As will be seen, a floating charge is postponed to certain other interests.

(2) A floating charge may be invalidated under section 322, *post*. [75]

Priority of charges (English law)

A company which has created a floating charge cannot later create another floating charge over some of the same assets ranking in priority to or *pari passu* with the original charge unless the provisions of the original charge allow this. [76]

On the other hand, since a company which has created a floating charge can, without the consent of the holders of the charge, deal with the class of assets in the ordinary course of business, it follows that the company can, in the ordinary course of business, create a later fixed charge, legal or equitable, over specific assets and with priority over the floating charge, [77] unless the floating charge provides that the company is not to create any mortgage or charge ranking *pari passu* with or in priority to the floating charge, in which case any fixed chargee taking *with notice of this provision* will be postponed to the floating charge. In spite of such a provision the holder of a specific charge will obtain priority over a floating charge on all the company's property if:

(1) taking a legal mortgage, he obtains his mortgage without notice of the provision, even though he has notice of the debentures [78]—the maxim "where the equities are equal the law prevails" will apply; or

---

[75] *Post*, p. 571.

[76] *Re Automatic Bottle Makers Ltd.* [1926] Ch. 412 (C.A.).

[77] *Wheatley* v. *Silkstone, etc., Coal Co.* (1885) 29 Ch.D. 715.

[78] *English and Scottish Mercantile, etc., Co. Ltd.* v. *Brunton* [1892] 2 Q.B. 700 (C.A.).

(2) taking an equitable mortgage, he obtains the title deeds without notice of the debentures[79]—the maxim "where the equities are otherwise equal the earlier in time has priority" will not apply since the debenture holders left the title deeds with the company so as to enable it to deal with its property as if it was unincumbered, so that the equities are not equal.

Further, registration of a floating charge under the Companies Acts, *post*,[80] although constructive notice of the charge, is not notice that the charge contains a provision prohibiting the creation of subsequent charges with priority over the floating charge.[81]

The following also have priority over a floating charge:

(1) an execution creditor if the goods are sold by the sheriff,[82] or the company pays out the sheriff to avoid a sale,[83] or the creditor obtains a garnishee order absolute[84] (not a garnishee order nisi),[85] *before* crystallisation of the floating charge;

(2) a landlord's distress for rent levied before crystallisation[86];

(3) the rights of persons such as one who has sold goods to the company under a hire-purchase agreement by which the goods are still the property of such person[87];

(4) *after* crystallisation, certain *un*secured but preferential debts: sections 94, 319, *post*.[88]

On the other hand a floating charge may not be postponed to the holder of a *Mareva* injunction over the assets. Such an injunction prohibits the company from removing its assets outside the United Kingdom. The holder of the floating charge may apply to have the injunction set aside and will succeed if the holders of the injunction are unsecured creditors.[89]

---

[79] *Re Castell & Brown Ltd.* [1898] 1 Ch. 315.

[80] pp. 573 *et seq.*

[81] *Per* Eve J. in *Wilson* v. *Kelland* [1910] 2 Ch. 306, at p. 313; *Dempsey* v. *Traders' Finance Corpn.* [1933] N.Z.L.R. 1258 (C.A.).

[82] *Re Standard Manufacturing Co.* [1891] 1 Ch. 627 (C.A.).

[83] *Heaton and Dugard Ltd.* v. *Cutting Bros. Ltd.* [1925] 1 K.B. 655.

[84] *Evans* v. *Rival Granite Quarries Ltd.* [1910] 2 K.B. 979 (C.A.).

[85] *Norton* v. *Yates* [1906] 1 K.B. 112.

[86] *Re Roundwood Colliery Co.* [1897] 1 Ch. 373 (C.A.).

[87] See *Re Morrison, Jones and Taylor Ltd.* [1914] 1 Ch. 50 (C.A.).

[88] pp. 592, 663.

[89] *Cretanor Maritime Co. Ltd.* v. *Irish Marine Management Ltd.* [1978] 1 W.L.R. 966 (C.A.).

Fixed securities and floating charges (Scots law)

Before 1961 any attempt by a Scottish company to create a floating charge was of no effect, since such a charge violated the principle of the common law expressed in the maxim *"traditionibus, non nudis pactis, dominia rerum transferuntur,"* *i.e.* "delivery, and not mere agreement, is required for the transfer of real rights."

"There is no principle more deeply rooted in the law than this, that in order to create a good security over subjects delivery must be given. If possession be retained no effectual security can be granted": *per* Lord Shand in *Clark* v. *West Calder Oil Co. Ltd.* (1882) 9 R. 1017, at p. 1033 (a case in which trustees for debenture holders to whom the company had assigned certain leasehold and moveable property in security were held to have no preference over the ordinary trade creditors of the company since no possession had followed on the assignation).

"The whole method of creating a floating charge . . . is absolutely foreign to our law": *per* Lord President Dunedin in *The Ballachulish Slate Quarries Co. Ltd.* v. *Bruce* (1908) 16 S.L.T. 48, at p. 51 (an attempt to create a floating charge in English form on the uncalled capital and other assets of a company was held to give a debenture holder no valid security).

A company registered in Scotland and having a place of business and assets in England borrowed money under debentures which were in English form and by which the company purported to create a floating charge over its whole undertaking, property and assets. *Held*, that no valid and effectual floating charge had been created even over the company's assets in England: *Carse* v. *Coppen*, 1951 S.C. 233.

"It is clear in principle and amply supported by authority that a floating charge is utterly repugnant to the principles of Scots law and is not recognised by us as creating a security at all. In Scotland the term 'equitable security' is meaningless. Putting aside the rare and exceptional cases of hypothec, we require for the constitution of a security which will confer upon the holder rights over and above those which he enjoys in common with the general body of unsecured creditors of a debtor, (*a*) the transfer to the creditor of a real right in specific subjects by the method appropriate for the constitution of such rights in the particular classes of property in question, or (*b*) the creation of a nexus over specific property by the due use of the appropriate form of diligence. A floating charge, even after appointment of a receiver, satisfies none of these requirements": *per* Lord President Cooper at p. 239.

Floating charges were introduced to Scots law by the Companies (Floating Charges) (Scotland) Act 1961, but there was no power under that Act to appoint receivers. Subsequently, on the recommendation of the Scottish Law Commission,[90] the Companies (Floating Charges

---

[90] *Report on the Companies (Floating Charges) (Scotland) Act 1961,* 1970 Cmnd. 4336.

and Receivers) (Scotland) Act 1972 was passed with the twofold purpose of:

(1) re-enacting with substantial modification the provisions of the Act of 1961; and
(2) making it competent under Scots law for receivers to be appointed.

Scottish floating charges and receivers have statutory definitions and statutory incidents which distinguish them in some respects from their English common law originals. The term "fixed security" is used in the statutory provisions to denote a security other than a floating charge.[91]

In the two following subdivisions of this chapter the sections referred to are, except where there is a statement to the contrary, those of the Companies (Floating Charges and Receivers) (Scotland) Act 1972.

Floating charges (Scots law)

The main characteristics of the Scottish floating charge are:

(1) It is a charge created by an incorporated company[92] "over all or any part of the property (including uncalled capital) which may from time to time be comprised in its property and undertaking."
(2) It may be created for the purpose of securing any debt or other obligation (including a cautionary obligation) incurred or to be incurred by, or binding upon, the company or any other person. It is therefore possible, for instance, for a subsidiary company to create a floating charge over its own property to secure a debt due by its parent company (another person), or for a subsidiary company to guarantee a debt due by its parent company and create a floating charge over its own property to secure its liability under the guarantee.
(3) On the commencement of the winding up or on the appointment of a receiver it attaches (provided it is not invalid under section 106A[93] or section 322[94] of the 1948 Act) to the property

---

[91] Companies (Floating Charges and Receivers) (Scotland) Act 1972, s.31.
[92] Floating charges may also be created by industrial and provident societies registered in Scotland: Industrial and Provident Societies Act 1967, as amended by the Companies (Floating Charges and Receivers) (Scotland) Act 1972, s.10.
[93] *Post,* p. 578.   [94] *Post,* p. 571.

then comprised in the company's property and undertaking. The term "crystallisation" is not a statutory term in relation to the Scottish floating charge.

(4) Once attached it has the same effect as if it were a fixed security over the property for the principal of, and any interest due or to become due on, the debt or obligation to which it relates. The security extends to interest stipulated for from the date of attachment until payment.[95]

(5) It is postponed to the rights of certain creditors[96]: section 1.

(6) It can be created by a Scottish company only by the execution, under the seal of the company, of an instrument or bond or other written acknowledgment of debt or obligation which purports to create a floating charge. There is no longer any statutory form as there was under the 1961 Act. An alternative to execution by the company itself is execution by an attorney who has been authorised for that purpose by writing under the company's common seal: section 2.

The document creating a floating charge may contain:

(*a*) provisions prohibiting or restricting the creation of any fixed security or any other floating charge having priority over, or ranking equally with, the floating charge; or

(*b*) provisions regulating the order in which the floating charge is to rank with any other subsisting or future floating charges or fixed securities over the property or part of it: section 5.

A floating charge may be altered by an instrument of alteration: section 7.

The advantage of a floating charge from the *company's* point of view is that the company can give security for a loan to it by charging property such as stock-in-trade and other moveables which it would be impracticable to deliver to the lender. Until the floating charge has attached to the property the company can, in the ordinary course of business, realise any of its assets without the consent of the creditor who is entitled to the benefit of the floating charge.

---

[95] *National Commercial Bank of Scotland Ltd.* v. *Liquidators of Telford Grier Mackay & Co. Ltd.*, 1969 S.C. 181, followed in *Royal Bank of Scotland Ltd.* v. *Williamson*, 1972 S.L.T. (Sh.Ct.) 45, and given statutory force by s.1(4).

[96] *Post*, p. 571.

From the *creditor's* point of view, the two disadvantages exemplified on page 565, *ante,* in relation to English law, apply also in Scots law, but for the protection of the creditor it is provided that a Scots company may be wound up by the court "if there is subsisting a floating charge over property comprised in the company's property and undertaking and the court is satisfied that the security of the creditor entitled to the benefit of the floating charge is in jeopardy." The security of the creditor is deemed to be in jeopardy "if the court is satisfied that events have occurred or are about to occur which render it unreasonable in the interests of the creditor that the company should retain power to dispose of the property which is subject to the floating charge": section 4.

Priority of charges (Scots law)

Where all or any part of a company's property is subject both to a fixed security and to a floating charge, the fixed security has as a general rule priority over the floating charge. This is always so if the fixed security is one arising by operation of law (*e.g.* by a statutory provision). If the fixed security is not of that nature (*e.g.* is a standard security over heritable property under the Conveyancing and Feudal Reform (Scotland) Act 1970), the order of ranking may be regulated by provisions in the document which creates the floating charge or in any instrument of alteration.

Where there are two or more floating charges, the charges as a general rule rank with one another according to the time of their registration with the Registrar,[97] and if received by the Registrar by the same postal delivery they rank equally with one another. Here again the order of ranking may be regulated by provisions in the document creating a floating charge or in any instrument of alteration. There is, however, the following statutory restriction on the priority which may be obtained: where the holder of a floating charge which has been registered receives written intimation of the subsequent registration of another floating charge over the same property or part of it, the preference in ranking of the first floating charge is restricted to security for:

> (*a*) the holder's present advances;
> (*b*) future advances which he may be required to make;

---

[97] *Post,* p. 574.

(*c*) interest due or to become due on advances within (*a*) and (*b*), above; and

(*d*) expenses or outlays reasonably incurred by the holder: section 5.

The following have priority over a floating charge:

(1) the rights of any person who has effectually executed diligence on the property or any part of it: section 1;

(2) the rights of persons such as one who has sold goods to the company under a hire-purchase agreement by which the goods are still the property of such person;

(3) certain *un*secured but preferential debts: 1948 Act, s.319.[97a]

Avoidance of floating charges

To prevent insolvent companies from creating floating charges to secure past debts to the prejudice of their general (unsecured) creditors, section 322 provides that where a company is being wound up a floating charge on the undertaking or property of the company created within 12 months before the commencement of the winding up is, unless the company was solvent immediately after the charge was created, invalid except to the amount of any cash paid to the company at or after the time when the charge was created and in consideration for the charge, with interest at five per cent. per annum or the rate prescribed by the Treasury.

Whether cash was paid at the time when the charge was created is a question of fact, and "a payment made on account of the consideration for the security, in anticipation of its creation and in reliance on a promise to execute it, although made some days before its execution, is made at the time of its creation within the meaning of the section."[98]

Moneys were advanced on the security of a floating charge to be created by a company, which was insolvent. The first advance was 54 days, and the last five days, before the charge was created. Five days after the charge was created the company went into liquidation. *Held*, (1) as the delay was not procured or suggested or acquiesced in by the lender, the payments were made at the time of the creation of the charge, and the charge was accordingly valid; (2) as the payments were made at the time of the creation of the charge,

[97a] *Post*, p. 663.
[98] *Per* Neville J. in *Re Columbian Fireproofing Co. Ltd.* [1910] 1 Ch. 758, at p. 765.

the charge could not be a fraudulent preference: *Re F. and E. Stanton Ltd.* [1929] 1 Ch. 180.

The words "in consideration for the charge" in section 322 mean "in consideration of the fact that the charge exists."

A company created a floating charge to secure its overdrawn current account with its bank. *Held*: (1) Every payment made by the bank to the company after the creation of the charge was "cash paid to the company" and was made in consideration of the charge. Consequently the charge was not invalid against the liquidator, and the bank was a secured creditor as to such payments. (2) The rule in *Clayton's Case*[99] applied. Each payment by the bank after the date of the charge was a provision of "new money" and there was nothing to displace the presumption that payments in by the company after the charge should be set in the first instance against the company's debt to the bank at the date of the charge: *Re Yeovil Glove Co. Ltd.* [1965] Ch. 148 (C.A.).

The effect of section 322 is merely to invalidate the charge, so that the creditor remains an unsecured creditor. If, therefore, the debt secured by a charge rendered void by that section is repaid by the company before the commencement of liquidation, the liquidator cannot recover it.[1]

Cash may have been paid to the company although it was only paid on condition that it be applied in paying a specified debt of the company.

Payments made direct to the company's creditors, though made on the company's behalf, have been held not to be within the phrase "cash paid to the company."[1a]

D. was a director of the company and a partner in the firm of D. & Co. who supplied goods to the company. The company owed D. & Co. £1,954 and D. & Co. refused to supply any more goods until this debt was paid. In March D., who wished to save the company, agreed to lend the company £3,000 on the security of a floating charge if the company would, out of this sum, pay £1,954 to D. & Co. This was done. The company was insolvent at the time. In July the company went into liquidation. *Held*, the floating charge was valid, the whole £3,000 being cash paid to the company: *Re Matthew Ellis Ltd.* [1933] 1 Ch. 458.

The cash must, however, have been intended to benefit the company and not certain creditors.

[99] (1816) 1 Mer. 572.
[1] *Re Parkes Garage* [1929] 1 Ch. 139.
[1a] *Libertas-Kommerz GmbH* v. *Johnston*, 1977 S.C. 191 (O.H.).

An insolvent company granted a floating charge to Z. to secure £900. The money was provided by D., for whom Z. was a nominee, and the same day as it was paid to the company the company paid £350 each to B. and S. for directors' fees and £200 to D., the amount guaranteed by D. in respect of the company's overdraft. Within 12 months the company went into liquidation. *Held*, the charge was invalid, as its object was to benefit B., S. and D. and not the company—in substance, no cash was paid to the company: *Re Destone Fabrics Ltd.* [1941] Ch. 319 (C.A.).

Fraudulent preferences

Any charge made by a company, within *six* months before the commencement of winding up, is void if it is a fraudulent preference of any of the company's creditors: section 320, *post*.[2]

REGISTRATION OF CHARGES

Charges created by a company are required to be registered (1) in the company's own register of charges, and (2) with the Registrar of Companies.

Registration in company's own register of charges

Section 104, applicable in England, provides that every *limited* company must keep at its registered office a register of *all* charges specifically affecting the property of the company and *all* floating charges on the undertaking or any property of the company. The register must give—

(*a*) a short description of the property charged;
(*b*) the amount of the charge;
(*c*) the names of the persons entitled thereto, except in the case of bearer securities.

There is a corresponding provision for Scotland in section 106I[3] but that section applies to *every* company and is not restricted to *limited* companies.

The omission to comply with section 104 or section 106I merely results in a fine on every officer who is knowingly a party to the omission. The validity of the charge is *not* affected.

[2] p. 637.
[3] ss.106A–106K are set out in the Schedule to the Companies (Floating Charges and Receivers) (Scotland) Act 1972.

Every company must keep a copy of every instrument creating a charge required to be registered under section 104, section 106I, or under sections 95 and 97 (for Scotland, sections 106A and 106C), *post*, at the registered office of the company. In the case of a series of uniform debentures a copy of one of the series is sufficient: sections 103, 106H.

These copies, and also the company's register of charges, are open to the inspection of any creditor or member of the company without fee for at least two hours each day during business hours. The register of charges *only* is similarly open to the general public on payment of a fee not exceeding five pence: sections 105, 106J.

Registration with Registrar

There are some differences between the registration requirements imposed on English companies by the 1948 Act and those imposed on Scottish companies by the Companies (Floating Charges and Receivers) (Scotland) Act 1972.

Registration in England

Section 95 provides that prescribed[4] particulars of certain specified charges *created* by companies registered in England, together with the instrument, if any, creating them, must be delivered to the Registrar within 21 days after their creation. The object of registration is to protect the grantee of the charge.[5]

The charges to which the section applies are:

(*a*) A charge to secure an issue of debentures.
(*b*) A charge on uncalled share capital.
(*c*) A charge created or evidenced by an instrument which, if executed by an individual, would require registration as a bill of sale.[6]
(*d*) A charge on any land or any interest therein.

The general rule is that a deposit of title deeds by a company to secure a debt, whether owed by the company or a third party, creates

---

[4] See the Companies (Forms) Regulations 1979, S.I. 1979/1547, reg. 6.
[5] *Per* Bankes L.J. in *National Provincial Bank* v. *Charnley* [1924] 1 K.B. 431 (C.A.) at p. 442.
[6] See *Stoneleigh Finance Ltd.* v. *Phillips* [1965] 2 Q.B. 537 (C.A.); *cf. R. A. Barrett & Co. Ltd.* v. *Livesey* (1981) 131 N.L.J. 1213.

an equitable charge on the land, despite section 40 of the Law of Property Act 1925, and not just a naked lien on the documents themselves, which charge is registrable under section 95 since it is contractual in nature even though created as a result of a presumption of law.[7]

On the true construction of sections 34, 35 and 36 of the Administration of Justice Act 1956, a charging order on specific land of a company obtained by a judgment creditor does not require registration under section 95.[8] (It must be registered under the Land Charges Act or the Land Registration Act, as the case may be, *post.*)

(*e*) A charge on book debts of the company.

If a company which has entered into hire-purchase agreements for the disposal of its products deposits the agreements as security for advances, there is a charge on the company's book debts.[9]

A charge on future book debts is registrable under section 95.[9] However, where the subject-matter of a charge at the date of its creation is the benefit of a contract which does not then comprehend a book debt, *e.g.* a contract of insurance, the contract cannot be brought within section 95 merely because it might ultimately result in a book debt.[10]

(*f*) A floating charge on the undertaking or property of the company.

(*g*) A charge on calls made but not paid.

(*h*) A charge on a ship (or aircraft[11]).

(*i*) A charge on goodwill, on a patent or a licence under a patent, on a trademark or on a copyright or a licence under a copyright.

A land charge for securing money created by a company on or after January 1, 1970 (other than a floating charge) must also be registered under the Land Charges Act 1972 to the same extent as such a charge

---

[7] *Re Wallis & Simmonds (Builders) Ltd.* [1974] 1 W.L.R. 391, distinguishing *London and Cheshire Insce. Co. Ltd.* v. *Laplagrene Property Co. Ltd.* [1971] Ch. 499 (unpaid vendor's lien created by law not registrable). And see *post,* p. 581. In *Wallis & Simmonds* there was no lien on the title deeds having a separate existence and the charge was void for non-registration.

[8] *Re Overseas Aviation Engineering (G.B.) Ltd.* [1963] Ch. 24 (C.A.).

[9] *Independent Automatic Sales Ltd.* v. *Knowles & Foster* [1962] 1 W.L.R. 974.

[10] *Paul & Frank Ltd.* v. *Discount Bank (Overseas) Ltd.* [1967] Ch. 348.

[11] See Mortgaging of Aircraft Order 1972 (S.I. 1972 No. 1268), art. 16(2).

created by an individual.[12] In the case of land the title to which is registered, a charge created by a company must also be protected by an entry on the land register under the Land Registration Act 1925.[13]

The Jenkins Report[14] recommended that a charge on shares held by a company in a subsidiary should be registrable under section 95. The Committee found it anomalous that such a charge is not now registrable whereas a charge on the book debts or real property of one of a company's branches is registrable.

Registration in Scotland

For Scotland section 106A, corresponding to section 95, requires registration of prescribed[14a] particulars of certain specified charges created by companies, together with *certified copies* of any instruments creating the charges.

The section applies to the following charges:

(a) A charge on land wherever situated or any interest therein. Hence registration with the Registrar in Scotland is required of a charge created by a Scottish company over heritable property in England.[15]

(b) A security over the uncalled share capital.

(c) A security over incorporeal moveable property of any of the following categories—

(i) the book debts of the company;
(ii) calls made but not paid;
(iii) goodwill;
(iv) a patent or a licence under a patent;
(v) a trademark;
(vi) a copyright or a licence under a copyright.

(d) A security over a ship (or aircraft[16]).

(e) A floating charge.

A security over incorporeal moveable property not falling within any of the categories specified (*e.g.* shares in other companies) does

[12] Land Charges Act 1972, ss.3(7) and (8).
[13] s.25.   [14] Para. 306.
[14a] See the Companies (Forms) Regulations 1979 (S.I. 1979 No. 1547), reg. 6.
[15] *Amalgamated Securities Ltd., Petitioners*, 1967 S.C. 56.
[16] See Mortgaging of Aircraft Order 1972 (S.I. 1972 No. 1268), art. 16(2).

not require registration, and if particulars of such a charge have been registered the court will order their deletion from the register.[17]

It is to be observed that a charge to secure an issue of debentures which is the first in the English list is absent from the Scottish list. "For some inscrutable reason no corresponding provision has been made in regard to Scotland."[18]

In the 1961 Act no provision was made for re-registration of any instrument creating a charge,[19] or for registration of an instrument increasing the amount secured.[20] Consequently if at a later date the amount secured by a fixed charge was to be increased, the security had to be re-created from the beginning, a "cumbersome and expensive" practice for which the Scottish Law Commission suggested a remedy.[21] The 1972 Act accordingly provides that where the amount secured by a fixed charge is increased, a further charge is to be held to have been created, and that the registration provisions apply to that further charge.

A fixed charge on land cannot now be created in any form other than a "standard security" under the Conveyancing and Feudal Reform (Scotland) Act 1970. For the creation of a real right the standard security must be recorded in the Register of Sasines or registered in the Land Register of Scotland: 1970 Act, ss.9, 11; Land Registration (Scotland) Act 1979, ss.2, 3.

Section 106A provides that the date of creation of a floating charge is the date on which the instrument creating the floating charge is executed by the company, and the date of creation of any other charge is the date on which the right of the person entitled to the benefit of the charge becomes a real right, *e.g.* in the case of a standard security, the date of recording in the Register of Sasines.[22]

The registration provisions extend to any instrument of alteration under section 7 of the 1972 Act if the instrument:

> (*a*) prohibits or restricts the creation of any fixed security or any other floating charge having priority over, or ranking equally with, the floating charge; or

[17] *Scottish Homes Investment Co. Ltd., Petitioners,* 1968 S.C. 244.

[18] *Per* Lord President Clyde in the *Scottish Homes* case, above, at p. 248 (shares in other companies assigned to trustees in security for an issue of debenture stock).

[19] *Archibald Campbell, Hope & King Ltd., Petitioners,* 1967 S.C. 21.

[20] *Scottish and Newcastle Breweries Ltd.* v. *Liquidator of Rathburne Hotel Co. Ltd.,* 1970 S.C. 215 (O.H.).

[21] (1970) Cmnd. 4336, paras. 17, 18.   [22] See note 19 above.

(*b*) varies, or otherwise regulates the order of, the ranking of the floating charge in relation to fixed securities or to other floating charges; or

(*c*) releases property from the floating charge; or

(*d*) increases the amount secured by the floating charge.

Registration in England and Scotland

In the case of a series of debentures containing, or giving by reference to another instrument, a charge to the benefit of which the debenture holders are entitled *pari passu,* it is sufficient if the following particulars are registered—

(*a*) the total amount secured by the series;

(*b*) the dates of the resolutions authorising the issue of the series and the date of the covering deed, if any, by which the security is created;

(*c*) a general description of the property charged;

(*d*) the names of the trustees, if any, for the debenture holders; and

(*e*) in the case of a Scottish floating charge, a statement of the restrictions, if any, on the company's power to grant further securities ranking prior to or equally with the floating charge;

together with the deed (or in Scotland a copy of the deed) creating the charge or, if there is no deed, one of the debentures (or in Scotland a copy of one of the debentures) of the series: sections 95, 106A. The sections also require registration of the date and amount of each issue in the series but failure to do so does not affect the validity of the debentures.

Particulars of the amount or rate per cent. of the commission, allowance or discount on an issue of debentures must be registered: sections 95, 106A.

The register contains the following particulars—

(*a*) in the case of a series of debentures, the particulars set out *ante*;

(*b*) in other cases—

(i) the date of the creation of the charge;

(ii) the amount secured by the charge;

(iii) short particulars of the property charged;

(iv) the persons entitled to the charge; and

(v) in the case of a Scottish floating charge, a statement of the restrictions, if any, on the company's power to grant further securities ranking prior to or equally with the floating charge: sections 98(1), 106D(1).

It is the duty of the company to register the particulars required by section 95 or section 106A. Registration, however, may be effected by any person interested in the charge and the registration fees may be recovered from the company: sections 96, 106B.

On the registration of a charge the Registrar gives a certificate of registration which is conclusive evidence that the requirements of the Act as to registration have been complied with: sections 98(2), 106E. The particulars delivered to the Registrar may incorrectly state the property charged, or the amount or date of the charge, but if a certificate is given the grantee of the charge is protected. The certificate is conclusive evidence that the Registrar has entered the particulars in the register and that the prescribed, *i.e.* accurate, particulars have been presented to him.[23]

In the course of its business in 1960 a company bought properties. R., a shareholder, advanced money for each purchase and the company undertook to execute formal mortgages on demand. In 1961 the directors and R. agreed that the company should implement its undertakings, and memoranda of deposit of title deeds purporting to charge some of the properties with payment to R. of certain sums on demand were signed but not dated on June 5, 1961. On July 11 the memoranda were registered with the Registrar, the date of execution being given as June 23. On August 4 the company went into voluntary winding up. *Held*, (1) the charges were not void under section 95(1)—by section 98(2) the certificate of registration was conclusive that all the requirements of the Act had been complied with within 21 days of execution, although the particulars submitted for registration incorrectly stated the date of the charges; (2) they were fraudulent preferences of R. and so void under section 320(1)[24]: *Re Eric Holmes (Property) Ltd.* [1965] Ch. 1052, applied in *Re C. L. Nye Ltd.* [1971] Ch. 442 (C.A.).

"If a chargee fraudulently deceives the registrar, a creditor personally damaged by the fraud can take proceedings in personam": *per* Russell L.J. at p. 474. However, on the facts no one gave credit between the date by which registration should have been effected and the date when it was effected.

"It is . . . possible that there is some lacuna in the Act . . . inasmuch as the Act gives, apparently, protection where the cerificate is made upon the basis of particulars which are incorrect and might even be fraudulent": *per* Pennycuick J., at p. 1072.

---

[23] *Re. C. L. Nye Ltd.* [1971] Ch. 442 (C.A.).   [24] *Post*, p. 637.

To discover the exact terms of a charge one has to look at the document creating it (which document, or in Scotland a copy of which document, will have been filed) and not at the register.[25]

In England, a copy of the certificate of registration must be indorsed on every debenture or debenture stock certificate issued by the company and the payment of which is secured by the charge registered. The penalty for neglect is a fine: section 99. The Jenkins Committee saw no need for this section and recommended its repeal.[26] Under the 1972 Act there is no corresponding provision for Scotland.

When the debt for which any registered charge was given is satisfied, in whole or in part, or part of the property charged is released or ceases to form part of the company's property, the Registrar enters a memorandum of satisfaction or release on the register. The company is entitled to a copy of the memorandum: sections 100, 106F(1).

In Scotland the Registrar must not enter any such memorandum on the register unless either:

(*a*) the creditor entitled to the benefit of the floating charge, or a person authorised by the creditor, certifies as correct the particulars submitted to the Registrar with respect to the entry; or

(*b*) the court, on being satisfied that such certification cannot readily be obtained, directs the Registrar to make the entry: section 106F(2).

The register is open to public inspection: sections 98(3), 106D(2).

Effect of non-registration

If a charge which ought to be registered under section 95 or section 106A is not so registered—

(*a*) the company and every officer who is knowingly a party to the default, is liable to a default fine (ss.96, 106B);

(*b*) the charge is, so far as any security on the company's property is concerned, void against the liquidator and any creditor of the company, but without prejudice to the contract to repay the money secured, which becomes immediately repayable (ss.95,

---

[25] *Re Mechanisations (Eaglescliffe) Ltd.* [1966] Ch. 20, following *National Provincial Bank* v. *Charnley* [1924] 1 K.B. 431 (C.A.).

[26] Cmnd. 1749, para. 306.

106A). The result is that the holder of the charge is reduced to the level of an *unsecured* creditor.

In March the company gave T. a legal mortgage of specific land to secure £500. The mortgage was not registered. In December the company issued debentures secured by a floating charge on its undertaking and assets to J. to secure another £500. This charge was registered. *Held*, although J., when he took his security, had actual notice of T.'s mortgage, he nevertheless had priority over T.: *Re Monolithic Building Co.* [1915] 1 Ch. 643 (C.A.).

In order to secure repayment of a loan a company gave the lenders subcharges on properties and deposited deeds and documents (such as legal charges and charge certificates) "to the intent that" they might "be equitably charged." The charges were void for non-registration (as charges on land or on book debts) under section 95. *Held*, the lenders had no common law lien on the documents. The deposit was merely ancillary to the equitable charge, and the contractual right to retention of the documents was lost when the charges were avoided. The contract had no independent existence apart from the charge: *Re Molton Finance Ltd.* [1968] Ch. 325 (C.A.), applied in *Re Wallis & Simmonds (Builders) Ltd.* [1974] 1 W.L.R. 391.

Rectification of register

Under section 101 for England and section 106G for Scotland the court may, on application by the company or any person interested, extend the time for registration or rectify the register if—

    (*a*) the omission to register a charge within the required time or the omission or mis-statement of a particular with respect to a charge is—

        (i) accidental; or
        (ii) due to inadvertence or some other sufficient cause; or
        (iii) not of a nature to prejudice the creditors or shareholders; or;

    (*b*) on other grounds it is just and equitable to grant relief.

Sections 101 and 106G require the court to be satisfied with respect to certain matters before it orders an extension of time and, therefore, if serious issues of fact are involved it should arm itself with the best information and evidence available.[27] The section does not empower the court to grant interim relief.[27]

---

[27] *Re Heathstar Properties Ltd.* [1966] 1 W.L.R. 993. In *Re Heathstar Properties Ltd.* (*No. 2*) [1966] 1 W.L.R. 999, it was found that the omission to register was due to inadvertence and the time for registration was extended notwithstanding that an action was proceeding in which the validity of the charge was in issue.

If, on an application for late registration, it is shown either that a liquidation of the company is imminent or has actually occurred, the court is unlikely to order an extension of time. Further, if when a chargee discovers that, by mistake, he is unregistered he must apply without delay for an extension of time and not deliberately defer his application in order to see which course would be to his best advantage. Failure to do so will prejudice his application: *Victoria Housing Estates Ltd.* v. *Ashpurton Estates Ltd.*[27a]

Relief will usually only be granted "without prejudice to the rights of parties acquired prior to the time when [the charge is] actually registered."[28] This proviso protects rights acquired *against the company's property in the extension of time*,[29] so that a secured creditor whose charge is created and registered in such time will not lose priority.[30]

It is otherwise when the second charge is created and registered within the 21 day period allowed by section 95 for registration of the first charge, *e.g.* the second chargee's rights do not gain priority by reason of the proviso—such rights are acquired at the date of execution of the second charge.

On January 22 a company created two floating charges on its undertaking and property by issuing a first debenture to X to secure £10,000 lent by him to the company and a second debenture to Y to secure £5,000. The second debenture was registered on January 28 but, by mistake, the first was returned to X unregistered. On October 20, X applied under secton 101 for an extension of the time allowed for registration and on October 28 the court ordered an extension to November 11 with a proviso that the order was "without prejudice to the rights of any parties acquired prior to the time when the said debenture is to be registered." Also on October 28, Y appointed a receiver under the second debenture. The first debenture was registered on November 5 and a receiver appointed thereunder on November 8. On November 9, the company went into a creditors' voluntary liquidation.

Held, (1) Y's rights under the second debenture were acquired at the date of its execution and not at the expiration of the 21 days allowed by section 95 for registration of the first debenture (February 12), when the first debenture being then unregistered became void, nor in the ensuing period, during which it remained void, between the expiration of the 21 days and the date of its actual registration, and accordingly such rights did not gain priority over the first debenture by reason of the proviso to the court order; (2) although the

[27a] [1982] 3 All E.R. 665 (C.A.).
[28] *Re Joplin Brewery Co. Ltd.* [1902] 1 Ch. 79.
[29] *Re Ehrmann Bros. Ltd.* [1906] 2 Ch. 697 (C.A.).
[30] *Re Monolithic Building Co.* [1915] 1 Ch. 643 (C.A.), *ante.*

appointment by Y of a receiver crystallised his floating charge, Y did not thereby acquire rights but merely exercised a power acquired when the debenture was executed (*Watson* v. *Duff, Morgan and Vermont (Holdings) Limited* [1974] 1 W.L.R. 450).

"The effect of an order extending the time for registration under section 101, followed by registration within that extended time, is to constitute the charge valid *ab initio* subject only to such conditions as might be imposed by a judge giving the extended time": *per* Templeman J. at p. 454.

Unsecured creditors with no charge on the company's property do not qualify for the purposes of the proviso. However, if the company has gone into liquidation there will be, as a general rule, no benefit in obtaining an extension of time, as the unsecured creditors will then have acquired rights against the property of the company.[31] A very exceptional case has to be made out to justify the court ordering rectification of the register after the company has gone into liquidation and the rights of unsecured creditors have crystallised.[32] The court has no power under section 101 to delete a whole registration.[33]

A clear case for the exercise of the court's power was held to have been made out where a Scottish company had failed to register a charge created over heritable property in England.[34] In a sheriff court case an extension of time was granted where there had been a misunderstanding as to which party was to effect registration.[35]

Registration of charges existing on property acquired

If a company acquires any property which is already subject to a charge which, if created by the company, would have required registration under section 95 or 106A, *the company* must register particulars of the charge and a copy of the instrument creating or evidencing it within 21 days after the acquisition is completed. Default renders the company and every officer in default liable to a default fine (ss.97, 106C)

---

[31] *Re S. Abrahams & Sons* [1902] 1 Ch. 695.

[32] *Per* Buckley J. in *Re Mechanisations (Eaglescliffe) Ltd.* [1966] Ch. 20, at p. 36.

[33] *Per* Russell and Megaw L.JJ. in *Re C. L. Nye Ltd.* [1971] Ch. 442 (C.A.), at pp. 474, 476.

[34] *Amalgamated Securities Ltd., Petitioners*, 1967 S.C. 56, *ante*, p. 576; contrast *Archibald Campbell, Hope & King Ltd., Petitioners*, 1967 S.C. 21, *ante*, p. 577 in which a prayer for extension was held inept under the 1961 Act where the instrument creating the charge had already been registered and the company was seeking to re-register it for the purpose of securing an additional sum; see now s.106A(9) in the Schedule to the 1972 Act.

[35] *M. Milne Ltd., Petitioners* (1963) 79 Sh.Ct. Rep. 105.

but the validity of the charge is not affected. This is as it should be since the person entitled to the benefit of the charge will have no opportunity of ensuring that registration is effected.[36]

REMEDIES OF DEBENTURE HOLDERS

1. If a debenture confers no charge, a debenture holder is an ordinary unsecured creditor. Thus, if there is default in the payment of principal or interest he may (*a*) sue for the principal or interest and, after obtaining judgment, levy execution against the company,[37] or (*b*), as will be explained later,[38] petition for the winding up of the company by the court on the ground that the company is unable to pay its debts.

2. When a charge is conferred on the company's assets by way of security, and default is made in the payment of principal or interest, a debenture holder, or the trustees where there is a trust deed, may:

(*a*) sue for the principal or interest; or
(*b*) present a petition for the winding up of the company; or
(*c*) exercise any powers conferred by the debenture or the trust deed, *e.g.* of appointing a receiver of the assets charged, of selling the assets charged or of taking possession of the assets and carrying on the business; or
(*d*) if the debenture or the trust deed does not contain powers in that behalf, apply to the court for:
  (i) the appointment of a receiver or a receiver and manager; or
  (ii) an order for sale or foreclosure.

A debenture or trust deed will normally contain an express power to appoint a receiver of, or to sell, the company's assets charged by way of security. If there is no express power there will be an implied power under the Law of Property Act 1925, s.101,[39] if the debenture or trust deed is under seal. Failing an express or an implied power, an applica-

---

[36] Seventh Interim Report of the Australian Company Law Advisory Committee, para. 3.
[37] The Scots equivalent is "do diligence on the decree obtained."
[38] *Post*, p. 608.
[39] Not applicable to Scotland.

tion may be made to the court for the appointment of a receiver or an order for sale.

In England, where there are numerous debentures of the same class, a *debenture holders' action* is usually brought. This is brought by one debenture holder on behalf of himself and all other debenture holders of the same class as himself. In it a claim may be made for:

(1) a declaration that the debenture holders are entitled to a (first) charge on the property of the company;
(2) if there is a trust deed, the enforcement of the trusts;
(3) an account of what is due to the debenture holders;
(4) the enforcement of the charge by sale or foreclosure;
(5) the appointment of a receiver and manager.[40]

An order for foreclosure will only be made if all the debenture holders of the same class as the plaintiff are before the court.[41]

If the assets require immediate protection an application for the appointment of a receiver is made.[41]

In Scotland, prior to the Companies (Floating Charges and Receivers) (Scotland) Act 1972, there was no provision for the appointment of receivers, and this constituted a major difference between Scots and English law in the remedies available to the holder of a floating charge and in the procedure for enforcing the security. On the recommendation of the Scottish Law Commission[42] receiverships were introduced to Scotland by the Act of 1972. Though based in general on the English model, the Scottish provisions form a distinct self-contained code comprising Part II of the 1972 Act, and are given separate consideration below.

A receiver appointed either in England or Scotland may exercise his powers in the other jurisdiction so far as that is not inconsistent with the law applicable there: Administration of Justice Act 1977, s.7.

RECEIVERS (ENGLISH LAW)

A receiver takes possession of the property of the company over which he is appointed and realises it for the benefit of the debenture

---

[40] Palmer's *Company Precedents,* 16th ed., Pt. III, p. 498.
[41] *Re Continental Oxygen Co.* [1897] 1 Ch. 511.
[42] *Report on the Companies (Floating Charges) (Scotland) Act 1961* 1970, Cmnd. 4336, para. 38.

holder(s). He should not be confused with a liquidator. A liquidator is appointed with the object of winding up the company and terminating its existence whereas a receiver may be paid out, whereupon the company will resume business as before.

As shown above, a receiver may be appointed to enforce a charge given by a debenture or a trust deed (1) under a power contained in the debenture or the trust deed; or (2) by an order of the court.

Receiver appointed by the court

The court may appoint a receiver when—

(1) the principal or interest is in arrear[43]; or
(2) the company is being wound up[44]; or
(3) the security is in jeopardy.

A creditor obtained judgment against the company and was in a position to issue execution. There was no default in payment of debenture principal or interest. *Held*, the debenture holders with a floating charge on the undertaking and property of the company were entitled to the appointment of a receiver because the security was in jeopardy: *Re London Pressed Hinge Co. Ltd.* [1905] 1 Ch. 576.

The security is in jeopardy when there is a risk of its being seized and taken to pay claims which are really not prior to the debenture holders' claims. Accordingly a receiver was appointed where the company's works were closed and creditors were threatening actions,[45] where execution was actually levied by a judgment creditor,[46] where a creditor's winding-up petition was pending and compulsory liquidation was imminent,[47] and where the company proposed to distribute its reserve fund, which was its only asset, among its members.[48]

Mere insufficiency of security is not jeopardy where the company is a going concern, is not being pressed by its creditors and there is no risk of its assets being seized by its creditors.[49]

---

[43] *Bissill* v. *Bradford Tramways* [1891] W.N. 51.
[44] *Wallace* v. *Universal Automatic Machines Co.* [1894] 2 Ch. 547 (C.A.).
[45] *McMahon* v. *North Kent Ironworks* [1891] 2 Ch. 148.
[46] *Edwards* v. *Standard Rolling Stock Syndicate* [1893] 1 Ch. 574.
[47] *Re Victoria Steamboats Ltd.* [1897] 1 Ch. 158.
[48] *Re Tilt Cove Copper Co.* [1913] 2 Ch. 588.
[49] *Re New York Taxicab Co.* [1913] 1 Ch. 1.

Who cannot be appointed receiver

A body corporate is disqualified for appointment as receiver[50]: section 366. Also, an undischarged bankrupt is disqualified from acting as receiver or manager, unless he is appointed by the court: section 367. Where an application is made to the court to appoint a receiver and the company is being wound up by the court, the Official Receiver may be appointed (s.368) and, unless there are special circumstances, he or the liquidator will be appointed so as to avoid unnecessary expense and the possibility of conflict.[51]

Persons subject to a disqualification order under section 188 of the Companies Act 1948 or section 9 of the Insolvency Act 1976 cannot act as receivers.[52]

Appointment of manager

If the debentures give a charge over the company's "business" or "undertaking and property," a manager may be appointed. The same person is usually appointed receiver and manager. A manager is appointed to carry on the business with the object of selling it as a going concern and, therefore, when appointed by the court he is invariably appointed only for a limited time, usually three months. If he acts beyond the limited period, without an order extending the time, his expenditure will be disallowed.[53]

The conduct of a receiver and manager appointed by a debenture holder cannot be examined in misfeasance proceedings under section 333[54] but the company may apply for the appointment of an inspector to investigate his transactions under section 164.[55]

Time of appointment of receiver

A receiver is appointed when the document of appointment is handed to him by a person having authority to appoint and in circum-

---

[50] An attempted appointment of a body corporate is a nullity, and the body corporate does not thereby become an agent for the purposes of the Law of Property Act 1925, s.109, and the Limitation Act 1980: *Portman Building Society* v. *Gallwey* [1955] 1 All E.R. 227.

[51] *British Linen Co.* v. *South American and Mexican Co.* [1894] 1 Ch. 108 (C.A.).

[52] *Ante*, p. 331.

[53] *Re Wood Green Steam Laundry* [1918] 1 Ch. 423.

[54] *Re B. Johnson & Co. (Builders) Ltd.* [1955] Ch. 634 (C.A.), *ante*, p. 416.

[55] *Ante*, p. 418.

stances from which it may fairly be said that he is appointing the receiver and the receiver accepts the proffered appointment.[56]

Effect of appointment of receiver

When a receiver is appointed:

(1) Floating charges crystallise and become fixed. This prevents the company from dealing with the assets charged, without the receiver's consent.[57]

(2) When a receiver of the undertaking of the company is appointed, the directors' power of controlling the company is suspended. However, this does not prevent a director from pursuing an action on behalf of the company if the debenture holders' interests are not thereby threatened.[58] They cannot claim remuneration from the receiver unless he employs them, but they can still claim from the company any remuneration to which they are entitled.[59]

> ". . . a floating charge purporting to extend . . . to the whole of the assets and undertaking of a company, does not upon appointment of a receiver and manager thereunder, extend to fettering the capacity or power of the directors of the company to cause proceedings to be instituted in the name of the company challenging that debenture": *per* Street J. in *Hawkesbury Development Co. Ltd.* v. *Landmark Finance Pty. Ltd.* (1970) 92 W.N. (N.S.W.) 199, at p. 210.

(3) When the appointment is by the court, the company's servants are automatically dismissed, for which they may be entitled to damages for breach of contract although they may be employed by the receiver.[60]

As to the position where a receiver is appointed by the debenture holders, in *Re Foster Clark Ltd.'s Indenture Trusts*,[61] it was held that the sale by the receiver of the company's business to a subsidiary

[56] *R. A. Cripps & Son Ltd.* v. *Wickenden* [1973] 1 W.L.R. 944, applying *Windsor Refrigerator Co. Ltd.* v. *Branch Nominees Ltd.* [1961] Ch. 375 (C.A.).
[57] *Ante*, p. 563.
[58] *Newhart Developments* v. *Co-operative Commercial Bank* [1978] 2 All E.R. 896.
[59] *Re South Western of Venezuela, etc., Rlwy.* [1902] 1 Ch. 701.
[60] *Reid* v. *Explosives Co. Ltd.* (1887) 19 Q.B.D. 264 (C.A.).
[61] [1966] 1 W.L.R. 125.

operated as a dismissal of the company's employees. Plowman J. observed[62] that there appears to be no good reason in principle why an appointment out of court of a receiver who is the agent of the company should of itself determine contracts of employment made with the company, and this observation was applied in *Re Mack Trucks (Britain) Ltd.*[63] Further, in *Griffiths* v. *Secretary of State for Social Services*[64] it was held that the mere appointment out of court by debenture holders of a receiver and manager as agent of a company did not automatically terminate an employee's subsisting contract of employment with the company where the continuation of his employment was not inconsistent with the role and functions of the receiver and manager. And see *per* Lawson J. at pp. 845, 846.

(4) Every invoice, order for goods or business letter which is issued by or on behalf of the company or the receiver and on which the company's name appears must contain a statement that a receiver has been appointed: section 370.

(5) A receiver of the whole, or substantially the whole, of the company's property, appointed on behalf of the holders of debentures secured by a floating charge, must forthwith give notice of his appointment to the company: section 372(1).

(6) Within seven days after the appointment, the person who made or obtained the appointment must give notice of the fact to the Registrar who must enter it in his register of charges: section 102(1).

(7) Within a period of, usually, 14 days after the receiver gives the company notice of his appointment as required by section 372(1), above, a statement of the company's affairs must be submitted to him, giving particulars of the assets, debts and liabilities, the names and addresses of the creditors, the securities they hold, the dates when they were given and such other information as may be prescribed. The statement must usually be submitted by, and verified by affidavit of, one of the directors and the secretary or, if the receiver is appointed out of court, verified by statutory declaration of the same persons. In certain circumstances the receiver may require past or present

---

[62] At p. 132.
[63] [1967] 1 W.L.R. 780.
[64] [1974] Q.B. 468.

officers, persons who have taken part in the formation of the company or past or present employees, to submit and verify the statement: sections 372(1), 373.

(8) Within two months after the receipt of the statement, the receiver must send to the Registrar, and to the court if he was appointed by the court, a copy of the statement and of his comments thereon. He must also send to the Registrar a summary of the statement and of his comments thereon, to the company a copy of his comments or a notice that he does not see fit to make any comments, and to the trustees for debenture holders and to all the debenture holders a copy of the summary: section 372(1).

(9) When a receiver appointed under a power in an instrument ceases to act, he must give notice to the Registrar: section 102(2).

Position of receiver

A receiver appointed by the court is an officer of the court, and cannot sue or be sued without leave of the court.[65] By leave of the court an action can be brought against him by a person at whose instance he was appointed.[66] In the case of a receiver appointed under a power in a debenture or a trust deed the debenture usually provides that he is to be the agent of the company. Consequently the debenture holder(s) or the trustees are not liable for his acts. A receiver appointed out of court may apply to the court for directions in any matter concerning the performance of his functions: section 369(1).

A receiver appointed by order of the court is personally liable on contracts made by him in the course of his receivership. (A liquidator is not personally liable on contracts which he enters into as liquidator.[67])

B. was appointed receiver and manager by the court. He gave a signed order for goods, with the words "receiver and manager" appended to his signature. *Held*, he was personally liable to pay for the goods: *Burt, Boulton and Hayward* v. *Bull* [1895] 1 Q.B. 276 (C.A.).

---

[65] *Viola* v. *Anglo-American Cold Storage Co.* [1912] 2 Ch. 305; *Searle* v. *Choat* (1884) 25 Ch.D. 723 (C.A.).
[66] *L. P. Arthur (Insurance) Ltd.* v. *Sisson* [1966] 1 W.L.R. 1384.
[67] *Post*, p. 648.

The receiver is entitled to be indemnified out of the company's assets,[68] so far as they are sufficient.[69]

Contracts made by the company and current at the date of his appointment are not binding on the receiver personally, unless they become binding by a novation.[70] They remain binding, however, on the company, so that in the event of a breach the company will be liable for damages. The receiver must carry out the company's current contracts if not to do so would injure the company's goodwill,[71] but if the contracts can only be carried out by borrowing money ranking in priority to the debenture holders and are unprofitable, he need not carry them out.[72]

Under section 369(2) a receiver appointed under a power in any instrument is, to the same extent as if he had been appointed by the court, personally liable on contracts made by him in the performance of his functions except so far as they otherwise provide. He has the same right of indemnity as a receiver appointed by order of the court and he may also, as a condition of accepting the appointment, require an express indemnity from the debenture holders. On the commencement of a winding up of the company the receiver ceases to be the company's agent and his authority to bind the company ceases[73] but his powers with regard to the property charged are unaffected[74] so that he may continue to use the company's name for that purpose.[75]

In general a receiver appointed by a debenture holder may not petition to wind up the company—article 80 of Table A vests that power in the directors, subject to ratification by the members. Such a power, however, may be given expressly by the debenture.[76] If a receiver carries on an action after the company has been wound up by the court he may be liable to pay the costs of that action provided that he can recover them from his debenture holders.[77]

---

[68] *Re Glasdir Mines* [1906] 1 Ch. 365.
[69] *Boehm v. Goodall* [1911] 1 Ch. 155.
[70] *Parsons v. Sovereign Bank of Canada* [1913] A.C. 160 (P.C.).
[71] *Re Newdigate Colliery Ltd.* [1912] 1 Ch. 468 (C.A.) and see *Airlines Airspares Ltd. v. Handley Page Ltd.* [1970] Ch. 193.
[72] *Re Thames Ironworks Co. Ltd.* (1912) 106 L.T. 674.
[73] *Gosling v. Gaskell* [1897] A.C. 575; *Thomas v. Todd* [1926] 2 K.B. 511.
[74] *Gough's Garages Ltd. v. Pugsley* [1930] 1 K.B. 615.
[75] *Sowman v. David Samuel Trust Ltd.* [1978] 1 W.L.R. 22.
[76] *Re Emmadart Ltd.* [1979] 1 All E.R. 599.
[77] *Bacal Contracting Ltd. v. Modern Engineering (Bristol) Ltd.* [1980] 2 All E.R. 655.

The Court of Appeal has held that a receiver appointed by a debenture holder, but not as the agent of the debenture holder, owed a duty of care both to the borrower and to a guarantor of the debt to take reasonable care to obtain the best price that the circumstances permitted, and he also had a duty to exercise reasonable care in choosing the time for the sale. It further held that the debenture holder might be liable for the receiver's actions if it were shown that he interfered with the conduct of the receivership, even if the receiver was not his agent: *Standard Chartered Bank* v. *Walker* [1982] 1 W.L.R. 1410 (C.A.).[78]

The Jenkins Report[79] recommended that the court should be empowered to relieve a receiver appointed, *e.g.* under an invalid charge, from personal liability. At present, such a person is a trespasser and may incur heavy liabilities.

Borrowing by receiver

To enable the receiver to carry on the business of the company or to preserve the property of the company, the court can authorise the receiver to borrow sums ranking in priority to the debentures.[80]

Preferential payments

Section 94(1) provides that where, in the case of a company registered in England, either a receiver is appointed on behalf of the holders of debentures secured by a *floating charge*, or possession is taken by or on behalf of those debenture holders of any property subject to the charge, then, if the company is not at the time in the course of being wound up, the preferential debts, *i.e.* certain unsecured debts,[81] must be paid out of any assets coming to the hands of the receiver or other person taking possession in priority to any claim for principal or interest in respect of the debentures. The receiver is under a positive duty to pay the preferential debts of which he has notice out of any assets coming to his hand in priority to all other creditors.[82] If the receiver is appointed prior to a liquidation the

---

[78] Disapproving *Latchford* v. *Beirne* [1981] 3 All E.R. 705. [79] Para. 306.

[80] *Greenwood* v. *Algesiras Ry. Co.* [1894] 2 Ch. 205. (C.A.).

[81] *Post,* pp. 663 *et seq.* In this case the periods mentioned in s.319 run from the appointment of the receiver.

[82] *Inland Revenue Commissioners* v. *Goldblatt* [1972] Ch. 498, where, by the direction of and on the receipt of an indemnity from the debenture holder, the receiver transferred the assets of which he had taken possession to the company and he knew or ought to have known that the company would transfer them to the debenture holder without paying off the preferential creditors.

floating charge is not postponed to the costs of the winding up, only to the preferred creditors.[83]

The receipt of monies by the debenture holder with notice of a statutory duty under which the monies should have been applied in settlement of a prior claim makes the debenture holder directly liable to the preferential creditors as a constructive trustee.[83a]

At the date of the appointment of a receiver in 1940, a company owed £63 for rates. This was a preferential debt. In the following month a winding-up order was made but the receiver continued to carry on the business of the company. From time to time a demand was made upon him for payment of the £63 but no payment was made. In 1945 the receiver had £91 in hand but in 1948 he had no assets in hand and so informed the rating authority. *Held*, the receiver was liable in damages because section 94 was not merely a negative provision preventing the receiver from paying the debenture holders until after the preferential debts had been paid, but it also imposed a positive duty upon him to pay those debts out of any assets in his hands: *Westminster Corporation* v. *Haste* [1950] Ch. 442.

Any preferential payment made out of the assets secured by the floating charge can be recouped as far as may be out of the assets of the company available for payment of the general creditors: section 94(5).

Section 94(1) not only protects preferential creditors where a debenture holder takes possession of assets as mortgagee but also extends to cases where the debenture holder arrogates all the assets to himself with notice of the preferential creditor's claim and is guilty of wrongfully procuring and being a party to a breach of statutory duty.[83a]

If the debentures give a fixed charge on specified assets and a floating charge on the company's undertaking and assets, the *fixed charge* is not subject to the payment of the preferential debts.[84]

Remuneration of receiver

A receiver appointed by the court has the amount of his remuneration fixed by the court.

A receiver appointed under a power in the debentures has his remuneration fixed by agreement. The court may, however, on the application of the *liquidator*, fix the receiver's remuneration. Under this power the remuneration may be fixed retrospectively, and any

---

[83] *Re Christonette International Ltd.* [1982] 1 W.L.R. 1245.
[83a] See note 82 above.
[84] *Re Lewis Merthyr Collieries Ltd.* [1929] 1 Ch. 498 (C.A.).

excess paid before the making of the order must be accounted for: section 371.

Delivery of accounts

By the terms of his appointment the receiver may be required to render accounts to the debenture holders. Apart from any such duty, a receiver or manager of the whole or substantially the whole of the company's property, who is appointed on behalf of debenture holders with a floating charge, is obliged by section 372(2), every year and on his ceasing to act, to send to the Registrar, any trustees for the debenture holders, the company and all the debenture holders, an abstract in the prescribed form of his receipts and payments during the year, and the aggregate amounts of his receipts and payments during the time of his appointment. Section 372(3) contains a similar provision where a receiver is appointed under the powers contained in any instrument. Penalties are imposed in the event of default. Except where section 372(2) applies, a receiver appointed under a power in the debentures must, every six months and on his ceasing to act, deliver to the Registrar an abstract in the prescribed form of his receipts and payments. Penalties are imposed in the event of default: section 374.

In addition if the receiver is appointed as the agent of the company he must keep full accounts (*i.e.* fuller than those required under section 372(2)) and produce those accounts to the company when required to do so. This is because he is running the company on behalf of the directors and so is answerable to the company for his conduct of its affairs.[85]

The court may order the receiver to make any returns or give any notices which he is by law required to make or give: section 375.

RECEIVERS (SCOTS LAW)

The reasons for the introduction of the office of receiver to Scotland by the Companies (Floating Charges and Receivers) (Scotland) Act 1972[86] were:

---

[85] *Smiths Ltd.* v. *Madden* [1979] 3 All E.R. 842.
[86] A petition for the appointment of a judicial factor *ad interim* on the affairs of a limited company is competent at common law: *Fraser, Petitioner*, 1971 S.L.T. 146 (O.H.) (appointment made in a "position of chaos requiring urgently to be dealt with").

(*a*) to enable the fortunes of a company to be revived and thus prevent unnecessary liquidation;

(*b*) to strengthen the rights of a holder of a floating charge by making it possible for him to take possession of and realise the security without liquidation; and

(*c*) to lessen the difficulties which could arise from the difference between Scots and English law where a group of companies included both Scottish and English companies.[87]

In this part of this chapter the sections referred to are, except where there is a statement to the contrary, those of the Companies (Floating Charges and Receivers) (Scotland) Act 1972.

A receiver may be appointed by either the holder of a floating charge or the court on the application of the holder of a floating charge: section 11. The term "holder of the floating charge" is sufficiently widely defined as to include, in the case of a series of debentures, the trustees acting for the debenture holders under a trust deed, or, if there are no such trustees, specified majorities of the debenture holders: section 28(2).

Appointment by holder of floating charge

A receiver may be appointed by the holder of the floating charge on the occurrence of any event which, by the instrument creating the charge, entitles the holder to make that appointment, and, in so far as the instrument does not provide otherwise, on the occurrence of any of the following:

(*a*) expiry of 21 days after the making of a demand—which is unsatisfied—for payment of the whole or part of the principal sum secured;

(*b*) expiry of two months during which interest has been in arrears;

(*c*) making of an order or passing of a resolution to wind up the company;

(*d*) appointment of a receiver by virtue of any other floating charge created by the company: section 12(1).

The appointment is made by means of an "instrument of appointment," validly executed by the holder of the charge or by a person

---

[87] *Report on the Companies (Floating Charges) (Scotland) Act 1961*, 1970 Cmnd. 4336, paras. 37, 38.

having his written authority. A certified copy of the instrument of appointment must be delivered by the person making the appointment to the Registrar within seven days of its execution, and the Registrar enters particulars of the appointment in the register of charges. The receiver is regarded as having been appointed on the date of the execution of the instrument of appointment, and as from that date the floating charge, subject to sections 106A and 322 of the 1948 Act, attaches to the property and takes effect as if it were a fixed security. Failure without reasonable excuse duly to register the certified copy of the instrument of appointment attracts a fine of £5 for every day during which the default continues, but does not affect the validity of the appointment: section 13.

Appointment by court

The circumstances in which a receiver may be appointed by the court are the same as those for an appointment by the holder of the floating charge (*ante*, p. 595) except that for paragraph (*d*) there must be substituted:

(*d*) where the court is satisfied that the position of the holder of the charge is likely to be prejudiced if no appointment is made: section 12(2).

The application to the court for the appointment is by petition, which must be served on the company. A certified copy of the court's interlocutor making the appointment must be delivered by or on behalf of the petitioner to the Registrar within seven days of the date of the interlocutor or such longer period as the court may allow, and the Registrar enters particulars of the appointment in the register of charges. The receiver is regarded as having been appointed on the date of the interlocutor, and as from that date the floating charge attaches to the property and takes effect as if it were a fixed security. Failure without reasonable excuse duly to register the certified copy of the interlocutor attracts a fine of £5 for every day during which the default continues, but does not affect the validity of the appointment: section 14 and R.C. 218A.[88]

---

[88] "Section 3A—Receivers," consisting of R.C. 218A, was added to the Rules of Court by S.I. 1973 No. 145.

Who can be appointed receiver

The following are disqualified from being appointed as receiver:
(a) a body corporate;
(b) an undischarged bankrupt; and
(c) a Scottish firm: section 11(3)

It is permissible to have joint receivers: section 11(5).

Where there are two or more floating charges, the same person may be appointed receiver by virtue of both or all of them: section 16(7).

Powers of receiver

A receiver has the powers, if any, conferred on him by the instrument creating the floating charge, and in addition he has the extensive powers listed in section 15 in so far as these are not inconsistent with any provision contained in the instrument creating the charge. The statutory powers are such as to place the receiver in a position comparable to that of a receiver and manager in England, and include the following powers:

(a) to take possession[88a] and dispose of the company's property;
(b) to borrow money and grant security over the property;
(c) to appoint agents, employees and professional persons such as a solicitor and an accountant;
(d) to apply to the court for directions;
(e) to bring or defend legal proceedings in the name and on behalf of the company,[89] and to refer questions to arbitration;
(f) to insure the company's business and property;
(g) to use the company's seal and execute documents, including bills of exchange and promissory notes, in the name and on behalf of the company;
(h) to carry on the company's business so far as he thinks it desirable to do so;

[88a] It is a matter of controversy whether this empowers a receiver to take proceedings in his own name against debtors to the company without having acquired an assignation of the debts from the company: *McPhail* v. *Lothian Regional Council*, 1981 S.L.T. 173 (O.H.), not followed in *Taylor, Petitioner*, 1982 S.L.T. 172 (O.H.).

[89] It is not competent for the directors to raise actions in connection with the property which is within the receivership: *Imperial Hotel (Aberdeen) Ltd.* v. *Vaux Breweries Ltd.*, 1978 S.C. 86 (O.H.).

(*i*) to grant and take on leases;

(*j*) to present or defend a petition for the winding up of the company; and

(*k*) to do all things incidental to the exercise of his other powers: section 15(1).

The receiver may require to exercise only some of these wide statutory powers of management. It is a matter for his discretion as to which powers he will exercise and when he will exercise them. The company, through its directors, cannot interfere with the exercise by the receiver of his discretion by, for instance, raising actions which the receiver considers should not be raised.[89a]

The exercise by the receiver of his powers is subject to the rights of persons who have effectually executed diligence[90] before his appointment and to the rights of persons who hold fixed security or floating charges with prior or equal ranking: section 15(2).

A person transacting with a receiver has no duty to inquire whether any event has happened to authorise the receiver to act: section 15(3).

Precedence among receivers

Where there are two or more floating charges, a receiver may be appointed by virtue of each charge, but the receiver whose charge has priority of ranking is entitled to exercise the statutory powers to the exclusion of any other receiver. Where two or more floating charges rank equally and two or more receivers have been appointed by virtue of these charges, the receivers are deemed to be joint receivers. The powers of a receiver whose charge has a ranking postponed to that of another charge by virtue of which a receiver has later been appointed are, from the date of the later appointment, suspended so far as is necessary to enable the second-mentioned receiver to exercise his statutory powers, and they revive when the prior floating charge ceases to attach to the property: section 16.

[89a] *Imperial Hotel (Aberdeen) Ltd.* v. *Vaux Breweries Ltd.*, *supra*.

[90] An arrestment which has not been followed by a decree of furthcoming is not an "effectually executed diligence" for this purpose: *Lord Advocate* v. *Royal Bank of Scotland Ltd.*, 1977 S.C. 155.

Agency and liability of receiver for contracts

A receiver is deemed to be the agent of the company in relation to the property attached by the floating charge. Subject to that general principle, a receiver is personally liable on any contract entered into by him in the performance of his functions, except in so far as the contract otherwise provides, but he is entitled to be indemnified out of the property in respect of which he was appointed.

Contracts entered into by or on behalf of the company before the receiver's appointment continue in force, subject to the terms of the contract, after the appointment, but the receiver does not, merely by his appointment, incur personal liability on such contracts. Contracts entered into by a receiver whose powers are later suspended under section 16, *ante*, continue in force, subject to the terms of the contract, after that suspension: section 17.[91]

Remuneration of receiver

The remuneration to be paid to a receiver is fixed by agreement between the receiver and the holder of the floating charge, but where there has been no such agreement or the remuneration fixed is disputed by the receiver, the holder of any floating charge or fixed security, the company or the liquidator, it may be fixed instead by the Auditor of the Court of Session: section 18.

Preferential payments and distribution of monies

The 1972 Act provides that where a company is not at the time of the receiver's appointment in course of being wound up the debts which would be preferential payments in winding up[92] must be paid out of any assets coming into the receiver's hands in priority to claims of the holder of the floating charge. This applies only to debts which have been intimated to the receiver or have become known to him within six months after he has advertised for claims in the *Edinburgh Gazette* and

---

[91] See *Macleod* v. *Alexander Sutherland Ltd.*, 1977 S.L.T. (Notes) 44 (O.H.). (Decree of implement refused.) For judicial comment on the receiver's position in general and on the distinction between receivership and liquidation, see *Lord Advocate* v. *Royal Bank of Scotland Ltd.*, 1977 S.C. 155, and *Taylor, Petitioner*, 1982 S.L.T. 172 (O.H.).

[92] See note 81, above.

in a local newspaper. Payments made in accordance with these provisions must be recouped as far as may be out of the assets available for ordinary creditors: section 19.

The monies received by the receiver are distributed in the following order:

> (*a*) to the holder of any fixed security which ranks prior to or equally with the floating charge, persons who have effectually executed diligence on any part of the property, creditors to whom the receiver has incurred liability, the receiver himself in respect of his liabilities, expenses and remuneration, and preferential creditors entitled to payment under section 19, *ante*;
>
> (*b*) to the holder of the floating charge in or towards satisfaction of the debt secured by the floating charge; and
>
> (*c*) to any other receiver, to the holder of a fixed security over the property, and to the company or its liquidator, according to their respective rights and interests.

Where there is doubt as to the person entitled to a payment, or where a receipt or discharge of a security cannot be obtained for a payment, the receiver must consign the amount in a bank of issue in Scotland in name of the Accountant of Court for behoof of the person entitled to it: section 20.

Cessation of appointment

A receiver appointed by the holder of a floating charge may resign on giving one month's notice to:

> (*a*) the holders of floating charges over any part of the company's property;
>
> (*b*) the company or its liquidator; and
>
> (*c*) the holders of any fixed security over the particular property in respect of which the receiver was appointed.

A receiver appointed by the court may resign only with the authority of the court and on such terms and conditions as may be laid down by the court.

The holder of the floating charge by virtue of which a receiver was appointed may apply to the court for the removal of the receiver on cause shown.

On the cessation of his appointment a receiver is entitled to be indemnified out of the property subject to the floating charge for any expenses, charges or other liabilities incurred in the performance of his functions.

Except where the cessation of a receiver's appointment is due to his death or removal by the court, he must give notice of the cessation to the Registrar within seven days. Where the receiver has been removed by the court, the duty to give such notice lies on the holder of the floating charge. The Registrar enters the notice in the register of charges.

If, on the expiry of one month after cessation of a receiver's appointment, no other receiver has been appointed, the charge then ceases to attach to the property and becomes again a floating charge: section 22.

Powers of court

Under the 1972 Act the court may exercise certain powers in relation to receiverships, whether the receiver has been appointed by the holder of the floating charge or by the court:

(*a*) The court may give directions in connection with the performance by the receiver of his functions. The application to the court may be made either by the receiver or by the holder of the floating charge: sections 15(1), 23(1).

(*b*) The court may, on the application of the holder of the floating charge, remove the receiver on cause shown: section 22, *ante.*

(*c*) Where the property which is subject to the floating charge is also subject to another security or burden or is affected by diligence, and the receiver wishes to dispose of the property but is unable to obtain the necessary consent of the other parties, the court may, on the application of the receiver, authorise the disposal of the property free of the security or burden or diligence. A fixed security ranking prior to the floating charge must always be met or provided for in full, but in other respects the court has a discretion both as to whether it will authorise the disposal at all and as to the terms or conditions on which it does so. The right of any creditor to rank for his debt in the winding up of the company is not prejudiced by these provisions: section 21.

(*d*) Where the floating charge is discovered to have been invalid, the court has a discretion to relieve, in whole or in part, a person who has acted as receiver from personal liability for actings which, had his appointment been valid, would have been proper. The court also has a discretion to impose personal liability instead on the person by whom the invalid appointment was made: section 23(2).

(*e*) If the receiver makes default in delivering the documents or giving the notices which are required of him, *post*, the court may order him to make good the default within a specified time. Application to the court for this purpose may be made by any member or creditor of the company or by the Registrar. Similarly, if the receiver fails, on the liquidator's request, to render proper accounts of receipts and payments and to pay over the proper amount to the liquidator, the court may, on the liquidator's application, order the receiver to make good the default within a specified time: section 27.

Requirements as to notification and information

When a receiver is appointed:

(*a*) Every invoice, order for goods or business letter which is issued by or on behalf of the company or the receiver or the liquidator and on which the company's name appears must contain a statement that a receiver has been appointed: section 24.

(*b*) The receiver must forthwith send notice of his appointment to the company: section 25(1).

(*c*) Within a period of, usually, 14 days after the receipt by the company of the last-mentioned notice, a statement of the company's affairs must be submitted to the receiver. The statement must give particulars of the assets, debts and liabilities, the names and addresses of the creditors, the securities held by them, the dates when the securities were given and such other information as may be prescribed. It must usually be submitted by, and verified by the statutory declaration of, one of the directors and the secretary. In certain circumstances the receiver may require past or present officers, persons who have taken part in the formation of the company or past or present employees to submit and verify the statement: sections 25(1), 26.

(*d*) Within two months after the receipt of the statement, the receiver must send to the Registrar, and to the court if he was appointed by the court, a copy of the statement and of his comments thereon. He must also send to the Registrar a summary of the statement and of his comments thereon, to the company a copy of his comments or a notice that he does not see fit to make any comments, and to the holder of the floating charge, to the trustees for debenture holders and to all the debenture holders a copy of the summary: section 25(1).

(*e*) On the expiration of each year from the date of his appointment and also on his ceasing to act, the receiver must prepare an abstract in the prescribed form showing his receipts and payments during the year or other period and the aggregate amounts of his receipts and payments during all preceding periods, and must send this abstract to the Registrar, the company, the holder of the floating charge, any trustees for the debenture holders, all the debenture holders and also the holders of all other floating charges or fixed securities over property of the company: section 25(2).

Penalties are imposed for failure to comply with the requirements of sections 24 and 25.

CHAPTER 26

WINDING UP BY THE COURT

THIS chapter and the following three chapters deal with the winding up of a company, which may be—

(1) by the court; or
(2) voluntary; or
(3) subject to the supervision of the court (s.211),

and with the two kinds of voluntary winding up, namely—

(a) a members' voluntary winding up; and
(b) a creditors' voluntary winding up (s.283(4)).

It will be recalled that winding up by the court on the "just and equitable ground" was explained in Chapter 18. Chapter 27 (Contributories and Creditors) and Chapter 28 (Completion of Winding up by the Court), deal with winding up by the court as well as the present chapter. Chapter 29 is concerned with voluntary winding up and winding up under the supervision of the court. Winding up under supervision is unimportant in practice.

The diagram on page 605 may assist the reader to obtain an overview of winding up.

Section 353, which is explained in Chapter 28,[1] provides a method of dissolving a defunct company by striking it off the register without a winding up, and under section 208, *post*,[2] the court may order dissolution without winding up where there is a compromise or an arrangement, to facilitate a reconstruction or an amalgamation.

A company cannot in England be made bankrupt[3] or in Scotland be sequestrated.[4]

---

[1] *Post*, p. 668.   [2] p. 714.   [3] Bankruptcy Act 1914, s.126
[4] *Standard Property Investment Co. Ltd.* v. *Dunblane Hydropathic Co. Ltd.* (1884) 12 R. 328. A Scottish company could, however, be made notour bankrupt for the purpose of the statutory provisions relating to equalisation of diligences: *Clark* v. *Hinde, Milne & Co.* (1884) 12 R. 347; see now section 327. Whether a company may be notour bankrupt for the purposes of the Conveyancing and Feudal Reform (Scotland) Act 1970, Sched. 3, para. 9(2)(a) is doubtful. In *United Dominions Trust Ltd.* v. *Site Preparations Ltd.* (*No.* 1), 1978 S.L.T. (Sh. Ct.) 14 the provision was held to relate only to individuals; *contra, United Dominions Trust Ltd.* v. *Site Preparations Ltd.* (*No.* 2), 1978 S.L.T. (Sh. Ct.) 21.

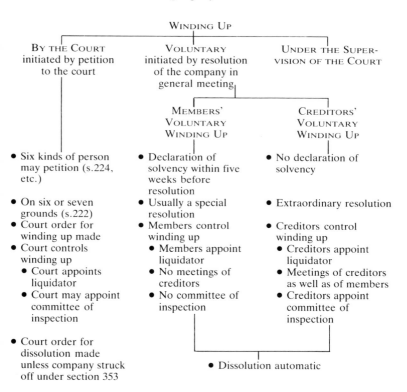

WINDING UP

| BY THE COURT initiated by petition to the court | VOLUNTARY initiated by resolution of the company in general meeting | UNDER THE SUPER-VISION OF THE COURT |

MEMBERS' VOLUNTARY WINDING UP   CREDITORS' VOLUNTARY WINDING UP

- Six kinds of person may petition (s.224, etc.)

- On six or seven grounds (s.222)
- Court order for winding up made
- Court controls winding up
  - Court appoints liquidator
  - Court may appoint committee of inspection

- Court order for dissolution made unless company struck off under section 353

- Declaration of solvency within five weeks before resolution
- Usually a special resolution
- Members control winding up
  - Members appoint liquidator
  - No meetings of creditors
  - No committee of inspection

- No declaration of solvency

- Extraordinary resolution

- Creditors control winding up
  - Creditors appoint liquidator
  - Meetings of creditors as well as of members
  - Creditors appoint committee of inspection

- Dissolution automatic

JURISDICTION TO WIND UP COMPANIES

In England

To obtain a winding up by the court, a petition must be presented to the court having the necessary jurisdiction. Section 218 provides that the courts having jurisdiction are—

    (1) the High Court, *i.e.* the Companies Court,[5] in the case of all companies registered in England;

    (2) Where the paid-up share capital does not exceed £120,000, the county court of the district in which the registered office is

---

[5] *Eastern Holdings v. Singer & Friedlander Ltd.* [1967] 1 W.L.R. 1017.

situate, provided that such county court has jurisdiction in bankruptcy.[6]

(3) Where the company is formed for working mines in the stannaries, the court exercising the stannaries jurisdiction, *i.e.* the county courts of Cornwall.[7]

In Scotland

The courts having jurisdiction are—

(1) the Court of Session, in the case of all companies registered in Scotland;
(2) where the paid-up share capital does not exceed £120,000,[8] the sheriff court of the sheriffdom in which the registered office is situate: section 220.

GROUNDS FOR WINDING UP BY THE COURT

Section 222 provides that a company formed and registered under the 1948 Act or an existing company, *i.e.* a company formed and registered under a previous Companies Act,[9] may be wound up by the court if—

(1) the company has by special resolution resolved to be wound up by the court[10]; or
(2) in the case of a public company first registered as such, no certificate of ability to commence business has been issued and the company has been registered for more than one year[11]; or
(3) the company does not commence business within a year after its incorporation, or suspends business for a whole year[12]; or
(4) the number of members is reduced below two; or

[6] See County Courts (Bankruptcy and Companies Winding-up Jurisdiction) Order 1971 (S.I. 1971 No. 656), amended by County Courts (Bankruptcy and Companies Winding-up Jurisdiction) (Amendment) Order 1971 (S.I. 1971 No. 1983) and the Insolvency Act 1976, s.1 and Sched. 1.
[7] As a result of the Lord Chancellor's direction under the Stannaries Court (Abolition) Act 1896.
[8] As amended by the Insolvency Act 1976, s.1 and Sched. 1.
[9] s.455.
[10] *cf.* s.278, *post*, p. 687, under which a company may pass a special resolution to wind up voluntarily.
[11] *Ante*, p. 183.
[12] *cf.* s.353, *post*, p. 672, under which a defunct company may be struck off the register and so dissolved without being wound up.

(5) the company is unable to pay its debts; or

(6) the court is of opinion that it is just and equitable that the company should be wound up. This part of the section was explained in connection with statutory protection of the minority.[13] It should be added that the power to wind up a company under this part is not confined to cases in which there are grounds analogous to those mentioned earlier in the section[14]; or

(7) in the case of a Scottish company, there is subsisting a floating charge over property comprised in the company's property and undertaking and the court is satisfied that the security of the creditor entitled to the benefit of the floating charge is in jeopardy.[15]

The Jenkins Report[16] recommended that section 222 should be extended to provide that a company may be wound up by the court if the event occurs on the occurrence of which the memorandum or the articles provide that it is to be dissolved, and section 278[17] should be correspondingly amended.

The Report[18] also proposed that the court should be empowered, on application by the Registrar, to order a company in persistent breach of its statutory duties, or being carried on for an unlawful purpose, to be wound up. This power could be execised where a company has failed to appoint the statutory minimum of directors.

Ground (3): Company not carrying on business

The period of a year is fixed by section 222, *ante*, so as to give the company a reasonable time in which to commence or resume business, as the case may be.

A winding-up order will only be made on this ground if the company has no intention of carrying on business.[19]

---

[13] *Ante*, p. 407.

[14] *Loch* v. *John Blackwood Ltd.* [1924] A.C. 783 (P.C.); *Symington* v. *Symingtons' Quarries Ltd.* (1905) 8 F. 121; *Baird* v. *Lees*, 1924 S.C. 83.

[15] Companies (Floating Charges and Receivers) (Scotland) Act 1972, s.4; for the meaning of "in jeopardy" see *ante*, p. 570.

[16] Para. 78.

[17] *Post*, p. 687.

[18] Para. 511.

[19] *Re Metropolitan Rlwy. Warehousing Co.* (1867) 36 L.J.Ch. 827.

A company was formed to build and use assembly rooms. Owing to a depression in trade in the neighbourhood, building was suspended for more than three years although the company intended to continue its operations when trade prospects improved. A shareholder presented a winding-up petition which was opposed by four-fifths of the shareholders. *Held*, the petition should be dismissed. Since the conduct of the majority was not unreasonable or something of which the minority had a right to complain, the wishes of the majority were not to be disregarded. It would have been different if business could not have been carried on or there was an intention to abandon the undertaking: *Re Middlesborough Assembly Rooms Co.* (1880) 14 Ch.D. 104 (C.A.).

If a company is formed to carry on business in England and abroad and has carried on business abroad, it will not be wound up merely on the ground that it has not started its business in England within the year if it intends to do so as soon as possible.[20] There is no need to wait a year if it is apparent within the year that the company cannot carry out the objects for which it was formed.[21]

Ground (5): Company unable to pay its debts

This is the ground on which a petition for a compulsory winding up is usually presented.

A company is *deemed* to be unable to pay its debts if—

(*a*) a creditor by assignment or otherwise, to whom the company is indebted in a sum exceeding £200[22] then due has served on the company, by leaving it at the registered office, a demand under his hand requiring the company to pay the sum so due, and the company has for three weeks thereafter neglected to pay the sum due or to secure[23] or compound for it to the creditor's satisfaction; or

(*b*) in England, execution issued on a judgment in favour of a creditor is returned unsatisfied in whole or in part; or

(*c*) in Scotland, the induciae of a charge for payment on an extract decree have expired without payment being made; or

(*d*) it is proved to the satisfaction of the court that *the company's*

---

[20] *Re Capital Fire Insurance Association* (1882) 21 Ch.D. 209.
[21] *Re German Date Coffee Co.* (1882) 20 Ch.D. 169 (C.A.), *ante*, p. 77.
[22] Substituted for £50 by the Insolvency Act 1976, s.1 and Sched. 1.
[23] The security must be a marketable security covering the amount of the debt: *Commercial Bank of Scotland Ltd.* v. *Lanark Oil Co. Ltd.* (1886) 14 R. 147.

contingent and prospective liabilities being taken into account, the company is unable to pay its debts: section 223.

A company has not neglected to pay a debt within (*a*), *ante*, if it bona fide disputes the debt, and consequently is not usually in such a case entitled to a winding-up order.[24] Where there is no doubt that the petitioner is a creditor for a sum which would otherwise entitle him to a winding-up order, a dispute as to the precise sum owed to him is not of itself a sufficient answer to his petition where the company is commercially insolvent in that it does not have assets presently available to meet its current liabilities.[25]

The period of three weeks' neglect required in (*a*), above, has been held to be a period of three clear weeks, excluding the day of service of the demand for payment and the day of presentation of the petition.[26]

It seems that in English practice an order will not usually be made even in cases (*b*) and (*d*), *ante*, unless the petitioner's debt is £200 or more, or the petition is supported by other creditors and the combined debt is £200 or more, since there must be circumstances which justify an inference that the company is insolvent.[27] Where a company refused to pay a debt of £35 on the ground that it was too small to be the foundation of a petition, an order was made.[28] The Scottish practice has been to apply the rule that "any creditor, whatever the amount of his debt, is entitled to a winding-up order, unless special circumstances exist for refusing it."[29]

The Insolvency Act 1976, section 1, empowers the Secretary of State to increase the minimum amount of the debt in section 223 above £200 by statutory instrument.

A company is unable to pay its debts if its acceptances have been dishonoured,[30] or it has informed a judgment creditor that it has no

---

[24] *Re London and Paris Banking Corporation* (1874) L.R. 19 Eq. 444; *Cuninghame v. Walkinshaw Oil Co. Ltd.* (1886) 14 R. 87; *W. & J. C. Pollok v. Gaeta Pioneer Mining Co. Ltd.*, 1907 S.C. 182. Where it is doubtful whether there is a bona fide dispute, the Scots court may sist the petition in order that the petitioners may constitute their debt: *Landauer & Co. v. Alexander & Co. Ltd.*, 1919 S.C. 492.

[25] *Re Tweeds Garages Ltd.* [1962] Ch. 406.

[26] See *Re Lympne Investments Ltd.* [1972] 1 W.L.R. 523.

[27] *Re Industrial Assurance Association* [1910] W.N. 245.

[28] *Re World Industrial Bank* [1909] W.N. 148.

[29] Per Lord Johnston in *Speirs & Co. v. Central Building Co. Ltd.*, 1911 S.C. 330, at p. 333.

[30] *Re Globe etc. Steel Co.* (1875) L.R. 20 Eq. 337; *Gandy, Petitioner*, 1912, 2 S.L.T. 276.

assets on which to levy execution,[31] or the petitioner has demanded payment of the sum due to him without success.[32] A company is not unable to pay its debts just because it is carrying on a losing business, if its assets exceed its liabilities.[33] However, a company may be unable to pay its debts where its assets exceed its liabilities if its assets are not presently available to meet its current liabilities.

PERSONS WHO MAY PETITION FOR WINDING UP BY THE COURT

Subject as below, a winding-up petition may be presented, on any of the grounds mentioned above, by any of the following parties—

(1) the company;
(2) a creditor;
(3) a contributory;
(4) in England, where, *e.g.* the company is already being wound up voluntarily, the Official Receiver (Companies Act 1948, s.224);
(5) the Department of Trade (Companies Act 1967, s.35; Insurance Companies Act 1974, s.46; Companies Act 1980, s.75[34]); or
(6) in England, in the case of a charitable company, the Attorney-General (Charities Act 1960, s.30).

A creditor

A compulsory liquidation is usually initiated by a creditor's petition. A secured creditor may petition but will normally rely on his security so that the petitioner is almost always an unsecured creditor. Where a petitioning creditor's debt is disputed on a substantial ground the court will usually restrain the prosecution of the petition as an abuse of the process of the court, even if the company appears to be insolvent.[35] This has been said to be a right if there is a genuine dispute as to whether the company owes the debt.[36] But the Court of Appeal have recently indicated that this practice must not be inflexible, particularly

---

[31] *Re Flagstaff, etc., Co. of Utah* (1875) L.R. 20 Eq. 268; *Re Douglas Griggs Engineering Ltd.* [1963] Ch. 19.
[32] *Stephen, Petitioner* (1884) 21 S.L.R. 764.
[33] *Re Joint Stock Coal Co.* (1869) L.R. 8 Eq. 146.
[34] *Ante*, p. 413.
[35] *Mann* v. *Goldstein* [1968] 1 W.L.R. 1091.
[36] *Stonegate Securities Ltd.* v. *Gregory* [1980] 1 All E.R. 241 (C.A.).

where the creditor may have difficulty in establishing his debt in other proceedings, *e.g.* where the company is a foreign company.[37]

A creditor whose debt is presently due and who cannot obtain payment normally has a right as between himself and the company *ex debito justitiae* to a winding-up order,[38] even if the company is being wound up voluntarily[39] or is in receivership.[39a] This is not displaced merely by showing that the company has appealed against the judgment giving rise to the debt,[40] or has a disputed claim against the petitioning judgment creditor which is the subject of litigation in other proceedings.[41] Where there is a cross-claim the matter is one for the discretion of the judge.[42]

The above rule applies only between the petitioning creditor and the company. As to all matters relating to winding up the court may have regard to the wishes of the creditors or contributories of the company, as proved by sufficient evidence, and may, for the purpose of ascertaining those wishes, direct meetings to be called, and in the case of creditors regard must be had to the value of each creditor's debt: section 346. This gives the judge a wide unfettered discretion to decide whether to make the order or not.

Where the company is insolvent the views of the creditors alone, as the only persons interested, are considered. In other cases the views of the contributories are considered.[43] Where there are different classes of creditors the wishes of those particularly interested will be given most weight and, in particular, where the company's assets are not entirely charged in favour of debenture holders the wishes of the unsecured creditors will be primarily considered. Where the assets are entirely charged in favour of debenture holders, if the petition of an unsecured creditor is opposed by the debenture holders the petitioner is entitled to a winding-up order unless the opposing creditors can show

---

[37] *Re Claybridge S.A.* (1982) 132 N.L.J. 415 (C.A.).
[38] See *Re Chapel House Colliery Co.* (1883) 24 Ch.D. 259 (C.A.); *Gardner & Co. v. Link* (1894) 21 R. 967.
[39] *Re James Millward & Co. Ltd.* [1940] Ch. 333 (C.A.); *Smyth & Co. v. The Salem (Oregon) Capitol Flour Mills Co. Ltd.* (1887) 14 R. 441.
[39a] *Foxhall & Gyle (Nurseries) Ltd., Petitioners,* 1978 S.L.T. (Notes) 29 (O.H.).
[40] *Re Amalgamated Properties of Rhodesia (1913) Ltd.* [1917] 2 Ch. 115 (C.A.).
[41] *Re Douglas Griggs Engineering Ltd.* [1963] Ch. 19.
[42] *Re L. H. F. Wools Ltd.* [1969] 3 All E.R. 882 (C.A.).
[43] If only a contributory opposes a petition it will usually be granted: *Re Camburn Petroleum Products Ltd.* [1980] 1 W.L.R. 86.

that there is no reasonable possibility of the unsecured creditors obtaining a benefit from a winding up.[44] The court must not refuse a winding-up order just because the assets of the company have been mortgaged to an amount in excess of those assets or there are no assets: section 225(1).

If the petition of an unsecured creditor is opposed by the majority in value of the unsecured creditors, although the court has a complete discretion under section 225(1), *ante,* to make or refuse an order and the fact of the majority opposition is not conclusive, if they oppose for good reason (*e.g.* because the assets exceed the liabilities and there are prospects of the company being able to continue business) their wishes will prevail in the absence of special circumstances making winding up desirable.[45] Similarly if the petition is opposed by only a minority of creditors this will normally not prevent the order being made although the wishes of the minority may prevail in special cases.[46]

If a company is being wound up voluntarily a compulsory order will not usually be made if the majority of the creditors want the voluntary liquidation to continue.[47] Where there are special circumstances the court may give effect to the wishes of the minority.[48]

Any assignee of a debt or of a definite part of a debt can petition,[49] unless a petition was presented in respect of the debt before the assignment.[50] A secured creditor can petition, and his security will not be prejudiced; the holder of bearer debentures can also petition.[51] It has been held that the holder of debenture stock secured by a normal trust deed cannot present a petition as he is not a creditor of the company,[52] the trustees being the proper persons to present the peti-

---

[44] *Re Crigglestone Coal Co. Ltd.* [1906] 2 Ch. 327 (C.A.); *Gardner's* case, *ante.*
[45] *Re Vuma Ltd.* [1960] 1 W.L.R. 1283 (C.A.); *Re P. & J. Macrae Ltd.* [1961] 1 W.L.R. 229 (C.A.). See also *Re A.B.C. Coupler Co.* [1961] 1 W.L.R. 243.
[46] *Re Southard & Co. Ltd.* [1979] 1 W.L.R. 1198 (C.A.).
[47] *Re Home Remedies Ltd.* [1943] Ch. 1; *Re B. Karsberg Ltd.* [1956] 1 W.L.R. 57 (C.A.); *Re J. D. Swain Ltd.* [1965] 1 W.L.R. 909 (C.A.); *cf. Pattisons Ltd.* v. *Kinnear* (1899) 1 F. 551 and *Elsmie & Son* v. *The Tomatin, etc., Distillery Ltd.* (1906) 8 F. 434.
[48] *Bell's Trustees* v. *The Holmes Oil Co. Ltd.* (1900) 3 F. 23; *Bouboulis* v. *Mann, Macneal & Co. Ltd.,* 1926 S.C. 637; *Re Southard & Co. Ltd.* [1979] 1 W.L.R. 1198 (C.A.).
[49] See *Re Steel Wing Co.* [1921] 1 Ch. 349.
[50] *Re Paris Skating Rink* (1877) 5 Ch.D. 959.
[51] *Re Olathe Silver Mining Co.* (1884) 27 Ch.D. 278.
[52] *Re Dunderland Iron Ore Co. Ltd.* [1909] 1 Ch. 446.

tion in such a case. However, it has been said that it is doubtful whether this decision can be supported.[53]

A contingent or prospective creditor can petition, but the court cannot hear his petition until he has given such security for costs as the court thinks reasonable and established a prima facie case to the court's satisfaction: section 224. It is enough if section 224 is satisfied by the time the petition comes on for hearing.[54]

A judgment creditor for more than [£250], who has issued a writ of *fi. fa.*, who is informed that the sheriff holds prior executions against the company so that a forced sale of the available effects will not satisfy all the executions and who is unaware that the company has paid the sheriff a sum to discharge the judgment debt, cannot petition for a winding-up order. The payment to the sheriff extinguished the debt, and the creditor is not a "contingent creditor" within section 224 just because in certain events under section 326(2)[55] his claim against the sheriff is subject to defeasance: *Re William Hockley Ltd.* [1962] 1 W.L.R. 555.

It has been held in England that a garnishor of a debt due from the company cannot petition, because he is not a creditor, a garnishee order only giving him a lien on the debt and not operating as a transfer of the debt,[56] and that a petition cannot be presented by a person with a claim against the company for unliquidated damages.[57] However, it may be that such persons can petition as "contingent or prospective creditors."[58]

A contributory

The term "contributory" means every person liable to contribute to the assets of the company in the event of its being wound up: section 213. As we shall see, it includes the present members and certain past members of the company: section 212.[59] A holder of fully paid-up

---

[53] Palmer's *Company Law*, 23rd ed., para. 85–13.
[54] *Re A Company* [1973] 1 W.L.R. 1566.
[55] *Post*, p. 659.
[56] *Re Combined Weighing Machine Co.* (1889) 43 Ch.D. 99 (C.A.).
[57] *Re Pen-y-Van Colliery Co.* (1877) 6 Ch.D. 477.
[58] In *Re A Company* [1973] 1 W.L.R. 1566 it was pointed out by Megarry J. at p. 1571 that the *Pen-y-Van* case was decided on section 82 of the 1862 Act which, unlike the present section 224, says nothing about contingent or prospective creditors and it is very doubtful whether it is an authority for the proposition that a claim for unliquidated damages will not support a petition.
[59] *Post*, p. 651.

shares in a limited company is a contributory and entitled to present a
winding-up petition.[60]

A contributory cannot present a petition unless—

(1) the number of members is reduced below two; or
(2) his shares, or some of them, were originally allotted to him or
have been held by him, and registered in his name, for at least
six months[61] during the 18 months before the commencement
of the winding up, or have devolved on him through the death
of a former holder: section 224.

The object of the latter provision is to prevent a person acquiring
shares to qualify himself to present a petition to wreck the company.

A shareholder whose calls are in arrear can petition, but he must first
pay the amount of the call into court.[62] If there is a genuine dispute as
to whether shares have been allotted to the petitioner the petition will
be dismissed.[63]

The court will not, as a rule, make an order on a contributory's
petition unless the contributory alleges and proves, at least to the
extent of a prima facie case, that there will be assets for distribution
among the shareholders,[64] or that the affairs of the company require
investigation in respects which are likely to produce a surplus of assets
available for such distribution.[65] The reason is that unless there are
such assets, the contributory has no interest in a winding up. The rule is
not affected by section 225(1), *ante*,[66] but does not apply where a
contributory's petition on the just and equitable ground[67] is based on
the company's failure to supply accounts and information about its

---

[60] *Re National Savings Bank Association* (1866) L.R. 1 Ch.App. 547; *Walker and Others, Petitioners* (1894) 2 S.L.T. 230 and 397 (O.H.).

[61] See *Re Gattopardo Ltd.* [1969] 1 W.L.R. 619 (C.A.), where an order was made that a name be entered on the register of members but the company was not a party to the proceedings and therefore was not bound to register the individual as a shareholder, and so the six months' period did not commence when the order was made.

[62] *Re Diamond Fuel Co.* (1879) 13 Ch.D. 400 (C.A.).

[63] *Re J.N. 2* [1978] 1 W.L.R. 183.

[64] *Re Rica Gold Washing Co.* (1879) 11 Ch.D. 36 (C.A.); followed in *Re Expanded Plugs Ltd.* [1966] 1 W.L.R. 514; *Black v. United Collieries Ltd.* (1904) 7 F. 18, *per* Lord Trayner at p. 20.

[65] *Re Othery Construction Ltd.* [1966] 1 W.L.R. 69, considering *Re Haycraft Gold etc., Co.* [1900] 2 Ch. 230 and *Re Newman and Howard, post.*

[66] *Re Othery Construction Ltd., supra.*

[67] *Ante*, p. 407.

affairs, so that he cannot tell whether there will be a surplus for contributories.[68] The jurisdiction of the court to order the winding up of a company on the just and equitable ground on a contributory's petition is very wide and depends upon a full investigation of the facts at the hearing. A contributory may rely on a report by Department of Trade inspectors to support his petition.[69] The Jenkins Report[70] recommended that a contributory's petition for winding up should not fail just because there are no assets available for contributories.

On a contributory's petition the court cannot properly determine the beneficial ownership of shares registered in the name of an opposing contributory but to which the petitioner raises an adverse claim. That is an issue which can only be determined in proceedings between the person claiming to have the interest in the shares as plaintiff and the registered owner as defendant.[71]

A petition by a contributory is uncommon. Such a petition which is opposed by the majority of the contributories will not be granted except where the conduct of the majority is something of which the minority have a right to complain.[72]

The right of a contributory to petition cannot be excluded or limited by the articles.

The articles provided that no winding-up petition could be presented without the consent of two directors, or unless a resolution to wind up was passed at a general meeting, or unless the petitioner held one-fifth of the share capital. None of these conditions was fulfilled. *Held*, the restrictions were invalid and a petition could be presented: *Re Peveril Gold Mines Ltd.* [1898] 1 Ch. 122 (C.A.).

In the case of the holder of a share warrant the shares are not "registered in his name," so that unless, *e.g.* he is an original allottee, he cannot petition.[73]

The trustee in bankruptcy of a bankrupt shareholder, where the trustee is not on the register of members, is not a contributory and

---

[68] *Re Newman and Howard Ltd.* [1962] Ch. 257.
[69] *Re St. Piran Ltd.* [1981] 3 All E.R. 270.
[70] Para. 503.
[71] *Re Bambi Restaurants Ltd.* [1965] 1 W.L.R. 750.
[72] *Re Middlesborough Assembly Rooms Co.* (1880) 14 Ch.D. 104 (C.A.), *ante*, p. 000; *Galbraith* v. *Merito Shpg. Co. Ltd.*, 1947 S.C. 446; *Re Tivoli Freeholds Ltd.* [1972] V.R. 445; *Re St. Piran Ltd.* [1981] 3 All E.R. 270.
[73] *Per* Chitty J. in *Re Wala Wynaad India Gold Mining Co.* (1882) 21 Ch.D. 849, at p. 853.

cannot petition.[74] In similar circumstances, it seems that the personal representative of a deceased shareholder is a contributory.[75] The Jenkins Report[76] recommended that section 224 should empower the trustee in bankruptcy or the personal representative of a contributory to petition the court for a winding up.

A person who may be required to repay an amount to an insolvent private company following a payment out of capital by that company for the purchase or redemption of its own shares under section 54 of the 1981 Act,[77] may petition to wind up the company on either the just and equitable or insolvency grounds, but no others: 1981 Act, s.58(7).

The Official Receiver

The Official Receiver can petition for a winding up by the court when a company is already in voluntary liquidation or is being wound up under the supervision of the court in England. An order will only be made if the court is satisfied that the existing liquidation cannot be continued with due regard to the interests of the creditors or contributories: section 224(2). It has been said that a strong case must be made out.[78] However, in the latest case,[79] it was said that to give the court jurisdiction under section 224 it must merely be satisfied on a balance of probabilities that the voluntary winding up cannot be continued with due regard to the interests of creditors or contributories.

---

[74] *Re H. L. Bolton Engineering Co. Ltd.* [1956] Ch. 577. (S.216(*a*), by which the trustee represents the bankrupt shareholder, does not come into effect until a winding-up order is made.) In the Scottish case *Ker, Petitioner* (1897) 5 S.L.T. 126 (O.H.), a trustee in bankruptcy was held entitled as a contributory to petition for the removal of a liquidator and for a supervision order.

[75] See *Re Norwich Yarn Co.* (1850) 12 Beav. 366; *Re Cuthbert Cooper & Sons Ltd.* [1937] Ch. 392, at p. 399, where Simonds J. assumed, without deciding, that such a personal representative is a contributory; *per* Wynn-Parry J. in *Re H. L. Bolton Engineering Co. Ltd.* [1956] Ch. 577, at p. 582; and *Re Meyer Douglas Pty. Ltd.* [1965] V.R. 638, where Gowans J. pointed out at p. 655 that in *Re Norwich Yarn Co.* the statutory definition of "contributory" included not only every member, but also every other person liable to contribute, whether as heir, devisee, executor or administrator of a deceased member. See also *Re Bayswater Trading Co. Ltd.* [1970] 1 W.L.R. 343, and *Howling's Trustees* v. *Smith* (1905) 7 F. 390.

[76] Para. 503.

[77] *Ante*, p. 252.

[78] *Re 1897 Jubilee Sites Syndicate* [1899] 2 Ch. 204. Such a case was made out in *Re Ryder Installations Ltd.* [1966] 1 W.L.R. 524.

[79] *Re J. Russell Electronics Ltd.* [1968] 1 W.L.R. 1252.

The Department of Trade

Where a petition for compulsory winding up is presented by the Secretary of State for Trade after he has reached the conclusion, as a result of investigations, that it is expedient in the public interest to wind up the company compulsorily,[80] his conclusion, without being decisive, ought to be given appropriate weight by the court; where there are circumstances of suspicion it is highly desirable that the winding up be by the court; and the passing of a resolution for voluntary winding up shortly before the petition is presented ought not to be allowed to put the voluntary winding up in an entrenched position which can only be demolished if the Secretary of State can show that voluntary winding up would be markedly inferior to compulsory winding up.[81]

A report of inspectors appointed by the Department is prima facie evidence on which the court may act in deciding to make a winding-up order on a petition by the Secretary of State.[82]

PETITION FOR WINDING UP BY THE COURT

In England the winding-up petition must be in one of the forms specified in the Companies (Winding-up) Rules 1949, as amended,[83] and set out—(1) the date of the company's incorporation, (2) the address of the registered office, (3) the capital, (4) the objects, and (5) the grounds on which the petitioner asks for an order to be made: rule 26.

The Companies (Winding-up) Rules 1949, which were made by the Lord Chancellor, with the concurrence of the President of the Board of Trade, under section 365(1), do not apply to Scotland. Under section 365(1) the Court of Session may by Act of Sederunt make general rules for carrying into effect the objects of the Act in relation to the winding up of Scottish companies.[84] Rules of Court, which were consolidated in 1965,[84] relate to Court of Session practice in general, but Chapter

---

[80] See p. 425, *ante.*

[81] *Re Lubin, Rosen and Associates* [1975] 1 W.L.R. 122.

[82] *Re Armvent Ltd.* [1975] 3 All E.R. 441.

[83] By the Companies (Winding-up) (Amendment) Rules 1957, 1962, 1967, 1971, 1972, 1975, 1977, 1978, 1979, 1980 and 1981.

[84] Acts of Sederunt regulating winding up are Sheriff Court Liquidations 1930 (S.R. & O. No. 234), as amended by Sheriff Court Liquidations 1948 (S.I. 1948 No. 2293), The Companies (Winding-up) Forms 1949 (S.I. 1949 No. 1065), and Rules of Court, consolidation and amendment 1965 (S.I. 1965 No. 321).

IV, sections 3, 3A and 3B, comprising rules 202–218B, is almost entirely devoted to winding-up procedure. In this work "R.C." denotes the Rules of Court 1965 as amended, whereas "r." denotes the Companies (Winding-up) Rules 1949 as amended. The contents of a petition for winding up by the Court of Session are prescribed by Rule of Court 202.

In England the petition must be presented to the Registrar of the court[85] who fixes a time and place for the hearing. Seven clear days, excluding Saturdays and Sundays,[86] before the hearing the petition must be advertised in the *London Gazette*. An error in the name of the company in the advertisements makes them absolutely void except where the error is a very trifling error in spelling.[87] The advertisement is an invitation to the creditors and contributories of the company to support or oppose the petition. The petition must first be served on the company at its registered office at least seven clear days before the advertisement. The form of the advertisement is set out and failure to comply with it may lead to the petitioner or his legal advisers paying the costs[88]: rules 27–29.

The petition must be verified by affidavit filed within seven days after the presentation of the petition: rule 30.[89] Where a contributory's petition is for the winding up of a private company on the ground of deadlock, evidence of his legal rights in the company must be given, *e.g.* the articles should be put in evidence.[90]

In the Court of Session the petition must be presented to the Outer House, where it is dealt with by a liquidation judge appointed by the Lord President: see R.C. 202.

In England it has been held (in a case where the Board of Trade presented the petition on the ground that winding up was expedient by reason of matters referred to in a report of inspectors appointed to investigate the affairs of the company) that when grave charges are levelled against individuals in a petition, the court will not be satisfied

---

[85] "Registrar," in the Companies (Winding-up) Rules, means the Registrar of the court.

[86] *Re Display Multiples Ltd.* [1967] 1 W.L.R. 571.

[87] Which it will normally be if four conditions are satisfied, as to which see *Re Videofusion Ltd.* [1974] 1 W.L.R. 1548.

[88] *Re Acoustic Transducer Co. Ltd., The Times*, November 12, 1980; *Re Shushella Ltd., The Times*, June 23, 1982.

[89] Altered by S.I. 1967 No. 1341.

[90] *Re Davis Investments (East Ham) Ltd.* [1961] 1 W.L.R. 1396 (C.A.).

with merely prima facie evidence. The petitioner must, if practicable, prove facts by the evidence of witnesses who have first-hand knowledge of the matters on which they give evidence.[91] However, in a later case it was held that the report of inspectors stands in a wholly different position from the ordinary affidavit evidence and represents the conclusions of a statutory fact-finding body, after hearing oral evidence and examination of books. The court is entitled to look at the report and accept it not as hearsay evidence but as material of a different character. At least where the report is not challenged by the company, the court does not have to be satisfied anew by evidence of the ordinary nature as to the facts found in the report.[92]

After the presentation of a petition in England, the petitioner or his solicitor must attend before the Registrar to satisfy the Registrar that the rules have been complied with. Unless this is done, no order will be made (r.33), *i.e.* no order in favour of the petitioner will be made—an order dismissing the petition with costs against the petitioner may be made.[93]

After the presentation of a petition (which has not been struck out or dismissed[94]) an application may be made to the court for the appointment of a *provisional liquidator*. In England the appointment may be made at any time before the making of a winding-up order, and the person usually appointed is the Official Receiver. In Scotland the appointment may be made at any time before the first appointment of liquidators: section 238. An appointment is made if the assets are in jeopardy,[95] or to avoid possible prejudice.[96] The provisional liquidator takes all the company's property into his custody or under his control (s.243), and after his appointment no legal proceedings can be com-

---

[91] *Re A.B.C. Coupler Co. (No. 2)* [1962] 1 W.L.R. 1236; not followed in *Re Travel & Holiday Clubs Ltd., post.*

[92] *Re Travel & Holiday Clubs Ltd.* [1967] 1 W.L.R. 711, where it was said (at p. 716c) that it is undesirable that inspectors who have conducted an inquiry should have to give evidence of their findings upon which they would be liable to be cross-examined. This case was followed in *Re S.B.A. Properties Ltd.* [1967] 1 W.L.R. 799. And see *Re Allied Produce* [1967] 1 W.L.R. 1469.

[93] *Re Royal Mutual Bldg. Socy.* [1960] 1 W.L.R. 1143.

[94] *Re A Company* [1973] 1 W.L.R. 1566.

[95] *e.g. Levy v. Napier*, 1962 S.C. 468, in which a deferred shareholder whose petition was opposed by the controlling ordinary shareholder averred that he was apprehensive that the proceeds of the sale of the company's business and assets were being depleted to his prejudice.

[96] *e.g. McCabe v. Andrew Middleton (Enterprises) Ltd.*, 1969 S.L.T. (Sh. Ct) 29.

menced or continued against the company without leave of the court: section 231. An interpleader summons to which the company is made respondent is a proceeding against the company.[97] The appointment of a provisional liquidator has the same result as the making of a winding-up order in that the board of directors of the company becomes *functus officio* and its powers are assumed by the liquidator,[98] but notwithstanding the appointment the board has some residuary powers, *e.g.* it can instruct solicitors and counsel to oppose the petition and, if a winding-up order is made, to appeal against it.[99] The board can also act in interlocutory proceedings, including a motion to discharge the provisional liquidator.

The court may also, after the presentation of a petition (which is still subsisting[1]) and before a winding-up order has been made, on the application of the company or of any creditor or contributory, stay or restrain any pending legal proceedings against the company: section 226. Section 226 is an exception to the rule[2] that proceedings pending in the Supreme Court cannot be restrained by injunction. The object of provisions such as sections 226 and 231 is "to put all unsecured creditors upon an equality, and to pay them *pari passu*."[3]

A petition cannot be withdrawn by a petitioner or be struck out by the court prior to the hearing merely because the petitioner's debt has been paid, or the parties have reached a compromise, but where it is an abuse of the process of the court and therefore bad in its inception, the court has jurisdiction to strike it out before the hearing.[4]

Hearing of petition

The company and any creditor or contributory may attend the hearing of the petition. For this purpose a person is a creditor if he is a creditor for a present debt, a prospective debt or a contingent debt. Whether a person is a contingent creditor depends on circumstances existing at the date of the hearing.[5]

---

[97] *Eastern Holdings* v. *Singer & Friedlander Ltd.* [1967] 1 W.L.R. 1017.
[98] *Post,* p. 630.
[99] *Re Union Accident Insce. Co. Ltd.* [1972] 1 W.L.R. 640.
[1] See note 94 above.
[2] In the Supreme Court of Judicature (Consolidation) Act 1925, s.41.
[3] *Per* Lindley L.J. in *Re Oak Pits Colliery Co.* (1882) 21 Ch.D. 322 (C.A.) at p. 329.
[4] *Re CDPD* (No. 001889 of 1975), June 16, 1975 (Templeman J.)
[5] *Re S.B.A. Properties Ltd.* [1967] 1 W.L.R. 799.

In England any creditor or contributory wishing to appear must give notice to the petitioner of his intention to appear, and state whether he intends to support or oppose the petition: rule 34 as amended.[6] Any affidavit in opposition to the petition must be filed within 14 days after the date on which the affidavit verifying the petition was filed. The petitioner can then file affidavits in reply within seven days: rule 36 as amended.[7] A summons can be taken out for the cross-examination of the deponents on their affidavits. If the company is in default in filing annual returns or other requisite documents, and it is sought to delay or avert the making of a winding-up order, by adjournment or otherwise, there ought usually to be before the court a sufficient indication that steps have been or will be taken for the prompt making good of the default.[8]

In Scotland persons intending to oppose, or otherwise appear in, the petition lodge answers. The induciae within which any answers must be lodged will have been stated in the advertisement of the petition: R.C. 202.

On the hearing of a petition the court may dismiss it, or adjourn the hearing conditionally or unconditionally, or make any interim order, or any other order that it thinks fit: section 225(1).[9]

The court may have regard to the wishes of the creditors or contributories: section 346.[10]

A petitioner can consent to his petition being dismissed, but he cannot withdraw it without leave of the court.

When a judgment creditor[11] is deprived of the right *ex debito justitiae* to a winding-up order because his petition is opposed by the majority of the creditors, the fair practice is to make no order as to costs.[12] The same is true where the petitioning creditor is not a judgment creditor but his debt is undisputed.[13] *Aliter* if the petitioning creditor acted unreasonably in presenting or prosecuting his petition,[14] or the com-

---

[6] By S.I. 1972 No. 1404.
[7] By S.I. 1979 No. 209.
[8] Practice Note (Companies Court) [1974] 1 W.L.R. 1459.
[9] *Ante*, p. 612.
[10] See also *Re Middlesborough Assembly Rooms Co.* (1880) 14 Ch.D. 104 (C.A.), and *Galbraith v. Merito Shpg. Co. Ltd.*, 1947 S.C. 446.
[11] Scots equivalent, a creditor who has obtained a decree.
[12] *Re R. W. Sharman Ltd.* [1957] 1 W.L.R. 774; *Re A.B.C. Coupler Co.* [1961] 1 W.L.R. 243.
[13] *Re Sklan Ltd.* [1961] 1 W.L.R. 1013.
[14] *Re A. E. Hayter & Sons (Portchester) Ltd.* [1961] 1 W.L.R. 1008.

pany is being wound up voluntarily and no evidence is filed on behalf of the petitioner beyond an affidavit verifying the petition.[15] In special circumstances costs may be awarded against one party, *e.g.* where the company failed to defend an action so that the plaintiff petitioned to wind up the company, on the petition being dismissed and the action set aside, the company was held liable for the costs of the petition.[16] Similarly where a petitioner was paid in full by the company, apart from his costs, the petitioner was unable to recover his costs because he had not complied with the rules as to advertisement of the petition.[16a]

If a judgment creditor[17] who petitions for the compulsory liquidation of a company which is in voluntary liquidation does more than allege the existence of the voluntary winding up he does so at his own risk as to costs.[18]

When a winding-up order is made, it is usual to order the costs of (1) the petitioner, (2) the company, and (3) one set of creditors and one set of contributories, to be paid out of the assets.

In England, three copies of the order must be sent by the court to the Official Receiver. Of these, one must be served on the company at its registered office. Notice of the order is given by the Official Receiver to the Department of Trade, which causes it to be gazetted, and to a local newspaper (r.42).[19]

A copy of the order must be sent by the company to the Registrar of Companies: section 230.

Section 9 (3) of the European Communities Act 1972 provides that the Registrar must cause notice of the receipt by him of the copy of the order to be published in the *Gazette*. The notice must state the company's name, a description of the document received and the date of receipt.

The court has power to stay a winding-up order either altogether or for a limited time, on such terms and conditions as it thinks fit, if an application is made to it by the liquidator or (in England) the Official Receiver or any creditor or contributory. In England the court may require the Official Receiver to furnish a report on matters relevant to

---

[15] *Re Riviera Pearls Ltd.* [1962] 1 W.L.R. 722.
[16] *Re Lanaghan Bros. Ltd.* [1977] 1 All E.R. 265. See also *Re M. McCarthy & Co. (Builders) Ltd. (No. 2)* [1976] 2 All E.R. 339.
[16a] *Re Shushella Ltd.*, *The Times*, June 26, 1982.
[17] See note 11 above.
[18] *Re A. & N. Thermo Products Ltd.* [1963] 1 W.L.R. 1341.
[19] For Scotland, see R.C. 205.

the application. A copy of any order made by the court under this provision must be sent to the Registrar: section 256. Such an order is not usually made unless all the creditors are paid or satisfied, but the court will have regard to commercial morality and not just to the interests of the creditors.[20] As a matter of practice a stay is never granted, and there are good reasons for the practice.[21]

An appeal from the making of a winding-up order in England may be brought within 21 days: R.S.C., Ord. 59, r.4. An order made by a Lord Ordinary in Scotland may be reviewed by the Inner House if a reclaiming motion is enrolled within 14 days: section 277.[22]

Where an order winding up a solvent company was made on a contributory's petition opposed by the company and another contributory, and the company appealed against the order, the company had to provide security for the costs of the appeal otherwise than from the company's assets. It would have been wrong, if the appeal failed, for the petitioner to be liable to bear any proportion of the costs of the appeal or of a liquidation. An order was made that security be provided by the directors or shareholders promoting the appeal: *Re E. K. Wilson & Sons Ltd.* [1972] 1 W.L.R. 791 (C.A.).

CONSEQUENCES OF A WINDING-UP ORDER

The consequences of the making of a winding-up order date back to an earlier date than that on which the order was actually made. This date is called the *commencement of the winding up* and is:

(1) the time of the presentation of the petition;
(2) where, before the presentation of the petition, the company was in voluntary liquidation, the time of the passing of the resolution for voluntary winding up (s.229).

The consequences of a winding-up order are:

(1) Any disposition of the property of the company, and any transfer of shares or alteration in the status of the members, after the commencement of the winding up, is void unless the court otherwise orders: section 227.

---

[20] *Re Telescriptor Syndicate Ltd.* [1903] 2 Ch. 174.
[21] See, *per* Plowman J. in *Re A. & B.C. Chewing Gum Ltd.* [1975] 1 W.L.R. 579, at p. 592.
[22] *e.g. Levy, Petitioner*, 1963 S.C. 46.

The effect of a winding-up order is to divest the company of beneficial ownership of its assets despite its continuance as legal owner.[23]

The object of section 227 is to prevent, during the period which must elapse before a petition can be heard, the improper alienation and dissipation of the property of a company *in extremis*. However, where a company is trading, the court can sanction transactions in the ordinary course of business—otherwise the presentation of a petition, whether well- or ill-founded, would paralyse the company's trade.[24] In the case of a solvent company the court will normally sanction a disposition which the directors consider to be necessary or expedient in the interests of the company for reasons which an intelligent and honest man could reasonably hold.[25]

Between the date of the presentation of the petition and the making of a winding-up order X advanced £1,200 to the company to enable it to pay wages due to the staff and took a debenture as security. X knew, at the time of the issue of the debenture, of the presentation of the petition. *Held*, the debenture was valid: *Re Park, Ward & Co. Ltd.* [1926] Ch. 828.

The court may order that a debenture taken after the commencement of the winding up is not void if the money is advanced, not for the payment of wages, but for the company's benefit to enable it to carry out its contracts and the lender has acted in good faith and with the honest intention of benefiting the company.[26]

Where the company has an overdraft on its bank account the court will freeze that account as at the date of the presentation of the petition by discontinuing all further dealings on the existing account and will require all subsequent dealings to be on a new and separate account.[27]

After the presentation of a petition, property may safely be transferred or payment made *to* the company,[28] but payments made *by* the

---

[23] *Ayerst* v. *C. & K. (Construction) Ltd.* [1976] A.C. 167.

[24] *Per* Lord Cairns in *Re Wiltshire Iron Co.* (1868) L.R. 3 Ch.App. 443, at p. 447; see also *United Dominions Trust Ltd., Noters*, 1977 S.L.T. (Notes) 56 (O.H.) (warrant to sell security subjects valid).

[25] *Re Burton & Deakin Ltd.* [1977] 1 W.L.R. 390.

[26] *Re Steane's (Bournemouth) Ltd.* [1950] 1 All E.R. 21, applied in *Re Clifton Place Garage Ltd.* [1970] 1 All E.R. 352 (C.A.).

[27] *Re Gray's Inn Construction Co. Ltd.* [1980] 1 W.L.R. 711 (C.A.).

[28] *Mersey Steel Co.* v.*Naylor, Benzon & Co.* (1882) 9 Q.B.D. 648 (C.A.); (1884) 9 App.Cas. 434; *Millar* v. *The National Bank of Scotland Ltd.* (1891) 28 S.L.R. 884 (O.H.).

company in respect of debts previously incurred must be refunded by the recipient.[29]

The word "disposition" in section 227 includes dispositions of a company's property whether made by the company or by a third party, or whether made directly or indirectly.[30]

The court may, under the section, authorise a disposition of a company's property after presentation of the petition notwithstanding that a winding-up order has not yet been made and will do so if the disposition will benefit creditors of the company if an order is made.[31]

Section 227 contains no express provision as to who can apply for the validation of dispositions. However, an applicant must have some discernible interest in the matter. The company can apply under the section. A shareholder has a sufficient *locus standi* to apply. A director may have a sufficient *locus standi*.[32]

The rule which makes transfers of shares and alterations in the status of members void operates for the benefit of the company and its creditors, not for the benefit of third parties, and so an assignation of shares, if duly intimated to the company, cuts out a subsequent arrestment of the shares.[33]

(2) As regards English companies and such property of Scottish companies as is situated in England, any attachment, sequestration, distress or execution put in force against the estate or effects of the company after the commencement of the winding up is void: section 228.[33a] As regards Scottish companies and such property of English companies as is situated in Scotland, any winding up is, as at the date of its commencement, equivalent to an arrestment in execution and decree of furthcoming, and to an executed or completed poinding, and also to a decree of adjudication of the heritable property of the company for payment of the whole of its debts: section 327.

[29] *Re Civil Service and General Store Ltd.* (1888) 57 L.J.Ch. 119; *M'Lintock v. Lithauer,* 1924 S.L.T. 775 (O.H.).

[30] *Re Leslie Engineers Co. Ltd.* [1976] 1 W.L.R. 292. But see *Re Mal Bower's Macquarie Electrical Centre Pty. Ltd. (in Liqdn.) etc.* [1974] 1 N.S.W.L.R. 254 to the effect that the section does not affect agencies such as a bank interposing between a company, as disponor, and the recipient of the property, as disponee.

[31] *Re A. I. Levy (Holdings) Ltd.* [1964] Ch. 19.

[32] *Re Argentum Reductions (U.K.) Ltd.* [1975] 1 W.L.R. 186.

[33] *Jackson v. Elphick* (1902) 10 S.L.T. 146 (O.H.).

[33a] A prior charging order nisi will not be confirmed after a liquidation: *Roberts Petroleum Ltd. v. Bernard Kenny Ltd., The Times,* February 15, 1983.

In spite of its plain words, section 228 is subject to the provisions of section 226, *ante*,[34] and section 231, *post*. Thus an order under section 231 validates, *inter alia*, sequestrations and executions which would otherwise be void under section 228.[35]

The effect of section 327 is to equalise diligence in Scotland by depriving any creditor who does diligence after the commencement of winding up (or within 60 days before that date) of the benefit which his diligence would otherwise have given him.[36] The section is not restricted by the provisions of section 231, *post*. Accordingly the court could not under section 231 sanction diligence contrary to section 327.[37] Section 327 has been held not to render ineffectual an arrestment executed within 60 days before the commencement of winding up but superseded, owing to payment of the debt, before that date.[38]

(3) After a winding-up order has been made or a provisional liquidator has been appointed, no action can be proceeded with or commenced against the company except by leave of the court: section 231.

The purpose of section 231 is to ensure that when a company goes into liquidation the assets are administered for the benefit of all the creditors.[39]

Notwithstanding the section, if a company in liquidation brings an action the defendant may, without leave of the court, set up a cross-demand for liquidated or unliquidated damages, but only as a set-off to reduce or extinguish the plaintiff's claim.[40]

Since "the court" is defined as "the court having jurisdiction to wind up the company" (s.455), an action brought in a Scottish court against a company registered in England requires to be sisted until leave of the English court has been obtained.[41]

---

[34] p. 620.

[35] *Re Lancashire Cotton Spinning Co.* (1887) 35 Ch.D. 656 (C.A.); *The Constellation* [1966] 1 W.L.R. 272.

[36] For an application of s.327(1)(*b*) (decree of adjudication), see *Turnbull* v. *Liquidator of Scottish County Investment Co. Ltd.*, 1939 S.C. 5.

[37] *Allan* v. *Cowan* (1892) 20 R. 36; see also opinion of Lord Trayner in *Radford & Bright Ltd.* v. *D. M. Stevenson & Co.* (1904) 6 F. 429, at p. 431.

[38] *Johnston* v. *Cluny Trustees*, 1957 S.C. 184.

[39] *Per* Widgery L.J. in *Langley Constructions (Brixham) Ltd.* v. *Wells* [1969] 1 W.L.R. 503 (C.A.), at p. 508.

[40] *Langley Constructions (Brixham) Ltd.* v. *Wells*, *supra*.

[41] *Martin* v. *Port of Manchester Insce. Co. Ltd.*, 1934 S.C. 143. And see *Coclas* v. *Bruce Peebles & Co. Ltd.* (1908) 16 S.L.T. 7 (O.H.).

(4) On a winding-up order being made in England, the Official Receiver by virtue of his office becomes provisional liquidator, and he continues to act until he or another person becomes liquidator: section 239.

(5) On a winding-up order being made, most of the powers of the directors cease,[42] and are assumed by the liquidator. Those which do not have been dealt with already.[43] Some of the duties of the directors cease, too, *e.g.* as to the mode of keeping the company's accounting records under what is now section 12 of the 1976 Act.[44] One of the duties which remains after the making of a winding-up order is the duty not to disclose confidential information.[45]

(6) On a winding-up order being made, the employees of the company are *ipso facto* dismissed,[46] and may be able to sue for damages for breach of contract, but an employee who continues to discharge the same duties and receive the same wages as before may be held to have entered by tacit relocation into a contract of service with the liquidator.[47] Where a liquidator re-engaged employees in order to complete certain contracts and thereafter dismissed them on the ground of redundancy, the employees were held, for the purposes of the Redundancy Payments Act 1965, to have been continuously employed by one employer (*i.e.* the company) from the dates of their initial engagement by the company down to the dates of their dismissal by the liquidator.[47a]

Every invoice, order for goods or business letter issued by or on behalf of the company or the liquidator, on which the company's name appears, must contain a statement that the company is being wound up: section 338.

---

[42] *Fowler* v. *Broad's Patent Night Light Co.* [1893] 1 Ch. 724.
[43] *Ante*, p. 624.
[44] *Ante*, p. 457.
[45] *Re Country Traders Distributors Ltd. etc.* [1974] 2 N.S.W.L.R. 135.
[46] *Chapman's Case* (1866) L.R. 1 Eq. 346, *ante*, p. 390; *Laing* v. *Gowans* (1902) 10 S.L.T. 461 (O.H.), *ante*, p. 390.
[47] *Day* v. *Tait* (1900) 8 S.L.T. 40 (O.H.).
[47a] *Smith* v. *Lord Advocate*, 1978 S.C. 259.

Appointment of special manager in England

When the Official Receiver becomes the liquidator, whether provisionally or otherwise, he may apply to the court for the appointment of a special manager of the company's business other than himself if the nature of the company's business or the interests of the creditors or contributories require it. The court can appoint the special manager with such powers, including any of the powers of a receiver or manager, as it thinks fit: section 263.

A special manager is appointed in almost all cases where the business of the company is to be carried on pending the appointment of a liquidator.

The special manager must give security to the satisfaction of the Department of Trade. His remuneration is fixed by the court.

PROCEEDINGS AFTER A WINDING-UP ORDER

1. Statement of company's affairs to be submitted to Official Receiver in England

Within 14 days after the appointment of a provisional liquidator or after the winding-up order, a statement of the affairs of the company must be delivered to the Official Receiver unless the court orders otherwise. This statement must be in the prescribed form, verified by the affidavit, and must show particulars of the assets, debts and liabilities of the company, the names, residences and occupations of its creditors, the securities held by them and the dates when they were given, and such other information as may be required.

The statement is made by one or more of the directors and by the secretary, or, if the Official Receiver so requires, by other persons, *e.g.* present or past officers of the company. The costs incurred in making the statement are allowed to the makers: section 235.[48]

The statement is open to the inspection of anyone stating himself in writing to be a creditor or contributory.

2. Report by Official receiver in England

Where a winding-up order is made the Official Receiver must, as soon as practicable after he has received the statement of affairs, submit a preliminary report to the court—

[48] See the 1967 Act, s.50.

(*a*) as to the amount of capital issued, subscribed and paid up, and the estimated amount of assets and liabilities;

(*b*) if the company has failed, as to the cause of the failure; and

(*c*) whether further inquiry is desirable as to any matter relating to the promotion, formation or failure of the company or the conduct of its business: section 236.

If he thinks fraud has been committed in or since the promotion or formation of the company, the Official Receiver may make a further report to the court and a public examination may be ordered under section 270, *post.*[49]

3. First meetings of creditors and contributories

The Official Receiver must summon separate meetings of the creditors and contributories of the company: section 239.

Unless the court otherwise directs, these first meetings of creditors and contributories must be held within one month, or, if a special manager has been appointed, within six weeks, after the winding-up order: rule 121.

The meetings are summoned by at least seven days' notice in the *London Gazette* and in a local paper; and at least seven days before the meeting notice must be sent by post to every creditor and contributory: rule 129.

The Official Receiver must send to the creditors and contributories a summary of the company's statement of affairs, including the causes of its failure, and any observations thereon he may think fit to make. The meetings are not invalidated by reason of any summary or notice not having been sent or received beforehand. The Official Receiver may also summon any director or other officer of the company to attend the meetings. The Official Receiver or his nominee is chairman at the meetings, and the procedure is regulated by the Companies (Winding-up) Rules 1949, rr.121–156. Any other meetings of creditors and contributories are summoned in the same way and regulated by the same procedure.

The object of these meetings is to decide whether to make application to the court to appoint a liquidator in the place of the Official Receiver and, if so, whether to apply for the appointment of a committee of inspection to act with him. If the meetings cannot agree, the court decides: sections 239, 252.

---

[49] p. 642.

Section 239 and the 1949 Rules do not apply to Scotland, but by section 252 when a winding-up order has been made by the court in Scotland, the liquidator must summon separate meetings of the creditors and contributories[50] of the company to decide whether or not an application is to be made to the court for the appointment of a committee of inspection to act with the liquidator, and if the meetings do not agree, the court decides.[51]

4. Appointment of liquidator

In England a liquidator may be appointed by the court, on application being made after the meetings of the creditors and contributories have been held. If the two meetings do not agree on the person to be appointed, the court will decide the difference and make such order as it thinks fit. If a liquidator is not appointed by the court, the Official Receiver is the liquidator: sections 237, 239. In Scotland a liquidator is appointed by the court, and is described by the style of "the official liquidator" of the particular company: sections 237, 241. The question of who is to be appointed liquidator is primarily a discretionary matter to be decided by the court which makes the order for winding up, and the exercise of that discretion is not lightly interfered with.[52]

Because liquidation is specialised work carrying heavy responsibilities and a liquidator in a compulsory liquidation is an officer of the court to whom various powers and duties imposed on the court itself are delegated, there has been a rule of practice for 30 years not to appoint an accountant of less than five years' standing. Although the rule is a good working rule, the overall discretion of the court remains.[53] Anyone who is subject to a disqualification order under section 188 of the 1948 Act or section 9 of the Insolvency Act 1976 cannot act as a liquidator.[54]

In England a person other than the Official Receiver who is appointed liquidator cannot act until he has given notice of his appointment to the Registrar of Companies and given security in the prescribed manner to the Department of Trade: section 240. In Scot-

---

[50] If the order has been made on the ground that the company is unable to pay its debts, a meeting of contributories need not be summoned: s.252(2) proviso.
[51] For Scotland, see R.C. 208, 210.
[52] *Steel Scaffolding Co. Ltd.* v. *Buckleys Ltd.*, 1935 S.C. 617.
[53] *Re Icknield Development Ltd.* [1973] 1 W.L.R. 537 (where exception was made).
[54] *Ante,* p. 332.

land all official liquidators must on their appointment find caution of such nature and amount as the court may direct: section 241 and R.C. 206.

In England, the appointment of a liquidator must be gazetted by the Department of Trade and advertised by the liquidator in such manner as the court directs, after security has been given: rule 58.[55]

Accounts of the liquidator's powers and duties will be found later in this chapter and in Chapter 28.[56]

5. Committee of inspection

The committee of inspection is appointed by the court after the meetings of the creditors and contributories have been held: section 252. It consists of creditors and contributories or persons holding general powers of attorney from creditors or contributories in such proportions as may be agreed on by the meetings or as, in the case of difference, is determined by the court, except that in Scotland if the winding-up order has been made on the ground that the company is unable to pay its debts, the committee consists only of creditors or persons holding general powers of attorney from creditors. The committee must consist of more than one individual.[56a] It will be shown[57] that the function of the committee is to assist and supervise the acts of the liquidator.

The committee meets at least once a month or oftener if required. The liquidator or any member of the committee may summon a meeting when he thinks necessary. The committee acts by a majority of the members present and a majority of the committee constitutes a quorum.

A person ceases to be a member of the committee if—

(*a*) he sends his resignation in writing to the liquidator; or
(*b*) he becomes bankrupt or compounds or arranges with his creditors; or
(*c*) he is absent from five consecutive meetings without leave of his fellow creditor or contributory representatives; or

---

[55] For Scotland, see R.C. 205.
[56] *Post*, pp. 646, 675.
[56a] *Souter, Petitioner*, 1981 S.L.T. (Sh. Ct.) 89.
[57] *Post*, p. 646.

(*d*) he is removed by ordinary resolution of the creditors, if he represents creditors, or of the contributories, if he represents contributories: section 253.

In a winding up in Scotland, the committee has, in addition to the powers and duties conferred and imposed on it by the Act, such of the powers and duties of commissioners on a bankrupt estate as may be conferred and imposed on committees of inspection by general rules: section 255. The committee has, *e.g.* a right of access to the liquidator's books and accounts: R.C. 209. [58]

A member of the committee of inspection is in a fiduciary position and cannot, *e.g.* buy any of the company's assets from the liquidator except by leave of the court: rules 161 *et seq.* [59]

THE PROPERTY OF THE COMPANY IN A WINDING UP BY THE COURT

Custody of company's property. Vesting in liquidator

When a winding-up order has been made, or a provisional liquidator appointed, the liquidator must take into his custody or under his control all the property to which the company is or appears to be entitled. In Scotland, if and so long as there is no liquidator, all the company's property is deemed to be in the custody of the court: section 243.

Winding up does not, as does bankruptcy or sequestration, operate as a *cessio bonorum* or transfer of property: the company's property remains vested in it as before. [60] The liquidator has therefore to get the property into his possession. Under section 244 the court may make an order vesting any of the company's property in him in his official name. Section 258 and, as regards England, section 273 and the Companies

---

[58] On R.C. 209 (*a*) and (*b*) see *Liquidator of Upper Clyde Shipbuilders Ltd.*, 1975 S.L.T. 39 (O.H.).

[59] For Scotland, see *Liquidators of North British Locomotive Co. Ltd.* v. *Lord Advocate*, 1963 S.C. 272 (O.H.), and *Brewis, Petitioner* (1899) 37 S.L.R. 669 (O.H.), approved in *Liquidators of Pattisons Ltd., Petitioners* (1902) 4 F. 1010.

[60] *Per* Warrington L.J. in *Re H. J. Webb & Co. (Smithfield, London) Ltd.* [1922] 2 Ch. 369 (C.A.), at p. 388; *per* Lord President Inglis in *Queensland Mercantile etc. Co. Ltd.* v. *Australasian Investment Co. Ltd.* (1888) 15 R. 935, at p. 939; *per* Lord Hailsham in *Alexander Ward & Co. Ltd.* v. *Samyang Navigation Co. Ltd.*, 1975 S.C. (H.L.) 26, at p. 47.

(Winding-up) Rules 1949, r.79, also contain wide powers to enable the liquidator to get the company's property into his custody.

The property to which the company is entitled and which the liquidator can accordingly take into his custody is:

(1) Property belonging to the company at the commencement of the winding up.[61]

(2) Subject as below, property against which execution has been issued by, or which has been attached by the diligence of, a creditor.

Restriction of rights of creditor as to execution or attachment where company being wound up in England

In the case of a company being wound up in England, section 325(1) provides that where a creditor has issued execution against the goods or lands of a company or has attached any debt due to it, and the company is subsequently wound up, he is not entitled to retain the benefit of the execution or attachment against the liquidator unless he completed the execution or attachment before the commencement of the winding up[62] or, if he had notice of a meeting at which a resolution for voluntary winding up was to be proposed, before such notice. A purchaser in good faith, under a sale by the sheriff, of goods on which execution has been levied acquires a good title to them against the liquidator. The section does not apply to a distress for rent by a landlord.[63]

An execution against goods is taken to be completed either by seizure and sale or by the making of a charging order,[64] and an attachment of a debt by receipt of the debt, and an execution against land by seizure, the appointment of a receiver or by the making of a charging order[64]: section 325(2) as amended by the Charging Orders Act 1979, s.4.

Where a judgment creditor issued a writ of *fi. fa.* in respect of the judgment and the sheriff seized the company's goods and, after a petition for a com-

---

[61] In Scotland this has been held to include heritable property which the company has come under a personal obligation to convey to a purchaser who has paid the purchase price to the company: *Gibson and Hunter Home Designs Ltd.*, 1976 S.C. 23.

[62] *Ante*, p. 623.

[63] *Re Bellaglade Ltd.* [1977] 1 All E.R. 319.

[64] Under section 1 of the Charging Orders Act 1979.

pulsory winding up had been presented (although this was unknown to the sheriff), sold them, when an order for winding up was made the sheriff had to hand over the proceeds to the liquidator.[65]

The phrase "the benefit of the execution" does not refer to "the fruits of the execution" but to the charge conferred on the creditor by the issue of execution.[66]

Where a creditor has issued a writ of *fi. fa.* against a company, money paid to the sheriff or his officers in order to avoid a sale and which remains in their hands at the commencement of the winding up is outside "the benefit of the execution" so that the liquidator is not entitled to such money as against the creditor.[66]

"The benefit of the attachment" means the right to take the necessary steps to complete it.

If a judgment creditor who has obtained a garnishee order obtains payment after receipt by him of notice of a meeting called for the winding up of the company, he must, subject to the court's discretion under section 325(1), proviso (c), *post*, account to the liquidator for the money.[67]

By section 325(1), proviso (c), the rights conferred by section 325(1), *ante*, on the liquidator may be set aside by the court in favour of the creditor. The basic scheme of the Companies Acts is that in a winding up unsecured creditors rank *pari passu* and an execution creditor who has not completed his execution at the commencement of the winding up is for this purpose in the same position as any other unsecured creditor. Section 325(1), proviso (c), gives the court a free hand to do what is right and fair according to the circumstances of the case,[68] but weighty reasons are necessary to justify the court in exercising its discretion under the proviso.[69]

Where a judgment creditor of a company refrained from levying immediate execution because of a promise of payment by a director, there being no dishonesty by the director, and the execution was not completed before the commencement of the winding up, the court refused to set the liquidator's rights aside. To allow the creditor to retain the benefit of the execution would have been contrary to the basic scheme of the Acts and unfair to the other

---

[65] *Bluston & Bramley Ltd.* v. *Leigh* [1950] 2 K.B. 548.
[66] *Re Walkden Sheet Metal Co. Ltd.* [1960] Ch. 170.
[67] *Re Caribbean Products (Yam Importers) Ltd.* [1966] Ch. 331 (C.A.); overruling *Re Rainbow Tours Ltd.* [1964] Ch. 66.
[68] *Re Redman (Builders) Ltd.* [1964] 1 W.L.R. 541.
[69] *Re Caribbean Products (Yam Importers) Ltd.*, *ante.*

creditors. During the year before the winding up the company was keeping its general body of trade creditors at bay and there was no reason why one execution creditor who had not completed execution should be preferred to the other creditors whether or not they had obtained judgment or commenced execution.[70]

On the other hand, where before the action the company stalled the creditors' claims by promises and defended the action by disputing a debt already admitted, the liquidator's rights were set aside.[71]

Duties of sheriff as to goods taken in execution

Section 326(1) provides that, subject to subsection (3), *post,* where any goods of a company are taken in execution and, before the sale thereof or the completion of the execution by the receipt or recovery of the amount of the levy, notice is served on the sheriff that a provisional liquidator has been appointed or a winding-up order made or that a resolution for voluntary winding up has been passed, the sheriff must, if so required, deliver the goods and any money seized or received in part satisfaction of the execution to the liquidator, but the costs of the execution are a first charge on the goods or such money and the liquidator may sell the goods or part of them for the purpose of satisfying the charge.

Money paid to the sheriff to avoid a sale is not money received in carrying out the execution, *i.e.* not money received in part satisfaction of the execution.[72]

Subject to subsection (3), where under an execution in respect of a judgment for a sum exceeding £250 the goods of a company are sold or money is paid to avoid sale, the sheriff must deduct the costs of the execution from the proceeds of sale or the money paid and retain the balance for 14 days, and if within that time notice is served on him of the presentation of a petition for winding up the company or of a meeting at which a resolution for voluntary winding up is to be proposed, and an order is made or a resolution is passed, as the case may be, he must pay the balance to the liquidator who is entitled to retain it as against the execution creditor: section 326(2), as amended by the Insolvency Act 1976, Sched. 1.

Where execution is issued against a company and money is paid to the bailiff to avoid a sale, the payment to the bailiff is payment to the sheriff and if

---

[70] See note 68 above.
[71] *Re Suidair International Airways Ltd.* [1951] Ch. 165.   [72] See note 66 above.

the 14-day period expires before he receives notice of a winding up the liquidator is not entitled to the money.[72]

If, after he has sold the company's goods but before he has handed over the proceeds of sale to the creditor, the sheriff receives notice of a meeting at which a resolution for *voluntary* winding up is to be proposed and at the meeting a resolution for *compulsory* winding up is passed, the sheriff is not bound to hand the proceeds to the liquidator.[73] If the sheriff receives notice, pursuant to section 293, of a meeting of creditors to appoint a liquidator, etc., he is taken to know that notices of a meeting of members have been sent out too, and the subsection is satisfied.[74]

Notice of a meeting for the proposal of a resolution for voluntary winding up was received by the sheriff's officer after he had taken possession of the company's goods and money was paid to him to avoid their sale. *Held,* there was no evidence that the sheriff had deputed to him the duty of receiving the notice and no reason to suppose it implicit in the duties of a sheriff's officer to inform the sheriff of the receipt of such notice, and it had not been served on the sheriff. The money was therefore properly paid to the execution creditor: *Hellyer* v. *Sheriff of Yorkshire* [1975] Ch.D. 16 (C.A.).

Section 326(3) provides that the rights conferred by the section on the liquidator may be set aside by the court in favour of the creditor.

In the section, the term "sheriff" includes any officer charged with the execution of a writ or other process (subsection (4)). This subsection is intended to cover persons who are in the equivalent situation, so far as execution is concerned, of the sheriff in respect of courts other than the High Court.[75]

Scottish companies, and property of English companies in Scotland

As regards Scottish companies and such property of English companies as is situated in Scotland, section 327 provides as follows:

(*a*) The winding up is, as at the date of its commencement, equivalent to an arrestment in execution and decree of furthcoming, and to an executed or completed poinding, and no arrestment or poinding of the funds or effects of the company executed on or after the sixtieth day before that date is effectual as against the liquidator except to the limited extent

---

[73] See note 65 above.
[74] *Engineering Industry Training Board* v. *Samuel Talbot (Engineers) Ltd.* [1969] 2 Q.B. 270 (C.A.).
[75] *Per* Russell L.J. in *Hellyer* v. *Sheriff of Yorkshire* [1975] Ch.D. 16 (C.A.), at p. 20.

that an arrester or poinder who is thus deprived of the benefit of his diligence is entitled to a preference for the expense bona fide incurred by him in his diligence.

C. brought an action of payment against a company and arrested the sum sued for in the hands of S., a debtor of the company. On the instructions of the company, S. paid the sum arrested to C. with the result that the arrestment was superseded. Later, but less than 60 days after the execution of the arrestment, an order was made for the winding up of the company, and the liquidator brought an action to recover the amount paid to C. *Held,* the only arrestments made ineffectual by section 327 were those which, but for it, would have been effectual at the commencement of winding up, and therefore the section did not apply to arrestments which had been withdrawn or superseded by payment of the debt before that date: *Johnston* v. *Cluny Trustees*, 1957 S.C. 184.

(b) The winding up is, as at the date of its commencement, also equivalent to a decree of adjudication of the heritable estates of the company for payment of the whole debts of the company, subject to any preferable heritable rights and securities which are valid and unchallengeable and subject to the limited right to poind the ground provided for in (c).[76]

(c) A poinding of the ground which has not been carried into execution by sale of the effects 60 days before the commencement of winding up is of no effect in a question with the liquidator unless the poinder holds a heritable security which is preferable to the right of the liquidator, in which case the poinding is available for the interest for the current half-year and for the arrears of interest for the preceding year, but for no more.

(3) Property used by the company to give a fraudulent preference to any of its creditors.

Fraudulent preference

Any conveyance, mortgage, delivery of goods, payment, execution or other act relating to property, made or done by or against a company

---

[76] For an instance of the application of provision (b), see *Turnbull* v. *Liquidator of Scottish County Investment Co. Ltd.* 1939 S.C. 5; on the interrelation of this provision and the Conveyancing and Feudal Reform (Scotland) Act 1970, s.24 (application to court for warrant to sell), see *United Dominions Trust Ltd., Noters*, 1977 S.L.T. (Notes) 56 (O.H.).

within six months before the commencement of its winding up, is void
if it is a fraudulent preference of any of the company's creditors:
section 320. "In this respect the company in liquidation is exactly in the
same position as an individual debtor under the Bankruptcy Acts."[77]

In *England* a payment will be a fraudulent preference if it is—

  (*a*) made with the dominant intention of giving the creditor a
        preference over the other creditors[78]; and
  (*b*) the voluntary act of the company. A payment made under
        pressure is not a fraudulent preference.[79]

> K. and his wife were the sole directors and shareholders of a company. The
> company's overdraft was guaranteed by K. On May 12 the directors were
> advised that the company was insolvent. Between May 12 and 21, payments
> were made into the bank extinguishing the overdraft, and on May 23 a
> winding-up resolution was passed. No trade creditors were paid between May
> 10 and 23. *Held*, a fraudulent preference: *Re M. Kushler Ltd.* [1943] Ch. 248
> (C.A.).

> M. and his wife were the sole directors and shareholders of a company. The
> company's overdraft was guaranteed by them. The company's overdraft was
> cleared without pressure from the bank. The company went into liquidation.
> M. believed at the time of payment that all the debts would be paid in due
> course even though they could not be paid as they became due. The Court of
> Appeal held that this was not sufficient to prevent the payment to the bank
> being a fraudulent preference: *Re F. P. & C. H. Matthews* [1982] 1 All E.R.
> 338.

> "Where the debtor company is unable to pay its debts as they arise, that
> circumstance seems to us to fall clearly within the words 'a preference over the
> other creditors.' The receiving creditor gets its money in full and the rest of the
> creditors are left with the risk that they may not be paid in full." *Per* Lawton
> L.J., at p. 342.

Where a creditor making an advance takes from the debtor a
promise to execute a charge on request the court will, in the absence of
other circumstances, infer that the purpose of the parties is to give the
creditor the right to be preferred on request. Such an arrangement,
although for value, is fraudulent and unenforceable, and when the
debtor creates the charge the court, in the absence of other circum-

---

[77] *Per* Lord Kinnear in *Bank of Scotland* v. *Liquidators of Hutchison, Main & Co.
   Ltd.*, 1914 S.C. (H.L.) 1, at p. 3.
[78] *Peat* v. *Gresham Trust Ltd.* [1934] A.C. 252.
[79] *Sharp* v. *Jackson* [1899] A.C. 419. And see *Re F.L.E. Holdings* [1967] 1 W.L.R.
   1409.

stances, will infer that the debtor's intention is to prefer the creditor. Where the creation of the charge is part of a wider arrangement, the debtor's intention must be determined in relation to the arrangement as a whole.[80]

If there is a fraudulent preference of a person interested in property charged to secure the company's debt, that person has the same rights and liabilities as if he were a surety for the debt to the extent of the charge on the property or the value of his interest, whichever is less: section 321. Thus, if a director has secured the company's overdraft, *e.g.* by deposit of the title deeds to his own property, but without undertaking personal liability, and the overdraft is discharged so as to amount to a fraudulent preference of him, and the bank has to repay the liquidator, the bank can sue the director, who can prove against the company.

The bankruptcy rule as to reputed ownership does not apply to companies.[81]

Fraudulent preferences (Scots law)

In Scotland fraudulent preferences may be reduced either at common law on the ground of insolvency or under the Bankruptcy Act 1696 (Scots Act 1696, c. 5), as amended by the Companies Act 1947, s.115(3), on the ground of notour bankruptcy.

At common law the challenger must prove that—

(*a*) the debtor was insolvent at the date of the transaction and continuously thereafter down to the date of the challenge;

(*b*) the debtor was aware at the date of the transaction that he was insolvent;

(*c*) the transaction was voluntary and in satisfaction or further security of a prior debt; and

(*d*) the transaction was to the prejudice of the debtor's other creditors.[81a]

The 1696 Act facilitated challenge of fraudulent preferences. Under that Act, as amended, the challenger must prove that—

---

[80] *Re Eric Holmes (Property) Ltd.* [1965] Ch. 1052, *ante*, p. 579.
[81] *Gorringe* v. *Irwell India Rubber Works Ltd.* (1886) 34 Ch.D. 128 (C.A.).
[81a] For a comprehensive review of the authorities, see *Nordic Travel Ltd.* v. *Scotprint Ltd.*, 1980 S.C. 1.

(*a*) the debtor is notour bankrupt;

(*b*) the transaction took place at, after, or within six months[82] before, notour bankruptcy;

(*c*) the transaction was voluntary and in satisfaction or further security of a prior debt; and

(*d*) the challenge is made by or on behalf of prior creditors or by a trustee in a sequestration.

Both at common law and under the statute the following are recognised as exceptions and are not reducible unless there is proof of fraudulent contrivance between debtor and creditor[82a]—(i) cash payments of debts actually due, (ii) transactions in the ordinary course of trade[82b] and (iii) *nova debita*, namely, new debts arising out of new transactions.

A transaction is not "voluntary" if the debtor is doing "the very thing which he is bound to do,"[83] such as implementing a prior obligation to grant a specific security provided that obligation is part of the original contract.[84]

The preference is equally challengeable whether conferred directly (*e.g.* where security is given to a creditor previously unsecured) or indirectly.[85]

An isolated and unprecedented assignation by an insolvent company cannot claim the protection afforded to transactions "in the ordinary course of trade," and is therefore reducible.[86]

The liquidator can sell or otherwise realise the property of the company (s.245).[87] In England it is his duty to collect the assets of the company and apply them in discharge of its liabilities: sections 257, 273; r.78. In Scotland it is for the court to cause the assets to be

---

[82] Substituted for 60 days by the Companies Act 1947, s.115(3).

[82a] Mere knowledge on the creditor's part of the debtor's absolute and irretrievable insolvency at the time of payment is not enough: *Nordic Travel Ltd.* v. *Scotprint Ltd., ante.*

[82b] See *Nordic Travel Ltd.* v. *Scotprint Ltd., ante.*

[83] *Taylor* v. *Farrie* (1855) 17 D. 639 at p. 649 (joint opinion).

[84] *T.* v. *L.,* 1970 S.L.T. 243 (O.H.).

[85] *Walkraft Paint Co. Ltd.* v. *Lovelock,* 1964 S.L.T. 103 (O.H.) (mandates given by the company to certain of its debtors to pay the favoured creditor); *Walkraft Paint Co. Ltd.* v. *James H. Kinsey Ltd.,* 1964 S.L.T. 104 (O.H.) (cheque from company's debtor endorsed by company to the favoured creditor).

[86] *Walkraft Paint Co. Ltd.* v. *James H. Kinsey Ltd., ante.*

[87] *Post,* p. 648.

collected and applied in discharge of the company's liabilities, there being no provision for delegation to the liquidator: section 257.

Private examination

After the making of a winding-up order or the appointment of a provisional liquidator, the court may examine on oath any officer of the company or person known or suspected to have in his possession any property of the company or supposed to be indebted to the company, or any person whom the court deems capable of giving any information as to the promotion, formation, trade, dealings, affairs or property of the company. The court may reduce his answers to writing and require him to sign them. He may be required to produce books and papers relating to the company. If a person summoned for examination does not appear, he may be apprehended and brought before the court for examination: section 268.

An order for an examination is usually made on the application of the liquidator,[88] but may be made on the application of a contributory. The examination is in private.

It has been said that the section is an extraordinary one giving an extraordinary power of an inquisitorial nature, enabling the court to direct the examination of a person who is not a party to any litigation, and that the process under the section is needed because of the difficulty in which the liquidator in an insolvent company is necessarily placed in that there are almost certain to be many transactions which are difficult to discover or to understand merely from the books and papers of the company.[89]

The section is not restricted either to information in existence at the date of commencement of the winding up, or to information acquired by persons connected with the company. Thus where an insurance company refused to pay a claim for fire insurance on the basis that it suspected arson the liquidator was able to persuade the court to summon an official of the insurance company and require production of various reports compiled by loss adjusters and specialist fire investigators *vis-à-vis* the fire.[89a]

---

[88] *e.g. M'Lintock* v.*Lithauer*, 1924 S.L.T. 775 (O.H.).
[89] *Per* Megarry J. in *Rolls Razor Ltd. (No.* 2) [1970] Ch. 576, at pp. 586 and 591–592.
[89a] *Re Highgrade Traders Ltd., The Times,* December 9, 1982.

While it is not a conclusive objection to an order for a private examination under section 268 that proceedings have been commenced against the person concerned, the court ought to act with very great care before ordering an examination of a person who is or who is about to be defendant to an action by the company in liquidation, lest the private examination may be said to be assisting the company to get a favourable judgment.[90]

Public examination in England

In bankruptcy, the bankrupt must always undergo a public examination. When a company goes into liquidation, however, a public examination only takes place if an order for examination has been made. Where the Official Receiver has made a further report[91] to the court stating that in his opinion a *fraud* has been committed by any person in the promotion or formation of the company or by any officer of the company in relation to the company since its formation, the court may make an order for the public examination of such person: section 270.

The report must make out a prima facie case of fraud, *i.e.* it must not be flimsy or sketchy. The charge need not be such as would support civil or criminal proceedings. It need not attribute particular pieces of alleged fraud to particular individuals.[92]

The Official Receiver must take part in the examination, and the liquidator, or any creditor or contributory, may take part. Evidence is given on oath. At his own cost, the person ordered to be examined is furnished with a copy of the Official Receiver's report and he may employ a solicitor with or without counsel. Notes of the examination are taken down in writing and signed by the person examined and may be used in evidence against him: section 270.

The Jenkins Report[93] recommended that section 270 should empower the court to order public examination of directors of an insolvent company where there is some prima facie case of culpability. The Act does not at present provide a sufficient deterrent to dissuade directors from continuing the business of a company which they know to be hopelessly insolvent.

[90] *Re Bletchley Boat Co. Ltd.* [1974] 1 W.L.R. 630, and see *per* Brightman J. at p. 637.
[91] Under s.236, *ante*, p. 628.
[92] *Tejani* v.*Official Receiver* [1963] 1 W.L.R. 59 (P.C.).
[93] Para. 503.

Attendance of officers at meetings in Scotland

While the public examination required in sequestration[94] has no place in the liquidation of a company, the court in the compulsory winding up of a Scottish company has power to require any officer of the company to attend any meeting of creditors or of contributories or of a committee of inspection for the purpose of giving information as to the trade, dealings, affairs or property of the company: section 269.

Fraudulent trading

Section 332 provides that if in the winding up of a company it appears that business has been carried on with intent to defraud creditors or for any fraudulent purpose, the court, on the application of the Official Receiver, the liquidator or any creditor or contributory, may declare that any persons who were knowingly parties to the fraudulent trading shall be personally responsible, without limitation of liability, for all or any of the company's debts or other liabilities as the court may direct, *i.e.* shall lose the privilege of limited liability: section 332(1). Such persons are also liable to two years' imprisonment or a fine or both: section 332(3). A company need not be in liquidation before a prosecution can be initiated under subsection (3).[95]

In general it may be properly inferred that there is an intent to defraud creditors if a company carries on business and incurs debts when, to the knowledge of the directors, there is no reasonable prospect of the company being able to pay them.[96] The expression "parties to" in section 332(1) indicates no more than "take part in" or "concur in" and involves some positive steps. Mere omission by the secretary to give certain advice (that the company is insolvent and should cease to trade) is not being a party to carrying on the business in a fraudulent manner.[97] However, another creditor who, knowing of the circumstances, accepts money fraudulently obtained by the company may be liable to repay it even if he took no part in the fraudulent trading.[98]

---

[94] Bankruptcy (Scotland) Act 1913, s.83.
[95] 1981 Act, s.96.
[96] *Re William C. Leitch Bros. Ltd.* [1932] 2 Ch. 71.
[97] *Re Maidstone Buildings Provisions Ltd.* [1971] 1 W.L.R. 1085.
[98] *Re Gerald Cooper Chemicals Ltd.* [1978] Ch. 262.

It is not fraudulent trading to intend to prefer one creditor to another even if all could not be paid in full,[99] nor to sell goods which prove to be defective knowing that liability for such defects might not be met.[1]

The court may charge the liability of any person declared liable under section 332(1) on any debt due to him from the company, or on any charge on any assets of the company held by him, or any company or person on his behalf, or certain assignees from him or such a company or person: section 332(2).

It has been held that a claim by a creditor under section 332 is made on his own account and not under a trust for the other creditors or anyone else.[2] Nevertheless it is thought that the section can only result in an accretion to the assets of the company for distribution in due course of winding up.[3]

It is thought that the section does not involve lifting the veil of incorporation.[4]

The Jenkins Report[5] recommended that section 332 be extended to make directors, and others who have carried on the business in a reckless manner, personally liable for the company's debts.

Misfeasance proceedings

These were explained in connection with statutory protection of the minority.[6]

Disclaimer in case of company wound up in England

When any part of the property of a company which is being wound up consists of—(1) land burdened with onerous covenants[7]; or (2) shares or stock in companies; or (3) unprofitable contracts; or (4) property that is unsaleable, or not readily saleable, because it binds the possessor to the performance of an onerous act or to the payment of

---

[99] *Re Sarflax Ltd.* [1979] Ch. 592.
[1] *Norcross Ltd.* v. *Amos* (1981) 131 N.L.J. 1213.
[2] *Re Cyona Distributors Ltd.* [1967] Ch. 889 (C.A.).
[3] See *per* Russell L.J. in the *Cyona* case at p. 908.
[4] *Ante*, p. 24.
[5] See note 93 above.
[6] *Ante*, p. 416.
[7] In *Re The Nottingham General Cemetery Co.* [1955] Ch. 683, the land disclaimed could not be used except in accordance with contracts between the company and the holders of grave certificates.

money; the liquidator may, with the leave of the court, disclaim the property. The disclaimer must be made, in writing signed by the liquidator, within 12 months after the commencement of the winding up[8] or such extension of time as the court may grant or, if the liquidator was not aware of the property within one month after the commencement of the winding up, within 12 months after his becoming aware of it or such extended period as the court may allow: section 323(1).

A disclaimer operates to determine the rights and liabilities of the company in respect of the property disclaimed but does not, except for the purpose of releasing the company from liability, affect the rights or liabilities of any other person: section 323(2). The court will not allow a disclaimer which would cause substantial injury to other parties, *e.g.* a landlord entitled to sue another party on a guarantee of the rent due from the company.[9]

The liquidator cannot disclaim any property if notice in writing is served on him, by a person interested in the property, requiring him to decide whether he will disclaim or not, and he does not, within 28 days or the further period allowed by the court, give notice that he intends to apply for leave to disclaim. In the case of a contract, if the liquidator does not disclaim within such time, the company is deemed to have adopted it: section 323(4).

Any person who is, as against the liquidator, entitled to the benefit or subject to the burden of a contract with the company may apply to the court for an order rescinding the contract. The court may grant rescission on such terms as it thinks fit, including the payment of damages for breach of contract. Any damages payable to such person under the order may be proved for in the liquidation: section 323(5).

The court may, on the application of any person interested in disclaimed property, make an order for the vesting of the property in, or the delivery of the property to, any person entitled thereto, on such terms as the court thinks just: section 323(6).

Where the property is leasehold, a vesting order cannot be made in favour of any person claiming under the company, as underlessee or mortgagee, except—

(*a*) subject to the same liabilities and obligations as those to which the company was subject under the lease in respect of the property at the commencement of the winding up; or

---

[8] *Ante*, p. 623.   [9] *Re Katherine et Cie Ltd.* [1932] 1 Ch. 70.

(*b*) if the court thinks fit, subject only to the same liabilities and obligations as if the lease had been assigned to that person at that date: section 323(6).

Any person injured by a disclaimer is deemed a creditor of the company to the amount of the injury and may prove for the amount as a debt in the winding up: section 323(7).

Repudiation in case of company wound up in Scotland

By the common law of Scotland the liquidator may either adopt or repudiate current contracts, and if he repudiates them the company is liable in damages for breach of contract. If the liquidator does not within a reasonable time declare his intention to adopt a contract, he will be held to have abandoned it and to be liable in damages.[10]

Where the company is bound under two separate contracts with the same party, the liquidator is entitled to adopt one and repudiate with the other, and the other party to the contracts is not entitled to retain a sum due to the company under the contract adopted, either in security for the proper fulfilment of that contract by the company or in security for a claim for damages in respect of the contract repudiated.[11]

The main criticism of the common law in this connection is the possible uncertainty of the other contracting party as to his position. The Scottish Law Commission has recommended that that other party be entitled to require the trustee to elect whether to adopt or refuse to implement the contract within a specified period of, say, 28 days or such longer period as the court might allow.[12]

POWERS OF THE LIQUIDATOR IN A WINDING UP BY THE COURT[13]

Section 245 provides that:

(1) The liquidator (including a provisional liquidator[14]) in a winding up by the court has power, *with the sanction of the court or of the committee of inspection*:

[10] *Crown Estate Commissioners* v. *Liquidators of Highland Engineering Ltd.*, 1975 S.L.T. 58 (O.H.).

[11] *Asphaltic Limestone Concrete Co. Ltd.* v. *Glasgow Corpn.*, 1907 S.C. 463; see also *Gray's Trustees* v. *Benhar Coal Co. Ltd.* (1881) 9 R. 225.

[12] *Report on Bankruptcy and Related Aspects of Insolvency and Liquidation*, 1982 Scot. Law Com. No. 68, para. 10.26).

[13] See further *post*, p. 675.

[14] *Wilsons (Glasgow and Trinidad) Ltd., Petitioners*, 1912, 2 S.L.T. 330.

(*a*) To bring or defend actions and legal proceedings in the name and on behalf of the company.

It is a matter for his discretion whether he should litigate or not and so the court will not give guidance as to whether he should appeal to a higher court.[15] If the liquidator brings an unsuccessful action he is personally liable as to costs and these are not limited to the assets of the company.[16]

(*b*) To carry on the business of the company so far as may be necessary for beneficial winding up.

When a liquidator carries on the business of the company he does so as the company's agent[16a] and is not personally liable on contracts which he enters into as liquidator.

S. had a contract with the company to deliver cotton in monthly instalments from November, 1929, to August, 1930. The company went into liquidation and C. was appointed liquidator by the court in May, 1930. C. did not disclaim the contract, and arranged with S. that payment should be made after and not before delivery. The goods were delivered but not accepted by C. *Held*, C. was not personally liable for damages for non-acceptance: *Stead, Hazel & Co.* v. *Cooper* [1933] 1 K.B. 840.

In *Liquidator of Burntisland Oil Co. Ltd.* v. *Dawson* (1892) 20 R. 180, the court refused the liquidator's application to carry on the business for an indefinite period on the ground that the company's property could not then be sold except on ruinous terms but granted power to carry on for six weeks while the property was advertised for sale. However, in *M'Intyre, Petitioner* (1893) 30 S.L.R. 386 (O.H.) power was granted to carry on business until the time of the year when the company's property, which consisted of a hall let for public entertainments, could be sold to best advantage.

(*c*) To appoint a solicitor to assist him in his duties.

It is, however, the duty of the liquidator "to perform the business of the liquidation himself, and only to employ the law-agent in such matters as bring him into contact with the court, in such matters as involve conveyancing, and in such other matters as justify him in obtaining legal advice for his guidance."[17]

---

[15] *Note for Liquidator in Liquidation of S.S. "Camelot" Ltd.* (1893) 1 S.L.T. 358 (O.H.).

[16] *Re Wilson Lovatt & Sons Ltd.* [1977] 1 All E.R. 274.

[16a] See *Smith* v. *Lord Advocate*, 1978 S.C. 259.

[17] *Per* Lord Johnston in *Reekie* v. *Liquidator of Leith etc. Shipping Co. Ltd.*, 1911 S.C. 808, at p. 815.

(*d*) To pay any classes of creditors in full.

(*e*) To make any compromise or arrangement with creditors.

(*f*) To compromise all calls and liabilities to calls and other debts and liabilities.

In England, if there is no committee of inspection, the Department of Trade may, on the liquidator's application, give any authorisation required to be given by the committee: section 254. In Scotland, if there is no committee of inspection, the court may provide that the liquidator may exercise powers (*a*) and (*b*), above, without the sanction of the court: section 245(4).

If a liquidator does any of the acts listed in section 245 without the necessary sanction of the court or the committee of inspection he is personally liable although the court may retrospectively sanction such an act.[18]

(2) On his own responsibility and *without obtaining any sanction*, the liquidator can:

(*a*) Sell the property of the company.

(*b*) Do all acts and execute, in the name and on behalf of the company, all deeds and documents, and use the company's seal therefor.

(*c*) Prove, rank and claim in the bankruptcy, insolvency or sequestration of any contributory.

(*d*) Draw, accept, make and indorse any bill of exchange or promissory note in the name and on behalf of the company.

(*e*) Raise money on the security of the company's assets.

(*f*) Take out letters of administration to any deceased contributory and do any other act necessary for obtaining payment of money due from a contributory or his estate.

(*g*) Appoint an agent to do business which he cannot do himself.

(*h*) Do all such other things as are necessary for winding up the affairs of the company and distributing its assets.

In Scotland the liquidator has, subject to any general rules made by Act of Sederunt under section 365, the same powers as a trustee on a bankrupt estate under the provisions of the Bankruptcy (Scotland) Act

---

[18] *Re Associated Travel Leisure and Services Ltd. (in Liquidation)* [1978] 1 W.L.R. 547.

1913, including power to apply to the court for directions in connection with the exercise of his powers[19]: s.245(5).

The liquidator has power to vest in trustees for sale property which the company and he are competent to dispose of, if the trusts are framed so as to accord with his statutory duties as liquidator. Table A, article 135, contemplates such an arrangement.[20]

WINDING UP OF UNREGISTERED COMPANIES

Section 399 provides that an unregistered company may be wound up by the court if—

  (i) it is dissolved, or has ceased business, or is carrying on business only for the purpose of winding up its affairs; or

 (ii) it is unable to pay its debts; or

(iii) the court is of opinion that it is just and equitable that the company should be wound up.

The expression "unregistered company" includes any partnership, association or company with the exception of, *e.g.*—

  (i) a company registered under the Companies Acts; or

 (ii) a partnership, association or company with less than eight members which is not a foreign partnership, association or company; or

(iii) a limited partnership registered in England or Northern Ireland: section 398.

For the purpose of determining the court having jurisdiction in the winding up, an unregistered company is deemed to be registered in England or Scotland according to whether its principal place of business is situated in England or Scotland: section 399(3).

An unregistered company is deemed unable to pay its debts if—

  (i) a creditor, by assignment or otherwise, for at least £200 has served on the company a written demand for payment and the company has neglected to pay the same or to secure or compound it for three weeks;

---

[19] *Liquidator of Upper Clyde Shipbuilders Ltd.*, 1975 S.L.T. 39 (O.H.).
[20] *Re Salisbury Railway & Market House Co. Ltd.* [1969] 1 Ch. 349.

(ii) an action has been instituted against a member for any debt due from the company, or from him in his character of member, and written notice of the institution of the action has been served on the company and the company has not within 10 days paid, secured or compounded for the debt, or procured the action to be stayed, or indemnified the defendant against the action and against all costs, damages and expenses to be incurred by him by reason of the same;

(iii) in England, execution issued on a judgment in favour of a creditor against the company or any member thereof is returned unsatisfied;

(iv) in Scotland, the induciae of a charge for payment of an extract decree, registered bond or registered protest have expired without payment being made;

(v) it is otherwise proved to the satisfaction of the court that the company is unable to pay its debts: section 399(6), as amended by the Insolvency Act 1976, Sched. 1.

Section 402 extends section 226[21] (stay of proceedings against company) to proceedings against a contributory where the application to stay is by a creditor, and section 403 provides that where an order has been made for winding up an unregistered company, no action or proceeding shall be proceeded with or commenced against any contributory of the company in respect of any debt of the company, except by leave of the court.

The provisions of Part IX of the Act (sections 398 to 405) with respect to unregistered companies are in addition to and not in restriction of the provisions with respect to the winding up of companies by the court, and the court or liquidator has the same powers in the case of unregistered companies as in the case of the winding up of companies formed and registered under the Act: section 404.

---

[21] *Ante*, p. 620.

CHAPTER 27

CONTRIBUTORIES AND CREDITORS

As soon as may be after a winding-up order is made, it is the duty of the liquidator in England to—

   (1) settle a list of contributories;
   (2) collect the company's assets and apply them in discharge of its liabilities: sections 257, 273; rules 78, 80.

In Scotland it is for the court to settle a list of contributories and to cause the assets of the company to be collected and applied in discharge of the company's liabilities: section 257. Section 273, which provides for delegation of the court's power to the liquidator, and the Companies (Winding-up) Rules 1949 do not apply to Scotland.

CONTRIBUTORIES

A contributory is a person liable to contribute to the assets of a company in the event of its being wound up: section 213. Section 212 provides that on a winding up every present and past member is liable to contribute to the assets of the company to an amount sufficient for payment of its debts and liabilities, and the costs, charges and expenses of the winding up, and for the adjustment of the rights of the contributories among themselves. This is subject to certain qualifications, *post, e.g.* a past member is not liable to contribute if he ceased to be a member one year or more before the commencement of the winding up[1]: section 212(1)(*a*). This qualification does not apply in the winding up of an unlimited company which has re-registered as limited either under section 44 of the 1967 Act or section 7 of the 1980 Act.[2]

A fully paid shareholder in a limited company is a contributory so that where all debts have been paid in a voluntary liquidation the liquidator is jusitified in making calls on partly paid-up shareholders for the purpose of adjusting rights between them and the fully paid-up shareholders.[3]

---

[1] *Ante*, p. 623.
[2] *Ante*, p. 42.
[3] *Re Anglesea Colliery Co.* (1866) L.R.1 Ch.App. 555, followed, *e.g.* in *Paterson* v. *M'Farlane* (1875) 2 R. 490.

Where a private company which has purchased or redeemed its own shares out of capital under section 54 of the 1981 Act goes into liquidation within one year of such payment, and is found to be insolvent, the directors and the recipient are liable to contribute up to the amount of the payment to cover any insolvency. Such persons are not, however, governed by either section 212 or 224 and are not therefore true contributories : 1981 Act, s.58.[4]

The list of contributories

The list of contributories is in two parts, the A list and the B list. The A list consists of the members of the company at the commencement of the winding up, *i.e.* present members. The B list consists of persons who were members within a year before the commencement of the winding up. The B list is often not settled at all, and is never settled unless it appears that the A contributories are unable to satisfy their contributions.[5] The list must distinguish between contributories who are liable in their own right and those liable as representatives of others: section 257.

Procedure on settling the list in England (rr.80–85)[6]: The list contains (1) the address of each contributory, (2) the number of his shares, (3) the amount called up and (4) the amount paid up.

The liquidator appoints a time and place for the settlement of the list, and gives notice in writing to every person whom he proposes to put on it. At the time appointed, the liquidator settles the list after hearing any objectors. He then gives notice to every person whom he has finally placed on the list. The notice must inform that person that any application to remove his name must be made to the court within 21 days. After the expiration of 21 days no application to vary the list can be made, unless the court extends the time. The liquidator can, from time to time, vary or add to the list. This does not entitle him to reopen any question finally settled.[7]

The court may dispense with the settlement of a list of contributories where it appears that it will not be necessary to make calls on or adjust the rights of contributories: section 257. The distribution of surplus assets among the contributories does not of itself involve an adjustment of the rights of the contributories among themselves.[8] The court

---

[4] *Ante*, p. 252.
[5] See Palmer's *Company Precedents* (17th ed.), Pt. II, p. 400.
[6] For Scotland, see R.C. 211.
[7] *Re Westways Garage Co. Ltd.* [1942] Ch. 356.
[8] *Re Phoenix Oil, etc., Co.* [1958] Ch. 560.

should not exercise its discretion to dispense with a list of contributories if the company has a large number of shares held by a large number of shareholders.[9]

Liability of contributories

The liability of a contributory on the A list is limited to the amount unpaid on his shares: section 212(1)(*d*).

The liability of a contributory on the B list is further limited:

(1) No contribution is required from him exceeding the amount unpaid on the shares in respect of which he is liable as a past member: section 212(1)(*d*).

Example: C and D are the holders of £1 shares, 37½p paid. C transfers his shares to X and D transfers to Y. Within a year the company is wound up, and is insolvent. X pays up his shares in full, but Y pays nothing. No contribution will be required from C. A contribution will be required from D.

If there have been several transfers of the same shares within a year before the winding up, and the A list is exhausted, all the transferors will be placed on the B list at the same time. In such a case the primary liability is that of the latest transferor.[10]

(2) B contributories are not liable to contribute in respect of any debt or liability of the company contracted *after* they ceased to be members: section 212(1)(*b*).

The assets of the company, including the amount received from A contributories, are first applied *pari passu* in payment of the debts of the company, irrespective of the time when they were contracted.[11] The liability of the B contributories is therefore further restricted, because they are liable only for such of the company's debts contracted before they ceased to be members as have not been satisfied by the distribution of the company's other assets among the creditors generally. The B contributories may therefore not be fully called upon although the creditors are not paid in full.

The liquidator made calls on the B contributories of 1s. a share in 1925, and 1s. 6d. a share in 1927. The amount so realised exceeded by about £10,000 the

---

[9] *Re Paragon Holdings Ltd.* [1961] Ch. 346.
[10] *Humby's Case* (1872) 26 L.T. 936.
[11] *Morris' Case* (1871) L.R. 7 Ch.App. 200.

debts of the company contracted while the B contributories were members but the total of all the calls did not suffice to pay the creditors in full. The liquidator asked to retain the full amount of the calls on the B contributories as assets available for the creditors. *Held,* he could not retain the full amount, but must return the £10,000 to the B contributories: *Re City of London Insce. Co. Ltd.* [1932] 1 Ch. 226.

B contributions are part of the general assets of the company, and are not to be applied, preferentially or exclusively, to the payment of debts incurred before the B shareholders ceased to be members.[12]

(3) B contributories are not liable to contribute unless it appears to the court that the existing members are unable to satisfy their contributions: section 212(1)(*c*).

It is uncertain whether the liability of a B contributory is fixed at the date of a call on him or at a later date.[13] Thus it is uncertain whether such liability would be reduced by the purchase, after a call has been made on him, of debts incurred by the company before he ceased to be a member.

A member cannot claim any dividend in competition with any other creditor not a member of the company: section 212(1)(*g*). For the purposes of section 212(1)(*g*) the word "member" includes a past member.[14] This provision has been held not to apply to dividends which have been carried to an account current between the company and a member.[15]

The liability of a contributory creates a debt (in England of the nature of a specialty) accruing at the time when his liability commenced, but payable when a call is made: section 214.

If a contributory dies either before or after he has been placed on the list of contributories, his personal representatives are liable. They are not personally liable; they are liable in their representative character. In England, if they make a default in payment, proceedings may be taken for administering the estate of the deceased: section 215.

If a contributory becomes bankrupt, his trustee in bankruptcy represents him for all the purposes of the winding up and is a contributory

---

[12] *Webb* v. *Whiffin* (1872) L.R. 5 H.L. 711.
[13] See *Re Apex Film Distributors Ltd.* [1960] Ch. 378 (C.A.).
[14] *Re Consolidated Goldfields of New Zealand Ltd.* [1953] Ch. 689.
[15] *Liquidator of Wilsons (Glasgow and Trinidad) Ltd.* v. *Wilson's Trustees,* 1915, 1 S.L.T. 424 (O.H.).

accordingly. Calls already made and the estimated value of the bankrupt's liability to future calls may be proved against the estate: section 216.[16]

There are special provisions as to the liability of B contributories where a company has re-registered under sections 43 or 44 of the 1967 Act or section 7 of the 1980 Act.[17]

Calls on contributories

In England calls on contributories are made by the liquidator with the leave of the court or the sanction of the committee of inspection: sections 260 and 273, and rule 86. In Scotland calls are made by the court: section 260.

Procedure on making calls in England (rr.86–90)[18]: The liquidator summons a meeting of the committee of inspection by at least seven days' notice stating the proposed amount of the call and the purpose for which it is intended. If the winding up is in the High Court, notice of the intended call and meeting is advertised in a London newspaper; in other cases, in a local newspaper. The advertisement must state that any contributory may attend the meeting and be heard, or make a communication in writing, with reference to the call. At the meeting any representations made by a contributory, either personally or in writing, must be heard. The sanction of the committee is given by resolution passed by a majority of the members present.

If there is no committee of inspection, the liquidator must obtain the leave of the court. Even if the committee has refused its sanction, the court may grant leave.[19] The application for leave is made by summons served at least four days before the day appointed for making the call on every contributory proposed to be included in the call, but, if the court directs, notice may instead be given by advertisement.

When the liquidator is authorised to make a call, he must file with the Registrar the document making the call. He must also serve on each contributory included in the call a copy of the resolution or order with a notice of the amount due from him.

Payment of the call may be enforced by order of the court, made in chambers on summons by the liquidator.

Calls may be made either before or after the insufficiency of the assets has been ascertained. They are made for an amount necessary to satisfy the debts and liabilities of the company, and the costs of winding

---

[16] On the interpretation of this provision, see, *ante*, p. 616, note 74.
[17] *Ante*, pp. 41, 42.
[18] For Scotland, see R.C. 212 and s.275.
[19] *Re North Eastern Insurance Co.* (1915) 85 L.J.Ch. 751.

up, and for adjustment of the rights of the contributories among themselves. In fixing the amount regard is had to the probability that some contributories may fail to pay the call: section 260.

A debt due from the company to a contributory cannot be set off against calls, whether made before or after the winding up,[20] except—

(1) where all the creditors have been paid in full (s.259); or
(2) in the case of an unlimited company, where the debt is due to him on an independent dealing with the company and not due to him as a member in respect of dividend or profit (s.259); or
(3) where the contributory is bankrupt.[21]

A contributory on the list may be ordered by the court, at any time after the making of a winding-up order, to pay any money due from him to the company: section 259.[22] The court can also order the arrest of, and seizure of the movable personal property of, a contributory believed to be about to abscond or to remove his property with the object of evading payment of calls: section 271.

CREDITORS

In the winding up of an *insolvent* English company the English bankruptcy rules apply with regard to (1) the respective rights of secured and unsecured creditors, (2) debts provable, and (3) the valuation of annuities and future and contingent liabilities: section 317.

It has been held that the bankruptcy provisions as to priority are applicable, including the provision as to limitation of interest to five per cent. in the Bankruptcy Act 1914, s.66(1).[23]

Section 317 has no application once the liquidation throws up a surplus, whatever may have been the position at the commencement of the winding up.[24]

---

[20] *Grissell's Case* (1866) L.R. 1 Ch.App. 528; *Cowan* v. *Gowans* (1878) 5 R. 581; this has been held to be so where a shareholder deposited money with the company against calls: *Millar* v. *Aikman* (1891) 28 S.L.R. 955 (O.H.).
[21] *Re Duckworth* (1867) L.R. 2 Ch.App. 578.
[22] The effect of s.259 dies with the company when it is dissolved: *Butler* v. *Broadhead* [1975] Ch. 97.
[23] *Re Theo Garvin Ltd.* [1969] 1 Ch. 624.
[24] *Re Rolls-Royce Co. Ltd.* [1974] 1 W.L.R. 1584, in which Pennycuick V.-C. said, at p. 1591: "I reach this conclusion with some regret . . . because . . . it seems fair that a creditor should be compensated for being kept out of his money during the period of administration . . . and, again, because the difference in this respect between the winding up provisions and the bankruptcy provisions appears to be without logical foundation."

In the winding up of an *insolvent*[25] Scottish company certain provisions of the Bankruptcy (Scotland) Act 1913, namely, sections 45[25a] to 62 (which relate to voting and ranking for payment of dividends), section 96 (as to reckoning of majorities), and section 105 (as to interruption of prescription) apply, so far as is consistent with the 1948 Act: s.318.

Secured creditors (England)

A secured creditor is one who holds some security for a debt due to him from the company, such as a mortgage, charge or lien. He must give credit for the realised or estimated value of his security unless he surrenders it. Thus he may—

(1) realise his security and prove, as an unsecured creditor, for any balance due to him after deducting the amount realised; or

(2) value his security and prove, as an unsecured creditor, for any balance due after deducting the value of the security; or

(3) surrender his security and prove, as an unsecured creditor, for the whole debt; or

(4) where he is fully secured, rely on his security and not prove at all.

A secured creditor who has realised his security for less than the total amount of his debt, part of which is preferential,[26] can appropriate the proceeds of sale to that part of his debt which is not preferential, so that he can prove for the preferential part.[27]

If a secured creditor has valued his security, the liquidator may (*a*) redeem the security at that value, or (*b*) require the security to be sold. The creditor may, on the other hand, serve notice in writing on the liquidator requiring him to elect whether or not he will exercise either of these powers, and if the liquidator does not within six months thereafter signify his intention to elect, he loses his right to exercise the powers: Bankruptcy Act 1914, Sched. 2.

---

[25] The word "insolvent" is implied from the general nature of the statutory provision: see *Collins' Trustees* v. *Borland & Co. Ltd.*, 1907 S.C. 1287.

[25a] As substituted by Insolvency Act 1976, s.5(3).

[26] *Post*, pp. 663 *et seq.*

[27] *Re William Hall (Contractors) Ltd.* [1967] 1 W.L.R. 948.

The liquidator may also, within 28 days after a proof, require the creditor to give up the security on payment of the estimated value with an addition of 20 per cent.: Companies (Winding-up) Rules 1949, r.142.

If the creditor has made a mistake in the valuation of his security, he may amend it by application to the court. If he subsequently realises his security, the amount realised must be substituted for the amount in the proof: Bankruptcy Act 1914, Sched. 2.

It, at a meeting of creditors, a secured creditor votes in respect of his whole debt, he will be deemed to have surrendered his security, unless the court is satisfied that the omission to value it was due to inadvertence: rule 141.

Secured creditors (Scotland)

The rules of the Bankruptcy (Scotland) Act 1913, relating to secured creditors, are to the same general effect as the rules applicable in England.

For the purpose of *voting,* a secured creditor must value his security, deduct that value from his debt and specify the balance. If the estate over which the security extends has been sold, he must specify his free proceeds, deduct them and specify the balance. In either case he is entitled to vote in respect of the balance and no more, except that in questions as to the disposal or management of the estate which is subject to his security he is entitled to vote as a creditor for the full amount of his debt: 1913 Act, s.55.

The liquidator within two months after the exercise of a secured creditor's vote, or the majority in value of the other creditors at a creditors' meeting, may require the creditor to convey the security to the liquidator on payment of the specified value with an addition of 20 per cent. The creditor may correct his valuation provided at least 21 days have elapsed since the claim was voted on and he has not been required to convey the security to the liquidator: 1913 Act, ss.58, 96.

For the purpose of *ranking for dividends,* a secured creditor must value his security, deduct that value from his debt and specify the balance, and the liquidator is entitled to a conveyance of the security on payment of the specified value, or to reserve to the creditor the full benefit of the security. In either case the creditor is ranked for and receives a dividend on the balance and no more: 1913 Act, s.61.

Proof of debts

If the company is *solvent*, all debts payable on a contingency, and all claims against the company, present or future, certain or contingent, ascertained or sounding only in damages, can be proved: section 316.

In other respects the law and procedure applicable depend on whether the company is registered in England or Scotland.

English companies

The debts which can be proved in a liquidation when the company is insolvent are all debts and liabilities, present or future, certain or contingent, owing at the date of the commencement of the liquidation, except demands in the nature of unliquidated damages arising otherwise than by reason of a contract, promise or breach of trust: section 317; Bankruptcy Act 1914, s.30.

If the company is solvent, a claim for unliquidated damages for tort may be proved; if the company is insolvent such a claim is not excluded at the commencement of the winding up but only if, when the claimant comes in to prove the claim, it has not been liquidated by judgment. If the claim does become liquidated the claimant may receive payment out of the undistributed assets but he cannot disturb prior distributions to creditors.[28] Statute-barred debts cannot be proved.[29]

If a debt is owed in foreign currency it must be paid at the rate of exchange prevailing at the commencement of the liquidation and not at the date of payment.[30]

Where there have been mutual credits, mutual debts or other mutual dealings between the company and one of its creditors, an account is taken of what is due from one to the other, and the balance of that account and no more can be claimed or paid; Bankruptcy Act 1914, s.31.

A Co. borrowed money from B Co. on the security of bills of sale charging some machinery and providing for its insurance against fire. The policies were in the name of B, and A paid the premiums. The machinery was destroyed by fire and the insurance amounting to £1,600 paid to B. A then went into liquidation. £744 was owing to B on the bills of sale at the date of the fire, so that B had £856 in hand, but A owed B £2,099 unsecured book debts. *Held*, B could set off the £856 against the £2,099: *Re H. E. Thorne & Son Ltd.* [1914] 2 Ch. 438.

---

[28] *Re Berkeley Securities (Property) Ltd.* [1980] 3 All E.R. 513.
[29] *Re Art Reproduction Co. Ltd.* [1952] Ch. 89; *Re Overmark Smith Warden Ltd.*, *The Times*, 22/3/82.   [30] *Re Lines Brothers* (1982) 126 S.J. 205 (C.A.).

The holder of a life policy in an assurance company mortgaged the policy to the issuing company. On the company's going into liquidation the policy holder claimed to set off the value of the policy against his mortgage debt. *Held,* he was entitled to do so: *Re City Life Assurance Co. Ltd.* [1926] Ch. 191.

This statutory set-off cannot be excluded by agreement between the parties.[31]

A person is not entitled to set off against the property of a debtor where he had, when he gave credit to the debtor, notice of an available act of bankruptcy by the debtor: Bankruptcy Act 1914, s.31. The publication of notice of a meeting of creditors of a company under section 293[32] is analogous to the filing of a declaration of inability to pay debts under the bankruptcy legislation.[33]

How debts are proved (rr.91–118): The liquidator must fix a time within which creditors must prove their claims or be excluded from the benefit of any distribution made before those debts are proved.[34] The time fixed must be not less than 14 days from the date of the notice. The time must be advertised in a newspaper and notice given to every creditor whose claim has not been admitted, and to every preferential creditor whose preferential claim has not been admitted.

Proof is made by delivering or posting to the liquidator a claim to the debt or, if the liquidator so requires, an affidavit verifying the debt and (1) giving particulars of the debt and any vouchers by which it can be substantiated, and (2) stating whether the creditor is or is not a secured creditor. The liquidator must then examine the proof and within 28 days must in writing admit or reject it or require further evidence in support of it. If he rejects it, he must state in writing the grounds of his rejection, and the creditor may then, within 21 days, appeal to the court. On an application to reverse a decision of the liquidator in rejecting a proof, the court must approach the question *de novo,* and decide the claimant's rights in the light of the evidence before it, *i.e.* the court is not bound merely to express a view as to whether the liquidator was right or wrong.[35]

If a proof has been improperly admitted, the court may, on the application of the liquidator, a creditor or a contributory, and after notice to the creditor, expunge the proof or reduce its amount.

The liquidator must, on the first day of every month, file with the Registrar a list of all proofs he has received in the preceding month, distinguishing

[31] *Rolls Razor Ltd.* v. *Cox* [1967] 1 Q.B. 552 (C.A.).
[32] *Post,* p. 691.
[33] *Re Eros Films Ltd.* [1963] Ch. 565.
[34] Ss.264, 273. "Distribution" in r.106 includes a distribution to contributories: *Butler* v. *Broadhead* [1975] Ch.D. 97.
[35] *Re Kentwood Constructions Ltd.* [1960] 1 W.L.R. 646.

between those admitted, those rejected, and those standing over. Proofs admitted or rejected must be filed with the Registrar.

If, where the liquidator has advertised for claims, a creditor, whether it is his fault or not, does not put in a claim, then he is barred under section 264 and rule 106, *ante.* There is no room for the application of the principle in *Ministry of Health* v. *Simpson* [1951] A.C. 251.[36]

Scottish companies

Certain provisions of the Bankruptcy (Scotland) Act 1913, *ante,*[37] apply when the company is insolvent.

A creditor, if he is to be entitled to vote or draw a dividend, must produce at the meeting or to the liquidator the account and vouchers necessary to prove the debt, and either—

(*a*) a notice of claim in the form prescribed by the Notice of Claim (Scotland) Regulations 1977[38];
or

(*b*) in any case in which the liquidator so requires, an oath as to the verity of the debt and stating what other persons, if any, are, besides the company, liable for the debt; and also specifying any security which he holds: 1913 Act, s.45, as substituted by Insolvency Act 1976.

When the creditor's claim depends on a contingency which is unascertained at the date when the claim is lodged, the creditor may require the liquidator to put a value on the claim, and the creditor is then entitled to vote and draw dividends in respect of that value; otherwise such a creditor is not entitled to vote or draw a dividend: 1913 Act, s.49.

The court may fix a time within which creditors must prove their claims or be excluded from the benefit of any distribution made before those debts are proved: 1948 Act, s.264. They may, however, participate in later distributions.[39]

If a creditor's oath or claim is in some respect defective, the court or the liquidator must call upon the person concerned to rectify it, and if it is not rectified it must be disallowed. Where, however, the defect is due

[36] *Butler* v. *Broadhead* [1975] Ch.D. 97.
[37] p. 657.
[38] S.I. 1977 No. 1495.
[39] *Dickey* v. *Ballantine*, 1939 S.C. 783 (O.H.).

to some improper or fraudulent purpose or where other creditors would suffer loss as a result, an opportunity for rectification need not be given: 1913 Act, s.47.

Appeals against any deliverance by a liquidator on claims to vote and rank are made by note of appeal and must normally be presented to the appropriate court within seven days of the liquidator's deliverance: R.C. 214.

Order of application of assets

The effect of section 319 is that in a winding up the assets of the company are applicable in the following order:

(1) Costs, charges and expenses properly incurred in the winding up, including the remuneration of the liquidator.
(2) The preferential creditors.
(3) The other (ordinary) unsecured creditors.

Subject to what is said later about debts secured by floating charges being postponed to the winding-up costs and preferential unsecured debts, secured creditors may pay themselves out of their security and, as to any balance remaining unpaid, rank as ordinary or preferential unsecured creditors.[40]

In the event of the assets being insufficient to satisfy the liabilities, the court may make an order for payment of the costs, charges and expenses in such order of priority as it thinks just: section 267.

In England priority is regulated by the Companies (Winding-up) Rules 1949, rule 195.

Unless the court orders otherwise, the order of priority is:

(*a*) Fees and expenses properly incurred in preserving, realising or getting in the assets.
(*b*) Costs of the *petition*[41] including costs of those appearing on the petition whose costs are allowed by the court.[42]
(*c*) Remuneration of the special manager (if any).

---

[40] *Ante*, p. 658. See, *e.g. Re Mesco Properties* [1980] 1 W.L.R. 96.
[41] See *Re Bostels* [1968] Ch. 346.
[42] In *Re Bathampton Properties Ltd.* [1976] 1 W.L.R. 168 the company's costs were increased by its unsuccessful and unjustifiable opposition to the petition, and only its costs down to and including the first hearing, when it could have consented, were paid out of the assets.

(*d*) Costs and expenses of any person who makes the company's statement of affairs.

(*e*) Charges of a shorthand writer appointed to take an examination.

(*f*) Disbursements of the liquidator.

(*g*) Costs of any person properly employed by the liquidator.

(*h*) Remuneration of the liquidator.

(*i*) Expenses of the committee of inspection, if approved by the Department of Trade.

Where the company is a lessee, rent accrued due after the winding-up order is an expense of the liquidation if the liquidator retained the lease solely for the benefit of the liquidation, and not for the joint benefit of himself and the lessors.[43]

The winding-up costs have priority over the preferential debts and the claims of debenture holders under a floating charge and if necessary are paid out of property subject to the charge.[44] However, if a floating charge crystallised prior to the winding-up order it takes priority over the costs of the liquidation and is merely postponed to the preferred creditors under section 94.[45]

In Scotland there are no fixed rules corresponding to rule 195, above, it being left to the court, in the exercise of its discretion under section 267, to give such priority as it "thinks just" in the circumstances of each case.[46]

The *preferential debts* rank equally among themselves and must be paid in full, in priority to the other unsecured debts, unless the assets are insufficient to meet them, in which case the preferential debts abate in equal proportions: section 319(5)(*a*).

By section 319 (1) the preferential debts include:

(*a*) Rates and value added tax[47] which became payable by the company within 12 months next before the relevant date.

---

[43] *Re A.B.C. Coupler & Engineering Co. Ltd.* (*No.* 3) [1970] 1 W.L.R. 702; and see *Re Downer Enterprises Ltd.* [1974] 1 W.L.R. 1460, where an intermediate lessee paid the arrears of rent and was held entitled to the lessor's rights by way of subrogation.

[44] *Re Barleycorn Enterprises Ltd.* [1970] Ch. 465 (C.A.).

[45] *Re Christonette International Ltd.* [1982] 1 W.L.R. 1245.

[46] See *The Northern Distilleries Ltd.* (1901) 9 S.L.T. 213 (O.H.); *Edinburgh Pavilion Ltd.* (1906) 14 S.L.T. 61 (O.H.); *Robertson* v. *Drummond* (1908) 15 S.L.T. 1067 (O.H.).

[47] Finance Act 1972, s.41 and Finance Act 1976, s.22.

The expression "the relevant date" means, when the company is being wound up compulsorily, the date of the appointment of a provisional liquidator or, if no such appointment was made, the date of the winding-up order; if the company is or was being wound up voluntarily, it means the date of the passing of the resolution for winding up: section 319(8).

> (*b*) *Any* one year's assessment of assessed tax, *e.g.* corporation tax, assessed up to April 5 next before the relevant date.

Apart from these provisions as to taxes, Crown debts have no priority.[48] The Crown's priority is not limited to tax assessed in the year immediately before the winding up; the Crown may claim priority for any one year before that date.[49]

The Crown can choose different years for different preferential debts.

A company in a creditors' voluntary liquidation owed income tax and profits tax, so that any one year's arrears of each was a preferential debt. *Held,* the Inland Revenue Commissioners could choose one year's arrears in the case of the income tax and a different year's arrears in the case of the profits tax: *Lord Advocate* v. *Liquidators of Purvis Industries Ltd.,* 1958 S.C. 338 (O.H.).

> (*c*) Wages or salary (whether or not earned wholly or partly by way of commission) of a clerk or servant in respect of services rendered to the company within four months next before the relevant date, not exceeding £800[50] per claimant (subs. (2)).[51]

In England a full-time secretary is a "clerk or servant,"[52] but in Scotland a secretary, *semble* even if full-time, is not.[53] A managing director[54] is not a "clerk or servant," nor is a director as such. However, a director may, under power in the articles, be employed in a

---

[48] *Food Controller* v. *Cork* [1923] A.C. 647.
[49] *Re Pratt* [1951] Ch. 225.
[50] Substituted for £200 by the Insolvency Act 1976, s.1 and Sched. 1.
[51] These include other sums payable to employees by virtue of s.121 of the Employment Protection (Consolidation) Act 1978.
[52] *Cairney* v. *Back* [1906] 2 K.B. 746.
[53] *Scottish Poultry Journal Co.* (1896) 4 S.L.T. 167 (O.H.) (secretary and manager); *Clyde Football etc. Co. Ltd.* (1900) 8 S.L.T. 328 (O.H.); *Laing* v. *Gowans* (1902) 10 S.L.T. 461 (O.H.).
[54] *Re Newspaper Proprietary Syndicate Ltd.* [1900] 2 Ch. 349, although see Wallace & Young, *Australian Company Law & Practice*, pp. 798, 799.

salaried position with the company and so be a clerk or servant. Thus, where a director could be, and was, employed as editor of a periodical, he was a preferential creditor.[55]

A chemist engaged two days a week at a salary to work on formulae for perfumiers is a "clerk or servant."[56] A contributor, even a regular contributor, to a newspaper, even though paid by a fixed salary, is not.[57]

(*d*) Wages of a workman or labourer for services rendered within four months next before the relevant date, not exceeding £800[58] per claimant (subs. (2)).

(*e*) Accrued holiday remuneration payable to a clerk, servant, workman or labourer on the termination of his employment before or by the effect of the winding-up order or resolution.

(*f*) All the debts specified in section 153(2) of the Social Security Act 1975 and Schedule 3 of the Social Security Pensions Act 1975, *e.g.* national insurance contributions payable by the company as an employer within 12 months next before the relevant date, unless the winding up is a voluntary winding up for the purposes of reconstruction or amalgamation.[59]

Advances made by a third person to pay the wages or salary of any clerk, servant, workman or labourer employed by the company have the same priority as the persons whose wages are paid out of the money advanced: section 319(4). It is not necessary to prove that the advance of money was made in pursuance of any agreement if it was in fact made for the purpose of paying wages.[60]

A bank met cheques drawn by the company on its overdrawn wages account. *Held*, (1) the bank was advancing money for the purpose of paying wages and the resulting indebtedness was preferential under section 319(4), and cheques drawn on current account in favour of wages account transferred

[55] *Re Beeton & Co. Ltd.* [1913] 2 Ch. 279.
[56] *Re G.H. Morison & Co. Ltd.* (1912) 106 L.T. 731.
[57] See note 55 above.
[58] See note 50 above.
[59] The Department of Health and Social Security may also recover this money from the directors personally: *Re J. Burrows (Leeds) Ltd.* (1982) 126 S.J. 227.
[60] *Re Primrose (Builders) Ltd.* [1950] Ch. 561, where an advance by the bank for paying wages was made on current account on the bank's being satisfied that an amount equal to the advance would shortly be paid in. *Held*, the advance was preferential. See also *Re Rampgill Mill Ltd.* [1967] Ch. 1138, where the bank did not make it a condition of an advance that it should be so satisfied.

part of such indebtedness to current account; (2) the rule in *Clayton's* case applied to sums credited to current account so as to discharge the earliest of the debits on such account: *Re James R. Rutherford & Sons Ltd.* [1964] 1 W.L.R. 1211.

A "labour only" contract between a company and a sub-contractor is not a contract of employment for the purposes of section 319(4) and so advances by a third person to enable the company to pay the sub-contractor are not entitled to priority.[61]

So far as the assets of the company available for payment of general creditors are insufficient to meet them, the preferential debts have priority over the claims of debenture holders under a floating charge[62] created by the company and are paid out of any property subject to the charge: section 319(5)(*b*); Companies (Floating Charges) (Scotland) Act 1961, s.7(*b*).

In England if a landlord or other person has distrained on the company's goods within three months next before a winding-up order, the preferential debts are a first charge on the goods or the proceeds of the distress. The landlord or other person, however, has the same priority as the persons paid out of the proceeds: section 319(7).

If the court is to interfere with the rights of a person seeking to complete distress, there must be some inequitable conduct on the part of such person, and where a collector of taxes, relying on his right of distress under the Taxes Management Act 1970, distrained on the goods of a company for unpaid national insurance contributions, and had taken possession prior to the date of winding up, he was entitled to complete distress by sale and the fact that he obtained priority over other preferential creditors was not sufficient to justify the court's interference.[63]

The ordinary debts rank and abate equally *inter se*.[64]

It may be mentioned here that a sum of money paid into a company's bank account for behoof of the company's employees and which is at the date of the liquidation "clearly distinguishable and capable of being disentangled from the company's own funds" does not form part of the company's assets but must be paid to the employees.[65]

---

[61] *Re C. W. & A. L. Hughes Ltd.* [1966] 1 W.L.R. 1369.

[62] *Ante*, pp. 567, 571.

[63] *Re Herbert Berry Associates Ltd.* [1977] 1 W.L.R. 1437 (C.A.), where the winding up was a creditors' voluntary winding up.

[64] *Per* Lord Selbourne in *Black & Co.'s Case* (1872) L.R. 8 Ch. 254, at p. 262.

[65] *Smith* v. *Liquidator of James Birrell Ltd.*, 1968 S.L.T. 174 (O.H.).

Where a company fails to implement an agreement to purchase its shares under section 46 of the 1981 Act[66] or to redeem its shares under section 45 of that Act,[67] and the company subsequently goes into liquidation the vendor/shareholder may enforce the agreement as a creditor. This will not apply, however, if at any time between the date for purchase or redemption and the commencement of the winding up the company could not have fulfilled its obligation out of distributable profits.[68] In any event the amount so claimed is a deferred debt—paid after all other creditors and even preference shareholders if the shares in question are not preferred[69]: 1981 Act, s.59.

---

[66] *Ante*, p. 245.
[67] *Ante*, p. 244.
[68] *Ante*, p. 532.
[69] *Ante*, p. 248.

CHAPTER 28

COMPLETION OF WINDING UP BY THE COURT

WHEN the liquidator has collected the assets and received the proofs of the creditors, he proceeds to divide the assets among the creditors.

Procedure on declaring dividends (England): Not more than two months before declaring a dividend the liquidator must give notice to (1) the Department of Trade so that it can be gazetted, and (2) such of the creditors mentioned in the statement of affairs as have not proved. The notice must state the latest date up to which proofs must be lodged, which must be not less than 14 days from the date of the notice. A creditor wishing to appeal against the rejection of a proof must do so within seven days from the date of the notice. Immediately after the time for appealing has expired, the liquidator declares a dividend and gives notice to the Department of Trade, so that they can gazette it and to each creditor whose proof has been admitted. If it becomes necessary to postpone the declaration of a dividend beyond the limit of two months, the liquidator must give a fresh notice of his intention to declare a dividend to the Department of Trade but need not give notice to the creditors.

When a dividend is declared the liquidator must transmit a list of the proofs filed with the Registrar to the Department of Trade.

Dividends may at the request and risk of the person to whom they are payable be transmitted to him by post: rule 119.

Procedure on declaring dividends (Scotland): For the provisions of the Bankruptcy (Scotland) Act 1913 which apply, see *ante*, p. 658. See also R.C. 214.

If there is any surplus after the costs of the liquidation and the company's debts have been paid, the court must adjust the rights of the contributories among themselves and distribute any surplus among the persons entitled thereto: section 265. The section requires a court order before the liquidator can distribute surplus assets, whether or not an adjustment has to be made among the contributories.[1] It will be remembered that under normal articles preference shareholders are entitled to priority over ordinary shareholders in the return of capital.[2]

In England the order by which the liquidator is authorised to return capital to contributories contains a list of the names and addresses of

---

[1] *Re Phoenix Oil, etc., Co. Ltd. (No.2)* [1958] Ch. 565, where a list of contributories was dispensed with and the register of members was seven years out of date.

[2] *Ante*, p. 210.

the persons to whom the return is to be made, the amount payable to each, and particulars of any variation in the list of contributories which has arisen since the list of contributories was settled: rule 120.

For tax purposes a distribution on a winding up does not count as income of the shareholder who receives it, whether it consists of a return of capital or a share in surplus assets.[3]

If the liquidation is not completed within a year after its commencement, the liquidator must send to the Registrar of Companies, at such intervals as may be prescribed, a statement in the prescribed form and giving prescribed particulars as to the position of the liquidation: section 342. A copy of this statement can be inspected and sealed copies or extracts obtained: section 426 of the 1948 Act as amended by Schedules 2 and 3 to the 1976 Act and section 98 of the 1981 Act.

In the case of a company being wound up in England, if the liquidator has in his hands or under his control for six months money representing unclaimed or undistributed assets of the company, he must pay it into the Insolvency Services Account at the Bank of England. Any person entitled to the money may then apply to the Department of Trade, and the Department may, if the liquidator certifies accordingly, make an order for payment: section 343, as amended by Schedule 2 to the Insolvency Act 1976. The Insolvency Services Account is regulated by section 3 of the Insolvency Act 1976 and replaces the former Companies Liquidation Account.

In the case of a Scottish company, when the company has been wound up and is about to be dissolved, the liquidator must lodge in a joint stock bank of issue in Scotland in the name of the Accountant of Court all unclaimed dividends and unapplied or undistributable balances, and the deposit receipts for these sums must be sent to the Accountant. Within seven years the Accountant, if satisfied of a claimant's right, must grant him a warrant upon which the bank pays the amount due including any interest which has accrued. On the expiry of seven years from the deposit, the Accountant must hand over the receipt to the Secretary of State for Scotland, who then obtains from the bank payment of the whole remaining amount on behalf of the Crown: 1948 Act, s.344; Bankruptcy (Scotland) Act 1913, s.153; S.I. 1974 No. 1274.

---

[3] See *Pinson, op. cit.*, para. 14–40.

Dissolution of company

When the affairs of the company have been completely wound up, the court, if the liquidator makes an application in that behalf, must make an order that the company be dissolved. The liquidator must, within 14 days, send a copy of the order to the Registrar of Companies, who must make a minute of the dissolution in his books (s.274) and cause notice of the receipt by him of the order to be published in the *Gazette* (European Communities Act 1972, s.9(3)). However, because of the expense involved in an application to the court, the modern practice is for the liquidator not to apply for a dissolution order under section 274, but to apply to the Registrar to dissolve the company by striking its name off the register under section 353, *post*. After the liquidator is released under section 251 (which does not apply to Scotland), the Registrar waits two years before striking the company off. The idea is to minimise the possibility of striking off being prejudicial.

The Jenkins Report[4] recommended that a simple and inexpensive means of formally dissolving companies wound up by the court—on the lines of sections 290 and 300, *post*[5]—should be provided.

Subject to any order which may at any time be made by the court under section 352 or section 353, as qualified by section 108 of the 1981 Act, any property vested in or held on trust for a company immediately before its dissolution (excluding property held by the company on trust for any other person) vests in the Crown as *bona vacantia*: section 354. The Crown may disclaim such property by a notice signed in the case of property in England by the Treasury Solicitor (and in the case of property in Scotland by the Secretary of State for Scotland). The effect of such disclaimer is much the same as if the property had been disclaimed under section 323, *ante*.[6] The notice of disclaimer must be executed within 12 months after the vesting of the property came to the notice of the Treasury Solicitor or the Secretary of State for Scotland or, where any person interested in the property applies in writing to the Treasury Solicitor or the Secretary of State for Scotland requiring him to decide whether he will disclaim, usually within three months after

---

[4] Para. 503.
[5] *Post*, pp. 690, 693.
[6] p. 644; s.323 is not applicable to Scotland but, for the purposes of s.355, is deemed to be so.

the application. The notice of disclaimer must be delivered to the Registrar of Companies and registered by him, and copies must be published in the *Gazette* and sent to persons who have given the Treasury Solicitor or the Secretary of State for Scotland notice of their interest in the property: section 355 (S.I. 1974 No. 1274).

Where a company has been dissolved the court may, within two years, make an order declaring the dissolution void. Such an order may be made on the application of the liquidator or of any other person who appears to the court to be interested: section 352. An order may be made after two years if the application is made within two years.[7] A solicitor acting on behalf of a client with a claim against the dissolved company, and having neither a financial nor a proprietary interest, is not a "person . . . interested" within section 352.[8] A liquidator de son tort, *i.e.* a person who has never been a duly appointed liquidator of the company but who has, without lawful authority, been carrying on the liquidation of the company, is.[9] So too is a contributory in the liquidation.[10] The Inland Revenue may apply where an assessment for taxes has been made but the assessments were under appeal when the company was struck off the register under section 353, *post*.[11]

When a dissolution is declared void, any property of the company which vested in the Crown under section 354 remains the Crown's property. Instead the company will receive a cash payment equivalent to those assets. This payment will be equivalent to either the sum the Crown received or the value of any property which has since been disposed of by the Crown. This provision allows the Crown to dispose of such property without fear of a revival of the company: 1981 Act, section 108. An office copy of the order declaring the dissolution void must be delivered to the Registrar of Companies within seven days: section 352. Such an order does not validate proceedings taken on behalf of the company between the dissolution and its avoidance.[12]

---

[7] *Re Scad Ltd.* [1941] Ch. 386, approved of *obiter* in *Dowling, Petitioner,* 1960 S.L.T. (Notes) 76 (O.H.).
[8] *Re Roehampton Swimming Pool Ltd.* [1968] 1. W.L.R. 1693.
[9] *Re Wood and Martin (Bricklaying Contractors) Ltd.* [1971] 1 W.L.R. 293.
[10] *Re Thompson & Riches Ltd.* [1981] 2 All E.R. 477.
[11] *Re Belmont & Co. Ltd.* [1952] Ch. 10; followed in *Re Test Holdings (Clifton) Ltd.* [1970] Ch. 285. The Inland Revenue can also apply under s.353(6), *post*: *Re Avondale Hotel Southport Ltd.* (1951) (unreported).
[12] *Morris v. Harris* [1927] A.C. 252.

Thus it does not revive a misfeasance summons issued, but not served, before dissolution.[13]

It is incompetent for the court to declare the dissolution void for a limited purpose only.[14]

Grounds for declaring a dissolution void are that there are unsatisfied claims by creditors,[15] or the discovery of undistributed assets such as a sum wrongly paid to the Inland Revenue,[16] or to enable the liquidator to grant a title to property of the company sold since the dissolution.[17]

> A testatrix by her will gave a share of her residuary estate to a company but the company was dissolved before she died. An order under section 352 was refused because the share of residue did not belong to the company before dissolution. The next of kin therefore took the lapsed share as on a partial intestacy: *Re Servers of the Blind League* [1960] 1 W.L.R. 564.

Relief will not be granted automatically whenever a petitioner comes within section 352(1). The court has an absolute discretion and the petiton may be opposed, *e.g.* by the Official Receiver or the Treasury Solicitor. The delay between the dissolution and the petition is another factor in the court's exercise of its discretion.[18]

In very special circumstances the Court of Session in the exercise of its *nobile officium* may declare a dissolution void, although the application has not been made within the two years.[19]

DEFUNCT COMPANIES

By section 353, if the Registrar of Companies has reasonable cause to believe that a company is not carrying on business or is not in operation, he may, after carrying out a specified procedure, strike the company's name off the register, after which it is dissolved and sections 354 and 355, *ante*, apply.

---

[13] *Re Lewis & Smart Ltd.* [1954] 1 W.L.R. 755.

[14] *Champdany Jute Co. Ltd., Petitioners*, 1924 S.C. 209 (for the purpose of receiving a repayment from the Inland Revenue).

[15] *Re Spottiswoode, Dixon and Hunting Ltd.* [1912] 1 Ch. 410.

[16] *Champdany* case, *ante*.

[17] *M'Call & Stephen Ltd., Petitioners* (1920) 57 S.L.R. 480.

[18] *Per* Slade J. in *Re Thompson & Riches Ltd.* [1981] 2 All E.R. 477, 483.

[19] *Collins Brothers & Co. Ltd., Petitioners*, 1916 S.C. 620. Contrast *Kerr (Lord Macdonald's Curator Bonis) and Another, Petitioners*, 1924 S.C. 163, and *Forth Shipbreaking Co. Ltd., Petitioners*, 1924 S.C. 489.

The procedure under section 353 is:

(1) The Registrar sends to the company by post a letter asking whether the company is carrying on business.
(2) If no answer is received within one month, he sends within the next 14 days a registered letter, stating that if no reply is received within one month a notice will be published in the *Gazette* with a view to striking the company's name off the register.
(3) If no satisfactory reply is received he sends to the company by post and publishes in the *Gazette* a notice, stating that unless cause is shown to the contrary the company will be struck off after three months.
(4) If cause is not shown to the contrary, he strikes the company off and publishes notice thereof in the *Gazette*, whereupon the company is dissolved.

Striking the company's name off the register does not affect the liability of any director or member of the company, and the company may still be wound up by the court. If the company is to be wound up, it should first be restored to the register under section 353(6).[20]

Section 353(6) provides that if the company, or any member or creditor thereof, feels aggrieved by the striking off the register, it or he may, within 20 years, apply[21] to the court which, if satisfied that it is just that the company be revived, may order that the name of the company be restored to the register. A petition for restoration under section 353(6) should contain an outline explanation of why the company was struck off.[22] Upon an office copy of the order being delivered to the Registrar the company is deemed to have continued in existence as if its name had not been struck off. The court may, by the order, give directions for placing the company and all other persons in the same position as nearly as may be as if the company had not been struck off. This provision should be compared with section 352, *ante*, as to the persons who may apply for a court order and as to what the court may do by an order. A contributory may apply under either section although the time limits are different; 20 years under section 353(6) and two years under section 352(1).[23] The word "creditor" in subsection (6) extends to a plaintiff claiming damages under the Fatal Acci-

---

[20] *Re Cambridge Coffee Room Association Ltd.* [1952] 1 All E.R. 112. *Alliance Heritable Security Co. Ltd., Petitioners* (1886) 14 R. 34; *Beith Unionist Association Trustees, Petitioners*, 1950 S.C. 1.
[21] By petition: R.S.C., O. 102, r.5; R.C. 190.
[22] Practice Note (Companies Court) [1974] 1. W.L.R. 1459.
[23] *Re Thompson & Riches Ltd.* [1981] 2 All E.R. 477.

dents Acts 1846 to 1959, and having therefore an unqualified claim against the company.[24] The subsection does not authorise the insertion of such a clause as would put a creditor in the same position towards other parties as if the company *had* been struck off.[25]

To qualify as a "member or creditor" within section 353(6) an applicant for restoration must have been a member or creditor of the company at the date when it was dissolved.[26] However, the personal representative of a deceased shareholder has been held entitled to apply for restoration of a company's name to the register, and then for its winding up, even though he is not registered as a shareholder.[27]

On an application for restoration to the register, the court may only restore or refuse to restore and cannot, *e.g.* impose a penalty (beyond costs) as a condition of restoration.[28] It may, however, make the restoration conditional on the company's filing such statutory returns with the Registrar as are necessary to bring the company's file up to date.[29]

The restoration of the company to the register under section 353(6) validates retrospectively all acts done on behalf of the company between its dissolution and its restoration.[30] This should be compared with the effect of an order under section 352, *ante.* In one English case, where the petition was that of a contributory and there were assets available for the shareholders or creditors, as the case might be, the court directed that, as regards creditors whose debts were not statute–barred at the date of dissolution, the period between dissolution and restoration to the register was not to be counted for the purposes of any Statute of Limitations.[31] Where, *e.g.* a creditor peti-

---

[24] *Re Harvest Lane Motor Bodies Ltd.* [1969] 1 Ch. 457.
[25] *Re Lindsay Bowman Ltd.* [1969] 1 W.L.R. 1443, not following *Re Rugby Auto Electric Services* (No. 00973 of 1959 (December 14, 1959) unreported).
[26] *Re New Timbiqui Gold Mines Ltd.* [1961] Ch. 319.
[27] *Re Bayswater Trading Co. Ltd.* [19701] 1 W.L.R. 343.
[28] *Re Brown Bayley's Steel Works Ltd.* (1905) 21 T.L.R. 374; *Re Moses and Cohen Ltd.* [1957] 1 W.L.R. 1007.
[29] *Healy, Petitioner* (1903) 5 F. 644, followed in *Charles Dale Ltd., Petitioners,* 1927 S.C. 130.
[30] *Tymans Ltd.* v. *Craven* [1952] 2 Q.B. 100 (C.A.), applied in *Re Boxco Ltd.* [1970] Ch. 442 (Legal charge created by company after being struck off. Order for restoration made. Company put in same position retrospectively as if charge duly created and registered).
[31] *Re Donald Kenyon Ltd.* [1956] 1 W.L.R. 1397. *Aliter* where the company is already in liquidation: *Re Vickers & Bott Ltd.* [1968] 2 All E.R. 264n.

tions and there is no indication that other creditors might be unfairly affected by an order not containing a special provision as to the limitation of actions, no such provision will be inserted in the order.[32] In so far as the property of the company has passed to the Crown under section 354, *ante*, the provisions of section 108 of the 1981 Act apply and the Crown may validly dispose of those assets paying a cash sum in lieu on the company's revival, *ante*.

Where the company is in breach of its statutory obligations and at least one applicant is guilty of some default, the normal order for taxation of costs under R.S.C. Order 62, rule 28, should be on a common fund basis (instead of the usual order on a party and party basis).[33]

The Jenkins Report[34] recommended that the court be empowered, on application by the Registrar, to order a company to be struck off the register and dissolved where winding up would not be appropriate. It appears that in one case a company had no assets and its managing director was in receipt of National Assistance but section 353 was not applicable.

THE LIQUIDATOR IN A WINDING UP BY THE COURT

The liquidator in a winding up by the court is an officer of the court.[35]

Appointment

The liquidator is appointed in the manner set out in Chapter 26.[36]

Apart from the necessity for giving security, there is no statutory requirement as to his qualifications. A body corporate cannot be appointed liquidator: section 335. Subject to section 335, a liquidator's acts are valid notwithstanding any defects which may afterwards be discovered in his appointment or qualification: section 242.

The court may appoint as liquidator a person resident beyond the

---

[32] *Re Huntingdon Poultry Ltd.* [1969] 1 W.L.R. 204, distinguishing *Re Donald Kenyon, ante,* and *Re Rugby Auto Electric Services Ltd., ante.*
[33] *Re Court Lodge Development Co. Ltd.* [1973] 1 W.L.R. 1097.
[34] Para. 511.
[35] *Per* Megarry J. in *Re Rolls Razor Ltd. (No. 2)* [1970] Ch. 576, 586.
[36] p. 630.

jurisdiction of the court but such an appointment is made only where there is adequate reason.[37]

It is no objection to the appointment of a person as liquidator that he has been a director,[38] the secretary[39] or the auditor[40] of the company, but where there are to be joint liquidators it is not desirable, at least where creditors object, that both should be connected with the company.[40]

Anyone who is subject to a disqualification order under section 188 as amended by section 93 of the 1981 Act, or section 9 of the Insolvency Act 1976, as amended by section 94 of the 1981 Act, cannot act as a liquidator.[41]

Any person who gives, or agrees or offers to give, any member or creditor of the company any valuable consideration with a view to securing his own appointment or nomination, or to securing or preventing the appointment or nomination of someone else, as the liquidator, is liable to a fine: section 336.

Resignation

A liquidator may resign before the completion of the liquidation: section 242.

In England resignation is effected by summoning meetings of the creditors and contributories to receive the resignation. If both meetings, by ordinary resolutions, agree to accept the resignation, the liquidator files a memorandum with the Registrar and gives notice to the Official Receiver, and his resignation thereupon becomes effective. If either of the meetings does not accept the resignation, the liquidator reports to the court the result of the meetings and sends a report to the Official Receiver, and the court, on application by the liquidator or the Official Receiver, decides whether or not the resignation shall be accepted; rule 167.

In Scotland leave to resign was granted to an official liquidator where it was stated that there was nothing to recover from the estate,

---

[37] *Brightwen & Co.* v. *City of Glasgow Bank* (1878) 6 R. 244 (appointment as joint liquidator of accountant resident in London refused); see also *Barberton Development etc. Ltd., Petitioners* (1898), 25 R. 654, and contrast *Liquidators of Bruce Peebles & Co. Ltd.* v. *Shiells*, 1908 S.C. 692.

[38] *Liquidators of Bruce Peebles* case, *ante*; *Sanderson & Muirhead and ors., Petitioners* (1884), 21 S.L.R. 766.

[39] *Gilmour's Trustees* v. *Kilmarnock, etc., Investment Co. Ltd.* (1883) 10 R. 1221.

[40] *Argylls Ltd.* v. *Ritchie & Whiteman*, 1914 S.C. 915.

[41] *Ante*, p. 332.

and the liquidator's application was concurred in by substantially all the creditors and was unopposed.[42]

Removal

A liquidator may, on cause shown, be removed by the court: section 242. Grounds on which a liquidator may be removed include personal unfitness (due to, e.g. his character, his residence,[43] or his personal interest or involvement[44]), insanity,[45] prosecuting a claim against the wishes of a majority of the creditors where the company is insolvent,[46] or unwillingness to prosecute a claim, which should have been prosecuted, against directors with whom he was intimate.

"The words 'on cause shown' have not quite the effect of 'if the Court shall think fit.' Jessel M.R. said in *In re Sir John Moore Gold Mining Co.*,[47] 'they point to some unfitness of the person—it may be from personal character, or from his connection with other parties, or from circumstances in which he is mixed up—some unfitness in a wide sense of the term.' But, as pointed out by the Court of Appeal in *In re Adam Eyton, Ld.*,[48] this definition was not intended to be exhaustive, and if the Court is satisfied on the evidence that it is desirable in the interests of all those interested in the assets that a particular person shall not manage the assets, the Court has power to remove him, without there being shown any personal misconduct or unfitness."[49]

Cause must be shown: the court will not remove a liquidator merely because he is a shareholder and former director,[50] or because the majority of the creditors or of the contributories desire it.[51]

A vacancy in the office of liquidator appointed by the court is filled by the court: section 242.

Remuneration

A person other than the Official Receiver who is appointed liquidator is remunerated as the court directs: section 242.

[42] *Jamieson, Petitioner* (1877) 14 S.L.R. 667.
[43] *Skinner, Petitioner* (1899) 6 S.L.T. 388 (O.H.) (residence in England of sole liquidator).
[44] *Lysons v. Liquidator of the Miraflores Gold Syndicate Ltd.* (1895) 22 R. 605.
[45] *Re The North Molton Mining Co. Ltd.* (1886) 54 L.T. 602.
[46] *Re Tavistock Ironworks Co.* (1871) 24 L.T. 605.
[47] (1879) 12 Ch.D. 325 (C.A.) at p. 331.   [48] (1887) 36 Ch.D. 299 (C.A.).
[49] *Per Astbury J. in Re Rubber etc. Investment Trust* [1915] 1 Ch. 382, at p. 387; *Lyson's* case and *Skinner's* case, *ante*.
[50] *M'Knight & Co. Ltd. v. Montgomerie* (1892) 19 R. 501.
[51] *Ker, Petitioner* (1897) 5 S.L.T. 126 (O.H.).

If there is a committee of inspection in England the remuneration is fixed by the committee and is in the nature of a commission or percentage, of which one part is payable on the amount realised and the other on the amount distributed in dividend. If the Department of Trade is of opinion that the remuneration so fixed is too high, it may apply to the court, which will then fix the remuneration. If there is no committee of inspection, the remuneration will be on the scale of remuneration payable to the Official Receiver as liquidator, unless the court otherwise orders: rule 159.

A liquidator must not receive any gift, remuneration or consideration of benefit whatever, beyond the remuneration he is entitled to receive under the Act or the Rules: rule 160. He must not, whilst acting, purchase any assets of the company except by leave of the court: rule 161. He must not, without the court's sanction, purchase goods for carrying on the business if he would obtain part of the profit arising from the transaction: rule 162.

Where there are joint liquidators, their remuneration is distributed among them in such proportions as the court directs: section 242. The presumption is in favour of equality, but is displaced by evidence that the liquidators have not shared the responsibility and work equally.[52]

A liquidator is not entitled to renumeration out of the funds of a related company.[53]

Duties

A liquidator must:

(1) Take all the property of the company into his custody as soon as possible: section 243.

(2) In England, as soon as may be, settle a list of contributories,[54] collect the company's assets, apply them in discharge of its liabilities and distribute any surplus among the members according to their rights and interests in the company: sections 257, 265, 273; rule 78.

In Scotland he must perform such duties as will enable the court to exercise the functions mentioned: sections 257, 265; R.C. 211.

The word "liabilities" excludes claims which are not legally enforceable. Thus does not include arrears of tax claimed by a foreign state, even one which adheres to the Commonwealth.[55]

---

[52] *City of Glasgow Bank Liquidators, Petitioners* (1880) 7. R. 1196.
[53] *Taylor, Petitioner,* 1976 S.L.T. (Sh. Ct.) 82.
[54] But see, *ante,* p. 652.
[55] *Government of India* v. *Taylor* [1955] A.C. 491; *cf. Clyde Marine Insurance Co. Ltd.* v. *Renwick & Co.,* 1924 S.C. 113.

If the liquidator distributes the assets without making provision for the liabilities he is liable to pay damages to the unpaid creditors.

The company had a lease of premises expiring in 1938 at a yearly rent of £1,217 10s. The lease was assigned to M., and in 1933 the company went into voluntary liquidation. M. was insolvent and unable to pay the rent. The liquidator distributed the assets without making any provision for the company's liabilities under the lease. *Held*, the liquidator had committed a breach of his duty and was liable in damages to the lessor: *James Smith & Sons (Norwood) Ltd.* v. *Goodman* [1936] Ch. 216. (C.A.).

(3) In England, have regard to any directions given by resolution of the creditors or contributories at a meeting or by the committee of inspection. Directions of the creditors or contributories override those of the committee of inspection: section 246.

In Scotland it is the duty of the committee of inspection to act with the liquidator and advise him in the management of the company's affairs and the conduct of the liquidation: R.C. 209.

(4) In England, summon meetings of the creditors or contributories when directed by resolution of the creditors or contributories or requested in writing by one-tenth in value of the creditors or contributories; section 246. He may summon meetings on his own initiative whenever he wants to ascertain the wishes of the creditors or contributories: section 246.

In Scotland the committee or any member of it may apply to the court for an order on the liquidator to summon a meeting of creditors or contributories or both: R.C. 209. The liquidator may call a meeting of creditors on his own initiative: section 245 and Bankruptcy (Scotland) Act 1913, s.93.

For the court's power to have meetings of creditors or contributories summoned, see section 346, *ante*.[56]

(5) In England, keep, in manner prescribed, proper books. Any creditor or contributory may, subject to the control of the court, inspect such books: section 247.

The books to be kept are (*a*) the record book, and (*b*) the cash book
The record book contains a record of all minutes, all proceedings had and resolutions passed at meetings of the creditors or contributories, or of the

[56] p. 621.

committee of inspection, and all matters necessary to give a correct view of the liquidator's administration of the company's affairs, excluding documents of a confidential nature such as opinions of counsel affecting the interest of the creditors or contributories: rule 171.

The cash book contains entries made from day to day of the receipts and payments made by the liquidator: rule 172.

Where the liquidator carries on the business of the company, he must keep a distinct account of the trading and must incorporate in the cash book the total weekly amounts of the receipts and payments on that trading account: rule 176.

In Scotland the committee of inspection have a right of access to the liquidator's books and accounts: R.C. 209.

In both countries, after a winding-up order has been made, the court may order inspection of the company's books and papers by creditors and contributories and the books and papers are then not open to any further or other inspection: section 266.

Sections 246 and 247, *ante*, and sections 248 to 250, *post*, do not apply to Scotland.

(6) In England, pay all money received by him into the Insolvency Services Account[57] at the Bank of England. If the committee of inspection satisfy the Department of Trade that it is for the advantage of the creditors or contributories for the liquidator to bank with another bank, the Department must direct payments to be made into such other bank: section 248.

If a liquidator retains more than £100[58] for more than 10 days, then, unless he explains the retention to the satisfaction of the Department of Trade, he is liable to pay interest on the excess at the rate of 20 per cent. per annum, to disallowance of his remuneration, to be removed from his office and to pay any expense occasioned by his default: section 248.

No money must be paid into the liquidator's private banking account: section 248.

All payments out of the Insolvency Services Account are made in the manner prescribed by the Department of Trade: rule 169.

Payments out of a special bank account are made by cheque payable to

---

[57] Substituted for the Companies Liquidation Account by the Insolvency Act 1976, s.3 and Sched. 2.
[58] Substituted for £50 by the Insolvency Act 1976, s.1 and Sched. 1.

order, with the company's name on the face of it, signed by the liquidator, and countersigned by a member of the committee of inspection and such other person, if any, as the committee may appoint: rule 170.

(7) In England, send his accounts to the Department of Trade twice a year: section 249. These accounts may be audited by the Department: Insolvency Act 1976, s.2(1).

The cash book is audited by the committee of inspection every three months and the trading account is examined and certified by the committee once a month: rules 174, 176.

Six months from the date of the winding-up order, and thereafter every six months, until his release, the liquidator must send to the Department of Trade a copy of the cash book in duplicate, with vouchers and copies of the certificates of audit of the committee of inspection. With the first accounts he must send a summary of the statement of affairs, showing the amounts realised and the cause of the non-realisation of the unrealised assets. Every six months he must send a report upon the position of the liquidation. When the assets have been fully realised and distributed, the liquidator must send in his accounts immediately. The accounts are verified by affidavit: rule 175.

When the accounts have been audited by the Department, one copy is filed with the court. Each copy is open to the inspection of any person: rule 177.

A summary of the accounts must be prepared and a printed copy sent by post to every creditor and contributory: rule 178.

A liquidator is under the control of the Department of Trade and if he does not perform his duties properly the Department must inquire into the matter and take such action as they may think expedient. They may also (*a*) require him to answer any inquiries in relation to the liquidation, (*b*) apply to the court to examine him on oath, (*c*) direct a local investigation to be made of his books and vouchers: section 250.

(8) A court winding up involves more than a mere realisation of the assets and distribution of proceeds. The liquidator is an officer of the court, and as such he has public responsibilities to investigate past activities connected with the company and, in appropriate cases, to initiate such further proceedings, civil and criminal, connected therewith as the circumstances may dictate. It is his duty to discover not only breaches of the Companies Acts but also conduct falling short of the requisite standards of commercial morality.[59]

---

[59] *Re Allebart Pty. Ltd.* [1971] 1 N.S.W. L.R. 24.

There is no objection to a liquidator accepting funds or indemnities from creditors to enable a winding up to proceed, and indeed such practice is to be encouraged. However, a liquidator must decide himself what steps should be taken in the winding up and, where he draws upon the financial assistance of the creditor, it is incumbent upon him to ensure that he does not place in jeopardy his independence in the discharge of his duties. A liquidator should not permit a situation to develop in which it might appear that he has yielded up to any degree whatever his exclusive independent control in the decision-making processes and administration of a winding up.[59]

Powers

The liquidator's powers are set out in Chapter 26.[60]

The exercise of his powers is subject to the control of the court and any creditor or contributory may apply to the court with respect to such exercise: section 245(3). If, in England, any person is aggrieved by any act or decision of the liquidator, that person may apply to the court, which may make such order as it thinks just: section 246(5). The court has been held entitled, on an application under either section, to interfere in circumstances analogous to those in which it would interfere under the Bankruptcy Act 1914, s.80, *e.g.* where there is fraud, or the liquidator has not exercised a discretion bona fide, or he has acted unreasonably.[61]

In England the liquidator may apply to the court for directions in relation to any particular matter arising under the winding up: section 246. In Scotland the liquidator has the same right by virtue of section 245(5), since a trustee on a bankrupt estate may apply to the court for directions in connection with the exercise of his powers.[62] The right should be exercised in every case of serious doubt or difficulty in relation to the performance by the liquidator of his statutory duties. The omission to exercise it may lead the liquidator into serious liabilities.[63]

---

[60] p. 646.
[61] *Leon* v. *York-o-Matic Ltd.* [1966] 1 W.L.R. 1450; *Re Mineral Securities Australia Ltd.* (*in Liquidation*), *etc.* [1973] 2 N.S.W. L.R. 207.
[62] *Liquidator of Upper Clyde Shipbuilders Ltd.*, 1975 S.L.T. 39 (O.H.).
[63] See *Re Windsor Steam Coal Co.* (*1901*) *Ltd.* [1929] 1 Ch. 151, and *Re Home and Colonial Insurance Co. Ltd.* [1930] 1 Ch. 102, *post.*

Liability

A liquidator is not strictly speaking a trustee for the individual creditors or contributories, his position being that of agent of the company.

During a liquidation a claim was made by a contributory for damages for delay in handing over to the contributory his proportion of the surplus assets of the company. *Held,* in the absence of fraud, bad faith or personal misconduct, an action for damages would not lie against the liquidator at the suit of a creditor or contributory, the proper remedy being an application to the court to control the liquidator in the exercise of his powers: *Knowles* v. *Scott* [1891] 1 Ch. 717.[64]

On the other hand, for breach of any of his statutory duties the liquidator will be liable in damages to a creditor or contributory for injury caused to them.

A liquidator distributed the assets of the company without paying X, a creditor, who had no notice of the liquidation. The books of the company showed X to be a creditor but the liquidator made no attempt to communicate with X beyond issuing an insufficient advertisement for creditors. The company was dissolved. *Held,* the liquidator was liable in damages to X. The duty of the liquidator was not merely to advertise for creditors but to write to those of whom he knew and who did not send in claims: *Pulsford* v. *Devenish* [1903] 2 Ch. 625.

A liquidator should make provision for contingent claims of which he has notice, *e.g.* where the company, having assigned a lease, is under a contingent liability for the rent,[65] or where he knows of possible claims by workmen for injuries not covered by insurance.[66]

If a liquidator applies the company's assets in paying a doubtful claim, which turns out to be unfounded, without taking proper legal advice or applying to the court for directions, he will be liable to refund the amount paid on a misfeasance summons taken out by a creditor or contributory.[67]

In such a case, although the liquidator may be a trustee for the purposes of sections 30 and 61 of the Trustee Act 1925,[68] he is not

---

[64] *cf. Upper Clyde* case, *ante, per* Lord Grieve (Ordinary), at p. 40.
[65] *James Smith & Sons (Norwood) Ltd.* v. *Goodman* [1936] Ch. 216 (C.A.); *cf. Lord Elphinstone* v. *Monkland Iron, etc., Co. Ltd.* (1886) 13 R. (H.L.) 98.
[66] *Re Armstrong Whitworth Securities Co. Ltd.* [1947] Ch. 673.
[67] *Re Windsor Steam Coal Co. (1901) Ltd.* [1929] 1 Ch. 151 (C.A.).
[68] The point was left open in *Re Windsor Steam Coal Co. (1901) Ltd., ante.*

entitled to relief, because he has paid away money in his hands to the wrong person.

The Trustee Act 1925 does not apply to Scotland but there are corresponding provisions in the Trusts (Scotland) Act 1921, ss.3 and 32.

A liquidator, however, is not liable for admitting a proof of debt which is ill-founded, provided he exercises all due care beforehand. But a "high standard of care and diligence is required from a liquidator in a . . . winding up. He is of course paid for his services; he is able to obtain wherever it is expedient the assistance of solicitors and counsel; and, which is a most important consideration, he is entitled, in every serious case of doubt or difficulty . . . to submit the matter to the Court and to obtain its guidance."[69]

H. Co. made a reinsurance agreement with L. Co. which was invalid. On H. going into liquidation, L. tendered a proof which the liquidator ultimately accepted for £89,100, on which £38,000 was paid to L. in dividends. On learning that he should have disallowed the claim, the liquidator sued L. but the claim was dismissed, as no mistake of fact on the part of the liquidator was made. A creditor took out a misfeasance summons. *Held*, the liquidator was negligent in admitting so large a proof without taking legal advice or applying for directions, and was liable to pay compensation to the company: *Re Home and Colonial Insurance Co. Ltd.* [1930] 1 Ch. 102, *ante.*[70]

Where a liquidator has paid money to shareholders under an eror in law, caused, *e.g.* by an underestimation of tax liability, he is not entitled to recover it under the *condictio indebiti*, there being no special relationship between the liquidator and the shareholders such as to take the situation outside the general rule.[71]

Release (England)

When the liquidator has realised as much of the property of the company as he can, and has distributed the final dividend, if any, to the creditors, and made a final return, if any, to the contributories, or has resigned or been removed, he may apply to the Department of Trade for a report on his accounts to be prepared. After considering the report and any objections of the creditors or contributories, the

---

[69] *Per* Maugham J. in *Re Home and Colonial Insurance Co. Ltd.* [1930] 1 Ch. 102 at p. 125.
[70] p. 416.
[71] *Taylor* v. *Wilson's Trustees,* 1975 S.C. 146.

Department may grant or withhold his release, subject to an appeal to the High Court: section 251.

Before applying for his release, the liquidator must give notice of his intention to the creditors and contributories, and must send with the notice a summary of his receipts and payments. This release, when granted, is gazetted: rule 205.

The release, when granted, discharges the liquidator from all liability in respect of his conduct of the liquidation. It may, however, be revoked on proof that it was obtained by fraud, or by suppression or concealment of any material fact: section 251.

Discharge (Scotland)

A liquidator may be discharged by the court on his presenting a petition for that purpose. Failure of the liquidator to carry out statutory procedure (*e.g.* to call meetings of creditors and contributories as required by section 252 and Rule of Court 208, and to make up a list of contributories for settlement by the court under Rule of Court 211) is a ground for the dismissal of the petition.[72]

Section 251 does not apply to Scotland.

Summary of Procedure on Compulsory Liquidation

1. Petition presented.
   Provisional liquidator may be appointed.
   Court may stay legal proceedings.
   No transfer of property or shares, or alteration in status of
       members, unless court otherwise orders.
   No attachment, sequestration, distress or execution.
2. Winding-up order made.
   Official Receiver becomes provisional liquidator in England.
   No actions except with leave of court.
   Powers of directors cease.
   Servants dismissed.
3. Statement of affairs within 14 days of order in England.
4. As soon as practicable Official Receiver reports to court in England.
5. First meetings of creditors and contributories[73] within one month of order.

---

[72] *Lovat Mantle Manufacturers Ltd., Petitioners*, 1960 S.L.T. (Sh. Ct.). 52.
[73] Meeting of contributories may not be required in Scotland.

6. In England liquidator and committee of inspection, in Scotland committee of inspection, may be appointed.
7. List of contributories may be settled.
8. Assets collected.
9. Proofs of debts received.
10. Dividends paid to creditors.
11. Capital may be returned to contributories.
12. Company struck off register and dissolved.

CHAPTER 29

VOLUNTARY WINDING UP

FROM the point of view of the company itself, a voluntary winding up has many advantages over a compulsory winding up, the chief being that there are not so many formalities to be complied with. In consequence the great majority of liquidations are voluntary liquidations.

Initiation of voluntary winding up

Section 278 provides that a company may be wound up voluntarily:

(1) When the period, if any, fixed for its duration by the articles expires, or the event, if any, occurs, on the occurrence of which the articles provide that it is to be dissolved, and the company in general meeting passes a resolution (*i.e.* an *ordinary resolution*) to be wound up voluntarily.

(2) If it resolves by *special resolution*[1] to be wound up voluntarily.

A company can be wound up by special resolution without any reason being assigned.

(3) If the company resolves by *extraordinary resolution* that it cannot by reason of its liabilities continue its business and that it is advisable to wind up.

An extraordinary resolution is allowed here because time is of the essence since the company is insolvent and a special resolution would normally require a longer period of notice.[2]

At least 7 days' notice may have to be given of any meeting at which such a resolution is to be proposed, s.293(1), as amended by s.106 of the 1981 Act. This is to prevent the members acting quickly without the knowledge of the creditors in a creditors' winding up, *post*. It has been held, however, that shorter notice will not invalidate the resolution.[2a]

A resolution for voluntary winding up must be advertised in the *Gazette* within 14 days after it is passed: section 279. In Scotland, where failure to make timeous advertisement was due to inadvertence and no

---

[1] *Ante,* p. 323.   [2] *Ante,* p. 323
[2a] E. V. *Saxton & Sons Ltd.* v. R. *Miles (Confectioner) Ltd., The Times,* March 2, 1983.

prejudice had been suffered as a result of the failure, the Court of Session, in the exercise of its *nobile officium,* authorised the liquidator to make a belated advertisement, the expenses of the proceedings to be borne by the liquidator personally.[3]

Kinds of voluntary winding up

A voluntary winding up may be either (1) a members' voluntary winding up; or (2) a creditors' voluntary winding up: section 283.

MEMBERS' VOLUNTARY WINDING UP

A members' voluntary winding up takes place only when the company is solvent. It is entirely managed by the members, and the liquidator is appointed by them. No meeting of creditors is held and no committee of inspection is appointed. To obtain the benefit of this form of winding up, a declaration of solvency must be filed: section 283, as amended by section 105 of the 1981 Act.

Declaration of solvency

This is a statutory declaration made by the directors or, if there are more than two of them, by the majority, at a board meeting, that they have made a full inquiry into the company's affairs and, having done so, they have formed the opinion that the company will be able to pay its debts in full within a specified period not exceeding 12 months from the commencement of the winding up.[4] The declaration has no effect unless it is made within the five weeks immediately preceding the date of the passing of the winding-up resolution. It may even be made on that date providing that it precedes the resolution. The declaration must be filed with the Registrar within 15 days of the passing of the resolution. Further, the declaration has no effect unless it embodies a statement of the company's assets and liabilities as at the latest practicable date before it is made: section 283, as amended by section 105 of the 1981 Act. If there is something which can reasonably be described as "a statement of the company's assets and liabilities," then, even if it subsequently appears that there were errors and omissions, these will not prevent the statement from being a statement within section 283.[5]

---

[3] *Liquidator of Nairn Public Hall Co. Ltd., Petitioner,* 1946 S.C. 395.
[4] *Ante,* p. 623. [5] *De Courcy* v. *Clement* [1971] Ch. 693.

A director making a declaration of solvency without reasonable grounds is liable to imprisonment for six months, or a fine or both. If the debts are not paid or provided for within the period stated, he is presumed not to have had reasonable grounds: section 283(3). If a declaration is made in accordance with the section the winding up is a members' voluntary winding up: section 283(4).

The liquidator

Unlike the liquidator in a winding up by the court, a liquidator in a voluntary winding up is not an officer of the court.[6] He is the agent of the company, but not of the individual members.[6a] He is appointed, and his remuneration may be fixed, by the company in general meeting (s.285), and within 14 days he must give notice of his appointment to the Registrar of Companies and publish it in the *Gazette:* section 305.[7] He may be appointed at the meeting at which the resolution for voluntary winding up is passed. If there is no liquidator acting, the court may appoint one. The court may also, on cause shown, remove a liquidator and appoint another: section 304.[8] Where a person had been appointed liquidator without his knowledge and he declined to act, it was held that the appointment was invalid and there was therefore no need to remove him.[9] Anyone subject to a disqualification order under section 188 or section 9 of the Insolvency Act 1976 cannot act as a liquidator.[10]

If a vacancy occurs in the office of liquidator, whether by death, resignation or otherwise, the company at a general meeting, summoned by any contributory or by a continuing liquidator, may fill it: section 286.

Conduct of liquidation

Subject to section 291,[11] within three months after the end of the first and every succeeding year of the liquidation, the liquidator must

---

[6] *Per* Megarry J. in *Re Rolls Razor Ltd. (No.* 2) [1970] Ch. 576, 586.
[6a] See *Taylor* v. *Wilson's Trustees*, 1975 S.C. 146.
[7] *cf.* s.240, *ante*, p. 630.
[8] *cf.* s.242, *ante*, p. 677.
[9] *Liquidator of Highland, etc., Dairy Farms Ltd. & Another, Petitioners*, 1964 S.C. 1.
[10] *Ante*, p. 332.
[11] *Post*, p. 690.

summon a general meeting of the company and lay before it an account of his acts and dealings and of the conduct of the winding up during the preceding year: section 289.

Subject to section 291,[11] as soon as the affairs of the company are fully wound up the liquidator must call a general meeting of the company. This is done by advertisement in the *Gazette* at least one month before the meeting. At the meeting the liquidator must present an account of the winding up, showing how the winding up has been conducted and how the company's property has been disposed of. A copy of this account, together with a return of the holding of the meeting, must be sent to the Registrar within a week after the meeting: section 290. It is not necessary for the affairs of the company to be fully wound up before the liquidator can validly make his return, only that they should be fully wound up so far as the liquidator is aware.[12]

If a quorum is not present at the final meeting, the liquidator must make a return that the meeting was summoned but no quorum was present, and this has the same effect as a return of the holding of the meeting.

The Registrar must publish in the *Gazette* notice of the receipt of the return (European Communities Act 1972, s.9(3)).

If the liquidator of a company which is in a members' voluntary winding up forms the opinion that the company will not be able to pay its debts in full within the period stated in the declaration of solvency, he must forthwith summon a meeting of the creditors, and lay before it a statement of the company's assets and liabilities: section 288. The winding up then proceeds as if it were a creditors' voluntary winding up, and sections 299 and 300, *post,* apply to the exclusion of sections 289 and 290: section 291.

Dissolution

The company is automatically dissolved three months after the Registrar registers the return of the final meeting, unless the court makes an order deferring the date of dissolution: section 290.

Any undistributed property passes to the Crown (s.354), unless the Crown disclaims (s.355). Within two years after the dissolution, the court may declare the dissolution void: section 352.[13]

---

[12] *Re Cornish Manures Ltd.* [1976] 1 W.L.R. 807.
[13] *Ante,* p. 671.

CREDITORS' VOLUNTARY WINDING UP

If no declaration of solvency is filed with the Registrar, a voluntary winding up is a creditors' voluntary winding up: section 283(4). In such a case the company must give at least seven days notice of the meeting at which the resolution to wind up the company is to be proposed[13a] and must summon a meeting of its creditors for that day, or the day after. Notices of the meeting of creditors must be sent by post to the creditors at the same time, as notices of the meeting of the company are sent to the members, *i.e.* seven days before the meeting: section 293, as amended by section 106 of the 1981 Act. Thus the creditors may have time to consider whether they should attend the meeting.

Thus the management of a creditors' voluntary winding up is shared by the members and the creditors but the creditors have control—in effect they appoint the liquidator and decide the composition of any committee of inspection, as will be seen.

Notice of the meeting of creditors must be advertised in the *Gazette* and in two local newspapers circulating in the district in which the company's registered office or principal place of business is situate: section 293.

Meeting of creditors

The meeting of creditors is presided over by one of the directors nominated for that purpose by the directors: section 293. The business of the meeting is:

(1) To receive a full statement by the directors of the position of the company's affairs, together with a list of the creditors and the estimated amount of their claims: section 293.

(2) To appoint a liquidator: section 294, *post.*

(3) To appoint a committee of inspection: section 295.

The liquidator

The creditors and the company at their respective meetings may nominate a liquidator and, if different persons are nominated, the person nominated by the creditors is the liquidator, subject to any order made by the court. If different persons are nominated, any director, member or creditor of the company may, within seven days

---

[13a] Shorter notice will not invalidate the resolution: *Saxton's* case, note 2a above.

after the creditors' nomination, apply to the court for an order that the company's nominee be liquidator instead of or jointly with the creditors' nominee, or that some other person be liquidator: section 294. If the members nominate or appoint a liquidator and no meeting of creditors is held, although a creditors' voluntary winding up is contemplated, until something is done about it at the instance of the creditors the person nominated or appointed is the liquidator of the company.[14]

In England, rule 134 of the Companies (Winding-Up) Rules 1949 applies to the creditors' meeting so that the creditors' resolution appointing a liquidator must be passed by a majority in number and value of the creditors present and voting in person or by proxy.[15] For Scotland, see Companies Act 1948, s.318(*b*) which has the effect that any question at a creditors' meeting is determined by the majority in value of those present and entitled to vote.

Sections 304 and 305 and the provisions relating to disqualification orders, *ante*,[16] apply as regards the appointment of the liquidator.

Any vacancy, by reason of death, resignation or otherwise, in the office of a liquidator, other than a liquidator appointed by the court, may be filled by the creditors: section 297.

The liquidator's remuneration is fixed by the committee of inspection or, if there is no committee, by the creditors: section 296.

Committee of inspection

The creditors, at their first or any subsequent meeting, may appoint a committee of inspection of not more than five persons to act with the liquidator.[17] If they do so, the company in general meeting may appoint not more than five persons to act as members of the committee, but the creditors may resolve that these persons ought not to be members of the committee, and thereupon, unless the court otherwise directs, they cannot act on the committee: section 295. It will be recalled that there is no statutory maximum number of members of the committee of inspection in a compulsory liquidation.[18]

Subject as above, section 253, *ante*,[18] and in Scotland, also section 255,[18] apply to a committee of inspection appointed under section 295.

A member of the committee is in a fiduciary position.[18]

---

[14] *Re Centrebind Ltd.* [1967] 1 W.L.R. 377.
[15] *Re Caston Cushioning Ltd.* [1955] 1 W.L.R. 163.
[16] p. 689.   [17] *Post,* p. 697.   [18] *Ante,* p. 631.

Conduct of liquidation. Dissolution

Within three months after the end of the first and every succeeding year of the liquidation the liquidator must summon a general meeting of the company and a meeting of creditors, and lay before the meetings an account of his acts and dealings and of the conduct of the winding up during the preceding year: section 299.

When the liquidation is complete, the liquidator must, by at least one month's notice in the *Gazette,* call final meetings of the company and the creditors, and present his account. Within a week after these meetings, a copy of the account and a return of the holding of the meetings or a return that no quorum was present thereat must be filed with the Registrar (s.300), who must publish it in the *Gazette* (European Commmunities Act 1972, s.9(3)). The company is thereupon dissolved automatically three months after the registration of the account and the return: section 300. Sections 352, 354 and 355, *ante,* [19] apply as in the case of a members' voluntary winding up.

Summary of Differences Between Members' Voluntary Winding Up and Creditors' Voluntary Winding Up

Members' Voluntary Winding Up	*Creditors' Voluntary Winding Up*
(1) Declaration of solvency.	No declaration of solvency.
(2) Usually initiated by special resolution.	Initiated by extraordinary resolution. Seven days notice to be given.
(3) No meetings of creditors.	Meeting of creditors required whenever meeting of contributories held. Notice of both meetings to be sent out together.
(4) Liquidator appointed and his remuneration fixed by company in general meeting.	Liquidator, in effect, appointed by creditors and his remuneration fixed by committee of inspection or, if there is no committee, by creditors.
(5) No committee of inspection.	May be committee of inspection, appointed, in effect, by creditors.

CONSEQUENCES OF ANY VOLUNTARY WINDING UP

The commencement of a voluntary winding up is the date of the passing of the resolution for voluntary winding up: section 280. Even if the company is subsequently wound up by the court, the commence-

---

[19] p. 690.

ment of the winding up is the date of the passing of the resolution: section 229.

The consequences of a voluntary winding up are:

(1) As from the commencement of the winding up the company must cease to carry on business except so far as is required for its beneficial winding up, although the corporate state and powers continue until the company is dissolved: section 281. Notification that the company is in liquidation must be given on the company's documents on which its name appears: section 338.[20]

(2) No transfer of shares can be made without the sanction of the liquidator and any alteration in the status of the members is void: section 282 (*cf.* s.227, *ante*).[21] A transfer of debentures can, however, be made.[22]

(3) On the appointment of a liquidator the powers of the directors cease except so far as the company in general meeting or the liquidator (in a members' voluntary winding up), or the committee of inspection or, if there is no such committee, the creditors (in a creditors' voluntary winding up), sanction their continuance: sections 285, 296.

A voluntary winding up does not necessarily operate as a discharge of the company's employees; but if it takes place because the company is insolvent, it will operate as a discharge.

By a written agreement F. was appointed managing director of a company for five years certain. Before the expiration of the five years the company passed a resolution for voluntary winding up as it could not by reason of its liabilities continue its business. F. voted for this resolution. *Held*, the voluntary winding up operated as a wrongful dismissal of F. and a term could not be implied that if the company went into voluntary liquidation with the assent of F. he should lose his right to damages: *Fowler* v. *Commercial Timber Co. Ltd.* [1930] 2 K.B. 1 (C.A.).[23]

"An order for the compulsory winding up of a company puts an end to the employment of the managing director . . . and in my judgment the same result must necessarily follow where there is a resolution for the voluntary winding up of the company which depends upon the company being unable to meet its obligations": *per* Greer L.J., at p. 6.

[20] *Ante*, p. 626.   [21] p. 623.
[22] *Re Goy & Co. Ltd.* [1900] 2 Ch. 149.
[23] And see *Reigate* v. *Union Manufacturing Co. (Ramsbottom) Ltd.* [1918] 1 K.B. 592 (C.A.).

When the terms of the contract of employment are to be found in the articles, no damages for breach of contract are recoverable.[24] If the winding up is purely for the purpose of amalgamation it will not operate as a discharge.[25] After the commencement of the winding up the liquidator may continue the employment of the company's employees to wind up the company.[26] In doing so he is acting as manager of the company.[26a]

In England there is no statutory provision for the stay of actions and other proceedings against the company in the case of a voluntary winding up (*cf.* ss.226, 228, 231, *ante*),[27] but on an application under section 307, *post,*[28] the court has a discretion to stay proceedings.[29] Executions will usually be stayed when it is necessary to ensure the distribution of assets among the creditors *pari passu,*[30] but actions will not be stayed when there is a dispute as to liability, or when no advantage will be gained, *e.g.* no expense will be saved, by a stay.[31] Section 307 extends section 256 (power to stay a winding up), *ante,*[32] to a voluntary winding up.[33] Normally, a stay should not be granted unless each member consents or is bound not to object, *e.g.* because there is a scheme under section 206, or there is secured to him the right to receive what he would have received had the winding up proceeded to its conclusion.[33] A charging order nisi will not be confirmed after a winding up has commenced.[33a]

In Scotland, the provision now in section 307, *post,*[34] has been interpreted as not giving the court power to stay proceedings against the company,[35] and section 308 provides that, on the application of the liquidator of a Scottish company, the court may direct that no action or proceeding shall be proceeded with against the company except by

[24] *Re T. N. Farrer Ltd.* [1937] Ch. 352.
[25] *Midland Counties District Bank Ltd.* v. *Attwood* [1905] 1 Ch. 357.
[26] *cf. Day* v. *Tait* (1900) 8 S.L.T. 40 (O.H.).
[26a] *Smith* v. *Lord Advocate*, 1978 S.C. 259.
[27] pp. 619, 624, 625.
[28] p. 700.
[29] *Currie* v. *Consolidated Kent Collieries Corpn. Ltd.* [1906] 1 K.B. 134 (C.A.).
[30] *Anglo-Baltic Bank* v. *Barber & Co.* [1924] 2 K.B. 410 (C.A.).
[31] *Cook* v. *"X" Chair Patents Co. Ltd.* [1960] 1 W.L.R. 60.
[32] p. 624.
[33] *Re Calgary and Edmonton Land Co. Ltd.* [1975] 1 W.L.R. 355.
[33a] *Roberts Petroleum* v. *Bernard Kenny, The Times*, February 15, 1983.
[34] See note 28 above.
[35] *Sdeuard* v. *Gardner* (1876) 3 R. 577.

leave of the court. Section 327 (relating to diligence in Scotland)[36] applies to voluntary, as well as to compulsory, winding up.

DISTRIBUTION OF THE PROPERTY OF THE COMPANY IN A VOLUNTARY WINDING UP

The costs, charges and expenses properly incurred in a voluntary winding up, including the remuneration of the liquidator, are payable in priority to all other claims: section 309. Subject thereto the liquidator must apply the property[37] of the company first in paying the preferential debts[38] and then in discharging the liabilities of the company *pari passu:* section 302. Under this section the liquidator has a duty to inquire into all claims against the company.[39] Even where the company is solvent, statute-barred debts cannot be paid unless the contributories consent.[40]

Provision may be made for employees on the cessation of business if it is aproved by the members or otherwise in accordance with the articles either before or during the liquidation. Such payment must be made out of the assets available to the members. Any excercise of this power is not subject to section 302: 1980 Act, s.74.

If the company is insolvent the bankruptcy rules apply as well to a voluntary as to a compulsory winding up: sections 317, 318.[41] Subject as above the property of the company must be distributed among the members according to their rights and interests: section 302.

A contracting out of the provisions of section 302 is contrary to public policy.[42]

---

[36] *Ante,* p. 625.

[37] ss.325*, 326*, 320, 321*, 332, 333 and 323*, apply as in a compulsory winding up. And s.322 may apply in either a compulsory or a voluntary liquidation. ss. marked * do not apply to Scotland; s.327 applies to Scotland only.

[38] See s.319, *ante,* p. 663.

[39] *Austin Securities Ltd.* v. *Northgate and English Stores Ltd.* [1969] 1 W.L.R. 529 (C.A.) applying *Pulsford* v. *Devenish* and *Re Armstrong Whitworth Securities Co. Ltd.*

[40] *Re Art Reproduction Co. Ltd.* [1952] Ch. 89. The Scottish equivalent of "statute-barred" is "prescribed."

[41] *Ante,* p. 653.

[42] *British Eagle International Air Lines Ltd.* v. *Compagnie Nationale Air France* [1975] 1 W.L.R. 758 (H.L.), where the rules of the general liquidation prevailed over the International Air Transport Association clearing house arrangements and, despite such arrangements, the plaintiff company was entitled to recover the sums payable to it by other airlines for services rendered by it and not cleared through the I.A.T.A. system and vice versa.

In the result, the order of application of assets is the same as that in a compulsory liquidation.[43]

Powers and Duties of the Liquidator in a Voluntary Winding Up

In every voluntary winding up it is the duty of the liquidator to pay the debts of the company and adjust the rights of the contributories among themselves: section 303.

To enable him to do this the section provides that he may *without sanction*:

(1) settle a list of contributories;
(2) make calls;
(3) summon general meetings of the company for any purpose he may think fit;
(4) exercise all the powers of a liquidator in a compulsory winding up under section 245, except those mentioned below.

He may carry on the business of the company, if he reasonably thinks it is necessary for the beneficial winding up of the company. If he does so, those to whom he incurs obligations are entitled to be paid in priority to the creditors at the commencement of the winding up: *Re Great Eastern Electric Co. Ltd.* [1941] Ch. 241.[44]

In a members' voluntary winding up, *with the sanction* of an extraordinary resolution of the company, and in a creditors' voluntary winding up, *with the sanction* of the court or the committee of inspection or (if there is no such committee) a meeting of the creditors, the liquidator may:

(1) pay any classes of creditors in full;
(2) make any compromise or arrangement with creditors;
(3) compromise all calls and liabilities to calls and other debts and liabilities: section 303.

List of contributories

The rules relating to the settling of the list of contributories in a compulsory winding up, *ante*,[45] are not required to be observed by the

---

[43] p. 662.
[44] *cf. Day* v. *Tait* (1900) 8 S.L.T. 40 (O.H.).
[45] p. 652.

liquidator in a voluntary winding up, although as a general rule he should follow them. It is no defence, therefore, to an action for calls that notice has not been given to the contributory.[46]

Proof of debts

The liquidator in a voluntary winding up need not require the creditors to prove their debts. The debts may be proved in the same way as in a compulsory winding up, *i.e.* in England by delivering or posting to the liquidator an informal claim or an affidavit verifying the debt.[47] The liquidator may fix a date before which debts must be proved. In England there is no limit to the time within which a dissatisfied creditor may appeal to the court. In Scotland any application to the court under section 307[48] to have a liquidator's deliverance reversed or varied must normally be presented within seven days of the deliverance: R.C. 214.[49]

Dividends

Dividends are declared by the liquidator; in England the rules as to dividends in a compulsory winding up[50] have no application to a voluntary winding up. In Scotland section 318 makes certain provisions of the Bankruptcy (Scotland) Act 1913 applicable to *any* winding up of an *insolvent* company.[51]

Meetings

In an English voluntary winding up the Companies (Winding-up) Rules l949, rules 121–156, *ante*,[52] apply only to meetings of creditors in a creditors' voluntary winding up. In a Scottish voluntary winding up, Rule 208 of the Rules of Court 1965 applies, with some modifications, to all general meetings of creditors or contributories in *any* winding up: R.C. 210.

---

[46] *Brighton Arcade Co.v. Dowling* (1868) L.R. 3 C.P. 175.
[47] *Ante*, p. 659.
[48] *Post*, p. 700.
[49] See *Knoll Spinning Co. Ltd. v. Brown*, 1977 S.C. 291 (O.H.) (note of appeal dismissed).
[50] *Ante*, p. 668.
[51] *Ante*, pp. 657, 668.
[52] p. 618.

Remuneration

The rules[53] limiting the liquidator's remuneration and restricting his dealing with the assets and purchasing goods apply in a voluntary winding up.

Books of account

In an English creditors' voluntary winding up, the liquidator must keep such books as the committee of inspection or, if there is no such committee, the creditors direct. The books must be submitted to the committee of inspection or, if there is no committee, to the creditors as and when the committee or the creditors direct: rule 172. In Scotland the committee of inspection have right of access to the liquidator's books and accounts: R.C. 209.

Neither the English nor the Scottish rules contain provisions relating to the books of account in a members' voluntary winding up, but proper books should be kept. The Jenkins Report[54] recommended that in a voluntary winding up the liquidator's accounts should normally be required to be audited.

Unclaimed assets, dividends, etc.

The provisions of section 343 relating to unclaimed assets in England and of section 344 relating to unclaimed dividends, etc., in Scotland, apply as in a compulsory winding up.[55]

Information as to pending liquidations

Section 342, *ante*,[56] applies where a voluntary winding up is not concluded within one year.

Power to apply to court

In a voluntary winding up the liquidator, or any contributory or creditor, may apply to the court to determine any question arising in the winding up or to exercise any of the powers which the court could

---

[53] rr.160–162 (not applicable to Scotland).
[54] Para. 503.
[55] *Ante*, p. 669.
[56] *Ante*, p. 669.

exercise if the company were being wound up by the court: section 307.[57] This gives the liquidator in a voluntary winding up the same right to the guidance of the court as in a compulsory liquidation. For example, in England, if he is of opinion that fraud has been committed in the formation or promotion of the company or in relation to the company since its formation, he can obtain an order of the court for the public examination[58] of any promoter, director or other officer of the company concerned. Again, he can apply for an order for private examination.[59]

In 1971 a company went into voluntary liquidation. In 1976 it became apparent that it might be liable for claims in tort for negligence during its operations. In 1979, after the liquidators had started preparing the final accounts, solicitors warned the liquidators of the possible claims. The liquidators applied under section 307 for an order that they should distribute the final dividend to the members without regard to the claims on the basis of delay. Alternatively they sought an order that the claimants should bear the costs of the delay in distribution. Megarry V.-C. held that the test was whether in all the circumstances it was just to make either of the orders sought. Default or lack of diligence by either party was relevant and the court was less likely to facilitate a distribution among the members than among the creditors. In the circumstances, both orders would be refused: *Re R-R Realisations Ltd.* [1980] 1 All E. R. 1019.

Duty to report criminal offences

If the liquidator thinks that any past or present officer, or any member, of the company has committed a criminal offence in relation to the company, he must report the matter, in an English winding up, to the Director of Public Prosecutions, and in a Scottish winding up, to the Lord Advocate. The matter may then be referred to the Department of Trade, who have the same powers of investigating the company's affairs as in an investigation into the affairs of a company under

---

[57] For examples of applications under s.307, see *Liquidators of North British Locomotive Co. Ltd.* v. *Lord Advocate*, 1963 S.C. 272 (O.H.), *ante*, p. 632, *Smith and Another, Petitioners*, 1969 S.L.T. (Notes) 94 (O.H.) (as to exercise of directors' discretionary powers under a pension scheme) and *Liquidators of Highland Engineering Ltd.* v. *Thomson*, 1972 S.C. 87 (O.H.) (as to provisional liquidator's right to retain funds to pay his remuneration and expenses).

[58] *Re Campbell Coverings Ltd.* (*No.* 2) [1954] Ch. 225. As to public examination in a compulsory winding up in England, see s.270, *ante*, p. 642. For Scotland, see s.269, *ante*, p. 643.

[59] As in *Re Rolls Razor Ltd.* (*No.* 2) [1970] Ch. 576. As to private examination in a compulsory winding up, see s.268, *ante*, p. 641.

sections 164 or 165: section 334, as amended by section 92 of the 1981 Act.

Section 334 lacks the force of section 236[60] in a compulsory winding up—in such a winding up section 236 imposes on the Official Receiver a duty to submit a preliminary report to the court as to the cause of the failure of the company and as to whether further inquiry is desirable into the cause of failure or the conduct of the business; and there is also provision for further reports as to frauds.[61] The English court has been held not entitled, under section 334, to order either a public examination under section 270 or a private examination under section 268.[62]

COMPULSORY LIQUIDATION AFTER COMMENCEMENT OF
VOLUNTARY LIQUIDATION

A voluntary liquidation does not bar the right of any creditor or contributory to have the company wound up by the court: section 310. A creditor of a company in voluntary liquidation is entitled *ex debito justitiae* as between himself and the company to a compulsory winding-up order.[63] However, the court is bound to have regard to the wishes of all the creditors,[64] and if the majority favour the continuance of the voluntary liquidation an order will not be made unless the petitioner can show special circumstances.[65] A contributory must satisfy the court that the rights of the contributories will be prejudiced by a voluntary winding up: section 310. What the Secretary of State must show when he is the petitioner has been dealt with already.[66]

When a voluntary winding up is superseded by a compulsory winding up, all proceedings in the voluntary winding up are deemed to have

---

[60] *Ante*, p. 628.
[61] *Per* Megarry J. in *Re Lubin, Rosen and Associates Ltd.* [1975] 1 W.L.R. 122, at p. 128.
[62] *Re Campbell Coverings Ltd.* [1953] Ch. 488 (C.A.); however, see *Re Campbell Coverings Ltd. (No. 2)* [1954] Ch. 225, *ante*.
[63] *Re James Millward & Co. Ltd.* [1940] Ch. 333 (C.A.); *Gardner & Co. v. Link* (1894) 21 R. 967.
[64] *Re Home Remedies Ltd.* [1943] Ch. 1; *cf. Pattisons Ltd. v. Kinnear* (1899) 1 F. 551 and *Elsmie & Son v. The Tomatin etc. Distillery Ltd.* (1906) 8 F. 434.
[65] *Re B. Karsberg Ltd.* [1956] 1 W.L.R. 57 (C.A.); *Re J. D. Swain Ltd.* [1965] 1 W.L.R. 909 (C.A.); for special circumstances, see *Bouboulis v. Mann, Macneal & Co. Ltd.*, 1926 S.C. 637.
[66] p. 617.

been validly taken unless the court, on proof of fraud or mistake, thinks fit to direct otherwise: section 229, *ante*.[67]

ARRANGEMENTS WITH CREDITORS IN A VOLUNTARY WINDING UP

Under section 306[68] a company which is about to be, or is being, wound up voluntarily, may make a binding arrangement with its creditors if the arrangement is—

(1) sanctioned by an *extraordinary* resolution of the company; and
(2) acceded to by three-fourths in number and value of the creditors, *i.e.* all the creditors, not just those voting.

Any creditor or contributory may, within three weeks from the completion of the arrangement, appeal to the court against it, and the court may confirm or vary the arrangement as it thinks just. A composition by the company with its creditors with the intention of making the company solvent and preventing a winding up is not an "arrangement" within the meaning of the section.[69]

Summary of Procedure

Members' Voluntary Winding Up

1. Notice of meeting to pass special resolution for voluntary winding up sent out.
2. Declaration of solvency made (may be on the day of the meeting).
3. Declaration of solvency filed with Registrar.
4. Resolution (usually special) passed and liquidator appointed.
   Company ceases to carry on business except for winding up.
   Corporate existence continues.
   No transfer of shares without liquidator's consent.
   Powers of directors cease.
5. Resolution filed wih Registrar.
   Gazetted within 14 days.
   Notice of liquidator's appointment gazetted and registered within 14 days.

---

[67] p. 694.
[68] *cf.* s.206 (*post*, p. 709), s.245 (*ante*, p. 648) and s.303 (*ante*, p. 697).
[69] *Re Contal Radio Ltd.* [1932] 2 Ch. 66; for a Scottish instance of a s.306 arrangement, see *Gillies* v. *Dawson* (1893) 20 R. 1119 (O.H.).

6–10. As for 7–11 in a compulsory winding up, *ante*.[70]
11. At end of each year, meeting of company summoned and liquidator's account submitted.
12. Final meeting advertised by at least one month's notice in the *Gazette*.
13. Final meeting held and liquidator's account presented.
14. Return of holding of meeting and copy account filed with Registrar.
15. Company automatically dissolved three months after return registered.

Creditors' Voluntary Winding Up

1. Notice of meeting to pass extraordinary resolution for voluntary winding up sent out at least seven days prior to the meeting.
   Notice of meeting of creditors sent out at the same time as the notices of the members' meeting and advertised.
2. Extraordinary resolution passed. Consequences, as in 4 above. Employees dismissed.
3. Liquidator and committee of inspection appointed by creditors.
4. Resolution filed with Registrar.

Other proceedings as in members' voluntary winding up but meetings of creditors are summoned in addition to meetings of the company.

WINDING UP SUBJECT TO SUPERVISION OF COURT

When a company has passed a resolution for voluntary winding up, the court may order that the winding up shall continue subject to such supervision of the court, and with such liberty for creditors, contributories, or others to apply to the court, and generally on such terms and conditions, as the court thinks just: section 311. However, as has been said,[71] supervision orders are rarely made now because under section 307, *ante*,[72] in a voluntary winding up creditors can apply to the court to determine questions and to exercise any power which the court could exercise in a compulsory winding up.

In England, a winding up under supervision resembles a voluntary winding up in that the Official Receiver is never liquidator. It differs from a voluntary winding up in that the order invariably directs the liquidator to file with the Registrar every three months a report of the position of, and the progess made with, the winding up of the company, and also orders the costs to be taxed.[73] In Scotland, in any

---

[70] p. 686.
[71] *Ante*, p. 604.
[72] p. 698.
[73] See Companies (Winding-Up) Rules 1949, Appendix, Form 18.

winding up (including a voluntary winding up) which lasts for more than one year the liquidator must send half-yearly statements to the Registrar.[74]

Although the court will have regard to the wishes of the creditors or contributories (s.346),[75] it has an absolute discretion as to the granting of a supervision order and a creditor is not entitled to such an order as of right, but must show some special cause, *e.g.* that there is danger of preference being created or that there is some impropriety, actual or threatened, in the conduct of the liquidation.[76]

A petition for the continuance of a voluntary winding up subject to supervision is, for the purpose of giving the court jurisdiction over actions, deemed to be a petition for winding up by the court: section 312. Consequently the court has the section 226[77] power to stay proceedings against the company, and under section 231[78] actions are stayed when the supervision order is made. For the purposes of sections 227 and 228[79] winding up subject to supervision is deemed to be a winding up by the court: section 313.

One advantage of a supervision order is that where such an order is made, the court may appoint an additional liquidator or remove an existing liquidator and appoint another in his place. A liquidator so appointed is in the same position as if he had been appointed in a voluntary winding up: section 314.

In England a supervision order must be advertised by the petitioner in the *London Gazette* within 12 days and served on such persons and in such manner as the court directs; rule 42. In Scotland an order must be advertised once in the *Edinburgh Gazette* within 14 days: R.C. 205

The effect of a supervision order is to allow the liquidator to wind up the company as in a voluntary winding up, subject only to any restrictions imposed by the order. The liquidator can exercise all the powers of a liquidator in a voluntary winding up, but in those cases in which he requires sanction in a voluntary winding up[80] he requires the sanction

---

[74] R.C. 213 and Form 35.
[75] *Ante*, p. 610; *e.g. Wilson* v. *Hadley* (1879) 7 R. 178.
[76] *Crawford* v. *A. R. Cowper Ltd.* (1902) 4 F. 849; *cf. Macquisten* v. *Adam etc. Co. Ltd.* (1896) 23 R. 910 (order granted to a creditor whose claim amounted to four-fifths of the company's debts).
[77] *Ante*, p. 618.
[78] *Ante*, p. 624.
[79] *Ante*, pp. 622, 623; s.228 does not apply to Scotland; s.327 relating to diligence in Scotland applies to any winding up.
[80] *Ante*, p. 698.

of the court (instead of the sanction of an extraordinary resolution of the company), or where before the order the winding up was a creditors' voluntary winding up, the sanction of the court or the committee of inspection or, if there is no committee, a meeting of the creditors: section 315.

The section also provides that various sections applicable to a compulsory liquidation, which are set out in the Eleventh Schedule, are not to apply to a winding up under supervision, but subject to those exceptions a supervision order is for almost all purposes deemed to be an order for winding up by the court.

The commencement of a winding up subject to the supervision of the court is the date of the resolution for voluntary winding up: section 229.[81]

The Jenkins Report[82] stated that the provisions of the Act relating to winding up under supervision serve no useful purpose and should be repealed.

---

[81] *Ante*, p. 622.
[82] Para. 503.

CHAPTER 30

RECONSTRUCTION AND AMALGAMATION

NEITHER of the words "reconstruction" and "amalgamation" has any definite legal meaning. A reconstruction is where a company transfers its assets to a new company with substantially the same shareholders. An amalgamation is the merger of two or more companies into one. This occurs, *e.g.* where a company acquires the assets of or the shares in two or more companies whose shareholders are issued with the appropriate number of shares in the new company.

In this chapter the procedures applicable to reconstructions and agreed amalgamations; *i.e.* where all the companies concerned are in agreement, are set out. The alternative, an often contested form of amalgamation, is referred to as a "take-over"; *i.e.* the acquisition of shares in one company by another company. Such take-overs are the subject of Chapter 31, *post*.[1]

Both a reconstruction and an amalgamation in the sense used in this chapter may be effected (1) under section 287 or section 298, or (2) under sections 206 to 208.[2] The third EEC Directive on Company Law[2a] will require slight amendments to the procedure under sections 206 to 208.

RECONSTRUCTION OR AMALGAMATION UNDER SECTION 287

Under section 287 a company (1) which is in a members' voluntary winding up; (2) may transfer or sell the whole or part of its business or property to another company, whether a company within the meaning of the Act or not; and (3) may pass a special resolution authorising the liquidator to receive as consideration cash or shares, policies or other like interests in the transferee company for distribution among the

---

[1] p. 717.
[2] For examples of amalgamation, see *Head (Henry) & Co. Ltd.* v. *Ropner Holdings Ltd.* [1952] Ch. 124. *Governments Stock, etc., Investment Co. Ltd.* v. *Christopher* [1956] 1 W.L.R. 237, *ante*, p. 132, *Rights and Issues Investment Trust Ltd.* v. *Stylo Shoes Ltd.* [1965] Ch. 250, *ante*, p. 111, and *Clydesdale Bank Ltd., Petitioners*, 1950 S.C. 30.
[2a] Adopted on October 9, 1978, O.J. 1978 L295/36.

members of the transferor company according to their rights and interests in that company. The sanction of the court is unnecessary. The sale may be to a foreign company.[3] However, it must be to a company and not to a speculator who hopes to form a company to take over the assets.[4]

The following procedure might be adopted under section 287. A meeting of the transferor company is summoned in order to pass resolutions for reconstruction or amalgamation. At the meeting, resolutions are passed for the voluntary winding up of the company, the appointment of a liquidator, and giving authority to the liquidator to enter into an agreement with the transferee company on the terms of a draft submitted to the meeting. The agreement provides that the transferee company shall purchase the assets of the transferor company, except a sum retained by the liquidator to discharge its liabilities, that the consideration shall be the allotment by the transferee company to the liquidator or his nominees of shares, fully or partly paid up, in the transferee company, that the liquidator shall give notice to the shareholders of the transferor company of the number of shares to which they are entitled, and the time within which they must apply, and that failure to apply for shares within that time shall preclude their rights to any shares.

A reconstruction scheme provided that shareholders in the old company should apply for shares in the new company within ten days after being given notice requiring them to apply, and that the liquidator should dispose of all shares not applied for. On June 12 the liquidator sent out notices requiring application for shares in the new company to be made before June 25. P., a shareholder in the old company, applied on August 24. *Held*, P. was not entitled to an allotment of shares in the new company, or to any other relief: *Postlethwaite* v. *Port Philip, etc., Gold Mining Co.* (1889) 43 Ch.D. 452.

Instead of the liquidator being authorised to dispose of all shares not applied for by the members of the transferor company, an underwriting agreement may be made in respect of such shares.[5] If the agreement is silent as to the disposal of the proceeds of sale of the shares not applied for, the proceeds must be distributed among the members of the transferor company who have not applied for shares in the transferee company.[6]

---

[3] *Re Irrigation Co. of France* (1871) L.R. 6 Ch.App. 176.
[4] *Bird* v. *Bird's Patent, etc., Sewage Co.* (1874) L.R. 9 Ch.App. 358.
[5] *Barrow* v. *Paringa Mines (1909) Ltd.* [1909] 2 Ch. 658.
[6] *Re Lake View Extended Gold Mine Co.* [1900] W.N. 44.

Shares may be given directly to the members of the transferor company instead of being applied for in the manner explained above.

Protection of dissentient members

A sale or arrangement under section 287 is binding on all members of the transferor company, whether they agree to it or not: section 287(2). However, a member who (1) did not vote in favour of the special resolution, and (2) expressed his dissent from it in writing addressed to the liquidator and left at the registered office within seven days after the passing of the resolution, may require the liquidator either to abstain from carrying the resolution into effect or to purchase his interest at a price to be determined by agreement or arbitration: section 287(3). Subsection (4) below shows that the election is that of the liquidator. The Jenkins Report[7] recommended that members who vote in favour of the resolution should be able to express dissent.

A transferee of shares whose transfer was not registered when the special resolution was passed may be entitled to have the register of members rectified and to dissent from the resolution.[8]

If the liquidator elects to purchase the member's interest, the purchase money must be paid before the transferor company is dissolved, and be raised by the liquidator as is determined by special resolution: section 287(4). The agreement usually provides for the retention by the liquidator out of the assets of the transferor company of a sum to cover the interests of the dissentient shareholders.

The articles cannot deprive a member of his statutory right to the value of his shareholding if he dissents.[9]

Protection of dissentient creditors

The liquidator must pay the creditors of the transferor company in the usual way in a winding up. If, however, the creditors conceive that they will be prejudiced by the transfer of all the company's assets to the transferee company, they may petition for a compulsory winding up or a supervision order. Section 287(5) provides that the special resolution for reconstruction shall not be valid if, within a year, an order is made

---

[7] Para. 503.
[8] *Re Sussex Brick Co.* [1904] 1 Ch. 598 (C.A.).
[9] *Payne* v. *The Cork Co. Ltd.* [1900] 1 Ch. 308.

for winding up the company by or subject to the supervision of the court, unless the court sanctions the resolution.

Application of section to other forms of winding up

Section 287 is limited by its terms to a members' voluntary winding up. It also applies, however, to a creditors' voluntary winding up, except that in this case, in addition to the special resolution of the company, the scheme must be sanctioned by the court or the committee of inspection: section 298.

In the case of a compulsory liquidation the court can, under section 245,[10] sanction a scheme which could be carried out by a liquidator under section 287, and no special resolution will be required.[11]

Sale under power in memorandum

The memorandum of association may give power to a company to sell its undertaking for shares in another company. If, however, the whole of the undertaking is to be sold and the proceeds are to be distributed among the shareholders, the procedure laid down in section 287, including the provisions for the protection of dissentient shareholders and creditors, cannot be excluded.[12]

SCHEME OF ARRANGEMENT UNDER SECTION 206

Where there is no reconstruction or amalgamation

A company cannot validly make any conveyance or assignment of all its property to trustees for the benefit of its creditors: section 320(2). Under section 306[13] an arrangement with its creditors can be made by a company when it is about to be or is in course of being wound up voluntarily, and in a winding up by the court the liquidator can make arrangements with the company's creditors under section 245,[14] but in both these cases liquidation is either in progress or in contemplation. Under section 206 a company can enter into a compromise or arrange-

---

[10] *Ante*, p. 646.
[11] See *Re Agra and Masterman's Bank* (1866) L.R. 12 Eq. 509n.
[12] *Bisgood* v. *Henderson's Transvaal Estates Ltd.* [1908] 1 Ch. 743 (C.A.); *cf.* *Waverley Hydropathic Co. Ltd. Petitioners*, 1948 S.C. 59.
[13] *Ante*, p. 702.
[14] *Ante*, p. 647.

ment with its creditors, or its members, or any class thereof, without going into liquidation. It can therefore be used for an agreed merger of two companies subject to the requirements of the section as to consent of the members and the court.

The proper way to distribute the assets of a company otherwise than strictly in accordance with creditors' rights is by a scheme of arrangement under section 206 which binds all creditors, and not by an agreement of compromise under section 245[14] which would deprive non-assenting creditors of the court's protection and prevent them from expressing their views.[15]

Section 206 provides that a compromise or arrangement will be binding on the company and the creditors or class of creditors or the members or class of members, as the case may be, if:

(1) The court, on the application in a summary way of the company or of any creditor or member of the company (or, if the company is being wound up, of the liquidator), orders a meeting of the creditors or class of creditors, or of the members or class of members, to be summoned.

The application for the meeting or meetings in England is by originating summons (R.S.C., Ord. 102, r.2) and in Scotland by petition to the Inner House (R.C. 190).

(2) The compromise or arrangement is agreed to by a majority in number representing three-fourths in value of those present and voting either in person or by proxy at the meeting.

(3) It is sanctioned by the court.

The application for sanction is by petition: R.S.C., Ord. 102, r.5; R.C. 190.

The word "company" in sections 206 and 207[16] means any company liable to be wound up under the Act: section 206(6). Thus it includes a company formed and registered under the 1948 Act, an existing company (in effect, a company formed and registered under a previous Companies Act), or an unregistered company.[17]

The word "arrangement" has a very wide meaning, and is wider than the word "compromise."[18] An arrangement may involve deben-

---

[15] *Re Trix Ltd.* [1970] 1 W.L.R. 1421.
[16] *Post.*
[17] s.398, *ante,* p. 649.   [18] *Re Guardian Assce. Co.* [1917] 1 Ch. 431 (C.A.).

ture holders giving an extension of time for payment, accepting a cash payment less than the face value of their debentures,[19] giving up their security in whole or in part, exchanging their debentures for shares in the company[20] or in a new company,[21] or having the rights attached to their debentures varied in some other respect,[22] creditors may take cash in part payment of their claims and the balance in shares or debentures in the company; preference shareholders may give up their rights to arrears of dividends,[23] agree to accept a reduced rate of dividend in the future, or have their class rights otherwise varied[24] (the use of section 206 to vary class rights has already been dealt with[25]). Or the members of a company in liquidation may agree with the company to seek or not to oppose a stay of the winding up, whereunder the members will give up their existing right to have all the proceeds of the company's assets distributed among them and instead be remitted to their contractual rights under the articles.[26] It even includes a scheme whereby the shareholders transfer their shares to another company, since that affects the contractual arrangements between the shareholders and their company so that there is an "arrangement" between them.[27]

Section 206 itself provides that the expression "arrangement" includes a reorganisation of the share capital of the company by the consolidation of shares of different classes or by the division of shares into shares of different classes. The word "compromise" implies some element of accommodation on each side. It is not apt to describe a total surrender. Similarly, the word "arrangement" implies some element of give and take.[28]

Where an arrangement under section 206 is essentially a scheme for the purchase by an outsider of all the issued shares of a company the

---

[19] *e.g. The Philadelphia Securities Co.* v. *The Realisation, etc., Corpn. of Scotland Ltd.* (1903) 11 S.L.T. 217 (O.H.).
[20] *e.g. Gillies* v. *Dawson* (1893) 20 R. 1119 (O.H.).
[21] *Re Empire Mining Co.* (1890) 44 Ch.D. 402.
[22] *e.g. Wright & Greig Ltd., Petitioners,* 1910 1 S.L.T. 353.
[23] *e.g. Balmenach-Glenlivet Distillery Ltd., Petitioners,* 1916 S.C. 639.
[24] *City etc., Trust Corporation Ltd., Petitioners,* 1951 S.C. 570.
[25] *Ante,* p. 216.
[26] *Per* Megarry J. in *Re Calgary and Edmonton Land Co. Ltd.* [1975] 1 W.L.R. 355, at p. 363.
[27] *Re Savoy Hotel Ltd.* [1981] 3 All E.R. 646.
[28] *Re N.F.U. Development Trust* [1972] 1 W.L.R. 1548.

scheme will not be sanctioned unless that company consents. Such consent may be expressed by the members in general meeting or by the board of directors.[29] It cannot be used therefore for a contested take-over or merger. Even if the take-over or merger is an agreed one the court will not allow the provisions of section 209, which require the outside purchaser to acquire 90 per cent. of the shares before he may compulsorily acquire the remainder,[30] to be circumvented by the use of section 206 where the necessary resolution under section 206 can only be passed with the assistance of votes of the wholly-owned subsidiary of the taking-over company.[31]

The meaning of the term "class" has been considered already.[32] The interests of a wholly-owned subsidiary of a company which is taking shares in another under a scheme of arrangement, when the subsidiary holds shares in the other, are different from those of the other ordinary shareholders in the other company and therefore the subsidiary is in a different class from the other ordinary shareholders and separate meetings must be held to approve the scheme.[33] Separate class meetings are required whenever the parties are not all on an equal footing, *e.g.* where some creditors are secured and others unsecured.[34]

It is the responsibility of the petitioners to see that the class meetings are properly constituted, and if they fail the court has no jurisdiction to sanction the arrangement.[35]

As to (1) *ante,* where a meeting of creditors or members is summoned under section 206, with every notice of the meeting there must be sent a statement explaining the effect of the compromise or arrangement and, in particular, stating any material interests of the directors in any capacity and the effect thereon of the compromise or arrangement in so far as it is different from the effect on the like interests of other persons. If the meeting is summoned by advertisement, a similar statement, or a notification of the place where such a statement may be

---

[29] But not all such schemes will fail, see *Re National Bank Ltd.* [1966] 1 W.L.R. 819; *The Singer Manufacturing Co. Ltd.* v. *Robinow,* 1971 S.C. 11 (scheme to enable parent company to acquire remaining 7·3 per cent. shareholding in subsidiary held competent).

[30] *Re Savoy Hotel Ltd., supra.*

[31] *Re Hellenic & General Trust Ltd.* [1976] 1 W.L.R. 123.

[32] p. 209.

[33] See note 31, above.

[34] *La Lainière de Roubaix* v. *Glen Glove etc. Co. Ltd.* 1926 S.C. 91.

[35] See note 31, above.

obtained, must be included. Where the compromise or arrangement affects the rights of debenture holders the statement must give the like explanation as respects the trustees of a deed for securing the issue of debentures as it is required to give as respects the directors: section 207.

Section 207 must be faithfully complied with: the court "has no discretionary power to dispense with the procedural requirements of section 207."[36] Thus a scheme will not be sanctioned if the explanatory statement, while stating that the company's assets have been revalued, does not give the amount of the revaluation,[37] or if a copy of the petition[38] or a copy of the scheme[39] has been sent without any further explanation. Material interests of directors must always be stated, even although those interests are in no way differently affected by the scheme from the interests of other persons.[40]

As to (2) *ante,* "three-fourths in value of the members or class of members" in section 206 refers to the size of the stake which each member has in the company. "The purpose is to prevent a numerical majority with a small stake outvoting a minority with a large stake, *e.g.* to prevent 51 members with one share each outvoting 49 members with 10 shares each."[41]

Any proper form of proxy may be used and it is not necessary to its validity that it should be sent to the company's offices before the meeting.[42] Directors who, pursuant to the court's order, receive proxies must use them whether they are for or against the scheme.[43]

As to (3) *ante,* before giving its sanction to a scheme of arrangement the court will see "First, that the provisions of the statute have been complied with. Secondly, that the class was fairly represented by those who attended the meeting and that the statutory majority are acting bona fide and are not coercing the minority in order to promote

---

[36] *Per* Lord Guthrie in *The Scottish Eastern etc. Trust Ltd., Petitioners,* 1966 S.L.T. 285, at p. 288.
[37] *Re Dorman, Long & Co. Ltd.* [1934] Ch. 635.
[38] *Rankin & Blackmore Ltd., Petitioners,* 1950 S.C. 218.
[39] *Peter Scott & Co. Ltd., Petitioners,* 1950 S.C. 507.
[40] *Coltness Iron Co. Ltd., Petitioners,* 1951 S.C. 476; contrast *Second Scottish Investment Trust etc., Petitioners,* 1962 S.L.T. 392.
[41] *Per* Brightman J. in *Re N.F.U. Development Trust Ltd.* [1972] 1 W.L.R. 1548, at p. 1553.
[42] *Re Dorman, Long & Co. Ltd.* [1934] Ch. 635; *La Lanière de Roubaix* v. *Glen Glove etc. Co. Ltd.,* 1926 S.C. 91.
[43] See note 41, above.

interests adverse to those of the class whom they purport to represent; and, Thirdly, that the arrangement is such as a man of business would reasonably approve."[44]

The court cannot sanction any arrangement involving transactions *ultra vires* the company.[45] Nor can the court approve under section 206 something for which a procedure is provided elsewhere by the Act, *e.g.* a reduction of capital.[46]

An order sanctioning a compromise or arrangement under section 206 has no effect until an office copy has been delivered to the Registrar of Companies. A copy of the order must also be annexed to every copy of the memorandum issued after the making of the order: section 206(3).

Where there is a reconstruction or an amalgamation.

Section 206, *ante*, can be used not only to effect arrangements with creditors and members, but also to carry out a scheme of reconstruction or amalgamation. One advantage of using section 206 to carry out such a scheme is that dissentient creditors are bound if the scheme is approved by the requisite majority. When the section is so used there is no statutory provision for the protection of dissentient members, and such members are bound by the arrangement if it is approved by the requisite majority. However, the court may, and usually will, as a condition of sanctioning the scheme, if it thinks it reasonable to do so, require dissentient members to be given the same rights as they would have had under section 287, *ante.*

In order to facilitate schemes of reconstruction and amalgamation, section 208 provides that when an application is made to the court under section 206 for the sanctioning of a compromise or arrangement, where the compromise or arrangement is for the purposes of a scheme for the reconstruction of a company or the amalgamation of two or more companies and the scheme involves the transfer of the whole or part of the undertaking or property of a company (called "a transferor

---

[44] *Per* Astbury J. in *Re Anglo-Continental Supply Co. Ltd.* [1922] 2 Ch. 723, at p. 736. See to the same effect, *per* Lindley L.J. in *Re Alabama etc. Rlwy. Co.* [1891] 1 Ch. 213 (C.A.), at p. 238. For adoption in Scotland, see *per* Lord President Dunedin in *Shandon Hydropathic Co. Ltd., Petitioners,* 1911 S.C. 1153 at p. 1155.

[45] *Re Oceanic Steam Navigation Co. Ltd.* [1939] Ch. 41.

[46] *Re St. James' Court Estate Ltd.* [1944] Ch. 6.

company") to another company (called "the transferee company"), the court may make an order providing for the following matters:

(1) The transfer to the transferee company of the whole or part of the undertaking and of the property or liabilities of a transferor company. An order so made cannot operate to transfer to the transferee company the benefit of a personal contract such as a contract of service between the transferor company and a person employed by it.[47] Further, a scheme under section 206, or an order under section 208 for giving effect to such a scheme, cannot transfer the office of executor from one bank to another; such an office of personal trust is incapable of assignment.[48]

(2) The allotting by the transferee company of any shares, debentures, policies or other similar interests in such company to the appropriate persons.

(3) The continuation by or against the transferee company of any legal proceedings pending by or against a transferor company.

(4) The dissolution, without winding up, of a transferor company.

(5) The provision to be made for persons who dissent from the scheme.

    This has been dealt with already.

(6) Any incidental matters.

An office copy of an order made under section 208 must be registered with the Registrar of Companies within seven days.

The word "company" in section 208 means a company within the meaning of the Act. Thus it means a company formed and registered under the Act or an existing company, in effect a company formed and registered under a previous Companies Act: section 455.

The Third EEC Directive

The Third Directive[49] deals with the regulation of mergers between public companies whereby all assets and liabilities of the acquired company are transferred to the acquiring company and the members of

---

[47] *Nokes v. Doncaster Amalgamated Collieries Ltd.* [1940] A.C. 1014.
[48] *In the Estate of Skinner (decd.)* [1958] 1 W.L.R. 1043.
[49] O.J. 1978 L295/36.

the acquired company receive shares in the acquiring company in return, with or without an additional cash payment. Thus it only applies to sections 206 to 208 and not to take-overs by the acquisition of shares. Implementation of the Directive will involve some amendments for public companies.

In particular the Directive requires the directors of both companies to draw up a "merger plan" covering details of the proposed merger, *e.g.* as to share exchange ratio. This will have to be sent to the Registrar.[50] It also requires "independent experts" to be brought in to examine the terms of the proposed merger, to draw up a written report for shareholders and, in particular, to state whether in their opinion the share exchange ratio is fair and reasonable.[51]

Implementation of this Directive will be by statutory instrument, and is expected shortly.

---

[50] Art. 6.
[51] Art. 10.

CHAPTER 31

TAKE-OVERS AND SUBSTANTIAL ACQUISITIONS OF SHARES

Many amalgamations take place without a scheme of arrangement under section 206 or a reconstruction under section 287 but by the simple method of one company acquiring a majority or the whole of the shares of another company from its shareholders. In such a case it is usual for the acquiring company (the offeror or transferee company) to make an offer (called a take-over bid) to the shareholders in the other company (the target or transferor company) to purchase their shares at a stated price and to fix a time within which the offer is to be accepted, with a condition that if a named percentage of the shareholders do not accept the offer, the offer is to be void. The offer is usually at a higher price than the current market price of the shares as quoted on the Stock Exchange and it may be in cash *(e.g.* £2 per share) or in kind *(e.g.* 2 of the offeror company's shares for each of the target company's shares). There are many economic reasons why such an offer is made. Sometimes more than one take-over bid is made for the same company so that there are rival bidders. As has already been seen[1] this form of amalgamation is the only practical form where the two companies do not agree to the merger.

There is little in the Companies Acts of relevance to such take-overs. Section 209 allows an offeror who has a 90 per cent. acceptance to compulsorily purchase the remaining 10 per cent. Section 209 is considered below. Otherwise the law of contract applies subject to certain statutory controls relating to monopolies and employee protection on take-overs. These are summarised at the end of this section. However it is fair to say that the most important controls on take-overs are those set out in the City Code on Take-overs and Mergers and administered by the City Panel, a "voluntary" self-regulatory code to which all who deal in shares on the Stock Exchange are subject.

---

[1] *Ante,* p. 712.

CITY CODE ON TAKE-OVERS AND MERGERS

The fifth edition of the City Code was published in February 1981.[2] It is administered by the City Panel which was instituted by the Bank of England and contains representatives of all the major City institutions, so that anyone in breach of its provisions is liable to fall foul of his own professional organization and may suffer penalties in consequence. In particular the Stock Exchange is represented, and withdrawal of a licence to deal on the Exchange is a potent threat against those dealing in shares on a take-over. The City Panel is part of a wider self-regulatory body, the Council for the Securities Industry (C.S.I), which produces other codes of conduct in relation to share dealings. The Code is constantly being revised and the Markets Committee of the C.S.I. is responsible for such revisions. The Panel also has a full-time executive which is available for advice at any time during the course of the bid, not as to the merits of the offer but as to procedure and conduct.

The full Panel will meet to decide on difficult points or where there is an alleged breach of the Code. There is a right of appeal from a Panel decision only if the Panel proposes to take disciplinary action *(e.g.* freezing the votes attached to certain shares) or if the dispute is as to the Panel's jurisdiction so that there is "serious hardship" to a company or individual. Appeals are to the Appeals Committee with a Law Lord as chairman.

Because the Code is not a statute it is not administered as such. There are no "cases" or strict interpretations of the wording. Proceedings before the Panel are formal but not legalistic. It is thus more flexible than a statute and can be adapted to changing circumstances, but there are many difficulties with such a code, *e.g.* the laws of defamation, enforcement, discovery of documents, etc. Often the threat of legal proceedings is sufficient to cause the Panel to suspend an investigation.[3] There are many who argue for self-regulation and many who argue against it.

The references in this chapter to Panel decisions and statements are to *The Journal of Business Law* which monitors the Panel on a regular basis.

---

[2] Copies may be obtained from the Secretary, Issuing Houses Association, Granite House, 101 Cannon Street, London EC4N 5BA.

[3] See Panel Report for the year to March 1978, p. 15.

Occasionally the Code is referred to in legal proceedings. In *Dunford & Elliott Ltd. v. Johnson & Firth Brown Ltd.*[4] one party to a bid sought an injunction to prevent the abuse of alleged confidential information in a take-over situation. Both Lord Denning M.R. and Roskill L.J. quoted the Code and used it as a guide to good commercial practice in an area where the court had a discretion. Again in *Re St. Piran Ltd.*[5] the court said that when considering whether to wind up a company on the just and equitable ground[6] the fact that the directors of a public company chose to flout the City Code or to ignore, without good reason, the consequent directions of the City Panel so that the minority shareholders were hurt by a withdrawal of the company's Stock Exchange quotation,[7] would be strong evidence in favour of granting the petition.

On the other hand the court has awarded injunctions preventing the Panel from issuing statements,[8] and the Panel has, on one occasion, had a battle of words with the Department of Trade following an inspectors' report under section 165.[9]

The Code is only applicable to public companies resident in the United Kingdom[10] and only where a take-over bid is concerned.[11]

The Code itself is divided into General Principles and Rules. The following is a summary of some of the more important parts of the Code.

General Principles

There are 14 general principles concerned with the provision of adequate and timely information to the shareholders so that all are to be treated equally, and the general responsibilities of the boards of directors of both the offeror and the offeree companies. General Principle 1 states that the spirit as well as the precise wording of the Code must be observed. This enables the Panel to find that there has

---

[4] [1977] 1 Lloyd's Rep. 505 (C.A.).
[5] [1981] 3 All E.R. 270.
[6] *Ante*, p. 407.
[7] This effectively prevents the shares being sold.
[8] Panel statement on *Sandstar Ltd. v. Graff Diamonds Ltd.* [1979] J.B.L. 274.
[9] Panel statement of May 14, 1979 [1979] J.B.L. 364.
[10] This includes the Isle of Man Panel statement on *Manx & Overseas Investments Ltd.* [1978] J.B.L. 184.
[11] Panel statement on *N.F.U. Development Trust* [1976] J.B.L. 162; *cf.* Panel statement on *Chaddesley Investments Ltd.* [1979] J.B.L. 271.

been a breach of the Code even though no specific provision was involved.[12]

The boards of both companies are required to act in the best interests of their respective shareholders. The offeree board should seek competent independent advice on receiving an offer and must not do anything to frustrate the offer without the general meeting's approval. In particular, rights of control must be exercised in good faith—minority oppression is "wholly unacceptable" (G.P.s 2, 4, 6 and 8).

General Principle 3 requires that the shareholders be put in possession of all the facts necessary for an informed judgment as to the merits of an offer and must have sufficient time to make an assessment and decision. No relevant information is to be withheld from them. No false market in shares is to be created—this can cause problems in relation to the disclosure of information about preliminary negotiations.[13] Rumour and speculation can drastically affect the quoted share price of a company (G.P.5).

The Rules

There are 42 Rules currently in the Code. Three were added to the 1981 edition on April 7, 1982 in response to a new device considered to be unsuitable.

(1) *The approach* (*Rules* 1–4)

An offer should be made first to the board of the offeree company or its advisers. The identity of the offeror if it is not the person making the bid should be disclosed at the outset and the offeree board is entitled to be satisfied that the offeror company will be in a position to implement its offer (either in cash or by shares) in full. The offeree board must circulate the independent advice it receives, usually from a Merchant Bank, to its shareholders.

(2) *Early stages* (*Rules* 5–10)

When a firm intention to make an offer is notified from a serious source a press notice must be issued immediately followed by a circular

---

[12] Panel statement on *Mount Charlotte Investments* v. *Gale Lister & Co. Ltd.* [1974] J.B.L. 310.

[13] Panel statement on *Rockwell International Corporation* v. *Wilmot Breedon (Holdings) Ltd.* [1979] J.B.L. 387.

to the shareholders. More difficult is the announcement of approaches which may or may not lead to an offer. Too early an announcement may kill the offer, too late and the market will have reacted in advance with all the possibilities of insider dealing by those with inside information.[14] Accordingly, an announcement, together with a temporary halt in dealings on the Stock Exchange, is normally expected either when negotiations have reached a point at which a company is reasonably confident that an offer will be made for its shares or when negotiations are about to be extended to embrace more than a small group of people. The responsibility is on the offeree company to make the announcement.[15]

The formal announcement of an intention to make an offer must include any conditions to which the offer is subject including the conditions as to acceptance levels, the ability to achieve a quotation for the new shares and the authority to issue those new shares[16] if a share for share offer is being made. Thus where a requirement as to the giving of a proxy vote was included in the offer documents but not in the original announcement the former were held to be void.[16a] If a formal offer is not forthcoming within 28 days after the announcement the offeror must be prepared to justify this to the Panel.[17] If necessary the Panel will take steps to enforce completion of the offer, *e.g.* by freezing the voting rights of shares already obtained.[18]

(3) *Board consideration of an offer* (*Rules* 11–13)

The directors must act in the interests of the shareholders as a whole.[19] There are special rules for "shut-out" bids, *i.e.* where an acceptance by the directors would give the offeror sufficient shares to make the bid a success.[20] All bona fide potential offerors must be given

---

[14] See *ante*, p. 442.
[15] See Panel statement on *Dickinson Robinson Group Ltd.* v. *Royal Sovereign Group Ltd.* [1978] J.B.L. 66; *Teachers (Distillers) Ltd.* v. *Allied Breweries Ltd.* [1978] J.B.L. 67; and *Balfour Ltd.* v. *Aurora Holdings Ltd.* [1979] J.B.L. 366.
[16] See *ante*, p. 165.
[16a] Panel statement on *Bassishaw Investment Ltd.* v. *UDS Group plc*, January 24, 1983.
[17] Panel statement on *Combined English Stores Ltd.* v. *David Greig Ltd.* [1974] J.B.L. 312.
[18] Panel statements on *St. Martins Property Ltd.* v. *Hays Wharf Ltd.* [1974] J.B.L. 312; *BSQ Securities Ltd.* v. *Court Hotels (London) Ltd.* [1976] J.B.L. 162.
[19] *cf. Gething* v. *Kilner* [1972] 1 W.L.R. 337, on such duties in a private company.
[20] Panel statement on *W. Henshall & Sons Ltd.* [1979] J.B.L. 46.

the same information on request as that given to a preferred offeror.[21] The offer document must disclose any arrangements between the offeror and offeree directors and state that consideration for the offer will be paid in full to each shareholder without any set-off, etc.

(4) *Formal documents* (*Rules* 14–20)

These rules elaborate General Principle 12 that all documents relating to an offer by either company must be treated with the same standard of care as if they were prospectuses[22] subject to the 1948 Act.[23] The rules also prescribe a minimum content of such documents including the social and employment consequences of the take-over.[24] Special care is required on profit forecasts and assets valuations put out by offeree companies as these may influence both the success and amount of the final offer.[25]

Prescribed information concerning directors' interests and those of the advisers must be set out including any dealings by directors during the previous 12 months. Copies of all documents relating to the bid must be sent to the Panel. The use of proxies as an integral part of a shareholder's acceptance of an offer is regarded as undesirable by the Panel.[25a]

(5) *Mechanics of the formal offer* (*Rules* 21–29, 42)

No offeror may acquire any voting shares of the offeree company for seven days after announcing the offer. The offeree board and shareholders must have time to consider. Further no offer which if accepted in full would result in the offeror holding over 50 per cent. of the voting shares can be declared unconditional unless acceptances are received or promised amounting to at least that amount.

Time limits are laid down within which each stage of the bid must be implemented and when public statements as to the results of the bid are

---

[21] Panel statement on *Scotia Investments Ltd.* [1975] J.B.L. 303.

[22] *Ante*, p. 129.

[23] See Panel statement on *York Trust Ltd.* v. *Greenwood & Batley Ltd.* [1978] J.B.L. 68.

[24] Panel statement on *British Investment Trust Ltd.* [1979] J.B.L. 161.

[25] Panel statements on *Crane Fruehauf Ltd.* [1978] J.B.L. 184; *Dunford & Elliott Ltd.* [1979] J.B.L. 159, and *Vantona Group Ltd.* v. *J. Compton Sons & Webb (Holdings) Ltd.* [1979] J.B.L. 160.

[25a] Panel statement on *Bassishaw Investments Ltd.* v. *UDS Group plc*, January 24, 1983.

to be made.[26] Partial bids are disapproved of and subject to special rules. No offeror may announce that it will not revise its offer until after the first date for acceptances has passed. This is intended to prevent undue pressure being put on the shareholders.

(6) *Dealings* (*Rules* 30–37, 40–41)

The most sensitive area surrounding take-over bids concerns the dealings in the shares of both companies during the course of the bid. Prior to the bid no party privy to the negotiations should deal in the shares. This is the most obvious area of insider dealing and has exercised the Panel greatly over the years. The prevalence of such dealings in fact led to the criminal offences in the 1980 Act for such transactions.[27]

After a public announcement the parties may, subject to what is said below, deal in the shares provided they make daily disclosure to the Stock Exchange and the press.

If the offeror or anyone acting in concert with him purchases shares on the market at above the offer price then that price must be increased to the highest price paid.[28] If 15 per cent of the shares are acquired for cash the offer must include a cash alternative, being the highest price paid for such shares.

Two specific problems have concerned the Panel in recent years. The first relates to persons who amass a significant holding of shares in a company without declaring a bid for the remainder. Since 1972 the Code has insisted that once a holding of shares is acquired above 30 per cent. of the voting rights of a company that holder should be required to make a general offer for the remainder. This has not always proved easy to enforce if either the holder refused to comply with the request[29] or indeed was unable to do so.[30] The usual sanctions are to freeze the votes on shares already acquired, to suspend the company's quotation on the Stock Exchange, to refer the matter to the Department of

---

[26] Panel statement on *Babcock & Wilcox Ltd.* v. *Woodall-Duckham Group Ltd.* [1973] J.B.L. 235.
[27] *Ante*, p. 446.
[28] See Panel statement on *Dalgety Ltd.* v. *Spillers Ltd.* [1980] J.B.L. 50.
[29] Panel statement on *St. Martins Property Ltd.* v. *Hays Wharf Ltd.* [1974] J.B.L. 312; *Ashbourne Investments Ltd.* [1975] J.B.L. 44 [1976] J.B.L. 259.
[30] Panel statement on *Gilgate Holdings Ltd.* [1980] J.B.L. 269.

Trade, or even to assist in a just and equitable winding up[31] by a shareholder.[32]

Currently the Code requires a mandatory bid by anyone who, together with persons acting in concert,[33] has acquired 30 per cent. or more of the current voting rights of a company, or who, owning between 30 and 50 per cent., has increased his holding by 2 per cent. within a year. This obligation applies to all members of a consortium and the bid must be on the highest terms paid by the holder. If the implementation of such an offer would require a resolution, *e.g.* to increase capital, no purchases may be made at all. Pending the posting of an offer no nominees of the potential offeror may be appointed to the offeree board and the votes already acquired are to be frozen. In exceptional circumstances the Panel may waive compliance with this obligation[34] (Rule 34). Persons who hold less than 30 per cent. of the shares are subject to other rules—*post.*

The second problem has been the reverse case. A bidder will make a "market raid" on the shares of one company and acquire a 30 per cent. holding either of shares or promises to transfer shares, at a high price, often in a matter of minutes. The company will then comply with Rule 34, above, and make a general offer at that price to the other shareholders. The objection to this practice is that it effectively deprives the offeree board of any chance to comment or advise on the merits of the bid. Thirty per cent. is regarded as almost effective control of a company. Accordingly Rules 40 and 41 apply.[35] They are intended to slow down the pace at which shareholdings over 30 per cent. are amassed.[36]

Thus no-one may acquire more than 30 per cent. of the shares of a company unless he has already made an offer for all the shares of a company. The only exceptions are where the purchase is from a single seller or the purchases are prior to and conditional on an agreed bid for the total shareholding of the company. On making such an offer no shares may be purchased for seven days by the offeror and anyone making an offer who holds less than 30 per cent. of the shares may not

---

[31] Panel statement on *St. Piran Ltd.* [1980] J.B.L. 358.
[32] Ante, p. 405.
[33] Panel statement on *Winchester London Trust Ltd.* [1976] J.B.L. 164.
[34] Panel statements on *London Tin Corporation Ltd.* v. *B. S. & W. Whitely Ltd.* [1976] J.B.L. 161; *Manx & Overseas Investments Ltd.* [1978] J.B.L. 184.
[35] Introduced on April 7, 1982.
[36] For holdings between 15 per cent. and 30 per cent. see *post,* p. 725.

acquire any further shares so as to take his holding above 30 per cent. until after the first date on which acceptances are to be counted—at least 21 days from the posting of the offer document.[37] The effect is to prevent control of a company passing in less than 21 days.

RULES GOVERNING SUBSTANTIAL ACQUISITIONS OF SHARES

The City Code on Take-overs only operates in a take-over situation[38] and this effectively commences either on an offer being made or a 30 per cent. holding of shares being amassed by one person or consortium.[39] In 1980, however, there was a series of "dawn raids" on the Stock Exchange where one person would acquire, in a matter of minutes, less than 30 per cent. of the shares of a public company but nevertheless a significant amount. The Council for the Securities Industry considered that such practices were undesirable for two reasons. First, the identity of the acquirer would often be disguised, *e.g.* by several linked companies each acquiring 5 per cent. of the shares on behalf of an unnamed person, and, second, it was obvious that only a few shareholders benefited from being able to dispose of their shares on a "dawn raid" at above market value. This opportunity was not available to the other shareholders.

The first problem was countered by pressure on the Government which led to the rules on share disclosures by shareholders or groups owning 5 per cent. or more of the shares of a public company introduced by the 1981 Act, sections 63 to 72.[40] The second problem, that of equal opportunity, was to be the subject of another self-regulatory code, the Rules Governing the Substantial Acquisition of Shares.[41] The City Panel[42] is responsible for administering this Code as the C.S.I. has no effective secretariat to do so.

The Rules apply to acquisitions of quoted shares in United Kingdom companies[43] within seven days amounting to 5 per cent. or more of the voting rights in any one company and which take the purchaser's

---

[37] Rule 22.
[38] *Ante*, p. 719.
[39] Rule 34, *ante.*
[40] *Ante*, p. 199.
[41] Introduced on December 11, 1980, and revised on April 7, 1982.
[42] *Ante*, p. 718.
[43] As defined in the City Code.

holding to 15 per cent. or more of that company's voting rights but less than 30 per cent., at which stage the City Code will come into operation.[44] Purchase by two or more connected or "concert" parties are regarded as purchases by a single purchaser.

Any acquisition caught by the Rules must now either follow the strict rules for partial bids set out in the City Code on Take-overs[45] or be acquired by means of a tender offer. Under this procedure the buyer makes a firm offer to buy a specified number of shares either at a fixed price or up to a maximum price. Shareholders then offer their shares by tender, in the latter case at any price up to the maximum specified. Shareholders are bound by their tenders and the purchaser and his associates must not deal in the shares during the tender period of at least seven days. Tenders must be advertised in two national newspapers and sent to the company and the Stock Exchange.

The effect of these rules is to check advances in shareholdings between 5 per cent. and 30 per cent.

Power to acquire shares of shareholders dissenting from scheme approved by majority

Section 209 provides that where—

(1) there is a scheme or contract involving the transfer of shares or any class of shares in a transferor company to a transferee company, whether a company within the Act or not;

(2) and within four months after it is made, the offer by the transferee company is approved by the holders of not less than nine-tenths in value of the shares whose transfer is involved (other than shares already held at the date of the offer by, or by a nominee for, the transferee company or its subsidiary);

(3) the transferee company may, within two months after the expiration of the four months, give notice in the prescribed form to any dissenting shareholder in the transferor company of its desire to acquire his shares;

(4) whereupon the transferee company is entitled and bound to acquire those shares on the terms approved by the approving shareholders unless, on application by the dissenting

---

[44] Rule 34, *ante.*
[45] Rule 27.

shareholder within one month from the date of the notice, the court orders otherwise.

The words "a scheme or contract involving the transfer of shares" include a scheme or contract involving the transfer of an absolute right to shares in a case in which by the terms of a trust deed securing convertible loan stock the effect of an offer to acquire the shares in a company is to entitle the holders of the stock to an allotment of shares, and approval "by the holders of not less than nine-tenths in value of the shares whose transfer is involved" includes approval by persons who have an absolute right to an allotment.[46]

The period of four months after the offer is a maximum period and the transferee company may prescribe a shorter period within which it must be approved.[47] If it does so, however, it usually reserves the right to extend the period up to the statutory maximum of four months.[48] Extension of the closing date for acceptance of an offer does not amount to a new offer and so the transferee company's right must be exercised within six months of the original offer.[49]

Section 209(5) provides that the expression "dissenting shareholder" includes a shareholder who has not assented to the scheme or contract and a shareholder who has failed or refused to transfer his shares in accordance with the scheme or contract. If the offer of the transferee company of a share for share exchange is accompanied by a cash offer from a third party and the transferee company wishes to exercise its rights of compulsory acquisition under section 209(1), a dissenting shareholder has an option to require the transferee to pay him the amount of cash he would have received had he accepted the offer of the third party.[50]

It has been held[51] that the word "court" in the section means the court with jurisdiction to wind up the transferor company.[52] The court will order otherwise and prevent the transferee company from acquiring the shares of dissentient shareholders only if it is satisfied that the

---

[46] *Re Simo Securities Trust Ltd.*[1971] 1 W.L.R. 1455.
[47] *Re Western Manufacturing (Reading) Ltd.* [1956] Ch. 436.
[48] *e.g. Musson* v. *Howard Glasgow Associates Ltd.*, 1960 S.C. 371; the right to extend the closing date need not be exercised within the original time limit: *per* Lord Sorn at p. 376.
[49] *Musson's* case, *ante.*
[50] *Re Carlton Holdings Ltd.* [1971] 1 W.L.R. 918.
[51] *Re Samuel Heap & Son Ltd.* [1965] 1 W.L.R. 1458 (C.A.).
[52] See ss.218, 220, *ante*, pp. 605, 606.

scheme is unfair to the general body of shareholders in the transferor company. There is normally a heavy burden of proof on the dissentients[53]—since the scheme has been approved by nine-tenths of the shareholders, prima facie it must be taken to be a fair one.[54] The test is one of fairness to the body of shareholders as a whole and not to individual shareholders, and it is not enough merely to prove that the scheme is open to criticism or capable of improvement.[55] It is not enough that the materials put before the shareholders were inadequate to enable them to form a just conclusion as to the acceptance or refusal of the offer.[56] Where there is a Stock Exchange quotation for the shares, prima facie that can be taken as the value of the shares.[57] The element of control of the transferor company, which would accrue to the transferee company from the acquisition of all the shares in the transferor company, is not to be taken into account in determining the value of the shares of a minority shareholder.[58] The dissentient shareholders, who are not satisfied with the price offered, cannot obtain an order for discovery so as to enable them to carry out an investigation into the value of the shares, unless there are special circumstances.[59]

However, if the dissentient shareholders show that in substance the transferee company is the same as the majority holding in the transferor company the onus is on the majority to satisfy the court that the scheme is one which the minority ought reasonably to be compelled to fall in with.

A and B were the two shareholders, each holding 50 shares, in the transferee company which offered to purchase the shares in the transferor company in which there were three shareholders, A and B, who each held 4,500 shares and who accepted the offer, and C, who held 1,000 shares and who dissented. *Held*, that C, by showing that the transferee company was, for practical purposes, equivalent to the holders of nine-tenths of the shares in the transferor company who accepted the offer, had, prima facie, shown that the case was one in which the circumstances were special and that the court ought

---

[53] *Re Sussex Brick Co. Ltd.*[1961] Ch. 289n; *Nidditch* v. *The Calico Printers' Assocn. Ltd.*, 1961 S.L.T. 282.

[54] The onus is the other way round under s.206, *ante: per* Templeman J. in *Re Hellenic & General Trust Ltd.* [1976] 1 W.L.R. 123, at pp. 130, 131.

[55] *Re Grierson, Oldham & Adams Ltd.* [1968] Ch. 17.

[56] *Re Evertite Locknuts Ltd.* [1945] Ch. 220.

[57] See *Re Press Caps Ltd.* [1949] Ch. 434 (C.A.).

[58] See note 55, above.

[59] *Re Press Caps Ltd.* [1948] 2 All E.R. 638.

to "order otherwise" within the meaning of section 209, and the majority had not shown that there was some good reason in the interests of the company (*e.g.* that the minority shareholder was acting in a manner highly damaging to the interests of the company) for allowing the section to be invoked for the purpose of enabling the majority to expropriate the minority: *Re Bugle Press Ltd.* [1961] Ch. 270 (C.A.).

The directors of an offeree company (*i.e.* a transferor company) have a duty towards their shareholders to be honest and not to mislead them. A shareholder in such a company may be prejudiced if his co-shareholders are misled into accepting the offer. A minority can therefore complain if it is being wrongfully subjected to the power of compulsory purchase as a result of a breach of duty by such directors.[60]

Where, after notice has been given to a dissentient shareholder, no application is made to the court or, if made, it is unsuccessful, the transferee company must send a copy of the notice to the transferor company together with an instrument of transfer executed on behalf of the transferee company and, on behalf of the shareholder, by a person appointed by the transferee company. The transferee company must also pay or transfer the money or other consideration to the transferor company, and is then entitled to be registered as the holder of the shares. The transferor company must pay any money received into a separate bank account, and must hold any money or other consideration received upon trust for the persons entitled to the shares in respect of which it was received: section 209(3), (4).

Section 209 does not apply, *e.g.* where one company acquires shares in another by purchase on the Stock Exchange, or where a "first come, first served" invitation to treat is made by one company to shareholders in another who then offer to sell their shares to the first company, or where an offer to purchase shares is made by an individual. It has been held that the Australian equivalent of section 209[61] does not apply where a "take-over" offer to purchase shares is made by a consortium of two or more companies jointly, or an offer is made to shareholders in two or more companies.[62] Of course, a group of companies can form a joint subsidiary which can make a take-over offer for shares in another company.

---

[60] *Gething* v. *Kilner* [1972] 1 W.L.R. 337, particularly at pp. 341, 342.
[61] Section 185 of the Companies Act 1961 as amended (N.S.W.).
[62] *Blue Metal Industries Ltd.* v. *Dilley* [1970] A.C. 827 (P.C.).

One-tenth of shares already held by transferee

Where, at the date of the offer, more than one-tenth in value of the shares or class of shares whose transfer is involved are held by, or by a nominee for, the transferee company or its subsidiary, section 209 does not apply unless:

(1) the transferee company offers the same terms to all the holders of the shares or each class of shares whose transfer is involved; and

(2) the holders who approve the scheme or contract, besides holding at least nine-tenths in value of the shares whose transfer is involved, are also not less than three-fourths in number of the holders of such shares: section 209(1) proviso.

The date at which a count has to be made to ascertain whether approving shareholders amount in number to three-fourths of the total holders is the most practical date and therefore the fraction must normally be calculated by reference to the total number of shareholders on the register at the offer date.[63]

Transferee acquires nine-tenths of shares

If the shares transferred under the scheme or contract, together with the shares held by, or by a nominee for, the transferee company or its subsidiary at the date of the transfer, amount to nine-tenths in value of the shares in the transferor company or of any class of such shares, the transferee company must, within a month after the transfer, give notice of that fact to the holders of the remaining shares, or of the remaining shares of the class, who have not assented to the scheme. Thereupon any such holder may, within three months after the notice, *require* the transferee company to acquire the shares in question on the terms on which, under the scheme, the shares of the approving shareholders were transferred, or on such terms as may be agreed, or fixed by the court on the application of either the transferee company or the shareholder: section 209(2).

[63] *Re Simo Securities Trust Ltd.* [1971] 1 W.L.R. 1455.

Other Provisions to be Borne in Mind When a Take-over Bid is to be Made

When a take-over bid is to be made, apart from the provisions of the Companies Act, the following should also be borne in mind:

(1) The Prevention of Fraud (Investments) Act 1958, section 14,[64] which restricts the channels through which circulars containing offers to sell or purchase shares (not being prospectuses within the meaning of the Companies Acts) may be distributed and so controls, *inter alia*, the distribution of take-over circulars.

(2) The Licensed Dealers (Conduct of Business) Rules 1960,[65] which were made by the former Board of Trade under section 7 of the Prevention of Fraud (Investments) Act 1958, and have statutory force only as regards licensed dealers, although they are observed generally.[66] These, *inter alia*, lay down certain requirements for the conduct of take-over offers and the contents of take-over circulars. For example, if an offer is conditional, the latest date on which the offeror may declare it unconditional must be specified, and if the offer relates to less than the total amount in issue of any class of securities it must be open to acceptance by all holders of the class and if too many acceptances are received they must be scaled down *pro rata*. Again, the bidder must be identified, and the extent of the offeror's interest in the securities of the offeree company must be given.

Fair Trading Act 1973

The Fair Trading Act 1973, which *inter alia* repealed, and re-enacted with amendments, the Monopolies and Mergers Act 1965, should be borne in mind because it enables the Secretary of State in certain circumstances to refer a merger to the Monopolies & Mergers Commission.

Sections 64 and 75 of the 1973 Act provide that where it appears to the Secretary of State that—

(1) two or more enterprises, at least one of which was or is carried on in the United Kingdom or by or under the control of a company incorporated here, have ceased to be distinct enterprises within the past six months or without notice to the Secretary of State or the Director General of Fair Trading, or are about to cease to be distinct enterprises; and

(2) either (*a*) as a result at least one-quarter of certain goods or services are or will be supplied in the United Kingdom by or to any one person, or by or to the persons by whom the enterprises are carried on; or (*b*) the value of the assets taken, or to be taken, over exceeds £15m.;

---

[64] *Ante*, p. 157.
[65] S.I. 1960, No. 1216.
[66] Jenkins Report, paras. 268, 269.

the Secretary of State may refer the matter to the Commission for investigation and report within, usually, six months (s.70).

If conditions (1) and (2) are fulfilled the Commission must decide whether the merger is against the public interest (s.69) and, if so, what action should be taken. If, according to the report as laid before Parliament, facts found operate against the public interest, the Secretary of State has the powers specified in Schedule 8 (s.73), *e.g.* he may prohibit bodies corporate from becoming interconnected bodies corporate, or provide for the division of any business by the sale of any part of the undertaking or assets or otherwise, or for the division of any group of inter-connected bodies corporate. For this purpose the Secretary of State may order, *inter alia,* the winding up of a company or the amendment of its memorandum and articles.

It is the duty of the Director General of Fair Trading to keep himself informed about actual or prospective mergers and to make recommendations to the Secretary of State as to action which it would be expedient for the Secretary of State to take (s.76).

"Enterprise" is defined in section 63 as the activities or any part of the activities of a business. Two enterprises are treated as ceasing to be distinct enterprises if they are brought under common ownership or control or either enterprise ceases to be carried on at all. The following enterprises are treated as being under common control—

(1) those of interconnected bodies corporate;
(2) those carried on by any two or more bodies corporate controlled by the same person or persons;
(3) that carried on by a body corporate and that carried on by the person or persons controlling the body corporate (s.65).

For the purposes of section 65 a person or group of persons able to control or materially to influence the policy of a body corporate, or that of a person carrying on an enterprise without having a controlling interest, may be treated as having control.

Associated persons, and any bodies corporate which any of them control, are treated as one person for the purposes of, *e.g.* section 65. Certain persons are deemed to be associated, *e.g.* an individual and that individual's spouse, and any relative, or spouse of a relative, of either (s.77).

By section 58 a transfer of a newspaper or of newspaper assets to a newspaper proprietor whose newspapers have an average circulation per day, with that of the newspaper concerned, of 500,000 or more copies is unlawful and void unless made with the written consent of the Secretary of State.

Industry Act 1975, Part II

The Industry Act 1975, Part II (sections 11–20), gives the Secretary of State power to prohibit the transfer or to acquire the undertaking if there is a serious and immediate possibility that control over an important manufacturing undertaking (as defined in section 11(2)) will pass to a person resident outside the United Kingdom and the transfer would be contrary to the national interest.

Section 11 provides that the powers conferred by Part II extend to changes of control of important manufacturing undertakings. Section 12 provides that there is such a change of control only in certain specified events, *e.g.* when a person not resident in the United Kingdom becomes able to exercise or control the exercise of 30 per cent. or 40 per cent. or 50 per cent. of the votes that may be cast at a general meeting of a body corporate carrying on the whole or part of the undertaking.

Transfer of Undertakings (Protection of Employment) Regulations 1981

These regulations apply where a person transfers a commercial undertaking to another person, *e.g.* on a take-over. The representatives of the employees who may be affected by the transfer must be informed by the transferor company and the transferee of the date of and the reasons for the transfer and its implementation for the employees.

If either company envisages taking measures in relation to the affected employees, it must enter into consultations with the representatives. Any employee dismissed because of a transfer may present a complaint of unfair dismissal.

INDEX

735